Anthony Blunt

GUIDE
TO
BAROQUE
ROME

GRANADA
London Toronto Sydney New York

To the Bibliotheca Hertziana
and to the memory of Wolfgang Lotz

Granada Publishing Limited
Frogmore, St Albans, Herts AL2 2NF
and
36 Golden Square, London W1R 4AH
866 United Nations Plaza, New York, NY 10017, USA
117 York Street, Sydney, NSW 2000, Australia
100 Skyway Avenue, Rexdale, Ontario M9W 3A6, Canada
61 Beach Road, Auckland, New Zealand

Published by Granada Publishing 1982

Copyright © Anthony Blunt 1982

British Library Cataloguing in Publication Data

Blunt, Anthony
Guide to Baroque Rome.
1. Architecture, Baroque – Italy – Rome
I. Title
724'.19   NA590

ISBN 0–246–11762–1

Typeset by Western Printing Services Ltd, Bristol

Printed in Great Britain by Mackays of Chatham Ltd

All rights reserved. No part of this publication may be reproduced, stored in a retrieval system, or transmitted, in any form or by any means, electronic, mechanical, photocopying, recording or otherwise, without the prior permission of the publishers.

Granada ®
Granada Publishing ®

CONTENTS

List of Plates iv

Preface vii

Introduction xiii

I THE CHURCHES 1

II THE PALACES 155

III THE VATICAN 201

IV THE VILLAS 205

V THE FOUNTAINS 225

VI MISCELLANEOUS BUILDINGS 243

VII THE ALBAN HILLS 259

Bibliography 271

Index of Artists 283

LIST OF PLATES

		page
1	Arms of the popes from Paul III to Clement XIV	xii
2	S. Agnese in Piazza Navona	4
3	S. Anastasia	8
4	S. Andrea al Quirinale. Plan	10
5	S. Andrea al Quirinale. Engraving by Falda	11
6	S. Andrea della Valle. Engraving by Piranesi	12
7	S. Andrea della Valle. Plan	13
8	S. Carlo ai Catinari	22
9	S. Carlo alle Quattro Fontane. Plan	23
10	S. Carlo alle Quattro Fontane. Engraving by Falda	23
11	SS. Carlo e Ambrogio. Plan	25
12	SS. Carlo e Ambrogio. Engraving after a medal	25
13	S. Chiara	29
14	S. Croce in Gerusalemme	32
15	SS. Domenico e Sisto. Engraving by Falda	34
16	SS. Domenico e Sisto. Engraving by Vasi	34
17	S. Francesca Romana	38
18	The Gesù. Plan	41
19	The Gesù. Vignola's design	42
20	The Gesù. Engraving of the façade as executed	44
21	The Gesù. Engraving by Falda	46
22	S. Giovanni in Laterano. Plan	52
23	S. Giovanni in Laterano. Engraving by Vasi	53
24	S. Gregorio al Celio	62
25	S. Ignazio	64
26	S. Ivo della Sapienza. Plan	66
27	S. Ivo della Sapienza. Engraving by Falda	67
28	S. Lorenzo in Panisperna	70
29	SS. Luca e Martina. Engraving by Falda	72
30	SS. Luca e Martina. Drawing by Martinelli	73
31	S. Maria in Campitelli. Engraving by Falda	83

32	S. Maria in Campitelli. Plan	84
33	S. Maria in Cosmedin	87
34	S. Maria Maggiore. Etching by Israël Silvestre	90
35	S. Maria Maggiore. Engraving by Vasi	91
36	S. Maria Maggiore. Bernini's project for the apse	92
37	S. Maria di Montesanto and S. Maria dei Miracoli	97
38	S. Maria di Montesanto. Plan	99
39	S. Maria dei Miracoli. Plan	99
40	S. Maria dell' Orazione e della Morte	101
41	S. Maria della Pace. Engraving by Falda	104
42	S. Maria della Pace. Plan	104
43	S. Maria della Pace. Engraving by Falda of interior	105
44	S. Maria in Vallicella and the Oratorio di S. Filippo Neri. Plan	114
45	S. Maria in Vallicella and the Oratorio di S. Filippo Neri. Engraving by Falda	115
46	S. Maria in Via Lata. Engraving by Falda	120
47	S. Maria in Via Lata. Engraving by Vasi	121
48	St Peter's. Plan	131
49	St Peter's. Engraving by Falda	133
50	St Peter's. Etching by Israël Silvestre	135
51	S. Rita da Cascia	141
52	S. Sebastiano fuori le Mura	144
53	S. Susanna	149
54	Palazzo Aldobrandini-Chigi	159
55	Palazzo Aste (Buonaparte). Engraving by Falda	161
56	Palazzo Aste. Engraving by Vasi	162
57	Palazzo Barberini. Plan of ground floor	163
58	Palazzo Barberini. Plan of first floor	163
59	Palazzo Barberini. Etching by Piranesi	164
60	Palazzo Borghese. Plan	167
61	Palazzo Borghese. Engraving by Falda	168
62	Palazzo Chigi-Odescalchi. Engraving by Falda	172
63	Palazzo Chigi-Odescalchi. Etching by Piranesi	173
64	Palazzo Colonna	174
65	Palazzo Corsini	176
66	Palazzo Pamphili (now Doria-Pamphili)	179
67	Palazzo Madama	184
68	Palazzo Mattei di Giove	185
69	Palazzo di Montecitorio	187
70	Palazzo Pamphili	189
71	Palazzo Pio di Savoia da Carpi	191
72	Palazzo del Quirinale	192
73	The Quirinal	192
74	Palazzo Spada	196
75	Palazzo dello Spirito Santo (Spada)	198

76	Vatican. Scala Regia	202
77	Villa Albani	208
78	Villa Altieri	209
79	Villa Benedetti	210
80	Villa Borghese	211
81	The gardens of Villa Colonna	213
82	Villa Ludovisi. Etching by Piranesi	216
83	Villa Ludovisi. Engraving by Falda	216
84	Villa Mattei (Celimontana)	217
85	Villa Pamphili. Engraving by Falda	218
86	Villa Pamphili. The fountain of Venus	219
87	Villa Patrizi	220
88	Villa Sacchetti (The Pigneto). Drawing by P. L. Ghezzi	221
89	Villa Sacchetti. Drawing by Hendrik van Lint	221
90	Villa Sforza ai Quattro Cantoni	222
91	Acqua Felice	229
92	Acqua Paola	230
93	The Barcaccia	231
94	The Quattro Fontane. Drawing by Lieven Cruyl	235
95	The Quattro Fontane. Engraving by Falda	236
96	The fountain in front of S. Maria in Trastevere	237
97	The Fontana di Trevi. Drawing by Lieven Cruyl	239
98	The Fontana di Trevi. Etching by Piranesi	239
99	Fontana del Tritone	240
100	Collegio di Propaganda Fide	247
101	The Dogana di Terra	249
102	Piazza Navona	252
103	Piazza di S. Ignazio	252
104	The Porto di Ripetta. Engraving by Falda	254
105	The Porto di Ripetta. Etching from *Varie Vedute di Roma*	254
106	Piazza di Spagna and the site of the Spanish Steps. Etching by Israël Silvestre	256
107	The Spanish Steps	256
108	Piazza di Spagna and the site of the Spanish Steps. Etching by Vincenzo Mariotti	257
109	Ariccia. Engraving by Falda	262
110	Ariccia, Church of the Assunta	262
111	Castel Gandolfo	263
112	Frascati. Greuter's general view	264/5
113	Frascati, Villa Aldobrandini	266
114	Frascati, Villa Mondragone	268
115	Frascati, Villa Torlonia	269

PREFACE

The purpose of this book is double. It aims first at providing a guide book which the visitor to Rome who is interested in the Baroque can carry round with him on his walks through the city; but it is also intended to be useful in the study for those who want to pursue the Baroque in a more leisurely way. The individual entries contain, therefore, what I hope is accurate information about the buildings and their contents, but also a lead or leads towards the sources from which this information is derived. Where possible I have given a reference to a good modern source, such as the volumes in the series *Le Chiese di Roma illustrate*, from which the interested student will be able to follow up his enquiries through the bibliographies supplied, but I have supplemented these by references to books and articles which were published since the volume in question appeared or which deal with individual problems not discussed in it. Where no reliable modern monograph exists I have referred to the old guide books to Rome, to the early biographies of artists, or to any other sources that seemed to me useful. I have also given references to the early guide books of Mola and Martinelli which have only been published within the last twenty years, and I have added references to the most important illustrated sources for the benefit of those who may want to use the book in the study rather than in the field.

One great problem was to decide what to include and what to leave out. As regards dates I have taken the Baroque to mean roughly the art of the period beginning with the election of Gregory XV as pope in 1621 and ending about the middle of the eighteenth century, but obviously precise limits of date cannot be laid down. The question of how late to carry the study was relatively easy to solve, because about the middle of the eighteenth century Roman Baroque architecture begins to wither away – mainly owing to the advent of neo-classicism, but partly perhaps because of the removal of Vanvitelli and Fuga to Naples in 1750 – and though clearly certain late-comers like Marchionni, the builder of the Sacristy of St Peter's and the Casino of the Villa Albani, had to be included, it was not difficult on the whole to decide what buildings should be excluded on the grounds that they belonged to the incipient neo-classical movement.

The question of where to begin was much more difficult. Obviously the immediate forefathers of Baroque architecture, who worked for Paul V and his nephew Scipione Borghese – Carlo Maderno, Flamineo Ponzio and Van Santen (Vasanzio) – had to be included, and it seemed to me sensible to put in as much as possible of the work of their immediate predecessors – Giacomo della Porta, Domenico Fontana and Giacomo del Duca – on the grounds that the first two created the Rome in which the inventors of the Baroque grew up, and the third was an important factor in the formation of Borromini's style. I have only mentioned the work of earlier artists when it is to be found in buildings which play an important part in the development of the Baroque, or which were enlarged or altered in the Baroque period and had therefore in any case to be discussed. So, for instance, Vignola's S. Andrea in via Flaminia is included as belonging to the first category, Perino del Vaga's frescoes in S. Marcello are mentioned because the church has to be discussed for its Baroque features, and even S. Sabina gets a mention because of its altarpiece by Sassoferrato and the chapel of St Dominic within the convent attributed to Borromini. I have even included the church and oratory of S. Giovanni Decollato and the Palazzo Sacchetti because they contain spectacular examples of Mannerist illusionist decoration which form a prelude to the work of the Alberti brothers and so lead on to Baroque decoration. I am aware of the fact that I have not been consistent in giving data about late sixteenth-century painting, but much of it is not really relevant to the Baroque, and I have tried to include as far as possible paintings of the last generation of Mannerists as well as the contemporaries and followers of Caravaggio and the Carracci.

The main emphasis in the book is on architecture. This is partly because of my own special interest in this aspect of Roman Baroque, but it has also a more objective basis, in that architecture was the master art in the Baroque age, and one of the most obvious characteristics of this period is the fusion of the three arts of architecture, sculpture, and painting under the dominant control of the first. The entries on individual churches therefore contain a fuller discussion of architecture than of the other arts. I have, however, as far as possible included information about the paintings and sculpture in the buildings discussed. In the case of the paintings I have taken a permissible short-cut by referring to Sir Ellis Waterhouse's lists in his *Roman Baroque Painting* (2nd edition, London, 1976) but they unfortunately do not cover some important painters of the eighteenth century, and do not refer to works in Roman churches by non-Roman artists. He has, however, kindly supplied me with many details from his notes and I have added others from old guide books and recent literature, but I am aware of the fact that my treatment of this aspect of the subject is a little summary. I have made no attempt to list paintings of the period in public or private collections in Rome, though I have referred – usually in a single sentence – to the great collections in buildings which come in for discussion, such as the Barberini, Corsini, Doria-Pamphili, Spada, and Rospigliosi Palaces, and the Villa Borghese. The problem of sculpture was more difficult because the modern literature on the subject is so incomplete, but here I have had the inestimable advantage of having been able to consult Dr Jennifer Montagu, the greatest expert on the subject, who generously offered to read through the whole manuscript and has not only saved me from making a number of howlers but has added much information of the greatest interest. Any facts based on unpublished documents discovered by Dr Montagu are marked with the initials J.M.

I said above that this book deals mainly with the churches of Rome. For this there are two reasons. The first is that the greatest achievements of the Roman Baroque were in ecclesiastical rather than in domestic architecture. There are of course palaces, such as the Mattei di Giove, Barberini, Chigi-Odescalchi, which attain a very high level of distinction, and others in which individual features stand out – the galleries of the Colonna and Pamphili palaces or Borromini's ceilings in the Palazzo Falconieri – but these cases are relatively rare, compared with the number of masterpieces among the churches. The second reason is that there are too many Baroque palaces in Rome and too little is known about them. The only general books on the subject (Callari and Torselli) are inadequate and though there are valuable monographs on some of the major palaces in many cases there is no information available. It seemed to me useless to load the book with entries such as 'Palace with fine door, probably early eighteenth century' which is often all that can be said in the present state of knowledge.

It was difficult to know how much practical information to add. The location of every monument has been given. These indications should make it possible for users of the book to find any building which interests them; but will they be able to get into it? Most Roman churches are open from early in the morning (6 or 7 a.m.) till mid-day and many reopen from about 3 p.m. onwards, but there are, as every student of Roman art knows, only too many which are only open on rare occasions, perhaps early on Sunday morning, but possibly for a late mass at mid-day, or perhaps only on the feast of the patron saint. It was tempting to include what information I had been able to collect on this subject, but careful examination showed that it goes out of date so rapidly that it can be more misleading than helpful. The new *Guide Rionali*, for instance, often give indications of when churches are open, but having made a check of about a dozen I found that two out of three were wrong – and the result was merely to add to one's sense of frustration. The only advice is 'Try, try again', and ask the advice of neighbours who may know where the *parocco* or the sacristan lives. Some Roman churches now have notices on their doors giving their times of opening, but the information is often misleading; for instance, they often forget to mention that the time-table does not apply in, say, August and September when the parish priest and the sacristan may be on holiday, or the monks in their country retreat.

In order to keep the price of the book as low as possible the illustrations have had to be kept to essentials. Plans of churches are given either when they are of particular interest or when the church contains a very large number of chapels or monuments which are difficult to locate. The other plates have been limited to a selection of engravings, mainly by Falda and Vasi, which supply information about the original appearance of churches which were later altered.

I have also added notes on some churches which no longer exist, but about which there is some visual evidence in the form of old photographs, engravings or, in one case, a foundation medal.

In the description of the interiors of churches I have followed a path starting from the entrance, going up the right wall or aisle, through the transepts (if they exist) and the choir and then down the left-hand side. The abbreviations *1 to R, 1 to L* mean first chapel or altar to the right or left. In churches of more complicated form – such as St Peter's or St John Lateran – a plan is added on which the various altars or monuments are marked with numbers.

I have visited – by which I mean been inside – almost all the churches covered in this handbook. In cases where I have failed to get into them during the preparation of the book I have qualified any comment I make about the interiors with the word 'apparently', which means that I have based my statement on what appears to be the best available evidence from written or verbal sources.

I have also been round all the major churches and a very large percentage of the smaller ones with the final typescript in my hand in order to make sure that I have supplied the answers to as many as possible of the questions which the student will ask and to check that objects which I mention are in the places where I describe them. As regards the first point I have not listed altarpieces or tombs about which no information seems to be available. About the second I have no doubt made mistakes, and I should be very grateful for any corrections which users of the guidebook may care to send me. The same applies to bibliographical references which I have done my best to check, but in which mistakes are certain to have arisen in the process of copying – mainly owing to my handwriting.

I have as far as possible noted whether the marbling in a church is composed of real marble or *scagliola*, or is painted. The distinction is important because it affects the whole appearance of a church and is not visible in a reproduction. The result is that certain churches – for instance S. Carlo al Corso or SS. Trinità degli Spagnuoli – appear in a reproduction to be magnificently decorated but in reality the 'marbling' is painted, with the result that instead of reflecting the light, it is completely dead and produces an effect of heaviness. The finest example of the effect of luminosity produced by real marbling is Bernini's S. Andrea al Quirinale, but it is also effective in less ambitious churches, such as S. Giovanni Calabita, S. Maria dell'Umiltà or S. Caterina da Siena a Magnanapoli.

I have incurred many debts of gratitude in the preparation of this book. Some of these have been acknowledged above, but I have also gained much by discussion with my colleagues in London University, particularly Howard Burns and Bruce Boucher. Constance Hill and the staff of the Conway Library and the Photographic Department of the Courtauld Institute have been consistently helpful over the making or obtaining of the photographs needed for the illustration of the book.

Above all I must thank Elizabeth Hasloch who has patiently and uncomplainingly typed and retyped the text, deciphering my additions and corrections and detecting many mistakes and inconsistencies, and has prepared the index of artists – a formidable task. Without her help the book would have remained an untidy bundle of notes and would certainly never have reached the publisher.

When it did reach the publisher I was lucky in that it fell into the hands of Moira Johnston who not only carried out the boring process of checking spelling, typography etc. but pointed out a shameful number of inconsistencies and ambiguities. I—and my readers—owe her a deep debt of gratitude for her acute and scholarly checking of the text and index.

It would not have been possible to write this book without the existence of the Bibliotheca Hertziana, with its unrivalled collection of modern books, periodicals and old guide books dealing with Rome, many of which are difficult to find in this country and even in other libraries in Italy. In fact it might be said that it is simply a distillation of their marvellous indexes arranged according to artists and individual monuments as well as by authors. It is for this reason, and also in gratitude for the kindness and hospitality that I have invariably received there over many years, that I dedicate this book to the Library, its foundress, those who built it up, and those who administer it today.

I should also like to express my particular gratitude to the late Wolfgang Lotz, who died suddenly while this book was in the press. During the many years when he was director of the Library he found time to discuss with me problems connected with Baroque architecture with which I was faced, always providing imaginative suggestions which cleared away many clouds and led me to a fuller understanding of the whole subject.

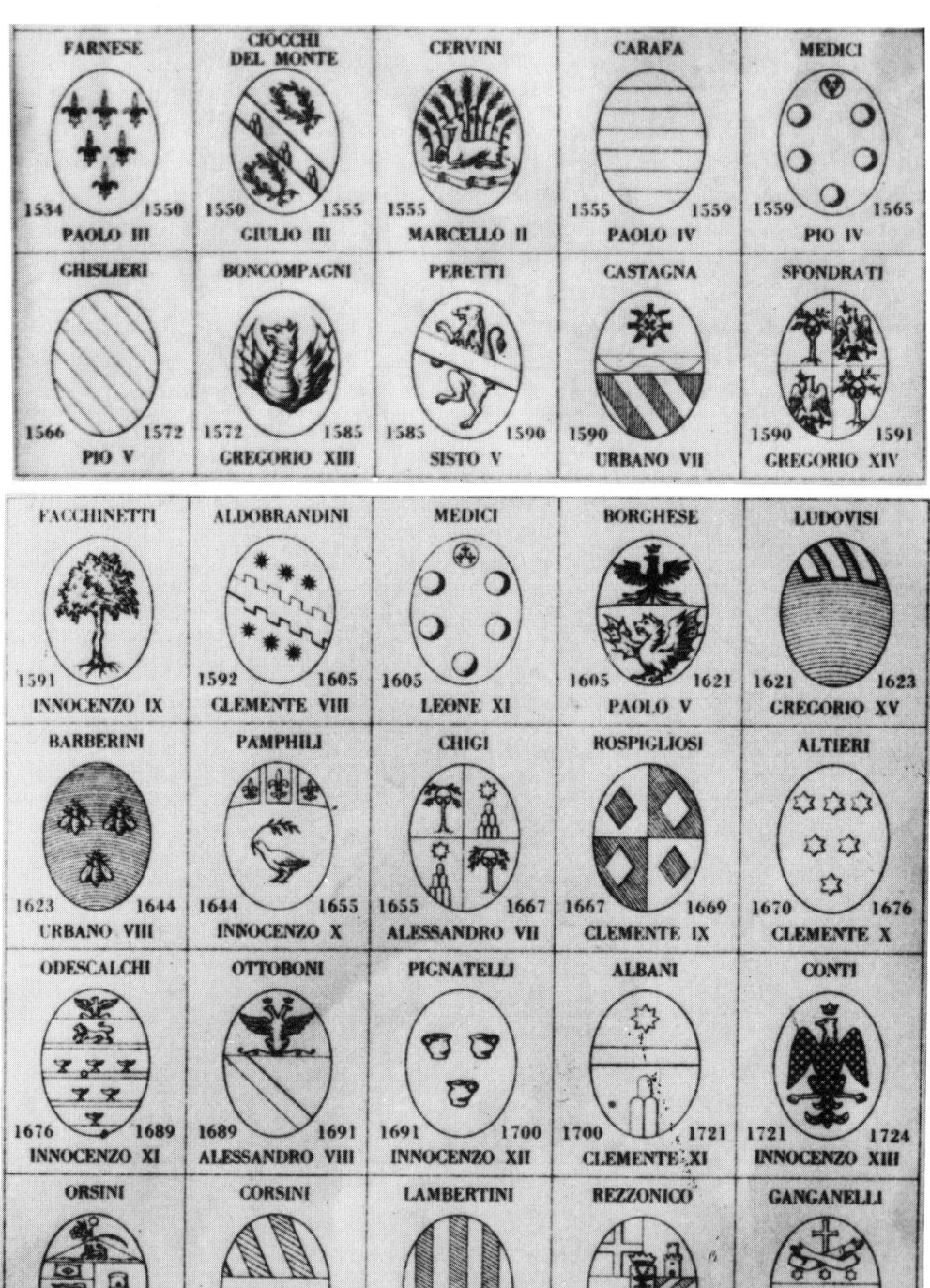

1. Arms of the popes from Paul III to Clement XIV.

INTRODUCTION

No two art historians use the word Baroque in quite the same sense, but, fortunately for the purpose of this book, almost all are agreed that the first great flowering of the style took place in Rome roughly in the period 1620–70, that is to say during the pontificates of Gregory XV Ludovisi (1621–3), Urban VIII Barberini (1623–44), Innocent X Pamphili (1644–55), and Alexander VII Chigi (1655–67). In this phase the Baroque reflected the religious atmosphere of the time, which was one of relaxed enthusiasm, even of triumph, after the austere period of the Counter-Reformation, marked by the doctrinal and administrative reforms of the Council of Trent (1545–63), and the establishment of the new Orders – the Jesuits, the Theatines, the Oratorians, and the Barnabites. The exuberant and rhetorical Baroque style exactly fulfilled the needs of the church in its new mood. Architects aroused astonishment in the pious by the grand scale of their buildings, the complexity of their forms, the dramatic effects of light which they introduced, and the richness of the marbles and gilded stuccoes with which they covered the walls and vaults of their churches. Painters and sculptors invented new formulas for rendering the ecstasies and sufferings of the saints and martyrs with strong dramatic and emotional effects, and Bernini, who was sculptor and painter as well as architect, combined all three arts into a single whole in his great masterpieces, the Baldacchino and the Cathedra Petri in St Peter's, the Cornaro chapel in S. Maria della Vittoria, and the church of S. Andrea al Quirinale.

Patronage depended essentially on the popes and their families. The popes were responsible for the grandest building schemes of the period; Urban VIII for the decoration of St Peter's and the building of the Palazzo Barberini; Innocent X for the building of S. Agnese, the lay-out of the Piazza Navona, and the restoration of the Lateran; Alexander VII for the colonnade of St Peter's and the Cathedra Petri within the church; but the papal nephews were patrons of almost equal importance. Cardinal Scipione Borghese built many churches (principally designed by G. B. Soria), Cardinal Francesco Barberini financed the building of SS. Luca e Martina by Cortona and many other churches (as well as the restoration of a number of early Christian churches), and his uncle, the more austere Cardinal Antonio, paid for the building of the Cappuccini, near the family palace, and a few other rather modest churches. These great princes of the church also built for their own pleasure. Cardinal Scipione Borghese built the Villa Borghese and another garden palace on the Quirinal (now the Palazzo Rospigliosi); Cardinal Ludovico Ludovisi built the Jesuit church of S. Ignazio and laid out the Villa Ludovisi; Cardinal Francesco Barberini and his brother Taddeo were largely responsible for the Palazzo Barberini; Cardinal Camillo Pamphili built the villa outside the Porta S. Pancrazio; Cardinal Flavio Chigi commissioned Bernini to design his palace on the Piazza S. Apostoli; and many other examples could be quoted. In addition, many of the Roman families who were not directly related to the popes but who were connected with the Vatican administration restored or enlarged their palaces. Fortunately it only needed a very small twist to adapt the rhetorical style invented for the church to satisfy the needs of the princes.

The new Orders also played an important part in the development of the Baroque. Their main Roman churches – the Gesù (Jesuits), S. Andrea della Valle (Theatines), Chiesa Nuova (Oratorians) and S. Carlo ai Catinari (Barnabites) – were built before the Baroque period but their decoration continued well into the seventeenth century; and many of them built second or third churches in the city (S. Andrea al Quirinale). The old Orders were less active in architecture, though the Dominicans built the important church of SS. Domenico e Sisto, the Carmelites S. Maria della Scala, and the Franciscans restored that of S. Francesco a Ripa and S. Maria d'Aracoeli.

The Baroque movement did not get going till the 1620s in sculpture and painting (Bernini, Lanfranco and Pietro da Cortona), and not till the mid-1630s in architecture (Borromini, Pietro da Cortona), but naturally it did not arise suddenly. Many architects, above all Borromini, looked back to the revolutionary inventions of the late Michelangelo for their inspiration, and Sixtus V (1585–90) foreshadowed much of the grand-scale urban development of the Baroque period with his lay-out of streets such as the Strada Felice (now via Sistina and via della Quattro Fontane), and his creation of piazzas centred on the ancient Egyptian obelisks which he erected at prominent points in the city (Lateran, Piazza del Popolo, St Peter's), and his architect, Domenico Fontana, in his vast blocks at the Lateran and the Vatican, worked on a scale which carried the grandeur of the Palazzo Farnese to the end of the century. In palace architecture Giacomo della Porta (1532/3–1602), the most successful architect of the pontificate of Clement VIII, broke with tradition by spacing the windows of his palaces unevenly, thus introducing an element of variety lacking in most palace fronts of the previous decades. Carlo Maderno (1556–1629) went much further in abandoning the tradition of flat wall-treatment which had been established by Vignola (1507–73), and in S. Susanna (1603) introduced a more varied treatment of the façade with a progression from pilasters to half-columns and then to full columns, thus concentrating attention on the central bay and creating a movement in depth which marks an important step towards the free movement of Baroque façade architecture. In the decoration of the gallery in the Palazzo Farnese, Annibale Carracci and his team of assistants replaced the artificial ingenuity of late-Mannerist fresco painting with a type of lucid illusionism which was to be the basis for the great Baroque decorative schemes of the seventeenth century (e.g. Cortona in the Palazzo Barberini, the Palazzo Pamphili, and the Chiesa Nuova). At the same time Caravaggio, by his investigations into the naturalistic rendering of detail and the dramatic use of light, was forging weapons of which Baroque painters were to make use in their representations of religious subjects. In sculpture the period was less inventive but the reliefs on the tombs in the two chapels – Sistine (1585–90) and Pauline (begun 1605) – in S. Maria Maggiore form a prelude to what was to come, and it is not without significance that the team of artists working in the latter included Pietro Bernini, father of Gianlorenzo.

The creators of Baroque architecture – Bernini, Pietro da Cortona and Borromini – were men of very different types. Bernini (1598–1680) was by far the most successful of the three and, apart from a few years of disfavour after the election of Innocent X in 1644, he enjoyed uniform and increasing success. He was not only sculptor, architect and painter, but wrote poetry, composed and produced plays and was a learned theologian, a man of deep piety and a close friend of the Jesuits. His architecture is essentially based on a sense of the dramatic and a brilliant exploitation of the combination of sculpture and architecture, with an almost painterly element of colour added by the use of gilding and coloured marbles. His architectural forms, however, even in such a vast scheme as the Piazza of St Peter's, are remarkably simple.

Curiously enough Pietro da Cortona (1596–1669), although he was himself a painter, made no use of fresco in the one complete building for which he was responsible, the church of SS. Luca e Martina, which is conceived entirely in huge travertine columns with the vault decorated in white stucco. His treatment of the wall is richly three-dimensional, and is based on the inset coupled columns of Michelangelo's Laurenziana Ricetto (he was a Tuscan by birth and early training) which he combined in the façades of SS. Luca e Martina and S. Maria della Pace with a convex form, curving sharply at the ends and almost flat in the middle, which is peculiar to him. At the Pace he also showed a magnificent sense of the theatrical combined with an ingenious solution of the complicated practical problems involved.

Borromini (1599–1667) was the only pure architect of the three. His works (S. Carlo alle Quattro Fontane, S. Ivo) are created in terms of wall and vault structures, producing complex combinations of spaces, often incomplete and leading one into another, the plans being frequently based on symbolical forms (S. Ivo). He was the one of the trio who really understood the late works of Michelangelo and developed them in a highly personal form, for instance using the incomplete forms of the Sforza chapel (S. Maria Maggiore) in his plans and the double pediment of the Porta Pia as the basis for his own favourite pediment form, as on the façade of the Oratory of S. Filippo Neri. However fanciful these forms may seem, they were in fact worked out on rigidly controlled geometrical systems, consisting usually of a combination of circles and equilateral triangles, and it is this severe discipline that gives to Borromini's buildings a quality of concentrated intensity lacking in the works of his great contemporaries. The same concentration is visible in the decoration of his churches. He never uses colour, and gilding only on rare occasions. His decoration is entirely in white stucco, but stucco moulded with a precision and sharpness of form which suggests the late eighteenth century rather than the Baroque age (cf. the niche heads in S. Carlino and S. Ivo, the bands of laurel and palms on the piers of the Lateran, or the palmettes on the ceilings of Palazzo Falconieri). The nervous intensity of Borromini's works was in part a reflection of his neurotic personality, which eventually led him to suicide.

While the centre of the stage was held by this trio, a great many buildings of a much more modest kind were being erected in Rome, so many indeed that it is possible to regard the Baroque – though artistically much more important – as numerically a minority movement. The most distinguished representative of this modest style was Giovanni Battista Soria (1581–1651) who in his three major church façades (S. Gregorio al Celio, S. Caterina da Siena, S. Carlo ai Catinari) invented a staid type, with two storeys of equal width, which is usually described as *retardataire* but should more properly be called 'non-Baroque' or even 'anti-Baroque', because there is some reason to think that there was a consciously anti-Baroque movement in architecture analogous to that of Poussin and Andrea Sacchi in painting (curiously enough Soria's patron in all these churches was Cardinal Scipione Borghese, the 'discoverer' of the young Bernini). In architecture this tradition was carried on by Giovanni Antonio de' Rossi (1616–95) who built several churches (S. Maria in Campo Marzio and S. Pantaleo) and the Palazzo Altieri for the family of Pope Clement X in a markedly severe style.

Between these two groups stood other architects who embraced some of the tenets of the Baroque but were not whole-hearted in their adherence to its methods. Carlo Rainaldi (1611–91) built the much admired church of S. Maria in Campitelli in a style which, though Baroque in the liveliness of the columnar treatment of the walls, shows no sense of the continuous movement of the real Baroque. Martino Longhi the Younger (1602–60) is principally famous for the façade which he added to the church of SS. Vincenzo e Anastasio which is Cortonesque in its coupling of inset columns and doubling of pediments, but completely avoids the curves favoured by the fully Baroque architects of the period. Antonio del Grande (active 1652–71), an architect who has not been sufficiently studied, built the gallery at the Palazzo Colonna, decorated by Coli and Gherardi (see below), and added a wing to the Palazzo Doria-Pamphili on the Piazza del Collegio Romano with an entrance vestibule designed to produce a fine vista up the staircase, an idea hinted at by Borromini in drawings but never fully realized by him in a building.

Painting in mid seventeenth-century Rome is dominated by Pietro da Cortona, who in addition to the great fresco cycles mentioned above painted altarpieces for many of the major Roman churches. His style was continued, though in a more restrained form, by his pupils, Guglielmo Cortese (1628–74), and Ciro Ferri (1634(?)–89), while the two Lucchese artists, Giovanni Coli (1638–81) and Filippo Gherardi (1643–1700), developed it in the direction of bolder Baroque forms. In the vault and dome of the Gesù the Genoese Giovanni Battista Gaulli, called

Baciccio (1639–1709), a protégé of Bernini, evolved an even bolder form of dramatically illusionist decoration, and in S. Ignazio the Jesuit Andrea Pozzo (1642–1709) created the grandest of all architectural false perspectives. At the same time many artists – such as Giacinto Gimignani (1611–81) and Sassoferrato (1609–85) – were working in a more restrained style both for churches and for private patrons, and others supplied the demand for genre paintings, landscapes and still-life, but these scarcely belong to the 'public' art with which this book is principally concerned.

Sculpture was dominated by Bernini, who after his brilliant beginnings in the representation of classical subjects for Cardinal Scipione Borghese (statues now in the Borghese Gallery) went on to create his great religious groups, such as the *St Theresa* in S. Maria della Vittoria and the *Blessed Ludovica Albertoni* in S. Francesco a Ripa, perhaps the most magnificent renderings of mystical experiences ever achieved. In the early part of the period the Fleming François Duquesnoy (1597–1643), a friend of Poussin, set up a much more classical style, which up to a certain point was continued, though blended with Baroque elements, by Alessandro Algardi (1598–1654).

Borromini and Cortona died in the late '60s and Bernini in 1680, and their place was taken by a generation of architects of lesser stature but great influence, of whom the most important was Carlo Fontana (1638–1714). He worked in Bernini's studio and inherited his unfinished commissions, but he had none of the imaginative fire of his master. He was an eclectic who combined features from the architecture of Borromini – particularly in the forms of doors and windows – with what he learnt from Bernini, to create a sort of moderate Baroque which turned out to be suited to non-Roman as well as to Roman patrons, and his studio became the Mecca of architects not only from other parts of Italy but from the Empire (Hildebrandt and the Asam brothers) and even England (Gibbs and probably Archer). His reputation was first established by the façade which he added to S. Marcello in 1682–3, and which became a model widely copied in all countries where the Baroque took root, and he became official architect to Clement XI Albani (1700–21) for whom he not only restored numerous churches but also built a granary and the huge Ospizio di S. Michele. At the same time, however, the Baroque line was continued by Antonio Gherardi (1644–1702), who built two dramatically conceived chapels, that of S. Cecilia in S. Carlo ai Catinari and the Cappella Avila in S. Maria in Trastevere.

In painting Carlo Maratta (1625–1713) occupied the same dominant position as Fontana in architecture and for the same reason: he produced a qualified Baroque style which suited the quieter mood of the turn of the century and was, like Fontana's, easily 'exportable'. His pupils dominated Roman painting during the first half of the eighteenth century.

In architecture this period was marked by a clear conflict between the classical tendency and a style for which Italian art historians have invented the word *barocchetto*, a much more satisfactory term than the word *rococo* applied to it by some American critics (notably Mallory), since the style is in fact an ingenious variant of Baroque, slightly less grandiose than that of the seventeenth century, and has nothing whatsoever in common with the true *rococo* of France or Southern Germany. Its most important representatives were Gabriele Valvassori (1683–1761), who in the façade of the Palazzo Doria-Pamphili on the Corso invented new variations on Borromini's window forms, and the Beneventan Filippo Raguzzini (*c.* 1680–1771), who was favoured by his compatriot Pope Benedict XIII (1724–30), and created the lively Piazza S. Ignazio; but the classical party triumphed in the greatest architectural competition of the period, that for the façade of the Lateran (1732) in which Alessandro Galilei came out victorious over his rivals who included Ferdinando Fuga (1699–1781) and Luigi Vanvitelli (1700–73). This victory was confirmed by the policy of the Florentine Pope Clement XII Corsini (1730–40) who employed Galilei to build his family chapel in the Lateran, in which Baroque exuberance is replaced by almost neo-classical restraint, verging on coldness.

Galilei died in 1736 and in 1750 Vanvitelli and Fuga were both called to Naples to work for Charles of Bourbon. The last Roman architect to employ a style which can in any sense be called Baroque was Carlo Marchionni (1702–86) who built the Sacristy of St Peter's and the villa in which Cardinal Alessandro Albani housed his great collection of ancient sculpture; but the Cardinal's taste and that of his librarian Winckelmann were soon to impose themselves on the art world in Rome, and the various pavilions in the gardens were built in a much more correctly classical style. The neo-classical movement had established itself, and soon the name of Bernini and Cortona and above all that of Borromini were to become synonyms for all that was contrary to good taste. It was not till the present century that this judgment was reversed and the genius of these artists was once again recognized.

I
THE CHURCHES

S. Adriano
In the Forum

Bibliography: Pugliese-Rigano, *Lunghi*, p. 67, pls 140–2; Varriano, 'The 1653 Restoration of S. Adriano al Foro Romano: new documentation on Martino Longhi the Younger', *Römisches Jahrbuch*, XIII, 1971, p. 287.

In Republican times this building housed the Senate. Under Honorius I (625–38) it was converted into a church. It was remodelled by Martino Longhi the Younger in 1653–6, but in the 1930s all the Baroque additions were removed. They are, however, recorded in photographs which are reproduced by Pugliese-Rigano.

The holy-water stoups with angels by Orfeo Boselli formerly in the church are now in that of S. Maria della Mercede, viale Regina Margherita (Boselli, *Osservazioni della Scoltura antica*, ed. Dent Weil, Florence, 1978, p. 29).

S. Agata dei Goti
Via Mazzarino

Bibliography: Pollak, I, p. 19; Roisecco, 1750, II, p. 582; Titi, 1763, p. 272; C. Huelsen et al., *S. Agata dei Goti*, Rome, 1924; Ferrari, *Lo Stucco*, pl. CXXIX; Buchowiecki, I, p. 279.

A church existed on the site from very early times, and at one moment in the 5th century it was occupied by the Arians. The mediaeval church was restored and decorated in the 17th century, but most of the additions then made were removed in a further restoration in 1933. The wooden ceiling was given in 1633 by Cardinal Francesco Barberini whose brother Cardinal Antonio completed the restoration of the church in 1636.

The façade dates from before 1750 and is attributed by Roisecco and Titi to Francesco Ferrari.

INTERIOR
The painting in the half-dome of the apse and those between the windows representing scenes from the life of St Agatha were attributed by Pascoli (*Vite de' pittori perugini*, Rome, 1732, p. 203), and in Titi (1763) to Paolo Gismondi, though some later critics have wrongly ascribed them to Cerrini (W).
Left aisle: Tomb (in stucco) of Cardinal Carlo Bichi (d. 1718) by C. de Dominicis (Mallory, *Rococo*, p. 131).

The usual entrance is at via Panisperna, 29.

S. Agata in Trastevere
Piazza Sonnino

Bibliography: U. Vichi, *Sant' Agata in Trastevere*, Rome, n.d.; Portoghesi, *Roma Barocca*, pls 326–9; Elling, pl. 33.

According to an inscription in the Sacristy the church was founded by Gregory II in 727, but it is first mentioned in 1192. It was given by Gregory XIII in 1575 to the Congregation of Christian Doctrine and rebuilt in 1710, on the designs of Giacomo Onorato Recalcati. The façade is dated 1748.

INTERIOR
Vault of nave: Girolamo Troppa, *St Agatha in Glory* (1711; W; Poensgen, fig. 53).
3 to R: Biagio Puccini, *Madonna del Rosario* (W).
High Altar: B. Puccini, *Martyrdom of St Agatha* (W).
3 to L: B. Puccini, *Crucifixion* (W).

S. Agnese in Agone (or in Piazza Navona)
Piazza Navona

Bibliography: Tessin, p. 162; De Brosses, II, p. 122; Magni, I, pls 63–6; Hempel, *Borromini*, p. 138; Lavagnino, *Altari*, p. 139; Fasolo, *Rainaldi*, p. 119; Eimer, *S. Agnese*; Portoghesi, *Borromini*, pls LXXIII–LXXIV, 123–31; R. Preimesberger, 'Bernini a S. Agnese in Agone', *Colloqui del Sodalizio*, series 3, 1970–2, p. 44; F. Trevisani, 'La Fabbrica di S. Agnese in Navona: estate 1653, *Storia dell' Arte*, 23, 1975, p. 61; Preimesberger, 'Das dritte Papstgrabmal Berninis', *Römisches Jahrbuch*, XVII, 1978, p. 159; Blunt, *Borromini*, p. 156; *Guide Rionali*, VI, 1, p. 36.

As an important part of his scheme to make the Piazza Navona into a monument to his family Innocent X planned to rebuild and greatly enlarge the church of S. Agnese, which at that time faced on to the via dell' Anima with its choir abutting on Piazza Navona. In 1652 Girolamo Rainaldi, assisted by his son Carlo, provided the first plan. This consisted of a Greek cross with rounded ends to the arms and large niches between them, a long rectangular vestibule and a straight façade articulated with large and small columns. In April 1653, as a result of the severe criticism which had been levelled at the design of the church, Girolamo Rainaldi resigned and the work was left in the hands of his son. In June, however, after some complicated manoeuvring, Carlo was replaced by Borromini. A drawing by Cortona in the Staatliche Sammlung, Munich, which was till recently thought to be connected with SS. Luca e Martina, is in

3

S. Agnese in Agone

2. *S. Agnese in Piazza Navona. Plan.*

fact for S. Agnese and shows that Cortona must have submitted a design for the church in 1652 or early in 1653. (The evidence for this will be set out in my forthcoming book on Cortona as an architect.)

By the time Borromini took over the interior had nearly reached the top of the pier niches and the façade had risen to a height of ten feet. Borromini had the façade pulled down and his final plan involved important changes: a concave façade enclosing a flight of oval steps and whole columns added at the corners of the main piers in the interior. Work went so fast that by the beginning of 1655 the dome was complete except for the lantern and the façade had reached the cornice, and in the interior the columns and pilasters were finished up to the capitals.

It has always been thought that the curved façade and the steps were the invention of Borromini, and Karl Noehles discovered a drawing (Eimer, I, fig. 91) which he believed was a copy of one which showed Borromini's new plan in one half and the Rainaldi plan in the other. Eimer however argues that the drawing shows Girolamo Rainaldi's original design together with a new design by his son. If this hypothesis is correct the oval steps and the concave façade would have to be credited to Carlo Rainaldi, but Eimer's arguments are not conclusive and the design with the concave façade has no parallel in the work of Carlo Rainaldi but is completely in accordance with Borromini's style.

In January 1655 Innocent X died and his nephew Camillo Pamphili was left to finish the church. Alexander VII appointed a commission under Cardinal Imperiali to supervise the building, but relations with the architect became strained, Borromini was accused of neglecting his duties, and in February 1657, in order to avoid being dismissed, he resigned. Carlo Rainaldi was called back to complete the church. In so doing he made considerable modifications in Borromini's design, reducing the height of the lantern and giving it eight columns instead of sixteen and taking away all the fantasy of Borromini's towers, which are recorded in a drawing (Hempel, pl. 90).

Preimesberger ('Bernini a S. Agnese in Agone') has shown that the completion of the church was not entirely due to Rainaldi. Camillo Pamphili died in May 1666 and control of the building was taken over by his widow Donna Olimpia. She appointed G. M. Baratta to supervise the architecture and in November added Cardinal Decio Azzolini to the commission who called in Bernini (his name appears in December). Bernini at once ordered work on the façade to be stopped and produced a new design for it. This involved abandoning Borromini's compound pediment which rose from the attic and replacing it by a straight pediment set against the attic. Above it was to be the coat of arms of Innocent X, supported by angels, and there were to be statues on the attic. Of all these features only two were carried out: the coat of arms and the statue of *S. Eugenia* by Andrea Baratta (1669; Garms, p. 68, document 253). In the interior Bernini made one important alteration: he removed those parts of the attic which ran over the niches on the main piers, thus enlarging the space for the pendentives, and he then caused the commission to fresco them to be given to his protégé Baciccio, and quite possibly supplied the iconographical programme – and perhaps even sketches – for them.

In the summer of 1668, however, the young Giambattista Pamphili, son of Camillo and Donna Olympia, came back to Rome after a tour abroad, took control and changed all his mother's plans. According to Preimesberger (who does not unfortunately quote the documents) he replaced Bernini by Cortona and his pupil, Ciro Ferri. Ferri began frescoing the dome in 1670.

Innocent X intended to erect his own tomb in the church. In one of Borromini's plans for the church made in 1653 he shows it at the end of the right transept in a semi-circular bay cut off from the church by four columns of green marble, with behind it a door leading to the adjacent college. In 1656 or 1657 – about the time that Rainaldi took over – it was decided to place the tomb in the left transept and to convert the right transept into a chapel in honour of St Agnes. While Borromini was in charge of the sculptor of the tomb was designated as Bernini's rival Algardi and on his death in 1654 the commission was passed on to his pupils, Domenico Guidi and Ercole Ferrata. In 1667 Bernini, who had just taken over control of the building, began to make his own plans for the tomb, with which two drawings at Windsor can be connected. The work was however not even begun, and in 1698 it was decided to put the tomb over the entrance door, set against a small oratory. The latter was constructed by Valvassori and the sculptured figures on the tomb were carved by G. B. Maini (finished in 1729).

The interior of the church was decorated under Rainaldi's (and for a short time Bernini's) direction by a series of sculptors and painters whose work almost completely destroyed the character of Borromini's interior by the richness of the gilding and the carved and coloured marbling and the luxuriance of the frescoes, but it is still possible to grasp the significance of the changes which Borromini made in the design of the piers by widening them through the addition of columns and thus giving them a monumentality which they would have lacked in Rainaldi's version.

INTERIOR

The dome showing the *Assumption* was frescoed by Ciro Ferri (begun 1670 and finished after his death in 1689 by his pupil Sebastiano Corbellini, 'non mezzanamente, ma male', according to Pascoli (*Vite*, I, p. 173)). The pendentives, representing *Justice, Peace and Truth, Faith and Charity, Temperance* and *Prudence*, were painted by the young Baciccio (1662–72; Enggass, *Baciccio*, pp. 9, 140).

In the half-domes over the altars on the piers of the dome are reliefs of angels, carrying the symbols of the saints to whom the altars are dedicated, executed by Ercole Ferrata after the designs of Ferri.

Over the central entrance door: Tomb of Innocent X (see above); figures of the pope and *Spiritual* and *Temporal Power* by G. B. Maini (finished 1729); Ferrari, *La Tomba*, pl. CLVI).
1 to R: Altar of S. Alessio by Giovanni Francesco Rossi (1660–3)
2 to R: Altar of S. Agnese, designed by Rainaldi in 1654; altered 1657–8; dedicated 1664; statue of the saint (1660) and the angels above (1660–2) by Ferrata.
Summer Sacristy: Built 1658 from Borromini's designs. A rectangular room with the corners cut off by curves, but here they are convex as opposed to the concave corners of Re Magi and S. Maria dei Sette Dolori. Vault frescoed by Paolo Gismondi, *St Agnes in Glory* (c.1664; W).
3 to R: Altar of S. Emerentia; relief by Ferrata (begun 1660).
High Altar: Ancient columns of *verde antico* bought by the pope in 1658; relief of the *Holy Family with St John* by D. Guidi (c.1683); angels and glory by Maini and F. Moderati (1721; Enggass, *Sculpture*, p. 177).
3 to L: Altar of S. Cecilia; relief by A. Raggi (1662–6; R. H. Westin, 'A. Raggi's Death of St Cecilia', *Art Bulletin*, LVI, 1974, p. 422); putti in half-dome by E. Ferrata (1670).
2 to L: Altar of *St Sebastian*; statue of the saint by P. P. Campi (1719; Enggass, *Sculpture*, p. 180).
1 to L: Altar of *St Eustace*; relief begun by Melchiorre Cafà (d.1667), finished by Ferrata. See plate 102.

S. Agostino
Via di S. Agostino

Bibliography: Titi, 1763, p. 400; A. Ronci, *S. Agostino in Campo Marzio*, Rome, n.d.; G. Urban, 'Die Kirchenbaukunst des Quattrocento in Rom', *Römisches Jahrbuch*, IX/X, 1964, p. 274; M. Breccia Fratedocchi, *S. Agostino in Roma, arte storia documenti*, Rome, 1980.

The site was given to the Augustinian Hermits in 1286 and a church was begun in the following year. It was rebuilt in 1483 by the French Cardinal d'Estouteville. The masons were Jacopo da Pietrasanta and Sebastiano Fiorentino. Vasari attributes the design to Baccio Pontelli, probably wrongly. The church was redecorated in 1747 by Vanvitelli who added the Sacristy. Restored 1856.

INTERIOR

On entrance wall: Jacopo Sansovino, *Madonna del Parto*.
On third pier left of nave: above, Raphael, *Isaiah* (1512); below: Andrea Sansovino, *Madonna and Child with St Anne* (1512). This group was moved by Vanvitelli to the third chapel left but in 1981 the niche was reopened and restored and the group replaced in its original position below the Raphael.

The two angels holding the holy waterstoups are by Cosimo Fanzago (*Raphael*, 1651; *Gabriel*, 1660). A third smaller angel in the left aisle is also attributed to him (A. Nava Cellini, 'Un documento Romano per Cosimo Fanzago', *Paragone*, 105, 1958, p. 17).

Right aisle
3 to R: Decorated by G. B. Contini; altarpiece, G. Brandi, *S. Rita da Cascia* (W); frescoes by P. Locatelli.
4 to R: Apse fresco: G. Vasconio, *Assumption*; over altar: G. B. Cassignola, group of *Christ giving the Keys to St Peter*, which originally stood in a niche in one of the nave piers.
Beside door to Sacristy: Tomb of Cardinal Enrico Noris (d.1704) by F. Maratta (Enggass, *Sculpture*, p. 116).
Sacristy: By Vanvitelli; altar: Romanelli (possibly copy after), *St Thomas of Villanova* (W).
Right transept: Altarpiece by Guercino, *Sts Augustine, John and Jerome* (1637-8); on walls scenes from the life of *St Augustine* by Lanfranco (W).
On the left wall: Tomb of Cardinal Giuseppe Renato Imperiali (d.1737) by Paolo Posi, statues by Pietro Bracci. The tomb executed in 1741 (De'Rossi, *Architettura Civile*, II, pl. 52; Magni, I, pl. 57; Gradara, *Bracci*, p. 103; Ferrari, *La Tomba*, pl. CLXVI).
Chapel to right of High Altar: *S. Nicola da Tolentino:* Vault frescoes by G. B. Ricci and A. Lilio; altarpiece by Tommaso Salini.
High Altar: By Orazio Torriani (1628). The two angels by Giuliano Finelli after Bernini's design; the first work of Bernini to be executed entirely by studio assistants (Wittkower, *Bernini*, p. 191).
Over doors in choir: Pairs of putti, those on the right by Bracci (Gradara, *Bracci*, p. 24), those on the left by Pincellotti.
Second chapel to left of High Altar: *Buongiovanni* (Sts Augustine and William): On walls and vault paintings by Lanfranco of scenes from the lives of the two saints (between 1616 and 1623; W; Gloton, pl. XIX).
Over the entrance to the chapel: Tomb of Cardinal Lorenzo Imperiali by Domenico Guidi (c.1673).
Left transept: (Pamphili Chapel) *Cappella di S. Tommaso di Villanova*: Decorated 1660-9 by G. M. Baratta (De' Rossi, *Architettura Civile*, II, pl. 15; Eimer, *S. Agnese*, II, fig. 277). The figure of St Thomas was begun by Melchiorre Cafà but the whole group was finished after his death in 1667 by Ercole Ferrata who also executed the angels and God the Father over the pediment. Reliefs on the side by Andrea Bergondi (R. Preimesberger and M. Weil, 'The Pamphili Chapel in S. Agostino', *Römisches Jahrbuch*, XV, 1975, p. 183).
Left wall: Monument to Giuseppe Eusanio by C. Rusconi (Enggass, *Sculpture*, p. 98).
5 to L: G. Brandi, *St John of Sahagun* (before 1674; W).
4 to L: *Marliani*: Altarpiece: Girolamo Muziano, *S. Apollonia*; walls and vault frescoes by Francesco Rosa.
3 to L: Altarpiece: Sebastiano Conca, *S. Chiara da Montefalco* (Voss, p. 622).
2 to L: *Cappella Pio:* Designed by Bernini (1643-9). Vault fresco by Abbatini (W); tombs in the manner of Bolgi (Nava Cellini, *Paragone*, XIII, 147, p. 29). The altar originally had an *Assumption* by Giacinto Gimignani which was removed by Vanvitelli and replaced by Andrea Sansovino's *Madonna and Child with St Anne* (Fagiolo dell' Arco, *Bernini*, cat. 92; Lavin, *Bernini*, pp. 54, 193).
1 to L: *Cavaletti*: Caravaggio, *Madonna dei Pellegrini* or *Madonna di Loreto* (1603-5; Kitson, p. 99).

The cloister and the vestibule which originally opened on via della Scrofa (now accessible from the via dei Portoghese) are by Vanvitelli (1746-56; Vasi, *Magnificenze*, pl. 123; Magni, II, pl. 101 and Pane in De Fusco *et al.*, *Luigi Vanvitelli*, Rome, 1973, p. 62, and A. Schiavo, 'L'Opera di L. Vanvitelli nel convento e nella chiesa di S. Agostino in Roma', *Studi Romani*, XXII, 1974, p. 316). On the staircase is a statue of Benedict XIV by G. B. Maini (1750). In the ex-refectory, leading out of the vestibule on the via della Scrofa, is a fresco of the *Feeding of the Five Thousand* by Gregorio Guglielmi.

SS. Alessio e Bonifazio all'Aventino
Via S. Sabina

Bibliography: Titi, 1674, p. 66; Letarouilly, pl. 150 (266); L. Zambarelli (Chiese di Roma, 9).

The foundation of the church probably goes back to the fourth century. It was originally dedicated to St Boniface but the name of S. Alessio was added by Honorius III in 1217. In 1426 it was given by Martin V to the Hieronymite Hermits. At the end of the 16th century it was in a dangerous condition and was restored in 1582. In 1750 it was completely remodelled by Tommaso de' Marchis who preserved the original plan of the church, including the atrium but left nothing of the mediaeval building visible except the campanile.

In the vestibule is a stucco statue of Benedict XIII (dated 1756).

INTERIOR
Right aisle: Tomb of Eleonora Buoncampagni, wife of Giovanni Battista Borghese, Principe di Sulmona (d.1695). This was moved here in 1936 from the church of S. Lucia dei Ginnasi which was demolished when the via delle Botteghe Oscure was widened in 1935. The tomb was originally set up in 1702–3 to the design of G. B. Contini, the figure sculpture being by Andrea Fucigna (Hager, 'Il monumento alla Principessa Eleonora Borghese di G. B. Contini e A. Fucigna', *Commentari*, XX, 1964, p. 109).
Right transept: Ciborium by D. Ferrerio.
High Altar: 1582–1603.
Chapel to left of choir: Built by Carlo Murena (1763); monument to Cardinal Guidi del Bagno by Domenico Guidi.
Left aisle: J. F. de Troy, *S. Girolamo Emiliani*.
1 to L: (Lavagnino, *Altari*, p. 209): Marble group showing St Alexis lying dead under the staircase under which he lived for seventeen years; attributed to Andrea Bergondi.

S. Ambrogio della Massima
Via S. Ambrogio

Bibliography: Totti, p. 175; Mola, p. 89; Hibbard, *Maderno*, p. 138.

Now attached to a Benedictine congregation, the church was rebuilt in 1606, probably from the designs of Maderno, though the dome was built by Orazio Torriani. It has suffered much from heavy restoration in the 19th century. It still contains, however, some good 17th-century altars, though most of the original paintings have been removed. In the pendentives of the dome are four *Virtues* by Francesco Cozza (W).
2 to R: Marble statue of *St Benedict* by Orfeo Boselli after a stucco model by François Duquesnoy (Boselli, *Osservazioni della scultura antica*, ed. P. Dent Weil, Florence, 1978, f. 144v).
High Altar: By G. P. Morandi (with modern painting).

S. Anastasia
Via di S. Teodoro

Bibliography: Totti, p. 154; Martinelli, p. 14; Mola, pp. 81, 182; Falda, *Nuovo teatro*, III, p. 28; De'Rossi, *Architettura Civile*, III, pl. 43; G. M. Crescimbeni, *L'Istoria della Basilica di S. Anastasia*, Rome, 1722; F. Cappello, *Brevi Notizie . . . di S. Anastasia di Roma*, Rome, 1722; Titi, 1763, p. 78; Pollak, I, p. 20; Ferrari, *Lo Stucco*, pl. CXLVI; Mallory, *Notizie*, p. 103; Portoghesi, *Roma Barocca*, pl. 411; *Guide Rionali*, X, 4, p. 30.

A church stood on the site probably since the 4th century but was rebuilt from 1606 onwards at the expense of Cardinal Sandoval y Royas. The façade, which is of extreme severity, was constructed in 1636 after the portico was destroyed by a cyclone in 1634. It bears the arms of Urban VIII. Martinelli ascribes the façade to Luigi Arigucci, but Titi, Cappello and Crescimbeni say it is by Domenico Castello (payments are recorded to both). Mola attributes it in one passage to Arigucci and in another to Castello.

INTERIOR
Restored by Cardinal Nuñez da Cuña in 1722 to the design of Carlo Gimachi, a Maltese amateur architect (Titi, 1763). In ceiling: Michelangelo Cerruti, *Martyrdom of S. Anastasia*.
1 to R: P. F. Mola, *The Baptist* (Cocke, *Mola*, p. 60, No. 54).
Right transept: F. Trevisani, *S. Toribio* (W).
Chapel to right of choir: L. Baldi, scenes from lives of *S. Carlo Borromeo* and *S. Filippo Neri* (W).

3. *S. Anastasia*. Engraving by Falda, datable 1667–9, the inscription to which includes the attribution of the façade to Bernini, a legend which was preserved in many later guide-books.

Choir: L. Baldi, frescoes on vault and behind High Altar, *Adoration of the Shepherds* (W).

The High Altar was remade by Borromini with the ciborium set against a semi-circular colonnade, but his work was replaced by the existing structure in 1696. Beneath it is the marble figure of S. Anastasia, begun by Francesco Aprile and finished after his death by Ercole Ferrata (d.1686; Donati, *Artisti ticinesi*, fig. 426). Tombs of the members of the Febei family by Tommaso Ripoli set up in 1684 (Cartari-Febei).

Chapel to left of choir: F. Chiari, *The Burial of S. Anastasia*.

Left transept: L. Baldi, *Madonna of the Rosary* (W).

S. Andrea delle Fratte
Via Capo le Case

Bibliography: Falda, *Nuovo teatro*, I, pl. 9; Letarouilly pl. 142 (265); Magni, I, pl. 59; M. d'Onofrio (Chiese di Roma, 116); Hempel, *Borromini*, pp. 167ff.; J. Zänker, 'S. Dorotea in Rom und verwandte Kirchenbauten', *Architectura*, IV, 1974, p. 165; F. A. Salvagnini, *La Basilica di S. Andrea delle Fratte*, Rome, 1967; Portoghesi, *Borromini*, pls 178–89; id, *Roma Barocca*, pls 161–8; Blunt, *Borromini*, p. 195.

A church dedicated to St Andrew with an Augustinian convent attached existed on the site by 1370. It then passed to the Scottish community but after the Reformation was given to the Confraternita del SS. Sacramento, who still reside in it. The church became a parish in 1584 and in 1585 was given by Sixtus V to the Minims. The rebuilding was begun in 1604 (Hibbard, *Licenze*, p. 100) on the designs of Gaspare Guerra but was interrupted owing to lack of funds in 1609. In 1612 the Marchese Ottavio del Bufalo, whose palace stood nearby, promised a large gift but died the next year when only a small part had been paid. In 1622 Guerra died when only the nave was finished. About 1653 the Marchese Paolo del Bufalo supplied further funds and Borromini was commissioned to complete the church. The campanile and the dome were finished by 1665 (when they appear in the engraving in Falda) but the projected lantern was never carried out. It seems probable that Borromini followed Guerra's designs in the plan of the transepts and choir, but the exterior of the dome and the campanile are entirely from his designs (drawing in the Albertina, Hempel, p. 169, fig. 61).

Borromini had several ancient models in mind when he was designing these features. The 'drum' which actually encloses the cupola, according to a system common in Lombardy since Bramante's dome of S. Maria delle Grazie, Milan, but rare in Rome, is close in its general configuration to the ancient tomb near Capua called *La Conocchia* (reproduced Blunt, *Borromini*, p. 78, fig. 26) though Borromini introduced an extra curve into the central section. The circular columnar section of the campanile is close to ancient works such as the choragic monument of Lysicrates in Athens. Though Borromini is unlikely to have known this, similar monuments are to be seen in Roman reliefs (Blunt, op. cit., p. 46, fig. 37). By contrast the top section is constructed of piers faced with the type of cherubim of which Borromini was so fond (cf. the Lateran and the niche on the façade of S. Carlino). There was to have been a lantern over the dome, which would have made the dome dominate the campanile in height as well as in bulk. In view of the roughness of the brickwork (particularly in the capitals) it is likely that Borromini intended to cover the dome with stucco.

The lower part of the façade dates from the period when Guerra was in charge, but the upper storey was built in 1826, probably according to his designs, owing to a bequest to the church from Cardinal Ercole Consalvi.

INTERIOR (entirely decorated with painted marbling)

Entrance wall (right): Tombs of Livia del Grillo (d.1746) and her daughter (d.1750) by Francesco Queirolo (1752).

1 to R: *Baptistery*: Altarpiece of the *Baptism* by L. Gimignani (1683; W).

2 to R: *S. Carlo Borromeo and S. Francesca Romana*: Altarpiece: *St. Michael* by L. Gimignani; frescoes by Cozza (*Vision of S. Francesca and S. Carlo during the Plague*; W).

3 to R: *S. Francesco di Sales e Beata Giovanna de Valois*: Altarpiece: *Saint François de Sales*, by Marcantonio Romoli; left wall: tomb of Cardinal Carafa by Paolo Posi.

Right transept: *Cappella di S. Francesco di Paola*: Altar by F. Barigioni (1726–36); altarpiece by Paris Nogari; putti with cross and perhaps also angels supporting the painting by G. B. Maini.

The dome and apse were frescoed by P. A. Marini, c.1700 (D' Onofrio wrongly ascribes the pendentives to Cozza). The subjects are the *Redemption*, the *Multiplication of Loaves and Fishes*, and the *Fathers of the Church*.

Ante-Sacristy: Cozza's altarpiece from the chapel of SS. Francesca Romana and Carlo Borromeo hangs here. Tombs of Monsignor Giuseppe Baviera (d.1756) and Monsignor Domenico Tomati (d.1711).

Chapel beyond Ante-Sacristy: (G. Odazzi, *S. Francesco di Paola* (c.1723; W).

Sacristy: On ceiling Giacomo Fuga, *S. Francesco di Paola*.

To right and left of the choir are the two angels carved by Bernini himself for the Ponte S. Angelo (1667–9, Wittkower, *Bernini*, p. 248; M. S. Weil, *The History and Decoration of the Ponte S. Angelo*, Pennsylvania State University Press, 1974, p. 46 and pls 45–51).

Apse: Right wall: G. B. Lenardi, *Burial of St Andrew*; over altar: L. Baldi, *Martyrdom of St Andrew*; left wall: Francesco Trevisani, *St Andrew tied to the Cross*.

Left transept: *St Anne*: Design of the chapel is attributed, on not very certain grounds, to Luigi Vanvitelli, though the chapel was not finished till the early 19th century (De Fusco and others, *Luigi Vanvitelli*, 1973, figs 195–9). Below the *mensa* is a recumbent statue of St Anne variously attributed to Camillo Pacetti and Giovanni Battista Maini. Neither attribution is certain, but it is an interesting variant on Bernini's *Blessed Ludovica Albertoni* in S. Francesco a Ripa.

4 to L: *S. Giuseppe*: Cozza, *St Joseph and the Christ Child* (1632; W).

2 to L: *Accoromboni*: On the walls of the chapel are marble portrait medallions of four members of the Accoromboni family, all of whom died in the 1620s or '30s. The medallions hang on white marble ribbons against a surface of Sicilian jasper and are in many ways reminiscent of the Spada Chapel in S. Girolamo della Carità and even more so of some of the unexecuted drawings for this and other Spada chapels, published by Portoghesi (*Borromini nella cultura europea*, figs 284ff.) and Heimbürger Ravalli (*Archivio Spada*, p. 75, figs 60ff.). The connection with the Spada designs is confirmed by the fact that the altar in the chapel was made by Giovanni Somazzi, called Il Moretto, a *maestro scarpellino* whose name occurs frequently as working for the Spada (Heimbürger Ravalli, pp. 48, 68, etc.), particularly in connection with the decoration of the chapel in S. Girolamo (ibid., p. 82). Portoghesi tentatively ascribes the Accoromboni chapel to Borromini, but now that it is generally recognized that the Spada chapel was not designed by him the basis for the attribution collapses. Whether Virgilio Spada or his brother Orazio, who seems to be responsible for the design, had a hand in the Accoromboni chapel is not clear, but it seems fairly certain that the decoration was carried out by Somazzi. The vault fresco is sometimes attributed to Guglielmo Cortese, but is not listed by Waterhouse.

Against entrance wall: tomb of Cardinal Carlo Leopoldo Calcagnini (d.1746) by P. Bracci (1748; Gradara, *Bracci*, p. 55).

CONVENT

The Doric cloister has an attractive garden and provides a good view of Borromini's dome. The frescoed lunettes illustrate scenes from the life of S. Francesco di Paola (some wrongly ascribed

to Cozza). On the second floor is a gallery with frescoes by Francesco Borgognone (brother of Guglielmo and Giacomo) and Christian Meder (between 1685 and 1729).
See plate 100.

S. Andrea al Quirinale
Via del Quirinale

Bibliography: Falda, *Nuovo teatro*, III, pl. 13; Tessin, p. 161, pls 83, 84; De'Rossi, *Architettura Civile*, I, pl. 107 and II, pl. 4; De Brosses, II, p. 310; Titi, 1763, p. 302; Magni, I, pls 53–4; Franco Borsi, *La Chiesa di S. Andrea al Quirinale*, Rome, 1967; Portoghesi, *Roma Barocca*, pls 62–9; Eimer, *S. Agnese*, II, figs 271–3.

In his biography of his father, Domenico Bernini tells us that the architect regarded this as one of his most successful works and that in his old age he sometimes came to sit here and enjoy it; and we may well endorse his judgment. Its plan is simple but original in having the short axis of the oval leading to the altar; its architecture is pure and conceived in almost unbroken surfaces of delicately coloured marble; and it contains one of the most brilliant examples of Bernini's device of carrying the action through the whole building: the martyrdom of the saint is depicted in the painting over the High Altar, he appears again in the round, rising to heaven, over the opening to the chancel, while the heavenly host awaits him round the base of the lantern, at the top of which hovers the dove of the Holy Ghost.

The Jesuit Noviciate was founded in 1566 on a site on the south side of what was then called the via Pia (via del Quirinale) opposite the garden of the Quirinal, and in 1658 Alexander VII approved an offer by Prince Camillo Pamphili, nephew of Innocent X, to build a new church. The commission was given to Bernini, and the church was completed by 1661.

The old church was at the north-west corner of the site but for the new one a site at the north-east was chosen. Eimer (*S. Agnese*, I, p. 328) has published a plan for the church based on a pentagon which may be the first design presented, but the attribution of the drawing which he published (pl. 271) to Bernini is open to doubt.

The site which was enclosed by the existing buildings was long and shallow which led Bernini to use an unusual plan consisting of an oval with the short axis leading from the door to the High Altar. From the Diary of Alexander VII (entries 226, 235, 238, 241, 331) we learn that Bernini discussed his plans with the pope on August 9, September 2, 1658 and August 8, 1659, and that on September 9, 1658 the architect submitted a model for the church. The entry (235) for September 2 refers to the fact that the church had been moved back in the new plan, which seems to imply that it may originally have been planned to stand right on the street.

In the first version the church was enclosed in a court separated from the road by a wall in which were two small gates, near the two ends. The basic features of the design were already established: there were to be four chapels on each side of the church, leaving a solid instead of a void, at each end of the long axis, but all the chapels as well as the chancel and the entrance bay were to be of uniform trapezoidal shape (with the outer wall curved) and there was to be no lantern. There is no elevation drawing of the façade but it is clear from the plan that it was to be flat and articulated with pilasters.

INTERIOR

On the floor is the inlaid marble tomb of Cardinal Sforza Pallavicini (d.1667). The stuccoes on the vault (1662–3) and the figure of St Andrew over the opening to the chancel are by Antonio Raggi. The Pamphili arms with two figures of Fame over the entrance door and the stuccoes in the dome over the High Altar are by Giovanni Rinaldi.

2 to R: *St Francis Xavier:* Baciccio: altar: *Death of St Francis Xavier* (1676); on walls: *St Francis Xavier Preaching and Baptizing* (1705–9; Enggass, *Baciccio*, pp. 25, 141).

3 to R: (Passion): G. Brandi, *Scenes from the Passion* (1675–82; W).

High Altar (Lavagnino, *Altari*, p. 89): Guglielmo Cortese, *Crucifixion of St Andrew* (1668) and fresco of *God the Father* in dome (W). The

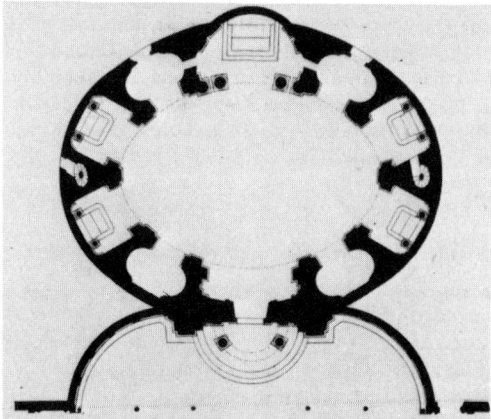

4. *S. Andrea al Quirinale. Plan.*

5. *S. Andrea al Quirinale. Engraving by Falda, showing the original form of the steps. On the right is the Manica Lunga of the Quirinal. In the distance the Piazza di Monte Cavallo with the horse-tamers, before the obelisk was set up by Pius VI. The buildings between S. Andrea and the Piazza were destroyed in the 18th and 19th centuries. Over them appears the belvedere of the Palazzo Rospigliosi-Pallavicini.*

tabernacle was made in 1697 and paid for out of a bequest from the General of the Order, Padre Oliva.

3 to L: *St Stanislas Kostka*: Altar: C. Maratta, *St Stanislas Kostka* (1679–87; W); wall frescoes by L. Mazzanti; vault by Giovanni Odazzi (W).

2 to L: *St Ignatius*: Giuseppe Chiari, fresco on vault of angels making music (after 1712; W).

Sacristy: Vault frescoed by Jean Delaborde (1669–70); Gloton, pl. LII).

In the Noviciate itself (access through the Sacristy) are the rooms lived in by St Stanislas. On the walls are water-colours (perhaps cartoons for tapestries) by Andrea Pozzo of scenes from the saint's life, and in the cell is the statue by Pierre Legros (1703) of the saint lying on his death bed, one of the most remarkable examples of Baroque illusionism in coloured marbles (Enggass, *Sculpture*, p. 138).

S. Andrea della Valle
Corso Vittorio Emanuele

Bibliography: Falda, *Nuovo teatro*, I, pl. 25; De' Rossi, *Prospectus*, pls 41–4; De'Rossi, *Architettura Civile*, III, pl. 38; De Brosses, II, p. 115; Magni, I, pls 20, 21; Hibbard, *Maderno*, p. 146; S. Ortolani (Chiese di Roma, 4); K. Schwager, 'Giacomo della Portas Herkunft und Anfänge in Rom', *Römisches Jahrbuch*, XV, 1975, p. 122; *Guide Rionali*, VIII, p. 72.

The design of this church, in spite of being the result of a series of compromises between the projects of different architects, each supported by his particular patron, is remarkably harmonious. On the other hand the decoration records the profound differences which existed within the arts in the first half of the 17th century, and Lanfranco's fresco in the dome – the first fully illusionist treatment of a dome to be painted in the 17th century – was a direct challenge to the classical principles illustrated by Domenichino's decoration of the vault of the choir, and was seen as such by contemporary critics (cf. below). Unfortunately the vault of the nave never received its intended decoration and the frescoes added in the early 20th century do not harmonize with either the purity of Domenichino or the Baroque exuberance of Lanfranco. It is not known how the architects involved in the original design of the church intended to treat the apse, but it is almost certain that there would have been a monumental marble altar enclosing a painted altarpiece. The existing arrangement with frescoes by Mattia Preti and his pupils between the pilasters bears some resemblance to a formula often adopted in the late 17th and early 18th centuries (cf. SS. Apostoli) though rarely quite so completely denuded of architecture, but in this case it was almost certainly dictated by lack of funds.

The Theatine Order, founded by S. Gaetano Thiene and confirmed by Paul III in 1540, was

S. Andrea della Valle

established at S. Silvestro al Quirinale in 1557. In 1586 the Order took possession of the Palace given to it by Donna Costanza Piccolomini on the site of the present church, and began planning a large church to the design of the Neapolitan architect Fabrizio Grimaldi. In 1588–9 Cardinal Alfonso Gesualdo offered to supply funds for the church but commissioned his architect, Giacomo della Porta, to make the plans. In the end Grimaldi was appointed architect, but his plans were subject to revision by della Porta. The old parish church of S. Sebastiano which stood on the site had to be pulled down (the parish was transferred to S. Susanna). The foundation stone of the new church was laid in 1591. The nave and first four chapels were constructed (1591–9) at first under the supervision of Francesco da Volterra (d.1594/5). In 1599–1600 a competition was held for the design of the façade but work had to be stopped for lack of funds. Gesualdo died in 1603 and his estate was not settled till 1605. In 1608 Cardinal Alessandro Peretti (Montalto), nephew of Sixtus V, agreed to complete the church and appointed Maderno as architect in charge. The nave was finished in 1621.

The problem of the façade is as complicated as that of the design of the church. It was begun in Maderno's lifetime and the plan of the lower storey must therefore be his. The design was, however, altered when it was being built, but critics are not agreed about the shares of Rainaldi and Fontana in the final form. Fasolo (*Rainaldi*, p. 243) emphasizes Rainaldi's share, but Noehles in his review of Fasolo (Noehles, *Fasolo*, p. 175) calls attention to the differences between Rainaldi's design of 1662 and the façade as built and attributes them to Fontana who was in charge in 1663. However Rainaldi was much the senior, and the character of the façade as it stands today is more in conformity with his style than with Fontana's.

The sculptures on the façade are by Ercole Ferrata (the angel standing on the lower storey where one would expect a volute, *St Andrew*, *The Blessed Andrew Avellino* and four putti), Domenico Guidi (*St Sebastian* and *St Gaetano of Thiene*), Cosimo Fancelli (*Hope* and *Prudence*) and were made according to the directions of Rainaldi (1664–6).

INTERIOR

The interior was heavily restored in 1905 when the pilasters were fluted and gilded, the angels in the spandrels added, the frieze and the vault of the nave decorated, and a new pavement was laid.

The vault of the choir was decorated (1624–8) by Domenichino, who executed the frescoes and designed the stuccoes, which were carried out by Jacques Sarrazin. The frescoes represent scenes from the life of *St Andrew* above and allegorical figures below (Voss, pp. 204, 510;

6. S. Andrea della Valle. Etching by Piranesi. In the distance on the left is faintly indicated the dome of S. Carlo ai Catinari.

Borea, *Domenichino*, p. 183). Drawings for the whole decoration are at Windsor (J. Pope-Hennessy, *The Drawings of Domenichino at Windsor Castle*, London, 1948, p. 73, Nos 752–4 and A. Blunt, *Supplement to the Catalogues of Italian Drawings at Windsor Castle*, London, 1971, p. 78, No. 160). The four Evangelists in the pendentives of the dome are also by Domenichino, but the dome itself was frescoed by Lanfranco in 1625–8.

Lanfranco's fresco in the dome, which is strongly influenced by Correggio's domes of the cathedral and S. Giovanni at Parma, is one of the earliest manifestations of the full Roman Baroque in ceiling painting and was seen as a novelty which shocked the conservative party but was vigorously defended by others (N. Turner, 'Ferrante Carlo's Descrizione della Cupola di S. Andrea della Valle', *Storia dell'Arte*, 12, 1971, p. 297, and A. Blunt, 'Gianlorenzo Bernini: Illusionism and Mysticism', *Art History*, I, 1978, p. 73).

In 1614 the tombs of the two Piccolomini popes, Pius II (1458–64) and Pius III (1503) were moved here from St Peter's – presumably to commemorate the fact that the church was built on the site of a palace given by Donna Costanza Piccolomini – and were built into the last piers of the nave, next to the crossing.

1 to R: *Cappella Ginetti* (De' Rossi, *Altari*, pls 38, 39; Magni, I, pl. 22; Donati, *Artisti ticinesi*, figs 382–7, 392, 393; Ferrari, *La Tomba*, pl. CLXXVIII): Begun in 1671 as the result of a bequest from Cardinal Marzio Ginetti on the designs of Carlo Fontana; opened in 1676 (Cartari-Febei) and consecrated in 1684. The statues of the Cardinal (left) and of *Fame* in the lunette and the relief over the altar (*Flight into Egypt*) are by Antonio Raggi. The statue of Cardinal Giovanni Francesco Ginetti (d.1691) on the right is by Alessandro Rondone. The tomb is first mentioned by Titi in 1721 (p. 137) but was probably set up before the end of the 17th century. The chapel is magnificently lined with marble, which even covers the dome and the pendentives, the earliest example of this practice introduced by Fontana (see also S. Maria del Popolo, Cappella Cybò).

2 to R: *Cappella Strozzi* (De' Rossi, *Altari*, pls 6, 7; Magni, I, pl. 25): This chapel is also richly marbled and contains bronze figures after statues by Michelangelo, cast in 1616, which is probably the date when the whole chapel was decorated.

Right transept: Lanfranco, *Vision of S. Andrea Avellino* (W).

Chapel to right of choir: *Confraternita del Divino Amore* (Crocifisso): Decorated in 1647

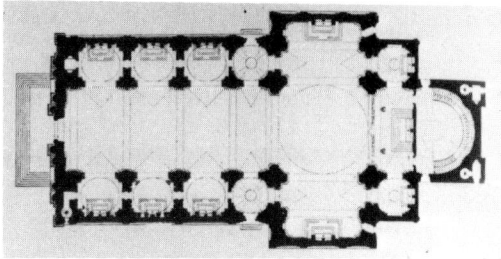

7. *S. Andrea della Valle. Plan.*

with fine black marble columns. According to Mola (p. 91) the altar, and therefore probably the whole chapel, are by Orazio Torriani.

Choir: Maderno planned a screen and High Altar to cut off the choir from the crossing (Hibbard, pl. 37a); but these were never built. The apse was frescoed in 1650–1 by Mattia Preti (W) with scenes from the life of *St Andrew*, and the decoration was completed with two frescoes on the side walls by Carlo Cignani (right) and Emilio Taruffi (left).

Left transept: Decorated 1764–70 by Mattia de Mare and Alessio d'Elia with scenes from the life of S. Gaetano (O. Michel, 'La Décoration de la chapelle de Saint Gaétan de Thiene à Sant'Andrea della Valle', *Regnum Dei*, 1972); the altar was erected in 1912.

4 to L: Tomb of Carlo Gaspare Thiene by Domenico Guidi.

2 to L: *Cappella Rucellai* (D'Onofrio, *Roma vista*, p. 677): Built 1603–5 by Matteo da Città di Castello (Martinelli, p. 19) for Orazio Rucellai; the angels are by Valsoldo.

1 to L: *Cappella Barberini* (Titi, 1686, p. 119; Magni, I, pl. 23; D' Onofrio, *Roma vista*, pp. 65, 145, 400): Begun in 1604 by Cardinal Maffeo Barberini, later Pope Urban VIII, in accordance with the will of his father, Francesco (d.1600), and consecrated in 1616. Attributed by Baglione (p. 178) and Martinelli (p. 19) to Matteo da Città di Castello, but according to Hibbard Maderno, and possibly even Ponzio, may have had a hand in the design. In 1612 Pietro Bernini made models for some putti which were carved by himself and his son, Gianlorenzo. The statue of *St Martha* is by Francesco Mochi, the *St John the Evangelist* by Ambrogio Buonvicino, and the *Magdalen* by Cristoforo Stati. Nicolas Cordier began a statue of *St John the Baptist* but did not complete it and the existing statue was carved by Pietro Bernini from a new block. The altarpiece (*Assumption*) and the vault frescoes are by Domenico Cresti, called Il Passignano.

In the little chapel of St Sebastian, attached to the Cappella Barberini, are statues of Carlo Barberini by Giuseppe Giorgetti (1665–7; Montagu, *Giorgetti*, p. 290) and Monsignor Francesco Barberini by Cristoforo Stati (Martinelli wrongly states that this statue is of Cardinal Antonio Barberini).

In the passage between the Barberini and the Rucellai chapels are medallions of Antonio Barberini and Camilla Barbadoa, parents of Urban VIII, by Tommaso Fedeli da Fossombrone (1627–9).

The monastic buildings to the left of the church were probably begun by Giuseppe Calcagni in 1602 and continued by Paolo Maruscelli after 1629 (Connors, *Oratory*, p. 108).

S. Andrea in via Flaminia

Bibliography: Baglione, p. 7; Falda, *Nuovo teatro*, III, pl. 37; Armellini, I, p. 231; Lotz, 'Die ovalen Kirchenraüme des Cinquecento', *Römisches Jahrbuch*, VII, 1955, p. 7; Ackerman-Lotz, p. 12; J. Coolidge, W. Lotz *et al.*, *La Vita e le Opere di Jacopo Barozzi da Vignola*, Vignola, 1974, figs 23–33.

Built 1550–3 by Vignola for Julius III as part of the scheme to develop the Valle Giulia and the area between it and the Tiber. The church is mentioned by Palladio (*Descritione de le Chiese di Roma*, Rome, 1554) but he does not name the author. The attribution goes back to Baglione.

This is the earliest surviving church built with an oval dome, though Peruzzi, a generation earlier, had left many designs for oval churches on paper. Vignola carried the idea a stage further in S. Anna dei Palafrenieri (see below) where the church itself is also oval.

S. Andrea in Vincis (destroyed)

Bibliography: Armellini, I, p. 683; M. J. Lewine, 'The Roman Church Interior 1527–1580' (Dissertation, Columbia University, 1960), p. 124.

The church stood in the old via di Tor de' Specchi, below the Capitol. A church stood on the site from the 15th century, but it was rebuilt in the 16th and again between 1735 and 1773. It was destroyed when the via del Mare was made in the 1930s but its façade is recorded in a photograph.

S. Andrea e Bartolomeo
Via S. Giovanni in Laterano

Bibliography: Guide Rionali, I, i, p. 96; G. Curcio, 'L'Ospedale di S. Giovanni in Laterano', *Storia dell'Arte*, 32, 1978, p. 23.

A small church attached to the Ospedale Lateranense (S. Salvatore), built in 1642 with a very simple front articulated by Ionic pilasters. The interior, which is in the shape of a trapezium, is of little interest, except for a fine 15th-century marble altar and floor.

Only open when funerals are taking place.

SS. Angeli Custodi (destroyed)

Bibliography: Armellini, II, p. 1246; G. Matthiae, 'Due chiesette romane del seicento', *Palladio*, V, 1941, p. 41.

Built on the via del Tritone for the Confraternity of the Angeli Custodi about 1675 to the design of Felice della Greca. The façade was by Mattia de' Rossi (before 1686) and the High Altar by Carlo Rainaldi (1681). Measured drawings and photographs are reproduced by Matthiae.

S. Angelo in Pescheria
Via del Portico d'Ottavia

Bibliography: Mola, p. 77; Titi, 1674, p. 96; Roisecco, 1745, I, p. 282; Buchowiecki, I, p. 384.

Founded in 770, and built into the ruins of the Portico of Octavia; restored in 1610, according to Mola by Giovanni Fontana, and again in 1700.

1 to R: G. B. Brughi, *St Lawrence*.

To the right is a small Oratory of the Pescivendoli or fish-sellers with a façade decorated with good 18th-century stucco work. It is secularized and in 1979 housed an antique shop. It contains the battered remains of frescoes by L. Baldi (1687; W) and some good stucco work of the same period.

S. Anna dei Bresciani. See SS. Faustino e Giovita (destroyed)

S. Anna dei Palafrenieri
Vatican City

Bibliography: M. Lewine, 'Vignola's Church of S. Anna dei Palafrenieri Rome', *Art Bulletin*, XLVII, 1965, p. 199; Lotz, *Die ovalen Kirchenräume*, p. 7; A. Cecinelli (Le Chiese di Roma, 110); J. Coolidge, W. Lotz *et al.*, *La Vita e le Opere di Jacopo Barozzi da Vignola*, Vignola, 1974, figs 86–91.

The church was built at the expense of the grooms (Palafrenieri) of the papal court. According to Vincenzo Danti in his life of Vignola prefixed to his edition of the latter's *Due Regole della Prospettiva Pratica* (Rome, 1583) the plans of the church were made by Vignola and put into execution by his son Giacinto. Probably begun about 1568 the church had reached the main cornice by 1576 when building ceased. The interior was altered in the 17th century when the door in the right wall was blocked and replaced by an altar. The upper part of the façade was added by A. Specchi between 1700 and 1725. The dome was built by Navone between 1744 and 1755.

The church marks a stage beyond S. Andrea in via Flaminia in the development of the oval ground plan. Here for the first time the plan of the church is oval, though it is enclosed in an outer rectangular shell. The interior is articulated with full columns set in niches and these are unequally spaced so that they form an alternation of wide and narrow bays. The exterior has Vignola's usual flat pilasters.

The interior was redecorated with painted marbling at the end of the 19th century. The frescoes by Ignazio Stern are negligible, and the Palafrenieri sold the only painting of importance that they ever owned, Caravaggio's *Madonna with St Anne*, which was paid for in April 1606 and sold to Cardinal Scipione Borghese in June of the same year.

Oratory of the SS. Annunziata (S. Spirito in Sassia)
Lungotevere Vaticano

Bibliography: Titi, 1763, p. 29; Venuti, 1767, p. 1223; Vasi, 1792, p. 597; Portoghesi, *Roma Barocca*, pls 422, 423; Elling, pl. 57.

The 1763 edition of Titi says that the Oratory was 'di nuovo rifabbricato', and a manuscript note in a copy in my possession adds 'col disegno di Pietro Passalacqua Siciliano'. These facts are confirmed by R. Venuti and Vasi. Passalacqua died in 1748, so Titi's use of the phrase 'di nuovo' suggests that the Oratory must be a late work. It was pulled down when the via della Conciliazione was laid out but was rebuilt, apparently exactly as it was, on a nearby site. In its general design the façade is close to that of S. Croce in Gerusalemme, which is, I believe, also due to Passalacqua.

The church has the form of a rectangle with rounded corners used by Borromini at the Re Magi and the Oratory.

SS. Annunziata a Tor de' Specchi
Via Teatro di Marcello

Bibliography: Guide Rionali, X, i, p. 54.

The church of the convent of Tor de' Specchi, founded in 1433 by Francesca Bussa di Leoni, later canonized as S. Francesca Romana (see the church of that name), was built at an uncertain date in the 17th century but was richly decorated as the result of a bequest received in 1668. The marbling shows some traces of the Neapolitan style introduced by Cosimo Fanzago in about 1650 (R. Bösel, 'Cosimo Fanzago a Roma', *Prospettiva*, 15, 1978, p. 37).

S. Antonio dei Portoghesi
Via dei Portoghesi

Bibliography: Mola, p. 63; Martinelli, p. 22; Rossi, 1697, p. 486; De' Rossi, *Architettura Civile*, III, pls 35–7; Magni, I, pls 13, 14; anon., *S. Antonio dei Portoghesi*, Rome, 1931; G. R. Ansaldi, 'La Fabbrica di S. Antonio dei Portoghesi a Roma', *Capitolium*, IX, 1933, p. 616; Pugliese-Rigano, *Lunghi*; Varriano, *Longhi*, p. 25.

The church was originally built under Eugenius IV in 1439–47 for the Portuguese colony in Rome but it was completely rebuilt in the 17th century. According to Mola the church was designed by Gaspare Guerra and the nave seems to have been finished before 1636, but the choir and transepts were only built much later. They were probably begun by Carlo Rainaldi who was in charge during the years 1674–6, though the work appears to have been completed by Cristoforo Schor who was in charge in 1686, when the choir and dome were still unfinished. The decoration of the interior was begun by 1692.

The most interesting feature of the church is the façade. The foundations were being laid in 1631 and it was described with admiration in 1636 and 1638 by the writers of two guide books, who ascribe it to Martino Longhi the Younger, an attribution which is confirmed by Martinelli and Mola. Work was, however, still being done on it in 1692, though this may have referred to sculpture only, since in that year the putto over the main door by Cristoforo Muti was paid for. De' Rossi says it was finished 'circa l'anno 1695'. There is reason to think that Longhi's design was followed in all essentials, and the façade can be regarded as in many ways a preparation for that of SS. Vincenzo e Anastasio, with which it has in common the unusual feature of winged cherubim instead of scrolls linking the two storeys.

INTERIOR

2 to R: *Cappella Cimini* (St John the Baptist) (Titi, 1686, p. 369): Designed by Cesare Corvara (1682–8). Altarpiece and lunettes by G. Calandrucci. Frescoes on walls by Ciccio Graziani and Nicolas Lorrain (*Scenes from the Life of the Baptist*). Tomb of G. B. Cimini (d.1683) often but wrongly attributed to Andrea Bolgi (Martinelli, 'Andrea Bolgi a Roma e Napoli', *Commentari*, X, 1959, p. 149).

Right transept: The altar is identical with that of the left transept, designed by Vanvitelli, but was apparently only set up in the last years of the 18th century. The commission for the altarpiece was given to Giuseppe Cades but when he died in 1799 he had only completed the *modello* for it. The actual altarpiece was executed by Luigi Agricola in 1801.

High Altar: Probably designed by C. Schor; altarpiece: Calandrucci, *Virgin and Child with St Anthony* (1687).

Left transept: Architecture designed in 1756 by L. Vanvitelli who had already left for Naples and was therefore assisted by Murena (A. Schiavo, *Archivio della Società Romana di Storia Patria*, XCV, 1972, p. 143 and J. Garms, *Römische historische Mitteilungen*, XVII, 1975, p. 187). Altarpiece: Zoboli, *Immaculata*, 1756 (Mallory, *Notizie*, p. 112). Tombs of members of the Sampaio family, said by Titi (1763, p. 400) to be by Pietro Bracci, but now shown to be by Filippo della Valle and to date from 1756 when this chapel was consecrated (Vernon Minor, 'Filippo della Valle's memoria to Sampaio: an attribution resolved', *Burlington Magazine*, CXVII, 1975, p. 659).

2 to L: Built in 1783 to the design of Francesco Navone.

S. Apollinare
Piazza S. Apollinare

Bibliography: Titi, 1763, p. 405; Vasi, *Magnificenze*, pl. 264; C. M. Mancini (Chiese di Roma, 93); Bianchi, *Fuga*, p. 75; Matthiae, *Fuga*, p. 79; Pane, *Fuga*, p. 104 and figs 84–97; Portoghesi, *Roma Barocca*, pls 430–3; Elling, pls 49, 52; Mallory, *Notizie*, 109ff.

The church was probably founded in the 7th century by Basilian monks. By 1284 a college of canons was attached to it. In 1574 the church and college were given by Gregory XIII to the German-Hungarian Jesuit College which held it till the Order was suppressed in 1775. In 1742 the foundation stone of the new church was laid by Benedict XIV who had promised to pay for the High Altar and the chancel. The architect was Ferdinando Fuga, some of whose drawings survive. The church was consecrated in 1748. The plan is unusual in having a large narthex for the use of the general public while the church itself could be cut off for the use of the college. The façade shows Fuga's rejection of the High Baroque style and his return to a flatter, more classical design. The outer bays end in curved blocks which were perhaps intended to support statues.

INTERIOR

The painting on the vault of the nave (the *Glory of S. Apollinare*) is by Stefano Pozzo (1746; Poensgen, fig. 47).

1 to R: Altarpiece: Lodovico Mazzanti, *S. Luigi Gonzaga*.

2 to R: Altarpiece: Giacomo Zoboli, *Holy Family* (1747).

3 to R: Statue of *St Francis Xavier* by Pierre Legros (1701–2; Enggass, *Sculpture*, p. 137).

High Altar: A rich structure of marble columns with gilt bronze capitals, between which are marble panels cut to make a symmetrical pattern. Altarpiece: Ercole Graziani, *Consecration of S. Apollinare* (1748).

3 to L: (St Ignatius): C. Marchionni, statue of *St Ignatius*.

1 to L: Placido Costanzi, *St John Nepomuk* (1742).

In the College attached to the church is a ceiling fresco by an imitator of A. Pozzo of the *Coronation of the Virgin*.

S. Apollonia (destroyed)

Bibliography: Titi, 1686, p. 35; Roisecco, 1750, I, p. 181; Vasi, *Magnificenze*, pl. 154; Armellini, II, p. 852.

The church, which stood in Trastevere opposite S. Margherita, was built in 1582 and consecrated in 1585 for the Tertiary Franciscan nuns. Its rather simple façade is recorded in the engraving by Vasi.

SS. Apostoli
Piazza SS. Apostoli

Bibliography: De' Rossi, *Architettura Civile*, III, pls 17–19; Letarouilly, pls 167, 168 (271, 272); Magni, I, pls 71, 72; F. Santilli (Chiese di Roma, 15); E. Zocca, *La Basilica dei SS. Apostoli*, Rome, 1959.

The church was probably founded in the 6th century and was given to the Franciscans by Pius II in 1463. It was restored by many popes, including Sixtus IV who added the portico probably to the designs of Baccio Pontelli. The upper floor was closed by Carlo Rainaldi who added the windows (1681; Noehles, *Fasolo*, p. 176). In 1701 it was decided that the church was in such a dangerous condition that it could not be saved and Francesco Fontana, son of Carlo, was commissioned to rebuild it but on the death of Francesco in 1708 his father took over. He was assisted by Niccolò Michetti who replaced him in 1712. The church was consecrated in 1724.

INTERIOR
Most of the marbling is painted. The fresco on the vault of the nave, *Christ receiving the Saints of the Franciscan Order*, is by Baciccio (1707; Enggass, *Baciccio*, pp. 100, 147). The apse fresco by Odazzi shows the *Fall of the Rebel Angels* (1709; W).

On the inner side of the façade four allegorical statues by P. Legros, G. Napolino, P. Papaleo, P. Monnot (after 1705; Enggass, *Sculpture*, pp. 85, 141).

Right aisle: 2nd pier left: Monument to Clementina Sobieski, wife of the Old Pretender, by Filippo della Valle (1737).
1 to R: (St Bonaventura): N. Lapiccola: *The Virgin and Child adored by S. Bonaventura and S. Andrea Conti*.
2 to R: (Immaculate Conception): Built from 1718 onwards by Sebastiano Rambotti; decoration completed 1774; restored 1858.
3 to R: *Cappella Odescalchi*: By Ludovico Rusconi Sassi (Titi, 1763, p. 215; Donati, *Artisti ticinesi*, fig. 328); altarpiece by Luti, *St Anthony of Padua* (1722; W); dome frescoes by Giuseppe Nasini (1722; W).
Apse: This is one of the earliest examples of an apse being constructed without a full altar, the altar being only marked by the flanking pilasters of the main order.
High Altar: Muratori, *Martyrdom of Sts Philip and James* (1726; W). The *Confessio* was excavated and decorated between 1873 and 1886.
End of left aisle: Monument to Clement XIV by Canova (1789).
Sacristy: Vault: *Ascension* by Sebastiano Ricci (1701).
3 to L: *Colonna* (S. Francesco): G. Chiari, *St Francis* (1726; W). Monument to Cardinal Carlo Colonna (d.1753) by G. B. Grossi (Verner H. Minor, 'Della Valle and G. B. Grossi revisited', *Antologia di Belle Arti*, 1978, p. 234) and Maria Lucrezia Rospigliosi Salviati (d.1740) by Bernardino Ludovisi.
2nd pier on left of nave: Pulpit by Sebastiano Cipriani (1736; Buchowiecki, I, p. 656).
2 to L: G. Cades, *St Joseph of Copertino*.
1 to L: F. Manno, *Deposition*.
See plates 62, 64.

S. Atanasio dei Greci
Via del Babuino

Bibliography: Totti, p. 343; Baglione, p. 80; Martinelli, p. 23; Falda, *Nuovo teatro*, III, pl. 19; Titi, 1674, p. 415; De' Rossi, *Prospectus*, pl. 60; Roisecco, 1750, II, p. 148.

Built in 1577–81 for members of the Eastern church who had joined the Roman church, partly with the intention that they should foster the union of the Eastern and Western churches. Totti ascribes the church to Martino Longhi the Elder but all the other early authorities attribute it to Giacomo della Porta. Roisecco says that the church was built by della Porta, but that the façade was added by Martino Longhi the Elder. This church ranks with S. Maria dei Monti among the most harmonious works of Roman architecture of the last decades of the 16th century. The interior is disturbed by the iconostatis inserted in 1876.

The façade is unusual in having two flanking towers, a form unusual in Rome at this date (but cf. SS. Trinità dei Monti).

Bambino Gesù
Via Urbana

Bibliography: Matthiae, *Fuga*, p. 19; Pane, *Fuga*, p. 56 and figs 35, 38; L. Bianchi, *Fuga*, pp. 35, 77; Elling, pl. 50; Garms (Chiese di Roma, 135).

Founded in 1671 for the Congregazione delle Zitelle del Bambino Gesù, mainly owing to the devotion of a pious servant of the Serlupi family, Anna Moroni, with the help of padre Cosimo Berlinzani, *parocco* of S. Maria in Portico.

In the early years of the 18th century it was planned to build a convent and a new church, and about 1708 the architect Alessandro Specchi was asked to produce designs, which survive in drawings but were never executed owing to lack of funds. In 1731 Clement XII made a generous donation and work was begun on a more modest project produced by Carlo Buratti, who, however, died the next year and was replaced by Fuga. It is not clear how far Fuga modified Buratti's designs, but the façade is characteristic of his style. It originally had a double flight of steps leading up to it.

The most interesting features of the interior are the six doors – two in the vestibule and four in the main body of the church – which incorporate interesting variations on Borrominesque forms, suggesting the authorship of Fuga.
Altar to R: D. M. Muratori, *St Augustine* (W).
Altar to L: Giacomo Zoboli, *S. Andrea Corsini*.

S. Barbara dei Librai
Off via dei Giubbonari

Bibliography: Titi, 1686, p. 82; Roisecco, 1745, I, p. 398; *Architettura minora*, II, pl. 17; G. Morelli, *La Chiesa di S. Barbara de' Librai*, Rome, 1924; *Guide Rionali*, VI, 2, p. 164.

The church, now secularized, was restored between 1674 and 1686 by Giuseppe Passeri. Externally it has good stucco figures of angels who support a niche containing a travertine statue of the saint by A. Parisi. The interior is said by Titi to be 'abbellita di Pitture' – and Roisecco lists them – but it is now ruined (W).

S. Bartolomeo all' Isola
Piazza S. Bartolomeo all' Isola

Bibliography: Mola, p. 81; Martinelli, p. 25; Titi, 1674, p. 61 and 1763, p. 58; *Guide Rionali*, XII, 1, p. 30.

The church goes back at least to the late 10th century but was badly damaged by a flood in 1557. It was rebuilt from 1583 onwards to the design of Martino Longhi the Elder at the expense of Cardinal Giulio Antonio Santorio. Titi says that the façade is by Martino Longhi the Elder, but it cannot be of such an early date and Mola is almost certainly right in stating that it was erected by Orazio Torriani (according to Buchowiecki in 1624–5).

INTERIOR
Drastically restored in 1852–68. The wooden ceiling dates from 1624 but was altered in the 19th-century restoration, when the painted panels were added.
2 to R: *S. Carlo Borromeo*: Frescoes by Antonio Carracci, probably painted 1608–12, heavily restored in the 18th century (L. Salerno, 'L'Opera di Antonio Carracci', *Bollettino d'Arte*, XLI, 1956, p. 30).
To the right of High Altar: *Orsini Chapel*: Built 1601 and frescoed by G. B. Mercati with scenes from the life of the Virgin.
3 to L: Much restored frescoes by Antonio Carracci representing scenes from the Passion (Salerno, loc. cit).
2 to L: Frescoes by Antonio Carracci of scenes from the life of the Virgin (Salerno, loc. cit.).

SS. Bartolomeo e Alessandro dei Bergamaschi (S. Maria della Pietà)
Piazza Colonna

Bibliography: Ferrari, *Lo Stucco*, pl. CXLII; U. Vichi, *SS. Bartolomeo e Alessandro*, Rome, 1965; Fasolo, 'Disegni inediti di un architetto romano del settecento', *Palladio*, N.S., I, 1951, p. 186; Salerno, *Via del Corso*, p. 199; Mallory, *Rococo*, p. 114.

The Confraternity of the Bergamasques was founded in 1539 but was not transferred to the present site till the 17th century. In 1729 it was decided to rebuild it on a larger scale and Raguzzini submitted a design. On the death of Benedict XIII in the next year Raguzzini lost the commission. An unidentified architect, who may be Valvassori, submitted new designs for an oval church but this was in fact not built. The early 19th-century guides attribute the existing church to Carlo de Dominicis, but as in 1733 he was still working in Raguzzini's studio this is unlikely. It is however probable that he completed the façade, adding the door and the curved pediment.

As built the church consists of a simple rectangular nave with side chapels. It was restored in the 19th century, from which time presumably dates the painted marbling. The college attached to the church was built by Valvassori from 1730 onwards.
2 to L: Aureliano Milani, *Beheading of St John the Baptist*.

S. Basilio
Via S. Basilio

Bibliography: Titi, 1686, p. 305; Roisecco, 1750, II, p. 300; *Guide Rionali*, II, 1, p. 62.

Built by Innocent XI for the Greek Catholic (Basilian) monks of Grottaferrata. A simple façade (dated 1683) of two almost equal storeys. The interior, which was restored in 1962, is dominated by the inconostatis and little of the 17th-century decoration remains visible.

S. Bernardino ai Monti
Via Panisperna

Bibliography: O. Montenovesi, 'La Chiesa di San Bernardino in Roma', *Archivi d'Italia*, S.II, IX, 1942, p. 79; Salerno, 'S. Bernardino ai Monti', *Palatino*, S.III, IX, 1965, p. 128.

A small church erected on the foundations of an ancient Roman circular building, and consecrated in 1625. The church, which was almost derelict, was restored in 1965.

In 1658 Domenico Caroli, brother of one of the nuns, Maria Chiara, left money to build a High Altar. Two years later Maria Chiara decided to have one made to the designs of Bernini, incorporating some columns and coloured marble already prepared by Pietro Vitale, but nothing came of this scheme.

INTERIOR
Frescoed dome by B. Gagliardi, *S. Bernardino received into Heaven* (Gloton, pl. XXV).
l to R: Giovanni de'Vecchi, scenes from the life of St Francis.
Over door to R: Giovanni de'Vecchi, *St Helen and St James.*
Apse: Frescoes by Clemente Maioli (1663).
Over door to L: G. Baglione, *St Elizabeth of Hungary, St Anthony and (?) St Agatha.*

S. Bernardo alle Terme
Piazza S. Bernardo

Bibliography: S. Ortolani (Chiese di Roma, 8).

The church was constructed in 1598–1600 within one of the circular chambers (*torrioni*) of the Baths of Diocletian for the Reformed Cistercians (Feuillants) whose prior was the Frenchman, Jean de la Barrière. This particular *torrione* and the area round it had formed part of the famous *vigna* laid out from 1535 onwards by Cardinal Jean du Bellay, the friend of Rabelais and Philibert de l'Orme.

The 'façade' formed by the door and flanking niches is decorated with light plaster work in the style current in about 1600, but the blind oval panels round the 'drum' which enclose the actual dome seem to date from the restoration of c.1670. The ancient coffered dome survived almost intact, but is now covered with stucco, probably dating from the restoration carried out after the church was occupied by the French in 1803.

INTERIOR
The eight statues of saints in the niches are by C. Mariani and Francesco Mochi.
l to R: G. Odazzi, *St Bernard* (c.1718; W).
To right of Choir: Portrait of Jean de la Barrière (over his tomb), traditionally ascribed to Sacchi, but the attribution is rejected by Sutherland Harris (*Sacchi*, p. 110).
Chapel to right of Choir: Nobili: *Stigmatization of St Francis* over the altar and the busts of members of the Nobili family are by G. A. Fancelli. Fine *scagliola* altar front.
Choir: Saraceni, *Madonna di Loreto* (1600–5).
l to L: G. Odazzi, *Madonna and Saints* (c.1710; W).

S. Biagio in Campitelli. See S. Rita da Cascia.
Via Montanara

S. Biagio della Pagnotta
Via Giulia

Bibliography: Vasi, *Magnificenze*, pl. 71; Titi, 1763, p. 419; *Guide Rionali*, V, 4, p. 52.

A church stood on this site from very early times, and was to have been rebuilt as part of the Palazzo dei Tribunali planned by Bramante for Julius II. This project, however, was not carried out, but the church was given its present façade in the 18th century by G. A. Perfetti (c.1730). The interior was completely altered in the 19th century.

S. Biagio e S. Cecilia dei Materassai. See Madonna del Divino Amore
Vicolo del Divino Amore

S. Bibiana
Via Giolitti

Bibliography: Pollak, I, p. 22; Martinelli, p. 29; Falda, *Nuovo teatro*, III, pl. 23; De' Rossi, *Architettura Civile*, III, pl. 40; De Brosses, II, p. 319; Fagiolo dell' Arco, *Bernini*, Cat. 34, 35; Wittkower, *Bernini*, pl. 189; Briganti, *Cortona*, pp. 167ff.

The church was founded in the 5th century and restored in 1220. In March 1624 the remains of S. Bibiana, her parents and sister were discovered under the High Altar of the church and Urban VIII immediately decided on a restoration of the church which was carried out in the years 1624–6. Bernini was commissioned to add a portico and façade and to carve the statue of the saint for the High Altar (in collaboration with G. Finelli). Over the colonnade of the nave are frescoes of scenes from the life of S. Bibiana between which are single figures of her relations who were martyred with her. Those on the right wall are by Ciampelli, those on the left wall by Cortona. The altarpiece at the end of the right aisle is by Cortona (*St Dafrosa*), that in the left is by Ciampelli (*S. Demetria*).

The church is important as being one of the earliest ventures of both Bernini and Pietro da Cortona into work of this nature, and one of the rare examples of their collaboration (another is the *Salone* of the Palazzo Barberini). In his frescoes Cortona came close to evolving a fully

Baroque formula, but in the façade Bernini uses a curiously dry idiom. The general design with a three-bay portico below is based on the façade of S. Sebastiano by Ponzio and Vasanzio, and can be traced further to a kind of loggia frequently found in the 16th century in the Veneto, for instance in Sansovino's S. Spirito in Isola (now destroyed) and Trissino's Villa at Cricoli; but the actual arches, cut out of the wall as if with a razor, without any mouldings, recall Vignola's colonnade in the Villa Giulia. What is original is the treatment of the central bay of the upper storey, used for displaying relics on particular holy days, which breaks through the upper entablature and forms a prominent central feature; but this feature does not seem to have been completely integrated into the design and almost gives the impression of having been slipped down over the façade as an afterthought. Bernini used a somewhat similar arrangement, but with much greater success, at S. Andrea al Quirinale.

The architecture of the High Altar is so different from that of the façade that it is hard to believe that both can have been designed by the same artist at the same time. The façade is thin and papery, conceived in flat surfaces broken only by pilasters; the altar has full columns, an entablature with a convex frieze and a rich and rather heavy pediment. The evidence as regards date is, however, final, since it appears in an engraving of the altar in Fedini's life of S. Bibiana which was published in 1627, and it is hard to believe that Bernini would have allowed anyone else to design it (unless it was Borromini who was working as his assistant at St Peter's, but it bears no resemblance to his work). It is more like altars of the previous generation such as Maderno's in the Cappella Salviati in S. Gregorio Magno, that in the Cappella Silvia in the grounds of the same church and that round Annibale Carracci's *St Margaret* in S. Caterina dei Funari.

S. Bonaventura al Palatino
Via di S. Bonaventura

Bibliography: Titi, 1686, p. 183.

Built by Cardinal Francesco Barberini in 1675 for a body of Spanish Discalced Zoccolanti but transformed in a restoration of 1839.

INTERIOR

1 to R: G. B. Beinaschi, *Crucifixion* (soon after 1675; W).
2 to R: G. Calandrucci, *Madonna with Saints* (before 1686; W).

2 to L: G. B. Beinaschi, *Annunciation* (soon after 1675; W).
1 to L: G. B. Beinaschi, *St Michael* (soon after 1675; W).

S. Brigida
Piazza Farnese

Bibliography: Mola, p. 63; Titi, 1674, p. 122 and 1763, p. 116; Roisecco, 1750, I, p. 622; *Guide Rionali*, VII, 2, p. 86.

Built in the 15th century for the Swedish colony in Rome on the site of a house in which St Bridget lived till her death in 1375. Rebuilt in 1614 (according to Mola by Francesco Peparelli) and restored by Cardinal Francesco Albani (begun before he became Pope Clement XI in 1700), who added the façade and commissioned B. Puccini to fresco the interior. According to the *Guida Rionale* Vasi states that the architect was Pietro Patriarca, but I have not been able to find any such attribution in the various editions of Vasi's guide to Rome. A Pietro Giacomo Patriarca is recorded as working for Cardinal Francesco Barberini in the late 1670s. He may be the man in question, but, if so, he is more likely to have been the builder than the designer of the church.

INTERIOR
Fresco on nave vault by B. Puccini, *St Bridget in Glory* (with arms of Clement XI). Tomb of Nicolai Bielve (d.1765) erected in 1768 by Pietro Camporese the Elder and Tommaso Righi.

S. Caio (destroyed)

Bibliography: Baglione, p. 129; Titi, 1686, p. 268 and 1763, p. 299; Armellini, II, p. 1015; *Guide Rionali*, II, 1, p. 35.

Built in 1635 on the site of via Milano on the orders of Urban VIII by Vincenzo della Greca and Peparelli. Pulled down in the late 19th century; the façade is recorded in a medal reproduced in the *Guide Rionali*, and in an engraving reproduced by Armellini.

S. Calisto
Via di S. Cosimato

Bibliography: Totti, p. 62; G. Mano, *Relazione sui lavori di restauro della Chiesa di S. Calisto a Roma*, Rome, 1938.

In 1608 Paul V granted the church and the adjacent palace to a body of Benedictine monks and both were reconstructed by Orazio Torriani.

INTERIOR
Completely restored in 1854 and again in 1938.
1 to R: The altar is ascribed by Baldinucci to Bernini. Fagiolo dell' Arco (*Bernini*, No. 161) accepts the attribution, but it is rejected by Mano and implicitly by Wittkower who does not mention the work. The altarpiece, *S. Maurus*, is by P. L. Ghezzi.

Cappuccini. See S. Maria della Concezione
Via Vittorio Veneto

Oratorio del Caravita
Via del Caravita

Bibliography: Pollak, I, p. 243; Buchowiecki, I, p. 722.

Founded by the Spanish Jesuit Father Pietro Gravita (Caravita) and built between 1631 and 1633. The latter date is on the frieze of the lower storey of the façade, an example of the severe style still current in Rome at that time. The upper storey appears to date from the 18th century.

INTERIOR
L. Baldi's frescoes on the vault of the vestibule survive though much restored (W), but the Oratory itself was completely repainted between 1858 and 1875 and retains nothing of its 17th-century character except some stucco decoration in the apse. The altarpiece of the *Holy Trinity with St Francis Xavier* is by Sebastiano Conca.

S. Carlo ai Catinari
Piazza Cairoli

Bibliography: Mola, p. 102; Falda, *Nuovo teatro*, I, pl. 24; Martinelli, p. 31; De' Rossi, *Prospectus*, pl. 48; De' Rossi, *Architettura Civile*, III, pls 23, 24; Vasi, *Magnificenze*, pl. 136; Magni, I, pls 25, 28; S. Ortolani (Chiese di Roma, 18); *Guide Rionali*, VIII, 1, p. 11.

In 1574 the Barnabites, an Order founded in 1532 in Milan by S. Antonio Zaccaria, established a house in Rome, when the monks were granted the little church of S. Biagio all'Anello. In 1611 the foundation stone of the new church, dedicated to the recently canonized S. Carlo Borromeo, was laid (Gigli, p. 23). The architect was Rosato Rosati of Macerata, who soon afterwards left Rome to return to his native city. The nave was finished by 1620, but the transepts and choir were not begun till after 1627, when a bequest from Cardinal G. B. Leni, which came through his executor, Cardinal Scipione Borghese, made the completion of the church possible. The façade was begun in 1636 and the choir was finished in 1646. According to Mola, Rosati intended to have a longer choir.

The façade was designed by G. B. Soria, who was undoubtedly chosen by Borghese, his best patron. It is a variant of the type used by him for two other churches commissioned by the Cardinal (S. Gregorio Magno and S. Caterina da Siena a Magnanapoli).

INTERIOR
The pilasters of the main order are of yellow *scagliola*. The angles of the crossing piers are of panelled marble and the walls of the transepts painted.

Over the doors in the entrance wall are frescoes of the life of S. Carlo by Mattia Preti and his brother Gregorio.

The dome was to have been painted by G. G. Semenza, a pupil of Guido Reni, but Cardinal Scipione Borghese insisted that Domenichino should replace him, and he executed the four pendentive frescoes of the *Cardinal Virtues* (*c*.1630; Borea, *Domenichino*, p. 187). In the event the dome was decorated with stuccoes, and Martinelli states that these were designed by Domenichino. The stucco decoration of the vaults of nave, choir and transepts is probably also after his designs. Like his wooden ceiling in S. Cecilia these stuccoes are based on a design at the end of Serlio's fourth book.

1 to R: *Costaguti*: Decorated by Simone Costanzi (1698); altarpiece: Lanfranco, *Annunciation* (W).

Right transept: Altar by Carlo Rainaldi; altarpiece: Giacinto Brandi, *Martyrdom of Sts Blaise and Sebastian*, replacing one by Cerrini (after 1674; W).

Chapel to right of High Altar (S. Cecilia) (Ferrari, *Lo Stucco*, pls. LXXXIXff.; Lavagnino, *Altari*, p. 165; Portoghesi, *Roma Barocca*, pls 200, 262, 263): Architecture (1695–1700) by Antonio Gherardi who also painted the *S. Cecilia* over the altar (before 1692, that is to say before the chapel was built; W). One of the most original late Baroque chapels in Rome, it has a cut-off dome, on which sit splendid music-making angels, and which leads to a rectangular chamber, lit by concealed windows. Gherardi also designed the Cappella Avila in S. Maria in Trastevere.

Choir: Fresco in the half-dome of the apse, Lanfranco, *S. Carlo Borromeo in Glory* (his last work, 1646–7; Voss, p. 526).

High Altar: In 1637 Cardinal Giovanni Battista Colonna bequeathed four ancient porphyry columns to be used for the altar, and in 1639 the

S. Carlo al Corso

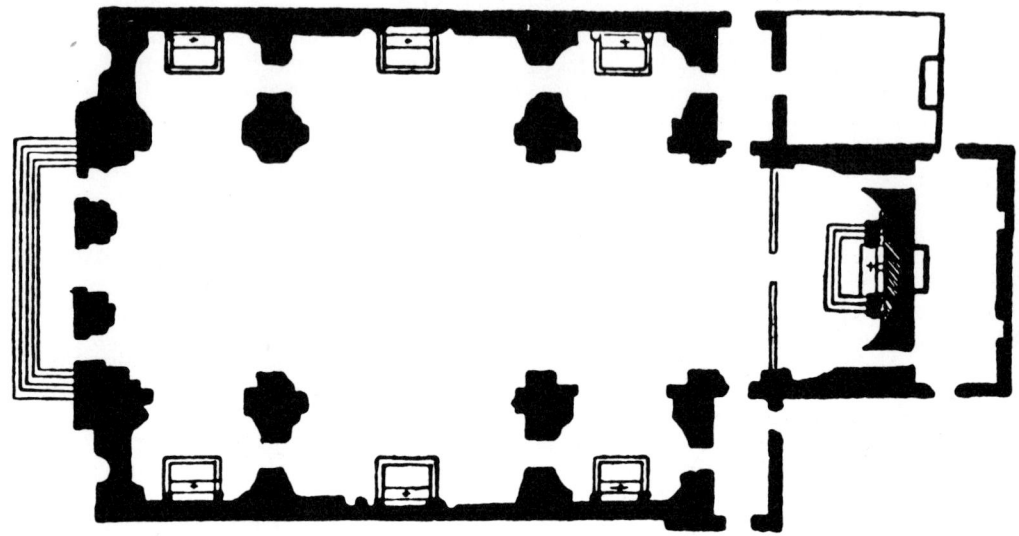

8. *S. Carlo ai Catinari. Plan.*

Contestabile Filippo Colonna bequeathed money for its construction, with the request that it should be designed by Girolamo Rainaldi, but as we know on the authority of Boselli, who carved the statues of the *Virtues* of Charity towards God and Charity towards one's neighbour over the altar after the designs of Martino Longhi the Younger, the actual altar was also designed by Longhi (Boselli, *Osservazioni della scultura antica*, ed. P. Dent Weil, Florence, 1978, ff. 61v., 80v., 156r.). Two altarpieces representing S. Carlo were painted in succession – by Gaspare Celio and Andrea Commodi – but neither was satisfactory, and the present altarpiece of *S. Carlo carrying the Holy Nail in Procession during the Plague* was painted by Cortona in 1667 (Briganti, *Cortona*, p. 268). The ciborium is by Simone Costanzi (1702). The two *cantorie* are by Carlo Fontana (1685).
Sacristy: Begun in 1640 (Eimer, *S. Agnese*, I, pp. 407, 409); fine marble *lavamano*, 1675; cupboards and holy water-stoups, 1690; bronze crucifix by Algardi, given c.1730 by Benedict XIII (Lavagnino, *Altari*, p. 35; Heimbürger Ravalli, *Algardi*, p. 160).
In passage behind High Altar leading from Sacristy to monastic buildings: Reni, *S. Carlo in Prayer* (originally on the inside of the façade) and Commodi's painting of *S. Carlo* originally on the High Altar.
2 to L: *Cappella Filonardi:* Built 1636 by Maruscelli and dedicated to the four Persian martyrs, Sts Marius, Martha, Habakkuk and Andofax. The altarpiece representing them is by Romanelli (now on side wall). The frescoes in the lunettes on the side walls are by Giacinto Gimignani (1641; W).
Left transept: A. Sacchi, the *Death of St Anne* (1648–9; W).
1 to L: *Cappella Cavallerini* (St Paul): Architecture by Mauro Fontana (1739–40); dome and wall frescoes by F. Mondelli (1746; Donati, *Artisti ticinesi*, fig. 324).
Former refectory: Giacinto Gimignani, *The Supper at Emmaus* (U. Verena Fischer, *G. Gimignani* (Dissertation, Freiburg, 1973), p. 182).

S. Carlo al Corso. See SS. Carlo e Ambrogio al Corso

S. Carlo alle Quattro Fontane
Via del Quirinale

Bibliography: Falda, *Nuovo teatro*, III, pl. 12; De' Rossi, *Architettura Civile*, I, pl. 101 and II, pls 18–26; De Brosses, II, p. 310; Magni, I, pls 60–2; Pollak, I, p. 36; Hempel, *Borromini*, pp. 32ff.; L. Steinberg, *S. Carlo alle Quattro Fontane*, New York, 1977; Portoghesi, *Borromini*, pls I–XXIX, 15–33, 204–13; Blunt, review of Portoghesi, *Burlington Magazine*, 1971, pp. 670ff.; C. P. Ridolfi, *S. Carlo alle Quattro Fontane*, Rome, n.d.; Blunt, *Borromini*, p. 52.

In 1611–12 the Discalced Spanish Trinitarians, whose function was to collect money to buy the freedom of Christians captured by the Moors, bought a small plot of ground on the south-west corner of the crossroads of the Quattro Fontane where Strada Pia met Strada Felice. The monks

S. Carlo alle Quattro Fontane

at first received some financial help from Cardinal Francesco Barberini, whose palace lay opposite, but he lost interest. Later they received help from the will of Pietro Soderini, and the Spanish Ambassador, the Marquis of Castelrodrigo, but he was recalled in 1660, and the building was not finished till after 1682 (when the accounts finish).

The commission to design the church and monastery was given to Borromini in 1634. He first built the cloister and monastic buildings behind it, but he must also have made a plan for the church at the same time, though he did not actually begin building it till 1637 when the cloister was finished. The drawings show that the cloister was conceived from the beginning almost exactly as it was executed, and they record only very small variations; but those for the façade of the monastic buildings facing the garden prove that Borromini tried out a number of projects. This façade was much altered in the 18th and 19th centuries when further blocks of monastic buildings were put up round the garden. For the latter Borromini made several projects which were never carried out.

The history of the church has been bedevilled by the fact that the generally reliable Hempel suppressed the most important drawings for it

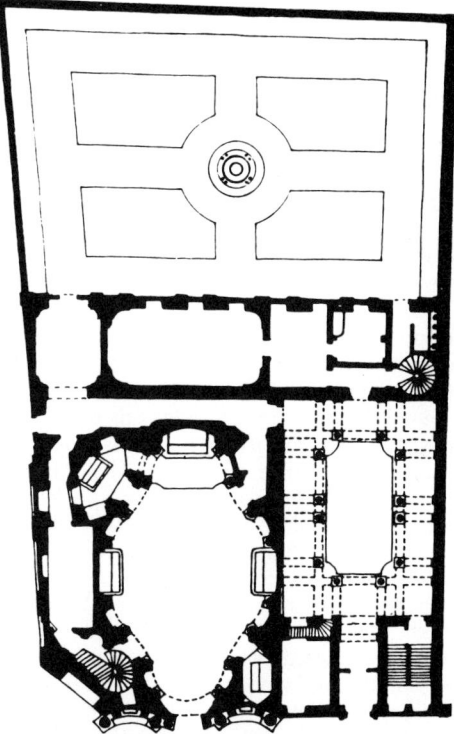

9. *S. Carlo alle Quattro Fontane. Plan.*

10. *S. Carlo alle Quattro Fontane. Engraving by Falda. On the extreme left is the Palazzo Albani (Mattei, Nerli). Next to the conventual buildings of S. Carlo is the small convent of SS. Giovacchino e Anna. Further on is the church of S. Andrea al Quirinale. Two of the four fountains at the crossroads are visible, that on the right being set in the Palazzo Galoppi, here shown before its restoration in the early 18th century.*

and published as studies for it four drawings (his figs 6–9) which, as has been shown by Steinberg, are certainly not for S. Carlino (they would not fit on the site) and are probably by Borromini's nephew, Bernardo Castello.

The four preparatory drawings (Albertina 171, 173, 175, 186; Portoghesi, figs VIII, IX, X, XII), though difficult to read owing to the degree to which they were reworked by the architect, show that originally he planned a church, abutting on the Strada Felice edge of the site, with two rectangular bays for the altar and the entrance and two semi-circular bays on the cross-axis. At a later stage, he moved the whole church some twenty feet to the west and flattened the bays on the cross-axis to parts of ovals and so was able to insert a sacristy between the church and the Strada Felice. The drawings also show that he was experimenting with designs for the façade as he developed the plan for the church, and it can be shown that he had reached the double S-curve on which it is actually based before he made the final plan for the church itself. It is therefore certain that, although the façade was not begun till 1665, it was planned in the 1630s and was not, as has often been said, a creation of Borromini's last years. At the time of his death only the lower storey was built and the upper part was completed by his nephew, almost certainly not according to his design, since it includes one motif – the oval painting supported by angels – which is taken directly from Bernini's altars at Castelgandolfo and in the Fonseca chapel in S. Lorenzo in Lucina. The statue of *S. Carlo Borromeo* over the door is by Raggi, those of *S. Giovanni de Matha* and *S. Felice di Valois*, the founders of the Order, by Sillano Sillani (1682), and the angels supporting the fresco are by G. C. Dono and F. A. Fontana (1676). The painting itself is by P. Giarguzzi. The capitals of the lower order were carved by Lorenzo Dini (1666). The stags' heads are by Simone Giorgi. The façade with the entrance to the cloister was executed in the very last years of Borromini's life. The original campanile was pulled down and replaced by the existing one by Bernardo Castello. The original campanile can be seen in a drawing by Lieven Cruyl (reproduced in plate 94).

S. Carlino with its monastic buildings, was Borromini's first independent commission, but it contains many of the essential features of his later and more mature works. The general plan makes brilliant use of a limited site of irregular shape; the cloister, at first sight simple and straightforward, is in fact extremely subtle in its variations on traditional forms; internally the church shows Borromini's inventiveness in the designing of a ground-plan and in the treatment of space with combinations of curves, convex and concave, with straight lines, and of a complete oval with parts of ovals covered by coffered part-domes of unusual flattened forms, the whole giving the effect of movement for which his architecture is famous. Externally this movement is even more apparent in the double S-curve of the plan of the façade, the stepped cupola and the re-entrant bays which enclose the lantern. It is characteristic of Borromini's style that the interior of the church should be decorated entirely in white stucco with only a few touches of gilding. The monk who wrote the history of the church soon after Borromini's death comments on the architect's ability to reduce the cost of the building without diminishing its beauty or its practical efficiency, and also on the care with which he guided all the individual craftsmen involved in the building. The beauty and consistency of the detail confirms his testimony.

INTERIOR

The statues in the niches are modern. The High Altar, by Pierre Mignard, represents S. Carlo Borromeo and the two founders of the Order praying to the Holy Trinity.

Chapel to left of High Altar: *Riposo* by Romanelli (1642; W).

The two side altars were given new paintings in the mid-19th century. The originals by Cerrini, *St Ursula* and the *Holy Family*, hang in the passage leading to the monastery.

The old sacristy is of little interest, but the present Sacristy (originally the refectory) has an unusual form with rounded corners. It is probable that the stucco decoration of the central field was added when the room was transformed into a sacristy. It contains the portrait of *S. Carlo Borromeo* by Orazio Borgianni, originally over the High Altar of the church (Nicolson, p. 25).

The lower church follows the upper one in plan, but it is much lower. The walls are flat and only articulated with pilaster bands, and the ridges of the vault are entirely without mouldings with the result that the space is even more sharply defined than in the upper church. To the left of the altar is a chapel, which Borromini may have intended as his own funerary chapel. It is small but contains some of Borromini's most beautiful play with curved surfaces and undulating architraves.

See plate 94.

SS. Carlo e Ambrogio al Corso
Via del Corso

Bibliography: *Prospectus*, pls 50–2; De' Rossi, *Architettura Civile*, III, pl. 27; Vasi, *Magnificenze*, pl. 140; Letarouilly, pls. 222 (286); Magni, I, pls 28, 81–5; G. Drago, L. Salerno (Chiese di Roma, 96); Salerno, *Via del Corso*, p. 146; J. L. Varriano, *The Roman ecclesiastical architecture of Martino Longhi the Younger* (Dissertation, University of Michigan, 1970); Buchowiecki, I, p. 312.

12. *SS. Carlo e Ambrogio al Corso. Engraving after a medal showing Onorio Longhi's original design for the façade.*

Built by the confraternity of the Lombards on the site of an earlier church dedicated to St Nicholas, which had been granted to them in the 15th century by Sixtus IV, and which had been replaced in 1513 by one dedicated to St Ambrose, patron saint of Milan. On the canonization of S. Carlo Borromeo in 1610 the confraternity decided to build a new and larger church of which the foundation stone was laid in 1612 and to the construction of which a large contribution was made by Cardinal Paolo Emilio Sfondrati, nephew of Gregory XIII and the restorer of S. Cecilia. The architect was Onorio Longhi and the church was continued after his death in 1619 by other architects, including his son Martino the Younger and Francesco Contini, who modified his design. His plan was of a mediaeval type very rare in Rome, a three-aisled church with side chapels, an ambulatory round the choir and transepts which did not project beyond the line of the chapels. In 1665 a panel of architects including Borromini and Pietro da Cortona were asked to examine the crossing piers and in 1668, after some strengthening had been carried out, the latter was commissioned to build the dome which, externally, is one of the most harmonious in Rome. In 1682–4 the façade was built, unhappily on the designs of the new benefactor of the church, Cardinal Luigi Omodei, who fancied himself as an amateur architect. The result was the present clumsy structure. Carlo Bizzacheri made a design for it, preserved in a drawing, but it was presumably rejected (Mallory, *Rococo*, p. 44; id., *Bizzacheri*, pp. 38, 45). Longhi's original design for the church is preserved in a medal struck by Paul V in 1612 and engraved in Claude du Molinet, *Historia summorum pontificum*, Paris, 1679, pl. 28, No. XIII. In his text (p. 148) du Molinet explicitly connects the medal with the church 'in via quae vulgò Cursus dicitur'. It seems fairly clear that Omodei knew this design and imitated it to the extent of using Longhi's general

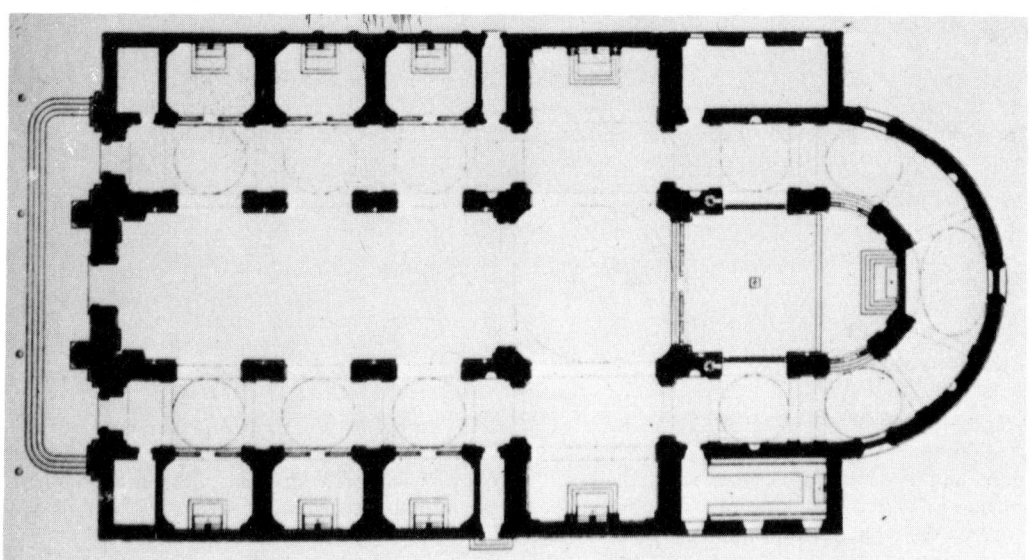

11. *SS. Carlo e Ambrogio. Plan.*

pattern with a colossal order enclosing two storeys of equal width, though he replaced Longhi's attic with the existing heavy pediment covering the whole width of the façade, introduced three doors instead of one, and abolished the high pedestals shown in Longhi's design which would have taken away the heaviness of the columns.

INTERIOR

The nave is vast but curiously inhuman. The effect of the whole is seriously affected by the very coarse painted marbling which probably dates from the 19th century. The vaults of nave, choir and transepts are decorated with fine gold and white stuccoes by G. A. and C. Fancelli after the designs of Cortona, probably modified by Ciro Ferri in the forms of the coffering (Ferrari, *Lo Stucco*, pls CXXVff.). They enclose a fresco of the *Fall of the Rebel Angels* by Brandi (Poensgen, fig. 30), who also decorated the apse (*St Charles among the plague-stricken*), the vault of the choir (*St Charles in Glory*), and the pendentives of the dome (*Prophets*). This work was unveiled in 1677 (Cartari-Febei). Reliefs of angels at the crossing are by C. Fancelli.

The inscriptions over the arches of the nave and the choir refer explicitly to the Old and New Dispensations and suggest that the church was conceived to represent the advance from the one to the other. This idea is rare in Roman churches but can be paralleled in a group of 18th-century Neapolitan churches (Blunt, 'The Temple of Solomon with special reference to South Italian Baroque Art', *Kunsthistorische Forschungen. Otto Pächt zu seinem 70 Geburtstag*, Salzburg, 1972, p. 258).

The vaults of the aisles and the ambulatory were decorated from 1677 onwards with a series of frescoes, representing various virtues, by L. Gimignani, G. Chiari, Garzi, Beinaschi, Troppa, and others, enclosed in stucco frames in the manner of Ciro Ferri. The statues in the aisles and ambulatory are attributed to F. Cavallini.

1 to R: right wall: Francesco Rosa, *Vision of St Henry* (before 1674; W); left wall: Morazzone, *Sts Ambrose and Charles*; wooden crucifix in the manner of Algardi (late 17th or early 18th century).
Right transept: Altar: 1769 with mosaic copy of Maratta's altarpiece in the Cappella Cybò in S. Maria del Popolo; statues of *Judith* by Pietro Pacilli and *David* by A. J. Lebrun.
High Altar: The original structure was by C. Fancelli and F. Cavallini (1677) but was replaced later; the painting (*Sts Ambrose and Charles in Glory*) by Maratta (1685–90).

Left transept: Altar built in 1929, as an exact copy of the right transept. The altarpiece by Tommaso Luini representing *God the Father adored by Angels* (1627–32) was originally designed for the High Altar and then stood over the altar of the right transept.
2 to L: Francesco Rosa, *S. Filippo Neri in Ecstasy* (before 1674; W).
1 to L: P. F. Mola, *St Barnabas preaching* (after 1652; Cocke, *Mola*, p. 60, No. 33).
Sacristy: Busts of Cardinals Ferdinando d' Adda and Luigi Omodei (d.1707) by A. Cornacchini (Enggass, *Sculpture*, p. 200); fine *lavamano* with dolphins (18th century).

To the left of the church is a building containing the premises of the Confraternity of S. Ambrogio which is attached to the church. Its cloister has windows and memorial tablets which are purely Cortonesque in style, but since they are dated 1679, that is to say ten years after Cortona's death, it is to be supposed that they were designed by Ferri. The door to the buildings of the Confraternity on the street to the left may well also be by him.

S. Caterina dei Funari
Via dei Funari

Bibliography: De' Rossi, *Prospectus*, pl. 67; Giovannoni, *Saggi sull'Architettura del Rinascimento*, 2nd ed., Milan, 1935, p. 179; Buchowiecki, I, p. 502.

The mediaeval church was given by Paul III in 1536 to Ignatius of Loyola who established here a house for poor girls run by himself in company with Gaetano da Thiene, Filippo Neri and Cardinals Federico Cesi and Gian Pietro Carafa (later Paul IV). The church was rebuilt in 1560–4. The traditional attribution is to Giacomo della Porta, but Giovannoni discovered the name of the real architect, Guidetto Guidetti, and the date 1564 on the frieze of the lower order of the façade. Guidetti is presumably also responsible for the belfry.

INTERIOR

(Accessible on the vigil and the feast of St Catherine, 24 and 25 November.)

This is one of the few Roman churches of its date to have survived without the addition of Baroque decoration and with its simple architecture and white walls gives a clear impression of what many of the late 16th-century churches (including the Gesù) and oratories originally looked like.
1 to R: Annibale Carracci (after?), *St Margaret* (c.1598; Posner, *Annibale Carracci*, London, 1971, p. 46).

S. Caterina della Rota
Piazza della Rota

Bibliography: Vasi, *Magnificenze*, pl. 111; Buchowiecki, I, p. 509; Salerno, *Via Giulia*, p. 444; Wasserman, *Mascarino*, p. 49; Elling, pl. 42; *Guide Rionali*, VII, 12, p. 46.

A church stood on the site since the 12th century, but it was replaced in the late 16th century by the present one almost certainly designed by Ottaviano Mascarino. The façade, which is in the lively style of the early 18th century, is first recorded in an engraving of 1756 by Vasi.
Nave: Fine carved and gilt wood ceiling with the arms of Sixtus V, moved here from the demolished church of S. Francesco a Ponte Sisto.

On the side wall to the right of the entrance G. Muziano, fresco of the *Rest on the Flight into Egypt*.
1 to L: G. A. Galli, called Lo Spadarino, *S. Valeria after her Decapitation*.

S. Caterina da Siena
Via Giulia, 163

Bibliography: Portoghesi, *Roma Barocca*, pl. 424; G. Zandri, 'Documenti per S. Caterina da Siena in via Giulia', *Commentari*, XXII, 1971, p. 415; Salerno, *Via Giulia*, p. 241; *Guide Rionali*, VII, 3, p. 36.

Originally built under Leo X for the Sienese colony, but rebuilt in 1766–70 by Paolo Posi. The façade is one of the latest Roman examples of a firmly curved concave design, which was at the time being superseded by flatter, more classical forms.

INTERIOR
1 to R: S. Monosilio, *St Bernard preaching* (1768).
2 to R: N. Lapiccola, *B. Bernardo Tolomei* (1769).
Apse: Fresco by Laurent Pécheux, *The Return of Gregory XI from Avignon* (1772).
High Altar: G. Lapis, *Marriage of St Catherine* (1768–9).
2 to L: Tommaso Conca, *Assumption* (1768–9; Voss, p. 622).
1 to L: D. Corvi, *The Fire in the Borgo* (1769; Voss, p. 664); tomb of Paolo Posi (d.1778) with bust by his pupil Giuseppe Palazzi.

Oval scenes from the life of St Catherine by Lapis (choir), P. Angeletti and E. Parrocel (nave), 1768–9. Feigned stucco decoration by T. Kuntz and G. B. Marchetti.

S. Caterina da Siena a Magnanapoli
Piazza Magnanapoli

Bibliography: Totti, p. 498; Mola, p. 94; Falda, *Nuovo teatro*, I, pl. 12 and III, pl. 16; Titi, 1674, p. 313 and 1763, p. 275; De' Rossi, *Architettura Civile*, III, pls 8–10; Magni, I, pls 102, 103; Lavagnino, *Altari*, pp. 29, 135; Buchowiecki, I, p. 515.

In 1563 Porzia Massimo (*née* Colonna) gave money to build a convent for the nuns of the Tertiary Franciscan Order, founded by St Catherine of Siena, who had previously been housed in the convent of the Minerva. The church was begun in 1620 to the designs of an unknown architect (Hibbard, *Licenze*, p. 101). According to Mola, G. B. Soria built the façade and 'parte della chiesa'. The choir was finished in 1631 and the church was consecrated in 1640. The façade probably dates from after 1638 (Hibbard, loc. cit.). The cutting of the via 24 Maggio and via 4 Novembre in the late 19th century involved lowering the level of the Piazza Magnanapoli and necessitated the construction of the steps leading up to the church. In the portico are stucco statues of *St Catherine* and *St Dominic* by G. F. Rossi.

INTERIOR
Over entrance fine nuns' choir and beside it two *coretti*.

Titi (1686, p. 250) records a series of early 17th-century altarpieces which were replaced in the late 17th and early 18th centuries by more up-to-date paintings. The choir was decorated before 1667 and the whole church was marbled with Sicilian jasper, probably in the late 17th century. The nave vault was frescoed by Luigi Garzi, *Glory of St Catherine* (before 1713; W).
1 to R: Benedetto Luti, *Communion of the Magdalen* (before 1721; W).
2 to R: Luigi Garzi, *Triumph of St Catherine* (probably after 1713; W).
3 to R: Decoration by Filippo Vasconi; altarpiece: Biagio Puccini, *St Dominic* (c.1720; W).
Over doors to sacristy and convent: Giuseppe Passeri, *Scenes from the life of St Catherine* (W); tombs of Giuseppe Bonanni (d.1648) and his wife Virginia (d.1650) by G. Finelli.
Choir: High Altar: Black marble columns, relief by Melchiorre Cafà of the *Ecstasy of St Catherine* (Titi, 1674, p. 314). The reliefs on either side were added by Pietro Bracci in 1755 (Titi, 1763, p. 480, and Gradara, *Bracci*, p. 107). Gilt bronze ciborium with lapis lazuli columns (1766). In lantern fresco of *God the Father* by F. Rosa (W).
3 to L: G. Passeri, *Madonna del Rosario* (W).
2 to L: Decorated by Giovanni Paolo Schor;

altarpiece: Fabio della Cornia, *Three Archangels*.
1 to L: Pietro Nelli, *St Nicholas*.
If shut apply at the Ordinariato militare (Chaplains to the Forces) d'Italia, 37 Salita del Grillo. See plate 16.

S. Cecilia
Via dei Vascellari

Bibliography: Vasi, *Magnificenze*, pl. 145; G. Matthiae (Chiese di Roma, 113) and *Fuga*, p. 78; Pane, *Fuga*, p. 98 and figs 74–6; Portoghesi, *Roma Barocca*, pl. 414.

Founded before the 5th century on the site of St Cecilia's house and restored by Paschal I (817–24); the portico and campanile added in the 12th century. In 1589 the body of the saint was discovered intact by Cardinal Paolo Emilio Sfondrati, nephew of Gregory XIV. This event led to a restoration of the church and to the commissioning of the statue of the saint from Stefano Maderno. In the early 18th century a further restoration of the interior was undertaken for Cardinal Francesco Acquaviva, whose name appears on the frieze of the portico, by Domenico Paradisi and Luigi Berettoni, who also remodelled the upper part of the façade. The vault was frescoed by S. Conca with a *Coronation of St Cecilia* in 1723–4 (Mallory, *Notizie*, p. 103; Voss, p. 620; Poensgen, fig. 40). In 1741–2 another member of the Acquaviva family, Cardinal Troiano, commissioned F. Fuga to build the façade on the street. Over the central arch are the arms of the cardinal, carved by Agostino Corsini.

In 1822 a survey of the church, ordered by Cardinal Giorgio Doria, showed that the columns of the nave were seriously out of the vertical and that the building was in danger of collapsing. As a result the architect F. Salvi was instructed to carry out a drastic restoration which involved enclosing the ancient columns in a series of piers betweeen round and flat headed openings (E. Bentivoglio, 'I progetti del XIX secolo per S. Cecilia', *Quaderni*, XVII-XIX, 1975, p. 133). This 'restoration' involved concealing the last features of the mediaeval building, except for the ciborium by Arnolfo di Cambio and the 8th-century mosaic in the apse (Cavallini's frescoes had been covered up in the restoration of 1725, and were not uncovered till 1901).

Portico: Tomb of Cardinal Sfondrati (d.1618) by Girolamo Rainaldi (Ferrari, *La Tomba*, pl. CIV; Hibbard, *Maderno*, p. 237).

INTERIOR
1 to R: *Cappella del Bagno*: Guido Reni, *Marriage* and *Martyrdom of S. Cecilia*, and landscapes by Paul Bril.
3 to R: Giuseppe Ghezzi, *St Benedict* (1676; W).
4 to R: L. Vanvitelli, *Appearance of the Angel to Sts Cecilia and Valerianus*.
Last chapel to right: Monument to Cardinal Rampolla by E. Quattrini (1929), a remarkable if unfortunate example of 20th-century neo-Baroque.
High Altar: The statue of the dead St Cecilia and the setting with gilt bronze angels are by Stefano Maderno (finished 1600; Lavagnino, *Altari*, pp. 9, 49; Nava Cellini, 'S. Maderno, F. Vanni e G. Reni a S. Cecilia in Trastevere', *Paragone*, 227, 1969, p. 18); on the wall behind the altar are busts of Innocent XII and Clement XI by G. Mazzuoli commissioned, probably in 1700, by Cardinal Francesco Acquaviva, whose career they had furthered. The busts stand on oval pedestals like those in Borromini's Re Magi.
2 to L: Baglione, *St Andrew*.
1 to L: Giuseppe Ghezzi, *Sts Stephen and Lawrence* (1676; W).

SS. Celso e Giuliano
Via Banco S. Spirito

Bibliography: Vasi, *Magnificenze*, pl. 109; G. Segni, C. Thoenes, L. Mortari (Chiese di Roma, 88); Fasolo, 'Del Borrominismo a Roma, I, Carlo de Dominicis', *Quaderni*, 4, 1953, p. 1; Portoghesi, *Roma Barocca*, pls 383–6; Mallory, *Rococo*, p. 136; *Guide Rionali*, V, 3, p. 36.

Founded probably in the 6th century when the relics of the two saints were brought from Antioch to Rome and deposited in S. Paolo fuori le mura. The old church was pulled down during the widening of the via dei Banchi by Julius II who in 1513 promised to build a new one. The designs supplied by Bramante are known from drawings but very little was actually built and that little was pulled down in 1733 when the present church was begun on the orders of Clement XII to the design of Carlo de Dominicis. Payments to him continued till 1743 though the structure seems to have been finished by 1735, the date on the façade.

The church is built on an oval plan with the shorter axis leading to the altar, as at S. Andrea al Quirinale, but with large chapels on the ends of the cross-axis. The façade, particularly in its upper part, shows interesting adaptations of Borrominesque ideas.

A note by P. L. Ghezzi, dated 1733, on a drawing of Cardinal Neri Corsini's villa at Anzio designed by Alessandro Galilei states that the latter was working on the church in 1733, but his share is not defined (S. Jacob, *Zeichnungen*, No. 798).

INTERIOR

The church has a nearly complete set of altarpieces dating from 1736–8.

1 to R: Gaetano Lapis, *Pope Cornelius with Sts Artemia and Januaria* (1737).
2 to R: Emanuele Alfani, *The Magdalen* (1736).
Choir: *High Altar:* Pompeo Batoni, *Christ in Glory* (1736–8; Voss, p. 651). To the right: Francesco Caccianiga, *St Celsus* (c.1736). To the left: Giacomo Triga, *Miracle of St Julian* (1736).
2 to L: Giuseppe Valeriani, *Madonna with St Liborius* (1736).
1 to L: Giuseppe Ranucci, *Baptism* (1736–7).

S. Cesareo
Via di Porta S. Sebastiano

Bibliography: G. Matthiae, *S. Cesareo 'de Appia'*, Rome, 1955; P. Tomassi, *San Cesareo in Palatio*, Rome, 1965; Buchowiecki, I, p. 525.

A church stood here from very early times, though it is first recorded in 1192. It was restored under Clement VIII between 1600 and 1603 by Cardinal Cesare Baronio. This restoration is an important example of the interest in the Early Christian church, in which Baronio, as a great ecclesiastical historian, played an important part (cf. SS. Nereo e Achilleo). The cosmatesque screens and *amboni* were preserved, though they were reconstructed to fit their new setting, and other fragments were used for the altar frontal.

The architect in charge of the restoration was probably Giacomo della Porta, though Buchowiecki quotes payments to Stefano Longhi and Battista Prata, who may only have been the executants. The decoration was in the hands of the Cavaliere d'Arpino and Francesco Zucchi.

The gilt and painted wooden ceiling dates from the same time and bears the arms of Clement VIII.

S. Chiara
Via S. Chiara

Bibliography: Baglione, pp. 48, 309; Vasi, *Magnificenze*, pl. 156; Titi, 1763, p. 153; A. Eschbach, *Le Séminaire pontifical français de Rome*, Rome, 1903; J. B. Frey, *Le Séminaire français à Rome*, Rome, 1919; *Guide Rionali*, IX, 2, p. 16.

According to Baglione the church was rebuilt to

13. S. Chiara. Engraving by Vasi, made before the church was remodelled in the 19th century.

the designs of Francesco da Volterra from 1582 onwards; the façade, which was added in 1627–8, is recorded in an engraving by Vasi. The convent buildings, designed by Carlo Maderno, are also shown in the engraving. Church and convent were completely rebuilt in the second half of the 19th century.

SS. Claudio e Andrea de' Borgognoni
Piazza S. Silvestro

Bibliography: Roisecco, 1745, II, p. 21; Titi, 1763, p. 350; Buchowiecki, I, p. 438; Elling, pl. 45; Valesio, p. 121.

The church of the Burgundian colony in Rome, mentioned by Titi in 1686, but rebuilt by the French architect, Antoine Dérizet, in 1728–31. An unexecuted plan for the church made by G. B. Contini in 1708 showed a curved convex central bay to the façade (H. Hager, 'Il Modello di L. Rusconi Sassi del Concorso per la facciata di S. Giovanni in Laterano', *Commentari*, XXII, 1971, p. 50, and fig. 9).

On the façade are statues of *St Andrew* by Luc-François Breton and *S. Claudio* by G. A. Grandjacquet (1771).

INTERIOR

Right transept: Altarpiece: Placido Costanzi, *S. Carlo Borromeo*.
Left transept: J. F. de Troy, *Resurrection*.

S. Clemente
Via S. Giovanni in Laterano

Bibliography: C. Cecchelli, Chiese di Roma, 25; J. Gilmartin, 'The Paintings commissioned by Pope Clement XI for the Basilica of San Clemente in Rome', *Burlington Magazine*, CXVI, 1974, p. 365; *Guide Rionali*, I, 2, p. 5.

One of the most famous early churches of Rome, built over the remains of a Mithraeum and other Roman buildings. It was rebuilt in the 12th century and although much work of this period is still visible – as well as Masolino's frescoes in the chapel of St Catherine – a good deal must have disappeared at the time of the restoration carried out in 1716–19 by Carlo Stefano Fontana for Clement XI, whose *monti* and star appear on the side door dated 1719 (Elling, pl. 31).

INTERIOR

The wooden ceiling dates from the restoration of Clement XI. It encloses a painting of the *Glory of St Clement* by G. Chiari. The paintings over the nave arcade illustrating scenes from the life of *St Clement* are by followers of Maratta – G. Odazzi, P. de Pietri, G. Piastrini, G. Triga, G. A. Crecolini, T. Chiari, P. L. Ghezzi and S. Conca.

Chapel at entrance end of right aisle (S. Domenico): Restored 1715; altarpiece and frescoes on side-walls: attributed to S. Conca, *Scenes from the Life of St Dominic*. Only that on the right wall is documented as being from the hand of Conca.

Chapel to left of High Altar: (Rosario): Altarpiece: S. Conca, *The Virgin giving the Rosary to St Dominic and St Catherine*.

SS. Cosma e Damiano
Via dei Fori Imperiali

Bibliography: Pollak, I, p. 116; Totti, p. 427; Mola, p. 103; G. Matthiae (Chiese di Roma, 59); P. Chioccioni, *La Basilica e il Convento dei SS. Cosmo e Damiano in Roma*, Rome, 1963.

The church is built in two Roman temples which were adapted to Christian worship by Pope Felix IV (526–30) who commissioned the celebrated mosaic in the half-dome of the apse. A project for restoring the church was produced for Urban VIII by Orazio Torriani in 1626, but between 1629 and 1633 this was replaced by one designed by Luigi Arigucci for Cardinal Francesco Barberini. (Mola however ascribes the remodelling to Domenico Castello.) The new work, apart from a fine gilt wood ceiling, and the High Altar by Castello, was of mediocre quality, but it was a manifestation of the interest shown by the popes of the early 17th century in restoring Early Christian churches.

INTERIOR

2 to R: Chapel of the Baglione family; paintings by G. Baglione: altarpiece: *St Peter and St John healing*; on the walls: *Adoration of the Magi* and *Presentation*.
3 to R: G. A. Galli, called Lo Spadarino, *St Anthony of Padua* (Nicolson, p. 50); frescoes on walls by Francesco Allegrini.
2 to L: Frescoes of *St Alexander* by Francesco Allegrini.

In the circular chapel attached to the west end of the church (originally the Temple of Romulus, son of Maxentius) is a huge and magnificent Neapolitan *presepe* or *crêche*, dating from the 18th century, with hundreds of little wooden figures enacting the *Adoration of the Magi*, which was given to the church in 1939.

SS. Cosma e Damiano
Via dei Barbieri

Bibliography: Roisecco, 1745, p. 189; *Guide Rionali,* VIII, 1, p. 32.

A small church built by the Guild of Barbers in 1722 to the designs of an architect called Carnevale and dedicated to Sts Cosmas and Damianus, the two brother apothecaries. For a period the parish of S. Elena was transferred here from the nearby church of that name which was demolished in the 19th century. It is decorated with good stuccoes, enclosing on the right wall a painting of the *Madonna and Child* carried by two angels and on the vault *Sts Cosmas and Damianus in Glory* by Giovanni Antonio Crecolini.
The Sacristan lives in the house to the left of the church.

S. Crisogono
Piazza Sonnino

Bibliography: Martinelli, p. 40; Mola, p. 58; Falda, *Nuovo teatro,* III, pl. 32; De' Rossi, *Architettura Civile,* II, pl. 42; Letarouilly, pl. 393 (353); Magni, I, pls 26, 27; Mandl, *Die Kirche des St Crisogonus in Rom,* Graz, n.d.; B. M. A. Ghetti (Chiese di Roma, 92).

The church is first recorded in 499, and was rebuilt in 1129. (The campanile survives.) In 1623 Cardinal Scipione Borghese undertook a complete renovation of the church, carried out by G. B. Soria, who added the carved wooden roof, replaced all the capitals of the re-used Roman columns, modified the entablature (into which he introduced the Borghese arms), inserted large windows in the clerestory, and redecorated the transepts and the arches at the crossing. On the frieze of the baldacchino is the date 1628. The portico and façade were also added by Scipione, whose name appears on the frieze of the portico with the date 1626 while his arms fill the centre of the pediment of the façade. Most early authorities ascribe this portico to Soria, but Mandl maintains that he was only the executant working on the designs of Sergio Venturi. The grille has the arms of Clement XI.

INTERIOR
In the ceiling is a copy of Guercino's *S. Crisogono in Glory.*
High Altar: Inscribed with the name of Cardinal Borghese and probably by Soria.
Chapel to right of High Altar: *Cappella Poli:* Attributed by Titi (1686, p. 461) and by De' Rossi (*Architettura Civile,* II, pls 13, 14) to Bernini and possibly based on a sketch by him, but executed entirely by assistants (1677–81; Fagiolo dell'Arco, *Bernini,* No. 243); tomb of Gaudenzio Poli (right; d.1679) and Fausto Poli (left; d.1653); vault fresco: G. Gimignani, *The Trinity,* much repainted (W).
To the left of the entrance: Tomb of Cardinal Giovanni Giacomo Millo (d.1757) by Pietro Bracci (Gradara, *Bracci,* p. 83).

S. Croce in Gerusalemme
Piazza S. Croce in Gerusalemme

Bibliography: Vasi, 1753, III, p. XIX and 1777, p. 207; Magni, I, pl. 101; S. Ortolani (Chiese di Roma, 106); Portoghesi, *Roma Barocca,* pls 409, 410, 415–20; Mallory, *Rococo,* p. 155; S. Negro, *Nuovo album romano,* Rome, 1964, pl. 160.

The church is said traditionally to have been founded by Constantine and it is certain that it existed in the 4th century. It was rebuilt by Lucius II in 1144, and of this building the campanile survives. In 1482 during a further restoration workmen discovered a box containing the label INRI from the Cross and this relic rapidly increased the popularity of the church. In 1495 Cardinal Bernardino Lopez de Carvajal became titular cardinal of the church and carried out extensive restoration, including the frescoing of the apse. His successor, Cardinal Francesco Quiñones, gave the splendid tabernacle, attributed to Jacopo Sansovino (1536). In 1561 Pius IV transferred the Carthusians who had previously held the monastery to S. Maria degli Angeli and gave S. Croce to the Cistercians who still serve it.

In 1602 on the orders of Archduke Albrecht Rubens painted three compositions of the *Crucifixion,* the *Descent from the Cross* and *St Helena.* These were removed when the church was restored in the mid-18th century (now at Grasse).

In 1741–4 a complete restoration of the church was carried out for Benedict XIV, including the stuccoing of the interior (leaving only the apse fresco) and the addition of a portico and façade (dated 1744).

All the guide books ascribe the church to Gregorini, except Vasi, who in 1753 attributes it to Gregorini and Pietro Passalacqua and in 1777 mentions Passalacqua alone. His first suggestion is confirmed by the only document so far available, a drawing in the Accademia di San Luca by Melchiorre Passalacqua with an inscription stating that the church was remodelled by his brother Pietro, 'unito con il Cavaliere Domenico Gregorini'. Mallory, who published

S. Croce in Gerusalemme

14. *S. Croce in Gerusalemme. Engraving by Vasi.*

the drawing, is inclined to give the lion's share of the work to Gregorini, but the similarity of the façade to Passalacqua's Oratory of the SS. Annunziata is so great – particularly in its use of a single order – that I should be inclined to regard this feature as being part of his contribution. There does not seem to be any parallel in the work of Gregorini for the impressive and unusual porch, an oval with its long axis across that of the church, but a very similar feature occurs in a drawing by Passalacqua, made for a competition at the Academy of S. Luca in 1713 (Mallory, figs 209, 210, and H. Hager, 'Il modello di L. Rusconi Sassi del concorso per la facciata di S. Giovanni in Laterano', *Commentari*, XXII, 1971, pp. 54 and 65, note 105).

Above the façade is a series of statues: angels by B. Ludovisi, *St Matthew* by C. Marchionni, *St John the Evangelist* by P. Verschaffelt, *St Luke* by A. Corsini, *St Mark* by G. B. Grossi (who also did the group of cherubim), *St Helena* by T. Brandini, *Constantine* by P. Lestache.

INTERIOR

Vaults of nave and transepts: Corrado Giaquinto, *The Virgin presenting Sts Constantine and Helena to the Trinity* (Poensgen, fig. 46) and the *Apparition of the Cross* (1744).

1 to R: Giovanni Bonatti, *The Head of S. Cesareo*.

2 to R: Carlo Maratta, *The Submission of Victor IV to Innocent II* (1656–9; W).

3 to R: Raffaelle Vanni, a *Vision of the Mother of St Robert* (W).

Choir: On the half-dome of the apse frescoes commissioned by Cardinal Carvajal from an unidentified Umbrian artist c.1500. On the walls frescoes by Corrado Giaquinto: *Moses striking the Rock* and *The Brazen Serpent*. In the apse monument to Cardinal Francisco Quiñonez (d.1540) with tabernacle by Jacopo Sansovino. The Baldacchino dates from the restoration by Gregorini and Passalacqua but incorporates the four columns of the mediaeval ciborium.

Lower Church: Cappella Gregoriana: Tomb of Cardinal Gioacchino Besozzi by Innocenzo Spinazzi (1755); marble relief of the *Pietà* by Archangelo Gonelli (1628–9).

3 to L: Luigi Garzi, *St Silvester and Constantine* (between 1675 and 1686; W).

1 to L: G. Passeri, *St Thomas* (between 1675 and 1686; W).

In the library of the monastery is a seated statue of *Benedict XIV* by Carlo Marchionni (J. Gaus, *Carlo Marchionni*, Graz, 1967, p. 140).

S. Croce dei Lucchesi
Via dei Lucchesi

Bibliography: Pollak, I, p. 124; De' Rossi, 1697, p. 362; U. Vichi, *S. Croce dei Lucchesi*, Rome, 1964; Elling, pl. 27.

A mediaeval church dedicated to St Nicholas which stood on this site was given in 1575 to the Capuchins and in 1631 to the Lucchesi who rebuilt it to the designs of Mattia de' Rossi at an undetermined date probably about 1670. The façade was built between 1695 and 1697.

INTERIOR (restored 1858–63)
The church, which consists of a single nave with three chapels on each side, is unusual in that the latter are separated from each other by broad piers containing little galleries (*coretti*).

The ceiling paintings are by Giovanni Coli and Filippo Gherardi, both of Lucca (1673–6): *Heraclius brings the Cross back from Persia*; *The Volto Santo of Lucca supported by Angels*; the *Sudarium supported by Angels* (W).
1 to R: *Fantinelli:* Lazzaro Baldi, *S. Zita* (*c*.1695; W).
2 to R: *Castagnori:* Altarpiece, *Immaculata*, by B. Puccini. On left wall D. M. Muratori, *S. Lorenzo Giustiniani* (after 1701; W).

S. Croce alla Lungara
Via della Lungara

Bibliography: Baglione, p. 181; Titi, 1686, p. 27; Guide Rionali, XIII, 1, p. 42.

Also called S. Croce della Penitenza. Founded in 1615 by the marchese Baldassare Paluzzi Albertoni as a convent for penitent women.

INTERIOR
The chapel was drastically restored in the 19th century when presumably the *Crucifixion* by Troppa, recorded by Titi and mentioned by Waterhouse, was removed.

Oratorio del SS. Crocifisso
Piazza dell'Oratorio

Bibliography: J. von Henneberg, 'An early work by Giacomo della Porta: The Oratorio del Santissimo Crocifisso di San Marcello in Rome', *Art Bulletin*, LII, 1970, p. 157; id., *L'Oratorio dell'Arciconfraternita del Santissimo Crocifisso di San Marcello*, Rome, 1974.

Built for the Confraternity of the SS. Crocifisso, which was founded in 1519 and attached to S. Marcello. The architect was Giacomo della Porta who was apparently making designs in 1561. Work on the actual building was begun in the next year and was finished in 1568. The oratory is of a simple rectangular form, with a carved wooden ceiling (1583–4) and walls frescoed from 1578 onwards with scenes connected with the discovery and exaltation of the Cross by Giovanni de'Vecchi, Niccolò Circignani (Il Pomarancio) and Cesare Nebbia. The most distinguished feature of the building is the façade which was traditionally ascribed to Vignola, but is in fact one of della Porta's most successful early works.

S. Dionigi alle Quattro Fontane (destroyed)

Bibliography: G. Matthiae, 'Due chiesette romane del seicento', *Palladio*, V, 1941, p. 39.

Built between 1619 and 1637 on via Felice (now via delle Quattro Fontane) near the Quattro Fontane. Pulled down in 1939 and replaced by a block of offices. Photographs of it are reproduced by Matthiae. The façade was designed by Giovanni Antonio Massi shortly before 1686 when the church was redecorated.

SS. Domenico e Sisto
Piazza Magnanapolo

Bibliography: Mola, p. 119; Falda, *Nuovo teatro*, I, pl. 12 and III, pl. 15; Tessin, p. 162; De' Rossi, *Architettura Civile*, III, pls 5–7; Vasi, *Magnificenze*, pl. 149; Magni, I, pl. 40; Pollak, I, p. 125; Wittkower, *Art and Architecture*, p. 539, note 25; B. A. Ontini, *La Chiesa di S. Domenico a Roma*, Rome, 1952; D'Onofrio, *Scalinate*, p. 259.

A church stood on this site from the late 10th century. In 1569 it was given by Pius V to the Dominican monks of S. Sisto Vecchio, which lay in a dangerously malarial part of the city.

The campanile, which was attached to the church, was built before 1574, probably by Giacomo della Porta, who was responsible for the choir of the new church and much of the convent. He was in charge certainly till 1591, and probably till his death in 1602, though little seems to have been done in the 1590s. He was replaced by Niccolò Torriani, brother of the better known Orazio Torriani, who completed the church, which was not consecrated till 1640. He added the façade in 1628, in the lower storey probably following della Porta, whose design is recorded in a view of Rome dating from 1625 (that is to say before the façade was actually begun, but this was quite normal) but altering the upper part so that the two storeys are now of the same width. The steps and probably the

SS. Domenico e Sisto

15. *SS. Domenico e Sisto. Engraving by Falda, showing the forecourt and steps as they were before the level of the Piazza Magnanapoli was lowered in the late 19th century. On the left is the Villa Aldobrandini.*

16. *SS. Domenico e Sisto. Engraving by Vasi, showing the Piazza Magnanapoli before its level was lowered and the original entrance gate to the monastery, destroyed at that time. On the left is one of the garden pavilions of the Villa Aldobrandini, rebuilt when the piazza was modified, and on the right the church of S. Caterina da Siena, the façade of which had to be altered by the addition of a double flight of steps when the level of the piazza was lowered.*

door were added in 1654–7. The effect of the steps was greatly damaged when the ground in front of the church was lowered in the late 19th century for the cutting of the via XXIV Maggio. As shown in old photographs the straight flight consisted of only seven steps and the façade would therefore have been viewed from a point only a little below the level of the bottom of the two curved flights. The present beetling effect is therefore not at all what the architect intended.

But who was the architect? The old attribution to Vincenzo della Greca has been disproved and it has been shown that he was only responsible for the door and the splendid steps, and it was then proposed that the design was made by Niccolò Torriani who is recorded as being in charge of the actual building, but it is difficult to believe that such an obscure architect was responsible for the drastic changes to della Porta's original design – necessitated by the fact that the nave was built higher than was intended by della Porta, if we can judge from the choir that he actually built – or for the impressive façade that we see today. Other architects are recorded as being involved in the building of the church, but only at a later date: Orazio Torriani (to whom D'Onofrio attributes the design) from 1630 to 1641, G. B. Soria from 1637 to 1651 and Vincenzo della Greca from 1651 to 1657, and in 1628 Carlo Maderno received a payment of 2 scudi, but apparently only for giving advice.

There is however one other important person involved in the story, Cardinal Scipione Borghese, who was protector of the convent during the relevant period. He seems to have been particularly fond of the façade with two storeys of equal width which appears on four churches for the building of which he was responsible: S. Sebastiano, S. Gregorio Magno, S. Carlo ai Catinari, and S. Caterina da Siena a Magnanapoli, the last next door to SS. Domenico e Sisto and being built at exactly the same time, 1625–30, and it seems possible that the alteration to the design was made at his suggestion. Furthermore, of the façades mentioned above all but that of S. Sebastiano were designed by Soria, and it seems not unlikely that, even though his name is not mentioned in the documents till later, he may have been the architect who actually designed the alteration. From the stylistic point of view there is nothing to be said against this hypothesis. On the façade are statues of Sts Thomas Aquinas and Peter Martyr by Stefano Maderno above, and Sts Dominic and Sixtus by Marc'Antonio Canini below.

INTERIOR
The pilasters are of *scagliola*.

Vault fresco: Domenico Maria Canuti and Enrico Haffner, *St Dominic in Glory* (1674–5); apse: *Ecstasy of St Dominic* and the *Virgin in Glory* (c.1672–4; W; Gloton, pls LIII–LV; Poensgen, fig. 56).

1 to R: *Cappella Alaleoni* (Lavagnino, *Altari*, p. 99): Marble group, *Noli me tangere*; commissioned in 1649 by Sister Maria Alaleoni from Bernini, who supplied the design and supervised the execution of the group by Antonio Raggi. The coloured background is a modern addition (De' Rossi, *Altari*, pl. 20; Wittkower, *Bernini*, p. 223).

3 to R: P. F. Mola, *The Picture of St Dominic carried to Soriano by the Virgin* (1648; Cocke, *Mola*, p. 60, No. 56).

High Altar: Attributed to Bernini by a diarist of 1652 and said by Fagiolo (*Bernini*, Cat. 87) to have been executed between 1636 and 1640. Not mentioned by Wittkower; stylistically quite unlike Bernini.

Chancel, end wall: Louis Cousin (Gentile): Scenes from the *Life of the Virgin*.

Chancel, right wall: Pietro Paolo Ubaldini, *St Dominic at the Battle of Muret* (1639; W).

Left wall: Cousin, *Miracle of St Dominic*.

Monks' choir: Frescoes by unknown artists (1605–6).

2 to L: Altarpiece: Francesco Allegrini, *St Catherine*.

1 to L: Altarpiece: Romanelli, *Madonna del Rosario* (1652; W).

If shut apply at College to right of church.

Domine Quo Vadis (S. Maria in Palmis)
Via Appia Antica

Bibliography: Pollak, I, p. 126; G. B. Lugari, 'Il Sacello "Domine Quo Vadis" sulla via Appia', *Nuovo Bollettino di Archeologia Cristiana*, VII, 1901, p. 5; Angeli, p. 367; Orbaan, I, p. 126.

Founded at a very early date (at the latest about 9th century) on the spot where St Peter escaping from prison is said to have met Christ and addressed to him the words which give its title to the church. It collapsed during a violent storm in January 1637 and was restored by Cardinal Francesco Barberini whose arms appear on the façade. This is composed of two pairs of giant pilasters supporting a straight broken pediment, a pattern very close to that of S. Egidio, which may have been designed by the same architect. The interior is simple and contains no works of art of importance.

S. Dorotea
Via S. Dorotea

Bibliography: Portoghesi, *Roma Barocca*, pl. 401; J. Zänker, 'S. Dorotea in Rom und verwandte Kirchenbauten', *Architectura*, IV, 1974, p. 165; Elling, pl. 51; *Guide Rionali*, XIII, i, p. 94.

Built 1751–6 on the site of a much earlier church, which had been given to the PP. Minori Conventuali of St Francis by Benedict XIII between 1727 and 1729. The architect was G. B. Nolli, author of the famous plan of Rome published in 1748. The façade is a simple but impressive composition of four giant composite pilasters on a simple concave plan. The interior, almost a Greek Cross in plan with an added apse, is dominated by the central space, covered not by a dome but a vault with four heavy ribs, a feature which in some ways recalls Piedmontese churches of the same period, such as Vittone's S. Chiara at Brà. The paintings on the vault date from 1931.

1 to R: Gioacchino Martorana, *S. Gaetano* and *S. Giuseppe Calasanzio*.
Right transept: L. Gramiccia, *St Anthony of Padua*.
3 to R: Gaspar von Prenner, *Immaculata*.
High Altar: Michele Bucci, *Sts Dorothy and Silvester*, enclosing an early painting of the Madonna.
3 to L: Bucci, *Crucifixion*.
Left transept: Liborio Marmorelli, *St Francis*.
1 to L: Vincenzo Meucci, *S. Giuseppe da Copertino*.

S. Egidio (S. Maria del Carmelo)
Via della Scala

Bibliography: Totti, p. 70; De' Rossi, *Prospectus*, pl. 69; Titi, 1674, p. 47; Roisecco, 1750, I, p. 173; Vasi, *Magnificenze*, pl. 147.

A small church originally dedicated to S. Lorenzo. In 1610 it was given to Agostino Lancellotti who established there a convent of Carmelite nuns and restored the church. It was restored again in 1630 by Filippo Colonna and dedicated to S. Maria del Carmelo. The façade is similar to that of Domine Quo Vadis and the two churches may have been designed by the same architect.

INTERIOR

Entrance wall: To right of door, tomb of Petronella Paolina Massimo (d.1663). To the left of the door, tomb of Marchesa Veronica Rondanini Origo by C. Fontana (Braham and Hager, p. 97).
High Altar: A. Camassei, *Virgin giving the Scapular to St Simon Stock* (c.1630; W).

S. Eligio dei Ferrari
Via S. Giovanni Decollato

Bibliography: E. Venier, G. Zandri, C. de Vita (Chiese di Roma, 127); *Guide Rionali*, XII, 1, p. 86.

Built 1561–2 by the guild of Iron-workers (Ferrari) but altered in the 17th and 18th centuries. The façade was rebuilt in 1905, apparently on the lines of the original one.

Over the door an organ-gallery of 1690. Fine gilt wood ceiling, 1604. The altars in the side chapels are dated between 1725 and 1764.
Apse and High Altar: Built by G. B. Mola, 1640–1; alabaster altar front by F. Poletti, 1727; altarpiece of the *Madonna and Child with Saints* by Sicciolante da Sermoneta.

In the Oratory (accessible from the choir) is a banner painted on both sides by Pompeo Batoni (1750). On one side is the *Virgin appearing to S. Eligius* and on the other the *Healing of St Ampelius*.
2 to L: A. Mattei, *St Ursula* (1764).
The authors of the other altarpieces are not known.

S. Eligio degli Orefici
Via di S. Eligio

Bibliography: C. L. Frommel, 'S Eligio und die Kuppel der Cappella Medici', *Stil und Ueberlieferung. Akten des 17ten Kongresses für Kunstgeschichte, Bonn, 1964*, Berlin, 1967; Buchowiecki, I, p. 680.

Begun to the designs of Raphael in 1516. The vaults and dome were reconstructed in the early 17th century, but the church remains one of the purest expressions of the ideals of Roman High Renaissance architecture.

INTERIOR

Right transept: Altarpiece: Romanelli, *Adoration of the Kings*; frescoes of sibyls in the spandrels (W).
Apse: Frescoes by Matteo da Lecce.
Left transept: Romanelli, frescoes of sibyls in the spandrels (W); fresco over altar: Giovanni de'Vecchi, *Adoration of the Shepherds*.

S. Eligio dei Sellari (destroyed)

Bibliography: Armellini, II, p. 838; *Architettura minora*, I, pl. 46.

The church stood in the piazza delle Gensole in Trastevere, near the Ponte S. Bartolomeo. It was built in 1740 to the designs of Carlo de Dominicis. From the old photograph reproduced by Armellini it seems to have been oval in plan with a convex façade of unusual design.

S. Eufemia (destroyed)

Bibliography: Vasi, *Magnificenze*, pl. 142; Titi, 1763, pp. 233, 476; Armellini, I, pp. 206, 211.

This church stood on the Forum of Trajan. It was rebuilt by Cardinal Baronio and Fulvio Sforza under Clement VIII. The façade was by Mario Arconio. The church was pulled down in the early 19th century in the course of the excavations carried out in the Forum of Trajan.

S. Eusebio
Piazza Vittorio Emmanuele

Bibliography: Vasi, *Magnificenze*, pl. 49; E. Iezzi, *La Chiesa di S. Eusebio all' Esquilino*, Rome, 1977; *Guide Rionali*, XV, p. 106.

A church stood on this site since the 4th century; in 1471 it was given to the Celestines by Sixtus IV. It was restored in the late 16th century and the façade was built by Carlo Stefano Fontana in 1711 (date on frieze), though without the steps which had to be added when the Piazza Vittorio Emmanuele was laid out and the ground lowered in 1873.

The façade is a variant of the type used by Ponzio at S. Sebastiano but with five bays instead of three. The church itself was almost completely rebuilt to the designs of Niccolò Picconi in 1753–9.

INTERIOR
The fresco on the vault of the nave is by A. R. Mengs (Titi, 1763, p. 227) with the assistance of Anton Maron, and represents the *Glory of S. Eusebius* (1757–8; Voss, p. 651; Poensgen, fig. 48).
Choir: Fine 16th-century choir-stalls (1586).
High Altar: By Onorio Longhi (Martinelli, p. 44).

S. Eustachio
Piazza S. Eustachio

Bibliography: Vasi, *Magnificenze*, pl. 113; Appetiti (Chiese di Roma, 82).

A church stood on this site at least since the 8th century, but by the middle of the 17th century it was in a dangerous condition. Various architects, including Borromini, were asked to produce designs for a restoration but nothing was done till 1700 when Cesare Corvara was entrusted with the job. The apse and the dome were built by Canevari in 1724 and the church was consecrated in 1730. The architecture of the church is undistinguished but it contains a few altars of interest.

2 to R: (Annunciation): O. Leoni, *Annunciation*.
Right transept: G. Zoboli, *St Jerome*.
High Altar: The altar is in the form of a sarcophagus, and was commissioned by Cardinal Neri Corsini, nephew of Clement XII, in 1739 and designed by Nicola Salvi. The candlesticks are by the same artist (1749). The apse fresco of the *Martyrdom of St Eustace* is by Francesco Fernandi, called Imperiali (Titi, 1763, p. 151).
Left transept: Giacomo Zoboli, *Visitation* (Titi, 1763, p. 151).
3 to L: (Cuore di Maria): Designed in 1771 by Melchiorre Passalacqua and carved by Agostino Penna.
2 to L: (S. Michele): Alessandro Sperone, 1716–19.
1 to L: B. Puccini, *St Julian* (c.1707; W).

SS. Faustino e Giovita (S. Anna dei Bresciani) (destroyed)

Bibliography: Coudenhove-Erthal, p. 21 and pl. 3; H. Hager, 'Le Facciate dei SS. Faustino e Giovita e di S. Biagio in Campitelli a Roma', *Commentari*, XXIII, 1972, p. 261; Tafuri, *Via Giulia*, pp. 233, 530; M. Myers, *Architectural and Ornament Drawings* (Metropolitan Museum), New York, 1975, p. 24.

Built in the 16th century as part of the Palazzo dei Tribunali, planned by Bramante for Julius II but never completed. In 1664 it was given a new façade by Carlo Fontana, known from drawings and engravings. The church was pulled down in 1890 when the Lungotevere was made.

S. Filippo Neri
Via Giulia

Bibliography: *Architettura minora*, I, pl. 29; M. Rotili, *Raguzzini*, p. 54; G. Lizzari, 'S. Filippo di via Giulia. Progetto di Sistemazione', *L'Urbe*, XXVI, 1963, p. 1; *Guide Rionali*, VII, 3, p. 16; Elling, pl. 41.

Built in 1728 by Raguzzini on the orders of Benedict XIII. The façade has a fine oval stucco bas-relief representing the *Virgin and Child appearing to St Philip*.

Now secularized, shut and threatened with demolition.

S. Filippo Neri, Oratory of. See S. Maria in Vallicella

S. Francesca Romana (S. Maria Nova)
Via dei Fori Imperiali

Bibliography: Mola, pp. 87, 110; Falda, *Nuovo teatro,* III, pl. 9; De' Rossi, *Prospectus,* pl. 73; De Brosses, II, p. 232; Magni, I, pl. 12; P. Lugano (Chiese di Roma, 1); Buchowiecki, III, p. 33.

Founded on the site of a Roman temple by Paul I (757–67) and dedicated to Sts Peter and Paul. The church changed hands several times, but in 1352 it was given to the Olivetans who held it till the suppression of 1873. In 1421 Francesca Buzzi de' Ponziani founded a congregation of Oblates in the church, and, when she was canonized, as S. Francesca Romana, in 1608, her name was added to that of the original dedication. The 12th-century campanile still stands but the church itself was remodelled between 1608 and 1615 by Carlo Lambardi (or Lombardo) who designed the façade, which is unusual for Rome in being an adaptation of Palladian motifs (S. Giorgio Maggiore and the Redentore). The church was restored in 1816–29 after being damaged by French troops in 1798. The date 1615 appears on the façade.

INTERIOR
The wooden roof dates from the 17th-century restoration.
Apse: Canini, *Martyrdom of six Saints* (before 1663; W).
Confessio (De' Rossi, *Altari,* pl. 29): S. Francesca Romana (d.1440) was first buried under the High Altar but when in 1634 her body was found there (Gigli, p. 179) it was decided to build a Confessio in honour of the saint. The original statues (1644–9) after Bernini were destroyed in 1798, but were replaced by copies. The relief of the saint by Ercole Ferrata survives in the crypt. The work was paid for by Donna Agata Pamphili, sister of Innocent X, who was a nun at Tor de' Specchi, a convent founded by S. Francesca (Wittkower, *Bernini,* p. 213; Fagiolo dell' Arco, *Bernini,* no. 124; Lavin, *Bernini,* pp. 58, 185).
4 to L: Vault of chapel copied exactly from a plate in Pozzo's *Perspectiva pictorum* (Gloton, p. 160, note 1 and plate LIX).
Sacristy: *Holy Trinity* by Brandi (W); *Tobias* attributed by Waterhouse to Cerrini; Pierre Subleyras, *St Benedict reviving a dead child* (1744; Voss, p. 644).
2 to L: Angelo Caroselli and Filippo Lauri, *The Mass of St Gregory.*

17. *S. Francesca Romana. Engraving by Falda. In the distance on the left is the Colosseum and on the right the Arch of Titus.*

S. Francesco d'Assisi a Monte Mario

Bibliography: L. Pallottino, 'Un'opera inedita di Pietro Passalacqua', *Palatino*, IV, 1960, p. 46; Elling, pl. 39b.

Built in 1669–76 as a result of a bequest from a priest named Bartolomeo Neri, for the benefit of those living on Monte Mario who had no nearby church, and made into a parish church in 1708. The façade was added in 1728–9, to the designs of Pietro Passalacqua. It is an unusually simple work for that architect but the funds available were limited.

S. Francesco di Paola
Piazza di S. Francesco di Paola

Bibliography: Pollak, I, p. 126; Totti, p. 479; Baglione, p. 181; Titi, 1674, p. 266 and 1763, p. 476; Roisecco, 1750, II, p. 493; Magni, I, pl. 70 (wrongly labelled S. Vincenzo di Paola); D. Taccone-Gallucci, *Monografia della Chiesa di S. Francesco di Paola in Roma*, Rome, 1916; Ferrari, *Lo Stucco*, pl. CXXXIII; Eimer, *S. Agnese*, I, figs 7–9; Buchowiecki, I, p. 718; Garms, No. 444; *Guide Rionali*, I, 2, p. 92.

The church was given to the Order of Minims, founded by S. Francesco di Paola, by Gregory XV in 1622. It was rebuilt between 1645 and 1650 to the designs of G. P. Moraldi (or Monaldi) at the expense of Donna Olimpia Aldobrandini-Pamphili, wife of Camillo, nephew of Innocent X. At this stage the lower half of the façade was built, but the upper part was only added at a much later date, though it is described as complete by Roisecco in 1750. The convent was being built by Domenico Castello when Baglione wrote in 1642.

INTERIOR
The interior was redecorated in 1760 from the designs of Luigi Berettoni, a pupil of Ludovico Rusconi Sassi, for the general of the Order, Francesco Zavarroni. It was restored in 1952 when the vault was given its present decoration. The altars in the side chapels are of blue *scagliola*.
1 to R: Altarpiece: Filippo Luzi, *Holy Family with St Anne*; vault: Onofrio Avellino, *St Anne* (1730–5; W).
2 to R: On walls and vault: Giuseppe Chiari, scenes from the life of *S. Francesco di Paola* (1726; W; Gloton, pl. XLIV).
3 to R: A. Crecolini, *St Francis of Sales*.
Choir: The bottom of the walls was covered with *cippolino* in 1952.
High Altar: Ciborium by G. A. de' Rossi (c. 1655; Eimer, *S. Agnese*, I, p. 123 and II, fig. 261); at the top of the altar wall: S. Pozzo, *Immaculata*.
Right wall: Tomb of Monsignor Lazzaro Pallavicini, erected in 1744 by Benedict XIV; designed by F. Fuga, bust by Agostino Corsini (Matthiae, *Fuga*, p. 50; Pane, *Fuga*, p. 115, fig. 101).
Left wall: Tomb of Giovanni Pizzullo (d.1646), attributed to Agostino Corsini.
Sacristy: Vault: Sassoferrato, *St Francis of Paola before the Virgin and Child* (1641; W); one of his finest works, set in a rich but severe stucco frame, a rare example of a pure *quadro riportato* from the mid-17th century. Lunettes by Agostino Masucci and Filippo Luzi.
Sala Capitolare: Altarpiece: Cozza, *Crucifixion* (W); walls: S. Pozzo, *Agony in the Garden* and *Carrying of the Cross*.
3 to L: (St Michael): Altarpiece: Stefano Perrugini, *St Michael*; oval panels on walls by Giacomo Triga.
2 to L: S. Pozzo: *B. Nicola dei Langobardi*; walls: *Adoration of the Kings* and *of the Shepherds*.
1 to L: Altar: O. Avellino, *St Joseph*; vault and walls: S. Pozzo, *Flight into Egypt* and *Dream of Joseph*.
If shut, ring at the door of the monastery to the left of the church.

S. Francesco a Ripa
Piazza S. Francesco

Bibliography: B. Pesci (Chiese di Roma, 49).

The church and monastery are built on the site of a hospital of S. Biagio in which St Francis stayed when in Rome, and which by 1229 was certainly in the hands of the Franciscans who rebuilt the church on a larger scale and still serve it today. In 1579 a theological college was attached to the church, adding greatly to its importance. The choir was rebuilt in 1603 by Onorio Longhi and the whole church was remodelled after 1682 by Mattia de' Rossi who added the meagre façade.

INTERIOR
Entrance wall: Tombs of Tommaso Raggi (d. c.1679) and his wife Ortensia Spinola (d.1672).
1 to R: *Cappella Ricci* (del Crocifisso): Pesci attributes this chapel to Carlo Fontana, but this seems not to be correct. The tomb of Cardinal Michelangelo Ricci (1682) is by Domenico Guidi.
2 to R: *Cappella di S. Giovanni da Capestrano*: Attributed to Carlo Fontana by Titi (1686, p. 39) who wrote while the chapel was in build-

ing. On the other hand in the *Aggiunta* to the edition of 1708 (p. 5) the chapel is attributed to Filippo Leti. In the 1763 edition no architect's name is mentioned. The paintings in the chapel representing scenes from the life of the saint are by Domenico Maria Muratori (c.1725; W).

3 to R: *Cappella Ludovisi* (S. Giuseppe): By Giovanni Corbelli (Titi, 1686, p. 39); altarpiece by Stefano Legnani (ibid.); frescoes by Giuseppe Passeri (W).

Right transept: *Cappella Pallavicini Rospigliosi* (St Peter of Alcantara and S. Pasquale Baylon) (Lavagnino, *Altari*, pp. 43, 199; Portoghesi, *Roma Barocca*, pl. 366). Begun by N. Michetti in 1710 from a model which still survives and is on loan to the Museo di Roma, Palazzo Braschi (F. Pansecchi, 'Il modello della Cappella Pallavicini Rospigliosi in S. Francesco a Ripa', *Bollettino dei Musei Comunali di Roma*, IX, 1962, p. 21); completed in 1725. Tombs of Maria Camilla Pallavicini and G. B. Rospigliosi (1713) and opposite, that of Stefano and Lazzaro Pallavicini, by G. Mazzuoli, 1715-19 (R. and J. Westin, 'Contribution to the late chronology of Giuseppe Mazzuoli', *Burlington Magazine*, CXVI, 1974, p. 36). Altarpiece by G. Chiari (W).

High Altar: Put up in stucco in 1737 and in marble in 1746 (Mallory, *Notizie*, p. 109; Fasolo, *Trastevere*, p. 102) by Antonio Rinaldi (Titi, 1763, p. 48). This is presumably the architect who was called to Russia in 1752 and worked later for Catherine the Great. It is not noticed in the article in Thieme-Becker which remarks that nothing is known of Rinaldi's works in Italy. Pesci gives the date 1746 for the High Altar and attributes it to Fra Secondo da Roma who may have executed it.

Sacristy: Remodelled by Mattia de' Rossi with fine wood work; bronze crucifix after Algardi.

4 to L: *Cappella Albertoni or della Cetera* (S. Anna): Lavagnino, *Altari*, pp. 27, 93. The structure dates from the 16th century (two frescoes survive from it) but the chapel was remodelled in 1622 by Giacomo Mola on the orders of the marchese Baldassare Paluzzi Albertoni who wished to honour his relative the Blessed Ludovica Albertoni. The frescoes are by Gaspare Celio (Gloton, pl. XIII). The cult of the Blessed Ludovica was confirmed in 1671 by Clement X who was related to the Albertoni family, and on this occasion Cardinal Angelo Paluzzi Albertoni commissioned Bernini to make a statue of the Blessed Ludovica (1671-4). This is one of the most moving renderings of a mystical ecstasy in Baroque art. It shows the Blessed Ludovica in the extreme state of mystical union with the divine, beyond even the tangible vision of St Theresa which Bernini evoked so vividly in the Cornaro Chapel at S. Maria della Vittoria (Wittkower, *Bernini*, p. 257 and Blunt, 'GianLorenzo Bernini: Illusionism and Mysticism', *Art History*, I, 1978, p. 67). The effect of the statue is marred by the fact that one of the side windows which light it is usually covered by a curtain. Bernini's original terracotta model for the statue was acquired in 1980 by the Victoria and Albert Museum (*Burlington Magazine*, CXXIII, 1981, p. 63). Baciccio's altarpiece of the *Virgin and Child with St Anne* was painted to complete the decoration of the chapel (1675; Enggass, *Baciccio*, pp. 24, 142).

On pier outside chapel: Tomb of Giulia Ricci, wife of the marchese Francesco Pallavicini, by E. Ferrata.

3 to L: *Cappella Mattei* (della Pietà): By Francesco Peparelli (Mola, p. 87) but heavily restored in 1882. On the left: tomb of Laura Frangipani Mattei (d.1635) by Andrea Bolgi (A. Nava Cellini, 'Ritratti di Andrea Bolgi', *Paragone*, XIII, 147, 1961, p. 24; Mola, p. 87); on the right: tomb of Cardinal Orazio Mattei (d.1686) by Lorenzo Ottoni (Enggass, *Ottoni*, p. 315).

2 to L: (Annunciation): Probably built about 1560; fresco over altar: F. Salviati, *Annunciation*; decoration of dome and side walls (dated 1614 and 1622) with frescoes by G. B. Ricci (Gloton, pl. XVIII).

Pier between 2 and 1 L: Tomb of Giuseppe Paravicini (d.1695) by C. Rusconi (Enggass, *Sculpture*, p. 97).

1 to L: (Immaculate Conception): Altarpiece: Martin de Vos, *Immaculate Conception*; on the left wall the *Birth of the Virgin* by Vouet (Crelly, *The Paintings of Simon Vouet*, New Haven, 1862, p. 208; *Caravaggeschi francesi*, exhibition catalogue, Villa Medici, 1974, No. 64). On the right wall the *Assumption*, attributed by Titi (1686, p. 40) to Antonio della Cornia, but which has recently been ascribed to Sandrart (C. Klemen, 'Sandrart à Rome', *Gazette des Beaux-Arts*, 1979, 1, p. 159).

On the wall outside the chapel: Tomb of Pietro Carcarasi (d.1716).

In addition to the monuments mentioned above the church contains a number of other late 17th- and 18th-century tombs of which nothing is known beyond what can be learnt from the inscriptions on them.

S. Francesco di Sales. See S. Maria della Visitazione (secularized)
Via S. Francesco di Sales

S. Galla. See **S. Maria in Portico**

S. Gallicano. See Miscellaneous Buildings, **Ospedale di S. Gallicano** Via S. Gallicano

Il Gesù
Piazza del Gesù.

Bibliography: De' Rossi, *Prospectus*, pls 18–20; Tessin, p. 161; De' Rossi, *Architettura Civile*, II, pls 2, 3; De Brosses, II, p. 108; Letarouilly, pl. 198 (282); Magni, I, pls. 73–8; P. Pecchiai, *Il Gesù di Roma*, 1952; J. Ackerman, 'The Gesù in the light of contemporary church design', in Wittkower and Jaffe, *Baroque Art: the Jesuit Contribution*, p. 15; Hibbard, 'Ut picturae Sermones', ibid., p. 29; C. P. Ridolfini, *Roma, Chiesa del Gesù*, Rome, 1975 (with useful plates); *Guide Rionali*, IX, 1, p. 38.

The Jesuit Order was approved by Paul III in 1540 and was given the little church of S. Maria della Strada near the palaces of the Altieri and Astalli families. In 1551 Nanni di Baccio Bigio (Nanni Lippi) was commissioned to design a larger church but owing to difficulties in collecting funds and in acquiring the necessary land nothing was built. In 1554 Michelangelo was asked to provide an alternative plan, but this is lost (the plan reproduced as Michelangelo's by Pecchiai (pl. III) and others is by Nanni Lippi, and only a small scribbled variant is by Michelangelo, see Ackerman, *Michelangelo*, II, Catalogue, p. 141).

In 1565 Francesco (St Francis) Borgia became general of the Order and a new patron appeared in the person of Cardinal Alessandro Farnese, who supplied funds generously, partly on the recommendation of his secretary, Giulio Folchi (buried in the first chapel to the right in the church), and with this help the complete site needed for the church was acquired.

At this time the architect of the Company was Giovanni Tristano, but Farnese imposed his architect, Vignola, who prepared the design, though Tristano remained in charge of the actual building operations. The foundation stone was laid in 1568; by the time of Vignola's death in 1573 the nave was structurally complete and the façade begun. Vignola's original design for the façade shown on the medal of 1568 had a high attic running the whole width of the building with a Serliana window in the middle under a broad pediment. This was immediately abandoned, and Vignola provided another design, but this too was rejected, and other architects including Galeazzo Alessi and Giacomo della Porta were asked to submit designs. Della Porta's was chosen and Vignola was only able to preserve his design for posterity by having it engraved by Mario Cartari (1573). The drawing made for the engraving, probably by

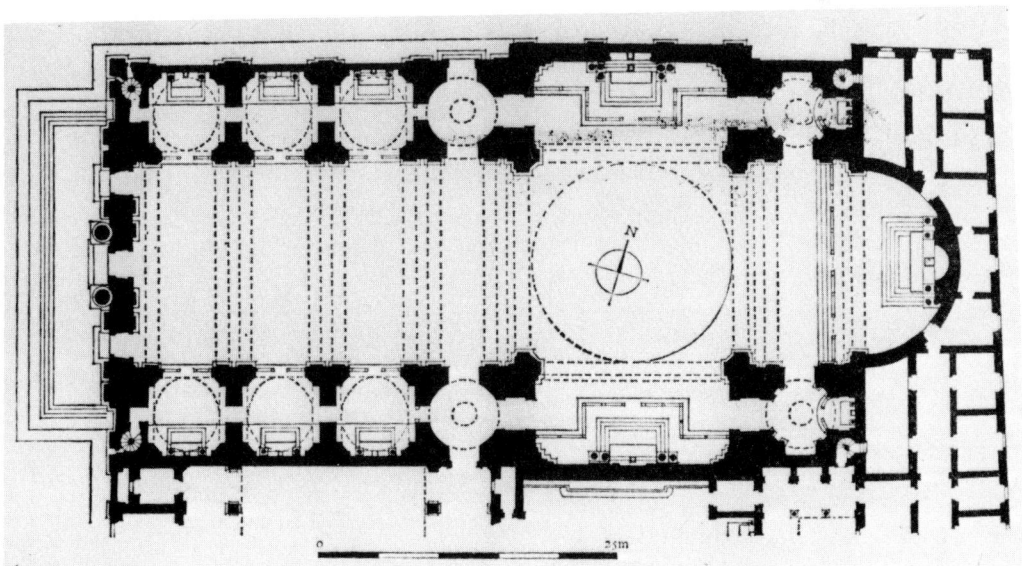

18. *The Gesù. Plan.*

19. *The Gesù. Engraving of Vignola's design for the façade.*

Giacinto Vignola after his father's design, is in the Kunstbibliothek, Berlin (cf. S. Jacob, *Italienische Zeichnungen der Kunstbibliothek Berlin*, Berlin, 1972, no. 22). The existing façade was finished in 1577, the panel with the Name of Jesus over the door being designed by Ammanati, and the choir and transepts were finished by 1582 when work on the High Altar was started. In 1583 the pendentives of the dome were frescoed by an artist named in the documents as 'Andrea' whose identity is uncertain, and the dome was begun by Giovanni de' Vecchi. The dome was left unfinished and all these frescoes disappeared when the church was decorated by Baciccio.

In its plan and structure the Gesù was more influential than any other Roman church of the later 16th century. It satisfied all the requirements of liturgy and ecclesiastical practice as laid down by the Council of Trent and the exponents of its doctrine, such as Carlo and Federico Borromeo. Its broad nave was suitable for preaching to large congregations; the choir was clearly cut off from the nave – as was not the case with centrally planned churches – and so emphasized the distinction between priest and laity; the long axis of the church was sufficiently emphasized to lead the eye firmly towards the altar; the chapels flanking the aisles provided for altars devoted to the worship of individual saints (and could also be sold to individual families); and the Sacristy was set far enough away from the apse to enable the priest carrying the host for the celebration of Mass to make an impressive procession to the High Altar. Vignola's design for the façade was also imitated all over Europe for several centuries – more actually than the façade as executed by Giacomo della Porta. It provided the ideal solution to the problem of binding into a single whole the higher central section covering the nave and the lower side section corresponding to the aisles, a problem which had exercised architects since the 15th century, when Alberti invented the earliest formula in the façade of S. Maria Novella in Florence.

As it was first conceived the interior of the church was to have been almost bare, the pilasters were of stucco, with capitals and bases of travertine, and the only marbling would have been on the altars and the inside of the entrance doors, with frescoes on the dome and pendentives only. It is shown in this state in Sacchi's painting of the centenary celebrations of 1639 (now in the Museo di Roma, Sutherland Harris, *Sacchi*, pl. 130) and in an engraving by de' Rossi. This simplicity was universal in early Jesuit churches and was laid down by Giuseppe Valeriano (who became the official architect of the Order after Tristano's death in 1565) in connection with the Jesuit churches in Genoa and Naples (Blunt, *Neapolitan Baroque and Rococo Architecture*, London, 1975, p. 38).

In this context it is worth emphasizing that the Jesuits, who are often regarded as the early protagonists of the Baroque, to the extent that in French the style was for long known as '*le style jésuite*', were in fact slow in taking it up. They never employed Borromini, and Bernini only built one church for them – the Noviciate of S. Andrea al Quirinale – and that not till the late 1650s. In fact it was not till Padre Giovanni Paolo Oliva was elected General of the Order in 1664 that a new policy in church building and decoration was inaugurated (F. Haskell, 'The Role of Patrons: Baroque style changes', in Wittkower and Jaffe, *Baroque Art: The Jesuit Contribution*, p. 51). He at once determined on a much grander scheme of decoration for the Gesù. For this purpose he enlisted the services of the most distinguished artists working in Rome at the time: Cortona for the chapel of St Francis Xavier; Maratta to paint its altarpiece; the Jesuit Guglielmo Cortese to fresco the apse; Baciccio to fresco the dome, pendentives and nave vault; and another Jesuit, Andrea Pozzo, to design the altar of St Ignatius. Cortese died in 1679 before he began his work, and in the event Baciccio replaced the earlier frescoes in the dome and pendentives and frescoed the vault of the nave with one of the most spectacular illusionist schemes in the whole of Baroque art.

The decoration of the chapels had been begun in 1584. (For an ingenious interpretation of the iconography of the early decoration see H. Hibbard, 'Ut picturae sermones', in Wittkower and Jaffe, *Baroque Art: the Jesuit Contribution*, p. 29). The first chapel to be decorated was the Cappella della Madonna in the left transept which stood more or less on the site of the old church of S. Maria della Strada and perpetuated its dedication, and in 1639 the left transept, dedicated to St Ignatius, was decorated by Cortona. All this work was, however, swept away in the later redecoration.

In 1767 the Jesuits were expelled from Spain and the Kingdom of the Two Sicilies, and money had to be raised to help the Fathers, for which purpose many of the precious objects in the treasury of the Gesù were sold. In 1775 the Company was finally suppressed by Clement XIV. The Fathers were, however, allowed to continue serving the church, but with the French occupation in 1798 almost everything of value in the church was either sold or carried off.

In 1814 Pius VII re-established the Company and an attempt was made to restore to the church some of its splendour and to complete the decoration of the apse (the High Altar was unfinished and the walls bare). This job was entrusted in 1841 to the architect Antonio Sarti by the General who was a Dutch Father called Jan Roothaan. Sarti made a new High Altar

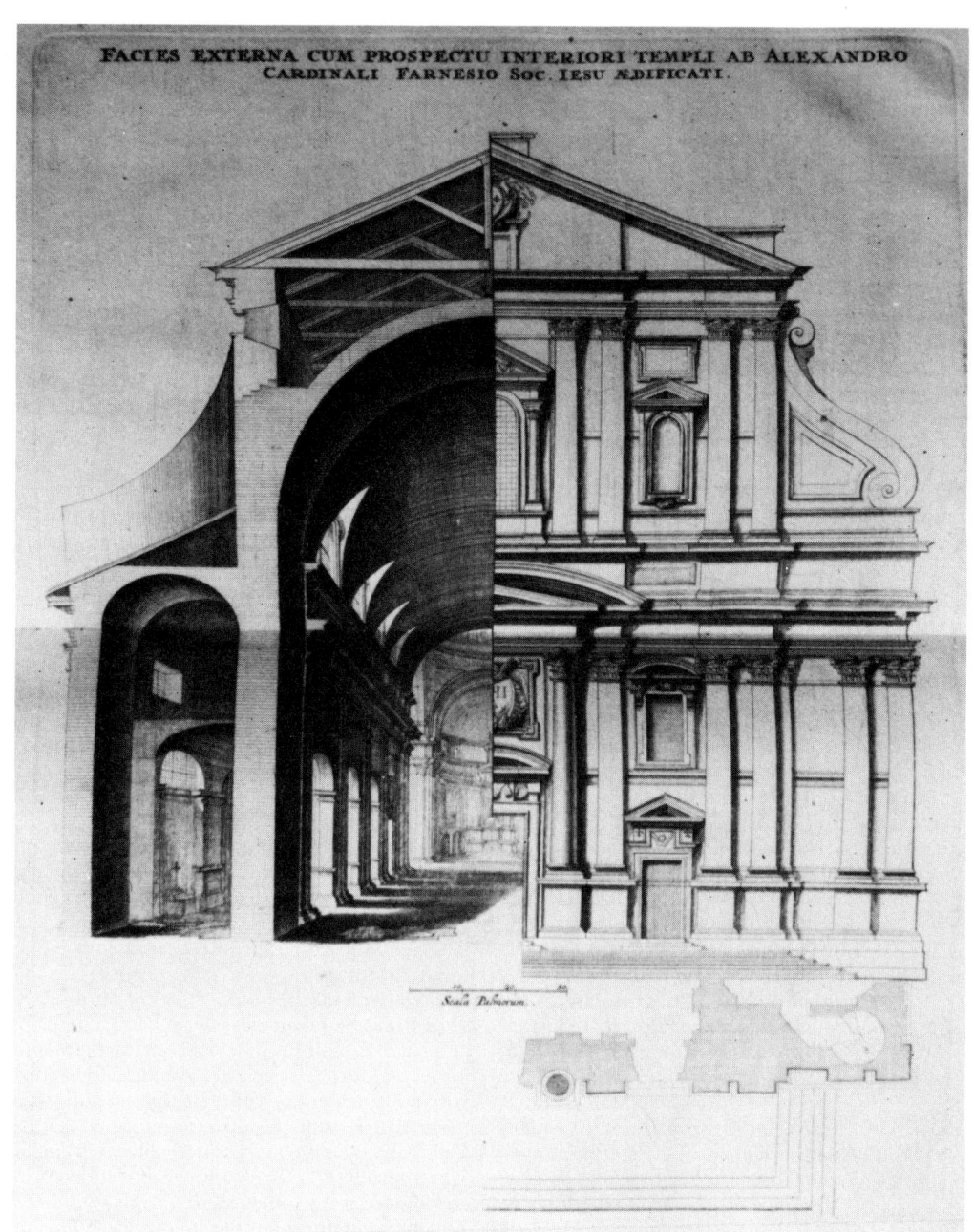

20. *The Gesù. Engraving by de'Rossi showing the façade as executed and the interior as originally intended before the late 17th-century decoration was added.*

(criticized at the time as being merely 'a door') and marbled the walls of the apse. In 1858 Prince Torlonia gave money to carry the restoration into the nave where the travertine and stucco of the pilasters and architrave were replaced by marble. The last traces of the original simplicity had vanished.

INTERIOR

Frescoes by Baciccio on the vault: nave, *Triumph of the Name of Jesus* (1676–9); dome, *Glory of Heaven* (1672–5); pendentives, *Evangelists, Fathers of the Church, Prophets and Law Givers* (1675–6); choir, *Choir of Angels* (c.1683); apse, *Adoration of the Lamb* (1680–3; Enggass, *Baciccio*, pp. 31, 135; Poensgen, fig. 31). The stucco decoration on the window embrasures and the frieze of putti are by A. Raggi (Donati, *Artisti ticinesi*, figs 397–406); the statues in the dome are by P. Naldini and others (Weil, *Ponte S. Angelo*, p. 142; Ferrari, *Lo Stucco*, pls LXXXIIff.).

A drawing at Düsseldorf (Dieter Graf, *Die Handzeichnungen von G. Cortese und G. B. Gaulli*, Düsseldorf, 1976, No. 241) shows that originally Baciccio intended to decorate the cove of the vault with circular panels supported by painted figures, which would have left a much narrower field for the main fresco and it was almost certainly Bernini who suggested the scheme as executed with a vast central fresco, extended outside the frame by clouds which appear to throw shadows on the gilt stuccoes of the cove. This device heightens the dramatic effect of the whole scene in which the light streaming from the IHS, signifying the name of Jesus, drives heretics and unbelievers out of heaven so that they seem to be hurtling down into the world of the spectator. Many of the frescoes and altarpieces in the side chapels are illustrated in Hibbard, op. cit.

1 to R: *Cappella Folchi*, later *Cerrini* (S. Andrea): Frescoes of scenes from the lives of various martyrs by Agostino Ciampelli (finished 1601).

2 to R: *Cappella Mellini* (the Passion): Frescoes of scenes from the Passion designed by G. Valeriano and executed by G. Celio (begun 1594).

3 to R: *Cappella Garzonio*, later *Vittorio* (degli Angeli): Altarpiece of the Trinity and vault fresco of the *Coronation of the Virgin* by Federico Zuccaro (mid-1590s).

Right transept: *Chapel of St Francis Xavier* (De' Rossi, *Altari*, pl. 47): Altar designed by Cortona in the last year of his life (1669), but executed after his death (finished 1679). The arms on the bases of the columns are those of Clement IX and Innocent XI. Altarpiece: Maratta, *Death of St Francix Xavier* (1674–9; W); vault frescoes by Andrea Carlone.

Chapel to right of High Altar: *Cappella Orsini Lisi* (del S. Cuore): Attributed to Giacomo della Porta (Titi, 1686, p. 150); vault frescoed by Baldassare Croce (1599); altarpiece of the Sacred Heart by Pompeo Batoni (1760).

Choir: High Altar: A. Sarti (1841). The original tabernacle ascribed to Giacomo della Porta is now in the Cathedral of Thurles (Co. Tipperary; see J. D. H. Masleck, 'The Original High Altar Tabernacle of the Gesù rediscovered', *Burlington Magazine*, CXII, 1970, p. 110). Pozzo designed two magnificent High Altars for the church, one of which he actually executed in false perspective for the ceremony of Quarant'ore but he was unable to carry out either in permanent form (Pozzo, *Perspectiva pictorum*, II, Rome, 1700, pl. 71). In 1755 a new ciborium was added by Giuseppe Silvestro, an artist who is only known from the drawings for this church and other buildings in Rome preserved in the Kunstbibliothek, Berlin (Jacob, *Zeichnungen*, Nos 811ff.).

To left: Bernini, bust of Cardinal Bellarmino (1622). It originally formed part of a larger tomb with allegorical figures by Pietro Bernini, which was destroyed in the restoration of 1841 (Wittkower, *Bernini*, p. 182). The tomb is usually ascribed to Girolamo Rainaldi, but Mola (p. 117) attributes it to Francesco Peparelli.

Chapel to left of Choir: Originally the left transept was dedicated to S. Maria della Strada but later it was devoted to St Ignatius and the dedication to the Virgin transferred to this chapel. It is attributed to Giacomo della Porta by Titi (1686, p. 152), but according to Pecchiai is by Valeriano.

Left transept: *Cappella di S. Ignazio* (Pozzo, *Perspectiva Pictorum*, II, Rome, 1700, pl. 60; Lavagnino, *Altari*, p. 169; Kerber, *Andrea Pozzo*, Berlin and New York, 1971, p. 140): this chapel was originally dedicated to the Crucifixion and given to Cardinal Giacomo Savelli, who commissioned Giacomo della Porta to design a rich decoration for it. However, work was interrupted by Savelli's death in 1587. In 1629 a gilt bronze urn to contain the remains of St Ignatius was executed after the designs of the Jesuit architect Orazio Grassi with decorative detail by Alessandro Algardi (Heimbürger Ravalli, *Algardi*, p. 130); E. Neumann, 'Das Figurenrelief an der Urne des Hl. Ignazio im römischen Gesù', *Pantheon*, XXXV, 1977, p. 318) but it was not actually installed till 1637, when Pietro da Cortona was commissioned by Francesco Giattino to design the altar frontal which was executed by Santi Ghetti, Giovanni

Pilotti and Francuccio Francucci (commissioned March 1636; J.M.). The urn was remade in 1737 incorporating parts of the original (J.M.). In 1696 the whole altar was replaced by a new one designed by Andrea Pozzo, one of the most sumptuous Baroque works in any Roman church. The statue of the saint is an early 19th-century reproduction, made in Canova's studio, of Pierre Legros' original statue which was of silver and was melted down on the orders of Pius VI. Right: *Triumph of Religion over Heresy* by Legros. Left: *Triumph of Faith over Paganism* by Jean-Baptiste Théodon. Above the Trinity by Bernardino Ludovisi and Lorenzo Ottoni (Enggass, *Sculpture*, pp. 67, 81, 107, 108, 120, 133, 153). The relief over the altar, showing *St Peter appearing to St Ignatius at Loyola* is by Lorenzo Merlini and the other reliefs are by Pietro Paolo Reiffi, René Frémin, F. Nuvolone, P-E. Monnot, A. de' Rossi and Merlini (for subjects see Enggass, *Sculpture*, p. 46). To the sides of the altar are two reliefs, *Paul III approving the Jesuit Constitution* by A. de' Rossi, and the *Canonization of St Ignatius* by Bernardino Cametti.

The bronze altar rail (1695–9) is of exceptional splendour. It was probably designed by Carlo Fontana and was modelled by Francesco Maglia, G. B. Antonini, P. Legros, A. de' Rossi, C. Lobelli and others (Enggass, 'The Altar-rail for St Ignatius's Chapel in the Gesù di Roma', *Burlington Magazine*, CXVI, 1974, p. 178).

3 to L: *Cappella Taro*, later *Arrigoni* (Trinity): Altarpiece: Francesco Bassano, *Holy Trinity* (1592); Frescoes by Ventura Salimbeni and others.

2 to L: *Cappella Cerri* (Hibbard, op. cit., p. 43): The chapel originally belonged to the Braghesi family, but passed to the Cerri about 1639 and was restored on the designs of Pietro da Cortona from 1640 onwards.

The frescoes belong to the earlier phase and are by Niccolò Pomarancio, but heavily restored in the 19th century. The chapel contains four allegorical figures, inserted by the Cerri: *Justice* by Cosimo Fancelli, *Fortitude* by Giacomo Antonio Fancelli, *Prudence* and probably *Temperance* by Domenico Guidi. It also contains four tombs by Pietro da Cortona, each designed to contain a bust. Right back: Monsignor Antonio Cerri (d.1642) with a bust executed in the studio of Algardi, possibly by Domenico Guidi, after one by the master which is now in the Manchester Art Gallery. Right front: Monsignor Carlo Cerri (d.1726) by Filippo della Valle; left back: Cardinal Carlo Cerri (d.1690) by Guidi. The fourth niche was filled in the 19th century with a bust of a member of a different family.

1 to L: *Cappella Morelli*, later *Ravenna* (S.

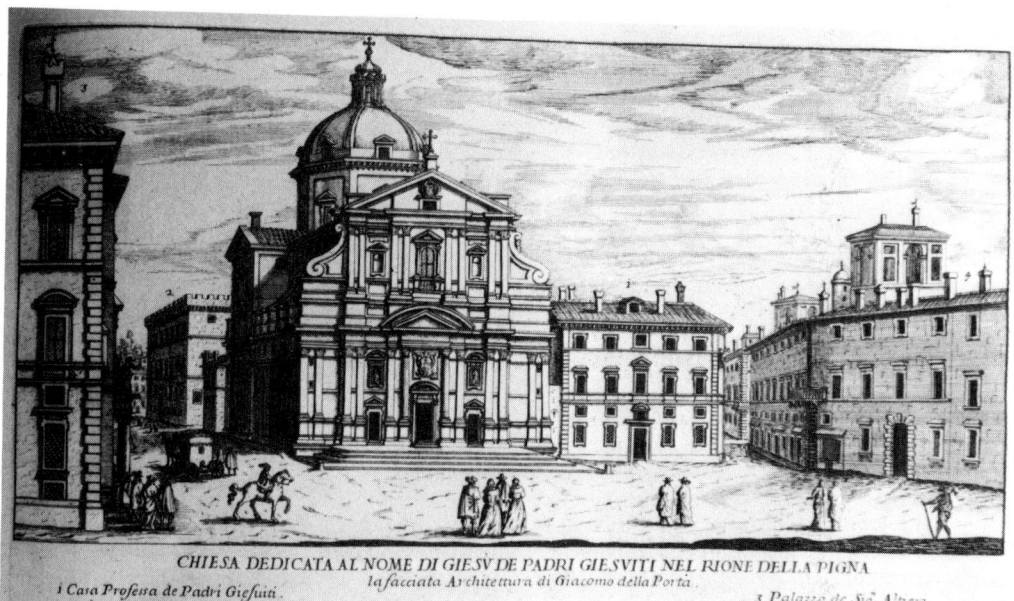

21. *The Gesù. Engraving by Falda. On the extreme left a corner of the Palazzo Altieri; in the distance the Palazzo Venezia; to the right of the church the Casa Professa of the Jesuits and on the extreme right the Palazzo Cenci-Bolognetti (Petrini) before its remodelling by Fuga.*

Francesco Borgia): Vault frescoes by Niccolò Circignani, called Il Pomarancio (*Pentecost* and allegorical figures); walls: frescoes by P. F. Mola (*Conversion of St Paul, St Peter baptizing in Prison* (Cocke, *Mola*, p. 59, No. 53); altarpiece: *St Francis Borgia in Prayer* by A. Pozzo, altered in the 19th century by the addition of the Japanese martyrs after their canonization in 1862 (W).

The church contains an important series of inlaid tomb slabs, of which the most interesting, in front of the altar rails to the right, is that of Carlo Pio, probably Cardinal Carlo Emmanuele Pio (d.1641). This was designed by Bernini about 1649–50, probably as a wall monument (a drawing for it exists at Holkham) but was eventually carried out as a floor slab, with the figures life-size, in brass inlaid in the marble, a technique very rare in Italy and much more frequent in northern Europe, particularly England, though it had gone out even there by this date. The result cannot be regarded as one of Bernini's triumphs, though as a smaller wall monument it might have been successful (Wittkower, *Bernini*, p. 271).

Casa Professa of the Gesù (to the right of the church): This contains the rooms of St Ignatius decorated with *trompe-l'oeil* frescoes begun by Giacomo Cortese in 1675 and finished by Andrea Pozzo between 1681 and 1686 (T. Venturi, *La Casa di S. Ignazio di Loiola a Roma*, Rome, 1924, and Kerber, op. cit., p. 50) and the chapel of Cardinal Odoardo Farnese by Girolamo Rainaldi (Fasolo, *Rainaldi*, p. 40).

Gesù e Maria
Via del Corso

Bibliography: Pollak, I, p. 130; Mola, p. 119; Titi, 1686, p. 349; De' Rossi, *Architettura Civile*, III, pls 33, 34; De' Rossi, *Altari*, pl. 48; Magni, I, pls 19, 35–7; Lavagnino, *Altari*, p. 149; Salerno, *Via del Corso*, p. 141; M. Fasolo, *Rainaldi*, p. 232; F. Trevisani, 'C. Rainaldi nella Chiesa di Gesù e Maria', *Storia dell'Arte*, XI, 1971, p. 163.

The church, which belongs to a house of Discalced Augustinian Friars, was built by an architect referred to as 'Carlo Butio Milanese', probably Carlo Buzzi, at the expense of Cardinal Scipione Borghese, the Principe di Sulmona and the Duca di Sangemini. The foundation stone was laid in 1633. In 1671–3 Carlo Rainaldi added the two western chapels and the façade and designed the decoration of the interior, including the High Altar; the church was consecrated in 1675 and the High Altar was unveiled in 1680 (Cartari-Febei). The façade is unusual in being a variant of Palladio's church façades with a smaller order playing against a larger one (S. Giorgio Maggiore, Redentore, S. Francesco della Vigna) which is rare in Rome (but cf. S. Francesca Romana and Bernini's Santuario at Ariccia) but in this case the small order is replaced by simple pilaster bands.

INTERIOR

Decorated with unusually rich marbling, partly of Sicilian jasper, the pilasters outlined in black and ranging from yellow through orange to red, except those flanking the chancel arch which are entirely in black.

Nave vault: G. Brandi, *God the Father receiving the Virgin into Heaven* (1686–7; W).

The most interesting feature of the church is the series of tombs of members of the Bolognetti family set in the four piers separating the side chapels (Donati, *Artisti ticinesi*, figs 427–32; Ferrari, *La Tomba*, pls CXLIXff.), which transform the whole church into a family chapel, a sort of oratory in which all the dead play their parts, an extension of the method employed by Bernini in his Cornaro and Fonseca chapels. The marble decoration and the tombs were finished in 1687 (Cartari-Febei).

Entrance wall (right): Tomb of Canon Camillo del Corno (d.1680), by Domenico Guidi.

1st pier right: Tomb of Pietro and Francesco Bolognetti by Francesco Aprile (De' Rossi, *Architettura Civile*, II, pl. 54).

2nd pier right: Tomb of Mario Bolognetti by Francesco Cavallini.

High Altar: G. Brandi, *Coronation of the Virgin* (between 1675 and 1686); angels in tympanum by P. Naldini; on either side marble statues of the two St Johns by Giuseppe Mazzuoli.

In the **monks' choir** is Lazzaro Baldi's painting, *The Virgin dividing her girdle between St Augustine and St Monica* (W).

3 to L: Memorials to Francesco and Flavia Bonelli, the latter by Bizzacheri (1691; Mallory, *Bizzacheri*, pp. 35, 45).

2nd pier L: Tomb of Giorgio Bolognetti, bishop of Rieti, who commissioned the whole scheme, by Cavallini (mentioned as not yet finished by Titi in 1686).

2 to L: G. Brandi, *Holy Family* (before 1663; W).

1st pier L: Tomb of Ercole and Luigi Bolognetti by Michele Maglia.

Over the tombs and in the window embrasures are stucco statues by Cavallini, M. Maglia and L. Ottoni.

Entrance wall (left): Tomb of Giulio del Corno (d.1662) by Ercole Ferrata with the assistance of Francesco Aprile.

S. Giacomo in Augusta. See next entry
Via del Corso

S. Giacomo degli Incurabili
Via del Corso

Bibliography: Falda, *Nuovo teatro*, III, pl. 26; De' Rossi, *Prospectus*, pls 56–8; Magni, I, pl. 19; P. Pecchiai and R. V. Montini (Chiese di Roma, 46); Salerno, *Via del Corso*, p. 128; Hibbard, *Maderno*, pp. 118ff.; M. Zocca, *La Cupola di S. Giacomo in Augusta*, Rome, 1945; Lotz, 'Die ovalen Kirchenräume', p. 58; Wittkower, *Italian Baroque*, p. 24; Buchowiecki, II, p. 34.

The hospital, also known as S. Giacomo in Augusta, owing to its proximity to the Mausoleum of Augustus, was founded in the 14th century by the terms of the will of Cardinal Pietro Colonna (d.1326). In 1515 Leo X raised it to an Arcispedale with the particular charge of looking after those suffering from syphilis which had been rampant in Italy since the 1490s. During the succeeding decades a number of distinguished architects, including Antonio da Sangallo the younger and Baldassare Peruzzi, made designs for a new building (plans reproduced by Buchowiecki), but nothing was done till the Florentine Cardinal Antonio Maria Salviati was put in charge.

Salviati first rebuilt the hospital, which runs in two wings between the Corso and the via di Ripetta, during the 1580s, and just before 1590 commissioned Francesco da Volterra to design the church. Volterra first planned a conventional Latin cross church, but soon abandoned it in favour of an oval scheme. The building was unfinished at the time of Volterra's death in 1594–5 and Maderno was appointed to replace him. Some parts of the building, including the upper part of the façade, have been attributed to him, but, though he unquestionably supervised the building of the façade and the dome, Hibbard has argued convincingly that he followed Volterra's design. The structure of the church was finished by 1601, and the steps in front of it were built in 1608 (Hibbard, *Licenze*, p. 106).

INTERIOR
The church marks an important step in the development of churches based on an oval plan in that the tall chancel arch, which breaks through the main entablature, gives a greater emphasis to the longitudinal axis than in Vignola's two oval churches (S. Andrea in via Flaminia and S. Anna dei Palafrenieri). Wittkower argues that the fact that the middle chapels – on the ends of the short axis of the oval – have higher arches than those which flank them (though they do not break through the entablature) establishes an emphasis on the cross-axis, but it is possible to see the succession of low–high–low arches as a variation on the normal regular repetition of equal arches which actually accentuates the movement of the eye towards the High Altar. The interior was restored in 1861 when the dome fresco was painted, and again in 1910 when the painted marble was added.

2 to R: (S. Francesco di Paola): Over the altar a relief of the Saint adoring the *Madonna dei Miracoli* by P. Legros (1716–19) who also did the stucco decoration (Enggass, *Sculpture*, p. 145); on the walls paintings by G. Passeri of the life of the Saint (1714; W).

Inside the hospital but accessible from the via di Ripetta is the small octagonal church of S. Maria Porta Paradisi, designed about 1523 by Antonio da Sangallo the Younger and executed by Giorgio da Coldrerio (Pecchiai and Montini, pp. 11ff., 62ff.). It was remodelled in 1644–5 by Giovanni Antonio de' Rossi (Spagnesi, *G. A. De Rossi*, pp. 32ff.). The stuccoes of the dome are by C. Fancelli and Domenico de' Rossi and the frescoes are ascribed by Waterhouse to Ubaldini, though the payments are to P. P. Naldini.

The High Altar is by F. Brunetti; that to the right (*Holy Family with St Anne (?) and St John the Baptist*) is traditionally ascribed to Lazzaro de' Rossi; that on the left (*Resurrected Christ*) is by Cosimo Fancelli. The tomb of Matteo Caccia (d.1644) and Dorotea Carelli (d.1650) is also by Fancelli, who presumably remodelled Jacopo Sansovino's tomb of Antonio de Burgos to match it.

To the north of this church, in the via di Ripetta, is another façade dated 1589, apparently also belonging to a church but in fact closing one of the wings of the hospital. As an engraving by Falda (Pecchiai and Montini, fig. 5) shows, this originally stood on the Corso, to the north of the church, though its exact function there is not clear. The two bays which at present close the wings of the hospital on the Corso are by Pietro Camporese the Younger and date from the Pontificate of Gregory XVI (1831–46). His wooden model for them is in the museum of the Ospedale di Santo Spirito.

S. Giacomo alla Lungara
Via della Lungara

Bibliography: Baglione, p. 181; Martinelli, p. 51; Titi, 1674, p. 38 and 1763, p. 33; Roisecco, 1750, I, p. 141; Vasi, *Magnificenze*, pl. 72; *Guide Rionali*, XIII, i, p. 46.

Founded by Pius IV as a convent for reformed prostitutes but given in 1628 by Urban VIII to the Augustinian nuns of S. Maria Maddalena delle Convertite al Corso, and rebuilt at the expense of Cardinal Francesco Barberini before 1642, probably to the designs of Luigi Arigucci working in collaboration with Domenico Castello.

INTERIOR
Choir: High Altar: G. F. Romanelli, fresco of *St James* (B. Kerber, 'Addenda zu G. F. Romanelli', *Giessener Beiträge zur Kunstgeschichte*, IV, 1979, p. 1).

Right wall: Monument to Ippolito Merenda, who died in 1636 and left 20,000 scudi for the convent. The tomb, which is entirely in white marble, consists of a skeleton holding a piece of drapery on which is incised the inscription celebrating the deceased. It was designed by Bernini on a commission from Cardinal Francesco Barberini but was executed by an assistant, probably in 1640–1 (Wittkower, *Bernini*, p. 211). For the skeleton cf. Bernini's tomb of Alessandro Valtrini in S. Lorenzo in Damaso; for the wind-swept drapery cf. the same monument and also that of the Blessed Maria Raggi in S. Maria sopra Minerva. This probably signifies the idea of death sweeping all away, as the wind blows away dead leaves (Blunt, 'Gianlorenzo Bernini: Illusionism and Mysticism', *Art History*, I, 1978, p. 67).

S. Giacomo degli Spagnuoli
Piazza Navona

Bibliography: Güthlein, *Familienarchiv Spada*, p. 219; *Guide Rionali*, VI, 1, p. 22.

Virgilio Spada records that when Innocent X was building his palace on the Piazza Navona and rebuilding S. Agnese the Spanish colony added a new – very simple – façade to their church.

In the 19th century the orientation of the church was changed and the main entrance is now from the Corso del Rinascimento.

SS. Gioacchino e Anna
Via del Quirinale, 24

Bibliography: Totti, p. 516; Titi, 1686, p. 269; De' Rossi, 1697, p. 670; Thieme-Becker; *s.v.*; Maruscelli.

Built for Reformed Spanish Carmelites, presumably in 1599, the date over the door, but rebuilt by Paolo Maruscelli (before 1638). The church has a central dome over a square substructure. Titi, writing in 1686, says the church had recently been redecorated, but this work was swept away in a drastic 19th-century restoration. It now belongs to the Belgian College. Entrance is through the rusticated door to the right of the church.

SS. Gioacchino e Anna
Via in Selci

Bibliography: Vasi, 1791, I, p. 211; Eimer, *S. Agnese*, I, p. 115; *Guide Rionali*, I, 2, p. 78.

Built 1774–80, on a simple Greek Cross plan, by Francesco Fiori for a body of Tertiary Franciscans founded in 1730. The altar, representing the Virgin with her parents, a good example of mid-18th-century Roman painting, has apparently only recently been inserted and the name of the author has not been vouchsafed.

S. Giovanni Calabita
Isola di S. Bartolomeo

Bibliography: Vasi, *Magnificenze*, pl. 173; L. Huetter, R. U. Martini (Chiese di Roma, 37).

A church dedicated to St John the Baptist stood on this site from Early Christian times, but the dedication was later changed to one to the Roman Martyr S. Giovanni Calabita. In 1584 Gregory XIII gave the church and the attached hospital to the Fatebenefratelli (an Order founded in the 16th century by the Portuguese St John of God) who reconstructed the church in 1640. Borromini was asked to produce plans for the façade (Albertina 356, 358, 359) and in 1644 Martino Longhi the Younger made designs for the façade but these were not carried out and the existing façade was built in 1711, probably by the architect Romano Carapecchia who worked mainly in Malta (J. Variano, 'Martino Longhi the Younger and the façade of San Giovanni Calabita in Rome', *Art Bulletin*, LII, 1970, p. 71). Between 1736 and 1741 the interior was given its present magnificent marble decoration, by Carapecchia, which was completed by a series of frescoes and paintings by Corrado Giaquinto. The result is one of the richest interiors of any 18th-century church in Rome. It was visited by Clement XII in 1742 (Mallory, *Notizie*, p. 108).

INTERIOR

Nave and choir vaults: Corrado Giaquinto, *Glory of St John of God* (1741–2), and *God the Father with the dead Christ* (Poensgen, fig. 45).
Sacristy: Vault fresco: *The Benefratelli ministering to the Sick* (attributed to Baldi or G. P. Schor).
2 to R: G. B. Lenardi, *Death of St John of God*.
Choir right: C. Giaquinto, *Martyrdom of Sts Marius, Martha, Audifax and Habbakuk*.
High Altar: A. Gennaroli, *The Virgin with St John of God*, enlarged at the top by C. Giaquinto.
Choir left: Giaquinto, *The Martyrs of Porto*.
2 to L: Giaquinto, *Death of St Anthony Abbot*.
In the hospital (apply in the Sacristy or at the door of the hospital to the left of the church):
Sala Capitolare: M. Preti, *Flagellation*.
Sala dell'Assunta: Magnificent stucco altar with painted curtain held by angels by B. Cametti, with the arms of Clement XI (1700–2; Pio, *Le Vite di Pittori Scultori et Architetti*, ed. Enggass, Vatican, 1977, p. 153, and review by E. Waterhouse, *Burlington Magazine*, CXXII, 1980, p. 202). Fine and unusual *scagliola* altar frontal.

S. Giovanni Decollato
Via S. Giovanni Decollato

Bibliography: V. Moschini (Chiese di Roma, 26); E. Lavagnino, *La Chiesa di Santo Spirito in Sassia*, Rome, 1962, p. 61; M. Hirst, 'Salviati's two Apostles in the Oratorio of S. Giovanni Decollato', *Studies in Renaissance and Baroque Art presented to Anthony Blunt on his 60th birthday*, London, 1967, p. 34.

The confraternity of S. Giovanni Decollato was founded in 1488 by a body of Florentines to attend those condemned to death. The church was begun almost immediately but not finished till the 1550s. The Oratory was built in 1535. The church contains a number of fine altarpieces of the mid and late 16th century, but the Oratory is much more remarkable for its frescoes which form one of the most complete examples of Mannerist illusionism. They were begun about 1536 by Jacopino del Conte, continued by Francesco Salviati and completed in the 1550s by Pirro Ligorio. They show one of the most ingenious schemes of Mannerist illusionism, with fictive architecture and figures apparently walking into the pictures from the real space of the chapel – devices which were to be widely employed by Baroque artists.

Within the buildings of the confraternity – and only shown on the feast day of St John the Baptist (August 29) – is a bronze group of the *Beheading of St John the Baptist* attributed to F. Duquesnoy (I. Toesca, 'A group by Duquesnoy', *Burlington Magazine*, CXVII, 1975, p. 668).

S. Giovanni dei Fiorentini
Via Giulia

Bibliography: De' Rossi, *Architettura Civile*, III, pls 25, 26; Magni, I, pl. 100; A. Nava, 'La storia della Chiesa di S. Giovanni dei Fiorentini', *Archivio della Romana Deputazione di Storia Patria*, LIX, 1936, p. 337; H. Siebenhüner, 'S. Giovanni dei Fiorentini', *Kunstgeschichtliche Studien für Hans Kauffmann*, Berlin, 1956, p. 174; E. Rufini, (Chiese di Roma, 39); Hibbard, *Maderno*, p. 142; Salerno, *Via Giulia*, p. 201; *Guide Rionali*, V, 4, p. 16.

The church of the Florentine community. After various projects had been submitted in 1518 the church was actually started in 1520 to the design of Antonio da Sangallo the Younger. After the Sack of Rome building stopped, when only part of the foundations of the nave had been built. In 1559 Michelangelo submitted plans for a centralized building, but these were not executed and in 1583 work was resumed under Giacomo della Porta on the original Latin Cross plan. By 1593 the nave was finished, but work had apparently stopped for lack of funds. In 1598–9 Maderno is mentioned as architect of the church, but little was done till 1610–14, when the church was finished. The transepts were being stuccoed in 1618. For the interior of the dome see Gloton, pl. XXI.

Maderno's main alteration to the earlier plans seems to have been to make the transepts and choir square-ended instead of apsed.

The façade was added by Alessandro Galilei in 1734 for Clement XII (Corsini). Reliefs: *St John preaching* by F. della Valle; *Baptism* by Bracci; *Visitation* by P. Benaglia; *Beheading of St John* by Scaramucci. Statues over entablature (left to right): *S. Maria Maddalena dei Pazzi* by S. Sanni; *S. Filippo Benizi* by F. Queirolo; *S. Pietro Igneo* by Simone Martines; *S. Bernardo degli Uberti* by G. Altobelli; *B. Eugenio Diacono* by C. (or P.) Pacilli; *S. Caterina dei Ricci* by G. Cornaro (all 1734–5); over the door: *Charity* and *Fortitude* by Filippo della Valle.

INTERIOR

The organ is said to have been made in 1673.
Right aisle: Bust of Clement XII by Filippo della Valle (1750) with inscription recording the building of the façade.

1 to R: D. Cresti, *St Vincent Ferrer preaching*.
2 to R: Altarpiece and fresco attributed to S. Pieri.
In passage to sacristy: Busts of Antonio Coppola (1612) and Antonio Cepparelli (1622) by Bernini (I. Lavin, 'Five new youthful sculptures by Gianlorenzo Bernini', *Art Bulletin*, 1968, p. 223). D'Onofrio (*Roma vista*, p. 106) thinks that the first bust is by Pietro Bernini.
3 to R: (S. Girolamo): Altarpiece: Santi di Tito, *The Penitent St Jerome* (dated 1599); right wall: Cigoli, *St Jerome writing the Vulgate*; left wall: Passignano, *The Building of S. Giovanni dei Fiorentini*.
4 to R: (S. Filippo Neri): Altarpiece: copy of Maratta's *S. Filippo Neri*.
Last pier right: Monument to marchesa Francesca Riccardi (d.1655) with bust by L. Merlini (c.1700) (Enggass, *Sculpture*, p. 122).
Right transept: Salvator Rosa, *Martyrdom of Sts Cosmas and Damian* (1669). Tombs of Ottaviano Acciaioli (d.1695; right) by Ercole Ferrata (Titi, 1763, p. 424) and Ottaviano Corsini (d.1641; left) by Algardi (Heimbürger Ravalli, *Algardi*, p. 105).
Chapel to right of choir: (Sacramento): Decorated by Matteo da Città di Castello (1612–14) with elaborately inlaid marble altar; right wall: Anastasia Fontebuoni, *Death of the Virgin*; left wall: Ciampelli, *Nativity*; dome fresco also by Ciampelli.
Choir: In the 17th century this was in effect turned into a family chapel by the Falconieri, whose palace stood at the end of Via Giulia and who were of Florentine origin (Pollak, I, p. 131; Blunt, *Borromini*, p. 201).

In 1634 Orazio Falconieri commissioned Pietro da Cortona to make the High Altar, the design for which is at Windsor (K. Noehles, 'Architekturprojekte Cortonas', *Münchner Jahrbuch der bildenden Kunst*, N.S. XX, 1969, p. 182, and *SS. Luca e Martina*, pp. 13, 29). Cortona is known to have made a full-scale model of it in wood, but no work seems to have been done on the marble altar itself. At some date between 1656 and 1664 Falconieri took up the scheme again, but this time he entrusted the execution of it to Borromini, in spite of the fact that Cortona was still alive.

For the High Altar Borromini used Cortona's design but modified it in several ways. He abolished the attic over the main order and continued the order itself to the full height available, thus producing a design commensurate with the unusual height of the nave and choir of the church. He replaced Cortona's simple curved pediment with one of his favourite compound forms (cf. Oratory façade), and moved the outer columns forward, giving them his most elaborate form of fluting (as in the fireplace in the Oratory). Francesco Mochi was originally commissioned to make a relief of the *Baptism* for the altar (now in the Museo di Roma) but this was never used and the existing group, in coloured marble, is by Antonio Raggi. The seated statues of *Fortitude* and *Justice* were added after Borromini's death, when he was succeeded by Cortona's pupil Ciro Ferri who completed the scheme (unveiled 1683, Cartari-Febei). *Fortitude* is by Leonardo Reti and *Justice* by an artist referred to by Titi in 1686 (p. 395) as Monsù Michele and was identified in the 1763 edition as Michel Anguier, but this cannot be correct, since he left Rome in 1651. He may possibly be Michel Maille, known in Italian as Michele Maglia.

On the two walls of the choir are monuments to the Falconieri family. These were begun by Borromini, but the crowning sections, which do not carry on the Borrominesque movement of the main order, were completed by Ferri (De' Rossi, *Altari*, pls 15, 16; De' Rossi, *Architettura Civile*, II, pl. 52). The right-hand tomb is that of Orazio Falconieri and his wife Ottavia Sacchetti, with a statue of *Charity* holding a portrait medallion, by Domenico Guidi. The left-hand tomb of Orazio's brother Cardinal Lelio (d.1648) has a statue of *Faith* by Ercole Ferrata. The other statues were added in the 18th century (Portoghesi, *Borromini*, pl. 198).

Orazio Falconieri also planned a mortuary chapel under the choir (Portoghesi, *Borromini*, pls 200–3; for measured drawings of this chapel and the tombs in the choir see G. Perugini, *Modelli Borrominiani in S. Giovanni dei Fiorentini*, Rome, 1961–2). From a drawing in Berlin (*Fünf Architecta aus fünf Jahrhunderten*, Kunstbibliothek, Berlin, 1976, No. 22) it is clear that Borromini was involved in the designing of the chapel, but as it stands it is far more Cortonesque than Borrominesque in character (compare the lower church of SS. Luca e Martina) and it must have been finished by Ferri after Borromini's death. It is worth noticing that the Doric columns have no bases and therefore correspond to the Roman Doric used by Borromini on the façade of the Palazzo di Propaganda Fide, but the floor of the chapel is not the original one and may have been raised, perhaps owing to flooding from the Tiber.

Drawings by Borromini for the Falconieri chapels are in the Kunstbibliothek, Berlin (Jacob, *Zeichnungen*, Nos 348–51).

In the pavement under the crossing, near the arch leading to the left transept, is the tomb of Carlo Maderno.

Chapel to left of High Altar: *Cappella Sacchetti* (Crocifisso): Paintings by Lanfranco: vault, *Christ in Glory* and the *Four Evangelists* (Gloton, pl. XX); lunettes and walls, *Scenes from the Passion* (W); bronze crucifix modelled by Prospero Antichi (Bresciano) and cast after his death in 1592 by Paolo Sanquirico.
Left transept: Altarpiece: Baccio Ciarpi, *Mary Magdalen* (W); monuments to Antonio Barberini (d.1559; right) after Bernini (before 1629; Wittkower, *Bernini*, p. 192), and P. F. de' Rossi (d.1673; left) by an unknown sculptor.
Left aisle: last pier left: Monument to Girolamo Samminiati (1733) by Filippo della Valle.
Last pier right: Monument to Alessandro Capponi (d.1746, monument set up the same year) designed by Fuga, sculpture by Michelangelo Slotz (Ferrari, *La Tomba*, pl. CLXXX; Matthiae, *Fuga*, p. 53).
5 to L: (St Francis): Altarpiece: Santi di Tito, *St Francis*.
4 to L: (St Anthony Abbot): Altarpiece: Ciampelli, *Death of St Anthony*; on walls: Giovanni Angelo Canini, frescoes of St Peter and St Paul (after 1659; W).
1 to L: *Montauto* (S. Sebastiano): Altarpiece: G. B. Vanni, *St Sebastian tended by the Holy Women*.

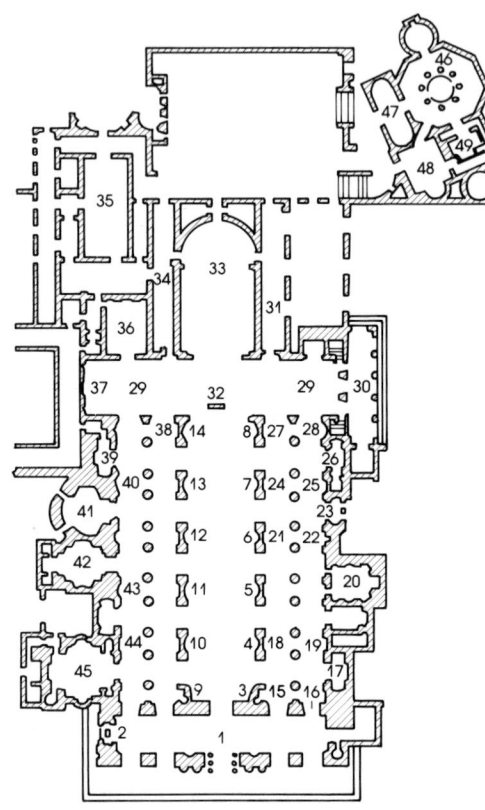

22. *S. Giovanni in Laterano*. Plan.

S. Giovanni dei Genovesi
Via dei Genovesi

Bibliography: Titi, 1763, p. 53; *Architettura minora*, I, pl. 39.

The church, which is attached to a hospital belonging to the Genoese community, was built in 1481 but completely remodelled in the 19th century. It still contains some paintings of the 17th and 18th centuries.
2 to L: G. Odazzi, *Madonna di Savoia*.
In the hospital is a fine 15th-century cloister.

S. Giovanni in Laterano
Piazza di S. Giovanni in Laterano

Bibliography: Titi, 1763, p. 210; De' Rossi, *Architettura Civile*, I, pls 64–70; Letarouilly, pls 225–8 (255–8); Magni, I, pls 92–5; Ortolani (Chiese di Roma, 13); *Guide Rionali*, I, 1, p. 22 and XV, p. 151; Buchowiecki, I, p. 61. For the early history of the church: R. Krautheimer et al., *Corpus basilicarum christianarum Romae*, Rome (Vatican), 1937–77, V, p. 1. For Borromini's restoration of the interior: Hempel, *Borromini*, p. 91; Portoghesi, *Borromini*, pls LVII–LXXII, 92–122; Heimbürger Ravalli, *Archivio Spada*, p. 217; Blunt, *Borromini*, p. 134; Güthlein, *Familienarchiv Spada*, pp. 206–17, 227–50. For the designs submitted for the façade; A. Prandi, 'A. Deriset e il concorso per la facciata di S. Giovanni in Laterano', *Roma*, XXII, 1944, p. 23; A. Schiavo, *La Fontana di Trevi*, p. 27; V. Golzio, 'La Facciata di S. Giovanni in Laterano', *Miscellanea Bibliothecae Hertzianae*, Munich, 1961, p. 458; H. Hager, 'On a project ascribed to Carlo Fontana for the façade of S. Giovanni in Laterano', *Burlington Magazine*, CXVII, 1975, p. 105; id., 'Il Modello di L. Rusconi per la facciata di S. Giovanni in Laterano', *Commentari*, XXII, 1971, p. 36; S. Jacob, 'Die Projekte Bibienas und Doris für die Fassade von S. Giovanni in Laterano', *Zeitschrift für Kunstgeschichte*, XXXV, 1972, p. 100; Mallory, *Rococo*, p. 112, note 16; Volker Hoffmann, 'Die Fassade von S. Giovanni in Laterano', *Römisches Jahrbuch*, XVII, 1978, p. 1. Much new information will be provided by Dr E. Kieven in her forthcoming monograph on Galilei (to be published by Zwemmer).

The Cathedral of Rome and first church of Christendom, founded by Constantine the

S. Giovanni in Laterano

Great on the property of the Plauti Laterani, a wealthy Roman family, and the barracks of the Equites Singulares. After being sacked and burnt a number of times it was rebuilt by Urban V (1362–70) and Gregory XI (1370–8), and restored by Martin V (1417–31). Finally it was remodelled by Borromini for Innocent X for the Holy Year of 1650. The Benediction Loggia on the north transept was built in 1586–9 by Domenico Fontana for Sixtus V.

The façade was built in 1733–5 by Alessandro Galilei who won a competition instituted by Clement XII in which all the leading architects of Rome took part. The statues on the top of the façade represent the two St Johns, and the doctors of the church (Ortolani lists the sculptors). Numbers refer to the plan.

VESTIBULE

The vestibule [1] contains an ancient statue of Constantine, set up here in 1737 to replace one of Clement XII [2]. The reliefs over the door with scenes from the life of the Baptist are by Filippo della Valle, P. Bracci, B. Ludovisi and G. B. Maini. The bronze doors dating from the reign of Diocletian were taken by Alexander VII from the Curia (later converted into the church of S. Adriano) and given to the Lateran in 1637, but they had to be enlarged to fit the door by the addition of the outer bands with stars. This operation was carried out by Girolamo Ferreri and other craftsmen between 1657 and 1661 to the design of Borromini. References to the installation of the doors occur in the *Diary* of the pope (entries 32, 34, 37, 168; also Güthlein, *Familienarchiv Spada*, p. 216).

INTERIOR

The carved wooden roof was begun under Pius IV in 1562 and finished under Pius V in 1567. It is ascribed to Pirro Ligorio.

The floor was originally laid by Martin V, the crowned column of whose arms (Colonna) appears three times in it. The sections under the arches of the nave have the arms of Innocent X and near the main door are those of Alexander VII. Payments to Borromini for it are recorded in 1654 (Güthlein, *Familienarchiv Spada*, II, p. 202).

In 1646 (Gigli, p. 278) Innocent X decided to restore the church which was in danger of collapsing and he gave the commission to Borromini with the condition that the work had to be finished by the Holy Year of 1650. The architect was also instructed to preserve as much of the old structure as possible, for reasons of piety, not on aesthetic grounds. In general the pope had no objection to the old parts being con-

23. *S. Giovanni in Laterano. Engraving by Vasi. On the right of the church is the Lateran Palace, and on the extreme right is the apse of the Triclinium of Leo III. In the distance the Ospedale delle Donne.*

cealed within the new but he insisted that some parts should be left visible. Borromini satisfied this demand by leaving the ovals, which now contain reliefs of the prophets added in the 18th century, open to show the old walls 'come gioia nell'anello, acciò resti e perpetua memoria la fabrica fatta da Costantino', as is recorded by Virgilio Spada (Heimbürger Ravalli, *Archivio Spada*, p. 220). Borromini pulled down the aisles, strengthened the walls of the nave (which were dangerously out of the vertical), removed one column out of three of the old arcade and embedded the remainder in his new piers. He produced three designs which are often said to have been made in succession but were actually alternatives presented simultaneously to the pope. He planned to vault the nave with a series of 'ribs' of which the first were to spring from the canted bays next to the main doors to the church and would have come down on the second pairs of pilasters along the nave. How he would have dealt with those which would have come down at the crossing is not clear, because his designs seem to show that he was going to preserve the colossal ancient granite columns which existed at that point in the old church and he would therefore not have been able to have canted bays.

The work was carried out at incredible speed in spite of difficulties which arose owing to Borromini's temperament, because though very practical and easy with his own workmen he was incredibly touchy about outside interference and on several occasions stopped work altogether till his grievancies were settled (Güthlein, pp. 238ff.). The structure was finished by the end of 1647, and most of the stucco decoration by October 1649, two months before the opening of the Holy Year. Borromini hoped to be able to continue his 'restoration' round the transepts and choir, but lack of funds – and after the death of Innocent X possibly lack of enthusiasm for the architect – frustrated the project. The result is that, though the articulation of the nave is one of Borromini's most mature achievements, the effect is incomplete because the huge pilasters clearly need to run on into a vault, and there is a complete break between the nave and the transepts and choir.

The detail of the interior is of superb quality. The bases of the nave pilasters have an almost Michelangelesque richness, whereas those of the aisles are much more delicate. The sides of the piers are decorated with bands of laurel and palm-leaves in Borromini's most crisp manner and the grey marble bases of the niches containing the statues of the Apostles are decorated with garlands of palm-leaves in the same style. The vaults of the aisles are peopled with a host of Borromini's favourite winged cherub heads.

After 1650 work was more or less suspended, though Borromini began to plan the project for bringing back into the church fragments of the mediaeval and Renaissance tombs which had been removed during the restoration of the building – some of which are recorded in summary drawings in the MSS of Virgilio Spada (Güthlein, *Familienarchiv Spada*, I, p. 230) – and incorporating them in settings of his own design. A few of the drawings connected with this project bear the arms of Innocent X but nothing was actually carried out till after his death and the actual monuments all bear the arms of Alexander VII (the project is mentioned a number of times in entries in Alexander's diary for 1658-9: entries 175, 314, 315, 345).

Borromini showed the utmost ingenuity in incorporating the old fragments and in producing designs which would fit the awkward spaces below the oval windows in the outer walls of the aisles. The tombs are engraved in De' Rossi, *Architettura Civile*, II, pls 37-44 and reproduced in Portoghesi, *Borromini*, pls 105-19.

The niches of the main piers of the nave are of grey marble and are flanked by columns of *verde antico* taken from the aisles of the old church. They contain statues of the Apostles, commissioned by Clement XI in 1703 and executed after the designs of Carlo Maratta between 1703 and 1718 by a team of sculptors under the general direction of Carlo Fontana (Enggass, *Sculpture, passim*; Braham and Hager, p. 86; M. Conforti, 'Planning the Lateran Apostles', *Studies in Italian Art and Architecture* (American Academy in Rome), Cambridge (Mass), 1980, p. 243). Statues: [3] **1 to R:** L. Ottoni, *Thadeus*; [4] **2 to R:** C. Rusconi, *St Matthew*; [5] **3 to R:** G. Mazzuoli, *St Philip*; [6] **4 to R:** P. Legros, *St Thomas*; [7] **5 to R:** C. Rusconi, *St James the Great*; [8] **6 to R:** P. E. Monnot, *St Paul*; [9] **1 to L:** F. Maratta, *Simon*; [10] **2 to L:** P. Legros, *St Bartholomew*; [11] **3 to L:** A. de'Rossi, *St James the Less*; [12] **4 to L:** C. Rusconi, *St John*; [13] **5 to L:** C. Rusconi, *St Andrew*; [14] **6 to L:** P E. Monnot, *St Peter*.

The reliefs over the niches, representing scenes from the Old and New Testaments, were executed in 1648-9 by various artists under the direction of Algardi (for details see Heimbürger Ravalli, *Algardi*, p. 171; Ferrari, *Lo Stucco*, pls CIVff.; Heimbürger Ravalli, *Archivio Spada*, p. 232). Between them are oval paintings with figures of Old Testament Prophets commissioned in 1718, by artists including G. Chiari, L. Garzi, B. Luti, D. M. Muratori, G. Nasini,

G. Odazzi, A. Procaccini and F. Trevisani (W).

RIGHT AISLE

Over the doors leading from the vestibule to the inner aisles are stucco panels with very elaborate curved and broken pediments put up by Cardinal Benedetto Pamphili in 1729 [15]. Beside them are doors by Borromini leading to small spiral staircases (De' Rossi, *Architettura Civile*, I, pl. 69). Over the doors leading from the vestibule to the outer aisles are stucco panels with the arms of Alexander VII designed by Borromini [16].

1 to R: *Cappella Orsini* [17]: One of the three chapels completely rebuilt by Borromini. The altar-rails show a variant of the form of balustrade with alternating balusters which he used in the cloister of S. Carlino and the gallery of the Oratory. Here in addition to making the balusters alternate in their vertical disposition, Borromini set them alternately with a flat face or a sharp edge facing into the aisle, thus introducing the maximum liveliness. Indeed the balusters seem almost to be rotating as one walks past them. Similar balustrades occur in the other two chapels which Borromini rebuilt (**4 to R** and **5 to L**). Altarpiece: *Madonna and Saints* by Placido Costanzi (Buchowiecki).

1st pier of nave [18]: Borromini, monument to Boniface VIII, incorporating four grey marble columns and a fragment of the Trecento fresco showing the pope proclaiming the Holy Year of 1300.

Between 1 and 2 to R [19]: Borromini, tomb of Cardinal Giulio Acquavivia (d.1574); incorporates statues of *Temperance* and *Prudence* by Isaia da Pisa from the tomb of Cardinal de Chiaves (see below).

3 to R: *Cappella Massimo* [20]: By Giacomo della Porta (1565–71; Schwager, 'Giacomo della Portas Herkunft und Anfänge in Rom', *Römisches Jahrbuch*, XV, 1975, p. 120). Its entrance had to be displaced when Borromini restored the church and he balanced the new door with a grille composed of the *monti* and stars of Alexander VII's arms. Altarpiece: *Crucifixion* by Sicciolante da Sermoneta.

3rd pier [21]: Borromini, monument to Alexander III in black and yellow marble with medallion of the pope by Guidi (1657–9; Diary of Alexander VII, entries 105, 286, 309, 362).

Between 3 and entrance to Palace [22]: Tomb of Cardinal Cesare Rasponi (d.1675) by Filippo Carcani.

Between 3 and 4 to R [23]: Bay containing the entrance to the Lateran Palace, bearing the date of the Holy Year 1650 and the arms of Innocent X (much criticized by Visentini, *Osservazioni*, p. 6). The swags with the Pamphili dove on the side walls and the leaves spread over the ceilings above the windows are to be found almost exactly repeated in Borromini's decoration of the Villa Giustiniani. The other side of the door, which also bears the arms of Innocent X, can be seen from the cloister of the Lateran Palace.

4th pier [24]: Borromini, monument to Sergius IV incorporating an earlier relief.

Between entrance to Palace and 4 to R [25]: Borromini monument to Cardinal Casate, conte di Giussano, in pale grey marble. It incorporates fragments of the mediaeval altar from the chapel of the Magdalen, which is surprising since it was Cardinal Bianco (see below) who was buried under this altar, not Cardinal Casate.

4 to R: *S. Giovanni Evangelista* [26]: L. Baldi, *St John on Patmos* (c. 1660–5; W).

5th pier [27]: Tomb of Cardinal Ranuccio Farnese, ascribed by Martinelli (p. 675) unconvincingly to Vignola. The statues are signed by Antonio Petrarca (Martinelli).

Between 4 to R and transept [28]: Borromini, monument to Cardinal Antonio Martinez de Chiaves, called the Cardinal of Portugal (d.1447), incorporating the sarcophagus and recumbent figures from his original tomb and three other 15th-century figures.

The transepts [29] were redecorated for Clement VIII under the direction of Giacomo della Porta and the Cavaliere d'Arpino between 1597 and 1601 in connection with the Holy Year of 1600. The lower parts of the walls have inlaid marbling, and the frescoes above are painted as feigned tapestries with the Aldobrandini arms in the borders. These represent scenes from the life of Constantine, including his conversion, the building of the Lateran and the Donation of land to the church. The organ case is by G. B. Montano (Martinelli, p. 64; Mola, p. 68); the two grey marble holy-water stoups, presumably dating from the mid-18th century, of asymmetrical Rococo designs, are of a type unusual in Rome. In the vestibule to the transept [30] (below the Benediction Loggia) is a statue of Henry IV of France by Nicolas Cordier, set up by Clement VIII to record his absolution and reception into the Roman church.

Corridor to the right of the Choir [31]: Tomb of Gabriele Filipucci by B. Cametti (Enggass, *Sculpture*, p. 154).

CROSSING

Under the crossing stands the Papal Altar at which only the pope can celebrate Mass [32]. Alexander VII planned to replace it in 1657. An entry in his *Diary* (No. 123 for 22.viii.1657) shows that Borromini, who had made designs for it (Hempel, *Borromini*, pl. 67, and De' Rossi, *Architettura Civile*, III, pls 48, 49), did not get the commission. The pope adds: 'si vuol morire di dolore'. In fact nothing was done at that time, but the baldacchino was reconstructed by Pius IX in 1851, incorporating parts of the original tabernacle.

CHOIR [33]
In 1763 Pope Clement XIII commissioned Piranesi to make designs for the remodelling of the choir of the church to complete the work undertaken by Borromini for Innocent X, but although the architect produced a set of brilliant drawings (in the Pierpont Morgan Library, New York) nothing was actually built and the project was abandoned in 1767 (J. Wilton-Ely, *Piranesi*, Arts Council Exhibition, 1978, p. 87; *The Mind and Art of Giovanni Battista Piranesi*, London, 1978, pp. 94ff.). In the event the choir was – disastrously – rebuilt and lengthened by Leo XIII in 1884.

Passage leading to Sacristy [34]: Tombs including those of the Cavaliere d'Arpino (1640) and Andrea Sacchi (1661), the latter probably by Pietro Paolo Naldini (Sutherland Harris, *Sacchi*, p. 32).

Sagrestia dei Canonici [35]: The end walls were frescoed by Agostino Ciampelli with scenes from the life of St Clement (*c*.1602–5) and the vault by Giovanni and Cherubino Alberti about 1600 with brilliant *quadratura* compositions (M. C. Abramson, 'Clement VIII's patronage of the Brothers Alberti', *Art Bulletin*, LX, 1978, p. 531). In a room off the sacristy is a monument to Louis XV.

Cappella Colonna [36]: According to Martinelli (p. 66) the architecture is by Girolamo Rainaldi. To left: tomb of Lucrezia Tomacelli (1625) designed by Teodoro della Porta with a bronze bust by Giacomo Laurenziano.

Left transept: Altar of the Holy Sacrament [37]: set up by Clement VIII for the Holy Year of 1600 to the design of Padre Paolo Olivieri who incorporated in his design four ancient Roman gilt bronze columns, of colossal size, said to have come from the temple of Jupiter Capitolinus. The tabernacle, made of semi-precious stones, is by Pompeo Targone. The silver relief of the *Last Supper* over the altarpiece was by Curzio Vanni but was melted down at the time of the French occupation in the 1790s and replaced in 1860 by a copy (Titi, 1763, p. 213 lists all the artists involved in the scheme). This was one of the first major altars to be devoted to the worship of the Holy Sacrament, a rite that became increasingly important during the 17th century.

LEFT AISLE
5th pier [38]: Tomb of Elena Savelli by Giacomo del Duca (1570; Benedetti, *Del Duca*, p. 77). The bronze medallions were cast by his brother Ludovico (Martinelli, p. 67); one of the few works in sculpture by this highly talented pupil of Michelangelo.

5 to L [39]: Guglielmo Cortese, *St Hilary* (W).
Between 5 and 4 to L [40]: Tomb of Cardinal Casanate; figure by P. Legros (1701–3; Enggass, *Sculpture*, p. 187).
4 to L: *Cappella Lancellotti* [41] (De' Rossi, *Altari*, pl. 45): The original chapel, probably built by Maderno, was pulled down on account of Borromini's restoration and the present one was built by G. A. de' Rossi, probably between 1674 and 1686 (Hibbard, *Maderno*, p. 124); stuccoes by Filippo Carcani (Spagnesi, *G. A. De' Rossi*, p. 104); altarpiece: B. Puccini, *St Francis*.

3 to L: *Cappella Santorio* (S. Severina) [42]: Designed by Onorio Longhi (Mola, p. 69; Martinelli, p. 66); tomb of Cardinal Giulio Antonio Santorio with bust by Finelli (1634; Nava Cellini, 'Giuliano Finelli, his monumental portrait sculpture', *Paragone*, XI, 131, 1960, p. 16).

Between 3 and 2 to L [43]: Borromini, monument to Cardinal Bernardo Caracciolo (d.1255) incorporating the recumbent figure from his original tomb.

Between 2 and 1 to L [44]: Borromini, monument to Cardinal Gerardo Bianco (d.1062), incorporating the incised slab from his original tomb.

1 to L: *Cappella Corsini* [45] (Ferrari, *La Tomba*, pls CLVIIIff.; C. Filippo, 'La Cappella Corsini nella Basilica Lateranense', *Carmelus*, XXI, 1974, p. 281; Enggass, *Sculpture*, pp. 16ff). The chapel was founded by Clement XII (Corsini) as a mausoleum for himself and other members of his family and built to the design of Galilei from 1734 onwards. It marks the transition from late Baroque to early neo-classicism (Enggass, *Sculpture* p. 16).

Right wall: G. Rusconi, *Fortitude*; Tomb of Cardinal Neri Corsini, uncle of the pope (d.1678); statues of the Cardinal, *Religion* and *Suffering* by Maini; G. Lironi, *Justice*.

High Altar: Mosaic after Reni's *S. Andrea Corsini in Prayer*; above, statues of *Penitence* and *Modesty* by B. Pincellotti; in lunette: A. Cornacchini, *S. Andrea appearing at the Battle of Anghiari*.

Left wall: Cornacchini, *Prudence*; Tomb of Clement XII (the ancient porphyry sarcophagus came from the portico of the Pantheon); bronze statue of the pope by Maini; *Abundance*

and *Magnificence* by C. Monaldi; *Temperance* by F. della Valle.
In the crypt of the chapel: *Pietà* by A. Montauti (1733–40).
To the left of the entrance to the church: Borromini, monument of Cardinal Riccardo Annibaldi della Molara, incorporating fragments probably by Arnolfo di Cambio.

The Baptistery

(S. Giovanni in Fonte) [46]: Founded by Constantine and rebuilt by Urban III (432–40). It was restored by Urban VIII and again by Alexander VII who commissioned Borromini to replace the roof, which was collapsing, and make the stucco frieze round the exterior of the building, which incorporates the keys and tiara of the papacy and the *monti* and oak-trees of the Chigi arms (Martinelli, p. 69; Blunt, 'Two neglected works by Borromini', *Römisches Jahrbuch*, 1982).

The frieze was restored in the late 1970s when one incomprehensible change was made in it: on one of the eight faces Borromini introduced instead of the tiara and keys a Chi-rho in a laurel wreath (visible in old photographs – e.g. one in the Biblioteca Hertziana) but in the restoration this was replaced by the tiara and keys which appear on all the other fronts.

INTERIOR
This was restored by Urban VIII, who commissioned Andrea Sacchi to paint scenes from the life of St John the Baptist round the drum of the dome (1636–45; Pollak, I, p. 132; Sutherland Harris, *Sacchi*, Nos. 54–61; Güthlein, *Familienarchiv Spada*, II, p. 201); the originals have been replaced by copies and are now in the Lateran Palace. Round the walls of the ambulatory are frescoes illustrating scenes from the life of *Constantine*, planned by Sacchi but mainly executed by other hands: Andrea Camassei, Giacinto Gimignani, C. Magnoni and the young Carlo Maratta (1639–49; Sutherland Harris, *Sacchi*, p. 84, cat. No. 53). The balustrade has the arms of Gregory XIII. The font was designed by Ciro Ferri and the bronze cover was commissioned by Cardinal Francesco Barberini and made by Carlo Spagna in 1677–8.

CAPPELLA DEI SS. SECONDA, RUFINA, CIPRIANO AND GIUSTINA [47]
Originally the narthex of the Baptistery.
Right bay: *Cappella Lercari* (SS. Seconda and Rufina): Decorated by L. Piccioni (1757); left of altar: fresco of the *Virgin with Christ and St John* by Sassoferrato; right: *St Philip Neri* by Guido Reni supported by stucco putti; tombs of Nicola Maria Lercari and Nicola Lercari (both d.1757).
Left bay: *Cappella Borgia* (SS. Cipriano and Giustina): Restored 1754. Tomb of Cardinal Alessandro Borgia (1767); altarpiece: *Martyrdom of S. Giustina*.

CAPPELLA DI S. VENANZIO [48]
Restored (after 1672) for the Ceva family by Carlo Rainaldi who designed the altar and the tombs which flank it: on the right Francesco Adriano Ceva and on the left Adriano Ceva. The tombs were executed by Cosimo Fancelli and the putti above them by Paolo Naldini. On the left wall a tablet to Cardinal Francesco Adriano Ceva (1650) by Borromini. The designer has used a particularly delicate selection of marbles, including the rare *pavonalezza*, for part of the frame and *rosso antico* for the red elements in the crowning feature, but the effect of the monument has been greatly damaged during the 20th-century restoration which, in order to reveal the Early Christian brickwork, removed the white stucco which provided an appropriate background for Borromini's carefully chosen materials and colours.

CAPPELLA DI S. GIOVANNI EVANGELISTA [49]
This chapel, notable for the 5th-century mosaics on its vault, was redecorated with fine stuccoes and marbling by Clement VIII.

The Scala Santa

Bibliography: Letarouilly, pl. 57 (246); A. Campanari and T. Amodei (Chiese di Roma, 72); C. D'Onofrio, *Scalinate*, p. 69; *Guide Rionali*, XV, p. 134.

This building incorporates the Sancta Sanctorum of the Early Christian Lateran Palace and the staircase approaching it which is supposed to have been brought from Pilate's palace in Jerusalem by St Helena. The original structure, dating from the time of Constantine, was remodelled by Nicholas III (1277–81) and again by Sixtus V when he pulled down the old Lateran Palace and built the new one to the designs of Domenico Fontana who was also responsible for the new setting of the Scala Santa and for the two chapels (S. Silvestro and S. Lorenzo) which flank the Sancta Sanctorum (finished 1589). Drastically restored 1852–6.

The Triclinium of Leo III

Bibliography: Matthiae, *Fuga*, p. 41; Pane, *Fuga*, p. 100 and fig. 77.

The apse represents the only surviving fragment of the hall in the papal palace attached to the Lateran and built by Leo III (795–816). It was saved when Sixtus V built the new palace. The mosaic was restored in 1625 by Cardinal Francesco Barberini who caused a book to be published in that year by Nicola Alemanni to celebrate the event (*De Lateranensibus parietinis ... restitutis*, Rome, 1625) and an aedicule to be built over it. Clement XII pulled down the monument while enlarging the square in front of the Lateran, but Benedict XIV had a copy made, based on the fragments still preserved at the time, and set it up at a point nearer the Scala Santa between 1741 and 1744. The architect was Fuga.

For the Lateran Palace, see p. 183.

S. Giovanni in Mercatello
(destroyed). See **SS. Venanzio e Ansovino**

S. Giovanni in Oleo
Via di Porta Latina

Bibliography: Hempel, *Borromini*, p. 182; Matthiae et al. (Chiese di Roma, 51, with S. Giovanni a Porta Latina); Portoghesi, *Borromini*, pls CXXXIX, 195, 196; M. L. Polidori, *Monumenti e mecenati francesi in Roma*, Viterbo, 1969, p. 59; Blunt, *Borromini*, p. 198.

In 1509 the Burgundian Benoît Adam built a small octagonal chapel on the site on which St John was supposed to have been plunged into boiling oil. Adam's arms and the date 1509 appear over the door. The architect was probably a member of the circle of Antonio da Sangallo the Younger. In 1658 (inscription inside the chapel) the chapel was restored by Borromini on the orders of Cardinal Francesco Paolucci. A drawing in the Albertina (Hempel, op. cit., pl. 119) shows that originally Borromini planned to make the roof curved and would have decorated the ribs with palm-branches. A second variant on the same drawing shows the roof stepped, but finally Borromini built a simple conical roof without either ribs or steps. The attic is decorated with palmettes and roses, the latter being an allusion to the arms of the patron. The frieze is typical of Borromini's late, almost classical decoration and is very similar to the one which he added to the Lateran Baptistery for Alexander VII.

INTERIOR
Baldi, frescoes of life of St John (*c.*1658; W).

S. Giovanni della Pigna
Piazza della Pigna

Bibliography: Totti, p. 387; Titi, 1674, p. 165, 1686, p. 132 and 1763, p. 155; Rossi, 1697, p. 524; *Guide Rionali*, IX, 2, p. 88.

A mediaeval church on the site was given by Gregory XIII in 1584 to the Confraternity of the Pietà dei Carcerati, who ministered to those in gaol. The church was rebuilt probably about 1690 by Angelo Torrone. The interior was wholly redecorated in the 19th century.

High Altar: Baldassare Croce, *St John the Baptist*; fresco above it: L. Garzi, *Pietà* (before 1686; W).

1 to R: G. Zoboli, *S. Eleutherius*.

SS. Giovanni e Paolo
Via SS. Giovanni e Paolo

Bibliography: S. Ortolani (Chiese di Roma, 29); B. M. Margarucci Italiani, *Il Titolo di Pammacchio, SS. Giovanni e Paolo*, Rome, 1967.

This church, which contains remarkable remains of ancient Roman and Early Christian frescoes, was disastrously 'restored' first for Cardinal Philip Howard in 1677 and later, by Antonio Canevari in 1715–18, for Cardinal Fabrizio Paolucci. Nothing of the mediaeval church is to be seen in the interior – except the Cosmatesque floor – and the Baroque remodelling is heavy and pedestrian. The wooden ceiling dates from 1598.

2 to R: M. Benefial, *S. Saturninus* (1716; Voss, p. 642).

3 to R: A. Milani, *S. Pammachius* (1716).

Apse: Frescoes: scenes from the martyrdom of Sts John and Paul; right by P. A. Barbieri; middle by G. Triga; left by D. Piastrini; half-dome by Niccolò Circignani, called Il Pomarancio (Gloton, pl. XII).

4 to L: T. Conca, *Crucifixion*.

3 to L: A. Milani, *St Joseph*.

2 to L: A. Milani, *The Martyrs from Scilium* (1716).

Vestibule to Sacristy: Busts of Fabrizio Paolucci and Innocent XII by Bracci (1725; Gradara, *Bracci*, p. 17) and Clement XIV and Pius VI by unknown artists.

SS. Giovanni e Petronio dei Bolognesi
Via del Mascherone

Bibliography: Salerno, *Via Giulia*, p. 489; Wasserman, *Mascarino*, p. 51; *Guide Rionali*, VII, 3, p. 58.

A mediaeval church on the site was given by Gregory XIII in 1581 to the Bolognese community who rebuilt it in the last years of the 16th century, almost certainly to the designs of the Bolognese architect Ottaviano Mascarino. It was restored in 1696–1700, the latter date being inscribed on the frieze.

INTERIOR
Altar to R: F. Gessi, *Death of St Joseph*.
High Altar: The original altarpiece was Domenichino's *Madonna with St John and St Petronio*, removed by the French in 1797 and now in the Brera. It is replaced by a copy.
Left transept: G. G. del Sole's *St Catherine* is now covered by an anonymous painting of the *Virgin*, brought from the Sacristy.

If shut, ring at No. 61 (to the left of the church).

S. Girolamo della Carità
Via di Monserrato

Bibliography: S. Papaldo (Chiese di Roma, 132).

The church originally belonged to the Franciscan Observants, but in 1524 it was handed over to the Arciconfraternita della Carità, a company of non-Roman nobles founded in 1519 by Cardinal Giulio de' Medici (later Clement VII) and approved by Leo X (L. Ponnelle and L. Bordet, *Saint Philippe Neri*, Paris, 1928, p. 119). The church was rebuilt by Domenico Castello – who is mentioned in the accounts in 1656 (Pollak in Thieme-Becker, *s.v.*) – and is said to have been finished in 1660. The façade has frequently been ascribed to Carlo Rainaldi and by Fasolo to Martino Longhi the Younger, but Noehles (*Fasolo*, p. 175) has shown that it was built, like the church, by Castello (Varriano, *Longhi*, p. 95).
1 to R: *Cappella Spada* (Hempel, *Borromini*, p. 182; Lavagnino, *Altari*, p. 119; Portoghesi, *Borromini nella cultura europea*, pp. 331ff. and *Borromini*, pls 190–4; Montagu, *Giorgetti*, p. 279; Heimbürger Ravalli, *Archivio Spada*, pp. 82ff., pls 68–87; and 'Supplementary Information concerning the Spada Chapel in S. Girolamo della Carità', *Paragone*, XXVIII, 329, 1977, p. 39; Blunt, *Borromini*, p. 207; R. Bösel, 'Cosimo Fanzago a Roma', *Prospettiva*, 15, 1978, p. 36).

The chapel was granted to Orazio Spada in 1595 and some restoration was carried out soon afterwards, but the whole chapel was redecorated in 1654–7 under the direction of Borromini's friend, Virgilio Spada, and his brother Bernardo to contain the tombs of two members of the family: Bernardino (right, by Cosimo Fancelli) and Giovanni (left, by Ercole Ferrata) and medallions of other members of earlier generations by Paolo Naldini and others.

The chapel was long attributed to Borromini on the authority of the old guide-books but recently discovered documents have shown that it is the invention of Virgilio Spada, who, as was his habit, submitted his designs to a number of professional architects, including Borromini, who supplied a drawing for the altar frontal which was not exactly followed.

The chapel has always stood out from Borromini's work – and indeed from Roman architecture of the period – on account of the very elaborate marble inlay with which its walls and floor are covered and which suggests a Neapolitan rather than a Roman origin (though the colours, yellow and brown, are more subdued than those in most Neapolitan *commessi*), and this has now been explained by the fact that the documents and Virgilio Spada's letters about the decoration of the chapel refer to the 'Cavalieri Cosimo', who is certainly the Neapolitan architect Fanzago, who was at that time in Rome working on the decoration of S. Lorenzo in Lucina, and to the craftsman actually executing the marble inlay called Giovanni Battista Scala, who is first referred to as 'Genovese', but later and correctly as 'Napoletano'.

The most remarkable feature of the chapel is the 'altar-rail' formed of two marble angels carrying a heavy piece of drapery – composed of sheets of jasper so ingeniously fitted together that at first sight the 'shroud' seems to be a single solid piece of the material. This is the work of Antonio Giorgetti, a pupil of Bernini. The wings of the right-hand angel are of wood and hinged to allow access to the chapel.
Right transept: Tomb of Conte Asdrubale di Montauto (Monte Acuto; d.1629) after a design by Pietro da Cortona (Titi, 1686, p. 95).
High Altar: By Carlo Rainaldi (Titi, 1686, p. 95). It contains a copy by Vincenzo Camuccini of Domenichino's *Last Communion of St Jerome* of which the original was removed by the French in 1797 and is now in the Vatican Gallery.
Chapel to left of High Altar: *Cappella Antamoro* (Lavagnino, *Altari*, p. 193; R. Preimesberger, 'Entwürfe Pierre Legros für Filippo Juvarras Cappella Antamoro', *Römische historische Mitteilungen*, X, 1966–7,

p. 203; Portoghesi, *Roma Barocca*, pls 394, 396; S. Boscarino, *Juvarra architetto*, Rome, 1973, p. 148; M. L. Myers, *Architectural and Ornamental Drawings*, catalogue of exhibition (Metropolitan Museum), 1975, p. 33; H. Millon, 'The Antamoro chapel in S. Girolamo della Carità', *Studies in Italian Art and Architecture* (American Academy in Rome), Cambridge (Mass.), 1980, p. 261): Dedicated to St Philip Neri who belonged to the Company before founding the Oratory. Designed by Filippo Juvarra and executed 1708–10; Juvarra's only work in Rome. The statues of the saint and the putti are by Pierre Legros.

The Oratory behind the church facing the Piazza S. Caterina della Rota was built between 1632 and 1635 by Peparelli (Pollak, I, p. 245). Over the entrance is an oval bas-relief of the dead Christ by Pietro Bracci (1734; Gradara, *Bracci*, p. 34).

particular talent of the architect, which is also shown in his decoration, as, for instance, in the Cappella Altemps in S. Maria in Trastevere.

INTERIOR

A single nave with shallow transepts and three chapels on each side, a spacious example of this familiar late 16th-century design. The vault of the nave and many other parts of the church were frescoed in the mid-19th century. The fresco in the dome (Gloton, pl. XLVIII) with fictive architecture is probably by Paolo Guidotti, and those in the choir – treated as imitation tapestries – are ascribed to A. Viviani and A. Lilio. All probably date from the first years of the 17th century.

On the entrance wall (to the right of the door) is the tomb of Paolo Gozzi (d.1660), almost as moving in its restraint as Bernini's monument to Fonseca in S. Lorenzo in Lucina. There is no record of who made the monument and no modern scholar has ventured on an attribution.

The paintings in **1** and **3 to R** and **3 to L** are by G. Puglia, called Il Bastaro.

Left transept: By the door to the Sacristy figure of the seated *St Jerome* by Francesco Grassia.

S. Girolamo degli Schiavoni
Via Ripetta

Bibliography: Mola, p. 81; Falda, *Nuovo teatro*, III, pl. 38; De' Rossi, *Prospectus*, pl. 64; Magni, I, pl. 11; G. Kokša (Chiese di Roma, 120, 121).

The church and hospital attached to it were founded in 1441 for the colony of Slavs – or Illyrians – who had fled from their countries in the face of the Turkish advance in the late 14th century, and it is now the church of the Croat colony. The church was begun in 1588 on the orders of Sixtus V, whose titular church it had been, probably to the design of Martino Longhi the Elder, though Mola says it was designed by Giovanni Fontana. The structure was apparently finished by the middle of 1589.

The façade, which is certainly by Martino Longhi the Elder, is characteristic of his style in its avoidance of all monumentality and its skilful treatment of the design in an almost unbroken plane. There are no columns or half-columns and only the flattest of pilasters, and the central section only breaks forward very slightly from the side bays. The pediment is unbroken and light in its mouldings. Longhi seems to have been defiantly reacting against Giacomo della Porta's façade of the Gesù, and even Vignola's unexecuted design for that church looks massive in comparison with his façade. In its delicacy and restraint it shows the

S. Giuliano dei Fiamminghi
Via del Sudario

Bibliography: Rossi, 1697, p. 510; Magni, I, pl. 26; *Guide Rionali*, VIII, 1, p. 50.

The church was rebuilt in *c*.1675 and apparently again in 1715. The façade, which must date from the 17th-century rebuilding and is probably by a Flemish architect, has rather elegant carved stone decoration round a niche which encloses a statue of St Julian by Jodocus Haerts (1631–4), preserved from an earlier church. Internally the church is of no architectural distinction. It probably dates from the 1715 campaign and appears to be by a Flemish architect.

The vault of the church was painted *c*.1717–18 by William Kent who offered to do the job without payment in order to establish his reputation in Rome (E. Croft-Murray, 'William Kent in Rome', *The English Miscellany*, I, 1950, p. 221).

The tomb of Vinoco de Valle is of some interest in showing the influence of the Neapolitan style introduced to Rome in about 1650 by Cosimo Fanzago (R. Bösel, 'Cosimo Fanzago a Roma', *Prospettiva*, 15, 1978, p. 37).

S. Giuseppe a Capo le Case
Via Francesco Crispi

Bibliography: Pollak, I, p. 144; Totti, p. 304; Titi, 1674, p. 372 and 1721, p. 364; Vasi, *Magnificenze*, pl. 146.

Founded in 1597 under the rule of the Discalced Carmelites for the care of poor girls and in 1619 placed under S. Giacomo degli Spagnuoli. The church was rebuilt in 1628 at the expense of Cardinal Marcello Lante. The façade is a severe design executed in fine brick, with the unusual arrangement of a Tuscan order over an Ionic. This may, however, be due to the fact that the two storeys appear to be of different dates, and there may originally have been a project for building the upper storey conventionally with a Corinthian order which was abandoned for reasons of economy, since a Tuscan order would be lower and would involve less elaborate detail than Corinthian. The same arrangement occurs on the façade of S. Maria di Grottapinta and on S. Maria in Publicolis. In the case of the latter the façade is all by a single hand, G. A. de' Rossi, and the architect must therefore have deliberately intended the arrangement.

The High Altar was designed by Bartolomeo Breccioli (Baglione, p. 347, and Martinelli, p. 57). It contains a ruined fresco of the *Dream of St Joseph*, painted by Andrea Sacchi and restored by Maratta. It was for a long period covered by a modern painting, but is now once again exposed to view.

Behind the altar (door on left of choir) is the nuns' choir off which leads a small Scala Santa with fine mid 18th-century stuccoes. The Scala Santa dates from about 1700 and is attributed by Donati (*Artisti ticinesi*, p. 326) to Carlo Stefano Fontana.

S. Giuseppe dei Falegnami
Forum

Bibliography: G. Zandri (Chiese di Roma, 118); D'Onofrio, *Scalinate*, p. 230; V. Tiberio, 'S. Giuseppe dei Falegnami', *Palladio*, XXI, 1971, p. 184; *Guide Rionali*, X, 1, p. 92.

The church of the Guild of Carpenters (*falegnami*), built over the Mamertine prison in which St Peter is supposed to have been incarcerated. Begun in 1597 from a design by G. B. Montano, a member of the Guild, whose reconstructions of ancient Roman buildings, published by his pupil, G. B. Soria, were to be of great influence on Baroque architects. The building was completed by Soria and Antonio del Grande, and the church was consecrated in 1663. The interior was restored and largely redecorated in 1880.

The façade, which was finished by 1602, has many features in common with Montano's designs for tabernacles, some of which are included in books of his works as published by Soria, particularly the unusual relation of the small upper storey to the tall lower one, and the two small pediments subsumed under the main pediment. The double staircase in front of the church was removed in 1932.

Over the door is an organ gallery by M. A. Ravasi (1691) and organ by F. Testa, with carved woodwork by G. B. Vannelli (1714).

Fine carved and gilt wooden ceiling with a relief of the *Nativity* by Montano (1612).
1 to R: Bartolomeo Colombo, *Death of St Joseph* (1648; W).
2 to R: *Chapel of St Anne: Holy Family* by G. Ghezzi (1692; W).
2 to L: *Cappella della Natività: Nativity* by C. Maratta (1651; W).
1 to L: *Flight into Egypt* copy after Maratta (the original is now in the Villa Chigi at Castelfusano).

The Oratory (accessible from the right aisle), added in 1627, has frescoes by M. T. Montagna (1631-7). The altar was designed by Tiberio Calcagni and the painting, *The Virgin with Sts Joseph and Joachim*, is by P. L. Ghezzi.
See plate 29.

S. Giuseppe alla Lungara
Via della Lungara

Bibliography: D. Vizzari, *La Chiesa di San Giuseppe alla Lungara*, Rome, 1966; Portoghesi, *Roma Barocca*, pls 397, 406; *Guide Rionali*, XIII, 1, p. 24.

Built for the Pii Operarii della Dottrina Cristiana, a body founded by the Neapolitan Carlo Carafa in 1600, which was established in Rome 1687. The present church was begun in 1730 on the design of Ludovico Rusconi Sassi, and was consecrated in 1734, but the pavement was not finished till 1736. At first sight the church appears to be an oval, but it is in fact a rectangle with its corners cut off. The vault was reconstructed in 1872 when the church was restored and the painted marbling added.
1 to R: Altar: N. Ricciolini, *Deposition* (1754).
High Altar: By F. Navone, c.1767; Mariano Rossi, *Dream of St Joseph* (between 1764 and 1774).
1 to L: Girolamo Pesci, *The Virgin, St Joachim and St Anne* (1754).

S. Gregorio al Celio
Via SS. Giovanni e Paolo

Bibliography: Totti, p. 143; Falda, *Nuovo teatro*, III, pl. 17; De' Rossi, *Prospectus*, pl. 71; Roisecco, 1750, I, p. 442; Vittorio Moschini (Chiese di Roma, 17); Magni, I, pl. 24.

Founded by Gregory the Great who converted his own house into an Oratory dedicated to St Andrew. A larger church was built, probably by Paschal II in 1108, on the site of the existing building. In 1573 the church and monastery were given to the Camaldolese, having previously belonged to the Benedictines. In 1595 Cardinal Antonio Maria Salviati began the restoration of the church which was continued by Cardinal Baronio (d.1607) (H. H. Brummer, 'Cesare Baronio and the convent of Gregory the Great', *Konsthistorisk Tidskrift*, XLII, 1978, p. 101) and finished by Cardinal Scipione Borghese, who was responsible for the restoration of the atrium and the building of the façade which has the date 1633 inscribed on it, but was not finished till 1642, nine years after the Cardinal's death. The architect was Giovanni Battista Soria – a protégé of Cardinal Borghese – who followed, with variations, the pattern which he had used at S. Carlo ai Catinari (Blunt, *The other side*, p. 65). In 1725–34 a further restoration of the interior of the church was begun by Fra Giuseppe Antonio Serratini and completed by Francesco Ferrari who is mainly responsible for its present appearance. The side chapels were not finished till 1757 and the main door of the church is dated 1772.

INTERIOR

In the ceiling painting of the *Triumph of Sts Gregory and Romualdus* by Placido Costanzi (1727; Mallory, *Notizie*, p. 104; Poensgen, fig. 42).

1 to R: John Parker, an English pupil of M. Benefial, *Sts Benedict, Sylvia and Gregory.*
2 to R: Francesco Mancini, *Pope Alexander III and St Peter Damianus*, (Titi, 1763, p. 74).
3 to R: Francesco Fernandi, called Imperiali, *The Death of St Romualdus* (Titi, 1763, p. 74).
Chapel to right of High Altar: *St Gregory*, attributed to Sisto Badalocchio (Titi, 1763, p. 74).
High Altar: Antonio Balestra, *Sts Andrew and Gregory* (1740; Mallory, loc. cit., p. 107).
Left aisle: *Cappella Salviati* (S. Gregorio): Built by Carlo Maderno, possibly on a design by Francesco da Volterra, though Hibbard (*Maderno*, p. 121) believes that it is entirely Maderno's invention. According to the inscription it was finished in 1600. Over the altar is a copy of Annibale Carracci's *St Gregory in Prayer* (the original of which was sold and was later at Bridgewater House). Frescoes by G. B. Ricci (Gloton, pl. XVI).
3 to L: *Fioravanti*: Altarpiece, F. Mancini, *Immaculata* (Titi, 1763, p. 75).
2 to L: *Gabrielli*: Pompeo Batoni, *Madonna with four Camaldolese saints* (ibid.); one of his earliest works (c.1735; Voss, p. 651).

24. S. Gregorio al Celio. Engraving by Falda, showing on the left the Oratories of St Sylvia and S. Andrea.

1 to L: G. B. Bonfreni, *S. Michael receiving a Crown from Christ* (c.1757).

In the grounds to the east of the church are three oratories:

1. S. Barbara: This incorporates part of a 3rd-century house and contains the table at which St Gregory is said to have served food to the poor – and also to an angel. Frescoes of scenes from the life of *St Gregory* by Antonio Viviani (1602). Statue of *St Gregory* by Nicolas Cordier (sometimes but wrongly said to have been begun by Michelangelo).

2. S. Andrea: Probably on the site of Gregory the Great's original oratory of S. Andrea. Rebuilt by Flaminio Ponzio in 1608 for Cardinal Scipione Borghese. Frescoes: right wall: Domenichino, *Flagellation of St Andrew* (Borea, *Domenichino*, p. 165); left wall: Reni, *St Andrew led to execution* (both painted in 1608; Voss, p. 507). These two frescoes were for long regarded as rivals, Reni's being more widely acclaimed, Domenichino's being admired by a group of more austere artists including Poussin. On the entrance wall chiaroscuro frescoes of *St Gregory* and *St Sylvia* by Lanfranco (W). Altarpiece: *Madonna* by Cristofano Roncalli, called Il Pomarancio. On either side frescoes of Sts Peter and Paul by Guido Reni.

3. St Sylvia: Restored in 1608 by Cardinal Scipione Borghese. A fine fresco with angels playing musical instruments by Guido Reni (1608; Gloton, pl. XV), an unusually illusionistic composition for this artist. Statue of *St Sylvia* by Cordier.

S. Gregorio a Ponte Quattro Capi
Via del Portico d'Ottavia

Bibliography: Roisecco, 1750, I. p. 222; Elling, pl. 43.

The church stands on the edge of the Ghetto and has over the door inscriptions in Latin and Hebrew directed against the Jews, and sermons designed for their conversion to Christianity were frequently preached here. The mediaeval church was replaced by the present building in 1729 on the orders of Benedict XIII to the design of Filippo Barigioni. Heavily restored in the 19th century.

1 to R: Andrea Casali, *St Philip*.
1 to L: E. Parrocel, *St Gregory*.

S. Ignazio
Piazza S. Ignazio

Bibliography: Pollak, I, p. 144; Falda, *Nuovo teatro*, III, pls 21, 22; Tessin, p. 161; De' Rossi, *Prospectus*, pls 24–6; De' Rossi, *Architettura Civile*, III, pl. 28; De Brosses, II, p. 110; Magni, I, pls 29, 30; D. Frey, 'Beiträge zur Geschichte der römischen Barockarchitektur', *Wiener Jahrbuch für Kunstgeschichte*, III, 1924–5, p. 11; Hibbard, *Maderno*, p. 232; G. Martinelli (Chiese di Roma, 97; unreliable on the history of the building); Thelen, *Borromini*, I, p. 39, II, pls C.32, 33; F. Calvo, *Chiesa di S. Ignazio di Roma*, Rome, 1968 (with useful plates); *Guide Rionali*, IX, 3, p. 24.

In 1626 Cardinal Ludovico Ludovisi decided to build a church for the Collegio Romano, at which his uncle, Gregory XV, had been a student. It was to replace the old church of the Annunziata and was to rival Cardinal Farnese's Gesù and Cardinal Montalto's S. Andrea della Valle. It was to be dedicated to St Ignatius who had been canonized by Gregory in 1622. Various architects were asked to submit designs, including Domenichino (J. Pope-Hennessy, *The Drawings of Domenichino at Windsor Castle*, London, 1948, No. 1741). The design chosen was almost certainly that of Orazio Grassi who was responsible for the wooden model made in 1628. His authorship is confirmed by Giovanni Simone Ruggieri in his account of the consecration of the church in his *Diario dell'anno del Santissimo Giubileo MDCL* (Rome, 1651, p. 177), where he writes: 'Intona il vespro il medesimo Padre Architetto di detta Chiesa, il Padre Horatio Grassi'. Maderno, however, was certainly consulted by Ludovisi and his project is recorded in a drawing by Borromini (Thelen, C.32 and Hibbard, pl. 100b). The church was opened for worship in 1650, but was then only built as far as the transepts.

INTERIOR

The nave arcade is unusual in that it consists of small columns – of Sicilian jasper – standing free from the main piers and forming a series of Serlianas.

The stucco frieze of putti on the entrance wall and over the first three chapels on either side and the inscription tablet on the entrance wall supported by figures of *Religion* and *Magnificence* were designed by Algardi.

The vaults were painted by Andrea Pozzo (Kerber, p. 54). The first part to be undertaken was the false perspective of the dome over the crossing (1684–5). This was painted on canvas and was damaged in 1891 when a powder maga-

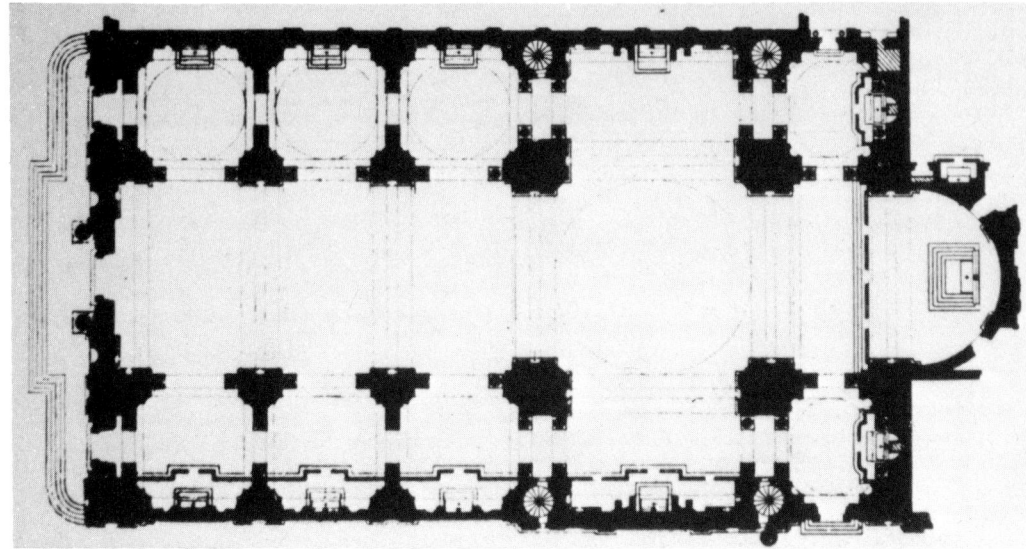

25. *S. Ignazio.* Plan.

zine near S. Paolo fuori le Mura exploded. It was restored in 1961–3. On the pendentives are four Old Testament figures: *Judith, David, Samson* and *Jael,* all of whom prefigured Christ. The half-dome of the apse shows *St Ignatius helping the Sick* (1685–8). Below are three paintings, also by Pozzo: over the altar *St Ignatius adoring the Trinity*; on the right *St Francis Borgia received into the Order*; on the left *St Ignatius sending St Francis Xavier to India.* On the vault over the choir *St Ignatius receives the call at the siege of Pamplona*; in that of the right transept: *S. Maria Maddalena dei Pazzi has a vision of S. Luigi Gonzaga.* The vault of the left transept was frescoed by L. Mazzanti (*Assumption*). Nave vault (by Pozzo) *The Glory of St Ignatius* with the effects of the Jesuits' mission in the four parts of the world shown on the cove (finished 1694). This is one of the most elaborate programmes of religious painting of the period, expounding the whole early history of the Society of Jesus. It is also one of the most dazzling pieces of illusionism in the whole of Baroque art, but it must be looked at from a point in the middle of the nave, seen from which all the perspective falls into place.

2 to R: *Sacripanto* (St Joseph): Originally built by Carlo Rainaldi for the Lancellotti family and decorated in 1712 by Niccolò Michetti for Cardinal Giuseppe Sacripanto (J. Pinto, 'An Early Design by Nicola Michetti: The Sacripanto Chapel in the Roman Church of S. Ignazio', *J.S.A.H.,* XXXVIII, p. 375); altarpiece: S. Pozzo, *Sts Joachim and Anna*; altarpiece: F. Trevisani, *Death of St Joseph*; frescoes by Luigi Garzi, Giuseppe Chiari and Trevisani (c.1712; W).

Right transept: Altar to S. Luigi Gonzaga by Pozzo (Lavagnino, *Altari*, p. 183; Kerber, p. 101). The relief is by Pierre Legros (Enggass, *Sculpture*, p. 144) and the marble angels on the balustrade are by Bernardino Ludovisi. The altar is second only to the altar of St Ignatius in the Gesù as an example of Roman Baroque sumptuousness.

Chapel to right of High Altar: Tomb of Gregory XV by Legros; *Religion* and *Munificence* by Etienne Monnot. In the four corners of the chapel allegorical figures by Camillo Rusconi: *Prudence, Temperance, Fortitude,* and *Justice* (Enggass, *Sculpture*, pp. 86, 95).

Chapel to left of Choir: Four allegorical statues: S. Giorgini, *Faith*; G. A. Lavaggi, *Hope*; F. Nuvolone, *Charity*: F. Rainaldi, *Religion* (before 1688; Enggass, *Sculpture*, p. 112). Stucco model by Giuseppe Rusconi for the statue of St Ignatius in the series of Founders in St Peter's executed by Giuseppe on the design of his master, Camillo Rusconi (Enggass, *Sculpture*, pp. 104, 208).

Sacristy: Ceiling fresco by the Fleming, Pierre Delattre, with a miracle of St Ignatius. Fine wooden cupboards.

Left transept: Carved decoration by F. Cerruti, c.1747 (A. Chiavo, *Archivio della Società Romana di Storia Patria*, XCV, 1972, p. 151); altar of the *Annunciation* by Filippo della Valle 1750; (Honour, 'Filippo della Valle', *Connois-*

seur, CXLIV, 1959, p. 175); marble angels on altar rails by Pietro Bracci (Gradara, *Bracci*, p. 59).

Attached to the church is the Cappella della Prima Primaria with frescoes by Giacomo Cortese (Jacques Courtois; F. A. Salvagnini, *I Pittori Borgognone Cortese (Courtois)*, Rome, 1936, p. 123).

For a design made by Andrea Pozzo for a temporary decoration in the choir of the church see S. Jacob, 'Zu zwei Architekturzeichnungen der Berliner Kunstbibliothek', *Römisches Jahrbuch*, XVI, 1976, pp. 299ff.

S. Ildefonso
Via Sistina

Bibliography: Titi, 1674, p. 371; Rossi, 1697, p. 395; Roisecco, 1750, II, p. 293; Buchowiecki, II, p. 220.

Founded in 1619 by the Spanish Augustinians. Titi in 1674 says that the church had just been rebuilt to the design of a Sicilian Dominican named Giuseppe Paglia (recorded 1662–82). The façade was added by Francesco Ferrari (before 1750). Buchowiecki gives 1667 as the date for the laying of the foundation stone.

The nave elevation consists of rather correct coupled Ionic pilasters but the vault is an imitation of Borromini's in the Re Magi (Collegio di Propaganda Fide).

1 to R: Marble bas-relief of the *Nativity* by the Palermitan sculptor Francesco Grassia.

The altars have fine *scagliola* frontals.

S. Isidoro
Piazza S. Isidoro

Bibliography: Mola, p. 102; Martinelli, p. 73; Magni, I, pl. 103; Aedan Daly (Chiese di Roma, 119); H. Quinn, *S. Isidore's Church and College of the Irish Franciscans*, Vatican City, 1959; Mallory, *Bizzacheri*, pp. 37, 46; id., *Rococo*, p. 42.

Founded in 1628 on the edge of the Villa Ludovisi by Spanish Discalced Franciscans. In 1625 under Luke Wadding it was taken over by Irish Franciscans to whom it still belongs. The church and monastic buildings are generally said to have been designed by Antonio Casone and finished by Mario Arconio, but Mola attributes the church to Domenico Castello. The steps and the portico are certainly by the latter, but the upper half of the façade was constructed by Carlo Bizzacheri in 1704–5. The statues in the niches of *St Patrick* and *St Isidore* are by S. Giorgini (Enggass, *Sculpture*, p. 112). The pediment is a sort of inversion of Borromini's at the Oratory, straight at the sides and curved in the middle.

INTERIOR

1 to R: *Cappella Alaleona* (S. Giuseppe): Decorated in 1652 by Maratta with stories from the life of St Joseph. The paintings on the walls have been replaced by copies (W).

2 to R: *Cappella Barberini* (S. Anna); Decorated by Castello; scenes from the life of *St Anne* by P. P. Ubaldini (before 1663; W).

Right transept: Tomb of Alfonso Mansanedo de Quiñones (d.1628) with a bust attributed to Giuliano Finelli (cf. A. Nava Cellini, 'Un Tracciato per l'attività ritrattistica di Giuliano Finelli', *Paragone*, 131, 1960, p. 13).

Chapel to right of High Altar: *Cappella de Sylva* (Immaculate Conception): The dedication of the chapel may be connected with the fact that Wadding first came to Rome with a mission sent by Philip III of Spain to promote the doctrine of the Immaculate Conception.

In 1661 the chapel was acquired by the de Sylva family and redecorated. It was dedicated in 1663. The painting over the altar is by Maratta and the decoration was commissioned from Bernini. It consists of portraits of the de Sylva family and allegorical figures of *Mercy* and *Truth* on one side, *Justice* and *Peace* on the other (Psalm 85). Draperies were later added to these figures. Drawings for the walls of the chapel by Bernini are known (Brauer and Wittkower, pp. 139–41, pls 103, 174), which show that the design is due to him but he seems to have had no share in the execution which appears to be largely by G. Cartari (Wittkower, *Bernini*, p. 244). The oval medallions with busts were inserted in the 18th century to replace coats of arms flanked by flying angels (De' Rossi, *Architettura Civile*, II, pls 16, 17). Fagiolo dell'Arco, *Bernini* (Cat. 190) points out that the reliefs with pairs of portraits do not appear in this engraving of 1699 and concludes that they too must be later.

High Altar: Andrea Sacchi, *The Virgin appearing to St Isidore* (1622–3) (cf. A. Sutherland Harris, *Andrea Sacchi*, p. 50, Cat. No. 6).

2 to L: *Cappella di S. Antonio:* Partly decorated about 1655 by Cosimo Fanzago who designed the marble inlay of the floor, the altar and the lower part of the walls. The decoration was completed in the 1680s by Carlo Bizzacheri (Mallory, *Bizzacheri*, pp. 31–45, and *Rococo*, p. 37; R. Bösel, 'Cosimo Fanzago a Roma', *Prospettiva*, 15, 1978, p. 29). Altarpiece: Cerrini, *Vision of St Anthony* (before 1663; W).

1 to L: *Cappella Ludovisi* (S. Croce): Frescoes in lunettes: Maratta, *Scenes from the Passion* (c.1655–7; W).

S. Ivo della Sapienza
Via della Sapienza

Bibliography: Pollak, I, p. 159; Falda, *Nuovo teatro*, I, pls 19, 20 and IV, pl. 49; Ferrerio, *Palazzi*, I, pl. 30; *Opera del Cavaliere Francesco Borromino*, Rome, 1720; De'Rossi, *Architettura Civile*, I, pls 98–100; Visentini, *Osservazioni*, pp. 23, 35; Magni, I, pl. 67; Rempel, *Borromini*, p. 114; Portoghesi, *Borromini nella cultura europea*, pls 46–74 and *Borromini*, pls L–LVI, 75–91; Thelen, 'Der Palazzo della Sapienza in Rom', *Miscellanea Bibliothecae Hertzianae*, Vienna, 1961, p. 285; *Ragguagli*, pp. 131, 225; L. Benevolo, 'Il tema geometrico di S. Ivo della Sapienza', *Quaderni*, 3, 1953; H. Ost, 'Borrominis römische Universitätskirche', *Zeitschrift für Kunstgeschichte*, 1967, p. 101; P. de la Ruffinière du Prey, 'Salomonic symbolism in Borromini's church of S. Ivo della Sapienza', ibid., XXXI, 1968, p. 215; E. Battisti, 'Il simbolismo in Borromini', *Studi sul Borromini*, I, p. 229; Portoghesi, *Roma Barocca*, pls 125–41; W. Hauptman, 'Luceat Lux Vostra coram hominibus', *J.S.A.H.*, XXXIII, 1974, p. 73; L. Benevolo, 'Il problema dei pavimenti Borrominiani in bianco e nero', *Quaderni*, 13, 1956, p. 1. (Borromini's note on the structure of the church is printed in *Ragguagli*, I, p. 151); R. Pacini, 'Alterazioni dei monumenti Borrominiani', *Ragguagli*, I, p. 315; V. Poulson, *The Iconography of Francesco Borromini's church of S. Ivo della Sapienza in Rome* (Dissertation, Oslo), 1976; M. Malmanger, 'Form as iconology. The spire of Sant'Ivo alla Sapienza', *Acta Instituti Romani Norvegiae*, VIII, 1978, p. 237; Blunt, *Borromini*, p. 111.

The Archiginnasio of Rome – later raised to the status of University – was founded by Boniface VIII in 1303 and moved to the site of the Sapienza under Eugenius IV (1431–47). In 1935 it was moved to the new University near S. Lorenzo fuori le Mura, though the University continues to serve the church. After 1935 the Archivio di Stato was installed in the main rooms, but they are now (1979) being expropriated so that the palace can be used as an extension of the Senate (see Palazzo Madama).

The present building was begun by Pirro Ligorio for Pius IV and was continued by Giacomo della Porta for his successors, whose arms appear on the arcades of the court. Borromini, who was appointed to the Archiginnasio in 1632, intended to make radical alterations to della Porta's façade, replacing his central door by two aligned on the cloisters, and he would have added an extra storey to della Porta's tower, but none of this was carried out. Della Porta planned a circular church at the end of the court (Thelen), but the building of the church did not start till 1643 under Borromini. The structure was finished in 1648, but the decoration of the interior was not begun till 1659, and the altar-piece of S. Ivo and other saints begun by Cortona about 1661 was finished after his death by G. V. Borghesi after 1674 (Briganti, *Cortona*, p. 265). The altar itself was erected by

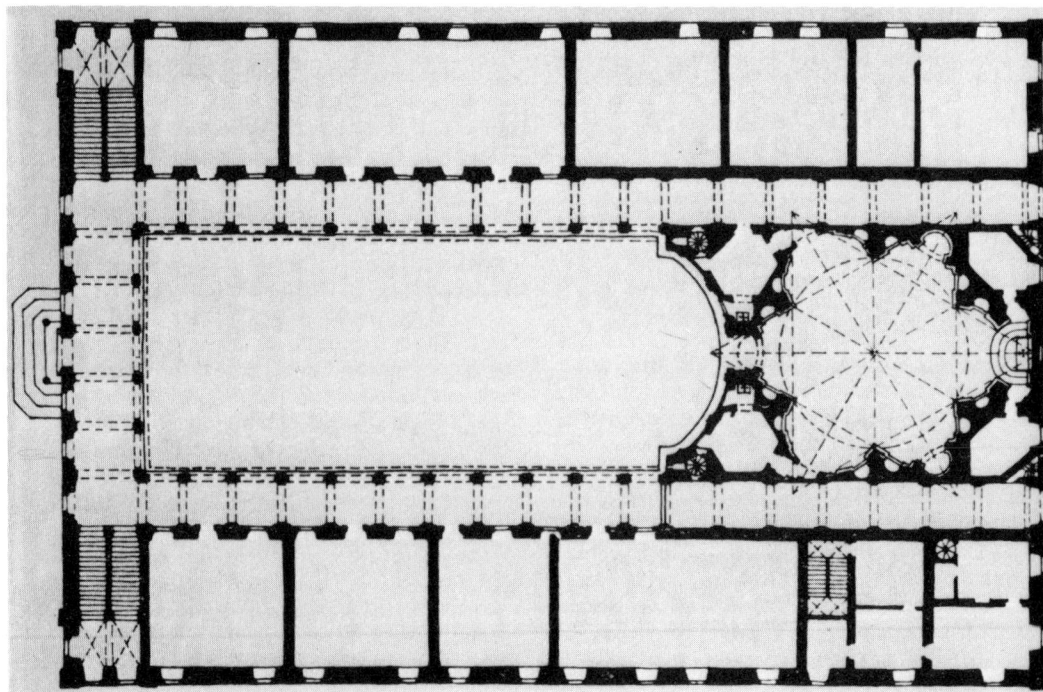

26. *S. Ivo della Sapienza. Plan, including the college.*

G. B. Contini in 1685, when the bay which contains it was altered and a window removed (see Pacini).

This is Borromini's boldest and most inventive building. All the features present in his earlier church of S. Carlo alle Quattro Fontane are here developed and given more mature expression. The church is brilliantly designed to fit a cramped site between the two existing blocks. The plan is formed by the intersection of two equilateral triangles. These form a six-pointed star (of Wisdom) and a central hexagon to each side of which a bay is added. Three of these are semi-circular, and the other three are triangles with their points cut off by convex arcs of circles drawn with the points of the basic triangles as centres. The structure of the building follows this plan up to the top of the dome, producing an effect of uniformity instead of the variety shown in the three stages of S. Carlino. In this scheme there is one small variation, carefully concealed. In the triangular bays the convex parts are continued up to and including the entablature, but above the windows the vault emerges concave, the change being concealed by the neutral character of the window, neither convex nor concave. The restoration of the 1960s gave back to the interior its whiteness, characteristic of Borromini, which had been destroyed by the painted marbling added in the 1850s, and the quality of the carefully thought-out detail can now be fully seen. The decoration of the dome includes the *monti*, stars and oak trees of Alexander VII's arms, but there are probably also allusions to the Temple of Solomon in the palms, cherubim and pomegranates (the last in the capitals of the pilasters). The symbolism of the interior has given rise to much discussion (see Ost, de la Ruffinière du Prey, Battisti, Hauptman, Poulson, and, for a summary, Blunt).

The exterior, designed to make a striking climax to the court in which the church stands, consists of a cylindrical element of six convex bays, which looks like the drum of the dome but in fact encloses the cupola and contains the solid masonry which takes the lateral thrust of the dome (the site did not allow space for buttressing). Above this is a convex stepped zone (cf. the Pantheon) up which run concave buttresses, ending in Ionic volutes supporting balls, a motif borrowed from Michelangelo's Porta Pia. The lantern consists of a series of concave bays between coupled columns, like some late antique 'temples' in reconstructions by Montanus (whether Borromini knew drawings of the circular temple of Baalbek is a matter of speculation, see Blunt, p. 39). Above this comes a spiral ramp reminiscent of a ziggurat, the symbolical meaning of which has led to even more specula-

27. *S. Ivo della Sapienza. Engraving by Falda of the east front, showing on the left the Palazzo Maccarani by Giulio Romano and in the distance on the right the dome and tower of S. Agnese in Piazza Navona.*

tion than the interior of the church (see the authors referred to in that context).

The Biblioteca Alessandrina (on the left side of the *cortile*) was added under Alexander VII. When it was restored full-scale drawings for the bookcases by Borromini himself were found on the walls behind the cases (cf. E. Re, *Biblioteca Alessandrina*, Rome, n.d., p. 11, and Portoghesi, *Borromini nella cultura europea*, pl. 72). At the end of the library is a tablet with an inscription and a bust of Alexander VII by Domenico Guidi (1660–1).

S. Lorenzo in Damaso
Piazza della Cancelleria

Bibliography: G. Urban, 'Die Kirchenbaukunst des Quattrocento in Rom', *Römisches Jahrbuch*, IX/X, 1961–2, p. 219; A. Schiavo, *Il Palazzo della Cancelleria e la Chiesa di S. Lorenzo in Damaso*, Rome, n.d.; *Guide Rionali*, VI, 2, p. 108.

Built 1486–95 by Cardinal Raffaele Riario, nephew of Sixtus IV, who also built the Palazzo della Cancelleria in which it is enclosed. The door was designed by Vignola and engraved, together with an unexecuted design for the door of the palace, at the end of his *Regola delle Cinque Ordini*.

INTERIOR
The church was restored and altered in the 17th and 18th centuries. The choir was remodelled by Bernini on the orders of Cardinal Francesco Barberini in 1640 (Pollak, I, p. 164; Fagiolo dell'Arco, *Bernini*, no. 89; and Portoghesi, *Roma Barocca*, fig. 60) and the *Confessio* was constructed in 1730 by Gregorini (Titi, 1763, p. 122; Portoghesi, ibid., p. 454) but both were completely transformed in the restoration by Giuseppe Valadier about 1814 and again by another in 1868. Finally the church was damaged by fire in 1939.
Entrance wall: Monument to Alessandro Valtrini (d.1634) designed by Bernini on a commission from Cardinal Francesco Barberini, and executed by assistants in 1640 (Wittkower, *Bernini*, p. 211; and Montagu, *Giorgetti*, p. 282, note 29). For the symbolism see the similar tomb of Ippolito Merenda in S. Giacomo alla Lungara.
On piers in vestibule: Statue of *S. Carlo Borromeo* by Stefano Maderno (Donati, *Artisti ticinesi*, fig. 339), and tomb of Giovanni Pacini (d.1567) attributed to G. A. Dosio.
1 to R: *Cappella Ruffo* (S. Nicola) (A. Schiavo, p. 105, pl. XXXV): The chapel was decorated by Nicola Salvi for Cardinal Tommaso Ruffo (consecrated 1743). The vault fresco of *God the Father in Glory* is by Corrado Giaquinto and the altarpiece of the *Madonna and Saints* is by Sebastiano Conca (Voss, p. 622). On the floor is the inlaid marble tomb-stone of Cardinal Ruffo (d.1753).
Right aisle: *1st pier of nave*: Monument to George Macdonald of Tuermont, Scottish secretary to Cardinal Francesco Barberini (d.1640).
End of left aisle: *Chapel of the Immaculate Conception*: Restored in 1634–5 by Cortona for Cardinal Francesco Barberini (Pollak, I, p. 163 and Del Piazzo, No. 154). The frescoes of the vault, which represented *God the Father in Glory*, were destroyed in one of the 19th-century restorations, but the fine stucco decorations remain. Passeri clearly states that Cortona was also responsible for the marbling of the walls.
1 to L: *Cappella Ottoboni* (Sacramento) (A. Schiavo, p. 104, pl. XXXIV): Decorated for Cardinal Pietro Ottoboni by Ludovico Rusconi Sassi (consecrated 1736). Vault frescoes by Andrea Casali.

In 1633 Cardinal Francesco Barberini commissioned Pietro da Cortona to design an *apparato* for the Quarant'Ore for the church, which is known from a drawing at Windsor (Noehles, *SS. Luca e Martina*, p. 14 and pl. 22).

S. Lorenzo in Fonte
Via Urbana, 50

Bibliography: Totti, p. 494; Titi, 1674, p. 308 and 1763, p. 269.

A small church rebuilt by Domenico Castello for Urban VIII. The interior was many times restored, lost in 1959–60 and now has little architectural character.

In a room adjoining the church is a bust of Urban VIII by Bernini (Wittkower, *Bernini*, p. 184).

S. Lorenzo in Lucina
Piazza S. Lorenzo in Lucina

Bibliography: L. Huetter and E. Lavagnino (Chiese di Roma, 27); Salerno, *Via del Corso*, p. 157; R. Bösel, 'Cosimo Fanzago a Roma', *Prospettiva*, 15, 1978, p. 29; *Guide Rionali*, III, 1, p. 92.

Originally built in the 4th or 5th century, according to one legend on the site of a temple of Diana Lucina, according to another founded by a Roman lady called Lucina. Rebuilt under Paschal II (1099–1118), to whose time the portico belongs. A parish church, it was handed over in 1606 by Paul V to the Chierici Regolari Minori, an Order founded by the Neapolitan Giovanni Pietro Carafa. Through this connection Cosimo Fanzago was invited by the Prior Raffaele Aversa – presumably from his name also a Neapolitan – to restore the church on the occasion of the Holy Year of 1650, at a time when he had taken refuge in Rome after the Masaniello revolt in Naples. The work, which was completed in 1652, involved an almost complete redecoration of the church, but most of it was swept away in a further restoration in 1857, leaving only the magnificent pulpit, the holy water-stoups and the pavement of the presbytery. The black and white marble pavement of the nave is dated 1734.

2nd pier R: Monument to Nicolas Poussin erected in 1829–30 by Chateaubriand.

3 to R: (S. Antonio da Padova): Architecture by C. Rainaldi (Mola, p. 115; Eimer, *S. Agnese*, I, figs 85, 86).

4 to R: *Cappella Fonseca* (Annunziata) (De' Rossi, *Altari*, pls 44, 50; J. Dobia, 'G. L. Bernini's Fonseca Chapel in S. Lorenzo in Lucina', *Burlington Magazine*, vol. CXX, 1978, p. 65): The chapel was designed by Bernini and executed probably in the early 60s (cf. Wittkower, *Bernini*, p. 256; mentioned by Mola (p. 116) in 1663). The bust of Gabriele Fonseca, doctor to Innocent X, was executed by Bernini, but the exact date of its execution is a matter of dispute. It was certainly begun by 1668, the date of Fonseca's death, but it was probably not finished till later. (Wittkower argues that it may only have been put in place after 1674 because Titi does not mention it in that year, but in fact it is also – unaccountably – omitted in all later editions.) The other three busts were added in the 18th and 19th centuries. The altarpiece (the *Annunciation*) by Lodovico Gimignani is a variant of Reni's painting in the Quirinal chapel (as is mentioned by Mola in 1663). On the right wall: Giacinto Gimignani, *Elisha pouring salt into the waters of Jericho in order to purify them* (1664), no doubt in allusion to the fact that Fonseca was much concerned with purifying the malarial waters of Rome and the Campagna. Bernini's bust of Fonseca, which is one of his most deeply felt late works, shows the doctor in impassioned prayer, gazing towards the altar (cf. Blunt, 'Gianlorenzo Bernini: Illusionism and Mysticism', *Art History*, I, 1978, p. 80). Curiously enough Specchi's engraving in de' Rossi's *Altari* (pl. 49) shows Fonseca's arms surmounted by an ecclesiastical hat, in spite of the fact that he was – *pace* Miss Dobia – a layman, and the arms in the chapel are surmounted by a knight's helm.

High Altar: By C. Rainaldi (1675) as a setting for the *Crucifixion* by Reni, bequeathed to the church by the marchese Angelelli.

5 to L: *Alaleoni* (S. Francesco and S. Giacinta Marescotti): Altarpiece: M. Benefial, *Death of S. Giacinta Marescotti* (1758); paintings on vault and side walls by Simon Vouet: vault: God the Father, angels and scenes from the life of the Virgin; right wall: *St Francis taking the Vow of Poverty*; left wall: *The Temptation of St Francis* (cf. W. R. Crelly, *The Paintings of Simon Vouet*, New Haven, 1962, p. 209).

2 to L: *S. Carlo Borromeo*, Carlo Saraceni (Nicolson, p. 87).

1 to L: *Baptistery*: By Giuseppe Sardi, between 1713 and 1721 (Portoghesi, *Roma Barocca*, pl. 332; Mallory, *Rococo*, p. 56). Paintings: Nasini, *Baptism* (before 1721); others by Antonio Crecolini.

Sala Capitolare: Onofrio Avellino, *Madonna* (W).

The convent attached to the church was rebuilt by C. F. Bizzacheri (1690–1700). It has a fine door on the via in Lucina (*Architettura minora*, I, pl. 41; Mallory, *Bizzacheri*, pp. 28, 45).

S. Lorenzo in Miranda
Via dei Fori Imperiali

Bibliography: Mola, p. 110; Titi, 1686, p. 179; Buchowiecki, II, p. 282; D'Onofrio, *Scalinate*, p. 272.

The temple dedicated by Antoninus Pius to the memory of his wife Faustina was converted into a Christian church at an early date. The *cella* was rebuilt in 1601–14 by Orazio Torriani who also built the lower half of the façade (the upper part was finished in the late 17th century). This architect was also involved in the restoration of the neighbouring church of SS. Cosma e Damiano; thirty-three drawings by him are in the Kunstbibliothek, Berlin (S. Jacob, *Italienische Zeichnungen der Kunstbibliothek Berlin*, 1975, Nos. 280ff.).

High Altar: Cortona, *Martyrdom of St Lawrence* (Briganti, *Cortona*, p. 240).

1 to L: Two stucco figures flanking the altar are attributed to Jacques Sarrazin after designs by Domenichino (cf. a note by Caylus in the *Mémoires inédits . . . des membres de l'Académie Royale de peinture et de sculpture*, Paris, 1887, I, p. 117, note 1); painting: Domenichino, *Holy Family* (much damaged) (Voss, p. 113).

S. Lorenzo fuori le Mura
Piazza Verano

Bibliography: G. Matthiae (Chiese di Roma, 89); C. F. Guglielmi, *Basilica di S. Lorenzo al Verano*, Milan, 1966.

One of the most important of the Early Christian basilicas but only relevant in the context of the Baroque through containing a certain number of tombs and paintings.

RIGHT AISLE
Inlaid marble tomb of Giuseppe Rondinini (d.1640) with mosaic portrait in exactly the style of that on the tomb of Ottaviano Ubaldini della Gherardesca in S. Maria sopra Minerva by G. B. Calandra and probably by the same hand.
Chapel to right: (S. Tarcisio): Altarpiece: Emilio Savonanzi, *S. Ciriaca burying a Martyr*; left wall: Giovanni Serodine, *Decapitation of St John the Baptist*, damaged in the bombing of 1943.

LEFT AISLE
Tomb of Michele Bonelli (d.1604).
Monuments to G. Aleandro and B. Guglielmi designed by Cortona. The monuments were commissioned by Cardinal Francesco Barberini in 1627 and they were originally intended to commemorate Guglielmi and John Barclay, who had been the cardinal's teachers in jurisprudence and letters. Both contained busts by Duquesnoy, but that of Barclay was stolen by his widow and is now in the Museo Tassiano at S. Onofrio. It was replaced by one of the Cardinal's secretary Gerolamo Aleandro by A. Giorgetti (cf. Noehles, *SS. Luca e Martina*, pp. 83ff., with reproductions of Cortona's drawings for the monuments; Montagu, *Giorgetti*, p. 280).

Between the monuments is a door leading to a staircase which goes down to the chapel of S. Ciriaca and the entrance to the catacombs. The chapel has an inscription with the date 1677, which is no doubt also that of the door and stairs.

S. Lorenzo in Panisperna
Via Panisperna

Bibliography: Totti, p. 494; Titi, 1674, p. 309 and 1763, p. 270; Rossi, 1697, p. 655; Vasi, *Magnificenze*, pl. 152; Hibbard, *Maderno*, p. 29; P. Tomassi, *Chiesa di S. Lorenzo in Panisperna*, Rome, 1967; C. Lotti, *Alma Roma*, 1973, XIV, 5/6, p. 14.

The church, which was rebuilt in 1575 perhaps by Francesco da Volterra, though the façade is dated 1684, stands at the end of a small forecourt

28. *S. Lorenzo in Panisperna. Engraving by Vasi showing the entrance to the church before the level of via Panisperna was lowered. In the background the domes of the Sistine and Pauline chapels of S. Maria Maggiore. On the extreme right the Palazzo Cimarra.*

now approached by a flight of steps and a gate built – very skilfully – in 1892 when the level of the via Panisperna was lowered.

The interior is dominated by the huge late 16th-century fresco of the *Martyrdom of St Lawrence* by Pasquale Cati on the altar wall, whereas the rest of the decoration dates from the mid-18th century. The vault of the nave is frescoed by A. Bicchierai with the *Apotheosis of St Lawrence* (1757; Mallory, *Notizie*, p. 112), who appears again in glory on a gilt relief on the vault of the choir. The altarpieces are all listed in the 1763 Titi but are not mentioned in 1745 by Roisecco who records a few 16th-century paintings which no doubt they replaced. The marbling is painted.

1 to R: Antonio Nessi, *S. Chiara*.
2 to R: Giovanni Francesco Romano, *Sts Crispin and Crispinianus*.
3 to R: Giuseppe Ranucci, *Immaculata*.
2 to L: Giuseppe Montesanti, *S. Brigit* (1757).
1 to L: Nicola Lapiccola, *S. Francis*.

S. Lorenzo in Piscibus (destroyed)

Bibliography: Armellini, II, p. 964; R. Battaglia, 'Due Architetti Borrominiani in San Lorenzo in Piscibus di Roma', *Bollettino d'Arte*, XXXI, 1937–8, p. 370.

This church in the Piazza Rusticucci was pulled down in 1938 when the via della Conciliazione was laid out. In 1659 it was given to the Scuole Pie (Scolopi). In 1672 it was altered by Francesco Massari, described as 'compagno del Borromini'. The façade was put up in 1733 to the designs of Giovanni Domenico Navone. It is shown in a drawing published by Armellini and was an imitation of a single bay of Michelangelo's Palazzo dei Conservatori. Navone added the portico, which was ingeniously designed to join the church to the Borgo Vecchio from which it was set back at a considerable distance. Battaglia gives the plan and good photographs of the interior.

SS. Luca e Martina
In the Forum

Bibliography: Pollak, I, p. 185; Falda, *Nuovo teatro*, III, pl. 5; De' Rossi, *Altari*, pls 17, 18; De' Rossi, *Architettura Civile*, I, pls 41, 42; Visentini, *Osservazioni*, p. 6; Magni, I, pls 46–8; Vasi, *Magnificenze*, pl. 42; Lavagnino, *Altari*, pp. 31; 103; Noehles, *SS. Luca e Martina*.

In 1588 the Accademia di S. Luca, which had been founded in 1577 as the academy of painters, sculptors and architects, was given possession of the small but ancient church of S. Martina in the Forum, built on the site of the Secretarium Senatus between the Forum Romanum and the Forum of Caesar, part of which is preserved in the foundations of the choir of the existing church. In 1589 the church was renamed S. Luca after the patron saint of painters; land adjacent to it was bought and a wooden model for a new church was made by Giovanni Battista Montano, who was lecturing at the academy on architecture at the time, but the money necessary to carry out these schemes was not forthcoming and nothing was done.

Noehles (pls 37, 38, 43) published various drawings which he identified as designs by Mascarino for the rebuilding of the church at this stage, but the attribution is in my opinion very doubtful. He also (pl. 61) published as being for this church a drawing by Cortona in Munich which can be identified as dating from the pontificate of Innocent X and as being, in my view, for S. Agnese in Piazza Navona. A design for a circular church which he also publishes (pls 48, 55) as being for SS. Luca e Martina is more problematic, but the identification is far from certain. These problems will be dealt with in my forthcoming book on Cortona as an architect.

In 1626 Cardinal Francesco Barberini, nephew of Urban VIII, was made protector of the academy and in 1634 Pietro da Cortona was elected principe. These two events led to the last and most important chapter in the history of SS. Luca e Martina. Cortona immediately decided to restore the crypt partly to strengthen the foundations of the church, which was in danger of collapsing, and partly in order to build there a tomb for himself, but also in all probability in the hope of finding the remains of S. Martina, which would be a sure way of attracting the interest and support of the pope (as at S. Bibiana). His hope was fulfilled. In November 1634 the pope visited the church to inspect the relics, and Cardinal Francesco Barberini undertook to pay for a new church.

A survey plan dating from before July 1635 shows that the foundations of the façade were already laid and the plans of the whole building must already have been completed. They must therefore have been made in the last months of 1634 or early in 1635. At first work proceeded quickly: the relics were buried again in the lower church in January 1635; the High Altar of the upper church was begun during the same year, and a drawing made by Cortona before he left for Florence in June 1637 (Noehles, pl. 91) shows that the apse was complete and the façade built as far as the entablature of the lower order.

There are no documents to show exactly

when the construction of the lower church was begun, but it is likely to have been started about 1635 and was in the main finished by 1647, but the sculptural decoration was not completed till much later.

Work on the church was held up for two reasons: Cortona was in Florence from 1639 till 1647, and Cardinal Francesco Barberini had to flee Rome and take refuge in Paris from the threats of Innocent X in January 1645. During the absence of Cortona work continued on the lower church under the direction of his nephew Luca Berrettini and largely at his own expense, but the construction of the upper church seems to have been halted till 1648 when Cardinal Francesco returned.

It was probably at this stage that Cortona produced his plan to enlarge the façade of the church to the width of the transept by adding two side bays either in the same plane as the central section (Noehles, pls 84, 86) or sloping back at 45° (ibid., pls 102, 103). This scheme was not carried out, presumably because the site could not be acquired, and in the event the façade was built as it appeared in the survey drawing of 1635.

By the time of Cortona's death in 1669 the construction of the church was complete, except for the top of the façade. This was finished under the direction of Angelo Torrone. The coat of arms was set up in 1671 and the angels supporting it, by Giuseppe Giorgetti, were put in place in 1673 (Montagu, *Giorgetti*, p. 391); the flaming urns were set up in the same year. It is not certain whether the façade was completed according to Cortona's final design or whether he intended to add a broad straight pediment over the existing curved one (as at S. Maria della Pace) and over the coat of arms, as Noehles (p. 109) convincingly suggests.

The external appearance of the church has suffered severely from the clearing of the area. In the early 19th century the excavation of the Forum lowered the level of the ground so that it is now completely dissociated from the church, which originally grew out of it but now stands on a macadamized street. In 1932 the buildings immediately surrounding it were pulled down to lay bare the ancient remains below them and at the same time the adjacent church of S. Adriano, built in the Republican Senate House, was stripped of its baroque decoration. The result of removing the houses which flanked the church was to emphasize the fact that Cortona had not been able to complete the façade and to make its unusual proportions even more conspicuous. The removal of the buildings round the apse made the dome more visible

29. SS. Luca e Martina. Engraving by Falda, showing the wings to the façade planned by Cortona. On the extreme left the Arch of Septimius Severus; beyond it the church of S. Giuseppe dei Falegnami; on the extreme right the façade of S. Adriano.

but necessitated the addition of much modern brickwork. As it stands now the church is in many ways awkward and naked.

The façade of the church is the earliest surviving example of Cortona's 'close-packed' designs, which he had employed earlier in secular architecture in the destroyed Villa del Pigneto, built for the Sacchetti. The columns of the lower storey and the pilasters of the upper are set under straight unbroken entablatures and the spaces between them are filled with panels which squeeze up against them and even overlap them. Cortona conceives of the wall as something to be carved out, almost like sculpture, an effect which is intensified by the choice which he has made of a particularly rough type of travertine.

INTERIOR

The decoration of the vault and dome was not finished at the time of Cortona's death in 1669, but was continued for many years under Luca Berrettini and Ciro Ferri, the latter being responsible for the stuccoes in the dome, which were still being worked on in 1679. It is not certain therefore that all the work was carried out according to Cortona's design. The question is of some importance, because it is generally said that Bernini borrowed from SS. Luca e Martina the idea of combining ribs and coffering for the decoration of a dome, which he applied at Castelgandolfo (1658–61) and his other later churches; but if in fact the decoration of the dome at SS. Luca e Martina was an invention of Ferri – and it has a certain softness which is more typical of him than of his master – then Bernini's churches may have been completed before SS. Luca e Martina. Cortona's priority, however, remains certain because he employed a simplified version of the same scheme in the dome of S. Maria della Pace on which he was probably working about 1656–7.

The reliefs of the four Evangelists in the pendentives were added in about 1735 from the designs of Giuseppe Rusconi who modelled one of them himself, the others being by Filippo della Valle and G. B. Maini.

The church – the only complete building by Cortona to survive – is in the form of a cross of which the arms are almost equal – the nave and choir being in fact slightly longer than the transepts – and is dominated by the heavy Ionic columns, typical of Cortona, which the architect has disposed in such a way that the walls are carved into a series of layers, ranging from the outer shell, behind the columns set into the walls of the choir, to the front layer formed by the entablature over the pilasters flanking the columns of the crossing piers. The

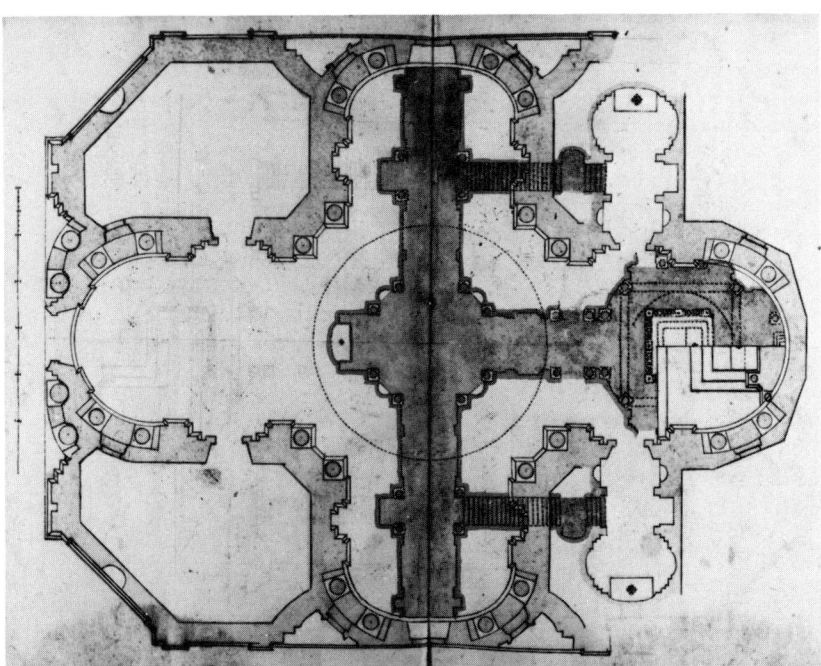

30. *SS. Luca e Martina. Drawing by Domenico Martinelli after Cortona (Bertarelli collection, Castello Sforzesco, Milan), showing the plan of the upper church superimposed on the lower. The plan of the upper church includes the extension to the façade planned by Cortona but not carried out.*

windows in the vaults and dome are composed of heavy Michelangelesque forms, typical of Cortona's work in the 1630s.

Immediately inside the main door (sharply criticized by Visentini) which has over it an inscription dated 1650, is a simple memorial slab to Cortona. To the right is a monument to the artist C. P. Balestra by Tommaso Righi (1776).
Right transept: Lazzaro Baldi, *St Lazarus* (1681; W), and tombs of Baldi and his sister, designed by the artist.
High Altar: Begun 1635 on a design by Cortona, the execution being in the hands of Luca Berrettini and Domenico Tavolaccio. The work was, however, interrupted and the altar was only completed after Cortona's death to a design slightly modified by Ciro Ferri. The altarpiece is a canvas of *St Luke painting the Virgin* traditionally ascribed to Raphael and presented to the Academy by Federico Zuccaro (now replaced by a copy). Below the *mensa* is the statue of the dead S. Martina by N. Menghini, a somewhat lumpish variant of Stefano Maderno's figure in S. Cecilia.
Left transept: Altar designed by Carlo Buratti (1722) perhaps incorporating elements from a design presented by Carlo Fontana in 1697; altarpiece: S. Conca, *Assumption* (Mallory, *Notizie*, p. 107).

In the Sacristy is a terracotta relief by Algardi of the *Ecstasy of the Magdalene*, a *bozzetto* for the relief now in Saint-Maximin (Provence).

Access to the lower church is through a small room to the left of the choir, which contains the tomb of the architect, G. B. Soria, a friend of Cortona, who was Principe of the Accademia di S. Luca in 1648 and died in 1651. The author of the bust is not known.

The lower church consists of two main chapels linked by a corridor. Over the altar of the first chapel is a relief by Algardi which originally represented the Holy Trinity, but has now lost the arched top which contained the Dove of the Holy Spirit (Heimbürger Ravalli, *Algardi*, p. 138). In the niches are the statues of four female saints: *S. Sabina, S. Teodora* and *S. Eufemia* by Cosimo Fancelli, and *S. Martina*, attributed to Pompeo Ferrucci.

In the inner chapel the altar containing the relics of S. Martina and designed by Cortona supports two alabaster reliefs also by Fancelli. In a shallow apse behind the altar is an Early Christian throne preserved from the old church. In a side chapel is a terracotta group by Algardi of S. Concordia, S. Epifania and a third unidentified saint (Heimbürger Ravalli, *Algardi*, p. 69). The lower church also contains a wall monument with a bust of Cortona begun by Bernardo Fioriti, and an inscription recording his bequest to the church.

In contrast to the upper church the inner chamber of the lower church is constructed of rich marbles and the altar is of elaborately worked gilt bronze. Cortona has set the four Ionic columns at the corners of the chapel on the diagonals, as Michelangelo had done in the Cappella Sforza, but he has softened the effect by setting them in shallow niches and flanking them with pairs of pilasters, whereas in the Cappella Sforza they project alone into the central space of the chapel. The pediments over the central panels are also Michelangelesque but Cortona has added mouldings in the field of the pediment which in the middle break forward into what seems to be the vestigial peak of another pediment.

The outer chamber is made of simpler materials and is much less ornate in detail. Eight Tuscan columns support the low vault in the centre of which is a broad stucco wreath of flowers and fruit surrounding an opening which allows a view straight up into the dome of the upper church.

S. Lucia del Gonfalone
Via dei Banchi Vecchi

Bibliography: Titi, 1763, p. 486; Vasi, 1791, II, p. 584; Donati, *Artisti ticinesi*, fig. 332; *Guide Rionali*, VII, 2, p. 11.

Built in 1761–5 to replace an earlier church belonging to the Compagnia del Gonfalone, the oldest Roman confraternity, founded in 1264 by St Bonaventura under the name of the Congregazione dei Raccomandati di S. Maria. The architect was Marco David and the patron Cardinal Flavio Chigi. The interior was heavily restored in the mid-19th century so that all that remains visible of the 18th-century church is the sober façade.

Oratory
Via del Gonfalone

Bibliography: Salerno, *Via Giulia*, p. 344.

Now used as a concert hall. Built in 1544–7 and decorated in the 1590s with one of the most complete cycles of late 16th-century frescoes surviving in Rome by Livio Agresti, F. Zuccaro, Cesare Nebbia and others (scenes from the Passion). The façade was built by Domenico Castello.

S. Lucia in Selci
Via in Selci

Bibliography: Baglione, p. 339; Titi, 1763, p. 242; Hibbard, *Maderno*, p. 136; Portoghesi, *Borromini nella cultura europea*, p. 205; *Guide Rionali*, I, 2, p. 72.

According to Hibbard begun by Maderno in 1603 for a convent of Augustinian nuns, and consecrated in 1619, though Baglione says that the convent was modernized by Felice Antonio Casone.

INTERIOR
A single nave with shallow side chapels, the form usual in the late 16th and early 17th centuries.
1 to R: Lanfranco, *Martyrdom of S. Lucy* (W).
2 to R: G. B. Speranza, *S. Augustine.*
High Altar: A. Fontebuoni, *Annunciation.* The grille over the *mensa* is by Borromini.
3 to L: G. B. Speranza, *St John the Evangelist giving Communion to the Virgin Mary.*
2 to L: *Cappella Landi*: Decorated by Borromini in 1637-9; altarpiece by Cavaliere d'Arpino. In this chapel Borromini uses for the first time a device which he repeats later in the cornice on the exterior of S. Ivo: he converts the egg-and-dart moulding into a series of cherubs' heads (the eggs) and wings (the darts).
Nuns' choir: B. Ciarpi, *Adoration of the Shepherds* and *Sts Ambrose, Lucy and Charles Borromeo.*

S. Luigi dei Francesi
Piazza S. Luigi dei Francesi

Bibliography: Totti, p. 360; Baglione, p. 81; Mola, p. 88; Martinelli, p. 80; Falda, *Nuovo teatro*, III, pl. 24; De' Rossi, *Prospectus*, pl. 37; De Brosses, II, p. 119; D'Armailhacq, *L'Eglise nationale de Saint-Louis des Français à Rome*, Rome, 1894; Magni, I, pl. 15; Cametti, 'Una divisione di beni fra i fratelli Giovanni, Domenico e Marsilio Fontana', *Bollettino d'Arte*, XXI, 1918, p. 177; M. L. Polidori, *Monumenti e Mecenati francesi a Roma 1492–1527*, Viterbo, 1969, p. 21; Giovannoni, 'Giovanni Mangone architetto', *Palladio*, III, 1939, p. 97; J. Lesellier, 'Jean de Chènevière', *Mélanges d'archéologie et d'histoire*, XLVIII, 1931, p. 233; Bousquet, *Recherches*, p. 119.

In 1478 the French colony acquired a small 14th-century church dedicated to S. Salvatore near this site. In the first years of the 16th century it was decided to build a new church which was to be dedicated to St Louis. This church which was designed by a French architect, Jean de Chènevière, was to be circular. It was never finished but a number of decorative panels from it were incorporated in the façade of the existing church, including two of salamanders, the emblem of Francis I, and the element which crowns the pediment of the existing church. The foundation stone of the church was laid by Leo X in 1518. Work on the church was suspended and it never rose more than about six feet above ground. The form of this church was no doubt suggested by Bramante's Tempietto, but it is interesting to notice that eight years earlier another northern patron, the Burgundian Benoît Adam, used a similar form, though octagonal instead of circular, for the little church of S. Giovanni in Oleo. The form was one mainly used for *martiria* to which class S. Giovanni belonged, but not S. Luigi. The reasons for the choice of this form for the church are unknown. Work on the church was abandoned in 1524.

At an unknown date – presumably after 1524 – Antonio da Sangallo the Younger produced a basilical plan which was not executed, and the church was actually begun on the plans of a little known architect, Giovanni Mangone. Mangone died in 1543 and it is not known who took over. The evidence about the completion of the church is somewhat confusing. Cametti has published documents which show that in the 1570s Giacomo della Porta was in charge with Domenico Fontana working under him. Mola says that the façade was begun by 'M.ro Gio: francese', no doubt meaning Jean de Chènevière, and adds that it was finished by della Porta, and both Baglione and Martinelli ascribe the façade to this architect. On the other hand Bousquet has shown that in 1585 Fontana was paid 300 scudi, and in 1588 220 scudi for his work on the façade, whereas della Porta was only paid 6 scudi per month, which suggests that Fontana was the actual designer and directing architect of the façade. A decision on stylistic grounds is difficult to arrive at, but the evidence seems to point to him rather than to della Porta as the designer. Della Porta never built a church with a façade composed, like S. Luigi, of two equal storeys, and though there is nothing precisely similar to be found in Fontana's work – he never built a complete church – the broad-shouldered squareness of S. Luigi recalls his style in general and has something in common with the external elevation of his Sistine Chapel at S. Maria Maggiore (Fontana, *Della Trasportatione dell'obelisco Vaticano*, Rome, 1590, p. 42). Further, the very heavy pediments over doors, niches and windows are closer to his manner than to that of della Porta as shown, for instance, at the Gesù, S. Maria ai Monti or S. Atanasio dei Greci. The two *ignudi* in the pediment were designed for the top of the Porta Pia but never set up there. They were tentatively ascribed by Schwager ('Die Porta Pia in Rom', *Münchner Jahrbuch*, XXIV, 1973, p. 59) to Daniele da Volterra, but documents published by Bousquet seem to show that they and the coat-of-arms which they support are by the French sculptor, Nicolas Pippe of Arras.

The church was consecrated in 1589, and when Fontana left Rome for Naples in 1594 his place was taken by Maderno who is recorded as receiving a payment of 10 scudi in 1606, and was still in charge in 1626, but since the building was by then complete his function was probably just to supervise its upkeep.

INTERIOR

The present appearance of the interior is due to a redecoration by Antoine Dérizet between 1756 and 1764 (for its original state see an engraving of 1665 reproduced by M. Fagiolo dell'Arco and S. Carandini, *L'Effimero barocco*, II, p. 277). The painting on the vault of the nave, *St Louis in Glory*, is by Natoire (1756; Mallory, *Notizie*, p. 112; Poensgen, fig. 49). The reliefs on the pendentives of the dome are by Maini, Filippo della Valle, N. Gillet and Simon Challe (1750–2).

Between 1 and 2 to R: Tomb of Charles Errard (d.1689), Director of the French Academy in Rome from 1666 to 1683.

2 to R: Domenichino, scenes from the life of St Cecilia (1616–17), one of the purest expressions of the classical tendency in early 17th-century Roman painting. Poussin drew on these frescoes in several of his compositions (Borea, *Domenichino*, p. 149).

Between 2 and 3 to R: Tomb of Nicolas Wleughels (d.1737) who was director of the French Academy from 1724 to 1737, by M. A. Slodtz (1738–40).

3 to R: Altarpiece: Etienne Parrocel, *The Blessed Jeanne de Valois*.

Between 4 and 5 to R: Tomb of Charles François Poerson (d.1725), director of the French Academy from 1704 to 1725.

End of right aisle (over door to Sacristy): P. Lestache, bust of Cardinal de la Grange d'Arguien (Enggass, *Sculpture*, p. 217).

High Altar: Francesco Bassano, *Assumption*.

End of left aisle: Bust of Cardinal Joseph François de la Trémouille (d.1720), sculptor unknown.

5 to L: *Contarelli* (St Matthew): Commissioned by Cardinal Matteo Contarelli. The vault was decorated by the Cavaliere d'Arpino, but on the walls and over the altar are canvases by Caravaggio (1599–1602). On the left wall the *Calling* of St Matthew, on the right his martyrdom, and as the altarpiece the Angel dictating the Gospel to him. The two side paintings were painted in 1599–1600. Caravaggio's first version of the altarpiece (now in Berlin) was painted in 1602 but was too brutal for the clergy of S. Luigi who sold it to the Marchese Vincenzo Giustiniani and commissioned Caravaggio to paint the much tamer version which we see in the chapel today, which was finished in the same year. These paintings were Caravaggio's first commission for a Roman church (Kitson, *Caravaggio*, London, 1969, p. 93).

4 to L: Frescoes mainly by Charles Mellin who obtained the commission in 1630 in a competition in which Poussin took part unsuccessfully. On the left wall Giovanni Baglione, *Adoration of the Kings* (Baglione, p. 404).

3 to L: *Cappella Benedetti*: Right wall: Lodovico Gimignani, *S. Louis* (1680; W); left: Nicolas Pinson, *Catherine de'Medici*.

Between 1 and 2 to L: Tomb of Pierre de Rochechouart by Nicolas Pippe (1593).

1st pier: Monument to Claude Lorrain by Paul Lemoyne (1836).

To the right of the church in the via Giovanna d'Arco is the Palazzo di S. Luigi built by Carlo Bizzacheri in 1709–12 to house a college attached to the church (Ferrari, *Lo Stucco*, pl. CLXVII; Mallory, *Bizzacheri*, pp. 36, 46 and *Rococo*, p. 46).

S. Macuto
Piazza di S. Ignazio

Bibliography: Vasi, *Magnificenze*, pl. 165; B. Pocquet du Haut-Jussé, 'L'Eglise Saint-Malo à Rome', *Mélanges d'Archéologie et d'Histoire*, XXXVI, 1916–17, p. 85; *Guide Rionali*, III, 2, p. 22 and IX, 2, p. 46; M. S. Lewine, *The Roman Church Interior 1527–1580* (Dissertation, Columbia University, 1960), p. 298.

The church was rebuilt in 1578 – possibly by Martino Longhi the Elder or Francesco da Volterra. Its original appearance is recorded in an engraving of 1589. It was restored in 1730 and again in the 19th century. It has a very simple façade with one unusual feature, a Serliana in the upper storey. This might be taken for a 19th-century insertion but it appears in Vasi's engraving.

The church contains two unusual altars, probably dating from the late 16th-century restoration, and in character Venetian rather than Roman.

The church now serves as the chapel of the Seminario (to the left) through which it can be visited.

Madonna del Divino Amore (SS. Biagio e Cecilia dei Materassai)
Vicolo del Divino Amore

Bibliography: P. Mancini, *La Chiesa della Madonna del Divino Amore in Campo Marzio*, Rome, 1976; Rotili, *Raguzzini*, p. 56.

The church belonged to the Corporation of Materassai (mattress makers) from 1575. It was rebuilt by Raguzzini in 1729–31. The façade is of great simplicity and the interior was drastically restored in 1874.

Altar to R: Sigismondo Rosa, *St Blaise healing a child.*
Altar to L: Placido Costanzi, *Sts Cecilia and Valeria.*

Madonna della Grazie (Madonella di S. Marco)
Piazza Venezia

Bibliography: E. Coudenhove-Erthal, p. 58; *Guide Rionali*, IX, 3, p. 122.

This chapel originally formed part of the Palazzetto Venezia and when this was pulled down and rebuilt on the other side of the Palazzo Venezia in 1911 it was moved to the right-hand end of the main front of the Palazzo. The altarpiece was put up in 1682 by G. B. Contini and the angels on either side are by Filippo Carcani. Coudenhove-Erthal suggests that Contini may have been working to a design by Carlo Fontana.

Madonna dei Monti. See S. Maria dei Monti
Piazza della Madonna dei Monti

SS. Marcellino e Pietro
Via Merulana

Bibliography: Vasi, *Magnificenze*, pl. 50; C. Cecchelli, E. Persico (Chiese di Roma, 36); Braham and Hager, p. 88; *Guide Rionali*, I, 2, p. 34.

A church with the dedication to these two martyrs probably stood on this site since the last years of the 4th century. A restoration was undertaken in 1703 by Carlo Fontana for Clement XI, but under Benedict XIV a completely new church was built in 1751–4 to the design of Girolamo Teodoli. The plan of the church – a Greek cross – and the façade are strictly classical but the architect allowed himself a flight of fancy in the stepped dome, which owes its origin ultimately to the Pantheon, but more immediately to Borromini's dome of S. Ivo.

INTERIOR
1 to right transept: F. Evangelisti, *St Gregory.*
High Altar: Gaetano Lapis, *Martyrdom of Sts Marcellinus and Peter.*
Left transept: Altarpiece: copy after Reni, *The Virgin with Sts Joseph and Theresa.*

S. Marcello
Via del Corso

Bibliography: De' Rossi, *Prospectus*, pl. 36; Tessin, p. 164; Magni, I, pl. 58; Coudenhove-Erthal, p. 51; Salerno, *Via del Corso*, p. 222; Zänker, 'S. Dorotea in Rom und verwandte Kirchen', *Architectura*, IV, 1974, p. 177; H. Hager, 'La Facciata di S. Marcello al Corso', *Commentari*, XXIV, 1973, p. 58; L. Gigli (Chiese di Roma, 131).

A church on the site is first mentioned in 418. Later it became the titular church of a Cardinal, and from 1369 it belonged to the Servites. The old church was destroyed by fire in 1519. Rebuilding was begun immediately on plans of Jacopo Sansovino and continued by Antonio da Sangallo the Younger after Sansovino's departure for Venice in 1526. The apse was added by Annibale Lippi in 1569 and the church was finished in 1592.

The façade was added in 1682–3 by Carlo Fontana (for the preliminary designs see Hager). Fontana has accepted the principle of the curved façade introduced by Borromini and Cortona in the 1630s but he has applied it in a simpler way. Instead of the double-S curve of S. Carlino or the play of convex against straight or concave of SS. Luca e Martina or S. Maria della Pace he planned his front on a single steady curve. The result proved enormously successful and the façade was probably more frequently imitated – often with variations – during the late 17th and 18th centuries than any other in Rome, except the Gesù (Juvarra's S. Cristina in Turin, the Neumünster in Würzburg, to quote two widely separated examples). S. Marcello seems to have been the first church façade actually built on this design but two architects had experimented with it on paper at an earlier date: Borromini for S. Carlino (Portoghesi, *Borromini*, pl. XXIX) and Martino Longhi the Younger for S. Giovanni Calabita in 1644 (J. Variano, 'Martino Lunghi the Younger and the façade of S. Giovanni Calabita in Rome', *Art Bulletin*, LII, 1970, p. 71).

The relief over the door showing *S. Filippo Benizzi renouncing the tiara* is by Antonio Raggi (1686). The statues representing S. Marcello and S. Filippo Benizi (below) and B. Gioacchino Piccolomini and Francesco Patrizi (above), and allegorical figures of *Faith* and *Hope* on the pediment are all by Francesco Cavallini (c.1683).

INTERIOR

Restored 1861–7. The ceiling was put up in 1592 at the expense of Monsignor Giulio Vitelli (d.1600), who also paid for the frescoes on the vault of the choir and the apse (by G. B. Ricci da Novara, who painted those on the entrance wall, 1613). The choir stalls were executed in 1612 and the pulpit, designed by Mattia de' Rossi and executed by Carlo Torriani, dates from 1673.

1 to R: *Cappella Alli-Maccarani*: Vault frescoed in early 17th century by Tarquinio Ligustri da Viterbo (Gloton, pl. XLIX); chapel decorated 1666; altarpiece: the *Annunciation* by L. Baldi (c.1686).

2 to R: *Cappella Muti-Bussi* (SS. Degna e Merita): Designed by Francesco Ferrari; vault fresco (*Glory* of the two saints) by Ignazio Stern; altarpiece and wall paintings of scenes from the lives of the two saints by P. A. Barbieri; chapel opened 1727 (Mallory, *Notizie*, p. 104); tombs of Giovanni Muti and his wife, Maria Colomba Vincentini, by Bernardino Cametti (1725; Ferrari, *La Tomba*, pls CXLIVff.; Enggass, *Sculpture*, p. 156). Brilliant variants in an 18th-century spirit of the ideas invented by Bernini in the Cornaro Chapel (S. Maria della Vittoria), and the Fonseca Chapel (S. Lorenzo in Lucina), and developed in the Bolognetti tombs in the Gesù e Maria.

3 to R: *Grifoni*: Frescoes by F. Salviati of scenes from the life of the Virgin (c.1562).

4 to R: (*Crocifisso*): *Creation of Eve* on vault by Perino del Vaga (before 1527); rest of vault by Daniele da Volterra and Tibaldi on Perino's designs. The Crucifix survived the fire of 1519; the screen which covers the Crucifix is by Luigi Garzi (before 1686; W); the tabernacle is by Bizzacheri (1691; Mallory, *Bizzacheri*, pp. 36, 45).

5 to R: *Paolucci* (S. Pellegrino Laziosi, a Servite): Restored between 1700–25 by L. Rusconi Sassi for Cardinal Fabrizio Paolucci (d. 1726), whose tomb by P. Bracci stands against the right wall (Gradara, *Bracci*, p. 23; H. Hager, 'Il Modello di L. Rusconi Sassi del Concorso per la facciata di S. Giovanni in Laterano', *Commentari*, XXII, 1971, p. 62, note 51); altarpiece and walls: A. Milani, scenes from the life of S. Pellegrino.

6 to L: (S. Filippo Benizi): Restored in 1725 by Cardinal Falconieri; altarpiece: P. L. Ghezzi, *S. Filippo Benizi, S. Alessio Falconieri and S. Giuliana Falconieri.*

5 to L: *Frangipane* (St Paul): Altarpiece: F. Zuccaro, *Conversion of St Paul*; walls: T. Zuccaro, scenes from the life of St Paul (1558); tombs of members of the Frangipani family: Antonio (d.1546) and his sons Curzio (d.1555), Mario (d.1569), Muzio (d.1588), Lelio (d.1605) and Roberto (1622), by Alessandro Algardi probably between 1630 and 1640 (Heimbürger Ravalli, *Algardi*, p. 95).

4 to L: (Sette Dolori): Restored and marbled in 1762 by Zanobi del Rosso, the sculptor being Alberto Fortini; altarpiece: P. P. Naldini, *Madonna Addolarata*; walls: D. Corvi, *Sacrifice of Isaac* and *Finding of Moses*.

3 to L: *Parisani*: Altarpiece: G. Triga, *Magdalen*; vault: G. P. di Francesco di Michelangelo del Colle, a pupil of Vasari, *Life of the Virgin* and *Prophets* (1551).

2 to L: *Massimo*: Begun in 1593, and finished in 1634 by F. A. Casone; altarpiece: A. Masucci, *Madonna and Saints*; walls: P. P. Naldini, scenes from the Passion.

To left of door: Tomb of Cardinal Giovanni Michiel and bishop Antonio Orso by Jacopo Sansovino.

S. Marco
Piazza S. Marco

Bibliography: F. Hermanin (Chiese di Roma, 30); G. Urban, 'Die Kirchenbaukunst des Quattrocento in Rom', *Römisches Jahrbuch*, IX/X, 1961–2, p. 125; *Guide Rionali*, IX, 3, p. 130.

Built on the site of the house belonging to Pope Mark I (337–40), the church was completely transformed in the second half of the 15th century by the Venetian Cardinal Pietro Barbo, later Pope Paul II, who also built the adjacent Palazzo Venezia, later the seat of the Venetian ambassador to the Holy See. The interior was redecorated in 1653–7 by Orazio Torriani on the orders of Niccolò Sagredo, and again by Filippo Barigioni in 1735–6 and 1743–9 at the expense of Cardinal Angelo Maria Querini when the columns veneered with Sicilian jasper were added.

The portico dates from the 15th-century restoration, as does the coffered wooden ceiling of the nave. The only visible remains of the mediaeval church are the mosaics in the apse and on the arch over it which date from the 9th century. The paintings on the walls of the nave which belong to the 1653–7 restoration, illustrate the lives of *Sts Abdon and Sennen*. Those on the right are totally ruined by damp.

4 to L: F. Chiari, *Translation of the Body of St Mark* (W).
3 to L: F. Allegrini, *Dedication of an Altar*.
2 to L: Canini, *St Mark approving the Plan of the Church* (W).
1 to L: Cortese, *St Mark crowned as Pope* (W).
  The stucco reliefs between the paintings representing scenes from the lives of the twelve Apostles were added c.1743–4 by C. Monaldi, P. Pacilli, J. Le Doux, S. Bercari, Andrea Bergondi and M. A. Slodtz (Ferrari, *Lo Stucco*, pls CXXXff.; Enggass, *Sculpture*, p. 187).
Right aisle: between 1 and 2 to R: Monument to Cardinal Francesco Pisani (d.1570) and Gerolamo Quirino (d.1571) with an unusual superstructure in the form of a temple façade.
2 to R: Altarpiece: Louis Cousin, called Luigi Gentile, *Virgin and Child with Saints*.
3 to R: Maratta, *Adoration of the Kings* (c.1656; W).
Between 3rd and 4th chapels: C. Fancelli, monument to Cardinal Cristoforo Vidman (d.1660).
4 to R: Altarpiece: Bernardino Gagliardi, *Pietà*; frescoes by the same.
Beyond 4th chapel: Monument to Francesco Erizzo (d.1700) by Francesco Maratta.
Before Cappella del SS. Sacramento: Monument to Cardinal G. B. Rubino (d.1707).
Chapel to the right of the choir: *Cappella del SS. Sacramento* (cf. V. Casale, 'Pietro da Cortona e la Cappella del Sacramento in S. Marco a Roma', *Commentari*, XX, 1969, p. 93): Casale states that the chapel was restored on the designs of Pietro da Cortona. He affirms that the artist's name occurs in the documents, but it does not do so in those that he quotes; and he attributes to him the two drawings for the chapel which he publishes but which are too weak to be from his own hand. He gives the date 1661 for the chapel but del Piazzo (No. 85) gives 1655 as the date of a drawing for the chapel, presumably one of those reproduced by Casale. The attribution of the decoration to Cortona is confirmed by the style and also by the fact that his nephew, Luca Berrettini, is recorded as being in charge of the work. Moreover the chapel is attributed to him by Titi (1763, p. 180) and Venuti (1767, p. 684). The frescoes on the walls, now almost completely obliterated by damp, are by Guglielmo Cortese. The altar is much earlier in style and is attributed by Venuti (p. 686) convincingly to Orazio Torriani.
Choir: Remodelled and decorated in 1735 by Barigioni who altered the shape of the last arches of the arcade. The High Altar (round a magnificent ancient porphyry bath) and the fine marbled structure which supports it are ascribed by Hermanin to Barigioni, but Venuti (1767, p. 686) says that they are by Michelangelo Specchi.
In apse: Romanelli, *St Mark* (badly damaged; W); on walls: frescoes by Cortese: right: *St Mark's Body dragged along the Ground*; left: *Martyrdom of St Mark* (W).
Left aisle: *before 4th chapel*: Carcani, monument to Cardinal Pietro Basadonna (d.1684); the statues by Filippo Carcani were being executed in 1686 (Titi, 1686, p. 436).
4 to L: Mola, *St Michael* (Cocke, *Mola*, p. 61, No. 59).
Between 4th and 3rd chapels: Monument to Cardinal Luigi Prioli (d.1720; Ferrari, *La Tomba*, pl. CLXXV).
Between 2nd and 1st chapels: Monument of Cardinal Marco Antonio Bragadin (d.1658). On the authority of Titi (1674, p. 201) this has always been ascribed to Raggi, but a document dated 1662 and published by D. L. Bershad (*Burlington Magazine*, CXIX, 1977, p. 114) shows that the commission was given to the *Scarpellino* Alessandro Vitale with the condition that the bust and the putti should be executed by Lazzaro Morelli.
Sacristy: Mola, *Portrait of Niccolò Sagredo*.

S. Margherita in Trastevere
Via della Lungaretta

Bibliography: Roisecco, 1750, I, p. 182; H. Hager, 'L'Intervento di Carlo Fontana per le chiese dei monasteri di Santa Maria e Santa Margherita in Trastevere', *Commentari*, XXV, 1974, p. 234.

Rebuilt in 1564 on the site of a 13th-century church, and again in 1678–80, to the design of Carlo Fontana by Cardinal Girolamo Gastaldi who also contributed to the completion of S. Maria dei Miracoli and S. Maria di Montesanto. Both façade and interior are typical of the severe side of Fontana's style, here manifesting itself at a very early date.

INTERIOR
The marbling is painted.
High Altar and the ovals beside it: Brandi, *St Margaret* (after 1686; W).
Altar to L: Baciccio, *Immaculate Conception* (c.1685; Enggass, *Baciccio*, pp. 29, 143).

S. Maria degli Angeli
Piazza delle Terme

Bibliography: Letarouilly, pl. 316 (300); Magni, I, pl. 13; G. Matthiae (Chiese di Roma, 87); J. Ackermann, *The Architecture of Michelangelo*, London, 1961, p. 123; R. de Fusco *et al.*, *Luigi Vanvitelli*, Naples, 1973, pls 173–92.

S. Maria degli Angeli

In 1561, partly at the instigation of a Sicilian priest called Antonio del Duca (uncle of the architect, Giacomo del Duca) who was passionately devoted to the worship of the angels, Pius IV decided to convert the vast tepidarium, which formed the central chamber of the Baths of Diocletian, into a church to be dedicated to S. Maria degli Angeli and to be controlled by the Carthusians of S. Croce in Gerusalemme. Such a conversion of a pagan building into a Christian church had been a regular practice in Early Christian times, but had lapsed for many centuries.

The remodelling of the church was placed in the hands of Michelangelo, who converted the building into a church with the minimum of construction. He chose to place the entrance and the High Altar on the shorter axis of the complex, leaving the main hall as a vast transept, at each end of which he enclosed a square space to form an entrance vestibule. In what had been the passage to the frigidarium he built a choir for the monks. He placed the High Altar, flanked by two columns, between this choir and the body of the church. This arrangement satisfied the demands of the Carthusians for complete seclusion from the laity, a demand which would not have been met by the alternative project for treating the great hall as a nave, since the choir would not have connected directly with the cloister, built over the frigidarium. Later – probably in 1565 when Pius declared the church a titular church – the altar was moved to the end of the choir which then became open to the church.

The interior was completely transformed in the 18th century. In 1700 and 1746 the two vestibules at the end of the great hall were closed and turned into chapels. In 1727 the bays opening off the hall were closed in order to provide wall space for the altarpieces from St Peter's which were being replaced by mosaics, and in 1749 Vanvitelli was commissioned to carry out a complete remodelling of the building. It is said that Vanvitelli suggested opening up these chapels again, but the Carthusians refused. To the existing eight ancient granite columns Vanvitelli added eight more (in *scagliola*) in the two bays on the short axis, and over the openings to these bays and to the chapels on the long axis he erected depressed arches imitating those used by Maderno in the aisles of St Peter's. He also redecorated the circular vestibule and added a very simple façade. This was removed in the restoration of 1909–13 when the present arrangement with two doors and a niche – totally unjustified archaeologically – was invented. Vanvitelli's impressive entrance door to the cloister is now within the Museo delle Terme.

INTERIOR
Vestibule: right: Holy-water stoup by G. B. de' Rossi. Tomb of Carlo Maratta (d.1713) designed (1704) by the artist himself; the bust by Francesco Maratta (before 1708; Enggass, *Sculpture*, p. 116); left: Monument to Salvator Rosa (d.1673), erected by his son; the bust and the putti representing painting and poetry by B. Fioriti.
Bay between Vestibule and Great Hall: right: Houdon, *S. Bruno*, 1766; left: Muziano, *Christ giving the Keys to St Peter*. This and a number of the altarpieces in the church were originally painted for St Peter's and were moved here when they were replaced by copies in mosaic.

GREAT HALL
Across the right half of this lies the meridian laid out by Francesco Bianchini for Clement XI in 1702.
In the right half:
1 to R: N. Ricciolini, *Crucifixion*.
2 to R: P-C. Trémolières after Francesco Vanni, *The Fall of Simon Magus*.
Chapel at end: Side walls: Trevisani, *Baptism by Water* and *Baptism by Desire* (W).
2 to L: F. Mancini, *A miracle of St Peter*.
1 to L: Girolamo Muziano, *St Jerome*.
Choir: Right wall: Romanelli, *Presentation* (1638–42) and Domenichino, *Martyrdom of St Sebastian* (Borea, *Domenichino*, p. 187).
Left wall: C. Maratta, *Baptism* (1696–8; W) and Cristofano Roncalli, called Il Pomarancio, *The Death of Ananias and Sapphira*; vault: A. Bicchierai and D. Seiter, *The Virgin in Glory*.
In the left half:
1 to R: P. Bianchi, *Immaculata*.
2 to R: P. Costanzi, *Resurrection of Tabitha*.
Chapel at end: Altar: Odazzi, after design by Maratta, *St Bruno* (soon after 1700; W); side walls: Trevisani, scenes from the lives of the Maccabees (1738–45; W); vault: A. Procaccini, *Evangelists* (soon after 1700; W).
Left wall of Great Hall: Pompeo Batoni, *Fall of Simon Magus* (Voss, p. 648); P. Subleyras, *The Mass of St Basil*.
Sacristy: Odazzi, *Rest on the Flight into Egypt* (Roisecco, 1750, II, p. 606); Off it the Sala dei Certosini with 18th-century frescoes and fine stalls. The *St Bruno in Glory* has been ascribed to Odazzi.

To the left of the church is a door with the arms of Gregory XIII who transformed part of the Baths into a granary in 1575, the architect being Martino Longhi the Elder (Wasserman, *Mascarino*, p. 83). Round the corner in via Parigi are the arms of Paul V connected with the same project and those of Clement XIII (dated 1764) on the entrance to the oil-store which he made there, apparently designed by Vanvitelli (reproduced by Pane in De Fusco et al., *Luigi Vanvitelli*, Naples, 1973, fig. 176).

Also to the left of the church is another door by Pietro Bracci, his only surviving architectural work (Gradara, *Bracci*, p. 94, pl. XXXII), which originally led to the Orphanage founded there by Clement XIII, whose arms it bears.

S. Maria dell'Anima
Via dell'Anima

Bibliography: Letarouilly, pls 68, 69 (251, 252); J. Lohninger, *S. Maria dell'Anima*, Rome, 1909; G. Urban, 'Kie Kirchenbaukunst des Quattrocento in Rom', *Römisches Jahrbuch*, IX/X, 1961/2, p. 73; *Guide Rionali*, V, 2, p. 62; G. Knapp and W. Hausmann, *S. Maria dell'Anima*, Münchengladbach, 1979.

Built as the German national church in 1431–3 but rebuilt between 1500 and 1523. It contains important 17th-century tombs and frescoes.

INTERIOR

1 to R: Saraceni, *S. Benno* (1618; Nicolson, p. 247).

2 to R: (S. Anna): Altarpiece: Giacinto Gimignani, *Virgin and Child and St Anne* (1640); frescoes by Giovanni Francesco Grimaldi; walls: *Story of Joachim*; vault: *Virgin and St Anne in Glory* (W); right wall: tomb of G. Savenier by Algardi (c.1648; Heimbürger Ravalli, *Algardi*, p. 123) and bust of Gualtiero Gualtieri by Ercole Ferrata; left wall: tomb of Cardinal Johann Walter Slusius (d.1687) attributed by D. Bershad to Domenico Guidi ('Domenico Guidi. Some new attributions', *Antologia di Belle Arti*, I, 1977, p. 18).

3 to R: *Fugger*: Giulio Romano's *Holy Family*, now over the High Altar, originally stood in this chapel; walls: frescoes by Sicciolante da Sermoneta.

3rd Pier: Tomb of Adraen Vryburgh by François Duquesnoy (1628).

Choir: Decorated by Paolo Posi; walls: frescoes by Ignazio Stern (Mallory, *Notizie*, p. 111); right wall: tomb of Hadrian VI by Peruzzi and others (1524–9); on left: Tomb of Prince Karl Friedrich of Jülich-Cleve (d.1575), by Nicolas Mostaert and Egidio della Riviera.

High Altar: Giulio Romano, *Holy Family*, the lower part repainted by C. Saraceni after being damaged in a flood in 1598.

Sacristy: Built by Paolo Maruscelli (1635–44; Martinelli, p. 87; Mola, p. 120); ceiling frescoed by Romanelli (1634–8); on walls: G. M. Morandi, *Annunciation* and *Marriage of the Virgin* (1682; W); Gilles Hallet, *Marriage of the Virgin*; G. Bonatti, *Annunciation* and *Visitation*.

4 to L: (Crocifisso): Frescoes by F. Salviati (finished 1550).

End of left aisle: Tomb of the archaeologist Luca Holste (or Holstenius), librarian to Cardinal Francesco Barberini (d.1661) by Antonio Giorgetti, erected 1663 (Montagu, *Giorgetti*, p. 281).

3rd pier: Tomb of Ferdinand van den Eynden by Duquesnoy (1633–40; Wittkower, *Art and Architecture*, p. 275).

1 to L: (St Lambert); Altarpiece: Carlo Saraceni, *The Martyrdom of St Lambert* (1618; Nicolson, p. 247); walls: frescoes by Jan Miel replacing those commissioned from Pietro Testa; tomb of Egidius Ursinus de Vivariis (d.1647) attributed to Finelli (Antonia Nava Cellini, 'Aggiunte alla ritrattistica berniniana e dell'Algardi', *Paragone*, 65, 1955, p. 26).

In addition the church contains a number of interesting 17th- and 18th-century tombs of which the authors are not known. Knapp and Hausmann give all the available data about them.

S. Maria Annunziata delle Turchine (destroyed)

Bibliography: Vasi, *Magnificenze*, pl. 157; Armellini, p. 280.

The church, which stood in via Sforza, was founded in 1675 by Camillo Orsini. The façade is shown in Vasi's engraving. The church was secularized in the 19th century and has now disappeared.

S. Maria Antiqua (S. Maria Liberatrice)
Forum

Bibliography: Falda, *Nuovo teatro*, III, pl. 27; Titi, 1686, p. 181 id., 1763, p. 205; Vasi, *Magnificenze*, pl. 54; W. de Grüneisen, *Sainte Marie l'antique*, Rome, 1911.

This Early Christian church was remodelled in 1617 by Onorio Longhi for Cardinal Marcello Lante. All his work was removed in a restoration of 1900 in order to reveal the Early Christian frescoes. The façade is recorded in engravings by Falda and Vasi, and the High Altar is reproduced from an old photograph in Pugliese-Rigano, *Lunghi*, pl. 154.

S. Maria in Aquiro
Piazza Capranica

Bibliography: M. D'Onofrio, C. M. Strinati (Chiese di Roma, 125); *Guide Rionali*, III, 2, p. 62.

Built by Cardinal Antonio Maria Salviati for the Orfanelli on the site of an earlier church from about 1583 onwards on the designs of Francesco da Volterra, but completed in 1620 after his death by Filippo Breccioli, working under Maderno (cf. Hibbard, *Maderno*, p. 121 and *Licenze*, p. 100).

The façade, begun in 1620, was designed by Breccioli to be of two almost equally broad storeys with small campaniles (his design is known from a drawing) but only the lower storey was built to his design and the upper one was added by P. Camporese the Elder in 1774. The interior was heavily restored in the late 19th century.

3 to R: *Cappella Ferrari:* On the side walls and the vault, frescoes by Saraceni (scenes from the life of the Virgin; Nicolson, p. 247).

2 to L: *Cappella della Pietà: Deposition, Crowning with Thorns, Flagellation* by followers of Caravaggio, the first by an unidentified 'Maestro Jacopo', the second probably by the Provençal painter, Trophime Bigot (J. Thuillier in 'La Peinture en Provence au XVIIe siècle', catalogue of exhibition in Marseilles, 1978, p. 3; J. P. Cuzin, 'Trophime Bigot in Rome: A Suggestion', *Burlington Magazine*, CXXI, 1979, p. 301; A. Blunt, ibid., p. 444).

2nd pier in left aisle: Tomb of Monsignor Carlo di Montecatini (d.1699).

S. Maria d'Aracoeli
Capitol

Bibliography: Padre Casimiro Romano, *Memorie istoriche della chiesa e convento di S. Maria in Araceli*, Rome, 1736; A. Colosanti (Chiese di Roma, 2); C. Pietrangeli, L. Salerno, 'L'Aracoeli', *Capitolium*, XL, 1965, p. 187; *Guide Rionali*, X, 2, p. 144.

The church, which is traditionally said to stand on the site of the altar at which the sibyl appeared to Augustus and foretold the birth of Christ, was originally built by the Benedictines in the 9th and 10th centuries but was given by Innocent IV in 1250 to the Franciscans who completely rebuilt it. It was frequently modified later and the steps leading up to it were added in 1348.

INTERIOR

The church was redecorated in honour of the victory of Lepanto, which was attributed partly to the skill of Marcantonio Colonna and partly to the intervention of the Virgin. A new roof was constructed by a Flemish wood-carver referred to as 'Flaminio Bolongier' – no doubt Flamen Boulanger – who also worked on the ceiling of S. Giovanni in Laterano. The ceiling incorporates allegorical allusions to the victory. The upper part of the nave walls was altered about 1686. Rectangular windows were inserted to replace the Gothic openings and oval frescoes were added between them by Odazzi and G. Passeri. This restoration was unveiled in 1690 (Cartari-Febei). Against a pier to the left is a fine wooden pulpit bearing the arms of Urban VIII.

ENTRANCE WALL

The wall contains four commemorative inscriptions. The one at the top spreading across the whole nave with the Barberini bees in a window of blue glass was erected in 1634–6 by the Senate in honour of Urban VIII and was designed by Bernini (Pollak, I, p. 165; Wittkower, *Bernini*, p. 206). Below to the left is one to Urban's brother, Carlo Barberini, put up on his death in 1630 and also designed by Bernini (Wittkower, ibid., p. 145). Over the door and to the right are tablets recording the Victory of Lepanto, set up in 1586.

1 to R: Frescoes by Pinturicchio (*c.*1485–6).

2 to R: Altarpiece: *Pietà* by Marco Pino; frescoes on walls by Cristofano Roncalli (Il Pomarancio).

Between 2 and 3 R: Statue of Gregory XIII by P. P. Olivieri.

5 to R: *Cappella Mattei* (S. Matteo): probably designed by Giacomo del Duca (Benedetti, *Del Duca*, p. 351); paintings of life of *St Matthew* by G. Muziano.

6 to R: (St Peter of Alcantara): Restored by G. B. Contini; stucco altarpiece and reliefs by M. Maglia (1682).

Bay leading to side door: Tomb of Cecchino Bracci based on designs by Michelangelo.

8 to R: (S. Pasquale Baylon): Frescoes on side walls, *Scenes from the Life of the Saint*, by D. Seiter (before 1686; W).

Right transept: *Savelli* (S. Francis): Restored in 1728 by F. Raguzzini for Benedict XIII (Rotili, *Raguzzini*, p. 56); altarpiece: *St Francis*, F. Trevisani (1729).

10 to R: (S. Rosa): Remodelled by Antonio Stanghellini (Titi, 1686, p. 169).

Chapel to right of High Altar: *Cappella Astalli* (SS. Sacramento; Portoghesi, *Roma Barocca*, pls 205, 206): Remodelled by Antonio Gherardi (Titi, 1686, p. 169) who also painted the altarpiece of the *Blessed Francesco Solano*; frescoes on the vault by Giuseppe Ghezzi (W). The whole chapel was damaged by restoration in 1882.

High Altar: Commissioned by the Senate in 1563. A drawing for it is in the Kunstbibliothek, Berlin (Jacob, *Zeichnungen*, No. 21).
Left transept: Shrine of St Helena (1605–24). Damaged by the French in 1797 and restored in 1833. The statue is modern.
Last pier of nave: Altar by F. Guidotti, 1682.
9 to L: *Colonna* (Madonna di Loreto): remodelled by Onorio Longhi (Baglione, p. 156).
8 to L: *Boccapaduli* (St Margaret): Redecorated in 1729 in honour of St Margaret of Cortona, who had been canonized in the previous year. The frescoes on the side walls (1732) are almost certainly by Marco Benefial, though they were credited at the time to his master, Filippo Evangelisti (scenes from the life of St Margaret; Voss, p. 641).
7 to L: *Tebaldeschi*: Altar by Carlo Rainaldi.
6 to L: *Orsini*: Altar by Onorio Longhi (1582–3); altarpiece: G. Muziano, *Ascension*.
5 to L: *Della Valle*: Altarpiece: G. Muziano, *St Paul*; frescoes on walls by C. Roncalli (Il Pomarancio).
4 to L: F. Trevisani, *Holy Family and B. Serafina Sforza* (probably after 1736).

S. Maria in Campitelli
Piazza Campitelli

Bibliography: Falda, *Nuovo teatro*, I, pl. 32; Titi, 1763, p. 83; Magni, I, pls 31–3; Ferrari, *Lo Stucco*, pls CXVIIff.; Wittkower, *Italian Baroque*, p. 9; Fasolo, *Rainaldi*, p. 147; Spagnesi, *G. A. De Rossi*, p. 115; Portoghesi, *Roma Barocca*, pls 221–30; Eimer, *S. Agnese*, II, figs 304–14; H. Hager, 'Zur Datierung des ovalprojekts von S. Maria in Campitelli', *Römisches Jahrbuch*, XI, 1967–8, p. 297.

A small church was built on this site by Paul V in 1619 but in 1657 Alexander VII approved the transfer to it of a holy image of the Virgin housed in the nearby church of S. Maria in Portico or S. Galla (now destroyed) which was said to have been responsible for the cessation of the plague the previous year. At the same time it was agreed that the church should be extended or rebuilt. Carlo Rainaldi was chosen as architect and at first produced a series of designs on an oval ground plan, but these were abandoned in favour of the one actually built which consists of a cross with nearly equal arms to which is added a square choir with an apse. The building was not actually begun till 1663. By this time Giovanni Antonio de' Rossi had been appointed joint architect with Rainaldi, but it does not seem likely that he exercised much influence on the design of the church as a whole.

Wittkower has pointed out that the plan is derived from north Italian models, such as Magenta's S. Salvatore at Bologna, but that Rainaldi translated it into Roman terms by the use of giant free-standing columns, the entablatures over which break forward to an almost uncomfortable extent. The most successful feature of the interior is the dramatic effect of the brilliantly lit dome over the choir – not, as was normal, over the crossing – as the climax to the

31. *S. Maria in Campitelli. Engraving by Falda showing on either side of the church the accommodation for the priests who served the church (that on the right either never executed or altered later). On the right of the piazza the Palazzo Capizucchi (extreme right) and the Palazzo Albertoni.*

church. The façade has a Baroque liveliness in its free treatment of the wall with inset columns and broken entablatures and pediments, but the movement is disjointed compared to the work of Borromini or Cortona. A feature peculiar to Rainaldi is the emphasis on the aedicules which dominate the centre of the design on both storeys.

INTERIOR

1 to R: Sebastiano Conca, *St Michael* (1735; Voss, p. 622).
2 to R: Luca Giordano, *St Anne, St Joachim and the Virgin*; angels by Lorenzo Ottoni (right) and Michele Maglia (left).
High Altar: (Lavagnino, *Altari*, pp. 39, 145); Spagnesi (p. 119) has shown that de' Rossi was responsible for the general design of the altar, with its Berninesque glory, in collaboration with G. P. Schor, though Rainaldi may have given some indication of what was wanted. Melchiorre Cafà made the wax model on Rossi's instruction and Ercole Ferrata was responsible for modelling the angels.
Choir (left wall): Baciccio, *Birth of the Baptist* (c.1698; Enggass, *Baciccio*, p. 143).
3 to L: *Capizucchi* (St Paul): Architecture by Mattia de' Rossi, 1685 (De' Rossi, *Altari*, pl. 10; Portoghesi, *Roma Barocca*, pl. 398); Lodovico Gimignani, *Conversion of St Paul* (before 1686; W).
2 to L: *Cappella Altieri*: Decorated by G. B. Contini (1693; Buchowiecki, II, p. 548); altarpiece supported by two angels by Giuseppe Mazzuoli.
1 to L: *Cappella Albertoni Altieri* (Portoghesi, *Roma Barocca*, pl. 399): Decorated by Sebastiano Cipriani (finished 1710); altarpiece, L. Ottoni, *Blessed Ludovica Albertoni* (1702–8); vault fresco, Giuseppe Passeri, *Assumption* (W); tombs by G. Mazzuoli: right, Laura Carpegna Altieri; left, Prince Angelo Altieri.

S. Maria in Campo Carleo (destroyed)

Bibliography: Vasi, *Magnificenze*, pl. 102; Armellini, I, p. 215.

The church, which stood since early times near the Forum of Trajan, was restored by Clement XIII in 1727. He presumably added the simple façade shown by Vasi. The church was pulled down in 1862.

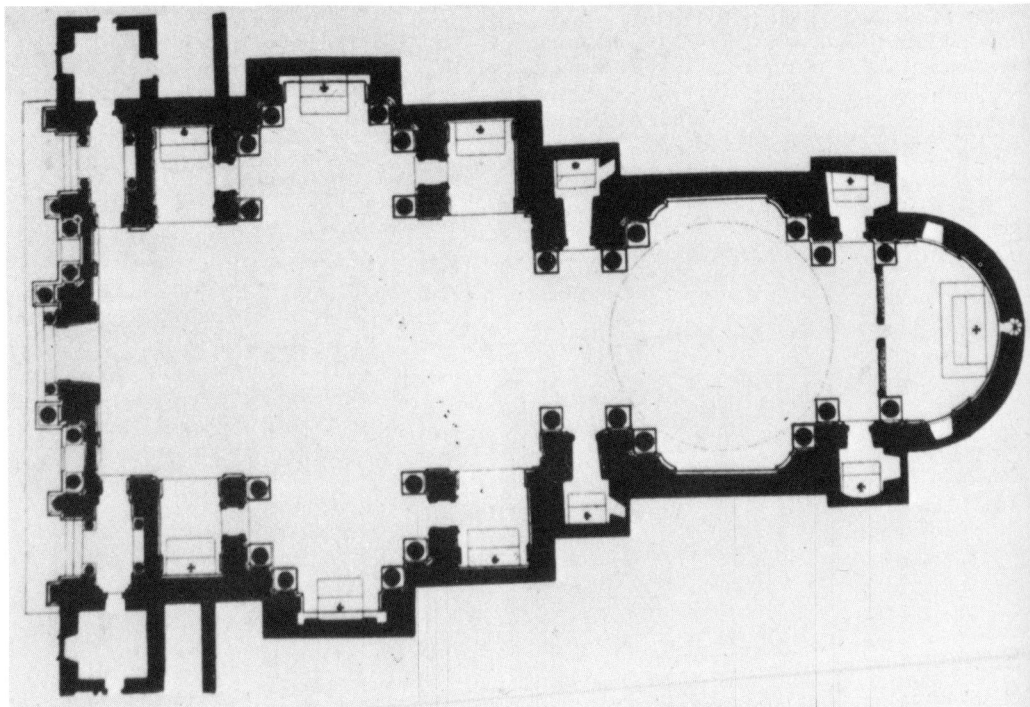

32. *S. Maria in Campitelli.* Plan.

S. Maria in Campo Marzio
Piazza di Campo Marzio

Bibliography: Vasi, *Magnificenze*, pl. 141; M. Bosi (Chiese di Roma, 61); G. Spagnesi, *G. A. De Rossi*, pp. 167ff.

Attached to a Benedictine convent of which the origin goes back at least to the 10th century. The existing church was begun about 1670 and finished in 1685, though the charming and unusual courtyard in front of it, one side of which contains a loggia, balancing the portico of the church, may have been begun earlier in the century. The architect of the church was almost certainly Giovanni Antonio de' Rossi whose name appears in the documents at the relevant period.

INTERIOR
Over the gallery: S. Conca, *Christ in the House of Martha and Mary* (Sestieri, Conca, XXI, p. 136).
Dome: Of unusual form, a type with flattened sides and ends, also used by de' Rossi in the Cappella delle Grazie at S. Rocco but not found in the work of any other major Roman architect of the period.
Right transept: P. Marini, *Life of the Baptist* (W).
2 to R: Garzi, *S. Gregorio Nazianzeno* (an oratory dedicated to him stood on the site from very early times).
Apse: An early example of the type of design which consists of two columns attached to the wall of the apse, without any central architectural element (cf. Fontana at SS. Apostoli); in half-dome: fresco, *Immaculata* by Placido Costanzi.
3 to L: (Crocifisso): Cast of a crucifix by Algardi.
Left transept: Baldi, *Three Scenes from the Life of St Benedict*.

S. Maria dei Cappuccini. See S. Maria della Concezione
Via Vittorio Veneto

S. Maria del Carmelo. See S. Egidio
Via della Scala

S. Maria del Carmine
Piazza Costaguti

Bibliography: Guide Rionali, XI, p. 50.

The chapel is now secularized but the porch composed of Tuscan columns stands against the back of the Palazzo Costaguti and is dated 1759. It is a variant of Cortona's porch of S. Maria della Pace.

S. Maria del Carmine alle Tre Cannelle
Vicolo del Carmine

Bibliography: Roisecco, 1745, II, p. 558; P. Mancini, 'La Chiesa del Carmine', *Alma Roma*, XV, 1974, 1/2, p. 31.

Built by Cardinal Odoardo Farnese for the congregation of S. Maria del Carmine and consecrated in 1605. The façade was added in 1750 from the designs of Michelangelo Specchi. The church was restored after a serious fire in 1772. The façade is an example of the increasing severity of style which became prominent in the mid-18th century.
Said only to be open on July 13–16 of each year.

S. Maria della Concezione (Cappuccini)
Via Vittorio Veneto

Bibliography: Pollak, I, p. 165; Mola, p. 101; Martinelli, p. 93; Vasi, *Magnificenze*, pl. 132; D. de Isnello, *Il Convento della SS. Concezione de'Padri Cappuccini in Piazza Barberini di Roma*, Viterbo, 1923; Buchowiecki, II, p. 559; Braham and Hager, p. 179; Brizzi, *Album di Roma*, Rome, 1980, pp. 62ff., 71, 80f.

Founded for the Capuchins by Cardinal Antonio Barberini, brother of Urban VIII, in 1626 and built to the austere design of Antonio Casone. Consecrated 1636. In 1890 the cutting of the new street, now Via Vittorio Veneto, involved the removal of the double flight of curved steps in front of the church and the destruction of the square in front of it. The façade was modified in 1925.

INTERIOR
Vault of nave: L. Coccetti, *Assumption* (1796).
1 to R: Guido Reni, *St Michael* (c.1632); on side wall: Honthorst, *Christ mocked* (Nicolson, p. 58).
2 to R: Left wall, Lanfranco, *Adoration of the Shepherds* (1631; W); altar: Mario Balassi, *Transfiguration*.

3 to R: Domenichino, *St Francis receiving the Stigmata* (Borea, *Domenichino*, p. 188).
4 to R: Baccio Ciarpi, *Agony in the Garden* (1632; W).
5 to R: Sacchi, *St Anthony revives a dead Man* (1631–3; Sutherland Harris, *Sacchi*, p. 70).
To left of choir: Monument to Alexander Sobieski (d.1714) by C. Rusconi (1727–8; Enggass, *Sculpture*, p. 103).
High Altar: Designed by P. Michele da Bergamo, altarpiece, copy of Lanfranco's destroyed *Immaculata*.
5 to L: Sacchi, *Vision of S. Bonaventura* (1634–6; Sutherland Harris, *Sacchi*, p. 78).
3 to L: Andrea Camassei, *Descent from the Cross* (c.1631; W).
2 to L: A. Turchi, *S. Felice da Cantalice*.
1 to L: Cortona, *St Paul recovers his Sight* (1631–2; Briganti, *Cortona*, p. 193).

In the monks' choir hang a number of unidentified 17th-century paintings.

Below the church (entrance from steps on right) is the cemetery composed of the bones of the Capuchins.

S. Maria della Consolazione
Piazza della Consolazione

Bibliography: P. Fernando da Riese (Chiese di Roma, 98); C. W. Brentano, *The Church of S. Maria della Consolazione in Rome* (Dissertation, University of California, 1967).

The church was begun, probably about 1470, to commemorate a miracle worked by an image of the Virgin below the Tarpeian Rock, and was attached to a hospital. Various chapels were added in the mid-16th century and the choir was built in 1581–5 to the designs of Giacomo della Porta. The architect in charge of the actual building was Martino Longhi the Elder who was probably responsible for the design of the nave which was rebuilt in the following years, incorporating some of the earlier chapels. He also built the lower storey of the façade. The upper one was not constructed till 1827 by the architect, Pasquale Belli, who may have been working after a drawing by Giuseppe Valadier. The addition has been made with such tact that it suggests that Valadier or Belli may have known of a drawing by Longhi. The door on the façade may be by Francesco da Volterra, who is recorded as working at the Consolazione just after Longhi's death in 1591.

INTERIOR
Three aisles separated by broad and open arches with light decoration typical of Longhi.

1 to R: *Cappella Mattei:* Decorated by Taddeo Zuccaro, 1553–6.
3 to R: *Cappella degli Affidati* (the Shepherds of the Forum): Built c.1632 by A. Ferreri and frescoed by Giovanni Baglione; altarpiece: *Adoration of the Kings*; side walls: *Adoration of the Shepherds* and *Assumption*.
Choir: The diamond-shaped coffering of the half-dome over the apse, based on that of the Temple of Venus and Rome in the Forum, is traditionally ascribed to Martino Longhi the Elder. The High Altar was also designed by Longhi.
Side walls: Cristofano Roncalli, called Il Pomarancio, right, *Birth of the Virgin*, left, *Assumption*.
Chapel at the end of the left aisle: Said to date from the second half of the 19th century, but is still in a semi-Baroque, semi-neo-classical style.
5 to L: *Cappella dei Vignaroli:* Antonio Circignani, called Il Pomarancio, *Marriage at Cana* and *Raising of Lazarus*. This and the following two chapels have fine late 16th-century stuccoes.
4 to L: *Cappella dei Pescatori:* Built about 1581, the altarpiece of *St Andrew* is by Marzio di Colantonio.
3 to L: *Cappella dei Garzoni degli Osti:* Decorated c.1600–10 with scenes from the life of the Virgin by Francesco Nappi.

S. Maria in Cosmedin
Piazza Bocca della Verità

Bibliography: Vasi, *Magnificenze*, pl. 56; G. Massimi, *S. Maria in Cosmedin*, Rome, 1953.

Built on the site of a temple of Ceres, the present church dates mainly from the 8th–13th centuries.

The façade was remodelled by G. Sardi in 1718 for Cardinal Annibale Albani (Mallory, *Rococo*, p. 54), but his work was removed in the 1890s when the church was restored to its mediaeval state. The façade is recorded in engravings and old photographs (Elling, pl. 32).

S. Maria delle Grazie alle Fornaci
Via Madonna delle Fornaci

Bibliography: Rossi, 1727, p. 85; Roisecco, 1750, I, p. 115; A. F. Caiola (Chiese di Roma, 109); Elling, pl. 44.

Founded in 1552 by the Guild of Brick-makers who had their kilns in this district. The existing

33. *S. Maria in Cosmedin. Engraving by Vasi showing the façade added by Sardi in 1718.*

church was begun in 1694 but was not completed till much later, by which time it had been handed over by Clement XI to the Trinitarians in 1720. According to a not very clear reference in Rossi the architect appears to have been Francesco Bufalini. As shown in the foundation medal of 1694 the façade of the church would have presented an interesting continuation of Seicento ideas (the dome and flanking towers of S. Agnese in Agone and the porch of S. Maria della Pace) but as built (the façade was finished in 1727, Valesio, p. 120), probably by an otherwise unknown architect Francesco Multò, it is an unfortunate adaptation of Borrominesque motifs, particularly in the pediment in which the architect has converted that of the Oratory into something which is both mean and lumpish.

The interior, which was still being finished in 1750 (Roisecco), is a typical but pedestrian example of the vernacular architecture of the period.

2 to R: O. Avellino, *Trinity* (1737; W).
High Altar: 1724–6 (modified in 1958).
3 to L: *Cappella Asnaghi* (1713): Altarpiece of the *Holy Family with St John* by Giuseppe Chiari (Pascoli, I, p. 214); dome fresco by Pietro de'Pietri; overdoors: N. Ricciolini, *Nativity* and P. Bianchi, *Rest on the Flight*.

S. Maria delle Grazie a Porta Angelica (destroyed)

Bibliography: Titi, 1763, p. 428; Vasi, *Magnificenze*, VI, p. XIII; Armellini, II, pp. 975, 1354.

The church which stood near the Porta Angelica was pulled down early in the present century. It was built in 1588 but rebuilt in 1618 at the expense of Cardinal Lante. The façade, shown in an engraving by Vasi, was like that of S. Sebastiano, with an open three-bay loggia below and a closed upper storey of equal width.

S. Maria di Grottapinta
Via di Grotta Pinta

Bibliography: *Architettura minora*, pl. 46; *Guide Rionali*, VI, 2, p. 170.

A small church which was in the gift of the Orsini, and is now secularized and used as a store. The façade, of extreme severity, has a lower storey with rather fine Ionic pilasters and above it an attic with Tuscan pilaster bands – perhaps an economy on a projected Corinthian order (cf. S. Giuseppe a Capo le Case).

S. Maria delle Lauretane
Via San Giovanni

Bibliography: *Architettura minora*, I, pl. 32; *Guide Rionali*, 2, p. 28.

The monastery was pulled down in the late 19th century, leaving only the façade of the church, attributed to Giuseppe Sardi.

S. Maria Liberatrice See S. Maria Antiqua
Forum

S. Maria di Loreto
Forum of Trajan

Bibliography: De' Rossi, *Prospectus;* Magni, I, pl. 9; Benedetti, *Del Duca*, pp. 115, 460, and Chiese di Roma, 100.

The church was begun in 1502 by Antonio da Sangallo the Younger, who constructed the building up to the bottom of the drum of the dome. After a long interruption it was completed by Giacomo del Duca, who built the campanile (1525) and the dome, and added the two side doors between 1573 and 1577 (H. Hager, *Römisches Jahrbuch*, XI, 1967–8, p. 243, note 107). In the doors and the windows of the dome he invented a number of variations on themes by his master Michelangelo (with whom he collaborated on the Porta Pia) which were to influence Borromini (Blunt, *Borromini*, pp. 15, 34). In the lantern he created a brilliant but fantastic structure which deeply shocked his successors and was never imitated.

INTERIOR
The choir was redecorated in 1628–30. The frescoes (*Birth* and *Death of the Virgin*) by the Cavaliere d'Arpino (1629). In the first niches are figures of angels by Stefano Maderno and in those nearer the altar figures of *S. Cecilia* by Giuliano Finelli (right) and *S. Susanna* by François Duquesnoy (1630; left). The latter was originally intended to be in the niche on the right, where she would have been looking towards the altar. On either side of the altar *St Domitilla* by Domenico de'Rossi and *St Agnese* by Pompeo Ferrucci. Duquesnoy's *S. Susanna* was long admired as the embodiment of a classical ideal, opposed to the Baroque of Bernini.
2 to R: (The Magi): Frescoes by Niccolò Circignani, called Il Pomarancio (*Adoration of the Kings*, etc.).

S. Maria della Luce
Via della Luce

Bibliography: Roisecco, 1750, I, p. 184; Vasi, 1777, p. 354; Melchiorri, p. 545; Fasolo, *Trastevere*, p. 70ff.; Portoghesi, *Roma Barocca*, pl. 367; D. Gallavotti, G. Testa (Chiese di Roma, 129); Mallory, *Rococo*, p. 105.

The church was originally called S. Salvatore in Corte. In 1595 it was made a parish church and in the late 17th century it was served by the Minims. In 1730 a miraculous figure of the Madonna in a nearby chapel was transferred to the church, the dedication of which was in consequence changed to S. Maria della Luce. Soon after this date the church was rebuilt (only the Romanesque apse and campanile survive from the earlier building), though the façade was never completed.

The documents show that building was taking place in the years 1738–41 and various altars were executed in the years 1752–4 which suggests that building probably continued till about 1750. In 1777 Giuseppe Vasi wrote that the church was not yet finished, but he was no doubt referring to the decoration, or to the absence of the façade.

The church is unusual in plan having an extra pair of transepts – smaller than the main transepts – next to the High Altar. This may possibly be dictated by the necessity of using the foundation or walls of the old church.

Roisecco and Melchiorri both name Valvassori as the architect and in the absence of other evidence their attribution must be accepted; but if it is correct the severe rectilinear planning of the church and the use of a flat trabeation over the openings to the side chapels (cf. Gregorini and Passalacqua at S. Croce in Gerusalemme) prove that Valvassori was a more classical architect than one would suppose from the works securely ascribed to him, such as the remodelling of the Palazzo Doria-Pamphili on the Corso. The almost neo-classical character of the decoration can be explained by the fact that it was mainly carried out from 1768 onwards.

INTERIOR
3 to R: Giovanni Conca, *Death of St Joseph* (1754).
4 to R: Labruzzi, *The Virgin with St Anne* (1753).
Apse: Sebastiano Conca, fresco of *God the Father*, before 1763; door of tabernacle (*The Saviour*) by the same artist (Voss, p. 622); frescoes on left wall: Onofrio Avellino, *S. Francesco di Paola*.
3 to L: Giovanni Conca, *SS. Francesco di Paola, François de Sales, and Jeanne de Valois* (1752; Mallory, *Notizie*, p. 112).

S. Maria Maddalena
Via della Maddalena

Bibliography: Vasi, *Magnificenze*, pl. 138; Magni, I, pls 104–7; L. Mortari, (Chiese di Roma, 104); Spagnesi, *G. A. De Rossi*, pp. 204ff.; Portoghesi, *Roma Barocca*, pls 258–61, 337, 338, 352; Mallory, *Rococo*, p. 67; *Guide Rionali*, III, ii. p. 36; Valesio, p. 123.

A church existed on the site from the 15th century onwards. In 1585 it was granted to Camillo de Lellis (beatified 1742, canonized 1746) founder of the Ministri degli Infermi. In 1673 a new church was begun to the designs of Carlo Fontana, but only the chancel and possibly the crossing were built. In 1680 the Palermitan architect, Paolo Amato, also produced a design for the church, but this does not seem to have been followed. There was then an interruption till the 1690s when work was taken up again with G. A. de'Rossi in charge, but he died in 1695 and the remainder of the church was apparently built by Carlo Quadri. The exact shares of the two architects are uncertain. The elongated octagonal nave, which fits awkwardly on to the chancel and crossing is not to be found in Rossi's churches, but the unusual manner in which the main arches cut into the entablature has a parallel in an early work, S. Maria in Publicolis. The lower part of the façade was built during the same campaign but the decoration was not finished till about 1735 (Ferrari, *Lo Stucco*, pls CXXVIIff.). The early guides attribute this decoration to Giuseppe Sardi, but Mallory has argued convincingly that this is stylistically impossible. She further points out that the coverings of windows and niches and the 'pediment' which covers the whole façade – some of the most fantastic variations on Borrominesque models to be found in Rome – are very close in character to the organ gallery over the entrance door (1765–6) of which, unfortunately the author is also unknown, though it is recorded that the organ itself is by Hans Conrad Wehrle and was finished in 1735.

INTERIOR
The nave vault was frescoed in 1732 by M. A. Cerruti (Mallory, *Notizie*, p. 105; Poensgen, fig. 43) with scenes from the life of the Magdalen. The dome fresco, showing the *Trinity in Glory*, is by Etienne Parrocel (1739). On the piers of the nave are niches with six allegorical statues connected with Confession of which the first on the left is signed by Monaldi (Enggass, *Sculpture*, p. 185). The others are probably by P. Marelli.

1 to R: Biagio Puccini, *S. Francesco di Paola* (W).

2 to R: (Madonna della Salute); Decorated by G. and G. B. Luraghi after designs by F. Ferruzzi (1718).

Right transept: *Cappella di S. Camillo*: The altar was executed by F. Rosa, F. Giardoni and V. Consalvi and the altarpiece painted by P. Costanzi in 1742, after the beatification of Camillo (Mallory, *Licenze*, p. 108), and the decoration of the chapel was completed after his canonization by E. Nicoletti in 1749. The vault was frescoed by S. Conca (1744; ibid, p. 109).

High Altar: Painting by M. Rocca (1698; Voss, p. 624); reliefs by F. Gesuelli (1756).

Sacristy: 1738–41 by C. Marchionni.

Left transept: *Chapel of S. Nicola da Bari*: Begun by Mattia de'Rossi in 1690, completed by Carlo Bizzacheri in 1694–6 (Mallory, *Bizzacheri*, pp. 32, 45; id., *Rococo*, p. 38); altarpiece: Baciccio, *S. Nicola da Bari* (c.1697–8; Enggass, *Baciccio*, pp. 96, 144).

2 to L: Luca Giordano, *S. Lorenzo Giustiniani* (1704); tombs of Antonio Farsetti (d.1677) and Matteo Farsetti (1704) by G. Mazzuoli.

1 to L: (Assumption): By Francesco Nicoletti.

The monastic buildings on the left of the church, which were probably designed by the Palermitan architect Paolo Amato, were begun in 1678 under his direction, but were finished by C. F. Bizzacheri in 1680–4 (Mallory, *Bizzacheri*, pp. 29, 45).

S. Maria Maggiore
Piazza S. Maria Maggiore

Bibliography: De Brosses, II, p. 319; Vasi, *Magnificenze*, pl. 48; Letarouilly, pls 304–11 (329–31); Magni, I, pls 86–91; E. Lavagnino and V. Moschini (Chiese di Roma, 7); G. Urban, 'Die Kirchenbaukunst des Quattrocento in Rom', *Römisches Jahrbuch*, IX/X, 1961–2, p. 96.

The church was founded in the 4th or 5th centuries and the main structure still dates from the 5th century. The portico added by Eugenius III (1145–53) was replaced in 1575 by one designed by Martino Longhi the Elder (Martinelli, p. 99; Mola, p. 75), recorded in a drawing by Carlo Fontana at Windsor (Braham and Hager, fig. 475), and this in turn was destroyed when Fuga built the present façade for Clement XII which was planned in 1735 and built in 1741 (Matthiae, *Fuga*, p. 75; Pane, *Fuga*, p. 84 and figs 61–71; for drawings see Bianchi, *Fuga*, p. 65). The statues include in the middle the *Virgin and Child* by G. Lironi (Enggass, *Sculpture*, p. 173) and the *B. Niccolò Albergati* on the right by Filippo della Valle. The block to the

S. Maria Maggiore

34. *S. Maria Maggiore. Etching by Israël Silvestre showing the church as it was about 1640. The mediaeval wall closing the nave is visible above the portico added by Martino Longhi the Elder. On the right is the wing of the Canonica built by Flaminio Ponzio; behind are the domes of the Sistine (right) and Pauline (left) chapels. In the foreground is the column set up by Maderno in 1613.*

right of the façade was built in the early 17th century by Flaminio Ponzio (Hibbard, *The Architecture of the Palazzo Borghese*, Rome, 1962, p. 46).

The apse which was added by Nicholas IV (1288–92) was transformed into a second façade (De'Rossi, *Architettura Civile*, III, pls 14–16) under Clement X by Carlo Rainaldi whose design was preferred to Bernini's much bolder and more Baroque scheme (Brauer and Wittkower, II, pl. 182a).

On the outside of the Cappella Paolina are statues set in niches: *St Luke* and *St Jerome* by Valsoldo, *St Matthew* by Mochi and *St Epaphra* and *St Matthias* by Stefano Maderno and Caporale (Dorati, 'Gli scultori della Cappella Paolina di Santa Maria Maggiore', *Commentari*, XVIII, 1967, p. 231).

Vestibule: Reconstructed by Fuga with the façade. On the right is a bronze statue of Philip IV of Spain by Girolamo Lucenti (1692) and on the walls four reliefs: Bernardino Ludovisi, *Giovanni Patrizi offers his riches to the Pope*; Pietro Bracci, *Pope St Flavius in the Council of 465* (1742); G. B. Maini, *The Madonna of St Luke*; Giuseppe Lironi, *Exarch Olympus and Pope Martin V* (Enggass, *Sculpture*, p. 174; Gradara, *Bracci*, p. 53).

INTERIOR

The character of the mediaeval church was completely transformed by later alterations. Only the 5th-century mosaics on the nave walls and over the choir arch and Jacopo Torriti's in the apse have survived more or less intact. The magnificent gilt-wood ceiling was put up for Alexander VI. The major changes were made by Fuga who regularized the spacing of the columns of the nave colonnade and gave them new bases, cut arches in the colonnade opposite the Sistine and Pauline Chapels, added the baldacchino and relaid the floor (dated 1750 in an inscription, but also containing a panel with the arms of Innocent X who may have carried out an earlier restoration on it). The result did not please Benedict XIV who had become pope while the work was in progress and said that Fuga had reduced the church to a ball-room.

On the right of the entrance, monument to Clement IX by Carlo Rainaldi: figure of the pope by D. Guidi, figures of *Faith* (C. Fancelli) and *Charity* (E. Ferrata). On the left, monument to Nicholas IV (d.1292; Ferrari, *La Tomba*, pl. CVII) executed by Leonardo Sormani for Cardinal Felice Peretti (later Pope Sixtus V) in 1574 (both Nicholas and Sixtus came from the Marches). The monument originally stood against the right wall of the choir.

Right aisle: end wall: Tomb of Costanzo Patrizi (d.1623) by Algardi (Heimbürger Ravalli, *Algardi*, p. 101).

1st chapel to right: *Baptistery*: Attributed to Flaminio Ponzio (Titi, 1686, p. 226). Font by Giuseppe Valadier (1825). Relief of the *Assumption* over altar by Pietro Bernini (Titi, ibid.), originally on the outside wall of the Cappella Paolina. Monument to Odoardo Santarelli by Algardi (1640–2; Heimbürger Ravalli, *Algardi*, p. 107). Bust in coloured marbles by Francesco Caporale of Antonio Nigrita, who came to Rome as ambassador of the King of Congo to Paul V and was converted to Christianity. The bust, which was traditionally ascribed to Bernini, was set up in 1628 (Pollak, I, p. 174). It is an important and early example of the revival in the 17th century of the ancient Roman practice of making polychrome busts or statues (for an earlier example see the tomb of Paul IV by Ligorio in the Carafa chapel in S. Maria sopra Minerva).

Sacristy: Fine wooden cupboards, apparently of the early 18th century.

2nd altar to right: Agostino Masucci, *Holy Family* (1723; W).

3rd altar to right: Stefano Pozzo, *S. Niccolò Albergati*.

2nd chapel right: *Cappella delle Reliquie:* Attributed to Fuga (Titi, 1763, p. 252).

4th altar right: P. Batoni, *Annunciation*.

3rd chapel right: *Cappella Sistina* (del Presepio) (cf. D. Fontana, *Della Trasportatione dell' Obelisco Vaticano*, Rome, 1590, p. 39; De' Rossi, *Altari*, pls 41, 42; K. Schwager, 'Zur Bautätigkeit Sixtus V in S. Maria Maggiore in Rom', *Miscellanea Bibliothecae Hertzianae*, Munich, 1961, p. 324): Built by Domenico Fontana for Sixtus V and begun in January 1585 three months before he was elected pope. It contains his tomb and that of Pius V whose confessor he was and who made him a cardinal. Titi (1686, p. 226) identifies the subjects represented in the reliefs and paintings of the chapel and names the artists involved (not always correctly). The chapel was restored in 1871.

The painted decoration embodies a complicated iconographical scheme with scenes from the life of the Virgin, ancestors of Christ, Jewish Kings and mediaeval saints. The reliefs on the tombs represent episodes in the lives of the popes, including Pius V giving the banner to Filippo Colonna before the Battle of Lepanto, and scenes illustrating actions of Charity, Justice, etc. (Fontana gives the inscriptions identifying all these scenes.) To the right and left of the entrance to the chapel are two small chapels dedicated to St Jerome and St Lucy, and leading out of the chapel (R) is a sacristy the vault of which is decorated with stuccoes and frescoes, including landscapes by Paul Bril.

In the middle of the chapel is the mediaeval Cappella del Presepio (some of the reliefs are by Arnolfo di Cambio) which was transported

35. *S. Maria Maggiore. Engraving by Vasi, showing the portico added by Fuga in 1741 and the left wing of the Canonica completed.*

bodily from another part of the church by Fontana (see his description and plates, p. 50). The tabernacle was designed by Fontana but the sculpture is due to G. B. Ricci and assistants.

The Cappella Sistina is one of the earliest examples of a chapel of its size being completely decorated with coloured marbles, including a small amount of inlay in the pilasters in the form of *monti* and stars in allusion to the Peretti arms.

End of right aisle: On right tomb of Cardinal Giovanni Pietro Moretti (d.1646); on left tomb of Cardinal Marcello Crescenzio (d.1587); on floor the family tomb of the Bernini family.

High Altar: (1749) The baldacchino, composed of four magnificent porphyry columns with gilt-bronze vines climbing round them, is Fuga's near-classical reply to Bernini's baldacchino in St Peter's.

Chapel to left of High Altar: Tombs of Girolamo Manili (d.1634) and Clemente Merlini (d.1642). The latter is attributed to Borromini by Martinelli (p. 107) who explains that the colours of the marbles of which the monument is composed are symbolical, the red for the strength of character and white for the purity of Merlini. The drawings of the tomb and of that of Manili, however, are certainly not by Borromini, but are more likely to be by Gregorio Spada, brother of Borromini's patron Virgilio (Heimbürger, 'Un disegno certo dell'Algardi e alcuni probabili da Gregorio Spada', *Paragone*, 237, 1967, p. 59). Nava-Cellini ascribes the bust of Merlini to A. Bolgi ('Ritratti di Andrea Bolgi', *Paragone*, XIII, 147, 1962, p. 32). The wreath surrounding it and many of the details of the monument are in the style of Borromini who may well have designed them for Spada. The bust of Manili is by Finelli (A. Nava-Cellini, 'Un tracciato per l'attività ritrattistica di Giuliano Finelli', *Paragone*, 131, 1960, p. 20).

Left aisle: 3rd chapel to L: *Cappella Paolina* (S. Maria ad Nives) (De'Rossi, *Altari*, pls 43, 44): The chapel, designed by Flaminio Ponzio, was planned by Paul V as a counterpart to the Cappella Sistina, but his intention was clearly to out-do his predecessor, and the chapel is in fact richer than its counterpart in its marbles and in its lavish use of sculptural decoration. The structure was finished by 1611 but the decoration continued till about 1615. For the sculpture see M. C. Dorati, 'Gli scultori della Cappella Paolina di Santa Maria Maggiore', *Commentari*, XVIII, 1967, p. 231. For the iconography of the frescoes see E. Mâle (pp. 24, 33). The authors of

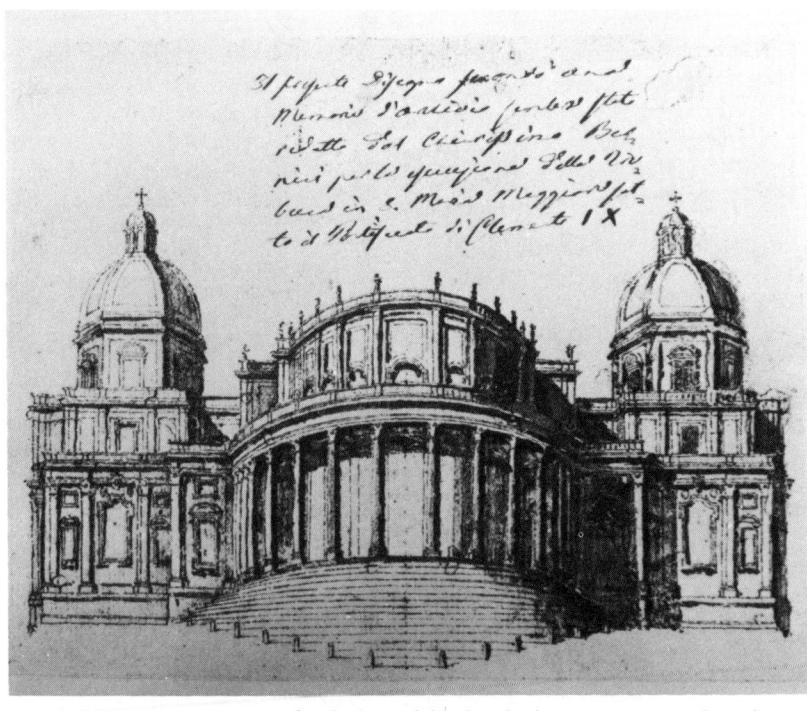

36. *S. Maria Maggiore. Bernini's project for the apse of the church (drawing, present whereabouts unknown).*

the frescoes are given in some detail by Titi in 1763 (p. 261; also A. M. Corbo, 'I pittori della Cappella Paolina in S. Maria Maggiore', *Palatino*, XI, 1967, p. 301).

It contains the tombs of Paul V and Clement VIII who made him a cardinal. The statues of both popes were originally by Silla Longhi, but that of Paul was found unsatisfactory and was replaced in 1612 by one begun by Nicolas Cordier who died the same year, leaving it unfinished (it is not known who completed it).

The subjects chosen for the reliefs on the tombs reflect the policy of both popes of reasserting the temporal power of the papacy. On Clement's tomb they represent the *Acquisition of Ferrara* (Ambrogio Buonvicino), the *Victory over the Turks at Graz* (Camillo Mariani and Mochi), the *Reconciliation of Philip II and Henry IV* (Ippolito Buzzi), and the *Canonization of Sts Hyacinth and Raymond* (G. A. Paracca, Il Valsoldo). Those on Paul's tomb show the *Fortification of Ferrara* (Buonvicino), the *Canonization of S. Carlo Borromeo and S. Francesca Romana* (Paracca), the *Reception of the Ambassadors of the King of the Congo* (Cristoforo Stati), and the *Coronation of the Pope* (Buzzi). The herms on the tomb of Clement are by Pietro Bernini, those on Paul's by Pompeo Ferrucci.

The central feature of the chapel is the Byzantine painting of the Virgin, traditionally attributed to St Luke, which was particularly venerated by the people of Rome. Girolamo Rainaldi made the original design for the altar, but this was modified by Antonio Tempesta. The painting is carried by gilt angels by Mariani. The two angels seated on the lower pediment are by Guillaume Berthelot, those standing on the upper pediment are probably after designs by Pompeo Targone. The relief in the pediment, showing the Miracle of the Snow (the foundation of the church), is by Stefano Maderno, who is also responsible for the putti in the marble frieze to the sides of the tombs. The painting was set up in 1613 (Gigli, p. 27).

The frescoes in the chapel were mainly carried out under the direction of the Cavaliere d'Arpino and Baglione, but that in the dome is by Cigoli and those round the tomb of Clement VIII are by Guido Reni and Lanfranco. They celebrate the virtues of the Virgin, expound the worship of holy images reaffirmed by the counter-Reformation theologians, and celebrate those who fought heresies. Mâle, in one of the earliest attempts to analyse this new iconography, gives a detailed account of these frescoes, which include stories of God's vengeance on the iconoclasts and of miracles wrought by images. The programme for the whole cycle of frescoes was prepared by two members of the Oratory who based their choice of subjects on the work of the great Oratorian historian of the early Church, Cardinal Baronius. The theme is carried on in Passignano's frescoes in the sacristy of the chapel.

The two side chapels are dedicated to two saints canonized under Paul V, S. Francesca Romana and S. Carlo Borromeo.

2nd chapel to left: *Cappella Sforza* (Ackerman, *Michelangelo*, London, 1961, I, 109, II, p. 122): Commissioned from Michelangelo in the last years of his life by Cardinal Guido Ascanio Sforza (d.1564). According to Vasari Michelangelo made the design but handed over the execution to Tiberio Calcagni. After his death in 1565 the chapel was completed by another architect, generally assumed – without any specific proof – to have been Giacomo della Porta. According to an inscription the chapel was finished by Cardinal Alessandro Sforza, brother of Ascanio. The tombs of the two cardinals stand in the curved side-bays of the chapel. That of Alessandro is dated 1582 and neither has any connection with Michelangelo.

Ackerman points out the poor quality of certain details (e.g. the capitals) as evidence for the fact that Michelangelo cannot have been responsible for the detail (which, it may be added, is not at all like della Porta's work), but the design of the whole is certainly due to Michelangelo.

The chapel contains many completely new features. The main piers are set on the diagonals of the crossing instead of on one or other of the main axes and the two apsed transepts are formed of arcs less than a semi-circle. With these innovations Michelangelo led up to features which were to be fundamental in Baroque architecture, above all the use of incomplete forms leading into one another.

The first architect who really understood these revolutionary features was Borromini who derived many ideas from them. He followed up Michelangelo's use of incomplete forms in the plans of the side chapels in S. Carlino and the canting of the columns at 45° in his monument to Cardinal Caracciolo in the Lateran (Blunt, *Borromini*, p. 29).

The façade of the chapel facing the aisle of the church was destroyed by Fuga, but is recorded in an engraving (Ackerman, I, pl. 73b). According to Ackerman it was designed after Michelangelo's death.

1st chapel to left: *Cappella Cesi-Massimi* (St Catherine): Attributed by Martinelli to Martino Longhi the Elder; altar: Sicciolante da Sermoneta, *Beheading of St Catherine*.

Right wall: Canini, *St Catherine disputing* (c.1660; W).
Left wall: C. Cesi, *Marriage of St Catherine*.
1st bay left: Tomb of Cardinal Agostino Favoriti (d.1682) with figures of *Faith* and *Fortitude* by Filippo Carcani (c.1685). The tomb is said to have been designed by Lodovico Gimignani (De'Rossi, *Architettura Civile*, II, pl. 48).

S. Maria ad Martyres (The Pantheon)
Piazza del Pantheon

Bibliography: V. Bartoccetti (Chiese di Roma, 47).

The temple, originally part of the Baths of Agrippa but rebuilt by Hadrian and dedicated to the seven major gods worshipped by the Romans, was converted into a Christian church and dedicated to S. Maria dei Martiri by Boniface IV in 609. Urban VIII removed the bronze supports in the portico to make the Baldacchino in St Peter's. In 1626 he caused two towers to be added to the façade (pulled down in 1883). These are generally ascribed to Bernini but the drawings for them are by Borromini and were made while he was still working for Maderno (Pollak, I, p. 178; Thelen, *Borromini*, p. 36; Hibbard, *Maderno*, p. 230; S. Bardini, *Quaderni*, 79–84, 1963, p. 53; and T. Thieme, 'Disegni di cantiere per i campanili del Pantheon', *Palladio*, N.S. XX, 1970, p. 73). The three left-hand columns of the portico were replaced under Urban VIII and Alexander VII, whose arms appear in their capitals.

INTERIOR
The attic was altered to its present form by Paolo Posi in 1747, but one section was restored to its original form in the present century.
1 to R: P. Naldini, bust of James Gibbs, possibly after a design by Pietro da Cortona (Noehles, *SS. Luca e Martina*, p. 106, note 23).
3 to R: Lorenzo Ottoni, *Virgin and Child with St Anne* (Enggass, *Ottoni*, p. 322).
High Altar: This includes some fragments of one designed by Alessandro Specchi, built 1715–25 and dismantled and rebuilt 1934. A preliminary design (not followed) is in the Kunstbibliothek, Berlin (Jacob, *Zeichnungen*, No. 746). To the left Francesco Moderati, *St Rasius* (1727); to the right Bernardino Cametti, *St Anastasius* (1725; A. Marday, 'Specchi's High Altar for the Pantheon and the Statues by Cametti and Moderati', *Burlington Magazine*, CXII, 1980, p. 30).
Niche beside 3 to L: Tombs of Raphael and Annibale Carracci.

Beside 2nd niche to L: Monument to Baldassare Peruzzi.
1 to L: On side walls: Paolo Benaglia, *Dream of Joseph*, and Carlo Monaldi, *Rest on the Flight into Egypt*.
1st niche to L: F. Cozza, *Adoration of the Shepherds and Kings* (1659–60; W).

S. Maria sopra Minerva
Piazza della Minerva

Bibliography: J. J. Berthier, *L'Eglise de la Minerve à Rome*, 1910; R. Spinelli (Chiese di Roma, 19); I. P. Grassi, *Basilica di S. Maria sopra Minerva*, Rome, n.d.; *Guide Rionali*, IX, 2, p. 52.

Founded in the 8th century on the ruins of a temple of Minerva Calcidica and given by Gregory XI (1370–8) to the Dominicans who rebuilt it on a much larger scale and in the Gothic style. It was frequently altered and restored, but in 1848–55 a disastrous attempt was made under the auspices of a Dominican father to restore it to its original state, which included encasing the Gothic piers in dark grey marble.

The façade was never completed. In 1725 a design for it was made by F. Raguzzini for Benedict XIII but it was not executed.

INTERIOR
1 to R: *Baptistery:* By Filippo Raguzzini (1724) but altered in 1850 (Rotili, *Raguzzini*, p. 31); bust of Cardinal Ladislao D'Aquileo (d.1621) by Francesco Mochi (cf. J. Hess, 'Nuovi aspetti dell'arte di Francesco Mochi', *Bollettino d'Arte*, XXIX, 1936, p. 309; I. Lavin, 'Duquesnoy's "Nano di Crequi" and two busts by Francesco Mochi', *Art Bulletin*, LII, 1970, p. 137).
2 to R: *Caffarelli:* Baciccio, *St Luis Beltran* (1671–4; Enggass, *Baciccio*, p. 144).
3 to R: *Cappella Colonna:* L. Baldi, *Scenes from the Life of S. Rosa of Lima* (c.1671; W).
3rd pier of nave: Monument to Carlo Emanuele Vizzanio (d.1661) by Domenico Guidi, put up by his son.
4 to R: *Capella Gabrielli:* Altar by Ciro Ferri (De'Rossi, *Altari*, pl. 28); altarpiece of St Peter Martyr by Ventura Lamberti (1688).
4th pier of nave: Monument of Alessandro Valtrini (d.1633), set up in 1637.
5 to R: (*Annunziata*): Decorated by Maderno probably after 1606 (cf. Hibbard, *Maderno*, p. 188); left wall: statue of Pope Urban VII (1590) by Ambrogio Buonvicino.
6 to R: *Cappella Aldobrandini* (Lavagnino, *Altari*, p. 15; Hibbard, *Maderno*, p. 133): Ceded in 1587 to Cardinal Ippolito Aldobrandini, later Clement VIII. In 1600 he decided to make

tombs for his parents and brother in it. The chapel was consecrated in 1611. The original architect was (almost certainly) Giacomo della Porta (possibly assisted by Girolamo Rainaldi) and on his death in 1602 he was (almost certainly) succeeded by Maderno who designed the altar in 1603 when Barocci's *Last Supper* was commissioned (delivered 1609). Giacomo della Porta must have been responsible for all the decoration up to the cornice but Maderno probably designed that of the vault. The figures of the pope's father (Silvestro) and mother are by Nicolas Cordier. The figures of *Prudence* and *Fortitude* on the former's tomb are by Ippolito Buzzi, and those of *Charity* and *Religion* on that of his mother (Luisa Deti) are by Cordier and Camillo Mariani respectively (cf. S. Pressouyre, 'Actes relatifs aux sculptures de la Chapelle Aldobrandini', *Bulletin de la société nationale des antiquaires de France*, 1971, p. 195). The *St Sebastian* is also by Cordier. On either side of the altar: Mariani, *St Peter* and *St Paul*.

The decoration of the walls is a fine early example of the use of coloured marbles. The vault and lunettes were frescoed by Cherubino Alberti in 1604 and 1609–10 respectively (C. M. Abramson, 'Clement VIII's Patronage of the Alberti brothers', *Art Bulletin*, LX, 1978, p. 540).

Right transept: (*Cappella Carafa*): Frescoed by Filippino Lippi; left wall: tomb of Paul IV designed by Pirro Ligorio and executed by G. B. Cassignola (cf. Ferrari, *La Tomba*, pl. CVI). An important early example of the revival of the use of coloured marbles in sculpture.

2nd chapel to right of High Altar: *Cappella Altieri:* Altarpiece, Maratta, *St Peter presenting five saints to the Madonna*; lunette by Baciccio (1671–2; Enggass, *Baciccio*, p. 145); tombs of Lorenzo Altieri and Cardinal Giovanni Battista Altieri (father and brother of Clement X) with busts by C. Fancelli (Buchowiecki, II, p. 720).

Chapel next the High Altar: *Cappella Capranica:* Paintings of the *Mysteries of the Rosary* by Marcello Venusti except for the *Crowning with Thorns* which is by Carlo Saraceni. Above is the organ made by Ennio Bonifazi (1633).

Choir: behind the High Altar: Tombs of Leo X and Clement VII by Antonio da Sangallo the Younger.

Pier to left of choir: Michelangelo, *Risen Christ*.

Passage to left of choir: over the door: Monument of Cardinal Carlo Bonelli by Carlo Rainaldi (*c*.1673) (Ferrari, *La Tomba*, pl. CLXXIV); left wall: tomb of Cardinal Alessandino Bonelli by Giacomo della Porta; right wall: tomb of Cardinal Domenico Pimentel (d.1653) designed by Bernini; the statues of the Cardinal, *Faith* and *Wisdom* are by E. Ferrata; *Justice* is by G. A. Mari and *Charity* by Raggi (Wittkower, *Bernini*, p. 227).

Passage to the Sacristy: Two statues of Virtues (*Faith* and *Religion*) by Tommaso della Porta which come from the tomb of Paul IV.

Sacristy: The altarpiece of the *Crufixion with Dominican Saints* and the fresco on the vault over it are by Andrea Sacchi (1637–8; cf. A. Sutherland Harris, *Sacchi*, p. 79). He may also have designed the doors. The author of the fresco on the vault of the sacristy itself is not documented, but is said by Martinelli (p. 110) to be 'Monsir Stella', that is to say the French artist Jacques Stella who worked in Rome from 1623 to 1635.

Behind the altar in the Sacristy is the room in which St Catherine of Siena died in the convent of the Minerva, which was moved to this place in 1637 and given an enclosing shell designed by Andrea Sacchi in a style of extraordinary classical delicacy (Harris, loc. cit., and Blunt, *The other side*). M. Fagiolo ('1638, una decorazione inedita', *Studi sul Borromini*, II, p. 201) has argued ingeniously that the reliefs on the structure were designed by Borromini, but though they bear some relation to his work on the Villa Giustiniani they do not actually seem to be of his invention.

In the Sala dei Papi between the Sacristy and the cloister is an over life-size unfinished marble statue of the *Virgin and Child*, traditionally ascribed to Bernini but probably by a Genoese sculptor of the later 17th century.

Left transept: (*S. Domenico*): Begun by Martino Longhi the Younger in 1649 but mainly built by Giuseppe Paglia in the 1670s, when the black and white marble columns were set up (Varriano, *Longhi*, p. 74). The chapel owes its present rich appearance to the decoration which it received from Filippo Raguzzini in the 1720s (Rotili, *Raguzzini*, p. 30). It contains the tomb of Benedict XIII designed by Carlo Marchionni with statues by Pietro Bracci (the pope and *Purity* or *Humility*, right) and Bartolomeo Pincellotti (*Religion*, left) (Gradara, *Bracci*, p. 35). The altarpiece of *The Virgin appearing to St Dominic* is by Paolo De Matteis. Opposite the tomb is a marble group of the *Virgin with the Child and St John* by Francesco Grassia, called Franco Siciliano (1670).

6 to L: A. Procaccini, *St Pius V* (W).

On 5th pier of nave: Monument to the Venerable Maria Raggi (d.1600) designed by Bernini and executed with the assistance of Antonio Raggi (cf. Wittkower, *Bernini*, p. 212; Lavin,

Bernini, p. 67; J. Bernstock, 'Bernini's Memorial to Maria Raggi', *Art Bulletin*, LXII, 1980, p. 243). The monument is usually dated 1643, but Bernstock has pointed out that the inscription refers to Lorenzo Raggi, who erected it, as cardinal which he only became in 1647. Documents quoted by her show that it was finished before 1653. The monument incorporates wind-swept marble drapery which no doubt symbolizes the idea of death sweeping men away as the wind carries off dead leaves, a theme which Bernini had already introduced in two earlier monuments, to Valtrini in S. Lorenzo in Damaso and Merenda in S. Giacomo alla Lungara (Blunt, 'Gianlorenzo Bernini: Illusionism and mysticism', *Art History*, I, 1978, p. 72). The effect of the monument has been greatly damaged by the addition of grey marble to the presumably travertine pier against which it should stand out in contrast.

Between 6 and 5 to L: Monument to Ottaviano Ubaldini della Gherardesca (d.1644), commander of the papal troops under Urban VIII with mosaic portrait by Giovanni Battista Calandra (A. Gonzales-Palacios, 'G. B. Calandra. Un mosaicista alla Corte dei Barberini', *Ricerche di Storia dell'Arte*, 1/2, 1976, p. 216). The tomb was erected by his widow, presumably in the year of his death, since Calandra died the same year. The putti are by Finelli.

4 to L: *Giustiniani* (St Vincent Ferrer): Altarpiece: Bernardo Castello, *St Vincent Ferrer at the Council of Constance* (after 1604).

Between 4 and 3 to L: Tomb of Giovanni Vigevano (d.1630). The bust is by Bernini but was probably made some time before the sitter's death, about 1620 (cf. Wittkower, *Bernini*, p. 175).

3rd pier of nave: Tomb of Fabio and Ippolito De Amicis (d. 1596 and 1651) designed by Pietro da Cortona (Titi, 1763, p. 161). The bust of Fabio is tentatively ascribed by Hibbard (*Bernini*, London, 1965, p. 66) to Camillo Mariani.

2 to L: *Cappella Naro:* This contains a number of tombs of members of the Naro family from the early 17th to the late 18th centuries. The most important is that of Cardinal Gregorio Naro. It has been attributed to various artists but the documents discovered by Lavin (*Bernini*, pp. 66, 182) prove that it was designed by Bernini and executed by the *scarpellino* Matteo Albertini in the years 1638-40, the bust of the cardinal being by G. A. Fancelli.

The bust of the cardinal's younger brother, Bernardino (d.1671), is by Andrea Bolgi (Nava Cellini, 'Aggiunte alle ritrattistica berniniana e dell'Algardi', *Paragone*, 65, 1955, p. 28 and 'Ritratti di Andrea Bolgi', ibid., 147, 1962, p. 24).

1st pier of nave: Monument to Raffaello Fabretti (d.1700) with bust by Rusconi (Enggass, *Sculpture*, p. 98).

Between 2 and 1 to L: Monument to Cesare Magalotti (d.1602).

The main building of the convent, to the left of the church, now contains offices connected with the Chamber of Deputies. Some of the rooms contain frescoes by Francesco Allegrini (F. Zeri, 'Gli affreschi dell Sant'Uffizio', *Antologia di belle arti*, 3, 1979, p. 266). In the cloister (late 16th century; accessible from the Sala dei Papi) is a small museum containing some chalices, vestments and lamps dating from the 17th and 18th centuries.

The wing originally containing the noviciate and running along the Via S. Ignazio was built by Paolo Maruscelli at the expense of Cardinal Antonio Barberini. It is now incorporated in the Biblioteca Casanatense which is housed in a vaulted hall, built in 1719, in the southern part of the range (Connors, *Oratory*, p. 109).

S. Maria dei Miracoli. See S. Maria di Montesanto
Piazza del Popolo

S. Maria di Monserrato
Via Monserrato, 15

Bibliography: Martinelli, p. 111; De' Rossi, *Prospectus*, pl. 66; S. Fernandez Alonso (Chiese di Roma, 103); Salerno, *Via Giulia*, p. 445; *Guide Rionali*, VII, 2, p. 32.

Built for the Spanish confraternity of S. Maria di Monserrato (founded in 1506) to the design of Antonio da Sangallo the Younger; begun in 1518 but not finished till the last years of the 16th century apparently still according to Sangallo's plans, except for the apse which was built by G. B. Contini in 1673-5. The façade was begun by Francesco da Volterra who built the lower storey in 1582-4, but the whole design is preserved in engravings in the early guide books (reproduced in the *Guide Rionali*). The upper storey was only built in 1926-8. The door with its freely designed group of the *Virgin and Child on the rock of Monserrato* must date from the early 18th century, but nothing seems to be recorded about it.

INTERIOR

The interior was completely redecorated in 1926-9, at the same time that the façade was completed.

1 to R: Annibale Carracci, *S. Diego di Alcala* (from the church of S. Giacomo degli Spagnuoli).
Room to left of Choir: Tomb of Cardinal Pedro de Montoya (d.1630) designed by Niccolò Torriani with bust by Bernini, one of his earliest works, executed in 1621 (originally in S. Giacomo; Wittkower, *Bernini*, p. 181). The room also contains other 17th-century tombs by unidentified artists.

S. Maria di Monterone
Via Monterone

Bibliography: Roisecco, 1750, I, p. 546; *Architettura minora*, I, pl. 99; Elling, pl. 22.

The mediaeval church was restored by Innocent XI (1676–89) when the present very simple façade was built. To the right of it is an interesting tall *barocchetto* façade covering premises attached to the church.
Choir: left wall: Tomb of Cardinal Stefano Durazzo, archbishop of Genoa (d.1667), with a skeleton holding a medallion with the portrait of the deceased.

S. Maria di Montesanto and S. Maria dei Miracoli
Piazza del Popolo

Bibliography: Letarouilly, pl. 233 (287); Golzio, *Archivi d'Italia*, VIII, 1941, p. 122; Magni, I, pl. 34; M. L. Casanova (Chiese di Roma, 58); G. Matthiae, *Piazza del Popolo*, Rome, 1946; Salerno, *Via del Corso*, p. 117; H. Hager, 'Zur Planungs- und Baugeschichte der Zwillingskirchen auf der Piazza del Popolo', *Römisches Jahrbuch*, XI, 1967/8, pp. 189ff.; Wittkower, *Italian Baroque*, pp. 9ff.; Braham and Hager, p. 64; Eimer, *S. Agnese*, I, figs 42–4; G. Ciucci, *La Piazza del Popolo*, Rome, 1974; Buchowiecki, II, p. 778 (with a summary of Hager's lengthy article).

Till the early 16th century the area within the Porta Flaminia, later called the Porta del Popolo, was an irregular space, marked by a monument, sometimes thought to be the tomb of Nero or Marcellus which stood near the point where the Via Lata (called the Corso since the time of Paul III) runs into the open area (this monument was destroyed in the first half of the 16th century). In 1518 on the orders of Leo X Raphael and Antonio de Sangallo the Younger laid out the Via Leonina (called the Ripetta since

37. *S. Maria di Montesanto (left) and S. Maria dei Miracoli (right). Engraving by Falda, showing the Piazza del Popolo as it was before the time of Valadier. In the foreground are the obelisk and fountain set up by Domenico Fontana in 1589 (the latter removed by Valadier). The engraving also shows the three streets leading off the piazza: the via Babuino (left), the Corso (middle) and the Ripetta (right). In the distance over the via Babuino is the SS. Trinità dei Monti and to its left the Villa Medici.*

the time of Clement XI) running down to the Porta Fluviale beside the Mausoleum of Augustus. In the Holy Year of 1525 the third street, called the Via Clemenza, was opened by Clement VII. It was completed by Paul III who renamed it the Via Paolina, and later it became the Via del Babuino. In 1573 Giacomo della Porta set up a fountain in the middle of the area (replaced in the early 19th century) and in 1589 on the orders of Sixtus V Domenico Fontana erected the obelisk brought by Augustus from Heliopolis to Rome and set up in the Circus Maximus. The area is marked as the Forum Populi in Bufalini's map of 1551 and as Piazza del Popolo in Tempesta's of 1593. A drawing published by Hager (fig. 136) shows the area c.1610.

In 1658 Alexander VII commissioned Carlo Rainaldi to build two churches flanking the opening of the Corso, both to be dedicated to the Virgin Mary. This scheme was designed to create a fine symmetrical effect for travellers arriving from the north along the Via Flaminia. The Piazza was given its present form between 1816 and 1820 by Giuseppe Valadier who added the two curved bays at the sides and the terraces leading up to the Pincio.

In 1658 there were two churches at the entrance to the Corso: to the left S. Maria in Montesanto served by Discalced Carmelites and on the right S. Orsola which was given by Alexander to the Tertiary Franciscan nuns, though the latter had its axis at right angles to the street and did not reach to the end of the block facing the Piazza. In order to make the execution of a symmetrical scheme possible more land had to be acquired and this caused delays.

Rainaldi, probably working in collaboration with the much younger Carlo Fontana, produced a design which included two almost identical circular domed churches with small apsed arms, of which the façades were to be articulated with pilasters. Later this design was modified and coupled columns replaced the pilasters. The foundation stones of the two churches were laid in 1661 and 1662 respectively. In the latter year an important change was made in the design by Rainaldi who planned to add the free-standing porticoes which are among the most unusual features of the church. In 1664 Fontana introduced a further modification by heightening the drums, thereby making the churches more impressive and improving the relationship of domes to porticoes. It was however Rainaldi who, probably in 1665, made the drastic decision to design the Montesanto on an oval plan, with the long axis leading to the altar, to make better use of the long but rather narrow site. Financial problems, coupled with the death of the pope in 1667 led to great slowness in the building of both churches, but in 1671 the newly created Cardinal Girolamo Gastaldi offered substantial help. At this stage Fontana replaced Rainaldi, but later he was made subordinate to Bernini. It was probably the latter who designed the adjustments needed to make the two domes – one oval and one circular – look as far as possible identical externally, by thickening the masonry of that of the Montesanto on the cross-axis and making both domes polygonal outside, that on the left having twelve sides, that on the right eight. As designed in 1662 the pediments over the porticoes were to stand against a high attic, but in the execution this was omitted. In 1674 Cardinal Gastaldi made a further gift of money so that work could start seriously on the Miracoli and in the following year Prince Camillo Pamphili made a further donation. In 1676 work started under the direction of Rainaldi although the inner dome of the Montesanto was finished under the direction of Bernini who was probably largely responsible for its decoration. The church was finished by Fontana to whom Rainaldi had handed over the effective control. Work on the Miracoli proceeded rapidly and in 1677 the interior of the dome was being stuccoed.

The statues on the attic of Montesanto are by Alessandro Rondone, Lazzaro Morelli, Sillano Sillani, Francesco (or Antonio) Fontana and others; those on the Miracoli are by Lorenzo Morelli, C. Fancelli, M. Maglia, 'Todesco' and Ercole Ferrata.

S. Maria di Montesanto

INTERIOR

(De' Rossi, *Architettura Civile*, III, pls 29, 30; Portoghesi, *Roma Barocca*, pl. 99.)

1 to R: *Cappella de'Rossi* (della Croce): By Alessandro Cassani (1677–9).
3 to R: *Cappella Vivaldi* (S. Anna): Architecture by Carlo Bizzacheri (1679, Mallory, *Bizzacheri*, pp. 31, 45; id., *Rococo*, p. 36); stuccoes by Pietro Paolo Naldini and painting by Niccolò Berrettoni (*Life of Joachim and Anna*, 1679–82; W).

CHOIR

(G. G. de'Rossi, *Altari*, pls 30, 31.)

High Altar: By Mattia de'Rossi (1677); angels by Filippo Carcani; right and left walls: stucco busts (after lost bronzes) of Popes Urban VIII (originally Innocent XI), Alexander VII, Clement IX and Clement X, after Girolamo Lucenti. The bust of Urban and possibly some of the others were originally after models by Bernini (Wittkower, *Bernini*, p. 186).
Sacristy: Biagio Puccini, *Deposition* (W).
3 to L: *Cappella Montioni* (St Francis): Architecture by Tommaso Mattei from a design by Carlo Fontana (1677–9); altarpiece: Maratta, *Virgin and Child with Sts James and Francis* (1686). Walls: Luigi Garzi, *St Francis*, and Daniel Seiter, *St James*. Vault: Giuseppe Chiari, *Assumption* (1686–7; W).
Sacristy of Cappella Montioni: Frescoes by Baciccio: vault: *Symbols of the Passion*; walls: *St James* (1691–2; Enggass, *Baciccio*, pp. 95, 145); altar: Giuseppe Chiari, *Deposition* (W).
2 to L: *Cappella Aquilanti* (S. Maria Maddalena dei Pazzi): Architecture by Carlo Rainaldi; stuccoes by L. Morelli; paintings: Lodovico Gimignani, *Scenes from the Life of S. Maria Maddalena dei Pazzi* (1680–6).

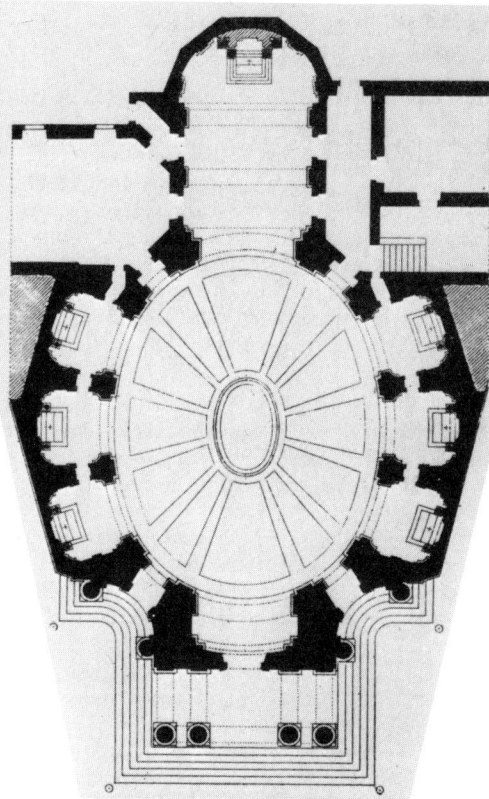

38. *S. Maria di Montesanto. Plan.*

39. *S. Maria dei Miracoli. Plan.*

S. Maria dei Miracoli

INTERIOR

(De' Rossi, *Architettura Civile*, III, pls. 31, 32.)

Over the choir arch: The arms of Cardinal Gastaldi by Antonio Raggi.
Choir: *High Altar:* Architecture by Carlo Fontana; sculpture by Raggi. At sides tombs of Benedetto Gastaldi (right) and Cardinal Girolamo Gastaldi (left; Donati, *Artisti ticinesi*, figs. 388–91, 394). Figure sculpture: on the right, Raggi, on the left, Girolamo Lucenti (De' Rossi, *Architettura Civile*, II, pl. 53).

S. Maria dei Monti (Madonna dei Monti)
Piazza della Madonna dei Monti

Bibliography: Totti, p. 475; Titi, 1674, p. 261; Martinelli, p. 111; Falda, *Nuovo teatro*, III, pl. 30; De' Rossi, *Prospectus*, pl. 72; Letarouilly, pl. 27 (241); Magni, I, pl. 6.

The church, which was attached to a convent which looked after non-Christian girls who intended to become converted to the Christian faith, was begun in 1580 to house a miraculous image of the Virgin. The architect was Giacomo della Porta and the church is one of the most complete examples of late 16th-century Roman architecture and decoration. The façade, of the familiar Roman type with a narrower upper storey joined to the wider lower one by scrolls, is treated entirely in pilasters and is an early and unusually harmonious example of the form.

INTERIOR
The church consists of a broad short nave, with three chapels on each side, a dominant domed crossing, shallow transepts and an apse, which contains a free-standing High Altar enclosing the holy image. The vault of the nave was frescoed by Cristofano Casolani (Poensgen, figs 23, 25) about 1620 with a composition of *The Ascension*, which is one of the first instances of an artist breaking with the traditional method of decorating a vault bay by bay by extending his main fresco to unite all three bays.

The dome has frescoes of scenes from the life of the Virgin by Casolani, Baldassare Croce and Paolo Guidotti (Gloton, pl. VIII). On the pendentives are the four Evangelists by Casolani. The half-dome of the apse is decorated with stuccoes enclosing frescoes by Casolani; below are frescoes by G. Gimignani (*Crucifixion, St Peter baptizing in Prison*, and *Christ appearing to the Virgin* (1676; W).
1 to R: (S. Carlo Borromeo): Altarpiece and frescoes of scenes from the life of *S. Carlo* by Giovanni Mannozzi (Giovanni da San Giovanni).
3 to R: side walls: Right, P. Nogari, *Christ carrying the Cross*, left, L. Mainardi, *Scourging of Christ*.
3 to L: (Nativity): Altarpiece: *Nativity*, by Girolamo Muziano; frescoes by Cesare Nebbia of scenes from the life of the Virgin.
1 to L: (Annunciation): Altarpiece: *Annunciation* by Durante Alberti (1588).

The noviciate attached to the church was built in 1635–9 at the expense of Cardinal Antonio Barberini to the designs of Gaspare de' Vecchi (Pollak, I, p. 207).

S. Maria in Monticelli
Via S. Maria in Monticelli

Bibliography: Vasi, *Magnificenze*, pl. 112; Braham and Hager, p. 180; Donati, *Artisti ticinesi*, fig. 327; *Guide Rionali*, VII, 1, p. 42.

The mediaeval church was restored for Clement XI in 1715 by Matteo Sassi and Giuseppe Sardi (an alternative project by Domenico Antonio de Sanctis is at Windsor, cf. Braham and Hager). In 1726 it was granted by Benedict XIII to the French Pères de la Doctrine Chrétienne. It was drastically restored in 1860.

INTERIOR
1 to R: Altar: Odoardo Vicinelli, *The Agony in the Garden*; right wall: attributed to Sacchi (but not mentioned by Harris): *Assumption*.
2 to R: Attributed to Antonio Carracci, *Flagellation*.
3 to R: G. B. Pacetti, *S. Ninfa*; left wall: E. Parrocel, *The Palermitan Martyrs*.
High Altar: 17th century; made of Sicilian marbles presented by Sicilian members of the Order. Tabernacle of 1727.
3 to L: Pacetti, *St John the Baptist preaching*.
1 to L: J. B. van Loo, *Flagellation:* left wall: G. Prinoti, *St Erasmus*.

S. Maria della Neve
Via del Colosseo

Bibliography: Roisecco, 1750, II, p. 490; Donati, *Artisti ticinesi*, fig. 258; *Architettura minora*, II, p. 15; Portoghesi, *Roma Barocca*, pl. 344; H. Hager, 'Il modello di L. Rusconi Sassi del concorso per la facciata di S. Giovanni in Laterano', *Commentari*, XXII, 1971, pp. 50 and p. 64, note 76; Mallory, *Rococo*, p. 63; *Guide Rionali*, I, 2, p. 104.

Originally called S. Andrea de Portogallo, this church, which belonged to the Confraternity of the Rigattieri (old clothes men), was rebuilt in 1706 to the design of Francesco Fontana. The façade is unusual in having a parapet over the pediment (cf. S. Pasquale Baylon).

The church contains three rather fine Baroque altarpieces, apparently without attribution.

S. Maria Nova. See S. Francesca Romana
Via dei Fori Imperiali

S. Maria dell'Orazione e della Morte
Via Giulia

Bibliography: Matthiae, *Fuga*, p. 13; Pane, *Fuga*, p. 42 and figs 26–32; H. Hager (Chiese di Roma, 79); Lavagnino, *Altari*, p. 197.

Built for the Confraternity of S. Maria dell'Orazione e della Morte to ensure Christian burial for those unable to afford to pay for it. Founded as an informal body in 1538 it was approved by Julius III in 1552. In 1572 they bought two houses in the via Giulia on the site of the present church. The first church was built in 1575–6 with a burial place beneath it. Designs for the existing church were presented by Ferdinando Fuga and approved in 1722, but the foundation stone was not laid till 1733 and it was only consecrated in 1738.

The site was small and awkward, because it was limited on the north (right) by the partywall of the Palazzo Falconieri which formed a slightly acute angle with the street. Remembering no doubt Borromini's solution at S. Carlo alle Quattro Fontane, Fuga chose an oval plan with the long axis running to the altar, round which he was just able to squeeze in four shallow chapels and a Sacristy (for the right-hand chapels the Confraternity had to acquire a narrow strip of land from the Falconieri).

The façade of the church is without curves in plan, but is richly articulated with pairs of full columns set between pilasters in a manner which recalls Cortona's SS. Luca e Martina and Martino Longhi the Younger's SS. Vincenzo e Anastasio, and the lines of the entablature and the tips of the pediment are broken consistently backward and forward at four points, corresponding to the junctions of the outer piers and central aedicules with the linking elements, an arrangement reminiscent of della Porta's Gesù façade. The interior is dominated by an order of Corinthian columns which support, over the entrances to the chapels, pediments broken like that over the choir opening in Bernini's S. Andrea al Quirinale. In the latter church the short axis leads to the High Altar, but the two plans have in common the fact that the cross axis of the oval ends in solids and not in the opening to a chapel. The design of the dome also owes much to S. Andrea.

This was Fuga's first church design for Rome and it shows that he was capable of making an impressive design from an intelligent choice of elements from the three 'Founding Fathers' of Roman Baroque architecture – Bernini, Borromini and Cortona. It remains one of the most accomplished buildings of the late 'classicizing' Baroque inaugurated in Rome by Carlo Fontana in the last decades of the 17th century.

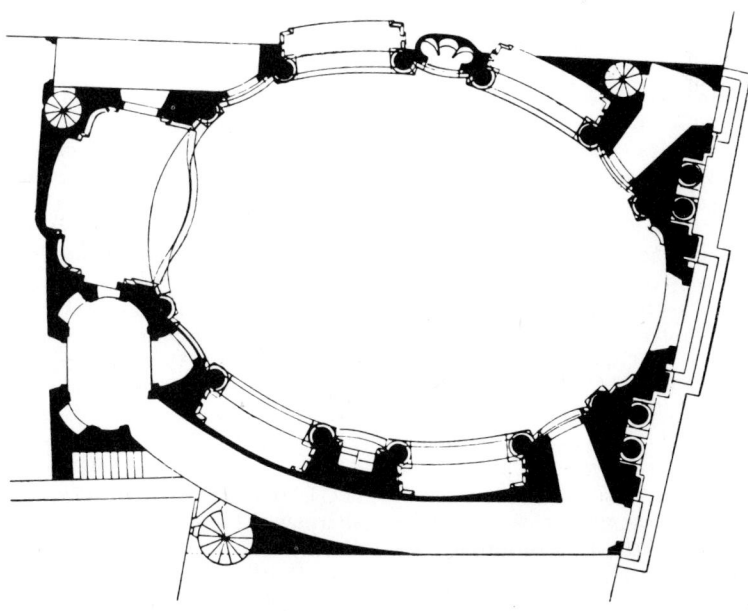

40. *S. Maria dell' Orazione e della Morte. Plan.*

INTERIOR

Between the two right-hand chapels: Lanfranco, *St Anthony Abbot and St Paul the Hermit*, fresco removed from the earlier church (W).

2 to R: (S. Michael): Architecture by Paolo Posi (1741); altarpiece: copy of Reni's painting in S. Maria della Concezione.

High Altar: Ferri, *Crucifixion*. An unusual work for the artist in that it shows a strong influence from Reni's painting of the same subject in S. Lorenzo in Lucina.

2 to L: P. L. Ghezzi, *S. Giuliana Falconieri receiving the Habit*, probably painted after her canonization in 1737.

Between 2 and 1 to L: Lanfranco, *S. Simon Stylites* (from the earlier church).

1 to L: Masucci, *Holy Family*.

S. Maria dell'Orto
Via Aniccia

Bibliography: Falda, *Nuovo teatro*, III, pl. 36; De' Rossi, *Prospectus*, pl. 65; Titi, 1763, p. 51; G. Giovannoni, *Saggi sull'architettura del Rinascimento*, second edition, Milan, 1935, p. 200; F. Fasolo, *S. Maria dell'Orto*, Rome, 1946; Ferrari, *Lo Stucco*, pls CXL ff.; L. Barroero (Chiese di Roma, 130); Portoghesi, *Roma Barocca*, pls 317–21; F. R. Milone, 'La facciata di S. Maria dell'Orto', *Quaderni*, XXII, 1976, p. 127; Colosanti, pls 165ff.

The church – with a hospital attached to it – was founded by the corporation of fruit growers in 1492. The documents give the essential dates connected with the building of the church, but only supply tantalizing indications of the artists involved. By 1525 the church was far enough advanced for some altars to be consecrated, and the whole structure was finished by 1563. The lower part of the façade was built in 1566–7, and the upper part was probably begun in 1568 and finished in 1579. Over the door to the Oratory is the date 1563, and the church was consecrated in 1585. In the early phases of the building no architect's name is given. Between 1556 and 1560 the name 'Guidetto' appears in the documents. This must be Guidetto Guidetti, the builder of S. Caterina dei Funari, but it is not clear whether he was the designer of the parts being built – probably the aisles and tribunes – or whether he was following the plan of the original architect. In 1560 'Rafaello' is mentioned as making a survey but he cannot be identified. In 1567 there is mention of 'Ms Jacinto' as taking measurements of the façade and this confirms the idea, originally put forward by Giovannoni on purely stylistic grounds, that the designer of the façade was Vignola, whose son and assistant was called Giacinto. The suggestion is confirmed by the fact – unknown to Giovannoni and Fasolo – that Martinelli names Vignola as the author (contemptuously rejecting the generally accepted attribution to Martino Longhi the Elder). The documents clearly state that drawings for the upper part of the façade were made by Francesco da Volterra, but it is so unlike him in style that it seems almost certain that he was following Vignola's design, at least in its main outlines. The whole façade is shown – though with the proportions falsified – in a woodcut by Girolamo Francini reprinted in Roman guide books from at least as early as 1589. The façade appears – more accurately – in Falda's engraving of the 1660s (it is often stated wrongly that the upper part of the façade dates from the 18th century).

There seems to be no solid evidence about the original designer of the church and it is at least possible that the design was altered during the course of execution. Some 17th-century writers of guide books attribute the design to Giulio Romano but this is unlikely, since he was only born in 1499. In general the indications of both date and authorship given in the guide books are confused and conflict with the facts known from the documents. It is, however, worth noticing that Palladio (*Descritione de la Chiese di Roma*) mentions the church in 1540, when it must have been still unfinished.

INTERIOR

The decoration of the interior which was begun by 1686 and finished in the first decade of the 18th century is described in detail in the 1763 Titi. The fresco of the *Assumption* on the vault of the nave is by Giacinto Calandrucci (W), and that of the *Immaculate Conception* over the crossing together with the pendentives is by Andrea and Giuseppe Orazi (1703) (Poensgen, fig. 36; Gloton, pl. XXXII). The stuccoes of the crossing and choir are by Simone Giorgini and Leonardo Reti. Those on the vault of the nave are more classical and probably later, possibly by Valvassori who is recorded as working in the church in the 1730s and later.

Right side aisle: Vaults frescoed by Andrea and Giuseppe Orazi.

1 to R: Taddeo Zuccaro, *Annunciation* (c.1561).

2 to R: Decorated probably by Luigi Barattone (1711) but altered later (1750) by Valvassori; altarpiece: Filippo Zucchetti, *Marriage of St Catherine*.

3 to R: Altarpiece: Giovanni Baglione, *Madonna and Saints*.

Right transept: Vault fresco: Calandrucci, *Re-*

surrection; walls: Niccolò Trometta, scenes from the Passion.
Over door to Oratory: A. Procaccini, *Pentecost* (W).

The Oratory has elaborate 18th-century decoration, including a carved ceiling and frescoes on the walls of a remarkable gaiety.

Apse: Frescoes next to altar: Zuccaro, *Nativity* and *Flight into Egypt, Visitation, Marriage of the Virgin* (the first by Taddeo, the two last perhaps by Federico); on side walls: Baglione, *Birth of the Virgin* and *Presentation*. The High Altar is datable to 1703 but was modified in 1755.
Left transept: Wall: Mario Garzi (son of Luigi), *St Francis*; walls and frescoes by N. Trometta, scenes from the life of the *St Francis*. Over door to Sacristy: A. Procaccini, *Joachim and Anna* (W).
Left aisle: Vault frescoes by D. Parodi.
3 to L: Frescoes by G. Baglione: over altar *Virgin with Sts Ambrogio, Carlo Borromeo and Bernardino* (c.1641).
2 to L: (St John the Baptist): Restored 1750 by Valvassori (Mallory, *Rococo*, p. 125); altarpiece: C. Giaquinto, *Baptism*; side walls: G. Ranucci, *Scenes from the Life of the Baptist* (1749).
1 to L: (St Sebastian): Baglione, *St Sebastian* (Nicolson, p. 20).

The hospital attached to the church, now dwelling-houses, is dated 1739. It is attributed by Fasolo to Luigi Barattone and by Barroero to Valvassori. It is probably by Valvassori who was architect to the confraternity at the time that it was built.

S. Maria della Pace
Piazza S. Maria della Pace

Bibliography: Falda, *Nuovo teatro*, I, pls 26–8; Titi, 1686, p. 384; id., 1763, p. 414; De'Rossi, *Architettura Civile*, III, pls 2–4; C. Fea, *Pro-Memoria per la venerabile chiesa di S. Maria della Pace*, Rome, 1809; Letarouilly, pls 63–6 (247–50); Magni, I, pl. 42; G. Urban, 'Die Kirchenbaukunst des Quattrocento in Rom', *Römisches Jahrbuch*, IX/X, 1961–2, p. 176; H. Ost, 'Studien zu Pietro da Cortonas Umbau von Santa Maria della Pace', ibid, XIII, 1971, p. 231; Portoghesi, *Roma Barocca*, pls 190–201; Güthlein, *Familienarchiv Spada*, pp. 190, 201.

A church called S. Maria della Virtù stood on this site in the 15th century and was granted to the Canons Regular of the Lateran. In 1482 Sixtus IV visited it to celebrate the peace which he had established after the troubles following on the assassination of Giuliano de'Medici in the Pazzi conspiracy, when he changed its name to S. Maria della Pace and ordered its reconstruction. The work was continued by his successor Innocent VIII. The author of the new church is said in the old guides to be Baccio Pontelli, but there does not seem to be any evidence to support this attribution. The cloister was built in 1500 by Bramante. In the first years of the 16th century Agostino Chigi, the banker and friend of Julius II, nephew of Sixtus IV, was granted a chapel in the church, and the link with the Chigi family led to the restoration of the church and the construction of the façade by Alexander VII in 1656–7, to the design of Pietro da Cortona.

The building of the façade was connected with the development of the area in front of the church (which continued till 1661) and this in turn involved consideration of the circulation of traffic. As a result of Alexander VII's interest the church became fashionable, particularly because it was possible to attend Mass there in the afternoon. On the other hand the approach to the church was difficult. The street leading to the front of the church from S. Tommaso in Parione was narrow and those on either side of the church were worse. That on the east passing below the apse of S. Maria dell'Anima would not admit a coach at all – and coaches had become *de rigueur* with the Roman nobility by the mid-17th century – and that on the left allowed passage for one, but not two, which led to quarrels over precedence. By pulling down some houses Cortona was able to make a symmetrical *piazza* of unusual shape (see plan) which made a fine approach to the church and allowed room for the turning of coaches, and he produced a design which brought the church and the adjoining streets into a single architectural unit.

The upper part of the façade of the church itself he articulated with an order of Corinthian pilasters and columns which are laid out on the same kind of curved plan that he had employed at SS. Luca e Martina, and below this he set a bold half-oval porch composed of massive Tuscan columns, which may have been inspired by a reconstruction of the Baths of Diocletian by Etienne Dupérac (Ost, p. 268, fig. 45), but the uneven spacing of the columns was inspired by Peruzzi's Palazzo Massimo alle Colonne. At the lower level he extended the line of the façade by a wall which contained an opening for the right-hand street which he balanced by a blind door. Above the wall he constructed two quarter-oval bays which mask the adjacent buildings, including the apse of S. Maria dell'Anima. The result was a brilliant solution to an extremely difficult problem. An unusual feature of the façade is that in the upper storey Cortona cut the very rough travertine that he chose as the material so

S. Maria della Pace

41. *S. Maria della Pace. Engraving by Falda, made as if the east half of the* piazza *had been removed. On the left is the Palazzo Gambirasi.*

42. *S. Maria della Pace. Plan. A drawing (Uffizi A. 3600) showing the upper level of the façade in lighter tone than the lower.*

that the 'graining' forms symmetrical patterns, thus giving an unusually rich texture to the surface. This technique was often used with marble but Cortona seems to be alone in applying it to the rough Roman stone.

The complicated and rather amusing story of the financial manipulations involved in the construction of the *piazza* is recounted by Hans Ost.

INTERIOR

The nave remains basically as it was in the 16th century except for the ribs on the vaulting and the window surrounds, which were added by Cortona. Over the arch leading to the octagon he added the arms of Sixtus IV and the figures of *Strength* and *Prudence* by C. Fancelli (a drawing for this exists at Windsor (Blunt and Cooke, *Roman Drawings at Windsor Castle*, London, 1960, No. 593); on the entrance wall are *Peace* and *Justice* also by Fancelli.

The alterations which he made to the octagonal section were more considerable. Here he extended to the ground the 15th-century pilasters which stood on high pedestals (recorded in drawings, Urban, fig. 181), preserving the original capitals. In the drum he transformed the earlier *bifori* into single windows, covered with typical Cortonesque hoods; and to the originally plain dome he applied a mixture of ribs and coffering which seems to be the earliest example of this combination of the two systems of dome articulation, and was later followed by Bernini

43. S. Maria della Pace. Interior looking from the octagon towards the entrance. Engraving by Falda.

at Ariccia and Castelgandolfo (cf. also SS. Luca e Martina). He preserved the 15th-century architect's rather unusual vertical division of the walls with spaces for large canvases over four of the chapels (over the other two are organs, one real, one sham to balance it). Only one of these paintings had been executed, Peruzzi's *Presentation of the Virgin*, painted about 1525, and Maratta, Raffaelle Vanni and G. M. Morandi were commissioned to fill the three remaining gaps.

1 to R: *Cappella Chigi:* Decorated by Raphael for Agostino Chigi with a fresco of the sibyls, left unfinished at his death, the upper part finished by Sebastiano del Piombo (M. Hirst, 'The Chigi Chapel in S. Maria della Pace', *Journal of the Warburg and Courtauld Institutes*, XXIV, 1961, p. 161). The chapel itself was altered under Alexander VII to the designs of Cortona, who inserted the bronze relief of the *Deposition* by Cosimo Fancelli and the kneeling statues of *St Catherine of Siena* (Fancelli) and *S. Bernardino* (Ercole Ferrata), both Sienese like the Chigi family, and reliefs of putti.

2 to R: *Cappella Cesi:* Built by Antonio da Sangallo the Younger (*c*.1525), the vault later decorated with stuccoes and frescoes designed by Sicciolante da Sermoneta. During the restoration under Alexander VII the chapel was slightly reduced in size in order to widen the Vicolo della Pace which runs along the right-hand side of the church, with the result that the vault decoration was truncated; two of the stucco *ignudi* vanished and one of the oval frescoes was replaced by a panel of architectural decoration clearly designed by Cortona. Altarpiece: C. Cesi, *Holy Family with St Anne*.

Octagon: In the lantern: F. Cozza, *God the Father* (W); on the walls: Maratta, *Visitation* (1656–7), Peruzzi, *Presentation of the Virgin*, Raffaelle Vanni, *Birth of the Virgin* and G. M. Morandi, *Death of the Virgin* (1657–71).

4 to R: (below the Peruzzi): *Cappella Olgiati:* Orazio Gentileschi, *Baptism* (before 1605; Nicoloson, p. 53); on walls, paintings by Bernardino Mei.

Choir: (Lavagnino, *Altari*, p. 53): Enlarged and rebuilt by Maderno for Gaspar Rivaldi (1611–14; Hibbard, *Maderno*, p. 189) as a setting for a miraculous image of the Virgin. On the pediment statues of *Peace* and *Justice* by Stefano Maderno; on walls: D. Cresti (Il Passignano), *Annunciation* and *Nativity*: on vault: Francesco Albani, *Assumption*.

3 to L (below the Morandi) (Presepe): Fresco (*Story of Adam*) and altarpiece (*Nativity*) by Girolamo Sicciolante da Sermoneta.

2 to L: Altarpiece: M. Venusti, *St Jerome*; above altar: F. Lauri, *Adam and Eve* (1668–70; W).

1 to L: Half-dome: B. Peruzzi, scenes from the Old and New Testaments.

S. Maria in Palmis. See Domine Quo Vadis
Via Appia Antica

S. Maria del Pianto
Via dei Calderari

Bibliography: Baglione, p. 365; Totti, p. 182; Martinelli, p. 121; Mola, p. 105; Titi, 1686, p. 83; id., 1763, p. 94; *Guide Rionali*, VII, I. p. 54.

The first part of the church, built to the designs of Niccolò Sebregondi, an architect from the Valtellina, was completed in 1612 when the miraculous image which gave its name to the Confraternity of S. Maria del Pianto was installed. The choir was added by G. B. Mola in 1642 and the nave was never built, but the executed parts of the church are impressive, simple and spacious. According to Martinelli the apse was decorated by Giacomo Mola.

1 to R: L. Baldi, *Virgin and Child with Saints* (before 1674; W).

Right transept: Tomb of Pompeo Palmieri, by G. B. Mola (1647).

S. Maria della Pietà. See SS. Bartolomeo e Alessandro dei Bergamaschi
Piazza Colonna

S. Maria del Popolo
Piazza del Popolo

Bibliography: Falda, *Nuovo teatro*, I, pl. 8; Letarouilly, pls 97, 98, 233–43 (287–98); Magni, I, pls 55, 56; E. Lavagnino (Chiese di Roma, 20); G. Urban, 'Die Kirchenbaukunst des Quattrocento in Rom', *Römisches Jahrbuch*, IX/X, 1961–2, p. 154; Wittkower, *Bernini*, p. 232; Fagiolo dell'Arco, *Bernini*, p. 160; E. Bentivoglio and S. Valtieri, *Santa Maria del Popolo*, Rome, 1976.

There is said to have been a church on this site since 1099, built over an ancient tomb, thought to be that of Nero, but the first certain documents refer to the consecration by Gregory IX in 1226 of a new church erected at the expense of the Roman people – hence its present name. It was served by a body of Augustinian Observants. It was rebuilt between 1472 and 1480 by an unknown architect for Sixtus IV (della

Rovere), but the apse is due to Bramante, working on the orders of Sixtus' nephew, Julius II (or possibly his predecessor Alexander VI). In about 1513 Raphael began the construction of the Cappella Chigi, commissioned by Agostino Chigi, the celebrated banker to Julius (who allowed him to quarter the della Rovere arms with his own), and between 1655 and 1657 another Chigi, Pope Alexander VII, commissioned Bernini to restore and embellish the church. This restoration included the alterations to the nave arcade and the interior of the entrance wall, and the addition of the shield and figures over the arch between the nave and the crossing (all in stucco), the organ and marble altars in the transepts.

Before Bernini's intervention the nave arcade consisted of the existing arches separated by columns with fragments of entablatures over them. Bernini linked the columns by a continuous entablature which, however, he had to bend because the arches – surprisingly – came above the level of the top of the entablature. The result was the present somewhat weak line which the architect has sought to work into the whole scheme by the addition of stucco figures of saints, which nearly reach up to the windows above, which he enlarged.

The sculptors involved in the execution of the scheme were Ercole Ferrata, G. F. Rossi, P. Naldini, G. A. Mari, A. Raggi, L. Morelli and G. Peroni (cf. Ferrari, *Lo Stucco*, pls XCVII ff.).

Bernini also added the curved half-pediments at the sides of the façade and the candelabra and Chigi *monti* on the central pediment.

For a view of the church before the façade was altered see J. Shearman, 'The Chigi Chapel in S. Maria del Popolo', *Journal of the Warburg and Courtauld Institutes*, XXIV, 1961, pl. 21a. For a project for a more complete transformation of the façade see S. Jacob, 'Zu zwei römischen Architekturzeichnungen der Berliner Kunstbibliothek', *Römisches Jahrbuch*, XIII, 1976, p. 291.

INTERIOR
1 to R: *Della Rovere:* Frescoes by Pinturicchio.
2 to R: *Cappella Cybò* (De'Rossi, *Altari*, pls 4, 5; Magni, I, pl. 56; Lavagnino, *Altari*, p. 157; H. Hager, 'La Cappella del Cardinale Alderamo Cybò in S. Maria del Popolo', *Commentari*, XXV, 1974, p. 47); Built in 1681–6 by Carlo Fontana for Cardinal Alderamo Cybò whose aim was to exceed in grandeur Raphael's Chigi chapel on the opposite side of the church. The chapel is one of the most ambitious pieces of marble decoration in Baroque Rome. As in the Cappella Ginetti in S. Andrea della Valle, Fontana has carried the marble beyond the entablature, in this case covering the barrel vault of the vestibule and the arms of the chapel. In spite of this obvious attempt at grandeur, however, the actual lines of the architecture are very simple. Altarpiece: C. Maratta, *The Virgin Immaculate with Sts Gregory, John Crysostom, John Evangelist and Augustine* (1686; W). Frescoes on side walls of first bay: Daniel Seiter, *St Lawrence* and *St Catherine*; dome fresco: Luigi Garzi, *Heavenly Glory* (W). Tombs: right, Alderamo Cybò (d. 1700); left, Lorenzo Cybò, both with busts by Francesco Cavallini (Donati, *Artisti ticinesi*, figs 433, 435).
4th pier L: Tomb of G. B. Pallavicini (d.1596).
4th pier R: Tomb of Cardinal Girolamo Albani (d.1591) by Valsoldo.
Right transept: Organ case designed by Bernini incorporating the della Rovere oak which the Chigi family were allowed to quarter. The organ itself was made in 1499–1500 by Stefano Pavoni, but was rebuilt for Alexander VII by Giuseppe Testa, who made a new organ to balance it in the left transept (G. and L. Bauer, 'Bernini's Organ-case for S. Maria del Popolo', *Art Bulletin*, LXII, 1980, p. 115). The marble altar is also from the design of Bernini. The altarpiece, *The Visitation*, is by G. M. Morandi (1659; W). The angels on this altar and the corresponding altar in the left transept are by E. Ferrata, G. A. Mari, Raggi and Arrigo Giardé, but their shares in the work are not clear.
2nd chapel to right of choir: (S. Rita da Cascia): On floor, tombstone of Cardinal Giovanni Battista Cicada with the arms in bronze in relief. The original state of the tomb is shown in a drawing at Windsor (cf. Blunt, *Supplements to the Catalogues of Italian and French Drawings*, London, 1971, No. 694).
Dome over crossing: Raffaelle Vanni, *The Virgin received into Glory* (1656–8; W).
Choir: The first bay of the choir is decorated with gold and white stucco reliefs, showing scenes from the early history of the church, which were commissioned through a bequest left by the Genoese Cardinal Antonio Sacchi (d.1627). The High Altar was paid for out of the same bequest. The choir was extended by Bramante and converted into a family mortuary chapel for the della Rovere family on the orders of Julius II. Vault frescoes by Pinturicchio; stained glass by Guillaume de Marcillat; tombs of Cardinals Ascanio Sforza (d.1505) and Girolamo Basso della Rovere (d.1527) by Andrea Sansovino. Fine 17th-century choir stalls.
1st chapel to left of High Altar: *Cappella Cerasi:* Founded and decorated in 1601. The

frescoes on the vault of the main body of the chapel are by G. B. Ricci da Novara, those on that of the choir by Innocenzo Tacconi after drawings by Annibale Carracci, who painted the altarpiece of the *Assumption*. On the side walls of the choir, Caravaggio, *Martyrdom of St Peter* and *Conversion of St Paul*. For an analysis of the relation of the paintings to architecture of the chapel, see L. Steinberg, 'Observations in the Cerasi chapel', *Art Bulletin*, XLI, 1959, p. 182.

2nd chapel to left of High Altar: G. Mazzoni, paintings and statue of *St Catherine*.

Left transept: Organ and altar from designs of Bernini; angels by Raggi (right) and Mari (left); altarpiece: Bernardino Mei, *Holy Family* (1659; W).

4 to L: *Cappella Soderini* (Crocifisso): Frescoes attributed to Pieter van Lint.

3 to L: *Cappella Millini:* Frescoes by Giovanni da San Giovanni (ruined); altarpiece: A. Masucci, *S. Nicola da Tolentino* (1745–50; W). Right wall: bust of Cardinal Savio Millini (d.1701) erected by himself in 1699 and executed by Pierre Etienne Monnot (cf. Enggass, *Sculpture*, p. 84). Left wall: monument to Cardinal Giovanni Garsia Millini, designed in 1637 by Alessandro Algardi in a markedly classical style, with half-length figure of the cardinal by the same artist. This form of tomb sculpture, consisting of a half-length figure with one hand holding a book and the other clutching his breast, was to become very popular. It was frequently used by Finelli and was adapted by Bernini in his Fonseca monument in S. Lorenzo in Lucina, and was widely used throughout the 18th century. To the left is the bust of Urbano Millini also by Algardi (cf. Heimbürger Ravalli, *Algardi*, p. 91). To the right is that of Mario Millini, often ascribed to Algardi, but without good reason. On floor, inlaid marble tomb of Cardinal Mario Millini (d.1760).

2nd pier of nave: Monument to Francesco Natale Rondinini (d.1657) with bust by Domenico Guidi.

2 to L: *Cappella Chigi* (J. Shearman, 'The Chigi Chapel in S. Maria del Popolo', *Journal of the Warburg and Courtauld Institutes*, XXIV, 1961, pp. 129ff.): Built and decorated by Raphael and his assistants for Agostino Chigi; begun about 1513. The altarpiece of *The Birth of the Virgin* is by Sebastiano del Piombo (finished by Salviati). The mosaics in the dome (*God the Father and the Planets*) are after the designs of Raphael, as are the statues in the niches of *Jonah* and *Elijah* which were executed by Lorenzetto who is also responsible for the altar frontal. The lunettes were frescoed by Francesco Salviati, and those in the side walls are by Raffaello Vanni: *David* and *Samuel with Eli*. In 1652 Bernini was commissioned by Cardinal Fabio Chigi (later Alexander VII) to complete the decoration of the chapel. In that year he added the oval medallions to the two obelisk-tombs and between 1655 and 1661 he made the two statues of *Daniel* and *Habakkuk* (cf. Wittkower, *Bernini*, p. 232).

Apart from the fact that it is one of the masterpieces of Renaissance art the Chigi chapel is important as foreshadowing many features of the Baroque, in particular the illusionism of the dome mosaics, the marble decoration of the walls, and the obelisks for the tombs. If, as has been plausibly suggested (Shearman), the painting over the altar was originally intended to be an *Assumption*, then Raphael would also have forestalled Bernini in the idea of continuing the action across the space of a church or chapel, since the Virgin would have been moving upwards towards the figure of God the Father in the cupola, as she does in Cortona's frescoes in S. Maria in Vallicella and as S. Andrea does in Bernini's S. Andrea al Quirinale.

Between 2 and 1 to L: Tomb of Maria Flaminio Chigi (d.1771) designed by Paolo Posi and executed by A. Penna, a flamboyant example of late-Baroque exuberance (Magni, I, pl. 56; Ferrari, *La Tomba*, pl. CLXXVI).

1st pier of nave: *Tomb of Francesco Mantica* (d.1614).

Entrance wall: Tomb of G. B. Ghisleni (d.1672) designed by himself with a highly naturalistic skeleton in yellow marble behind a bronze grille. Tomb of Maria Eleonora Buoncampagni Ludovisi (d.1745).

S. Maria Porta Paradisi. See S. Giacomo degli Incurabili
Via Ripetta

S. Maria in Portico (S. Galla) (destroyed)

Bibliography: Vasi, *Magnificenze*, pl. 177; Titi, 1763, p. 61; Armellini, II, p. 773; L. Pasquali, *S. Maria in Portico*, Rome, 1904.

The church stood in the via Montanara but was pulled down in the 1930s. It was remodelled in the 17th century by Mattia de'Rossi. The façade is recorded in an engraving by Vasi, reproduced by Armellini.

S. Maria del Priorato
Piazza dei Cavalieri di Malta

Bibliography: Magni, I, pls 136, 137; W. Körte, 'Giovanni Battista Piranesi als praktischer Architekt', *Zeitschrift für Kunstgeschichte*, II, 1933, p. 16; Wittkower, *Italian Baroque*, p. 247; M. Salmi, 'S. Maria del Priorato. Il consolidamento delle fondazioni', *Palladio*, XX, 1970, p. 157; Lavagnino, *Altari*, p. 215; Portoghesi, *Roma Barocca*, pls 469–75; J. Wilton-Ely, *The Mind and Art of Giovanni Battista Piranesi*, London, 1978, pp. 93ff.; Elling, pl. 60.

The Priory of the Knights of Malta was established on the site in 1568. The church was completely remodelled by Piranesi for Cardinal Giambattista Rezzonico, Grand Master of the Order and nephew of Clement XIII, between 1764 and 1766, as is shown by the account book preserved in the Avery Library of Columbia University and drawings in the Pierpont Morgan Library. The figures on the vault and the High Altar were made by Tommaso Righi. The entrance gate and the screen round the piazza in front of it are also by Piranesi who incorporated in their decoration many allusions to the military and naval prowess of the Knights of Malta. The chapel and the piazza are the only buildings actually designed and erected by Piranesi; they embody – particularly in their decoration – many of the most inventive features to be found in his drawings and etchings.

In the Casa del Vescovo: Sacchi, *St John Chrysostom offering a Dove to the Madonna and Child* (Sutherland Harris, *Sacchi*, p. 82).

S. Maria in Publicolis
Piazza Costaguti

Bibliography: Spagnesi, *G. A. De Rossi*, p. 27; *Guide Rionali*, VIII, 1, p. 24.

Built 1640–3 almost certainly by G. A. de'Rossi for Cardinal Marcello Santacroce, whose family were patrons of the church. This is the earliest work of an architect who represents the sober, non-Baroque trend in Roman architecture of the mid-17th century. The church is simple and traditional in plan, a rectangular nave with three shallow chapels on either side, but in the façade the architect has been bolder, if not always completely successful. The use of two storeys of equal width is common at this date, but the relation of the attic storey to the lower parts of the façade and the treatment of the pediments are clumsy. The fact that de'Rossi uses an Ionic order for the lower storey and a Tuscan for the upper is highly unorthodox, though the same arrangement is to be found on the façades of S. Giuseppe a Capo le Case and S. Maria di Grottapinta.

INTERIOR
To right of door: Tomb of Prince Scipione Publicola-Santacroce (d.1747) by G. B. Maini, from the design of G. P. Pannini (before 1750; Mallory, *Notizie*, p. 111).
1 to R: Raffaelle Vanni, *St Helena* (W).
Choir: High Altar: Vanni, *Birth of the Virgin* (W). On side walls monuments to the Publicola-Santacroce family with oval painted portraits by Alessandro Grimaldi (not Giovanni Francesco, as is often stated).
To left of door: Tomb of Antonio and Girolama Publicola (d.1707, 1727) by Lorenzo Ottoni (cf. Enggass, 'Ottoni', *Storia dell'Arte*, 15/16, 1972, p. 315); altarpiece: G. F. Grimaldi, *St Francis in Prayer* (1655; W).

S. Maria della Purificazione (destroyed)

Bibliography: Vasi, *Magnificenze*, pl. 155; Armellini, I, p. 267.

This church stood behind S. Pietro in Vincoli. It appears to have been founded in 1643 and was under the protection of Cardinal Francesco Barberini. It had a façade of five bays, the outer two not being linked to the inner ones by the usual scrolls.

S. Maria della Quercia
Piazza della Quercia

Bibliography: *Architettura minora*, I, pl. 31; A. Martini (Chiese di Roma, 67); Rotili, *Raguzzini*, p. 44; Portoghesi, *Roma Barocca*, p. 358; Elling, pl. 40.

The Corporazione dei Macellai (butchers) took possession of the mediaeval church of S. Nicola de Curte in 1523 but were not officially confirmed in its possession till 1532. Between that date and 1555 its dedication was changed to S. Maria della Quercia, in honour of the holy image of this name venerated in a church just outside Viterbo.

The foundation stone of the existing church was laid by Benedict XIII in 1727; it was opened in 1731 and consecrated in 1738. It was restored – rather drastically – in 1864.

All the early sources agree in ascribing the church to Filippo Raguzzini. The plan – a square with three semi-circular bays and a rectangular choir – is curiously archaic for the period, but Raguzzini used a similar but even simpler design for the chapel of the hospital of

S. Gallicano, a square with shallow rectangular side bays. The façade of S. Maria della Quercia is based – in plan – on an elaborate play of convex curves, as opposed to the concave curves of S. Gallicano. In elevation however the relation of the attic to the lower storey is somewhat clumsy. In the interior the only features to have survived from the original church are the elaborate 18th-century organ gallery, and the two side altarpieces; on the right Pietro Barbieri's *Baptism* and on the left the *Crucifixion* ascribed to F. Evangelisti but probably by his assistant M. Benefial.

S. Maria del Rosario sul Monte Mario
Monte Mario

Bibliography: Vasi, *Magnificenze*, VII, p. XXXIX; *Architettura minora*, pl. 76; A. Zucchi, *Roma domenica*, Florence, 1940, II, p. 40.

Built in 1628–9, but rebuilt to the design of Camillo Arcucci from 1659 onwards. In 1709 it was given to the Dominicans of S. Marco, Florence.

S. Maria della Scala
Via della Scala

Bibliography: Martinelli, p. 134; Mola, p. 61; Falda, *Nuovo teatro*, III, pl. 35; Titi, 1763, p. 41; De' Rossi, *Prospectus*, pl. 68; Wasserman, *Mascarino*, p. 56.

The church was begun in 1593 for the Casa Pia, founded by Pius IV in 1563 to care for reformed prostitutes. The documents prove that the architect was Francesco de Volterra, but Martinelli states that he only built the church up to the entablature and that it was finished by Mascarino. Mola says that it was built by Matteo da Città di Castello, who may well have been the mason in charge. The dome was built in 1607–10. Martinelli adds that the convent was mainly built by Bartolomeo Breccioli.

In 1597 the establishment passed to the Discalced Carmelites who finished the church (1610) and began the façade in 1624, apparently still following the designs of Francesco da Volterra (the upper storey, which is in stucco, is later). The relief over the door is by Silvio Valloni (Titi, 1763, p. 41).

INTERIOR

1 to R: Honthorst, *Beheading of St John the Baptist* (Nicolson, p. 58).

3 to R: Odazzi, *Scenes from the Life of St Joseph* (W).

Right transept: Redecorated in 1734 to the designs of G. P. Pannini who also designed the altar furniture; altarpiece by F. Mancini, *St Theresa* (1745; Mallory, *Notizie*, p. 109); stucco reliefs illustrating *Scenes from the Life of St Theresa:* oval ones below by M. A. Slodtz (right) and F. della Valle (left); those beside the window are by G. Lironi (cf. Enggass, *Sculpture*, p. 173).

High Altar: Tabernacle designed by Carlo Rainaldi and carried out in 1647 (F. Fasolo, 'L'Altar maggiore di S. Maria della Scala', *Fede e Arte*, VII, 1960, p. 302; Eimer, *S. Agnese*, I, fig. 26 and p. 147).

On the screen separating the Sanctuary from the choir: S. Giorgini, *St Theresa* and *St Joseph* (Enggass, *Sculpture*, p. 112).

Left transept: Tombs of Prospero Santacroce by Algardi (1641; Heimbürger Ravalli, *Algardi*, p. 111) and his mother, Livia Santacroce (d.1662), by Domenico Guidi (Weil, p. 148).

3 to L: *Cappella del Crocifisso:* recorded by Titi (1763) as decorated 'di nuovo' for Cesare Baldi by Filippo Zucchetti; marble groups of *St John of the Cross* by Pietro Papaleo.

2 to L: Attributed to Girolamo Rainaldi (1603–4) by Fasolo (*Rainaldi*, p. 48). Altarpiece: C. Saraceni, *Death of the Virgin*, painted before 1619 to replace Caravaggio's painting of the same subject now in the Louvre, which was painted for this church but rejected by the authorities on account of its naturalistic presentation of the subject (Nicolson, p. 87).

S. Maria dei Sette Dolori
Via Garibaldi

Bibliography: M. Bosi (Chiese di Roma, 117); Perugini, *Architettura di Borromini nella Chiesa di S. Maria dei Sette Dolori*, Rome, 1959–60 (with measured drawings); Portoghesi, *Borromini*, pls 70–4; Blunt, *Borromini*, p. 129; *Guide Rionali*, XIII, p. 110.

The Convent of Augustinian Oblates was founded in 1641 by Camilla Virginia Savelli, the wife of Pier Francesco Farnese, duke of Latera, and the church was begun in the same year. Borromini agreed to make the design but said that he was too busy – presumably with S. Ivo and the Oratory – to work out the details, which he handed over to Antonio del Grande. The structure was finished by 1646 and the decoration of the interior was begun in 1648, but was not finished till 1667 (by G. B. Contini, who designed the High Altar of S. Ivo).

The exterior, which is unfinished, is composed of an astonishingly rich and varied series of concave and convex forms executed in rough brick. This gives a rugged quality to the whole building, but it is so simple that we can be fairly certain that here, as at S. Andrea delle Fratte, Borromini would have plastered it. When he intended the brick to be left visible, as at the Oratory, he chose thin bricks and laid them with less mortar to make a smooth surface. The door – which is certainly not according to Boromini's design – leads into a small vestibule, square, but with each side curved, convex inwards. Beyond this is a cloister probably designed by Contini.

The church belongs to the small group of those designed by Borromini in the form of a rectangle with rounded corners, the others being the Oratory of S. Filippo Neri and the Re Magi in the Collegio di Propaganda Fide, but it differs from these in that it is articulated with columns instead of pilasters and has a shallow half-oval chapel in the middle of each side. The interior was disastrously repainted in 1845.

INTERIOR

High Altar: After Pordenone, *Deposition*.
Left-hand altar: Maratta, *St Augustine and the Child* (*c*.1655; W).

S. Maria del Suffragio
Via Giulia, 59

Bibliography: Titi, 1686, p. 391; Salerno, *Via Giulia*, p. 332; Fasolo, *Rainaldi*, p. 429; *Guide Rionali*, V, 4, p. 56.

The Confraternity of the Suffragio was founded in 1592. The church was built by Carlo Rainaldi between 1662 and 1669 (the latter date is inscribed on the frieze of the lower order of the façade). Rainaldi at first proposed an oval plan, but this was replaced by the existing design consisting of a rectangular nave with side-chapels.

INTERIOR

Decorated with painted marbling, presumably dating from the restoration of 1870.
1 to R: Walls and vault painted by G. B. Natali (Titi, 1686, p. 391).
2 to R: Right wall: Calandrucci, *Joseph's Dream*; left wall: Troppa, *Sacrifice of Abraham*; both before 1686 (W).
3 to R: Architecture by G. B. Contini; stucco decoration and tombs of members of the Marcacciona family (d.1673 and 1703) by Paolo Naldini (Titi, 1763, p. 420); paintings on side walls: G. Chiari, *Birth of the Virgin* and *Adoration of the Kings* (W); vault fresco attributed to N. Berrettoni.

High Altar: Designed by Rainaldi for a painting by Giacinto Brandi (Cartari-Febei) but this was replaced by one by G. Ghezzi, *Madonna del Suffragio* (1672; W); over it fresco of the *Assumption* by Beinaschi.
1 to L: Seiter, *Madonna with Sts Catherine and Hyacinth* (*c*.1685; W).
Oratory: Beinaschi, *Lazarus* and *Daniel* (originally on the walls of the choir).

S. Maria in Traspontina
Via della Conciliazione

Bibliography: Baglione, p. 91; Martinelli, p. 135; Falda, *Nuovo teatro*, III, pl. 34; Titi, 1686, p. 401; De'Rossi, *Prospectus*, pl. 63; Magni, I, pls 7, 8; Pollak, I, p. 184; C. Catena, *S. Maria in Traspontina*, Rome, 1954; Wasserman, *Mascarino*, p. 59.

The church was founded by Pius IV in 1563 but building was not begun till 1566 to the design of Salustio Peruzzi which was preferred to one by Vignola known from a drawing (E. Kieven, 'Eine Vignola Zeichnung für S. Maria in Traspontina', *Römisches Jahrbuch*, XIX, 1981, p. 245). In 1567 Peruzzi left for Austria and was replaced by Battista Ghioldo. In 1581 Ottaviano Mascarino took charge till 1587, when the church, still unfinished, was consecrated. The exact shares of the three architects involved cannot be determined in the present state of our knowledge, particularly in connection with the façade. Baglione and Martinelli, probably following him, however, state that it was begun by Peruzzi and that the upper half is by Mascarino, and this statement seems convincing. The choir, transepts, dome and Sacristy were finished in 1637 (Pollak, I, p. 184), the Sacristy being by F. Peparelli.

INTERIOR

The interior was decorated with *scagliola* marble and the vault decorated in 1845.
1 to R: Cavaliere d'Arpino, *St Barbara* (1597).
2 to R: (S. Canuto): Daniel Seiter, *St Canute* (before 1686).
This chapel and that of S. Elia (2 to L) show the influence of the Neapolitan style of marbling introduced about 1650 by Cosimo Fanzago (cf. R. Bösel, 'Cosimo Fanzago a Roma', *Prospettiva*, 15, 1978, p. 37).
5 to R: (St Albert): Antonio Circignani, scenes from the life of *St Albert*.
Right transept: Altar: Cerrini, *Christ and the Virgin appearing to S. Maria Maddalena dei Pazzi* (before 1674; W).
High Altar (De' Rossi, *Altari*, p. 27): Designed by C. Fontana in 1674 (Coudenhove-Erthal, p. 42); figures added 1695: *Elijah* by G. A.

Lavaggi, *Elisha* by V. Felici, *S. Angelo*, by A. Rondone, *St Albert* by M. Maglia.
Left transept: Vault: Puccini, *Intervention of S. Andrea Corsini at the Battle of Anghiari* (W; Gloton, pl. XXXIX); altarpiece: G. P. Melchiori, *S. Andrea Corsini.*
5 to L: (S. Angelo): G. B. Ricci, altarpiece and frescoes, scenes from the life of *S. Angelo.*
4 to L: A. Gherardi, *St Theresa* (W; *c.*1700).
2 to L: G. Calandrucci, *Scenes from the Life of Elijah* (1690; W; see above, **2 to R**).
Oratory: L. Garzi, *Christ preaching* (after 1715).

S. Maria in Trastevere
Piazza S. Maria in Trastevere

Bibliography: Martinelli, p. 136; C. Cecchelli (Chiese di Roma, 31, 32).

The Early Christian church was rebuilt by Innocent II (1130–43). It was restored probably by Martino Longhi the Elder and again by Clement XI who added the portico, and finally by Pius IX. Certain parts of the mediaeval church survive: the 12th-century campanile, the main colonnade of the nave, composed of reused ancient columns, the Cosmatesque pavement, the mosaics, and the ciborium.

The portico was designed by Carlo Fontana and built in 1701–2 (Braham and Hager, p. 77). The statues are by Théodon (*St Calixtus*), Michele Maglia (*St Cornelius*), Ottoni (*St Julian*) and Vincenzo Felici (*St Calapodius*).

INTERIOR
The carved wooden ceiling was designed by Domenichino (Mola, p. 58 and Bellori, p. 350) who also painted the *Assumption* in the middle of it (Voss, p. 513; Borea, *Domenichino*, p. 172; Colosanti, p. 157). The ceiling itself is composed of an unusually complicated series of geometrical shapes based ultimately on an engraving at the end of Serlio's fourth book.
Right aisle (near the side door): Tomb of Cardinal Pietro Marcellino Corradini (d.1743) by Filippo della Valle (H. Honour, 'Filippo della Valle', *Connoisseur*, CXLIV, 1959, p.172).
Chapel to right of High Altar: *Cappella della Strada Cupa:* Begun 1625 (Pollak, I, p. 184); architecture and stuccoes designed by Domenichino, who was only able to execute one painting, a putto, because of his departure for Naples in 1630 (R. Spear, 'The Cappella della Strada Cupa', *Burlington Magazine*, CXI, 1969, p. 12). The stucco figure below the painted putto is by Algardi (Heimbürger Ravalli, *Algardi*, p. 65).

On either side of the apse (which contains mosaics mainly dating from 1140, with the *Life of the Virgin* added by Cavallini) stand two tombs of members of the Altemps family, Cardinal Osio and Roberto, duca di Gallesi (d.1586), the latter attributed to Valsoldo.
Chapel to left of High Altar: *Cappella Altemps* (cf. B. Torresi, 'La Cappella Altemps in S. Maria in Trastevere', *Quaderni*, XXII, 1976, p. 95): Commissioned by Cardinal Marcus Psiticus Altemps (1533–95), whose family came from the Vorarlberg and who was a nephew of Pius IV and cousin of Carlo Borromeo. He played an important part in the religious reforms after the Council of Trent. The chapel was built between 1584 and 1589 by Martino Longhi the Elder to house a much venerated image of the Virgin. The walls and ceiling are decorated with light and delicate stuccoes, and with frescoes by Pasquale Cati. Those on the ceiling show scenes from the life of the Virgin, to whom the chapel is dedicated, but those on the walls are much more unusual in theme: one shows a sitting of the Council of Trent – probably the last – and the other Pius IV confirming the decrees of the Council. In the foreground of the former is a figure representing the papacy, surrounded by allegorical figures of Virtues. Over the altar and the door are frescoed portraits of Pius IV and the Cardinal.
5 to L: *Cappella Avila:* By Antonio Gherardi about 1680 (Titi, 1686, p. 37; De' Rossi, *Altari*, pls 34, 35; Ferrari, *La Tomba*, pl. CLVII; Portoghesi, *Roma Barocca*, pls 264, 267, 268) who also painted the altarpiece of *St Jerome* (W). This and the chapel of S. Cecilia in S. Carlo ai Catinari are the two boldest works by this artist who built little but is perhaps the most original architect of his generation. In this chapel he combines architectural forms based on Borromini, freely interpreted, in the false perspective over the altar, with a Berninesque use of concealed light and combination of sculpture and architecture in the cupola.
3 to L: A. Procaccini, *Sts Marinus and Calixtus* (W).
1 to L: (Baptistery): Built by Onorio Longhi (Martinelli, p. 136) and altered by Filippo Raguzzini (cf. Rotili, *Raguzzini*, p. 39).
Room behind Sacristy: G. Brandi, *Martyrdom of St Frederick.*

Behind the church (to the right) is the 18th-century *Canonica* (Elling, pl. 36; *Architettura minora*, p. 67) and in the adjacent vicolo del Piede the former Oratory of the Holy Sacrament, dated 1670 on the frieze (now a *trattoria*).

S. Maria in Trivio
Fontana di Trevi

Bibliography: Magni, I, p. 24; Benedetti, *Del Duca*, p. 155, pls 123–47.

About 1560 the church, which was formerly known as S. Giuseppe del Bufalo or S. Giuseppe Grande, was given to the Crociferi who between 1573 and 1575 rebuilt it to the designs of Giacomo del Duca, who was Michelangelo's assistant in some of his last works. When the Order of the Crociferi was suppressed by Alexander VII in 1656 the church buildings were handed over to the Padri Ministri degli Infermi (see S. Maria Maddalena), who installed their Noviciate in the monastic buildings.

Borromini, who seems to have been an admirer of del Duca, copied the façade in a drawing now in the Albertina (Rome, 141) and was, I believe, inspired by the pediment over the door to invent his own favourite form of pediment used for instance over the façade of the Oratory of S. Filippo Neri (cf. Blunt, *Borromini*, p. 39).

INTERIOR
The church consists of a single nave with shallow recesses for chapels, separated by Ionic pilasters which would no doubt originally have been white but now have coarse painted marbling. The whole interior was redecorated about 1670 to the designs of Antonio Gherardi, who painted the ceiling, made a new High Altar, and designed the stucco group of angels carrying the Cross over the chancel arch (T. Pickrel, 'Two Stucco Groups by Antonio Gherardi', *Antologia di Belle Arti*, 7–8, 1978, p. 216).

The ceiling (Mazzetto, 'La Pittura di Antonio Gherardi', *Bollettino d'Arte*, XXXIII, 1948, p. 162; Poensgen, fig. 54; Gloton, pl. XXXVI) is painted with scenes from the life of the Virgin arranged in an unusual scheme. Along the flat top of the ceiling are three canvases in a line, set in gilt frames, all seen *di sotto in sù* in a perspective view derived from Veronese. The cove of the ceiling is in fresco but is treated in a similar manner but with a greater effect of illusion, because the scenes are set against the sky which suggests that the space continues from one section to another. In the penetrations above the windows are pairs of angels, those at the end against the sky, but those in the middle panels against a gold ground.

Three of the altars in the nave have fine *scagliola* fronts, a fourth is in the passage to the cloister.
Sacristy: Vault fresco with putti carrying the cross, with an architectural perspective on the cove, possibly by an assistant of Gherardi.
Room between the Sacristy and the cloister: Vault fresco: Gherardi, *A Vision of St Philip Neri* (1677). The small cloister is neatly designed by del Duca to fit a confined space. The top storey is a later addition (*Architettura minora*, II, pl. 103).

S. Maria dell'Umiltà
Via dell'Umiltà

Bibliography: Baglione, p. 310; A. Cicinelli (Chiese di Roma, 111); Portoghesi, *Roma Barocca*, pl. 353; Pugliese-Rigano, *Lunghi*, p. 36; Braham and Hager, p. 86; Buchowiecki, III, p. 195.

Founded in 1601 as a Dominican convent by Francesca Baglioni Orsini. The church was rebuilt in 1641–6 to the design of Paolo Maruscelli (Baglione). The interior was originally simple, with one order of Doric pilasters and decoration in stucco only, but it was enriched with marbles – mainly Sicilian red and yellow jasper – and gilding in the first half of the 18th century. The façade was built in 1703 by Carlo Fontana, who is recorded as architect to the convent in 1681. Early drawings and engravings (Buchowiecki) show that it was a bold Baroque design with the inverted broken and curved pediment fragments used by Buontalenti in the Porta delle Suppliche in the Uffizi and by Bernini in the door in the Cappella del Crocifisso in St Peter's, but this heretical feature was removed when the church was restored under Pius IX and replaced by the existing pure rectilinear pediment. Over the door is a relief of the *Assumption* by Vincenzo Felici, a pupil of D. Guidi. The church is now part of the North American College.

INTERIOR
The decoration of the interior may have been begun by Carlo Fontana, who died in 1714, but it is so much richer than his other works that much of it must be attributed to Alessandro Dori who worked there after his death.

The fresco of the *Assumption* on the vault of the nave is dated 1726 and is probably by Cerruti (Poensgen, fig. 41). The stucco statues of virgin martyrs in niches around the nave are by A. Raggi (Donati, *Artisti ticinesi*, figs 407–13).

Over the entrance is a magnificent gilt wood gallery enclosing the nuns' choir.

The High Altar is by P. Maccarano from the designs of M. Longhi the Younger with bronze and marble angels by Orfeo Boselli (1643–6) (Martinelli, p. 96); altarpiece: A. della Cornia, *Assumption*.

2 to L: *Cappella Gaspardi*: Founded 1645; altarpiece: Francesco Allegrini, *St Michael* (Titi, 1686, p. 297).

1 to L: *Cappella Colonna*: Architecture: Pietro Vecchiarelli; stucco figures by Francesco Cavallini (Titi, 1686, p. 297; Donati, *Artisti ticinesi*, figs 437–40).

S. Maria in Vallicella (Chiesa Nuova) and the Oratory of S. Filippo Neri
Corso Vittorio Emanuele

The Oratory was founded by St Philip Neri in 1561 as an informal gathering of men of piety and goodwill, on the model of the Oratory of Divine Love founded some forty years earlier by S. Gaetano Thiene (Ponnelle and L. Bordet, *Saint Philippe Neri*, Paris, 1928, pp. 118ff.). In 1575 it was established as a Congregation by Gregory XIII, who handed over to them the church of S. Maria in Vallicella and the small Franciscan convent attached to it. The foundation stone of the new church was laid in the same year, but the buildings for the fathers were not finished till the middle of the 17th century.

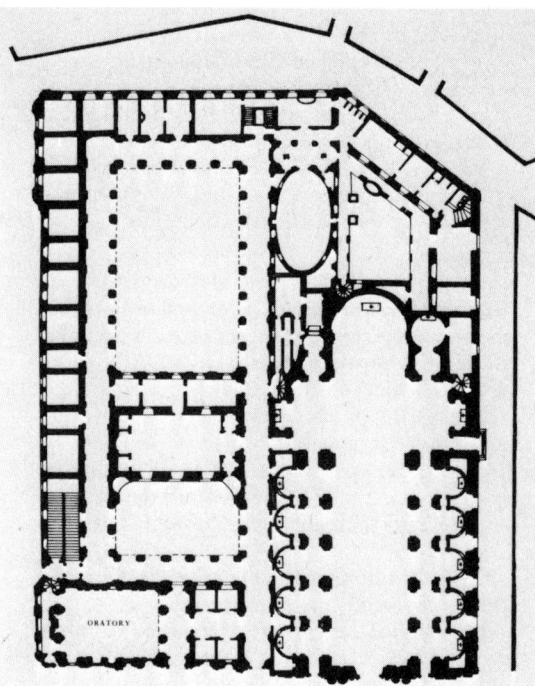

44. *S. Maria in Vallicella and the Oratorio di S. Filippo Neri. Plan.*

The church
Bibliography: Pollak, I, p. 423; De' Rossi, *Prospectus; Architettura Civile*, II, pls 5, 6; id., III, pls 20–2; Magni, I, pl. 41; M. Guidi, 'Francesco Borromino e le fabbriche dei Filippini in Roma', *Rassegna d'Arte*, XXI, 1921, p. 158; E. Strong, *La Chiesa Nuova*, Rome, 1923; M. T. Russo, 'Il contributo della Congregazione dell' Oratorio alla topografia romana', *Studi Romani*, XIII, 1965, p. 21; J. Hess, 'Contributi alla storia della Chiesa Nuova', *Kunstgeschichtliche Studien*, Rome–Vienna, 1967, I, p. 353; C. Gasbarri, *Santa Maria in Vallicella (Tesori d'Arte cristiana)*, Rome, 1968; R. Lefèvre, 'Il primo architetto della Chiesa Nuova', *Oratorium*, IV, 1973, p. 42; *Guide Rionali*, VI, 2, p. 10.

For the documents connected with Pietro da Cortona see Del Piazzo, pp. 19ff. For the history of the dome see H. Hager, 'La crisi statica della cupola di Santa Maria in Vallicella', *Commentari*, XXIV, 1973, pp. 300ff. For Cortona's decoration see Briganti, *Cortona, passim.*

The church was begun in 1575 to a design with a single nave, side chapels and a low drumless dome. The author of the plan was Philip Neri's favourite architect, Matteo da Città di Castello who built the nave and side chapels according to the original plan. He seems to have disappeared about 1582 and after an interval of four years Martino Longhi the Elder was put in charge of the building. At this point, probably owing to a large bequest from Cardinal Pierdonato Cesi, it was decided to give the church aisles, built on the site of the existing chapels, with small semi-circular chapels outside them. In 1588–90 Longhi added the choir and transepts, but he died the next year and the dome and vault of the nave were finished in 1591–4. In 1593 a competition was opened for designs for the façade – for which Longhi's original design (known from an engraving) was no longer suitable owing to the enlargement of the church – the winner being the little-known architect Fausto Rughesi, the candidate of the new patron, Monsignor Angelo Cesi, brother of the Cardinal. The façade bears the date 1605, but it was not in fact finished till the following year.

INTERIOR
In spite of the fact that the building and decoration of this church took over a century it is one of the most complete and harmonious Baroque interiors in Rome, though it is not at all as St Philip Neri intended it to be. Like the Gesù, on which the plan is based, it was to be almost completely plain with travertine or stucco pilasters and whitewashed walls, in accordance with Philip Neri's wishes (cf. Ponnelle and Bordet, p. 363). This spirit of austerity survived among the Oratorians till the 1630s when Borromini was instructed by the Fathers to use brick rather

than travertine on the façade of the Oratory, but in the 1640s their principles changed, as those of the Jesuits were to do twenty years later, and Pietro da Cortona was commissioned to design and execute the magnificent series of frescoes enclosed in gilt and white stucco which decorate the dome, the half-dome of the apse and the vault of the nave. In 1700 the scheme was further enriched by closing the *coretti* over the nave arcade and replacing them by stuccoes enclosing paintings by Daniel Seiter, Giuseppe Ghezzi and others (for a detailed account of the subjects represented in them and also of the complicated iconography of the frescoed vaults of the various side chapels see Strong, op. cit.).

Cortona's frescoes consist of the *Trinity* in the dome (1647–51), the four major prophets – *Isaiah, Jeremiah, Daniel* and *Ezechiel* – in the pendentives, the *Assumption of the Virgin* in the half-dome of the apse (1655–60), and the *Vision of St Philip* (1664–5) on the vault of the nave. The last is conceived as a *quadro riportato* but with a Venetian *di sotto in su* view point. It is supported by stucco angels by C. Fancelli and E. Ferrata and surrounded by high relief stucco decoration of Cortona's designing (Poensgen, fig. 29; Briganti, *Cortona*, pp. 248, 261, 267).

To the same phase belong the stucco allegorical figures in the window lunettes of the transepts and on the entrance wall, all by Fancelli except one – probably *Religion* – which is by Ferrata.

Over the entrance door: Daniel Seiter, *St John preaching* (W).

1 to R: (Crocifisso): S. Pulzone, *Crucifixion*.

2 to R: *Cappella della Pietà:* Altar: copy after Caravaggio's *Entombment* painted for the chapel in 1602–4, removed by the French in 1797 and now in the Vatican.

3 to R: (Ascensione); G. Muziano, *Ascension*.

4 to R: G. M. Morandi, *Pentecost* (W).

5 to R: *Cappella Amici:* Cerrini, *Assumption* (W).

Transepts: Late 17th- or early 18th-century organ (author unknown).

Chapel to right of choir: *Cappella Spada* (S. Carlo Borromeo): Commissioned by or in memory of Cardinal Bernardino Spada (d.1661), one of Borromini's patrons. Titi (1674, p. 132) ascribes it to Carlo Fontana, but Noehles (*Fasolo*, p. 176) shows that this is a mistake. According to Noehles the chapel was begun by Antonio Fontana but Camillo Arcucci (d.1667) was certainly involved at an

45. *S. Maria in Vallicella and the Oratorio di S. Filippo Neri. Engraving by Falda showing the square as laid out under Alexander VII.*

early stage (J.M.) and it was completed by Carlo Rainaldi who is no doubt responsible for the fine marbling. Altarpiece: Maratta, *Sts Charles and Ignatius adoring the Virgin* (begun 1674; W).

Choir: The original High Altar, constructed 1597 by St Philip, recorded in a painting of 1623 (Strong, pl. XXIV), was modified, probably to the design of Ciro Ferri who made the tabernacle, unveiled in 1681 (Cartari-Febei), but the crucifix at the top by the French sculptor named Guillaume Bertholet was incorporated into the later version (Lavagnino, *Altari*, p. 61; K. Noehles, 'Das Tabernakel des Ciro Ferri in der Chiesa Nuova zu Rom', *Miscellanea Bibliothecae Hertzianae*, Münich, 1961, p. 429; Incisa della Rocchetta, 'Del Ciborio di Ciro Ferri alla Vallicella', *L'Oratorio di S. Filippo Neri*, XIX, October, 1962, p. 1).

The three paintings over and on either side of the altar were executed by Rubens in 1606–8. The one over the altar was designed to enclose the holy image of the *Virgin and Child*, the two others represent (left) *St Gregory the Great with Sts Papianus and Maurus*, and (right) *St Domitilla with Sts Nereus and Achilleus*.

Rubens originally painted a single canvas to include the holy image and the saints but it was unsatisfactory because of the way in which it reflected the light. He therefore decided to paint the three existing pictures on slate, which makes their surface more matt. (He took the first canvas back to Antwerp with him; it is now in the Musée des Beaux-Arts at Grenoble.)

On the side walls of the choir over the *coretti* are oval panels of *God the Father* and the heavenly host by Lazzaro Baldi (1700; W).

Chapel to left of choir (Lavagnino, *Altari*, p. 57): Designed in 1600 by Onorio Longhi. The first section of the chapel, which is octagonal, has in its vault a painting of *St Philip* by C. Roncalli, called Il Pomarancio, and its walls are elaborately panelled with marble and semi-precious stones. The inner circular section has a dome, decorated with gilt and white stuccoes, designed by Pietro da Cortona in 1650 and finished in 1653, though the design may have been modified by Ciro Ferri (Incisa della Rocchetta, 'La Cappella di S. Filippo alla Chiesa Nuova', *Oratorium*, III, 1972, p. 49). Over the altar a mosaic copy of Reni's *S. Filippo Neri kneeling before the Virgin* (the original (1614) is in the inner chapel, see below). In 1922 the body of the saint was transferred from its original casket (see below) to its present glass enclosure.

Left transept: *Cappella della Presentazione:* Marbled and decorated in 1594 at the expense of Angelo Cesi, Bishop of Todi, a great benefactor of the Oratorians. The painting of the *Presentation* over the altar is by Barocci, for whom St Philip had a particular admiration.

Sacristy: Marble floor, 1640; over the altar: *St Philip Neri* by Algardi (1635–9; Heimbürger Ravalli, *Algardi*, p. 71; J. Montagu, 'Alessandro Algardi and the statue of St Philip Neri', *Jahrbuch der Hamburger Kunstsammlungen*, XX, 1977, p. 75). Over the door: bust of Gregory XV also by Algardi (Heimbürger Ravalli, ibid., pp. 104, 140). Ceiling fresco by Cortona of *Angels bearing the instruments of the Passion* (1633–4; Brianti, *Cortona*, p. 205).

From the passage near the Sacristy a door leads to the 'inner' chapels of St Philip Neri which incorporate the rooms in which he lived (transported from the old convent buildings to the east of the church). In the lower chapel, *St Philip in adoration* by Guercino; in the upper, the same subject by Reni. In the Sala Rossa on the ground floor a fresco by Niccolò Tornioli of *St Philip seeing a Vision during his Illness*. It also contains the urn in which the remains of the saint were enclosed till 1922 (A. Broschi, 'Il Borromini nelle Stanze di S. Filippo alla Vallicella', *Palatino*, S.IV, XII, 1968, p. 13).

5 to L: *Cappella Ruspoli* (dell'Annunziata): Built in 1591 and decorated for the brothers Alessandro and Orazio Ruspoli (cf. inscription on floor). The altarpiece representing the *Annunciation* is by Passignano. The frescoes on the vault incorporate a complex iconographical scheme alluding to the Virgin Mary in terms of Salomonic Wisdom (Strong, pp. 84ff.).

4 to L: *Cappella della Visitazione:* The altarpiece of the *Visitation* by Barocci was much loved by St Philip who was frequently found in a state of ecstasy in front of it.

3 to L: *Cappella della Natività:* Decorated in 1601 by Cardinal Silvio Antoniano (cf. inscription in floor), who acquired the chapel in 1590 (Strong, p. 97). The *Nativity* over the altar is by Durante Alberti and the frescoes of three saints in the half-dome over the apse are by Cristofano Roncalli, Il Pomarancio.

2 to L: *Cappella Ceva* (dei Re Magi): The painting over the altar, *Adoration of the Magi*, is by Cesare Nebbia. The chapel was acquired by Ponzio Ceva for his tomb in 1578, but the decoration was not finished till 1618 (cf. inscription on floor).

1 to L: *Cappella Cusano* (della Presentazione): Acquired and decorated by Cardinal Agostino Cusano, a friend of St Philip and St Charles Borromeo, who secured the relics of St Papianus and St Maurus for the church. The altarpiece, *The Presentation*, is by the Cavaliere d'Arpino.

The Oratory

Bibliography Borromini's own ideas – partly seen through the eyes of his friend, Virgilio Spada, the prior of the Oratorians – are to be found in the *Opus architectonicum*, published in Rome in 1725 with magnificent engravings of the whole building (facsimile edition, London, n.d.); on the text see Giovanni Incisa della Rocchetta, 'Un dialogo del P. Virgilio Spada sulla Fabbrica dei Filippini', *Archivio della Società Romana di Storia Patria*, XC, 1968, pp. 165ff.; Pollak, I, p. 437; Falda, *Nuovo teatro*, I, pls 21–3; De' Rossi, *Architettura Civile*, I, pls 85–97 and II, pl. 7; Magni, I, pl. 41; Hempel, *Borromini*, pp. 61ff.; Portoghesi, *Borromini*, pls XXX–XLIX, 37–65; Blunt, *Borromini*, p. 85; Connors, *Oratory*.

The history of the building of the Oratory is long and complicated but has been admirably set forth by Connors. The designers had to take account of the special nature of the establishment which was not an enclosed house, but one for priests who continued to live in the world and who, like their founder, practised preaching and disputation of an informal kind and attached great importance to the performance of religious music, often in semi-dramatic form. It was in these performances that the word Oratorio in its modern sense has its origin.

At first the accommodation for the fathers was on a small area to the east of the church, but it soon became apparent that this was inadequate, and after acquiring some further houses on that side they decided to expand to the west of the church.

The first designs for the *casa* were produced about 1621–3 by Mario Arconio but he was soon replaced by Paolo Maruscelli who, between 1620 and 1627, probably in collaboration with Virgilio Spada, who joined the Oratory in 1622, produced a series of plans which contained the essential elements of the house: Oratory, Library, rooms for the fathers. Work was begun in 1629 according to the last of Maruscelli's projects, the first parts to be built being the Sacristy, together with the section of the corridor which separated it from the church, and the rooms round the chapel, which had been attached to the room occupied by St Philip in the old *casa* to the east of the church, but which had been moved, stone by stone, to the new *casa* on the west. These were finished by 1634. In 1637 Borromini was appointed to complete the execution of the design. The circumstances which led to this appointment are not clear, because the competition referred to by most writers on the subject seems to have been an invention of the architect. The change was apparently made by the *preposito* (prior) Angeli Saluzzi, possibly on the advice of Virgilio Spada who had been invited to advise on the plan and who was to remain one of Borromini's keenest supporters (cf. S. Giovanni in Laterano).

Maruscelli had designed the *casa* round two cloisters, separated by the Sacristy, the larger (north) being for the accommodation of the fathers and the smaller for the more public rooms. The Oratory itself, to be used for preaching and musical performances, was to stand between the smaller cloister and the façade. Borromini was compelled to follow Maruscelli's general disposition, but he was able to introduce many modifications to individual parts of the building and so to impose his personality on them.

The first part of the complex to be built after he took over was the Oratory which was constructed in 1637–8, the vault fresco of the *Coronation of the Virgin* by Romanelli being painted in 1639–40 (removed 1788). Maruscelli had planned this as a simple rectangular space, but Borromini transformed it by putting curved pilasters in the corners which, like those on the side and end walls, lead to ribs, which are non-functional and purely decorative, but give the impression that the vault is almost like a ribbed dome. Further, he opened up the end walls with a series of arches, leading on the east to 'green rooms' for the musicians and galleries for distinguished visitors, and at the west to similar galleries (this time for musicians) and a bay for the High Altar. In 1652, after Borromini had left the Oratory, the altar was rebuilt and the columns and niches, which were originally, like the rest of the Oratory, of white stucco, were faced with coloured marbles.

Below the Oratory is a crypt once used as an overflow hall for concerts; it is linked to the main hall by two openings in the middle of the floor, covered by gilt bronze grilles.

The galleries in the Oratory are closed by balustrades of the complex form – on a triangular plan – used by Borromini in the cloister of S. Carlino. In this case he explains that he chose this type of baluster because it gave those sitting in the gallery a better view of what was happening below than if the balusters had been circular in plan. The main door to the Oratory itself from the vestibule leading off the main 'spine' of the building is of extraordinary richness, not in its ornament but in the depth and variety of its mouldings. There are two other doors, one in the middle of the north side leading to the small cloister, the other on the south side under the gallery, which on the exterior forms the central feature of the façade. The High Altarpiece is an *Assumption* by R. Vanni (W).

In designing the façade of the Oratory Borromini was hindered by the need to make it subsidiary to that of the church. He was instructed to use pilasters and to work mainly in brick. To conform with these instructions but at the same time make his façade effective he designed it on a slightly concave curve – almost like a sheet of metal bent under pressure. He also paid great attention to the brickwork which is composed of very thin bricks laid with the minimum of mortar between them. In a passage in the *Opus architectonicum* Borromini explained his intention in doing this: how wonderful it would be, he exclaims, if one could construct a whole façade out of a single piece of terracotta; but since this was not feasible he made the front as smooth and fine-grained as possible.

The Oratory is probably the first curved front to be actually completed in Rome, since that of SS. Luca e Martina, though begun in 1636, was not finished till much later, and that of S. Carlino, though designed in the 1630s, was not begun till 1665.

It has been suggested by Wittkower that the unusually shaped pediment is based on the old façade of Milan Cathedral, but this is unconvincing, since the Milanese gable was composed of an ogee curve, whereas an essential feature of the Oratory pediment is that it consists of a combination of straight and curved sections. The latter is more likely to be a development from Michelangelo's combination of straight and curved pediments on the Porta Pia, the intermediate stage being the design for the door of S. Maria in Trivio by Giacomo del Duca (Blunt, *Borromini*, p. 34). The relation of the façade to the Oratory is curious, since the axis of the latter runs parallel to the façade and not, as the visitor is led to expect, at right angles to it, and the main door leads not into the Oratory itself, but, as we have seen, into the vestibule below the gallery.

The next section of the *casa* to be built (1638–41) covered the area behind the apse of the church to the north. Originally this was to include the library as well as the refectory but when it was decided to move the former to a position over the Oratory Borromini had greater freedom in redesigning the buildings for this area, and in the refectory and the Sala di Ricreazione above it he produced two rooms of unusually inventive design. The refectory was originally to be of simple rectangular form, but Borromini eventually changed it into a long oval, using the corners thus created for serving rooms and a small spiral staircase. Another argument in favour of the oval, according to the architect, was that it was more convenient for the fathers who normally engaged in disputations while having their meals.

The refectory is now used for amateur theatricals (it was once a cinema), but in the anteroom is preserved one of the beautiful *lavamani*, almost Gothic in its form, with a tank to hold the water in the form of a tulip. Over the refectory is the Sala di Ricreazione with a huge and superb fireplace, made out of a piece of white marble found in building the foundations of the Oratory, with a Doric frieze of which the metopes contain Oratorian symbols, and from which hangs a fringe of marble tassels.

This building campaign also included parts of the north cloister in which Borromini employed a giant order of Composite pilasters. This was to be continued round the small south cloister which, together with the main entrance between the church and the Oratory, was built between 1641 and 1644. The articulation of the cloister was complicated by the fact that the windows in Maruscelli's Sacristy were irregularly disposed, but Borromini got over this difficulty by an ingenious use of half-blind openings. The *forestaria* for guests was introduced over the entrance and the rooms of the porter.

During the first years of Innocent X's pontificate no building was done on the *casa*, partly no doubt because Spada, who had been appointed almoner to the pope, was engaged on other projects, including the remodelling of the Lateran, but in 1647 work was begun on the north-west part of the building, including the clock-tower.

Soon after this difficulties began to arise between Borromini and the fathers, and in 1652 he was replaced as architect by Camillo Arcucci. In 1656–7 Spada made an energetic and ingenious attempt to have him reinstated, but he failed. The *casa* was, however, finished by Arcucci according to Borromini's plans, except for certain decorative details, between 1659 and 1662, when the west wing, including the main staircase, was built.

The staircase is approached through an opening flanked by two ancient Roman columns, found during the excavation for the foundations of the building, but which Borromini had to extend to make them of the required height by adding bands of lotus-leaves at the bottom – a device which he derived from a type of ancient column (cf. a set in S. Prassede). The staircase itself has both flights covered by a single vault, a form unusual in Rome at this date but already common in Venice. On the first landing is the life-size stucco model for Algardi's *Meeting of Leo I and Attila* in St Peter's (Heimbürger Ravalli, *Algardi*, p. 149).

After Borromini's departure small additions

were made to the buildings to the north-east of the church by Carlo Rainaldi between 1669 and 1674, when a new thoroughfare, the via della Chiesa Nuova, was opened partly on the site of the fathers' first *casa*. Various changes to the building were made, of which the most serious was the closing of the arcades in the two cloisters. In the 19th century rooms were built on to the north side of the Sacristy, thus reducing the size of the larger cloister, and many other small alterations were made. Generally speaking, however, the actual building has survived almost intact, though many parts of it have been put to unworthy uses.

The buildings of the Oratory, to which the entrance is to the left of the church, are now divided up between various authorities. The Oratory itself is used for concerts, and can sometimes be visited through the good offices of the *portiere* – an uncertain factor; the library which is on the second floor and contains the Biblioteca Vallicelliana is generally accessible; the first floor, which contains the Sala di Ricreazione, is occupied by the Archivio Capitolino. In another room on this floor is the plaster model of the *Miracle of St Agnes* in S. Agnese in Piazza Navona, executed from Algardi's model after his death by Guidi and Ferrata (Heimbürger Ravalli, *Algardi*, p. 173). See plate 75.

S. Maria delle Vergini
Via delle Vergini

Bibliography: Totti, p. 292; Martinelli, p. 127; Titi, 1674, p. 357; id., 1763, p. 326; Rossi, 1697, p. 377; Vasi, *Magnificenze*, pl. 144; Portoghesi, *Roma Barocca*, pl. 396; Buchowiecki, III, p. 241.

A charitable foundation for young girls, founded in 1593 on the Quirinal, was moved to the present location by Cardinal Scipione Borghese because he wanted the site for the palace which he proposed to build (now the Palazzo Rospigliosi). According to Martinelli the church was originally built by Peparelli, and according to Titi in 1674 it was being enlarged at that time. De' Rossi in 1697 says that the church was finished that year, including the façade, and that the High Altar was designed by Mattia de' Rossi, to whom the 1763 Titi ascribes the whole church.

INTERIOR
Built on a Greek Cross plan, unusual in Rome in the 17th century. The vault was frescoed by L. Gimignani, *The Glory of Heaven* and the *Glory of the Trinity* (1682–3; W).
1 to L: Altarpiece: G. B. Mercati, *Noli me tangere*.

S. Maria in Via
Largo Chigi

Bibliography: Mola, p. 95; Magni, I, pl. 11; C. Cecchelli (Chiese di Roma, 14).

A church has stood on this site since the 10th or 11th century. In 1513 it was given by Leo X to the Servite Fathers who still administer it. The building of the present church was apparently begun in 1579 and Tempesta's plan of Rome of 1593 shows it complete except for the upper half of the façade. It is traditionally attributed to G. della Porta but Mola says that it is by Onorio Longhi. It conforms to the standard form of small Roman church of the late 16th century with a single nave and side chapels, in this case rather deep. Baglione ascribes the lower storey of the façade to della Porta but the archives of the Servites mention the name of Martino Longhi the Elder. The upper part is traditionally ascribed to Carlo Rainaldi (Fasolo, *Rainaldi*, p. 429). It is certainly higher than would have been intended by the original architect, and, with its double pediment and huge scrolls, somewhat crushes the lower storey.

INTERIOR
The choir was lengthened at the expense of Cardinal Bellarmin from 1604 onwards. The fresco on the vault of the nave, representing *The First Mass of S. Filippo Benizi*, was painted by G. D. Piastrini in 1722–3 (W; Mallory, *Notizie*, p. 103), which may give the date for the decoration of the whole nave.
2 to R: *S. Filippo Benizi*: Built 1626. Frescoes and altarpiece by Tommaso Luini and Antonio Circignani, Il Pomarancio.
3 to R: *Aldobrandini* (Annunziata): Altarpiece: Cavaliere d'Arpino, *Annunciation*.
4 to R: *Crocifisso*: Built in 1608 by the architect Carlo Lombardo (or Lambardi) as his own chapel. Frescoes by Francesco Lombardo and Cherubino Alberti.

S. Maria in Via (Oratory of the SS. Sacramento)
Piazza Poli

Bibliography: Magni, I, pl. 107; Portoghesi, *Roma Barocca*, pl. 421; Mallory, *Rococo*, p. 146; P. Mancini and G. Scarfone, *L'Oratorio del SS. Sacramento di S. Maria in Via*, Rome, 1973; Mallory, *Notizie*, p. 105.

S. Maria in Via Lata

Built in 1727–30 by Cardinal Pietro Ottoboni for the Confraternity of the SS. Sacramento founded in 1576, the architect being Domenico Gregorini. As built the Oratory was flanked by two identical blocks of secular buildings, but the one on the right was pulled down in the late 19th century for the widening of the via del Tritone. The façade is a good example of the moderate Baroque of which Gregorini was one of the most competent exponents in the early 18th century. Internally the Oratory is a rectangle with rounded corners, like Borromini's chapel of the Collegio di Propaganda Fide. It was twice restored and wholly repainted in the 19th century. It now belongs to the Corporation of Travel Agents.

INTERIOR

The High Altar was made in 1843 to the design of Luigi Maria Valadier, son of Giuseppe. Over it hangs the *Holy Family* by F. Trevisani (1729; W).

S. Maria in Via Lata
Via del Corso

Bibliography: Falda, *Nuovo teatro*, I, pl. 17; Vasi, *Magnificenze*, pl. 44; L. Cavazzi, *La Diaconia di S. Maria in Via Lata*, Rome, 1908; Magni, I, pls 43, 44; Pollak, I, p. 184; Salerno, *Via del Corso*, p. 246; Wittkower, *Art and Architecture*, p. 244; Buchowiecki, III, p. 255; C. Bertelli and C. Galassi Paluzzi (Chiese di Roma, 114); R. Bösel, 'Cosimo Fanzago a Roma', *Prospettiva*, 15, 1978, p. 29; *Guide Rionali*, IX, iii, p. 48.

At a very early date a chapel was established in the remains of a Roman house in which St Paul was supposed to have stayed while awaiting trial. In 1049 the church over it was rebuilt and this was in turn replaced by another in 1491. In 1594 various alterations were made which included raising the High Altar to its present level.

In 1636–43 the choir was reconstructed and decorated to the design of Bernini for Francesco d'Aste and his wife whose tombs stand in it (Lavin, *Bernini*, pp. 50, 169). Between 1650 and 1655 the nave was redecorated by Cosimo Fanzago and though part of his work was altered or swept away in a further restoration of

46. *S. Maria in Via Lata. Engraving by Falda showing the façade of the church as built by Cortona. On the extreme right is a palace, later absorbed into the Palazzo de Carolis, with the Fontana del Facchino. To the left of the church is the Palazzo Pamphili (formerly Aldobrandini, now Doria-Pamphili) before it was regularized by Valvassori in the 18th century. Beyond it, on the corner of the Piazza Venezia is the Palazzo Aste (later Buonaparte) and in the distance the Palazzetto Venezia (moved in the 1920s to a position to the west of the Palazzo Venezia).*

1863, much of it survives, including the wooden roof, the decoration of the upper part of the walls with the windows, the encasing of the columns with Sicilian marble, the organ, the doors in the aisles and probably the bronze angels standing on the altar-rails.

In 1658 Pietro da Cortona was commissioned to build the vestibule and façade. The lower storey was finished by 1661 when Cortona showed Alexander VII the model of the upper storey (*Diary of Alexander VII*, 564, 577, June–July, 1661). It was finished in 1663 and Cortona immediately produced plans for the campanile (ibid., 693, 13 June 1663). The grille was put in place in March 1663 (ibid., 808).

Cortona also restored the lower church which was visited by the pope on 31 March 1665. In so doing he preserved as much of the Early Christian church as possible, an example of the interest taken in the 17th century in the holy places of the early church.

The façade (dated 1662) is the latest of Cortona's works of this kind. In one way it is the simplest, because it does not incorporate any curves, a feature probably due to the fact that it had to be aligned to a long row of palaces facing on the relatively narrow Corso. It contains, however, several novelties, in particular the breaking of the entablature over the upper order into the pediment, a device which Cortona could have known from Roman – and perhaps Hellenistic – examples (for instance, the arch at Orange). The interior of the portico with its massive columns standing against the wall of the church recalls the vestibule to the Sacristy of S. Spirito in Florence (by Giuliano da Sangallo and Cronaca) and reminds one of Cortona's Tuscan origin. A curious feature is that the coffering of the barrel-vault seems to continue behind the arches enclosing the apsed ends of the portico. Over the door is a relief of the *Virgin* by Cosimo Fancelli.

INTERIOR

The marble pavement is inlaid with heraldic elements from the arms of Aldobrandini and Pamphili and must therefore date from the time of Camillo Pamphili and his wife Olimpia Aldobrandini (married in 1647).

The organ is by Caterinazzo of Subiaco (1652).

Entrance wall: Monument to Cardinal Maurice

47. *S. Maria in Via Lata. Engraving by Vasi, showing the Palazzo Pamphili (Doria-Pamphili) as remodelled by Valvassori, and on the extreme right a corner of the Palazzo de Carolis with the Fontana del Facchino still in its original position.*

of Savoy set up in 1637, near Pietro da Cortona in style. A. Masucci, *Baptism*.
Before 1st altar: Masucci, *Annunciation*.
1 to R: G. Brandi, *St Andrew adoring his Cross* (1685; W).
Between 1 and 2 to R: Pietro de'Pietri, *Adoration of the Shepherds*.
2 to R: G. Ghezzi, *St Joseph adored by St Nicholas of Bari and St Blaise* (1686; W).
Beyond 2 to R: Pietro de'Pietri, *Presentation*; G. D. Piastrini, *Madonna of the Rosary*; A. Masucci, *Adoration of the Kings*.
High Altar: Set up between 1636 and 1643 to the design of Bernini (De' Rossi, *Architettura Civile*, III, pl. 47). On either side, tombs of the d'Aste family, the bronze bust of G. B. d'Aste being probably by Giuliano Finelli and that of his wife Clarice Margana probably by Andrea Bolgi (A. Nava-Cellini, 'Ritratti di Andrea Bolgi', *Paragone*, XIII, 1962, 147, p. 30).
Chapel to left of High Altar: Giovanni Odazzi, *Madonna with Saints* (W).
Between this chapel and 2 to L: Masucci, *Marriage of the Virgin*; Pietro de'Pietri, *Presentation of the Virgin*.
2 to L: P. L. Ghezzi, *St Paul baptizing S. Sabina*.
Between 2 and 1 to L: Pietro de'Pietri, *Birth of the Virgin*.
Sacristy: The vaulting has grisaille frescoes imitating stucco, apparently dating from the 18th century.
1 to L: Pietro de'Pietri, *Madonna with Saints*.
Before 1 to L: A. Masucci, *Joachim and Anna*.
Entrance wall: G. D. Piastrini, *Christ appearing to the Apostles*.
Lower Church: Doors and grilles by Cortona. At the top of the steps leading to the church, monument to Atanasio Ridolfi by Cortona. The bust probably dates from about 1640, but the sculptor is not known. Over the altar in the lower church, relief of *Sts Paul, Peter, Martial and Luke* by Cosimo Fancelli. On the left wall a fragment of a fresco painted by an assistant of Cortona probably over the remains of a mediaeval fresco.

S. Maria della Visitazione (S. Francesco di Sales)
Via S. Francesco di Sales

Bibliography: Guide Rionali, XIII, 1, p. 34.

The church was probably built by G. B. Contini. It is now part of the prison of Regina Coeli and is therefore not conveniently accessible.

S. Maria della Vittoria
Via XX Settembre

Bibliography: Baglione, p. 308; Falda, *Nuovo teatro*, III, pl. 10; Tessin, p. 162; De'Rossi, *Prospectus*, pl. 70; Vasi, *Magnificenze*, pl. 148; Magni, I, pls 49–52; G. Matthiae (Chiese di Roma, 84); Hibbard, *Maderno*, pp. 140ff; Guide Rionali, XVII, p. 11.

Founded 1607 by the Carmelites of S. Maria della Scala as a training college for missionaries. Originally dedicated to St Paul, after a small chapel on the site. The church was built between 1610 and 1612 and the design is attributed to Maderno by Baglione (p. 308). In 1622 its name was changed to S. Maria della Vittoria in honour of an image which was said to have caused Tilly to win the Battle of the White Mountain in 1621 and which was given to the church the next year. It perished in 1833 in a fire which destroyed the apse of the church.

In Maderno's time the interior was plain and devoid of marbling or stucco. At some date before 1663 G. D. Cerrini painted the frescoes of the dome and vault. The vault was stuccoed in 1675, the pilasters covered with Sicilian jasper between 1705 and 1714, and the floor marbled in 1740.

The façade was built by G. B. Soria between 1625 and 1635 and paid for by Cardinal Scipione Borghese. It is Soria's earliest and least original church façade, but it was conditioned by the proximity of Maderno's S. Susanna (from which it was originally separated by a palace on the site of the Largo di S. Susanna). Soria has followed the main lines of Maderno's design but has inserted an awkwardly heavy curved pediment over the main door. He has also copied one unusual feature of S. Susanna, the introduction of a balustrade on the pediment, but surprisingly he has given this a form of interlaced mouldings, apparently otherwise unknown in Rome, which was used at about the same time in France by François Mansart and which Soria could have known from engravings in Jacques Androuet du Cerceau's *Plus excellents Bastiments* (e.g. at Verneuil).

INTERIOR

Frescoes in nave and dome by Giovanni Domenico Cerrini: *Victory of the Virgin over heretics* and *St Paul in Glory* (before 1663; W). Poensgen wrongly ascribes them to the brothers Orazi.

The organ gallery over the entrance is by Mattia de'Rossi (1677; Cartari-Febei).

2 to R: *Cappella Merenda* (S. Francesco): Decorated c.1630 by Mario Arconio; altarpiece: Domenichino, *Madonna and Child with St Francis* (Voss, p. 513).

3 to R: *Cappella Vidoni:* Monuments to Cardinal Girolamo Vidoni (d.1632) and his nephew Giovanni Vidoni (d.1626) by Ferrucci.

Right transept: *Cappella Capocaccia* (S. Giuseppe): Decorated by G. B. Contini in 1694 to balance Bernini's Cornaro Chapel opposite. Over the altar, the *Vision of St Joseph* by Domenico Guidi; on the side walls reliefs of the *Adoration of the Shepherds* and the *Flight into Egypt* by P. E. Monnot (1695–9; Enggass, *Sculpture*, p. 82). Frescoes on vault by Bonaventura Lamberti.

Passage to Sacristy: Monument to Cardinal Sebastiano Antonio Tanari (d.1724) by Fuga set up in 1744 with a bust by Agostino Corsini (Matthiae, *Fuga*, p. 80; Pane, *Fuga*, p. 115, fig. 100); opposite is a relief of the *Assumption of the Virgin* by Pompeo Ferrucci (c.1626).

Choir: Rebuilt after the fire of 1831, but contains a painting of the *Ecstasy of St Paul* by Honthorst (Nicolson, p. 58).

Left transept: *Cornaro Chapel* (St. Theresa): Decorated by Bernini for Cardinal Federico Cornaro; begun soon after 1644, architecture finished by 1647 (De'Rossi, *Altari*, pls 21, 22; Wittkower, *Bernini*, p. 216; Lavagnino, *Altari*, pp. 25, 83; Portoghesi, *Roma Barocca*, pls 48–57; Blunt, 'Gianlorenzo Bernini: Illusionism and Mysticism', *Art History*, I, 1978, p. 73; Lavin, *Bernini*, passim.). The central group shows the vision of St Theresa when an angel appeared ad pierced her heart with a spear. This represents the second stage of mystical experience, beyond the act of prayer controlled by the will shown in Bernini's statue of Fonseca in S. Lorenzo in Lucina, but less complete than the total abandon of his Blessed Ludovica Albertoni in S. Francesco a Ripa, because though the will has withdrawn the senses are still active. On the side walls of the transept members of the Cornaro family – all deceased except for the Cardinal himself who appears second from the right in the right-hand relief – are shown disputing some theological point – no doubt connected with the saint's vision. The chapel encompasses a range of different worlds from the heaven in the frescoed vault (by Abbatini after a sketch by Bernini) through the visionary world of St Theresa and the material world of the Cornaro family, living and dead, to purgatory, represented by the two panels of inlaid marble in the pavement showing two skeletons, one in hopeful prayer, one in despair.

The chapel is one of Bernini's most inspired works and a brilliant expression of the fusion of the arts which was among his most personal contributions to the Baroque. The group of St Theresa and the angel expresses with unparalleled intensity the mystical experience which played such an important part in 17th-century religious life, and the combination of architecture, painting and sculpture – the last carried to the highest point of illusionism in the imitation of silks and velvets in marble – intensifies the dramatic effect of the whole, and adds conviction to the dramatic unity which Bernini imposes on the different elements – divine, human and infernal – which makes the chapel one of the great masterpieces of Baroque art.

3 to L: *Cappella Gessi:* Founded by Cardinal Berlingherio Gessi (d.1639). The architecture is by Algardi (Passeri, p. 352), who was also responsible for the figures of *Justice* and *Prudence* over the entrance arch to the chapel and the figurative parts of the stucco decoration of the vault. The frescoes on the vault, now much damaged, are by Giovanni Francesco Grimaldi (W) who may have designed the general scheme of the decoration. Altarpiece: Guercino, *Trinity* (c.1642). Right: portrait of Cardinal Bernardino Gessi by Reni.

2 to L: Nicolas Lorrain, *St John of the Cross*. See plate 53.

S. Marta
Piazza del Collegio Romano

Bibliography: Falda, *Nuovo teatro*, I, pl. 18; De' Rossi, *Architettura Civile*, III, pl. 41; H. Hager, 'L'Intervento di Carlo Fontana per le chiese dei monasteri di S. Marta e S. Margherita in Trastevere', *Commentari*, XXV, 1974, p. 225; *Guide Rionali*, IX, 1, p. 76.

In 1546 Ignatius Loyola founded on this site a hospice for 'Malmaritate', i.e., unhappily married women. In 1561 the hospice was transferred to S. Chiara and the buildings were handed over to the Augustinian nuns, who built a church, which was consecrated in 1570. Between 1671 and 1674 the church was remodelled by Carlo Fontana who had become the architect to the community and whose daughters were members of it.

The church was widened by the addition of chapels and the new vault was higher than the old. Fontana designed a new façade but this was not executed. The vault was frescoed by Baciccio with the *Glory of S. Marta* with allegorical figures by Girolamo Troppa in the corners (about 1672; Enggass, *Baciccio*, pp. 18, 146). The stuccoes are by Leonardo Lombardo. All the altarpieces were removed in the 19th century when the convent was turned into a police barracks. In 1961 the church was restored and is now used as a concert hall.

S. Marta in Vaticano (destroyed)

Bibliography: Vasi, *Magnificenze*, pl. 166; Titi, 1721, p. 29; Armellini, *Chiese*, II, p. 939; G. Bossi, *La Chiesa di S. Marta al Vaticano*, Rome, 1883; Wasserman, 'Santa Marta al Vaticano', *Capitolium*, XXXVI, 9, 1961, p. 23; Wasserman, *Mascarino*, p. 64.

The church stood near the Sacristy of St Peter's. It was built in 1538 but rebuilt by Mascarino in 1582 and restored by Clement XI, who added a new façade, presumably that shown in the engraving by Vasi reproduced by Armellini.

S. Martino ai Monti
Via Lanza

Bibliography: Titi, 1686, p. 218; Letarouilly, pls 252, 253 (308, 309); Magni, I, pl. 45; E. Boaga, 'La Basilica di S. Martino ai Monti', *Capitolium*, XXXI, 1956, p. 280; G. C. Miletti and S. Ray, 'Filippo Gagliardi e il rifacimento di S. Martino ai Monti', *Palatino*, XI, 1967, p. 3; *Guide Rionali*, I, 2, p. 42.

A church stood here since Early Christian times and was rebuilt by Sergius II (844–7). In 1559 it was given to a body of Carmelite monks. The interior was restored in the mid-17th century by the prior, G. A. Filippini, the architect being Filippo Gagliardi. The façade is dated 1676.

INTERIOR
The wooden ceiling was given by S. Carlo Borromeo. The *Confessio* was ascribed to Pietro da Cortona by Bottari in 1754 (*Dialoghi sopra le tre arti del Disegno*, ed. Parma, 1845, p. 85). And the attribution was repeated by Muñoz (*Pietro da Cortona*, Rome, 1921, pl. XXVII) and others but the documents show that it is by Gagliardi. It is in fact a feeble imitation of Cortona's idiom, entirely lacking his feeling for monumental form, and the columns, which look like *cippolino*, are hollow and made of stucco.

The frescoes on the aisle walls were painted between 1647 and 1651 by Gaspard Dughet, brother-in-law of Nicolas Poussin, except for three on the left wall (the first and last which are views of St Peter's and St John Lateran by Filippo Gagliardi and one near the middle of Pope Silvester holding the council of AD 324 in S. Martino) and two on the right wall (the 2nd and 3rd from the entrance) which are by Grimaldi. The themes are principally taken from the story of Elijah, traditionally the founder of the Order, and of various saints connected with it. The idea of representing such scenes in a series of frescoed landscapes may have been suggested by the similar series in S. Vitale, dating from the first decades of the 17th century.

For a full discussion of the subjects and their sources see J. J. Bardel, 'Gaspard Dughet and San Martino ai Monti', *Storia dell'Arte*, 26, 1976, p. 45; for the dating and attribution of the frescoes see A. Sutherland, 'The Decoration of S. Martino ai Monti', *Burlington Magazine*, CVI, 1964, pp. 58, 111, and J. Heideman, 'The dating of Gaspard Dughet's frescoes in S. Martino ai Monti', ibid., CXXII, 1980, p. 540. The figures in the fresco representing *Herodias' vision of the Cross* (5th on right) are probably by Pietro Testa.

3 to R: Fabrizio Chiari, *St Martin* (1645; W).
4 to R: Giovanni Angelo Canini, *St Stephen* (?1646; W).
3 to L: G. A. Canini, *Trinity* (1644; W).
2 to L: G. Muziano, *St Albert*.
1 to L: Testa, *S. Angelo Carmelitano* (1645–6; W).

The statues in the nave are by Paolo Naldini.

SS. Michele e Magno
To the south west of the Piazza of St Peter's (Largo degli Alicorni)

Bibliography: M. Mosi and P. Becchetti (Chiese di Roma, 126).

A church stood on this site at least since the 9th century but after many restorations it was completely rebuilt and decorated by Benedict XIV and Clement XIII between 1756 and 1759, the architect being Carlo Murena. At this time it belonged to a college of canons directly dependent on St Peter's. Apart from the fine mediaeval campanile it has no architectural features of interest.

INTERIOR
High Altar: N. Ricciolini, *Sts Gregory and Magnus*.
Altar to L: Lugwig Stern, *Sts Peter and Paul*.
End of left aisle: Tomb of Anton Raphael Mengs (d.1779) by Vincenzo Pacetti.

SS. Nereo e Achilleo
Via delle Terme di Caracalla

Bibliography: J. Urban, 'Die Kirchenbaukunst des Quattrocento in Rom', *Römisches Jahrbuch*, IX/X, 1961–2, p. 91; G. Matthiae, 'Tre Chiese all' inizio dell'Appia', *Capitolium*, XLIV, 1969, p. 154.

A church was recorded on the site in the 4th century but was many times restored and was rebuilt for the Holy Year of 1475. When Cesare Baronio was made a cardinal in 1596 with this as his titular church he restored it, preserving as much as possible of what had survived of the early church (cf. S. Cesareo), including the baldacchino, altar front and screens which date from the 13th century. The frescoes in the interior are by Niccolò Circignani, called Il Pomarancio.

S. Nicola in Arcione (destroyed)
Bibliography: Guide Rionali, II, 1, p. 112.

The mediaeval church which stood on the site of via del Traforo was rebuilt several times, last in the mid-18th century by Girolamo Teodoli. It was pulled down in 1907 when the *traforo* was cut under the Quirinal, but its façade is recorded in an old photograph reproduced in the *Guida Rionale*.

S. Nicola in Carcere.
Via del Teatro di Marcello

Bibliography: G. B. Proja (Chiese di Roma, 112); Vasi, *Magnificenze*, pl. 118.

Built on the ruins of three Roman temples, parts of which are built into the existing structure. The ruins were converted into a Christian church probably in the 9th century. It was restored many times, but the interior owes its present appearance largely to Cardinal Federico Borromeo who decorated the apse and built the present High Altar, and Cardinal Pietro Aldobrandini, nephew of Clement VIII, who added the façade. The church was heavily restored and redecorated with frescoes under Pius IX, who replaced the old wooden ceiling with the present one. The façade by Giacomo della Porta, dated 1599, is unlike any other in Rome. Its form was partly dictated by the narrowness of the site – till the via del Mare, now the via del Teatro di Marcello, was opened up in the 1920s the church was squeezed between houses and faced on to a narrow street – which led the architect to articulate it with two tall fluted Ionic columns with Michelangelesque capitals and a rich entablature over which is a low attic. The stucco bas-reliefs are exceptional for the period, though they recall those by Pirro Ligorio on the Villa Pia in the Vatican gardens, and their character led one critic to make the – unfounded – suggestion that they were added in the 18th century by Piranesi.

INTERIOR
Restored several times, last in 1865.
Chapel at end of right aisle: *Aldobrandini* (Sacramento): Giovanni Baglione, Old Testament scenes prefiguring the Eucharist.
High Altar: The altar itself is composed of a magnificent ancient sarcophagus of green porphyry. The Baldacchino was set up in the restoration of 1865 but incorporates the four re-used ancient columns which stood beside the mediaeval altar.

S. Nicola degli Incoronati (destroyed)

Bibliography: C. P. Planca Incoronati, 'La Chiesa di S. Nicola degli Incoronati in Roma', *Archivio della R. Deputazione romana di storia patria*, LXI, 1938, p. 193.

This church stood from the 12th century onwards in piazza Padella, off via Giulia. It was rebuilt in 1680–1 with an unusual façade of a single bay flanked by Tuscan pilasters and crowned by a broken pediment of which the curved sections end in volutes, which is recorded in a drawing reproduced by Incoronati.

S. Nicola dei Lorenesi
Via dell'Anima

Bibliography: Titi, 1763, p. 410; F. Bonnard, *Histoire de l'église de Saint-Nicolas de la Confraternité des Lorrains à Rome*, Rome, 1932; Ferrari, *Lo Stucco*, pls CXXIff.; M. de Dumast, *L'Eglise Saint Nicolas des Lorrains à Rome*, Rome, n.d.; Mallory, *Notizie*, pp. 106ff.; *Guide Rionali*, VI, 1, p. 76; Bousquet, *Recherches*, p. 125.

The Confraternity of the colony of Lorrainers living in Rome was originally established in the church of S. Luigi dei Francesi, where it enjoyed the use of the second chapel to the left, but in 1622 the church of S. Nicola in Agone was allotted to it by Gregory XV. This was replaced by the existing church, which was built in 1635–6, ironically exactly at the moment when Lorraine was losing its independence and being absorbed into France by Louis XIII and Richelieu. The identity of the architect has been established by M. Jacques Bousquet (see note in Dumast) as the Lorrainer François du Jardin, called Francesco Giardini in Rome, where he lived at least from 1625 to 1661, of whom little is known. The façade, however, indicates that he must have been trained in Rome, and he must have formed his style on the study of Giacomo della Porta, whose works it closely resembles.

In 1731 the painter Corrado Giaquinto, a native of Bari, of which Nicholas was the patron saint, offered to fresco the vault of the nave and choir and the dome (Poensgen, fig. 44; Gloton, pls XXXIII, XLV), his first important commission in Rome (unveiled 1733; Mallory, *Notizie*, p. 100), paid for by the chaplain, Domenico

Fabri, who was responsible for the complete decoration of the church, including the marbling of Sicilian jasper (1746). Giaquinto also painted for the walls on either side of the space under the dome two large canvases representing scenes from the life of *St Nicholas* (one now replaced by a copy). Fabri may also be responsible for commissioning the four large stucco reliefs with similar subjects on the walls of the nave by Giovanni Battista Grossi.
High Altar: Nicolas Lorrain, *St Nicholas*.
2 to L: Nicolas Lorrain, *St Catherine*.

S. Nicola dei Prefetti
Via dei Prefetti

Bibliography: Vasi, *Magnificenze*, pl. 106; G. Drago (Chiese di Roma, 55).

A small church of early but uncertain date, which for a short time, about 1525, housed S. Gaetano and the first Theatines (before the building of S. Andrea della Valle). In 1567 it was given to the Dominicans of S. Sabina by Pius V. The façade, which dates from before 1674, is unusually chaste in design. The interior, wholly restored in the 18th and again in the late 19th century, is of little interest.

S. Nicola da Tolentino
Via S. Nicola da Tolentino

Bibliography: Totti, p. 297; Falda, *Nuovo teatro*, III, pl. 14; Titi, 1686, p. 302; 1686, p. 302 and 1763, p. 334; De' Rossi, *Architettura Civile*, III, pls 11–13; Bertolotti, *Artisti modenesi a Roma*, Bologna, 1882, p. 147; Magni, I, pls 38, 39; Fasolo, *Fede e Arte*, XI, 1963, p. 66; H. Hager, 'Il modello di C. Rusconi Sassi del Concorso per la facciata di S. Giovanni in Laterano', *Commentari*, XXII, 1971, p. 61; Eimer, *S. Agnese*, II, figs 268–70; Buchowiecki, III, p. 407; *Guide Rionali*, II, 1, p. 44.

Founded in 1614 by Discalced Augustinian Friars. The church was built at the expense of Don Camillo Pamphili from 1654 onwards and the architect was Giovanni Maria Baratta, brother of Bernini's pupil, Francesco Baratta, and himself a pupil of Algardi. The effect of the façade, which was begun in 1655 (J.M.), has been altered owing to the fact that extra steps had to be added to the flight approaching it when the level of the street was lowered in the late 19th century.

INTERIOR
The pilasters of the nave are of a purplish-grey substance, apparently a kind of composition of marble fragments. Holy water-stoups by G. M. Baratta (1664).

On vault, over entrance: P. Naldini, *St William of Aquitaine* (Weil, *Ponte S. Angelo*, p. 142).
Over High Altar: *S. Chiara di Montefalco* by G. B. Ferrabosco who also made ten stucco angels, probably the putti in the window embrasures (J. M.).
1 to R: Altarpiece: F. Laurenzi, *St Nicholas*; on walls: G. V. Borghesi, *Birth of the Virgin* and *Christ crowning the Virgin*. An unusual altar frontal of inlaid marble, partly in relief.
3 to R: (Sts Gertrude and Lucretia): Altarpiece and walls by Pietro Paolo Ubaldini, scenes from the lives of the two saints (before 1665; W).
Right transept: Altar with arms of Prince Camillo Pamphili; altarpiece: Baciccio, *St John the Baptist* (c.1670; Enggass, *Baciccio*, p. 147); stuccoes by Ercole Ferrata.
Dome: Giovanni Coli and Filippo Gherardi, *St Nicholas in Glory* (1670–1; W; Gloton, pl. XXIX); pendentives: Ubaldini, *Obedience, Poverty, Chastity* and *Humility*.
High Altar: *Vision of St Nicholas* (De' Rossi, *Altari*, pls 25, 26). The altar and the sculpture were designed by Algardi just before his death in 1654 but were largely executed by pupils, the relief of *God the Father* and the figure of *St Nicolas* being by Ercole Ferrata and the *Virgin, St Augustine* and *St Monica* by Domenico Guidi. Algardi here makes skilful use of a deep curved niche which enables him to treat his figures in full relief (J. Montagu, 'Alessandro Algardi's Altar of S. Nicola da Tolentino and some related models', *Burlington Magazine*, LXII, 1970, p. 282).
Chapel to left of High Altar: *Cappella Buratti*: Built by G. B. Mola. Pietro Paolo Ubaldini, altarpiece of *Virgin and Child and Saints Matthew and Cecilia* and on the walls scenes from the lives of these saints (W).
3 to L: On walls: right, G. Cades, *Holy Family* (1790), left, P. Raffaele, *Annunciation*.
2 to L: *Cappella Gavotti* (De' Rossi, *Altari*, pls 23, 24; A. Muñoz, *Pietro da Cortona*, Rome, 1921, pls XXV, XXVI; Lavagnino, *Altari*, p. 107; Briganti, *Cortona*, p. 270): Founded under the will of Giovanni Battista Gavotti (d.1661), the chapel was begun by Cortona in 1668 (Wittkower, *Art and Architecture*, p. 504) and opened in 1677 (Cartari-Febei). Cortona also began the vault fresco which was finished by Ciro Ferri in 1669 (W). Altar relief of the *Miracle of the Madonna of Savona* by Cosimo Fancelli; *St John the Baptist* by Antonio Raggi, *St Joseph* by Ercole Ferrata. Below the statues are the tombs of Giovanni Battista (left) and Carlo Gavotti (right), with busts in oval frames over marble sarcophagi, that of G. B. Gavotti being

by Cosimo Fancelli. Lunette of *St Philip Neri* by Ferrata. This is one of Cortona's last works of architecture, characterized, like the façade of S. Maria in Via Lata and the dome of S. Carlo al Corso, by a grand simplicity and monumentality compared with an early church such as SS. Luca e Martina.

The church and monastic buildings attached to it now belong to the Armenian community. If shut, apply at door of monastery on left.

SS. Nome di Maria
Forum of Trajan

Bibliography: A. Martini and M. C. Casanova (Chiese di Roma, 70); W. Oechslin, 'Contributo alla conoscenza di Antoine Dérizet', *Quaderni*, 16, 1969, p. 47; Jacob, *Zeichnungen*, No. 793.

On the defeat of the Turks and the raising of the Siege of Vienna in 1683 Innocent XI, who had actively supported the Emperor Leopold I and John Sobiecki, declared a new feast dedicated to the Holy Name of the Virgin to whose intervention he attributed the success against the Turks, and at the same time a Confraternity was founded with the same title. This was at first housed in the church of S. Stefano del Cacco, but was moved to that of S. Bernardo on the Forum of Trajan in 1694. In 1728 the Confraternity undertook to build a new church on a site adjacent to S. Bernardo and designs were put forward, but nothing was done. In 1735 the Protector of the Confraternity, Cardinal Lodovico Pico della Mirandola, insisted on the choice of the Frenchman Antoine Dérizet as the architect. The foundation stone was laid in 1736, and the church was consecrated in 1741. Dérizet's first plans recorded in drawings in the Kunstbibliothek, Berlin, were for a church with a low dome. Later it was decided to introduce a tall double dome with a drum, but Dérizet's foundations were discovered to be too weak to carry this and the church was finally built with a single dome.

Dérizet, though born in Lyons and trained in Paris, went to Rome when he was 26 and spent the rest of his life there, and there is nothing specifically French about the church (except the shape of the windows in the drum of the dome) which stands as a rather mediocre example of the classical wing of Roman architecture in the second quarter of the 18th century. The statues at the base of the drum are by a group of Roman artists, whose names are given by Martini and Casanova (p. 57), among them being M. A. Slodtz's *St Matthew*. On the inside of the dome is a series of stucco reliefs of the *Life of the Virgin* by various artists including Slodtz and Maini who is responsible for the *Annunciation*.

The chancel was added by Mauro Fontana after 1750.

INTERIOR
All the marbling is painted.
1 to R: Antonio Nessi, *S. Luigi Gonzaga*.
2 to R: Agostino Masucci, *St Anne and the Virgin* (1757).
3 to R: Stefano Pozzo, *Death of St Joseph* (1755; Mallory, *Notizie*, p. 112).
Choir: Built by Mauro Fontana (after 1750); High Altar by Andrea Bergondi.
2 to L: (S. Bernardo): N. Ricciolini, *The Virgin appearing to St Bernard.*
1 to L: L. Masucci, *Sts Peter and Paul.*

S. Omobono
Via della Consolazione

Bibliography: G. Matthiae (Chiese di Roma, 56).

The church is built on the site of an ancient Roman temple and incorporates part of its walls. It was originally dedicated to S. Salvatore, but the dedication was changed to S. Omobono (a Cremonese saint) at some date soon after 1573 when it was granted to the Corporation of Tailors, who remodelled it. It was frequently restored and the interior is now of no architectural interest.

INTERIOR
1 to R: Vincenzo Milone, *St Francis* (1767).
Apse: Pietro Turini, *Christ in Glory* (1510).
1 to L: G. A. Galli, called Lo Spadarino, *S. Omobono giving his clothes to a beggar.*

S. Onofrio
Salita di S. Onofrio

Bibliography: L. Huetter and E. Lavagnino (Chiese di Roma, 40); G. Urban, 'Die Kirchenbaukunst des Quattrocento in Rom', *Römisches Jahrbuch*, IX/X, 1961–2, p. 79; *Guide Rionali*, XIII, p. 156

The church was founded in 1419 and largely decorated in the 15th century, but it contains some work of the 17th and 18th centuries.

Portico to right of entrance (Borea, *Domenichino*, p. 161): Domenichino, three scenes from the life of *St Jerome*.
Cappella del Rosario (at end of Portico): Built in 1620 by Cardinal Maffeo Barberini, later Pope Urban VIII. Over door: Baglione, *Sibyls*.
Passage to cloister: Tomb of Marchese Giuseppe Rondinini.
Cloister: Frescoed lunettes, some by the Cavaliere d'Arpino.

Museo Tassiano: Devoted to the memory of the poet Tasso who died in the monastery in 1595. It includes the bust of John Barclay by François Duquesnoy, originally in S. Lorenzo fuori le Mura.

INTERIOR
2 to R: (Madonna di Loreto). Built in 1604 by Cardinal Madruzzi; frescoes: G. B. Ricci da Novara; altarpiece: Annibale Carracci, *Madonna of Loreto*.
Sacristy: Trevisani, *S. Giovanni Gambacorta* (W).
Apse: Frescoes by a follower of Pinturicchio.
3 to L: Tomb of Cardinal Filippo Sega (d.1596). The tomb is attributed to Domenichino, but this appears to be due to a confusion in the early guide-books and biographies of the artist.

S. Orsola. See Conservatorio di S. Cecilia
Via Vittoria

S. Pancrazio
Piazza S. Pancrazio

Bibliography: M. Cecchelli (Chiese di Roma, 124).

A church on this site dating probably from the 5th century was pulled down in 1609 and replaced by a new building which was restored between 1662 and 1665 and again in 1673 by the Discalced Carmelites to whom it had been given by Alexander VII. In one of these restorations it received its decoration of unusually delicate stucco putti and swags and the eight stucco bas-reliefs in the aisles representing scenes from the lives of S. Pancrazio and other saints. The frames between the swags over the main arches and the carved and gilt roof were presumably intended to contain frescoes.

S. Pantaleo
Piazza S. Pantaleo

Bibliography: Spagnesi, G. A. De Rossi, pp. 193ff.; id. (Chiese di Roma, 94); Guide Rionali, VI, 1, p. 112.

A church stood on this site since 1216. It was dedicated to S. Pantaleo, patron saint of doctors, and was at one stage attached to an English college. In 1622 it was given to the Fratelli delle Scuole Pie (founded 1614). In 1681 the church was rebuilt to the design of G. A. de' Rossi on the orders of Cardinal Gaspare Carpegna, protector of the Order. De' Rossi prepared several preliminary plans which are preserved in drawings (Spagnesi, pls 98–105). These proceed from a circular church to a rectangle with rounded corners and finally to a simple rectangle with side chapels – a plan which minimized the number of houses that had to be demolished to clear the site. The façade was added by Giuseppe Valadier in 1806.

The vault of the nave was frescoed in 1687–92 by Filippo Gherardi (Coli, his usual collaborator, died in 1681), the subject being the *Triumph of the name of Mary* (W; Gloton, pl. LVI; Poensgen, fig. 33).

On the entrance wall, monument to Aurora Berti (d.1720) by L. Merlini (Enggass, *Sculpture*, p. 122).
High Altar: Begun in 1748 by Nicola Salvi but left hardly begun at the time of his death. Vanvitelli was asked to complete it and eventually in 1762 sent from Naples a design for the sarcophagus under the *mensa* (De Fusco and others, *Luigi Vanvitelli*, Naples, 1973, p. 76 and fig. 193). The bas-relief was inserted in the 19th century.

S. Paolo fuori le Mura

The great Early Christian basilica, founded by Constantine, was destroyed by fire in 1823, only the apse and transepts being saved. In the left transept, next to the apse, is the Cappella del Coro, which is attributed in all the guide-books and many text-books to Maderno, but Hibbard (*Maderno*, p. 208) has shown that it dates from the early 18th century.

S. Paolo Primo Eremita
Via A. de Pretis

Bibliography: De'Rossi, 1727, p. 694; Titi, 1763, pp. 65, 70; Vasi, *Magnificenze*, pl. 122; Vasi, 1777, p. 138; M. Vasi, 1814, p. 183; Ladislao Toth, 'Contributi alla storia di S. Paolo I Eremita', *Atti del II° Congresso Nazionale di Studi Romani*, 1931, II, p. 371; F. A. Salvagnini, *I Pittori Borgognoni*, Rome, 1936, p. 159; A. Schiavo, *Capitolium*, XXXVI, 1961, 3, p. 8; Buchowiecki, III, p. 531.

The house was given by Alexander VII to a body of Polish and Hungarian hermits in 1667. The church, which was begun in the following year, was replaced by the existing one designed by Clemente Orlandi in 1767–8. When the Pauline Order was abolished Pius VI gave the house and church to a conservatory for girls, but later the church was deconsecrated and given to the University of Rome. It contained a statue of *St Paul* by Bergondi and a painting by

Guglielmo Cortese of two guardian angels, but these were removed in 1883 and sold.

The façade consists of a narrow, slightly concave bay between tall pilasters, betweeen which is a flattened version of Bernini's portico of S. Andrea al Quirinale.

S. Paolo alla Regola
Via S. Paolino alla Regola

Bibliography: Titi, 1686, p. 435 and 1763, p. 100; Vasi, *Magnificenze*, pl. 131; Roisecco, 1750, I, p. 592; P. G. Parisi, *S. Paolo alla Regola*, Rome, 1931; Buchowiecki, III, p. 534; Elling, pl. 34; *Guide Rionali*, VII, 1, p. 32.

The church belongs to the Tertiary Franciscans of Sicily. Titi states in 1686 that the church was being rebuilt to the designs of Padre Giovanni Battista Bergonzoni (or Borgonzoni or Borgognone), a Bolognese Franciscan. The façade was designed by Giacomo Ciolli and executed by Giuseppe Sardi; it was finished in 1721.

INTERIOR

1 to R: (Rosalia): Altarpiece: attributed to M. Rossi, *Virgin and Three Female Saints;* on right wall: Biagio Puccini, *St Erasmus* (W).
Right transept: M. Rocca, *St Francis* (Voss, p. 624).
2 to R: Altarpiece: G. B. Lenardi, *St Francis.*
3 to R: On wall: Puccini, *S. Bonaventura* (1708; W); bronze crucifix, attributed to Francesco Mochi. This attribution is unconvincing, but the crucifix is an impressive work of that period.
Apse: L. Garzi, *Scenes from the life of St Paul* (W).
3 to L: On wall: Puccini, *Madonna with St Clare* (W).
Left transept: G. Calandrucci, *Holy Family with St Anne;* frescoes by Monosilio (1747; W).
1 to L: Altarpiece: Calandrucci, *Vision of St Anthony* (W); on walls: G. Diol, scenes from the *Life of St Anthony.*

S. Paolo alle Tre Fontane
Via Laurentina

Bibliography: Baglione, p. 81; Totti, p. 118; Titi, 1686, p. 55.

Three churches were erected on the site of St Paul's execution to mark the founts which sprang up when his decapitated head bounced on the gound. That of SS. Vincenzo e Anastasio has retained its mediaeval aspect but that of S. Paolo was rebuilt by Cardinal Pietro Aldobrandini in 1600. The third church, the dedication of which, Scala Coeli, records the vision seen here by St Bernard of souls walking up a ladder to Heaven, was rebuilt in 1582 by Cardinal Alessandro Farnese. Baglione and Titi attribute the two latter churches to Giacomo della Porta.

S. Pasquale Baylon (SS. Quaranta Martiri)
Via di S. Francesco a Ripa

Bibliography: Vasi, *Magnificenze*, pl. 160; Portoghesi, *Roma Barocca*, pls 343, 345; Mallory, *Rococo*, p. 61; G. Cannizzaro, *La Chiesa dei SS. Quaranta Martiri e di S. Pasquale Baylon*, Rome, 1977; Elling, pl. 58.

The site was given to the Spanish Padri Minori Osservanti Scalzi in 1736, but the church was not built till 1744–7 to the designs of G. Sardi, who also constructed the attached monastery. The façade is unusual in having a parapet running over the pediment (cf. S. Maria della Neve), a device which may ultimately go back to Maderno's S. Susanna and Soria's S. Maria della Vittoria.

INTERIOR

The interior is one of the liveliest in Roman architecture of the mid-18th century, and is unusual in the breaking of the main entablature by the insertion of oval *coretti.*
Vault fresco: M. Panaria, *Glory of S. Pietro d'Alcantara.*
1 to R: G. Sorbi, *S. Diego.*
2 to R: L. Krahe, *S. Pietro d'Alcantara.*
3 to R: S. Monosilio, *S. Pasquale Baylon.*
Right of High Altar: M. Panaria, *S. Giovanni di Prado.*
High Altar: L. Tosi, *SS. Quaranta* (1747; Mallory, *Notizie*, p. 110).
2 to L: G. Sorbi, *St Francis.*
1 to L: F. Preciado de la Vega, *Holy Family.*

S. Pietro in Montorio
On the Janiculum

Bibliography: Falda, *Nuovo teatro*, III, pl. 31; Magni, I, pl. 96; B. Pesci, E. Lavagnino (Chiese di Roma, 23); *Guide Rionali*, XIII, 1, p. 124.

The mediaeval church was given to the Franciscans by Sixtus IV in 1472 and was rebuilt in the last decades of the 15th century with the help of Ferdinand and Isabella of Spain, possibly to the designs of Baccio Pontelli. It has always remained under the protection of the Spanish sovereigns. Bramante built the circular Tempietto which stands in the cloister on the supposed spot where St Peter was crucified. It was finished in 1502 and Bramante intended it to be enclosed in a circular cloister. The lower chapel was restored in 1736, but the stuccoes appear to date from about 1600.

INTERIOR

1 to R: Sebastiano del Piombo, *Flagellation* based on a design by Michelangelo (1516–24); in the half-dome of the apse *Transfiguration* by the same.
2 to R: Altarpiece: N. Pomarancio, *Madonna della Lettera.*
3 to R: Frescoes by Michelangelo Cerruti.
Over 2 and 3 to R: School of Pinturicchio, *The Theological Virtues* and *Four Sibyls.*
Right transept: *Cappella del Monte* (S. Paolo): Designed by Vasari, sculpture by Bartolomeo Ammanati; altarpiece: Vasari, *Conversion of St Paul*; tombs of two del Monte cardinals, uncles of Julius III, who commissioned the chapel; over the tombs are niches with allegorical figures of *Religion* and *Justice.*
High Altar: Originally contained Raphael's *Transfiguration*, now in the Vatican. The apse now contains a copy of the *Crucifixion of St Peter* by Guido Reni.
Left transept: *Cappella Ricci* (S. Giovanni Battista): Commissioned by Cardinal Giovanni Battista Ricci who built and decorated the Palazzo Sacchetti in via Giulia. The architecture is an almost exact copy of the del Monte chapel in the right transept. The whole scheme was directed by Daniele da Volterra who painted the altarpiece of the *Baptism* and provided designs for the statues of Sts Peter and Paul in the niches over the tombs, which may have been executed by Leonardo Sormani, called Leonardo Milanese.
4 to L: *Cappella della Pietà:* Built in 1615–20, with fine stuccoes in the dome; altarpiece: D. van Baburen, *Deposition*; on walls and lunettes, paintings by David de Haan (Nicolson, pp. 18, 56). There does not seem to be any evidence for the attribution of the chapel to Maderno which has been proposed.
2 to L: *Cappella Raimondi* (St Francis) (De' Rossi, *Altari*, pls 8, 9; Lavagnino, *Altari*, p. 77; Lavin, *Bernini*, p. 22). Built by Bernini, probably between 1638 and 1648 (Wittkower, *Bernini*, p. 213). Over the altar a high relief of *St Francis in Ecstasy*, one of the first examples of Bernini's use of concealed lighting. On the right wall is the tomb of Monsignor Girolamo Raimondi (d.1628) and on the left that of Monsignor Francesco (d.1638). In both cases the deceased is shown alive and praying in the niche above but also as a corpse in the sarcophagus, a device common in northern Europe in the late Middle Ages but extremely rare in Italy, particularly in the 17th century. The tombs and the sculptures were all designed by Bernini, but were executed by members of his studio. The reliefs on the sarcophagi by Niccolò Sale are of particularly fine quality. One represents the dead rising at the Last Judgment; the other shows three scenes of which only one, *Confirmation*, is clearly identifiable, the second being a burial and the third a Bacchic dance based on Poussin's *Bacchanal in front of a Herm of Pan* in the National Gallery, London. On the vault, fresco of *St Francis* by Romanelli surrounded by grisailles by Abbatini (W).
1 to L: Giovanni de'Vecchi, *St Francis.*

S. Pietro in Vaticano

Bibliography: the literature on St Peter's is so vast that only the books and articles relevant to the Baroque period can be mentioned here. For the history of the church before this period the most convenient summary is to be found in Heydenreich and Lotz, *Architecture in Italy 1400–1600*, Pelican History of Art, London, 1974, pp. 157, 173, 198, 254, 270. For a fuller account see F. Wolff-Metternich, *Die Entstehung der Peterskirche zu Rom im 16. Jahrhundert*, Vienna-Munich, 1972. For the visitor to the church the three volumes by C. Galassi-Paluzzi in the *Chiese di Roma* series (74, 76, 77) are still the most convenient guide, but see also Buchowiecki, I, p. 103. For the main documents dating from the Baroque period, see Pollak, II. Of the old books illustrated with engravings dealing with the architecture – and to some extent with the tombs and paintings in St Peter's – the most useful are the following: Domenico Fontana, *Della Trasportatione dell'Obelisco Vaticano*, Rome, 1590; Martino Ferrabosco, *Architettura della Basilica di S. Pietro in Vaticano*, Rome, 1684; Carlo Fontana, *Templum Vaticanum*, Rome 1694; Filippo Bonanni, *Numismata Summorum Pontificum*, Rome, 1696; De Brosses, II, p. 157. For the description of individual works of art see also Agostino Taja, *Descrizione del Palazzo Vaticano*, Rome, 1750; Giovanni Pietro Chattard, *Nuova Descrizione del Vaticano*, Rome, 1762–7 and Erasmo Pistolesi, *Il Vaticano descritto*, Rome, 1829. For plates see Magni, I, pls 105–35.

Books and articles dealing with the contribution of the various artists concerned with the building and decoration of the church will be quoted in the text below.

The history of the church before the Baroque period may be summarized briefly as follows. In 1506 Julius II laid the foundation stone for a church to replace the old Constantinian Basilica on the design of Bramante in the form of a Greek cross. From the beginning there were proposals to build the church on a Latin-cross plan on the grounds that it was more suitable liturgically, and that it would more completely

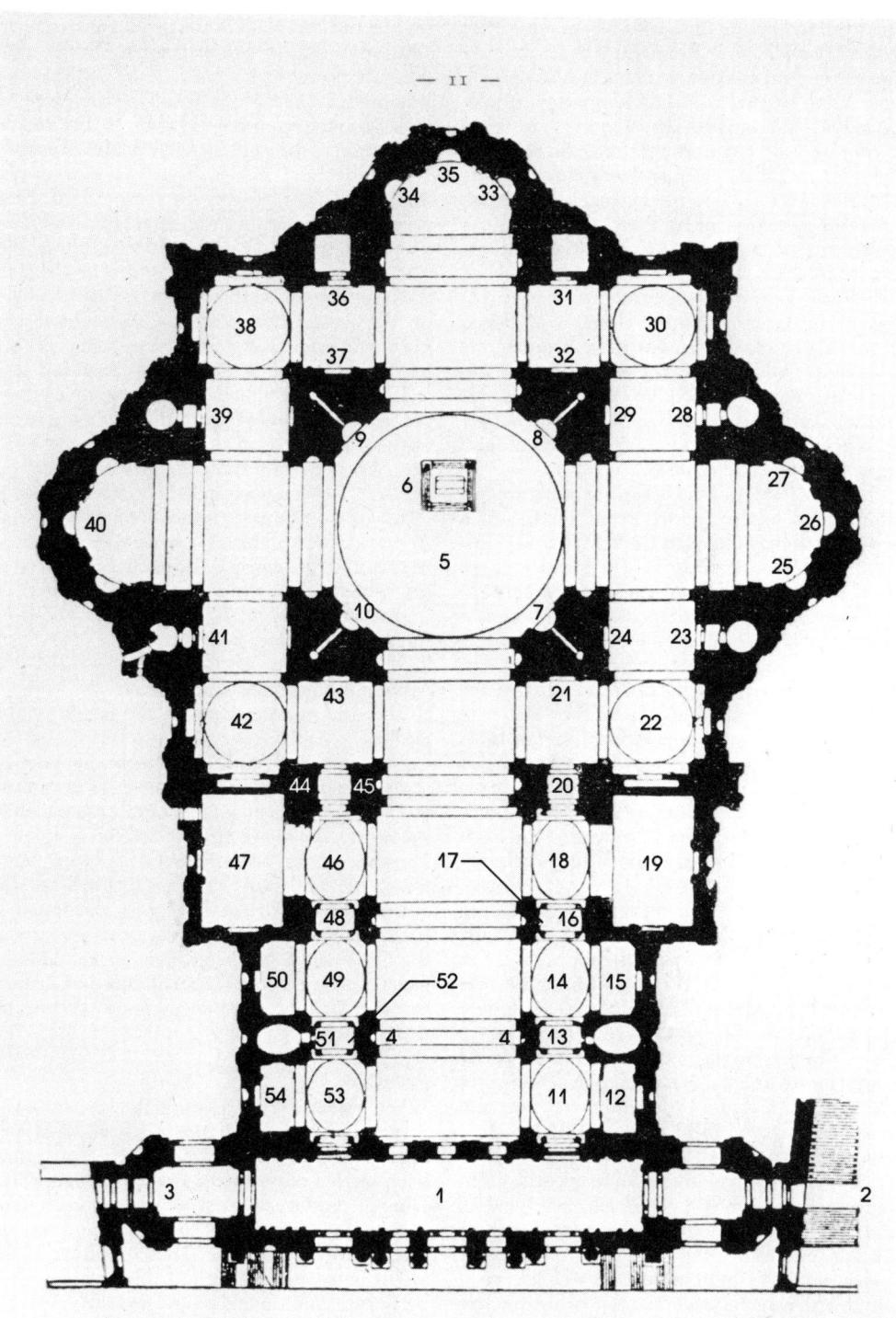

48. St Peter's. Plan.

incorporate the site of the old basilica, but they were rejected. After Bramante's death in 1514 the church was continued under the direction of various architects, including Raphael, who produced several variants on Bramante's original centralized plan. Antonio da Sangallo prepared a model on a different plan but almost nothing of this was carried out. Michelangelo, who took over the direction of St Peter's on Sangallo's death in 1546, made radical alterations in Bramante's design, but retained the Greek cross. Three arms of the cross were completed according to his plans, and the dome was begun according to his design, but there is much dispute about whether in its existing form it follows the outline which he projected or one modified after his death by Giacomo della Porta, who completed the building of the dome and built the two small domes.

In 1605 Paul V, after long and acrimonious discussions, finally decided to add a nave which was built to the designs of Carlo Maderno (Hibbard, *Maderno*, pp. 65, 155). The addition of the nave finally sacrificed Michelangelo's conception of a great dome supported by a compact Greek cross church, closely related to it in its proportions, and meant that from nearby the dome is almost completely obscured by the façade of the church. This was built by Maderno and the existing structure was finished in 1614. It does not however represent Maderno's complete intention. He planned to have two towers and in order that they should not obscure the small domes he extended the front by two bays beyond the width of the church itself. In the event the towers were never built, because when in 1640 Bernini begun to construct the one on the left it was realized that the foundations were too weak to support it. On the death of Urban VIII in 1644 this failure was exploited by Bernini's enemies – including Borromini – and Bernini was removed from his post. The present aedicules with clocks were a compromise erected by Giuseppe Valadier in the first years of the 19th century (Brauer and Wittkower, p. 37, and Fagiolo Dell'Arco, *Bernini*, Cat. No. 84).

The visitor is strongly urged to take the lift to the roof where he will get an excellent view of the main and subsidiary domes, as well as a fine distant prospect of the city.

See plate 48, the numbers on which correspond with those given in the following descriptions.

Portico [1] (Hibbard, *Maderno*, pp. 160ff.): Begun by Maderno in 1608; the vault was constructed 1611; stucco decoration by G. B. Ricci begun 1618. In its general form, with five doors leading into the church, the portico provides an allusion to that of Old St Peter's. On the right the Porta Santa with a putto in the pediment by Borromini. The bronze doors in the centre by Filarete come from the old church. The stucco decoration of the vault includes figures of canonized popes and scenes from the *Acts of the Apostles*. The relief over the central door, *Feed my Sheep*, by Bernini, was originally (1646) set up over the door on the inside of the church, but was moved to its present position in 1649. In theme it echoes Ambrogio Buonvicino's relief on the façade representing *Christ giving the keys to St Peter*, and the theme of papal authority deriving from St Peter was continued in a statue of *St Peter* which Maderno removed from the old church and set up at the point where the portico impinged on the entrance to the Vatican. When Bernini built the new entrance and the Scala Regia it was replaced by the equestrian statue of Constantine (set up 1669; Wittkower, *Bernini*, p. 251). This [2] can now be seen from the portico through glass doors. It is balanced at the other end of the portico by the statue of Charlemagne [3] by A. Cornacchini (1730–5; Enggass, *Sculpture*, p. 260).

What remains of Giotto's fresco of the *Navicella (St Peter walking on the waters)* is over the middle door on the inside of the façade.

The Benediction Loggia over the portico (only accessible from the Vatican) was vaulted in 1612. It now contains Maratta's cartoons for the mosaics in the interior of St Peter's. In 1619 Lanfranco was commissioned by Paul V to fresco the vault and walls but this project was abandoned by Urban VIII who decorated it with stuccoes (Lanfranco's cartoons are now in the Quirinal; E. Schleier, 'Les Projets de Lanfranc pour le décor de la Sala Regia du Quirinal et pour la loge des Bénédictions', *Revue de l'Art*, 7, 1970, p. 40).

INTERIOR

When Maderno came to build the nave the basic decoration of the structure had been fixed owing to the fact that Bramante's coffering had been carried out over the first bays in the three arms of the Greek cross which had been constructed by him and his successors and this set the pattern for the nave. The decoration of the arches between the nave and aisles was designed by Bernini and carried out by an army of assistants from 1645 onwards for Innocent X with portraits of the popes from St Peter to Benedict I. In the spandrels are allegorical figures of Christian virtues (begun 1599–1600, completed 1647–9; Enggass, 'New attributions in St

Peter's: the spandrel figures in the nave', *Art Bulletin*, LX, 1978, p. 96), and over the middle arch are the arms of Innocent X supported by Fame (Wittkower, *Bernini*, p. 216). The piers were decorated by Clement XI after the designs of Carlo Fontana (Braham and Hager, p. 217). In the niches between the pilasters are statues of founders of the monastic Orders, begun in 1706 but still being executed in the 20th century. Some are listed by Enggass (*Sculpture*, pp. 139, 181, 182, 186, 191, 203). The tombs of the popes are engraved in De' Rossi, *Architettura Civile*, II, pls 29–34.

Against the first piers of the nave [4] are holy water-stoups of colossal size (1722–5) by G. Lironi, F. Moderati, G. B. de' Rossi and A. Cornacchini (Magni, I, pl. 119; Enggass, *Sculpture*, p. 202).

Crossing [5]: When Paul V died in 1621 the crossing still had a provisional altar over the supposed tomb of St Peter, but the *Confessio*, or chapel under the altar, designed by Maderno, was complete (1615–17). The crossing itself was decorated by Bernini on the orders of Urban VIII. The scheme involved the construction of a Baldacchino over the grave of St Peter, and the decoration of the four piers (Lavin, *Bernini*, p. 19).

Baldacchino [6]: Designed by Bernini and executed 1624–33 (Wittkower, *Bernini*, p. 189). For the iconography see H. Kauffmann, 'Berninis Tabernakel', *Münchner Jahrbuch*, VI, 1955, p. 222. For the complicated question of the origin of the design and the share of Borromini in it see I. Lavin, *Bernini and the Crossing of St Peter's*, New York, 1968, H. Thelen, *Die Enstehungsgeschichte der Hochaltararchitektur von St Peter in Rom*, Berlin, 1967, and W. Chandler Kirwin, 'Bernini's Baldacchino Reconsidered', *Römisches Jahrbuch*, XIX, 1981, p. 141. Kirwin's important discoveries about the actual methods by which the Baldacchino was constructed will be published in the Acts of the Bernini Congress held in Rome in January 1981.

Crossing piers: In the niches designed by Bernini stand statues connected with the four principal relics: the Veil of St Veronica (statue [9] of the saint by Francesco Mochi, 1629–32); fragment of the Holy Cross found by St Helena (statue [8] by Andrea Bolgi, 1630–9); the Spear of St Longinus (statue [7] by Bernini, 1630–9); and the Head of St Andrew (statue [10] by François Duquesnoy, 1629–40). The relics themselves are now preserved in the Loggia over St Veronica.

Above the niches are four galleries designed by Bernini incorporating symbols of the four relics and eight of the Salomonic columns from the screens surrounding the High Altar in the old church (see below, under **Sacristy**).

The Baldacchino and the decoration of the piers are the first manifestations of Bernini's

49. *St Peter's. Engraving by Falda showing Bernini's planned third wing to close the piazza. In the distance on the right the Nicchione di Belvedere.*

genius as a decorator and as a *metteur-en-scène*. In the Baldacchino he solved the problem of constructing an altar which would not be dwarfed by Bramante's colossal order of pilasters by making his columns of dark bronze and giving them the twisted form of the columns which had stood in front of the altar in Old St Peter's and were traditionally believed to have come from the Temple of Jerusalem. In the galleries in the four piers he incorporated eight of these columns and made a crucial innovation by setting the angels bearing the relics against a background of coloured marble inlay which imitates a yellow sunset sky with purple clouds, the colours of which are echoed in the gilt of the half-domes over the reliefs and the purple marble of the balustrade. This is one of the first examples of the Baroque fusion of the arts, architecture blending with sculpture and using the means proper to painting such as colour and the naturalistic rendering of clouds against a sunset sky.

In the late 17th and early 18th centuries all the painted altarpieces, which had suffered badly from damp, were removed and replaced by mosaic copies. The originals are now in the Vatican Gallery and S. Maria degli Angeli.

RIGHT AISLE

1st bay [11]: Mosaic of St Peter over the Holy Door after a design by Ciro Ferri (1675); vault mosaics (*Mysteries of the Cross, Sibyls,* and *Prophets*) after designs by Pietro da Cortona (before 1669; cupola) and Ferri (1669–71).

1st chapel [12]: Originally *Cappella del Crocifisso* but called *Cappella della Pietà* since Michelangelo's *Pietà* was placed there. The door on the right is by Bernini. In it the artist developed the theme of inverted curved half-pediments which was first used by Buontalenti in the Porta delle Suppliche in the Uffizi. Frescoes by Giovanni Lanfranco of the *Triumph of the Cross* and scenes from the Passion (1629–32).

1st pier L [13]: Monument to Queen Christina of Sweden (d.1689), erected 1696–1702, designed by Carlo Fontana (Braham and Hager, p. 56); relief of *The Queen abjuring Protestantism* by J. B. Théodon (Enggass, *Sculpture*, p. 68).

2nd bay [14]: Dome and lunette: mosaics of Old Testament martyrs after designs of Cortona.

2nd chapel [15]: *Cappella di S. Sebastiano* (70): Mosaic after Domenichino's *St Sebastian*.

2nd pier R [16]: Tomb of Innocent XII. Innocent was first buried in a simple tomb designed by Carlo Fontana which stood between the first and second chapels on the right aisle (Braham and Hager, p. 51), but in 1746 it was decided to give him a grander monument and the present tomb, designed by Fuga, was set up (Matthiae, *Fuga*, p. 53). The statues of *Charity* and *Justice* are by Filippo della Valle.

2nd pier L [17]: Monument to Countess Matilda commissioned by Urban VIII as a tribute to the great supporter of the temporal power of the papacy. Designed by Bernini and executed by members of his studio (1633–7; Wittkower, *Bernini*, p. 201). The relief on the sarcophagus shows the Emperor Henry IV kneeling before Gregory VII at Canossa.

3rd bay [18]: Mosaics of subjects referring to the Eucharist after Cortona (Briganti, *Cortona*, p. 252).

3rd chapel [19]: *Cappella del SS. Sacramento*: Grille and doors designed by Borromini (1626; Hempel, *Borromini*, p. 11). The artist has introduced one curious detail: hung over the corners of the pedestals supporting the grille on either side of the actual doors are a rosary and a necklace with a little oval medal, worked in the bronze in a highly naturalistic manner (Maurizio Fagiolo, 'L'Attività di Borromini da Paolo V a Urbano VIII', *Studi sul Borromini*, II, pl. 8, and Scarfone, 'Ex-voto Borrominiano (?) nella Basilica di S. Pietro in Vaticano', *Strenna dei Romanisti*, XXXVIII, 1977, p. 372). The significance of these details is not clear; but Professor Kirwin has discovered similar features on the base of the Baldacchino.

Fresco over the altar, the *Holy Trinity*, by Cortona (1628–31; Briganti, *Cortona*, p. 187). Ciborium and angels by Bernini (1673–4) for Clement X (De'Rossi, *Architettura Civile*, II, pls 27, 28; Wittkower, *Bernini*, p. 260 and K. Noehles, 'Zu Cortonas Dreifaltigskeitgemälde', *Römisches Jahrbuch*, XV, 1975, p. 169). The stuccoes on the vault are attributed by Donati (*Artisti ticinesi*, p. 341 and figs 303, 304) to Giovanni Casolano and Simone Daria.

On right wall mosaic copy of Domenichino's *Ecstasy of St Francis*, flanked by two more of the Salomonic columns said to come from the Temple of Jerusalem.

3rd pier R [20]: Monument to Gregory XIII, commissioned by Cardinal Giacomo Buoncampagni and erected 1715–21 to replace an earlier tomb by Prospero Antichi (known from a drawing, reproduced by Noehles, *SS. Luca e Martina*, p. 81) of which the volutes were incorporated in the new monument. The programme was provided by a Theatine father, Alessandro Salarolo. Figures of *Religion* and *Magnificence*: relief of the *Reform of the Calendar by Gregory*. The general design was given by Camillo Rusconi, though the relief was probably designed by Bernardino Cametti and certainly executed by Carlo Francesco Mellone (Enggass, *Sculpture*, p. 102; F. den Broeder, 'Early Eighteenth-Century Sculpture in Rome', *Burlington Magazine*, CXX, 1978, p. 542).

Ambulatory [21]: Mosaic after Domenichino's *Mass of St Gregory*.

Cappella Gregoriana [22]: Decorated under Gregory XIII; a fine example of the early use of coloured marbles. Dome mosaics after Girolamo Muziano.

Passage to transept: right [23]: Tomb of Benedict XIV (11) by P. Bracci and assistants (1759; Gradara, *Bracci*, p. 72); statues of *Wisdom* and *Disinterestedness* (a rarely represented virtue).

Left pier [24]: Mosaic of *St Basil* after Subleyras.

Right transept: Mosaic altarpieces: *St Wenceslas* [25] (Caroselli), *Sts Processus and Martinianus* [26] (Valentin), *St Erasmus* [27] (Poussin, 1627–8).

Passage to Cappella di S. Michele: right: Tomb of Clement XIII [28] (by Canova, 1784–92); **left:** Mosaic of *St Peter walking on the Water* [29] (after Lanfranco, 1625).

Cappella di S. Michele [30]: Mosaics of saints in cupola after Sacchi (1631), Pellegrini (1636–7) and Romanelli; altarpieces: mosaics after Reni's *St Michael* and Guercino's *S. Petronilla*.

Passage to the Tribuna (apse) [31]: Tomb of Clement X [31] by Mattia de'Rossi; unveiled 1686 (Cartari-Febei). The sculpture is by Ercole Ferrata, Giuseppe Mazzuoli, and Lazzaro Morelli. The relief shows the opening of the Porta Santa for the Holy Year of 1675 (Ferrari, *La Tomba*, pl. CLXIV). Opposite [32]: mosaic of *Peter raising Tabitha* after Placido Costanzi (1757).

Tribuna (apse): Tomb of Urban VIII [33] by Bernini (1627–47) (Wittkower, *Bernini*, p. 198; Fagiolo dell'Arco, *Bernini*, No. 63).

In 1627 Urban VIII decided to move the tomb of Paul III [34] by G. della Porta, which stood in the Cappella Gregoriana and to set up his own tomb to balance – and excel – it.

The monument to Urban VIII is Bernini's first major tomb (the earlier ones were simply busts in niches) and it shows his inventiveness in *concetti*, use of materials, and dramatic treatment of gestures and draperies. The commanding figure of the pope is in dark bronze, partly gilt, as are the sarcophagus, the figure of Death emerging from it, and the tablet on which he writes the name of the pope. The allegorical figures of *Charity* and *Justice* are in white marble. Originally the left breast of *Charity* was uncovered, but stucco drapery was added, probably in the very end of the 17th century. It is shown in its original state in an engraving in Filippo Bonanni (pl. 35). This tomb was the model which was to be imitated with variations for almost all the papal tombs in St Peter's till it was replaced by Canova with a neo-classical type in the tomb of Clement XIII (see above).

50. *St Peter's. Etching by Israël Silvestre, showing the basilica before the construction of Bernini's colonnade and with the one tower partly built to his design but pulled down under Innocent X.*

The Cathedral Petri [35]: Designed by Bernini and executed 1657–66 on the order of Alexander VII as a setting for the wooden throne believed to have been the Chair of St Peter (now shown in the Museo Storico, see below) and as the climax to the progression from the nave, through the Baldacchino to the altar in the apse of the church.

The 'Chair' is supported by colossal figures in partly gilt bronze, representing four of the Fathers of the Church – Sts Ambrose, Augustine, Athanasius and John Chrysostom. Above the chair is an oval window of golden yellow glass with the dove of the Holy Spirit at its centre, surrounded by a gilded stucco setting of rays and putti. On the chair itself is a relief illustrating Christ's words to St Peter 'Feed my sheep'. The whole structure is therefore a dramatic testimony to the continuity of the Catholic church based on the charge to St Peter, continued by the tradition of the Fathers and guided by the Holy Ghost.

Passage to the Cappella della Colonna: right: Tomb of Alexander VIII [36], designed by Angelo de'Rossi and executed with the help of assistants (1700–25); allegorical figures of *Religion* and *Prudence*; relief of the canonization of five saints (Enggass, *Sculpture*, p. 164; F. den Broeder, 'Early 18th century sculpture in Rome', *Burlington Magazine*, CXX, 1978, p. 542); opposite: mosaic of *Peter healing a lame man* after Francesco Mancini [37].

Cappella della Colonna or **di S. Leo** [38]: Mosaics in vault representing symbols of the *Virgin* and *Saints* after Andrea Sacchi (1631–2) and Giovanni Francesco Romanelli (1643–4; W); relief of *The Encounter of Leo the Great and Attila* by Algardi (1646–50; Heimbürger Ravalli, *Algardi*, p. 146). The stucco life-size *modello* for the relief is on the staircase of the Oratorio di S. Filippo Neri.

Passage to transept: right: Tomb of Alexander VII [39], by Bernini, executed 1671–8 (Wittkower, *Bernini*, p. 254); allegorical figures of *Justice* and *Prudence* behind and *Charity* and *Truth* in front, executed by members of Bernini's studio (for details see Wittkower, loc. cit.). The tomb is a variant of Bernini's earlier monument to Cardinal Pimentel with the pope kneeling instead of sitting. It is exceptional among Roman tombs in being constructed over a door (leading actually to a passage out of the church), a pattern familiar in Venice which Bernini had adopted in an unexecuted design for a tomb for the Doge Giovanni Cornaro, father of Cardinal Cornaro who commissioned the Cornaro chapel in S. Maria della Vittoria (Blunt, 'Two drawings for Sepulchral Monuments by Bernini', *Essays in the History of Art presented to Rudolf Wittkower*, London, 1967, p. 230).

Left transept: Altarpiece (left) with mosaic after Guido Reni's *Crucifixion of St Peter* [40].

Sacristy [41]: Built by Carlo Marchionni for Pius VI (1776–84) after previous projects had been abandoned (H. Hager, *Filippo Juvarra e il concorso di modelli del 1715 . . . per la nuova Sacrestia di S. Pietro*, Rome, 1970; J. Gaus, *Carlo Marchionni*, Graz, 1967, p. 67).

Attached to the Sacristy is the Museo Storico which contains not only important Early Christian ivories and Antonio Pollaiuolo's tomb of Sixtus IV but the life-size plaster model for one of Bernini's angels in the Cappella del SS. Sacramento, and much 17th- and 18th-century altar plate.

Cappella Clementina [42]: Decorated under Clement VIII; altarpiece: mosaic after Sacchi's *Miracle of St Gregory* (1625–7) and Raphael's *Transfiguration* [43].

Passage to left aisle: right [44]: Monument to Leo XI designed by Algardi (1634–50; Heimbürger Ravalli, *Algardi*, pp. 82, 144); figures of *Liberality* and *Majesty*; left [45]: monument to Innocent XI, designed by Maratta (finished 1701); figures of *Religion* and *Justice* and bas-relief of the *Liberation of Vienna from the Turks* by Monnot (Enggass, *Sculpture*, p. 83).

3rd bay [46]: Mosaics of prophets after designs by Ciro Ferri (1681), Maratta (1700–4) and Marcantonio Franceschini. The cartoons by the last are in the Palazzo della Cancelleria (F. R. Di Federico, 'The Mosaic decoration in the Chapel of the Choir in St Peter's', *Storia dell'Arte*, 32, 1978, p. 71).

3rd chapel: *Cappella del Coro* [47]: Grille by Borromini (1626; Hempel, *Borromini*, p. 11); decorated in 1622; the stuccoes are ascribed to G. B. Ricci.

Between 3 and 2 to L: Antonio and Piero Pollaiuolo, Tomb of Innocent VIII [48].

2nd bay [49]: Mosaics after Maratta on the theme 'Deposuit Superbos' (He hath put down the mighty from their seat; 1677–1708).

2nd chapel: *Cappella della Presentazione* [50]: Altarpiece: mosaic after Romanelli, *Presentation of the Virgin*.

Passage to 1st chapel: right: Tomb of Maria Clementina Sobieska (1739), wife of the Old Pretender [51], designed by F. Barigioni; sculpture by Pietro Bracci (Gradara, *Bracci*, p. 45); left: Tomb of the last Stuarts by Canova [52].

1st bay [53]: Mosaics of scenes of *Baptism* and the four continents after designs of Trevisani (1710–45).

1st chapel: *Baptistery* [54]: The font designed by C. Fontana and executed 1692–9 (for drawings at Windsor cf. Braham and Hager, p. 39); on walls mosaics of three scenes of Baptism: *Baptism of Christ* (after Maratta, 1696–8); *St Peter baptizing Sts Processus and Martinianus* (after G. Passeri, 1709–11), and *St Peter Baptizing the Centurion Cornelius* (after A. Procaccini, 1710; W).

The crypt of the church (*Grotte Vaticane*) is open to visitors (entrance under the statue of *St Longinus* [7] in one of the crossing piers) but it contains little of interest to the student of the Baroque.

The Piazza

Bibliography: C. Thoenes, 'Studien zur Geschichte des Peterplatzes', *Zeitschrift für Kunstgeschichte*, XXVI, 1963, p. 97; D'Onofrio, *Acque e Fontane*, p. 316; *Obelischi*, p. 11. For Bernini's schemes see Brauer and Wittkower, p. 64; Wittkower, 'The Third Arm of Bernini's Piazza S. Pietro', *Italian Baroque*, pp. 53, 61; T. Kitao, *Circle and Oval in the Square of St Peter's*, New York, 1973 (see also reviews of his book by H. W. Kruft in *Kunstchronik*, 28, 1975, p. 270; G. Bauer in *Art Bulletin*, LIX, 1977, p. 641; and C. Thoenes in *Zeitschrift für Kunstgeschichte*, XL, 1977, p. 324); A. G. Marino, 'Il Colonnato di Piazza San Pietro: dell'architettura obliqua di Caramuel al "classicismo" berniniano', *Palladio*, XXIII, 1973, p. 81; T. Thieme, 'La Geometria di Piazza San Pietro', ibid., p. 129; H. W. Kruft, 'The Origin of the Oval in Bernini's Piazza S. Pietro', *Burlington Magazine*, CXXI, 1979, p. 796.

In the Middle Ages before the Vatican became the regular residence of the popes the area between St Peter's and the Tiber which was enclosed within the walls of Leo IV (847–55) was sparsely inhabited and the only ancient road was one which ran from the Mausoleum of Hadrian (the Castel S. Angelo) and passed just south of the basilica. By the end of the 15th century two straight roads – the Borgo Vecchio and the Borgo Nuovo – had been laid out (the latter by Alexander VI who also built the corridor along the top of the Leonine wall to form a direct link between the Vatican and Castel S. Angelo), and Nicholas V (1447–55) began to systematize the approach to the church by building the Benediction Loggia, but the area below the broad flights of steps was completely irregular. The main approach to the Vatican was through a clock tower built by Martino Ferrabosco for Paul V (1616–17).

In 1656 Alexander VII announced his intention of developing the whole area in front of St Peter's and Bernini was asked to supply designs. The site was awkwardly restricted by the Vatican buildings to the north, the corridor running down to Ferrabosco's clock-tower and various palaces and ecclesiastical buildings on the periphery of the area. In addition the piazza had to be designed so that the pope could be visible to as many people as possible when he gave the blessing either from the Benediction Loggia of St Peter's or from his apartment in the block added by Sixtus V to the Vatican. Finally, the colonnade had to provide a covered way for processions, particularly that on the Feast of Corpus Christi. A further complication was the presence of the obelisk set up by Domenico Fontana for Sixtus V in 1585–6, and a fountain built by Maderno (1613).

Bernini's first plan is not preserved but from descriptions it appears to have been composed of a trapezium, based on building a wing to correspond with the corridor to the clocktower but the lines of these wings were to be extended to the edge of the Borgo. This plan was rapidly changed for one in which the area in front of the church was made into a square, in front of which were planned two semi-circular arcades, with a straight *terzo braccio* between their ends (a drawing for this scheme is published by Kitao, fig. 15). This scheme was developed in 1657 with arcades articulated by single pilasters, but this design was soon changed in favour of one with colonnades. This change was probably made because, since the outer circumference of the covered way was larger than the inner, the outer arches would have to be wider than the inner and would therefore have to be made either taller or depressed. In the earlier versions of the colonnade scheme the columns were coupled and dispersed uniformly round the whole curve; they were then replaced by single columns, and a cross-axis was established by introducing a projecting frontispiece in the middle of each arc.

From an early stage the oval design was referred to as a 'teatro' and it was clearly meant to reflect the shape of a Roman amphitheatre. Various medals struck during this phase of the design show the oval, with the *terzo braccio* straight at first but curved in the later versions. Maderno's fountain was moved to its present position and a second one added to balance it. In the final design the colonnade takes the form of an oval, as distinct from the earlier shape which consisted of two semicircles linked up by a rectangular area.

This oval is drawn according to the method laid down by Serlio (Book I). This was based on two circles, the circumference of each passing through the centre of the other. The ends of the oval were formed by arcs of these circles and the middle section by circles drawn with their centres at the points of intersection of the two main circles (Borromini used the same construction at S. Carlo alle Quattro Fontane). (Kitao appears to be wrong in saying that 17th-century architects knew how to construct the true ellipse and his diagram of the 'string-method' of drawing such a figure (pl. 52) has no basis – as he implies – in Serlio.) The particular form of oval used by Bernini and Borromini is specially praised by Serlio for its *dolcezza* and was described by the geometers of the time as *ovato perfetto* (G. Pomodoro, *Geometria Prattica*, Rome, 1599, pl. XXVIII).

In the first (arcaded) schemes the wings were to contain first one and then two 'aisles', but in the final scheme there are three, of which the middle one is wider than the others to accommodate the processions.

In the final project of 1667 Bernini intended to set the *terzio braccio* back to the east of the line of the main colonnade, so that it would have formed a sort of propylaeum. Carlo Fontana, in an unexecuted project, planned to remove the *terzio braccio* still further east, and may therefore have to take the blame for instigating the plan which led to the destruction of the buildings along the *spina* of the Borgo and the opening up under Mussolini of the via della Conciliazione.

At an early stage in the development of the scheme for the Piazza criticisms were made of Bernini's designs and a counter-proposal was put forward (Wittkower, *Italian Baroque*, p. 61).

Bernini was influenced in his design for the oval colonnade by ancient models, particularly Dupérac's reconstruction of the area round the Vatican (cf. Kruft). For the covered way round the Piazza he may also have thought of the Aviary of Marcus Varro as shown restored in an engraving in J. Lauri's *Antiquae Urbis Splendor* (1621), but he no doubt also had in mind the fact that the ancient road leading past St Peter's was a covered way.

The statues on the oval part of the colonnade were planned by Bernini who in some cases made drawings for them but they were executed by various members of his studio (A. Haus, *Der Petersplatz in Rom und sein Statuenschmuck* (Dissertation, Freiburg im Breisgau, 1979); for a brief account see Fagiolo dell'Arco, *Bernini*, No. 166; some individual statues are mentioned by Enggass, *Sculpture*, pp. 70, 154, 177, 180, 205; they are listed by Buchowiecki, I, p. 132).

S. Pietro in Vincoli
Piazza S. Pietro in Vincoli

Bibliography: G. Matthiae (Chiese di Roma, 54); *Guide Rionali*, I, 2, p. 80.

The origin of the church goes back to the 4th century. The columns of the arcade re-used from a Roman temple are of green marble and date from the 1st century AD, but the interior was transformed – not very happily – by Francesco Fontana (1705) who constructed the depressed ceiling in the centre of which is a fresco by G. B. Parodi of the *Miracle of the Chains* (those of St Peter which are preserved in the church). The portico in the façade dates from 1471–83 and the upper storey was added in 1570–8.

INTERIOR
Right aisle: Monument to Cardinal Lanfranco Margotti (d.1611). This monument has frequently been ascribed to Domenichino, but the attribution is due to a confusion in the early guide-books and biographies of the artist. Further on is the monument to Cardinal Girolamo Agucchi (d.1605), erected by his brother Monsignor Giovanni Battista Agucchi, author of an important treatise on painting. The monument was designed by Domenichino who painted the portrait of the dead man above the inscription and actually carved the two rams' heads himself (Martinelli, p. 166).
1 to R: Attributed to Guercino, *St Augustine*.
Right transept: Tomb of Julius II by Michelangelo.
Left aisle: Monument to Mariano Vecchiarelli (d.1639) with yellow marble skeletons, designed by Pietro Vecchiarelli and executed by two Neapolitan sculptors (Titi, 1686, p. 216).

Monument to Cardinal Cinzio Aldobrandini (d.1610) erected 1705 by C. Bizzacheri (Mallory, *Bizzacheri*, pp. 35, 45; id., *Rococo*, p. 41; 'The Cardinal Cinzio Aldobrandini tomb in S. Pietro in Vincoli', *Antologia di Belle Arti*, 7/8, 1978, p. 323).
Antesacristy: Domenichino, *Liberation of St Peter* (1604; Borea, *Domenichino*, p. 159).

SS. Pietro e Marcellino. See SS. Marcellino e Pietro
Via Mentana

S. Prassede
Via S. Prassede

Bibliography: B. M. Apolloni Ghetti (Chiese di Roma, 66); *Guide Rionali,* I, 2, p. 56.

The church, built in the 9th century and famous for its mediaeval mosaics, contains some Baroque works of interest. On the walls of the nave frescoes of scenes from the Passion by B. Croce, G. Balducci, G. Massei and P. Nogari (1594–1600).
1 to R: (Rosario): Right wall: G. D. Piastrini, *B. Tesauro Beccaria* (W); left wall: Angelo Soccorsi, *S. Pietro Igneo (Aldobrandini)* (c.1717).
2 to R: Frescoes on walls by Guglielmo Cortese; right: *Sts Joachim and Anna*; left: *Adoration of the Kings*; on vault: *God the Father and four Saints.* Lunettes by Ciro Ferri (before 1659; W).
Last pier to left in right aisle: Bust of Bishop G. B. Santoni (d.1593) by Bernini (erected by his nephew between 1613 and 1616; Wittkower, *Bernini,* p. 173; D'Onofrio, *Roma vista,* p. 114). The heads in the decorative reliefs are also by Bernini.
Apse: *SS. Prassede and Pudenziana* by Domenico Muratori (1735; W); High Altar: commissioned by Cardinal Pico della Mirandola in 1730; architecture: Francesco Ferrari; four angels by Giuseppe Rusconi (Enggass, *Sculpture,* p. 208).

Against the walls of the choir are eight ancient columns of an unusual type with bands of lotus-leaves, which probably inspired Philibert de l'Orme to invent his banded columns for the 'French order', and were imitated by Borromini in the columns leading to the staircase at the Oratory.
Sacristy: A. Ciampelli, *S. Giovanni Gualberti*; Guglielmo Cortese, *S. Giovanni Gualberti*; attributed to Giulio Romano, *The Flagellation,* showing the column preserved in the Cappella di S. Zeno (**3 to R**).
3 to L: *Cappella Olgiati:* By Martino Longhi the Elder (Martinelli, p. 166); frescoes by the Cavaliere d'Arpino (Gloton, pl. L; Poensgen, fig. 24).
2 to L: E. Parrocel, *S. Carlo Borromeo during the Plague at Milan;* walls: L. Stern, *S. Carlo in meditation* and *in ecstasy.*
1 to L: Altarpiece: A. Severoni, *St Peter* (1717); wall frescoes by the same artist: right: *Sts Emerentia and Agnes*; left: *St John the Baptist.*

S. Prisca
Via S. Prisca

Bibliography: Titi, 1686, p. 60; Buchowiecki, III, p. 629.

A church stood on this site since the late 5th or early 6th century. It was restored for the Holy Year of 1600 by Cardinal Benedetto Giustiniani who added the fine brick façade dated 1600, to the design of Carlo Lambardi. The church was restored in the 1930s and later.
INTERIOR
Sacristy: Detached fresco: Odazzi, *Immaculata.*
Apse: Probably decorated between 1719 and 1734.
High Altar: D. Cresti, *St Peter baptizing S. Prisca.*

S. Pudenziana
Via Urbana

Bibliography: R. U. Montini (Chiese di Roma, 50).

An Early Christian church which is chiefly famous for its apse mosaic (4th-5th century). It also contains, however, important works of later periods.
2 to R: *Chapel of the Madonna della Misericordia:* On the walls *Birth of the Virgin* and *Birth of Christ*; vault: the *Virgin in Glory* by Lazzaro Baldi (1690; W).
3 to R: *Chapel of S. Bernardo:* On the walls *St Catherine of Siena* and *St Benedict* by Michele Cippitelli (c.1700).
Passage to Sacristy: L. Gimignani, *Assumption.*
Choir: Oval dome with frescoes of *Christ surrounded by the Heavenly Host* by Niccolò Circignani, called Il Pomarancio (Gloton, pl. XI). High Altar: *Glory of Sta Pudenziana* by Bernardino Nocchi, painted in 1803, a remarkable example of how late the full Baroque still survived in Rome.
To left of High Altar: *Chapel of St Peter: The Giving of the Keys* by G. B. della Porta.
1 to L: *Cappella Caetani* (De'Rossi, *Altari,* pls 36, 37; Magni, I, pl. 10; A. C. Beccarini, 'La Cappella Caetani nella Basilica di S. Pudenziana in Roma', *Quaderni,* XXII, 1976, p. 143): Begun 1590 by Francesco da Volterra and finished after his death by Maderno in 1601 (Hibbard, *Maderno,* p. 127). The splendid marbling –

mainly in dull green and yellow – is by G. B. della Porta and Valsoldo; the dome has fine stuccoes enclosing mosaics after the designs of Federico Zuccaro. Altar: relief of the *Adoration of the Kings* by P. P. Olivieri and C. Mariani (begun before 1599). Right wall: tomb of Filippo, duca Caetani (d.1614); figures of *Fortitude* by G. A. Mari and *Temperance* by C. Malavista; left wall: tomb of Cardinal Enrico Caetani, figures of *Prudence* by 'Adamo Lorenese' (presumably Adam Claude Brefort) and *Justice* by a pupil of Domenico Guidi.

SS. Quaranta Martiri. See S. Pasquale Baylon
Via di S. Francesco a Ripa

SS. Quattro Coronati
Via dei SS. Quattro Coronati

Bibliography: R. M. Apollonj Ghetti (Chiese di Roma, 81).

Founded in the 4th century and frequently enlarged and rebuilt, the last time by Paschal II in 1111. Restored in 1914 and now containing no works of the Baroque period except the apse frescoes by Giovanni da San Giovanni representing the *SS. Quattro Coronati* (Sts Severus, Severianus, Carpophorus and Victorius) in the glory of heaven (1630).

SS. Quirico e Giulitta
Via Tor de' Conti

Bibliography: Architettura minora, II, p. 89; M. Bosi (Chiese di Roma, 60); Rotili, *Raguzzini*, p. 105; Mallory, *Rococo*, p. 126.

A small but ancient church restored on the orders of Benedict XIII probably by Filippo Raguzzini between 1728 and 1733. The façade incorporates a 15th-century door. The convent was built by Valvassori in 1750–3 (to whom Rotili also ascribes the building of the church).

The door at 31 via S. Maria ai Monti appears to be by Valvassori and was apparently the main entrance to the convent.

Re Magi. See Miscellaneous, Collegio di Propaganda Fide
Via di Propaganda Fide

S. Rita da Cascia (also called S. Biagio in Campitelli)
Via Montanara

Bibliography: Falda, *Nuovo teatro*, I, pl. 11; De' Rossi, *Architettura Civile*, III, pl. 44; Coudenhove-Erthal, p. 21; H. Hager, 'Due opere giovanili di Carlo Fontana', *Commentari*, XXIII, 1972, p. 263; Elling, pl. 54; *Guide Rionali*, X, 1, p. 66.

The church was originally built at the foot of the Aracoeli Steps, but was pulled down in the clearance round Piazza Aracoeli in 1928 and re-erected on its present site in 1940. In the process it lost most of its interior decoration. For its appearance before it was moved see *Capitolium*, XL, 1965, pl. 78, after p. 214.

The church was built by 1653. The architect is unknown (Hager has suggested that it may be Felice della Greca, but he was only born c.1626). The most interesting feature of the church is the façade, added by Carlo Fontana, to whom the whole church is usually, but wrongly, ascribed (he was only born in 1638). The lower part of the façade has a door, and niches with false perspective soffits (cf. the top loggia at Palazzo Barberini) and the upper storey breaks back in concave bays in a highly original manner (cf. Bernini's design for the Cornaro tomb, Wittkower, *Bernini*, p. 216). The exact date at which the façade was built is uncertain, but it must be before 1667 since it has the *monti* of Alexander VII and it must have been at least designed before 1665 since it appears in plate 11 of Falda's *Nuovo teatro*, published that year, though one must bear in mind the fact that engravers often showed incomplete buildings as if they were finished.

S. Rocco
Via di Ripetta

Bibliography: Mola, p. 113; L. Salerno, G. Spagnesi, *La Chiesa di S. Rocco all'Augusteo*, Rome, 1962; Spagnesi, *G. A. De Rossi*, p. 36.

The church was built in 1500–2 for the Confraternity of S. Rocco, founded in 1499. It was dedicated to St Martin and had its entrance at the east end. To it was attached a hospital administered by the Confraternity. The church was rebuilt between 1645 and 1680. During the first year the work was conducted by Pietro Maraldi and another unidentified architect who may have been Girolamo Rainaldi (Mola), but they do not seem to have achieved much, and the church is really the creation of G. A. de' Rossi, who took over in 1646. The alignment of the church was reversed so that the façade came

51. S. Rita da Cascia. Engraving by Falda, showing the church in its original position below the steps leading up to S. Maria d'Aracoeli. To the right are the steps leading up to the Capitol.

above the Porto di Ripetta. The façade was added by Giuseppe Valadier in 1834. The interior was extensively restored in 1852, when the nave vault was frescoed and the sham marbling added.

INTERIOR
In the aisles de'Rossi has copied the depressed arches used by Maderno in the aisles of St Peter's, a detail typical of his non-Baroque tendencies.

To right of Choir: *Cappella delle Grazie* (1655–7): Traditionally ascribed to Niccolò Menghini but in fact by G. A. de'Rossi. The rich marbling may be part of a later restoration carried out in 1722. The dome of the chapel has an unusual oval form, with flattened sides and ends, used also by de'Rossi in S. Maria in Campomarzio. Monument to Angelo Parracciani, who completed the decoration of the chapel in 1683. Dome: fresco of the *Assumption* by G. A. Carosi (1657).
High Altar: Designed by G. A. de'Rossi, executed by Gioseppe Giorgetti (1673; Montagu,

Giorgetti, p. 292); altarpiece: Brandi, *St Roch received into Heaven* (W).
Sacristy: Built 1651 by G. A. de'Rossi; altar: Baciccio, *Virgin and Child with Sts Roch and Anthony Abbot* (1663–6; Enggass, *Baciccio*, pp. 15, 47); vault: Cozza, *Madonna appearing to St Roch* (W); Antonio Amorosi, *S. Francesco di Paola*.
3 to L: in dome: F. Rosa, *Scenes from the life of St Anthony of Padua* (1663, W); altarpiece: G. Preti, *St Anthony*.
See plate 105.

SS. Rufina e Seconda
Piazza S. Rufina

Bibliography: Armellini, pp. 850, 1426.
A church has stood on this site since very early times. It was restored in 1602 but was recently stripped back to its original state. It contains the tomb of Bianca Maria Nerli (d.1697).

S. Sabina
Via S. Sabina

Bibliography: F. Darcy (Chiese di Roma, 63–4).

Built in the 5th century, the interior was decorated by Domenico Fontana in 1587 but these later additions were removed in the present century and the church was restored to what remained of its original form. It contains, however, some 17th- and 18th-century paintings and monuments.
Apse fresco: Taddeo Zuccaro, *Christ in Glory*.
Right aisle (near entrance): Tombs of Cardinal Alessandro Bichi (d.1657) and his brother Celio (d.1657).
Cappella di S. Giacinto: Altar: L. Fontana, *St Hyacinth*; on walls: Federico Zuccaro and assistants, frescoes of scenes from the life of St Hyacinth (1600).
Left aisle: *Cappella Elci* (S. Caterina): Tomb of Princess Eleonora Borghese by G. B. Contini and A. Fucigna (Hager, 'Il monumento alla Principessa Eleonora Borghese', *Commentari*, XX, 1969, p. 110). Wall and dome frescoes: scenes from the life of *St Catherine* by Odazzi (W; Gloton, pl. XXXI). Altarpiece: Sassoferrato, *Marriage of St Catherine* (W; 1643), one of his most beautiful works, though too small in scale for this setting into which it was inserted to replace a painting by Morandi (see below).

Within the convent are two chapels, one in the cell occupied by St Dominic, the other in that of Pius V when a monk in the monastery.

The chapel of St Dominic was attributed to Borromini in the 1765 edition of Roisecco's guide (p. 256) and Hempel (*Borromini*, p. 185) hesitantly accepts the attribution, though he points out that the marble wall decoration with Ionic pilasters is quite unlike Borromini's style. He also says that according to the inscription in the chapel the decoration was finished in 1669, that is to say, two years after Borromini's death. Actually it says it was *executed (aptari et exornari fecit)* in that year, and being a very small work, it is unlikely to have taken longer than one year. Moreover in the last years of his life Borromini was so ill that he was hardly in a state to undertake even a small job such as this. The stucco decoration on the vault has many features in common with Borromini's late style, particularly the rosettes and bands of oak-leaves, and the most likely solution seems to be that it was executed by the architect's nephew, Bernardo Castello, on the basis of drawings by his uncle.

The chapel of Pius V was decorated in 1710 with very elaborate stucco work, including naturalistic garlands of flowers and fruit which recall those on the vault of S. Maria dell'Orto. The altarpiece of St Pius V is by D. Muratori.

In the museum in the convent is the *Madonna del Rosario* by G. M. Morandi, originally the altarpiece of the Cappella Elci.

Oratory of the SS. Sacramento. See S. Maria in Via (Oratory of)
Piazza Poli

S. Salvatore in Campo
Piazza S. Salvatore in Campo

Bibliography: Totti, p. 211; Martinelli, p. 170; Titi, 1721, p. 116; Roisecco, 1745, I, p. 344; Pollak, I, p. 193; Elling, pl. 77.

Rebuilt in 1639 by Francesco Peparelli for Cardinal Francesco Barberini.

The church does not apparently contain any works of art of interest.

S. Salvatore delle Coppelle
Via delle Coppelle

Bibliography: Mallory, *Rococo*, p. 140; L. Lotti, *San Salvatore alle Coppelle*, Rome, 1976.

Now the church of the Rumanian Catholic community.

The rebuilding of the church, which took place in 1738–9, is attributed in the early guides to Carlo De Dominicis. The façade is of unexpectedly classical simplicity for him.

INTERIOR
Completely altered in the 19th century.
Left aisle: Tomb of Cardinal Giorgio Spinola (d.1739) signed by Bernardino Ludovisi and dated 1744.

S. Salvatore in Lauro
Piazza S. Salvatore in Lauro

Bibliography: Totti, p. 251; Baglione, p. 99; Titi, 1763, p. 407; *Architettura minora*, I, pl. 86; Wasserman, *Mascarino*, p. 191; E. Fanano (Chiese di Roma, 52); *Guide Rionali*, V, 1, p. 62.

The old church, which belonged to the Celestine Canons regular of S. Giorgio in Alga, Venice, was burnt in 1591. Rebuilding began immediately and two 17th-century writers, Totti (1638), and Baglione (1642), attribute the new church to Mascarino, though Totti in the 'Emendationi e aggiunte' writes: 'il disegno è del Padre Massimano', and in the 1652 edition the name of Mascarino is discarded altogether. The attribution to Mascarino in fact seems very insecure. First there are no drawings for the church among the vast number which he bequeathed to the Accademia di S. Luca and which cover almost every building with which he was connected. Secondly the nave, with its bold coupled columns – single shafts of travertine – reminiscent of Palladio, is quite unlike his dry and timid style. In fact on entering the church one has the impression of being in Venice rather than Rome, and it seems likely that a design for the church was sent from the parent house, presumably by a follower of Palladio.

In the first building campaign only the nave was built. When the Celestines were suppressed in 1668 the church was handed over to the Marchigian community in Rome. At the end of the 17th century plans were made for completing the building and in 1727 the transepts and choir were added by Lodovico Rusconi Sassi. The interior was much altered by restoration in 1792 and 1861 when the present façade was built.

INTERIOR

1 to R: *Paroni*: Architecture by Carlo Bizzacheri (c.1694; Mallory, *Bizzacheri*, pp. 31, 45; id., *Rococo*, p. 38); putti by Camillo Rusconi (Enggass, *Sculpture*, p. 96); paintings by Giuseppe Ghezzi: altar: *Pietà*; side walls: *S. Giacomo della Marca, S. Nicola da Tolentino* (W).
2 to R: Alessandro Turchi, *Madonna with Saints*. The tombs of the marchese Girolamo Pallavicini Montoro (d.1645) and Monsignor Giovanni Castellani (d.1646) were set up many decades after their deaths and are ascribed in the *Guida Rionale* – though on what evidence is not clear – to Mario Asprucci.
3 to R: Cortona, *Adoration of the Shepherds* (1628–30; Briganti, *Cortona*, p. 183).
High Altar: Originally designed by L. R. Sassi with a painting by Giovanni Peruzzini which was removed in 1792 (now in the Sacristy) when the existing *Glory* by Vincenzo Pacetti was added. The putti over the pediment, by Pietro Paolo Campi (Enggass, *Sculpture*, p. 181), belong to the original altar; on either side (in transepts) tombs of Cardinals Simonetti and Marefoschi, designed by Girolamo Teodoli with sculpture by Carlo Monaldi (1756; Mallory, *Notizie*, p. 173).
4 to L: *Tiracoda*: Altarpiece: A. Massarotti, *St Lutgard*.
1 to L: Altarpiece: A. Grammatica, *Freeing of St Peter*.
Sacristy: Borgianni, *Lamentation over the dead Christ* (fresco; Nicolson, p. 25).

To the left of the church is a late 15th-century cloister.

S. Salvatore ai Monti
Via Madonna dei Monti

Bibliography: Totti, p. 476; Vasi, *Magnificenze*, pl. 169; Vasi, 1791, p. 344; Buchowiecki, III, p. 830.

A small church, next to the conventual buildings of S. Maria ai Monti. Façade dated 1762. The interior is not apparently of interest.

S. Salvatore in Onda
Via Pettinari

Bibliography: Salerno, *Via Giulia*, p. 505

A small church recorded since the early 12th century. At some date before 1684 a project was put forward by G. Tommasini to rebuild the church nearer the Tiber and so make a worthy end to the via Giulia (the plan and elevation are reproduced in Salerno). The scheme was not carried out, and the church retains much of its mediaeval character, in spite of a restoration dating from 1864.

S. Sebastiano fuori le Mura
Via Latina

Bibliography: Mola, p. 76; Martinelli, p. 26; A. Ferrana (Chiese di Roma, 99).

Built by Constantine over a famous catacomb which was believed to have contained the bodies of St Peter and St Paul. The church also covered the tomb of St Sebastian. From 1431 onwards it was served by the Cistercians. In 1609 Cardinal Scipione Borghese began a complete remodelling of the church on the designs of Flaminio Ponzio. According to Martinelli he built the church as far as the cornice and at his death in 1613 it was completed by Vasanzio. The façade, however, which is dated 1612, is by Ponzio.
4 to R: *Cappella Albani* (S. Fabiano): Built by Clement XI (Albani) between 1706 and 1712 to the designs of Carlo Fontana: over the altar, statue of *S. Fabiano* by Pietro Papaleo (Enggass, *Sculpture*, p. 76); fresco on right wall by Giuseppe Passeri, *St Sylvester baptizing Constantine* (W); left wall, P. L. Ghezzi, *S. Fabiano and the Emperor Philip*.
1 to L: *St Sebastian*: Commissioned in 1672 by Cardinal Francesco Barberini and designed by Ciro Ferri; statue of the dead Saint by Giuseppe Giorgetti (Montagu, *Giorgetti*, p. 287).

52. *S. Sebastiano fuori le Mura.* Etching by Piranesi.

S. Sebastiano al Palatino
Via di S. Bonaventura

Bibliography: Pollak, I, p. 193; L. Gigli (Chiese di Roma, 128); Gigli, p. 119.

A church stood on this site from very early times and played an important part in the 10th-12th centuries owing to its dependence on the Frangipani family (frescoes of the late 10th century survive in the apse). It was restored by Luigi Arigucci in 1630 on the orders of Cardinal Francesco Barberini and the first Mass was said in January 1631.
Choir: Frescoes by B. Gagliardi, *St Sebastian, God the Father* and four *Virtues* (Gloton, pl. LI).
Left wall: A. Camassei, *Martyrdom of St Sebastian* (1633; W).

SS. Sergio e Bacco
Piazza Madonna dei Monti

Bibliography: Buchowiecki, II, p. 328.

A church is recorded on this site since about 800. In 1641 it was given to a body of Basilian monks and was rebuilt in 1741–5 to the design of Francesco Ferrari. The façade was rebuilt in 1880.

The church contains (left wall) an altar by Ignazio Stern.

S. Silvestro in Capite
Piazza S. Silvestro

Bibliography: Vasi, *Magnificenze*, pl. 153; J. S. Gaynor and I. Toesca (Chiese di Roma, 73); Hibbard, *Maderno*, p. 125; I. Lavin, 'Decorazione barocca in S. Silvestro in Capite', *Bollettino d'arte*, XLII, 1957, p. 44.

The church was founded by Paul I in 761 and till 1285 was served by Benedictine monks. In that year it was given to the Clares who served it till it was suppressed in 1871. In 1885 it was handed over to English Pallottini fathers.

Of the mediaeval building only the 12th/13th- century campanile and parts of the outer walls survive, though the forecourt presumably replaced an earlier atrium of the same type. In 1518 Pietro Soderini offered a new altar, the design of which was submitted to Michelangelo, though the existing altar shows none of the characteristics of his style. In 1591 a design for a new church was submitted by Francesco da Volterra and building began two years later. In 1594/5 Volterra died and was succeeded by Maderno, who modified his predecessor's plans, adding a third chapel to each side of the nave and making the transepts narrower, so that Volterra's oval dome had to be elongated. The building was finished in 1596 and consecrated in 1602. The decoration continued till 1604.

In 1680, when Carlo Rainaldi was the architect of the church the nuns decided on a new campaign of decoration. This was continued after Rainaldi's death in 1691 by Mattia de'Rossi, Lodovico Gimignani and Domenico de'Rossi.

In 1680-4 Giacinto Brandi painted the *Assumption* on the vault of the nave (unveiled 1685; Cartari-Febei; Poensgen, fig. 55), and the side chapels were decorated under the direction of Gimignani, the whole work being finished in 1696 (W). The dome over the crossing, which was frescoed by Cristofano Roncalli before 1605, belongs to the early campaign of decoration. Of the statues on the façade *St Silvester* is by Lorenzo Ottoni (between 1702 and 1708; Enggass, *Ottoni*, p. 320), *Pope St Stephen I* by M. Maglia, *St Francis* by V. Felici and *St Clare* by G. Mazzuoli.

INTERIOR

The interior is interesting as a complete decorative scheme dating from the last two decades of the 17th century. The organ was probably designed by C. Rainaldi. Some of the stucco putti are by C. Rusconi (Enggass, *Sculpture*, p. 96), and those over the altars are by Lorenzo Ottoni (1696; Enggass, *Ottoni*, p. 320).

1 to R: *Cappella Tedallini* (St Anthony): Decorated by Giuseppe Chiari.

2 to R: *Cappella Savelli* (San Francesco): Altarpiece, O. Gentileschi, *St Francis* (Nicolson, p. 53); walls and vault frescoed by Luigi Garzi, *Scenes from the life of St Francis* (c.1695; W).

3 to R: *Spirito Santo*: Decorated by Giuseppe Ghezzi: altarpiece *Pentecost*; walls: *John baptizing the People* and the *Baptism of Christ*; lunettes: *St Gregory* and *Pope Paul I* (W).

Right transept: *Cappella Colonna*: Altarpiece,

Baccio Ciarpi, *Madonna with Saints* (c. 1622; W).

Confessio: Constructed in 1906.

Apse: Paintings of *S. Silvestro* and *St Stephen I* (pope) ascribed by Roberto Longhi to Orazio Borgianni.

2 to L: (SS. Giuseppe and Marcello): Decorated by Lodovico Gimignani with scenes from the *Life of the Virgin* (1697).

1 to L: *Cappella Timotei-Salvetti*: Decorated by Francesco Trevisani with scenes from the Passion (C. R. di Federico, 'Trevisani and the decoration of the Crucifixion chapel in S. Silvestro in Capite', *Art Bulletin*, LIII, 1971, p. 52).

S. Silvestro al Quirinale
Via 24 Maggio

Bibliography: Titi, 1674, p. 317; Vasi, *Magnificenze*, VII, p. LV; Buchowiecki, III, p. 866; E. Iezzi, *S. Silvestro al Quirinale*, Rome, 1975.

Founded in the 11th century, the church belonged in the 16th century to Dominican nuns. Vittoria Colonna lived in the convent and it was there that she held her conversations with Michelangelo. In 1555 Pius IV gave the church to the Theatines who rebuilt it (consecrated 1584). The two chapels nearest the façade were cut off in 1877 when the via 24 Maggio was cut through at the present low level, and the existing façade dates from the same time. A drawing in the Ashmolean for a projected façade of the church identified as being by G. A. Dosio after Guglielmo della Porta, probably made in the late 1550s, was published by Carolyn Valone ('Paul IV, Guglielmo della Porta and the rebuilding of S. Silvestro al Quirinale', *Master Drawings*, XV, 1977, p. 243).

INTERIOR

The nave arcade and pilasters are decorated with painted marbling. Wooden ceiling dating from the time of Pius V.

End wall (originally the entrance): Tombs of Cardinal Federico Cornaro by Domenico Fontana, put up by Gregory XIV in 1591 (Donati, *Artisti ticinesi*, fig. 51), and Prospero Farinaci (d.1618), the latter made as an exact pair to the first. Between them a bas-relief of the *Baptism* (19th century).

2 to R: Giacinto Gimignani, *Pius V and Cardinal Alessandrino* (W).

Right transept: Antonio Barbalonga, *Vision of SS. Gaetano and Andrea Avellino*.

Choir: The pilasters are of real marble. The *trompe-l'oeil* frescoes on the vault were begun by Giovanni Alberti (apse over high altar, cf.

Martinelli, p. 172), continued after his death (1601) by his brother Cherubino (d.1615), and completed by Padre Matteo Zaccolini who taught Domenichino perspective and whose writings on the subject Poussin studied (M. D. Abromson, 'Clement VIII's patronage of the Brothers Alberti', *Art Bulletin*, LX, 1978, p. 353). Right wall: B. Betti (a Theatine father), *Christ among the Doctors*; left wall: Lazzaro Baldi, *S. Gaetano of Thiene*.

Monks' Choir: On the end wall: Zaccolini and Giuseppe Agellio, *Constantine sending for St Silvester*. Below, *St Peter* and *St Paul* by Stefano Pozzo. The authors of the other paintings are not known.

Left transept: *Cappella Bandini:* By Mascarino (1579) (Wasserman, *Mascarino*, p. 45); statues of *St John the Evangelist* and *The Magdalen* by Algardi (Heimbürger Ravalli, *Algardi*, p. 66), *St Joseph* and *St Martha* attributed, but without good reason, to Mochi by V. Martinelli ('Contributi alla scultura del Seicento, I, Francesco Mochi a Roma', *Commentari,* II, 1951, p. 224). Tondi in pendentives by Domenichino: *David, Judith, Solomon, Esther* (1628; Borea, *Domenichino*, p. 186). Monuments to Cardinal Ottavio Bandini (d.1629), with bust by G. Finelli, and Pietro Antonio and Cassandra Bandini (d.1588, 1582).

1 to L: Polidoro da Caravaggio, *St Catherine of Siena* and *The Magdalen*, the earliest pure landscapes in Roman art, executed in an imitation of the ancient technique of encaustic painting.

The church contains an interesting series of inlaid marble tomb slabs of the 17th and 18th centuries.

A door in the left transept leads to a terrace, originally the cemetery, with a small oratory dating from the first half of the 18th century.

S. Simeone Profeta (destroyed)

Bibliography: C. Cecchelli, 'Necrologia di S. Simeone profeta', *Urbe*, V, 1940, no. 9, p. 5.

The church stood in the Piazza Lancellotti and was restored about 1610 by Orazio Lancellotti. In the 19th century it was secularized and it was pulled down about 1940.

S. Sisto Vecchio
Via di Porta S. Sebastiano

Bibliography: G. Matthiae, 'Tre chiese all'inizio dell'Appia', *Capitolium*, XLIV, 1969, p. 154; Rotili, *Raguzzini*, p. 40; C. Sterpi et al., *San Sisto Vecchio a Porta Capana*, Rome, 1975; Elling, pls 38, 39a; Mallory, *Notizie*, p. 103.

A church stood on this site since the 4th century, but was several times restored or rebuilt. It was originally basilical in plan but towards the end of the 16th century it was reduced to its present form with a single nave, and the apse and wooden roof were constructed. A further restoration, which gave the church its present appearance, was carried out by F. Raguzzini for Benedict XIII and completed in 1725.

Spirito Santo (destroyed)

Bibliography: Titi, 1686, p. 208; Roisecco, 1750, p. 566; Vasi, *Magnificenze*, pl. 142; Armellini, I, p. 212.

Founded in 1432 for a body of Augustinian nuns and restored in 1582. The façade is shown in Vasi's engraving.

Spirito Santo dei Napoletani
Via Giulia

Bibliography: Mola, p. 120; Titi, 1763, p. 464; Salerno, *Via Giulia*, p. 392; Wasserman, *Mascarino*, p. 71; *Guide Rionali*, VII, 3, p. 24.

An earlier church on the site was presented to the Neapolitan colony by Gregory XIII in 1574. Ottaviano Mascarino made a number of elaborate plans for the church, some based on an oval with an arcade of coupled columns, but the church was ultimately built on a simple rectangular plan, possibly but not certainly by Mascarino. In about 1649 the façade was built by the Neapolitan architect Cosimo Fanzago (Rossi, 1727, p. 259; Braham and Hager, p. 71; R. Bösel, 'Cosimo Fanzago a Roma', *Prospettiva*, 15, 1978, p. 29) but this was replaced by the existing façade in the mid-19th century.

INTERIOR
Remodelled by C. Fontana in 1666–8 and again in 1702–8 (Braham and Hager, p. 71). The dome was frescoed by G. Passeri (much damaged; W). The church was completely restored in the mid-19th century.

Right wall: Tomb of Cardinal G. B. de Luca probably designed by Fontana (1690–3) with figures by D. Guidi (Braham and Hager, p. 73). **1 to R:** Bonaventura Lamberti, *S. Francesco di Paola* (Titi, 1763, p. 464).
3 to L: Luca Giordano, *Martyrdom of St Januarius*.
1 to L: D. M. Muratori, *St Thomas Aquinas*, after 1727 (W).

S. Spirito in Sassia
Borgo S. Spirito

Bibliography: E. Lavagnino, *La Chiesa di S. Spirito in Sassia*, Rome, 1962.

The Confraternity of S. Spirito in Sassia was founded in the 12th century mainly to administer a hospital. The hospital was greatly enlarged by Sixtus IV who built the nucleus of the existing structure which was extended in the late 16th century by Ottaviano Mascarino. The church was built between 1538 and 1545 by Antonio da Sangallo the Younger, and the façade was completed by Ottaviano Mascarino during the pontificate of Sixtus V, following Sangallo's design.

INTERIOR
Carved wooden ceiling dating from the 16th century, but restored by Pius IX. In 1582 Jacopo Zucchi was commissioned to fresco the whole church on a programme devised by P. Ignazio Danti, but only a part of the scheme was carried out (Gloton, pl. X; E. Pillsbury, 'Jacopo Zucchi in S. Spirito in Sassia', *Burlington Magazine*, CXVI, 1974, p. 434).

From the point of view of the Baroque two features are of particular interest. First, the second altar right has Salomonic columns which are extremely rare in church architecture till they were introduced by Bernini in the Baldacchino of St Peter's; secondly, Zucchi's frescoes in the apse constitute an unusually bold piece of illusionism, particularly in the use of architecture in the scene of *Pentecost* and in the fact that the action is spread over the two frescoes on the wall and on the half-dome, so that the light emanating from the Holy Ghost in the upper zone flows down into the lower.

The steps to the High Altar were laid in 1749 (Mallory, *Notizie*, p. 111). Ciborium by 'Monsu Lorenzo Tedesco' (Titi, 1763, p. 27; Lavagnino, *Altari*, pp. 41, 163).
Sacristy: Fine wooden cupboards; vault frescoed with scenes connected with the *Holy Spirit* by G. Abbattini (W; Poensgen, fig. 32).

To the left of the church, stretching down to the Tiber, are the buildings of the hospital, begun under Sixtus IV, later enlarged and altered and in the present century in part put back to what was believed to be their original condition.

The main entrance is in the Palazzo del Commendatore, immediately to the left of the church, which was built by Ottaviano Mascarino in the last years of the 16th century (Baglione, p. 99; Martinelli, p. 253; Ferrerio, *Palazzi*, II, pls 56–8).

From a second cloister (to the left) a passage leads to the Quattrocento block containing two large wards between which is an octagonal chapel (visible from the outside) containing a Baldacchino persistently but wrongly ascribed to Palladio. It dates from the late 16th century, but was altered under Clement VIII (reproduced, with the attribution to Palladio, by E. Lavagnino, 'Una novità palladiana', *Bollettino del centro internazionale di studi di Architettura Andrea Palladio*, 1962, p. 52 and figs 14–20). The writer produces no solid evidence for the attribution which is based on 18th-century guide-books.

Beyond this cloister is the museum which contains a pharmacy with 17th-century blue and white maiolica drug jars and a wooden model for one of the wings of the Ospedale degli Incurabili made by Camporesi in 1833 (see S. Giacomo degli Incurabili).

Of the two doors constructed by Bernini (cf. Fagiolo dell'Arco, *Bernini*, No. 193), one was destroyed in the present century and the other, slightly altered, was reconstructed in the via dei Penitenzieri, which runs along the side of the church, leading to the Porta di S. Spirito.

Under Benedict XIII Fuga added a wing and a cemetery with a chapel dedicated to the Madonna del Rosario, but this was destroyed when the 20th-century additions to the hospital were made (Armellini, II, p. 807; Pane, *Fuga*, p. 100; Matthiae, *Fuga*, p. 43).

Oratory of S. Spirito in Sassia. See Oratory of the SS. Annunziata
Lungotevere Vaticano

S. Stanislao dei Polacchi
Via delle Botteghe Oscure

Bibliography: Totti, p. 389; Titi, 1686, p. 159 and 1763, p. 183; G. Marincola-Mauro, 'La Chiesa di S. Stanislao dei Polacchi', *Alma Roma*, XV, 1974, p. 62; Buchowiecki, III, p. 927.

A mediaeval church on this site was granted to the Polish community by Gregory XIII in 1578 and was rebuilt between 1580 and 1582. The present church dates from 1729–35 and is by Francesco Ferrari.

INTERIOR
The vault was frescoed with the *Glory of St Stanislas* by Ermengildo Costantini (1774–7; Poensgen, fig. 50).
1 to R: F. Smigliewicz, *St Casimir* (1765–7).
2 to R: T. Kuntz, *Bishop Stanislas of Cracow*.
High Altar: A. Grammatica, *St Stanislas and St Hyacinth*.
2 to L: S. Czechowicz, *St Hedwiga*.
1 to L: S. Monosilio, *St John Kanty* (1767).

S. Stefano del Cacco
Via S. Stefano del Cacco

Bibliography: Totti, p. 395; Martinelli, p. 177; Titi, 1674, p. 186; *Guide Rionali*, IX, 1, p. 82.

The mediaeval church was restored in 1607 and again in 1725. The façade presumably belongs to the latter campaign.

INTERIOR
Right aisle: Attributed by Vasari to Perino del Vaga, *Pietà*.
Choir: Frescoes by Cristofano Casolani: in the middle, the *Martyrdom of St Stephen*, to the right, *S. Francesca Romana*, to the left, *S. Carlo Borromeo*; the altars have good *scagliola* frontals.
Sacristy: G. Odazzi, *St Nicholas of Bari* and a *Scene of martyrdom* attributed to G. M. Morandi (W).

Stimmate di S. Francesco
Via dei Cestari 21

Bibliography: Mola, p. 122; Titi, 1721, p. 165 and 1763, p. 165; Pascoli, III, p. 534; Vasi, *Magnificenze*, pl. 179; F. Fasolo, 'Il progetto di G. B. Contini per S. Francesco delle Stimmate', *Bollettino del Centro Nazionale di Studi di Storia dell'Architettura*, IV, 1945, p. 13; *Guide Rionali*, IX, 2, p. 98.

An earlier church on the site was given by Clement VIII in 1597 to the Congregation of the Stigmata of St Francis, founded in 1594. The church was rebuilt from 1708 onwards to the designs of G. B. Contini, though the vestibule and façade were added a little later (before 1721) by A. Canevari. The author of the statue of *St Francis* over the door is not known.

INTERIOR
Single nave with side chapels. The corners of the nave are rounded as in Borromini's chapel of the Collegio di Propaganda Fide. Fresco on vault of nave: Garzi, *St Francis in Glory* (c.1720; W; Poensgen, fig. 39).
1 to R: Vault: Odazzi, *Symbols of the Passion* (after 1726); right wall: M. Benefial, *Flagellation* (Voss, p. 642); left wall: D. Muratori, *Crowning with Thorns* (1731; W).
High Altar: Trevisani, *St Francis receiving the Stigmata* (c.1720; W); over it stucco group of angels by Pietro Bracci (Gradara, *Bracci*, p. 82).
3 to L: F. Trevisani, *St Anthony of Padua* (after 1720; W).
1 to L: Brandi, *The Forty Martyrs* (from the old church, before 1663; W).

SS. Sudario dei Piemontesi
Via del Sudario

Bibliography: Titi, 1686, p. 112; U. Vichi, *La Chiesa del SS. Sudario dei Piemontesi di Roma*, Rome, n.d.; Fasolo, *Rainaldi*, p. 193.

The Confraternity of the SS. Sudario, called after the Holy Shroud preserved in Turin, was founded in 1597. The church was begun in 1604 to the design of the Piedmontese architect, Carlo di Castellamonte, and finished in the following year. In 1657 it was decided to enlarge the church and in the next year work was begun under the direction of Carlo Rainaldi. It was however soon suspended and the main remodelling of the church took place between 1682 and 1692 (Rainaldi died in 1691).

INTERIOR
The choir is decorated with Sicilian jasper, the nave with unusually fine *scagliola*. The vault was repainted at the restoration of 1874, but the church retains much of its Baroque character.
High Altar: A. Gherardi, *The Dead Christ with Angels* (1682; W) with a fine stucco group of *God the Father and Angels* over it designed by him but executed by Pietro Mantinovese (T. Pickard, 'Two stucco groups by A. Gherardi', *Antologia di Belle Arti*, 7/8, 1979, p. 216).
Sacristy: Baldi, *Nativity* and *Circumcision* (c.1690; W).
For Sacristan ring bell on door to left of church.

S. Susanna
Via XX Settembre

Bibliography: Falda, *Nuovo teatro*, III, pl. 11; De' Rossi, *Prospectus*, pl. 62; Vasi, *Magnificenze*, pl. 148; Magni, I, pls 17, 18; Pollak, I, p. 265; Hibbard, *Maderno*, pp. 38–43, 110–14.

A church of basilical form stood from a very early date on this site which incorporated the remains of a Roman house, said to be that of Pope Caius (282/3–95/6), uncle of St Susanna, and the scene of her martyrdom. It underwent frequent restorations, including one under Sixtus IV in 1475–7 when the nave arcades were probably removed.

Cardinal Girolamo Rusticucci, who became titular cardinal of the church in 1570, had certain alterations carried out by Domenico Fontana notably in the chapel of St Lawrence (left transept; after 1580), which is frescoed by G. B. Pozzo (d.1589).

In 1586 Sixtus V gave the church to Cistercian nuns, who rebuilt the convent to the design of Francesco da Volterra. In 1589 the parish of S.

53. S. Susanna. Drawing by Israël Silvestre (Witt Collection, Courtauld Institute). On the left S. Susanna, and to the right S. Maria della Vittoria. Between them is a palace which was replaced by one of somewhat fantastic design in the late 19th century, demolished when the present piazza was made in the 1930s, thus bringing the two façades into more abrupt juxtaposition. To the right of S. Maria della Vittoria is the Acqua Felice, erected by Sixtus V, and on the edge of the drawing is visible the door to the vigna of Cardinal du Bellay, which still stands incorporated in later buildings.

Sebastianello was transferred to the church of S. Susanna, since its site was needed for the construction of S. Andrea della Valle. S. Susanna thus became the centre of a new parish in the recently built up area on the top of the Quirinal. A nuns' choir was built behind the apse of the existing church.

In 1593 a complete remodelling of the church was undertaken by Rusticucci. In the first document Domenico Fontana is mentioned as architect with Carlo Maderno, but his name does not appear again, and the existing church is the work of Maderno, though he used the outer shell of the old church.

The chancel was begun in 1593, the stuccoes being by Francesco de'Rossi and his sons. The High Altar was commissioned in 1596 from Matteo da Città di Castello and de'Rossi, with a painting of the martyrdom of the Saint by Tommaso Laureto. The frescoes in the apse and choir, executed in 1595–7, are by Cesare Nebbia and Paris Nogari. The triumphal arch over the choir is dated 1595 and the gilded wooden roof of the nave was erected in 1593–4.

The *confessio* below the choir, which contained the relics of St Susanna, was remodelled in 1595 to include the Cardinal Rusticucci's tomb, an early example of the Counter-Reformation cult of Early Christian martyrs.

The carved and gilded wooden ceiling of the nave was commissioned in 1596. (A drawing for it by Maderno survives.) The two arches spanning the church were removed at the time and the buttresses cut down to their present height, to support the statues of prophets attributed to Giovanni Antonio Paracca, called Valsoldo. The contract for the frescoes of the nave was signed by the Bolognese Baldassare Croce in 1598. They represent scenes from the life of the Old Testament Susanna.

The contract for the façade was signed in 1597 and it was finished in 1603. The statues represent *Sts Susanna* and *Felicita* (attributed to Valsoldo) and *Caius* and his brother *Gabinus* (attributed to Stefano Maderno).

The façade marks an important step towards the Baroque type of façade. Though the walls are all in parallel planes the architect has contrived a strong emphasis on the central bay by the movement forward of the wall, the increase in the plasticity of the order (pilaster to half column to full column) and the increasing richness of the sculpture.

The foundation stone of the conventual buildings was laid by Cardinal Francesco Barberini in 1638 (Pollak, I, p. 206).

S. Teodoro al Palatino
Via di S. Teodoro

Bibliography: Braham and Hager, p. 79

A circular church founded not later than the mid-6th century but rebuilt under Nicholas V. Restored for Clement XI (1702–4) by C. Fontana, who planned drastic alterations which were however forbidden by the pope who was anxious to preserve as much as possible of the earlier building. The church was again restored in the 1720s and 1780s when the altars were rebuilt, and Fontana's work was further modified in two 19th-century restorations (1825, 1851).

S. Tommaso di Canterbury. See Miscellaneous, Collegio Inglese
Via Monserrato

S. Tommaso in Formis
Behind S. Maria in Domnica

Bibliography: P. P. Antonio dell'Assunta and Romano di S. Teresa, *S. Tommaso in Formis*, Isola dei Liri, 1927.

A small mediaeval church attached to a hospital, rebuilt in 1663 on the orders of Alexander VII. It contains two stucco altars of that period.

S. Tommaso in Parione
Via di Parione

Bibliography: Totti, p. 229; Titi, 1674, p. 137 and 1763, p. 129; De'Rossi, 1697, p. 240; Vasi, *Magnificenze*, pl. 110; Roisecco, 1750, II, p. 9; M. Lumbroso and A. Martini, 'Due chiese romane dedicate a S. Tommaso', *Fede e Arte*, IX, 1961, p. 428; Elling, pl. 19; *Guide Rionali*, VI, 1, p. 21.

Consecrated in 1139 but rebuilt in 1581. De' Rossi ascribes the rebuilding to Francesco da Volterra, and later writers repeat this attribution. It belonged to the Confraternity of public scribes. It has a simple 17th-century façade and is apparently of little interest internally.

1 to L: G. Passeri, *Immaculata* (before 1686; W).

If closed, apply to the sacristy of S. Maria in Vallicella.

SS. Trinità dei Monti
Piazza Trinità dei Monti

Bibliography: Falda, *Nuovo teatro*, III, pl. 18; C. Salerno, *Piazza di Spagna*, Rome, 1967; *Chiesa e convento della SS. Trinità dei Monti in Roma*, Rome, 1968; Bousquet, *Recherches*, p. 127.

Founded by Charles VIII, King of France, for the Order of Minims created by S. Francesco di Paola. The church and convent were begun in 1502 in a French Gothic style (still visible in the vault over the crossing). The façade of the church was mainly built in 1570 (the date on the tower), but the door and the towers were not finished till 1587. The whole is traditionally ascribed to Giacomo della Porta, but the attribution is not supported by documentary evidence. The steps were added by D. Fontana for Sixtus V.

INTERIOR

The chapels were mainly decorated in the mid-16th century. The most important are the following:

1 to R: *Altoviti:* Scenes from the life of *St John the Baptist*.

3 to R: *Della Rovere:* Daniele da Volterra and assistants, *Assumption, Presentation* and *Massacre of the Innocents*.

4 to R: *Cappella Orsini:* Paris Nogari, frescoes of scenes from the Passion; tomb of Cardinal Rodolfo Pio da Carpi (1568) by Leonardo Sormani; tomb of Cecilia Orsini (1585).

7 to R: *Cappella Châteauvilliers:* Decorated for Cardinal Châteauvilliers, French ambassador to Leo X. Frescoes by an unknown Sicilian artist: on vault, *Sibyls and prophets*; on walls scenes from the life of *St Gregory the Great*.

High Altar: The two angels are by Jean de Champaigne (1676) but the rest of his sculpture has been removed (De' Rossi, *Architettura Civile*, III, pl. 52).

Sacristy and Antesacristy: Built by B. Breccioli (1617–22); in the latter, stucco decoration with the arms of France and Navarre, apparently late 17th century.

8 to L: F. Zuccaro, *Coronation of the Virgin*.

7 to L: *Cappella Pucci:* Frescoes begun for Cardinal Pucci by Perino del Vaga in 1523 (*Visitation, Isaiah* and *Daniel*), but left unfinished. In 1563 Giacomo Caucho, bishop of Corfù, commissioned Taddeo Zuccaro to complete the work, but he died when he had only painted the *Death of the Virgin* and *God the Father supporting the dead Christ*. In 1589 Federico Zuccaro completed the *Assumption* which had been begun by Taddeo, and painted the lunette of *Augustus and the Sibyl*.
2 to L: Daniele da Volterra, *Deposition*.
Convent: *Parlatorio:* Quadratura ceiling, early 17th century.
Refectory: Frescoed by A. Pozzo (1694; B. Kerber, *Andrea Pozzo*, Berlin and New York, 1971, p. 75).
Cloister: Astronomical table by E. Maignan (1637).
Corridor: Anamorphic frescoes – i.e. designs in steep perspective – by J. F. Nicéron representing *St John on Patmos* and *St Francesco di Paola as a hermit*.

A room in the upper part of the convent was decorated by Clérisseau for Thomas Lesueur, a scientifically minded Father, with an illusionist effect of ruins and landscape.
See plates 106–8.

SS. Trinità dei Pellegrini
Piazza dei Pellegrini

Bibliography: Titi, 1674, pp. 121, 414 and 1763, p. 103; Roisecco, 1745, I, p. 305; Vasi, *Magnificenze*, pl. 126; Magni, I, pl. 108; Elling, pl. 35; S. V. Rocca (*Chiese di Roma*, 133); *Guide Rionali*, VII, 1, p. 26; S. Vasco Rocca, 'Alcune note sulla chiesa della SS. Trinità dei Pellegrini in Roma', *Storia dell'Arte*, 38/40, 1980, p. 285.

The mediaeval church of S. Benedetto in Arenula was granted by Paul IV in 1558 to a confraternity which had been founded in 1540 by Filippo Neri and his confessor, Persiano Rosa, to provide lodgings for pilgrims and the sick, and originally met in S. Girolamo della Carità (L. Ponnelle and Louis Bordet, *Saint Philippe Neri*, Paris, 1928, p. 59). The church was rebuilt between 1587 and 1597 to the designs of Martino Longhi the Elder. The façade was not executed at this time, but the projected design is recorded in a drawing by G. P. Maggi, probably based on Longhi's ideas. The new church was consecrated in 1616 and rededicated to the Trinity and St Benedict. At this stage the interior was entirely articulated with pilasters, but in 1690 cracks appeared in the dome and Giovanni Battista Contini added eight travertine columns at the crossing which carried supporting arches. The existing façade, which is a skilful variant of Carlo Fontana's S. Marcello, was added by Francesco de Sanctis in 1722–3. The statues of the four *Evangelists* on it are by Bernardino Ludovisi.

INTERIOR
The church was heavily restored in the years 1847–53 when the columns and pilasters were covered with yellow *scagliola*, and the vault and much of the walls repainted.
Dome: In lantern, fresco of *God the Father* by Guido Reni; in the pendentives the four *Evangelists* by G. B. Ricci (after 1612).
1 to R: *Lucatelli:* Decorated soon after 1630.
3 to R: (S. Giovanni Battista de'Rossi): Frescoes by G. B. Ricci.
Right transept: Altar with marble figures of St Matthew and the angel. The figure of St Matthew was commissioned from J. C. Cobaert in 1587 for the Contarelli chapel in S. Luigi dei Francesi but was rejected when it was submitted in 1602. The angel was added by Pompeo Ferrucci when the group was set up in the Trinità in about 1615. The altar frontal was given in 1731.
Sacristy: Jacopo Zucchi, *The Mass of St Gregory*, and an anonymous painting showing *St Philip Neri caring for pilgrims*.
Choir: Decorated by Antonio de'Battisti. The High Altar, designed by Domenico Pozzi in 1624 but remodelled in the 19th century, contains Guido Reni's painting of the *Holy Trinity* (1625). On either side of the altar are magnificent candlesticks by Orazio Censore (1616).
Left transept: G. B. Ricci, *St Joseph and St Benedict*, incorporating an earlier miraculous image (1613); altar frontal 1731.
3 to L: (St Gregory the Great): B. Croce, *St Gregory freeing souls from Purgatory*.
2 to L: Altarpiece: Cavaliere d'Arpino, *Madonna with Sts Augustine and Francis*; vault and lunette frescoes by B. Croce.
1 to L: Guglielmo Cortese, *Madonna with Sts Charles Borromeo, Dominic Guzman, Philip Neri and Felix of Cantalice* (1677).

To the left of the church (now a shop) is the old refectory of the hospital (of which the remainder was pulled down in 1940), with a series of memorials to popes, and a door above which is a bust of St Philip Neri in a setting designed by Cosimo Fanzago (R. Bösel, 'Cosimo Fanzago a Roma', *Prospettiva*, 15, 1978, p. 29). The setting for the bust of Innocent X was designed by Algardi. Both busts – as well as most of the others in the room – are plaster casts after bronze originals. The bust of Urban VIII is after Bernini.

SS. Trinità degli Spagnuoli
Via Condotti

Bibliography: Vasi, *Magnificenze*, pl. 129; P. C. Blanco (Chiese di Roma, 28); Mallory, *Notizie*, p. 111.

Founded in 1733 by the Spanish Trinitarians and built to the design of the Portuguese architect Emanuele Rodriguez, Giuseppe Sardi being in charge of the actual construction. The plan is an oval with the long axis leading to the High Altar and with six side-chapels. The façade is on a slightly concave curve, like that of S. Marcello, and culminates in a complicated and not altogether harmonious system of broken pediments, one curved, one rectilinear. The group over the door is by P. Pacilli.

The effect of the interior is seriously damaged by the coarse painted marbling.
Vault fresco: Gregorio Guglielmi, *Glory of S. Giovanni de Matha* (1748).
1 to R: G. Paladino, *St Catherine* (1750).
2 to R: Side walls: Casali, *S. Giovanni de Matha and S. Felice de Valois* (1779 and 1775).
3 to R: Casali, *Our Lady of Sorrows* (1776) and on side walls *Christ falling under the Cross* and *The Flagellation*.
Choir: High Altar: C. Giaquinto, *Trinity*; the remainder of the decoration by Antonio Velázquez.
3 to L: F. Preciado de la Vega, *Immaculata* (1750).
2 to L: Walls: Casali, *S. Giovanni de Matha*.
1 to L: Benefial, *St Agnes* (1750; Voss, p. 642).
Sacristy: Over door: G. Sibilla, monument to Diego Morcillo (1760); the door itself is by Cortosi after the design of Marco David who designed the whole decoration of the sacristy (1758); vault fresco, Gregorio Guglielmi, *St Ambrose*.

SS. Vincenzo e Anastasio
Fontana di Trevi

Bibliography: Martinelli, p. 185; Mola, p. 104; Falda, *Nuovo teatro*, III, pl. 25; De' Rossi, *Architettura Civile*, III, pl. 39; Passeri, p. 230; Magni, I, pl. 16; Pugliese-Rigano, *Lunghi*, p. 45; Varriano, *Longhi*, p. 377.

The church was given by Paul V in 1612 to the Hieronomites, who began to build the monastery in 1614. In 1640 Urban VIII, who was planning a new Fontana di Trevi, issued a brief allowing the monks to rebuild their church. According to Borromini, correcting Martinelli, the architect was Gaspare de'Vecchi (d.1643). It is possible that Cardinal Mazarin may have financed this operation, but his certain contribution was the building of the façade begun by Martino Longhi the Younger in 1646 and probably finished by 1650. Mola says that he also built part of the church. According to Passeri Longhi intended to have the panels on either side of the door filled with bas-reliefs. The choir was added in the 1760s by Giuseppe Ferroni who also apparently redecorated the nave.

INTERIOR
High Altar: Francesco Rosa, *The Martyrdom of Sts Vincent and Anastasius* (W).

The monastic buildings (entrance in via del Lavatore, 38), about which no documents have been published, appear to date from the early 18th century, and the door (*Architettura minora*, II, pl. 80; Elling, pl. 66), vestibule and steps leading to the cloister show a rare understanding of Borromini's method of design. It is known that Bizzacheri worked on the building and the design of this part may be due to him (Varriano in Mallory, *Bizzacheri*, p. 45).
See plate 97.

SS. Venanzio e Ansovino
(destroyed)

Bibliography: Titi, 1721, p. 97; Roisecco, 1750, I, p. 318; Vasi, *Magnificenze*, pl. 116.

The church, also called S. Giovanni in Mercatello, which stood below the steps leading up to the Capitol, was given in 1675 to the Community of the Camerinesi by Clement X, who had been bishop of Camerino, and who paid for its restoration to the designs of Antonio Liborio Raspantini. It was pulled down in the 19th century but its façade is recorded in Vasi's engraving.

S. Vitale
Via Nazionale

Bibliography: L. Huetter and V. Golzio (Chiese di Roma, 35).

A church has stood on the site since the early 5th century. It was rebuilt by Sixtus IV in 1475. In 1598 it was given by Clement VIII to the Jesuits and attached to their noviciate of S. Andrea al Quirinale. They set up four altars supported on marble columns, those of the two nearest the apse being ancient columns re-used. They decorated the walls with a bold scheme of illusionist frescoes, articulated with pairs of fictive giant

Ionic columns flanking the altars. Between the pairs the wall is divided into two zones: above are fictive niches with figures of prophets and below landscapes with scenes of the martyrdom of hermit saints. The artists involved are not known, but the fictive architecture suggests the style of Giovanni and Cherubino Alberti and the landscapes that of Paul Bril. Indeed the whole scheme is a reflection of that worked out by these artists on a more ambitious scale for the Sala Clementina in the Vatican, and although the exact dates do not seem to be recorded the scheme can safely be assigned to the first two decades of the 17th century. This dating is confirmed by the fact that Andrea Commodi, who painted the fresco in the apse, left Rome to return to Florence in 1614.
1 to R: G. B. Fiammeri, *Virgin martyrs.*
2 to R: Attributed to Fiammeri, *Assumption.*
3 to R: A. Ciampelli, *Stoning of S. Vitale.*
Apse: A. Commodi, *Road to Calvary, Beheading of St Protasius* and *Flagellation of St Protasius.*
3 to L: A. Ciampelli, *Martyrdom of S. Vitale.*
1 to L: Fiammeri, *Holy Confessors.*

SS. Vito e Modesto
Via S. Vito

Bibliography: Vasi, *Magnificenze,* pl. 126; P. Odescalchi, *Notizie dei nuovi lavori eseguiti nella chiesa dei Santi Vito e Modesto,* Rome, 1837; Armellini, pp. 1002, 1473.

An Early Christian church stood on this site, next to the arch of Gallienus. It was rebuilt by Sixtus IV in 1477. The Baroque façade is shown in Vasi's engraving, but this was removed in the 19th century. The interior was stripped of all decoration at some date after the Second World War.

II
THE PALACES

The literature on the palaces of Rome is much less satisfactory than that on the churches. There are only two general books on the subject, by Callari (*Palazzi di Roma*, second edition 1944) and Torselli (*Palazzi di Roma*, Rome, 1965), which give little information about the buildings and, of that little, part is misleading. In the last twenty years a number of well-illustrated and often well-documented books have been published on the great palaces – usually at the expense of the institutions which now occupy them – and also some useful volumes covering individual streets or areas, such as the Corso, the Piazza Navona and the via Giulia; but for the less well-known palaces the best information is to be obtained from the *Guide Rionali* (see below p. 272) which are particularly strong on the history of the families to which the palaces belonged, and give reasonably reliable information on the architects involved insofar as that is available in printed sources. It is said that a complete survey of the palaces of Rome is to be undertaken by the Cenno dei Romanisti which will be of great value, but many of the problems involved could only be solved by years of search in the archives of individual families and those of their lawyers deposited in the Archivio di Stato.

In the following entries palaces belonging to families whose names begin with de' or del are listed under D.

Many of the major palaces and villas (Barberini, Braschi, Capitoline, Carpegna, Corsini, Doria-Pamphili, Spada, Villa Borghese) contain museums and are open to the public at the usual times. Others, which are the seats of banks or commercial bodies, can often be visited if application is made to the secretary or some other person in authority. Those which are occupied by embassies (Farnese, Pamphili) are no longer normally accessible to the public, owing to the fear of terrorism, and can only be visited through direct contact with a member of the embassy staff. Palaces which belong to government departments (Chigi- Aldobrandini, Consulta, Giustiniani, Madama, Montecitorio, Quirinal) are even more difficult of access.

Some palaces are occupied by academies or other institutions and in these cases admission is usually granted, though it is wise to apply in advance.

Many of the palaces are still in private hands and are not accessible except through personal contacts, but some – not all – of the owners will allow serious students to visit their houses if they can show that they particularly need to do so in connection with their work.

Palazzo Albani (Mattei, Massimi, Nerli, del Drago)
Via Agostino de' Pretis

Bibliography: Baglione, p. 82; Bellori, MS. annotation to Baglione, ibid.: Ferrerio, *Palazzi*, II, pls 11–13; Rossi, 1697, p. 686; 1707, p. 717 and 1725, p. 160; P. Ferri, *Roma ampliata*, Rome, 1725, p. 146; Roisecco, 1739, p. 134; Rossini, *Mercurio Errante*, Rome, 1750, p. 82; Martinelli, *Roma ricercata*, Rome, 1750, p. 173; id. *Roma ornata*, p. 246; Titi, 1763, p. 300; Letarouilly, pl. 169 (133); Wasserman, *Mascarino*, p. 139; Torselli, p. 8.

The palace was built at the cross-roads of the Quattro Fontane for Muzio Mattei probably about 1587–90. (It is visible in Tempesta's map of 1593.) Baglione ascribes it to Giacomo della Porta, but Bellori in a manuscript note says 'del Fontana', that is to say Domenico Fontana, and this is confirmed by Martinelli (*Roma ornata*) who explicitly rejects the attribution to della Porta. Mascarino also made drawings for it and may be responsible for the original design.

The palace belonged to Cardinal Camillo Massimi, the friend and patron of Poussin, and after his death in 1677 it was bought by Cardinal Francesco Nerli (d.1707). It is recorded as belonging to him in Ferrerio's *Palazzi di Roma*, which was probably published about 1680, and in the 1697 and 1707 editions of M. A. and P. de'Rossi's *Descrizione di Roma Moderna*. This fact is repeated in the reprints of 1708 and 1719, though the cardinal died in 1707, but in the 1725 edition of the same guide the palace is stated to have been bought by the three nephews of Clement XI, of whom one, Cardinal Alessandro Albani, established there the great collection of ancient sculpture and drawings by 16th and 17th century artists (now in the Royal Library at Windsor Castle) and a magnificent library which was under the direction of Winckelmann.

Cardinal Alessandro greatly enlarged the palace. Muzio Mattei had built a single block of nine bays on the Strada Felice and five on the Strada Pia, with a five-bay loggia at the back facing on to a garden. Ferrerio's plan, which was made when the palace belonged to Cardinal Nerli, shows to the right – that is to say along Strada Felice – a further area which contained a broad double flight of steps – probably part of a garden – leading to a pavilion behind which was another small garden.

Cardinal Albani closed the loggia on the first floor and converted it into a gallery, and built three wings round the court, in one of which he constructed a spacious staircase. He also extended the main front on Strada Felice by building over the area occupied by Nerli's open staircase and apparently beyond it to incorporate a palace which had belonged to the duca Bonelli. Ferri in 1725, Roisecco in 1739, Rossini in the *Mercurio Errante* of 1750, and the editor of the 1750 edition of Martinelli say that the architect of these alterations was Filippo Barigioni but Titi (1763) ascribes them to Alessandro Specchi, and his name has generally been accepted by later writers.

The plan in Letarouilly does not correspond exactly with any part of that in Ferrerio but represents the part built by Cardinal Albani over Cardinal Nerli's garden.

The rooms in the early part of the palace have stucco friezes incorporating the Mattei arms. The rooms decorated for Cardinal Albani have ceilings frescoed by Giovanni Odazzi with allegorical compositions of the *Virtues*, and the gallery was painted by Giovanni Paolo Pannini (cf. A. Clark, 'State of studies: Roman eighteenth century Art', *Eighteenth Century Studies*, IX, p. 106).

In the mid-19th century the palace was bought by Maria Christina, widow of Ferdinand VII of Spain, who built a ball-room over part of Nerli's garden (the rest of it is now covered by a garage). She bequeathed the palace to her son-in-law the Principe del Drago, to whose descendants it still belongs. It is now the seat of the British Council in Rome.
See plates 10, 94.

Palazzo Albertoni (Spinola)
Piazza Campitelli 2

Bibliography: Baglione, p. 82; Ferrerio, *Palazzi*, II, pl. 39; Martinelli, p. 247; Magni, II, pl. 35; *Guide Rionali*, X, I, p. 40.

Begun by Giacomo della Porta and finished by Girolamo Rainaldi who added the door, over which is the lion passant of the Albertoni Arms.
See plate 31.

Palazzo Aldobrandini-Chigi
Piazza Colonna

Bibliography: Diary of Alexander VII, passim; Falda, *Nuovo teatro*, I, pls 14, 15 and IV, pl. 27; Ferrerio, *Palazzi*, II, pl. 14; De'Rossi, *Architettura Civile*, II, pls 53–61; De Brosses, II, p. 47; Salerno, *Via del Corso*, p. 181; R. Lefèvre, *Il Palazzo degli Aldobrandini e dei Chigi*, Rome, 1964; id., 'Della Porta e Maderno a Palazzo Chigi', *Palladio*, N.S. XXI, 1971, p. 15; and id., *Palazzo Chigi*, Rome, 1973 (with good plates); Hibbard, *Maderno*, p. 215; *Guide Rionali*, III, 2, p. 54.

54. *Palazzo Aldobrandini-Chigi. Engraving by Falda. The engraving shows the whole of the Piazza Colonna with the column of Marcus Aurelius and the fountain erected by Giacomo della Porta. The north side of the piazza is occupied by the Palazzo Aldobrandini-Chigi. On the extreme right, on the Corso, is visible a corner of the Palazzo Verospi. To the left of the Palazzo Aldobrandini-Chigi is the Palazzo Montecitorio, of which the middle section is still unfinished. The west side of the piazza is occupied by a palace used by the attendants of the Ludovisi family, which Alexander VII intended to pull down and replace by one for his own family, designed by Cortona. On the extreme left is a corner of the Palazzo del Bufalo Ferraioli.*

Baglione and Totti ascribe the palace to Giacomo della Porta, but Borromini, in a note to Martinelli, says that it was built by Maderno, and this is confirmed by the fact that the complete site did not come into the possession of Cardinal Pietro Aldobrandini, nephew of Clement VIII, till 1618. It is however possible that della Porta produced a plan for the previous owner, Fabrizio Fossano, between 1588 and 1597. The palace was completed and transformed by Alexander VII, to whom it was sold in 1659. His architect was Felice della Greca who is responsible for the façade on Piazza Colonna. Of the existing building the only detail that can be firmly ascribed to Maderno is the door on the Corso. The palace is now the seat of the Presidenza del Consiglio.

Palazzo Alessandrino. See Palazzo Valentino
Piazza SS. Apostoli 119

Palazzo Almagià (Ludovisi, Ottoboni, Perettini, Trano)
Via del Corso and Piazza S. Lorenzo in Lucina

Bibliography: Hibbard, *Maderno*, p. 217; Salerno, *Via del Corso*, p. 162; *Guide Rionali*, III, 1, p. 82.

Originally built in the 13th century as the palace of the titular cardinal of S. Lorenzo in Lucina, on which it abuts, it was sold in 1624 by Urban VIII to Michele Peretti, Principe di Venafro, who reconstructed it on a grand scale to the designs of Maderno. Later it passed to the Ludovisi, Ottoboni (1690) and Trano families. In 1898 the palace was sold to the Almagià family who remodelled it, leaving only a small section of the old palace visible on the exterior on via in Lucina.

The vault of the Gallery was decorated with frescoes by François Perrier, commissioned by Michele Peretti, and representing *Aurora, Juno and Aeolus*, the *Birth of Venus* and *Venus in the Forge of Vulcan*, and landscapes by Giovanni Francesco Grimaldi, flanked by figures of *Virtues* by Ruggieri (E. Schleier, 'François Perrier a Roma', *Paragone*, XXXVII, 217, 1968, p. 45).

Palazzo Altemps
Via S. Apollinare

Bibliography: Baglione, p. 68; Mola, p. 127; Martinelli, p. 231; Ferrerio, *Palazzi*, II, pls 18, 19; Titi, 1763, p. 406; Percier and Fontaine, *Palais*, IV, pl. 23; Letarouilly, pl. 169 (133); *Guide Rionali*, V, 1, p. 24; M. F. Milone, 'Palazzo Riario Altemps', *Quaderni*, XXIV, 1977–8, p. 13.

The palace was built about 1480 for Cardinal Girolamo Riario, but was remodelled entirely after 1578 for Cardinal Marcus Psiticus (Marco Sittico) Altemps of the Austrian family of Hohenems, nephew of Pius IV, by Martino Longhi the Elder. It has an impressive court with a loggia of five arcades – originally open – at each end, with fine and elaborate stucco decoration in the spandrels of the arches dating from 1585–9. On the keystones of the arches on the ground floor is the ram rampant of the Altemps arms. The palace is now the seat of the Spanish College.

In a room on the first floor are frescoes by Romanelli representing *Europa*, *Aurora*, *Galatea* and *Amphitrite*, all prudishly repainted (W). In the chapel of S. Aniceto are frescoes by Antonio Circignani, called Il Pomarancio.

Palazzo Altieri
Piazza del Gesù

Bibliography: Falda, *Nuovo teatro*, IV, pls 28, 29; Ferrerio, *Palazzi*, II, pl. 38; De'Rossi, *Architettura Civile*, I, pls 119–23; Tessin, p. 178, pls 90, 91; De Brosses, II, p. 112; Visentini, *Osservazioni*, p. 33; Magni, II, pls 56, 57; Spagnesi, *G. A. De Rossi*, p. 69; Schiavo, *Palazzo Altieri*, Rome, 1964; *Guide Rionali*, IX, 1, p. 56.

The Altieri owned a palace on this site since at least the early 16th century but in the mid-17th century Giambattista Altieri, brother of Emilio, who became Pope Clement X, decided to rebuild it on a grander scale. At this stage the left hand part of the palace, facing on the Piazza del Gesù, was built, but later, from about 1670 onwards, it was enlarged by G. A. de' Rossi by extending the building along the site opposite the Gesù itself. This addition was largely financed by Cardinal Albertoni, uncle of Gaspare Albertoni, the pope's adopted nephew. Carlo Fontana was asked to produce a design, which was rejected, presumably because it would have involved pulling down much of the existing palace, and instead Albertoni adopted Rossi's project which left the existing buildings and added a second court to the east. The amount of money spent on this building by Albertoni caused a scandal in Rome and the pope dissociated himself from the project.

The Palazzo Altieri is G. A. de'Rossi's most important work, in which he demonstrates his opposition to the Baroque innovations of Bernini, Borromini and Cortona, and his determination to cling to principles established in the last decades of the 16th century. On the façade the windows are evenly spaced, and de' Rossi does not even allow himself to use the alternation of straight and curved pediments which had been current practice in Rome for more than a century. The elevations of the courtyard – with the exception of some slightly Borrominesque windows in the upper storey – are equally austere, and the staircase, though grand in conception, is positively dry in its treatment of detail.

INTERIOR
The main *salone* has a ceiling fresco by Carlo Maratta in honour of Clement X, representing the *Triumph of Clemency* (1674–7; W). Maratta intended to complete it by adding frescoes on the cove according to a programme by Bellori recorded in a manuscript in the Vatican Library. A number of drawings exist for the project which was never carried out owing to the death of the pope (J. Montagu, 'Bellori, Maratti and the Palazzo Altieri', *Journal of the Warburg and Courtauld Institutes*, XLI, 1978, p. 334).

The ceiling of the Salone Rosso (*Allegory of Passionate Love*) is by Niccolò Berrettoni; that in the Salone Verde is by Francesco Cozza and Andrea Carlone (*The Seasons*). Another room has a ceiling fresco by D. M. Canuti with a *quadratura* setting by Haffner. The Sala degli Specchi was frescoed by Fabrizio Chiari in 1675 (*The Chariot of Apollo;* W).

A *Gabinetto di Toeletta* on the *piano nobile* of the second court is one of the most completely rococo rooms in Rome. These rooms all belong to the part of the palace occupied by a bank; others at the right and left ends of the main front with frescoed and stuccoed ceilings are let off to shops which can sometimes be penetrated.

See plate 56.

Palazzo Antamoro (Strada)
Via della Panetteria 15

Bibliography: Falda, *Fontane*, III, pl. 28; Magni, III, pl. 27; Wittkower, *Bernini*, p. 267; D'Onofrio, *Acque e Fontane*, p. 448; Fagiolo dell'Arco, *Bernini*, No. 218.

In the court of the palace is a fountain, probably made after a design by Bernini. In his time the palace belonged to Paolo Strada, cameriere segreto to Clement IX. The pope's arms were originally displayed on the fountain but were later replaced by those of the Antamoro family who bought the palace in the 18th century. The palace has a fine door which probably also dates from the time of Paolo Strada, but the façade was remodelled in the 19th century and the court in the mid-20th century.

Palazzo Astalli
Via d'Aracoeli 2

Bibliography: Pascoli, I, p. 317; Letarouilly, 40 (34); Spagnesi, *G. A. De Rossi*, p. 202; C. Pietrangeli, 'Il Palazzo Astalli', *Capitolium*, XVIII, 1968, p. 6; *Guide Rionali*, X, 1, p. 9.

Originally built in the 16th century, the palace was completely remodelled by G. A. de' Rossi from 1672 onwards. In 1930–2 parts of it were demolished to make way for the broadened via di San Marco. The frescoed ceilings were destroyed. Its original appearance and some of the frescoes are recorded in drawings and old photographs reproduced by Pietrangeli and in the *Guida Rionale*. It is now of no interest architecturally.

Palazzo Aste-Buonaparte
Piazza Venezia

Bibliography: Falda, *Nuovo teatro*, I, pls 16, 17 and IV, pl. 48; Ferrerio, *Palazzi*, II, pls 28, 29; De' Rossi, *Architettura Civile*, I, pls 135–7; De Brosses, II, p. 108; Visentini, *Osservazioni*, p. 27; Letarouilly, pl. 111 (88); Salerno, *Via del Corso*, p. 256; Spagnesi, *G. A. De'Rossi*, p. 60; *Guide Rionali*, IX, 3, p. 94.

Built by G. A. de'Rossi between 1658 and 1665 for the brothers Giuseppe and Benedetto d'Aste. The site was small and narrow and de' Rossi invented for it an unusual plan with a long narrow vestibule running right through the length of the building, connecting with a side entrance and ending in the staircase. The windows show a mixture of Borrominesque and Cortonesque features. From 1815 to 1838 it belonged to Madame Mère, mother of Napoleon. The exterior was restored in 1979 in a particularly unattractive and quite un-Roman colour.

See plate 46.

55. *Palazzo Aste (later Buonaparte). Engraving by Falda. Beyond the Palazzo Aste (right, on the corner of the street) is a series of small palaces, then come the Palazzo Grazioli (Gottifredi), and in the distance the dome of S. Andrea della Valle. On the left is the Palazzo Venezia. The street depicted is now the via del Plebiscito.*

56. *Palazzo Aste. Engraving by Vasi representing the same view as Falda's engraving shown in plate 55 with the Palazzo d'Aste on the extreme right. The main differences are that the irregular buildings to the west of the Palazzo d'Aste have been replaced by the new wing of the Palazzo Pamphili, and that the Palazzo Altieri has been extended towards the east, so that it now features prominently in the view.*

Palazzo Avila
Via di Montegiordano 2

Bibliography: *Guide Rionali*, V, 2, p. 42.

A small 17th-century palace built by the Avila family who also built the chapel of that name in S. Maria in Trastevere. Its most interesting feature is the door above which are the eagles of the Avila arms. They also occur in the cornice, interspersed with roses and fleurs-de-lys.

Palazzo Baldinotti-Carpegna
Via delle Botteghe Oscure

Bibliography: De'Rossi, *Architettura Civile*, I, pl. 131; Spagnesi, *G. A. De'Rossi*, p. 202.

Built by G. A. de'Rossi, but pulled down and rebuilt with alterations when the via delle Botteghe Oscure was opened up in the 1930s.

Palazzo Balestra. See Palazzo Muti Papazzuri
Piazza SS. Apostoli

Palazzo Barberini
Via Quattro Fontane

Bibliography: G. Tetius, *Aedes Barberinae*, Rome, 1642 and 1647; Falda, *Nuovo teatro*, IV, pls 17, 20; Ferrerio, *Palazzi*, I, pls 7, 8; Tessin, p. 165; De'Rossi, *Architettura Civile*, I, pls 35–52; III, pls 7, 8; De Brosses, I, p. 58; Venuti, 1767, I, p. 219; Percier and Fontaine, *Palais*, IV, pls 81, 82; Letarouilly, pls 181–6 (140–5); Magni, II, pls 42–6; Pollak, I, p. 251; Brauer and Wittkower, p. 27; Blunt, 'The Palazzo Barberini', *Journal of the Warburg and Courtauld Institutes*, XXI, 1958, p. 256; Hibbard, *Maderno*, p. 222; Thelen, *Borromini*, p. 54 (cf. also the present writer's review, *Kunstchronik*, March, 1969, p. 87); P. Waddy, 'Michelangelo Buonarroti the Younger. Sprezzatura and Palazzo Barberini', *Architectura*, V, 1975, p. 101, and 'The Design and Designers of Palazzo Barberini', *J.S.A.H.*, XXXV, 1976, p. 151; Blunt, *Borromini*, p. 33; M. A. Lavin, *Seventeenth-Century Barberini Documents and Inventories of Art*, New York, 1975; P. Magnanimi, P. Macoratti, F. Palazzesi, 'Il rilievo planimetrico di Palazzo Barberini', *Antologia di belle arti*, 4, 1977, p. 364; *Guide Rionali*, II, 1, p. 126; Brizzi, *Album di Roma*, Rome, 1980, pp. 51–84.

The architectural history of the Palazzo Barberini is extremely complicated and in many points obscure. The earlier part of the history, up to the beginning of the actual construction of the existing palace, has been disentangled, but the shares of the various architects involved in the planning and construction of the palace remain hard to determine.

In 1625 Urban VIII bought a palace and a *vigna* belonging to Duke Alessandro Sforza between the Piazza Grimani (now Piazza Barberini) and the via Pia (via XX Settembre), and gave it to his nephew Taddeo, who determined to build on the site a palace worthy of the newly acquired importance of the Barberini family.

Various projects for the palace were submitted, including one by Michelangelo Buonarroti the Younger, but the scheme proposed by Carlo Maderno was finally adopted. Levelling of the ground began in 1627, but the actual building was not started till December 1628, two months before Maderno's death. Maderno was replaced by Bernini, who took over his assistant, Borromini. The latter had played an important part – exactly how important is difficult to determine – in the final shaping of Maderno's design, and he continued to play a similar role under Bernini, who at this date had little experience in architecture (and had been assisted by Borromini in the construction of the Baldacchino of St Peter's).

It seems fairly certain that the general plan of the palace is due to Maderno, though he incorporated some ideas from earlier proposals, such as the unusual atrium, but the actual drawings made at this time are mostly from the hand of Borromini. All 17th-century authorities agree that the square staircase in the left wing was designed by Bernini and the oval one in the right wing by Borromini, though the latter is only an adaptation of a late 16th-century type to be found in Mascarino's staircase in the Quirinal and Flaminio Ponzio's in the Palazzo Borghese. These two staircases were intended to be open to the sky and are so described by Philip Skippon who saw them in 1663 (*An account of a Journey through . . . Italy . . .*, London, 1733, p. 667).

Borromini is also responsible for the windows on the top floor in the bays between the loggia and the wings, and he may have had a hand in the final design of the false perspective windows in the top floor of the loggia (the drawing for these is certainly from his hand) though these are a development of Maderno's door to the staircase in the Palazzo Mattei di Giove. The doors and the fireplace in the *salone* are the result of collaboration between Bernini and Borromini, and some of the unpublished drawings in the Albertina show, I believe, Borromini's design in red chalk with Bernini's corrections in ink. The central pavilion of the garden façade is a modification by Bernini of Maderno's rather heavy composition, recorded in a drawing at Windsor, though the actual drawings in each case are probably by Borromini.

The Palazzo Barberini differs from most of the great Roman palaces in that it consists of a solid block with projecting wings instead of being planned round a central court. The reason for this is no doubt that, being situated in a large *vigna*, it has something of the character of a villa, and therefore it was logical to turn to the most famous of Roman villas, Peruzzi's Farnesina, as a model. The planning of the building was complicated by the necessity of incorporating the existing Sforza palace, which is partly

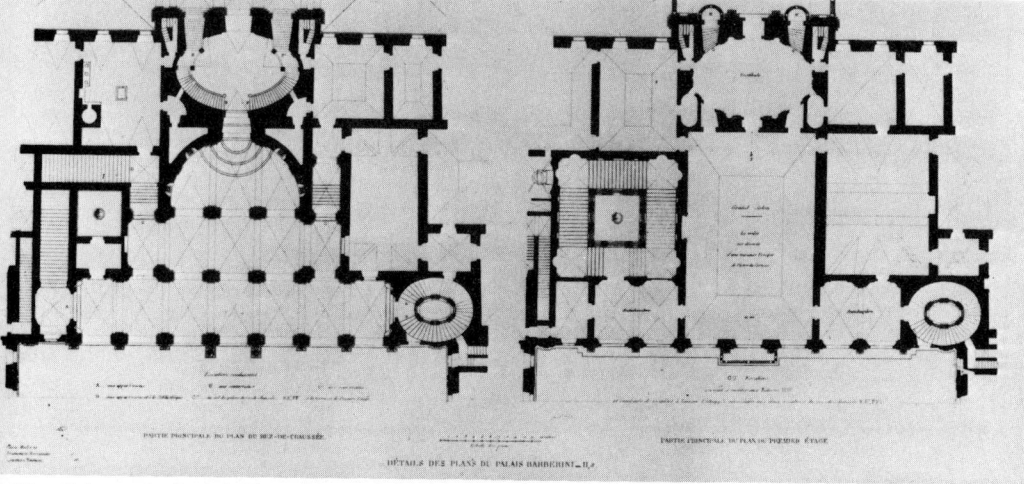

57. *Palazzo Barberini. Plan of ground floor.*   58. *Palazzo Barberini. Plan of first floor.*

enclosed in the north wing of the present palace, but runs back along the north side of the garden.

The palace was structurally complete by the mid-1630s but the decoration and furnishing of the interior continued for many years. Work was interrupted in 1645 when Taddeo Barberini and his brother Cardinal Francesco, who had come to live in part of the palace, had to flee from Rome after the death of Urban VIII and the election of Innocent X, but it was taken up again in 1648 after the reconciliation of the Barberini family with Innocent. In 1677 (Cartari-Febei) a carriage-way was cut from the atrium through to the garden, an arrangement which had important implications for the approaches to the palace. Originally the main approach was through the door next to the Quattro Fontane, which brought the visitor to the entrance on the *piano nobile* in the middle of the garden façade. This led into the oval vestibule and so directly to the *Salone*, off which the two main apartments opened. Alternatively he could come in from the piazza Grimani, through the stables and along the terrace on the north side of the palace – which was used for *feste* – and so arrive at the ground floor of the great loggia. From here he could go directly to the two summer apartments, which were on the ground floor, or up one of the two staircases to the apartments on the *piano nobile*. With the new carriage-way, however, he could drive straight through the main block of the palace and so reach the door leading to the oval vestibule. The piercing of the carriage-way, however, destroyed the closed character of the atrium and involved some awkward changes in the garden front. In 1865–7 the approach was changed again. The wall which separated the palace from houses facing the via Felice (via Quattro Fontane) which had only a small undecorated gate, was pulled down and replaced by the existing piers and railings. Its original state is shown in an etching in Piranesi's *Varie Vedute* of 1748, which is repeated in the 1767 edition of Venuti. The result was that the façade which had been designed to open on a small garden became the principal approach to the palace.

When the palace was first being planned Pietro da Cortona submitted a design, but it was rejected on the grounds that it was too expensive. The plan is not recorded but the design for the façade with the loggia is known from a drawing on the Florentine art-market in 1980 and a partial drawing in the Uffizi (Thelen, I,

59. *Palazzo Barberini. Etching by Piranesi showing the west façade before the present grand approach on this side was laid out in the 1860s.*

pl. 52). A further drawing, at Chatsworth, probably represents the interior of the loggia. These drawings will be published and discussed in my forthcoming book on Cortona as an architect. Cortona was also responsible for several buildings connected with the palace. These include the entrance gate near the Quattro Fontane (probably built c.1627; Hibbard, *Licenze*, p. 112) and the fountain adjoining it (visible in an unfinished state in a drawing by Lieven Cruyl in the Albertina, dated 1665, but shown complete by Falda in his *Fontane* of 1691), and the wall closing the terrace on the north side of the palace, behind which the theatre was later built. The exact date of this wall is not known but it appears in an engraving in Totti's guide of 1638. It is also safe, I believe, to ascribe to Cortona the door in the north façade just to the right of the theatre and some at least of the windows on the *piano nobile* of the garden front, particularly those immediately next to the central pavilion, which have a very unusual combination of curved and straight pediments, not to be found in either Bernini or Borromini, but appearing in exactly the same form in Cortona's stucco decoration of the Sala di Venere at the Palazzo Pitti (M. Campbell, *Pietro da Cortona at the Pitti Palace*, Princeton, 1977, pl. 22).

INTERIOR

The rooms on the *piano nobile* of the north wing formed part of the Sforza Palace, and several of them have the Sforza eagle in the stucco frames of the ceiling frescoes. The stuccoes are in the style current in Rome about 1610–20, to be found, for instance, in Maderno's Palazzo Mattei di Giove. Many of the rooms were, however, redecorated for Taddeo Barberini, who used them for his winter apartment. The first that the visitor enters has a ceiling painting by Andrea Camassei of the *Hierarchy of Angels* (probably before 1632; W). To the right is a room with Sacchi's *Divina Sapienza* (1629–31), off which opens the chapel decorated by Cortona with the assistance of Romanelli (1631–2; Briganti, *Cortona*, p. 195). In the corridor at the end of the wing are two frescoes by Cortona or a member of his studio, one representing a *Sacrifice to Juno*, the other an episode in the life of Caeculus which took place at Praeneste, that is to say Palestrina, the principality which had recently been acquired by Taddeo Barberini (Briganti, *Cortona*, p. 204). A restoration of this room carried out in 1978 has shown that this gallery was constructed out of two rooms and that the frescoes by Cortona were inserted in the end walls at the same time. The exact date when this operation was carried out is not known. In the middle of the vault are the arms of the Falconieri family.

The vault of the *Salone* was decorated between 1633 and 1639 with a vast fresco by Pietro da Cortona in honour of Urban VIII as the agent of Divine Providence, with the bees of the Barberini arms prominently displayed in a laurel wreath at the top of the composition (Briganti, *Cortona*, p. 196). On the cove are scenes from classical mythology symbolizing the achievements of the pope's regime. For a discussion of the symbolism of the central section of the fresco see W. Vitzthum, 'A comment on the Iconography of Pietro da Cortona's Barberini Ceiling', *Burlington Magazine*, CIII, 1961, p. 427. The fresco is one of the first and yet one of the most complete manifestations of Baroque decorative painting in Rome, with its combination of illusionism and glowing colouring. The spectator is supposed to imagine that the actual coved ceiling has been removed and replaced by an entablature supported at the corners by four piers composed of atlantes and stucco reliefs, through which the eye passes to the sky in which float allegorical figures symbolizing the virtues of the pope. It is typical of Baroque Rome that Divine Providence should be identified not only with the papacy but with the reigning pope and his family, symbolized by the bees of his arms.

The oval vestibule next to the *Salone* (still part of the officers' club which occupies a considerable section of the palace) is discussed and illustrated by G. Magnanimi, 'Palazzo Barberini: la sala ovale', (*Antologia di Belle Arti*, I, 1977, p. 29). It was constructed between 1633 and 1639 and was decorated with niches containing ancient Roman statues and busts.

The rooms on the ground floor of the north wing which formed Prince Taddeo Barberini's Summer Apartment (now occupied by the officers' club) were decorated in the 1670s with ceiling frescoes with stories from classical mythology illustrating an allegorical theme based on an exhortation to virtue by the examples of *Ulysses* (Giacinto Camassei), *Apollo* (*Parnassus* by Andrea Camassei, actually painted earlier in 1631–2 and now lost), *Bellerophon* (Giuseppe Passeri) and themes taken from a poem by Urban VIII (J. Montagu, 'Exhortatio ad virtutem', *Journal of the Warburg and Courtauld Institutes*, XXXIV, 1971, p. 366).

Most of the *piano nobile* of the palace is occupied by the Galleria Nazionale d'Arte antica, but the rooms in the south wing which belong to the officers' club have important Seicento paintings. A museum of Settecento art is being arranged in the rooms of the second floor of the south wing, which were redecorated for the marriage of the Barberini heiress, Cornelia Costanza, to Giulio Cesare Colonna di Sciarra, Principe di Carbognano, in 1728 (Golzio, *Palazzi*, figs 49–52).

See plate 94.

Palazzo Barberini alla Giubbonara
Piazza del Monte di Pietà

Bibliography: Totti, p. 211; Hibbard, *Maderno*, p. 222; D'Onofrio, *Roma vista*, p. 49.

Bought in 1584 by Francesco Barberini, uncle of the future Urban VIII who inherited it from him in 1600. It was altered by Flaminio Ponzio between 1600 and 1603 and by Maderno in 1621. In 1623 the newly elected pope gave the palace to his brother Carlo who continued work on it under the direction of Maderno from 1624 to 1627. In the early 1640s further alterations were made by Francesco Contini, who moved the entrance from the via dei Giubbonari to the piazza in front of the Monte di Pietà. In 1684 it was bought by the Gabrielli family (Cartari-Febei).

It contains an interesting semicircular staircase and, on the ground floor facing the piazza, some rooms with fine stucco ceilings in the same style as the early rooms in the Palazzo Barberini alle Quattro Fontane. It is now occupied by the Istituto Magistrale 'Vittoria Colonna' and other institutions.

Palazzo Bentivoglio. See Palazzo Rospigliosi-Pallavicini
Via XXIV Maggio

Palazzo Bernini
Via della Mercede 11 and 12

Bibliography: D'Onofrio, *Roma vista*, p. 139; Elling, pl. 93.

When Pietro Bernini settled in Rome in 1606 he bought a house opposite S. Maria Maggiore (via Liberiana 24, on the corner of the via di S. Maria Maggiore) where Gianlorenzo lived till 1639, when he moved to the via Mercede, to a site on the corner of the via del Collegio di Propaganda Fide. He replaced the small and decaying buildings on the site and built a palace, which still exists, though much altered in the 19th century. It contains a ceiling and some frescoes which date from the 17th century.

Though Bernini owned the whole site now occupied by Nos 11 and 12 via della Mercede he lived with his family in the house which is now No. 11.

It must have been galling for Bernini when in the 1650s his rival Borromini, whose architecture he hated, erected immediately facing his palace two of his most eccentric buildings, the dome and tower of S. Andrea delle Fratte and the Collegio di Propaganda Fide, the latter of which involved pulling down Bernini's chapel.

Palazzo Bonelli. See Palazzo Valentino
Piazza SS. Apostoli 119

Palazzo Borghese
Piazza Borghese

Bibliography: Falda, *Nuovo teatro*, III, pl. 38 and IV, pls 12, 13; Ferrerio, *Palazzi*, II, pls 22–4; Tessin, p. 171; De Brosses, II, p. 42; Percier and Fontaine, *Palais*, IV, pl. 87; Magni, II, pls 17–21; Letarouilly, pls 175, 176 (136, 137); Hibbard, 'The architecture of the Palazzo Borghese', *Memoirs of the American Academy in Rome*, XXVII, 1962, p. 1; id., *Maderno*, p. 191; Golzio, *Palazzi*, figs 53–71, pls IV, V.

The plot was bought in 1560 by Monsignor Tommaso del Giglio who began building immediately on the site of the present palace on the Piazza Fontanella di Borghese. His activities were interrupted by absences from Rome but at the time of his death in 1578 the front block of the palace was mainly built, though it was still unroofed, and the court was begun. The architect is unknown but Hibbard tentatively proposed the name of Vignola, who was a Bolognese like Giglio.

In 1586 the palace was bought by the Spanish Cardinal Pedro Deza, who set about completing the building under the direction of Martino Longhi the Elder, but at the Cardinal's death in 1600 only one wing, on the via di Monte d'Oro, had been built and the court was still unfinished. Longhi was responsible for the cornice on the main façade and probably for the design of the court. On his death in 1591 he was succeeded as architect by his pupil, Flaminio Ponzio.

In 1604 the palace was bought by Cardinal Camillo Borghese, and has remained in the possession of his family ever since. On his election as Pope Paul V in 1605 he gave the palace to his two brothers, Giovanni Battista and Francesco, but continued to direct building operations, Ponzio being still in charge. By 1612 the court

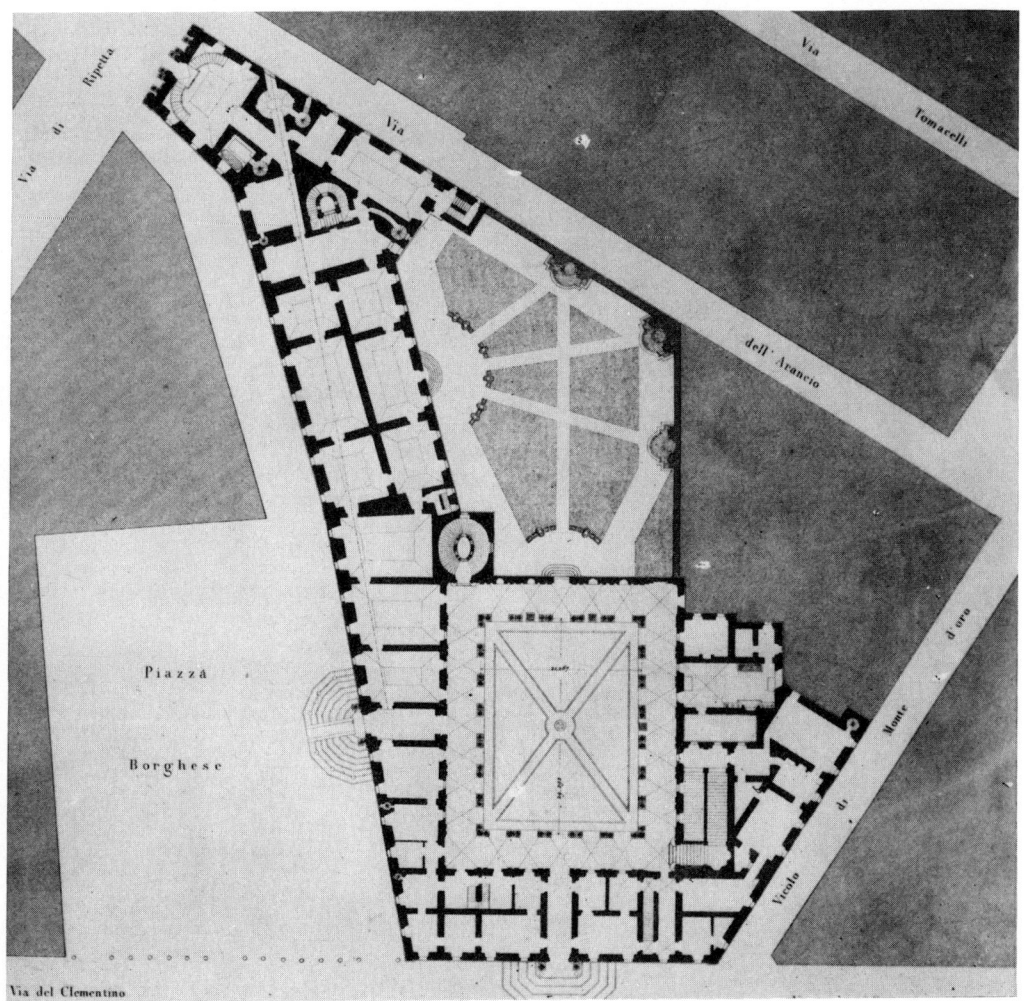

60. *Palazzo Borghese. Plan.*

was complete and a wing had been built along the Piazza Borghese leading to the Tiber, including an oval spiral staircase. In 1612–14 this wing was enlarged, leading to a garden which extended right down to the Ripetta. On the death of Paul V in 1621 his nephew, Cardinal Scipione Borghese, came to live in the palace and paid for its completion. He replaced the old garden with a loggia and a hanging garden. Ponzio died in 1613 and the work carried out for Cardinal Scipione was the responsibility of Vasanzio and Maderno, though their precise shares cannot be determined.

In the 1670s Carlo Rainaldi carried out extensive alterations for Prince Paolo Borghese. He reconstructed the wing along the Piazza Borghese leading to the Tiber, and created within it a circular chapel and a magnificent gallery with stucco allegories on the history of Rome and busts of the emperors. The decoration of the gallery was devised by Giovanni Francesco Grimaldi, who also decorated the end room overlooking the port of Ripetta. The reliefs in the gallery are by Cosimo Fancelli (cf. Hibbard, 'Palazzo Borghese Studies: II. The Galleria', *Burlington Magazine*, CIV, 1962, p. 9).

Rainaldi also laid out the garden, one of the most complete and best-preserved Baroque gardens in Rome (cf. also Palazzo del Grillo), but the elaborate stucco fountains were designed by Giovanni Paolo Schor and the models were made by Cosimo Fancelli (Falda, *Fontane*, III, pls 11, 12; Magni, III, pls 24, 25; Hibbard, 'Palazzo Borghese Studies, I: the garden and its fountains', *Burlington Magazine*, C, 1958, pp. 205, 252; Portoghesi, *Roma Barocca*, pls 233–5).

61. Palazzo Borghese. Engraving by Falda showing one of the fountains in the garden.

Architecturally the most interesting feature of the palace is the court with its two floors of arcades – which would originally both have been open – supported on pairs of Doric and Ionic columns. The arcades at the end of the court serve to link the two wings of the palace at first and second floor levels and also form a magnificent approach to the garden which lies behind them.

Another unusual feature is the oval spiral staircase in the left-hand corner of the court; next to the arcade leading to the garden. This is based on Mascarino's staircase of similar shape in the Quirinal, which itself is a Mannerist variant of Vignola's monumental circular staircase at Caprarola.

The two upper mezzanine floors facing the piazza formed the summer apartment of Princess Borghese. They were decorated from 1671 onwards under the direction of Giovanni Paolo Schor and Carlo Rainaldi with frescoes by Gaspard Dughet, Filippo Lauri, Luigi Garzi, Ciro Ferri and others (M. N. Boisclair, 'La Décoration de deux mezzanines du Palais Borghèse à Rome', *Racar*, III, 1976, p. 7). In an apartment on the second floor, facing the court, off the spiral staircase, is a *salone* with frescoed walls and ceiling representing the four continents (M. Trionfi Honorati, *Antichità Viva*, IV, 4, 1965, p. 79).

Opposite the palace, on the Piazza Borghese, is another built in 1624–7 by Antonio de Battisti, Bolini, Venturi and G. B. Soria, but it is not certain which of them was responsible for the design (Hibbard, *The Architecture of the Palazzo Borghese*, Rome, 1962, p. 73). The palace was taken as a model by Maruscelli for the Oratory of S. Filippo Neri and the Palazzo del Bufalo (Connors, *Oratory*, p. 117).

See plates 104, 105 and Palazzo Rospigliosi-Pallavicini.

Palazzo Bossi
Via di Monserrato 154

Bibliography: Salerno, *Via Giulia*, p. 376; *Guide Rionali*, VII, 2, p. 18.

The 16th-century palace which stood on this site was rebuilt in the early 18th century. The architect is not known, but the disposition of the vestibule and staircase shows that he had a gift for creating interesting spaces enclosed by curving walls or covered by arches of unusual shapes. The façade has a fine rusticated door running into a curved element which joins it to the window above.

The palace was restored in the 20th century when the façade was redecorated in a pseudo-16th-century style, and a part of the vestibule was cut off on the left, leaving it unsymmetrical.

Palazzo Braschi
Corso Vittorio Emanuelle II

Bibliography: Letarouilly, pls 196, 197 (150, 151); C. Pietrangeli and A. Ravaglioli, *Palazzo Braschi*, Rome, 1967; Colosanti, pls 188ff.

Although the palace, built for Pius VI (Braschi) from 1790 onwards, belongs to the neo-classical period it must be mentioned in the context of the Baroque, partly because certain features in it – such as the staircase and the oval vestibule – have strong echoes of earlier Baroque buildings, and partly because the Museo di Roma which it houses contains paintings, sculpture and drawings – and even old photographs – which are intimately connected with the history of Baroque Rome. These include paintings of *feste* in the Palazzo Barberini and in the Piazza Navona, and the beautiful model for the cappella Pallavicini in the church of S. Francesco a Ripa.

Palazzo Buonaparte. See Palazzo Aste (Buonaparte)
Piazza Venezia

Palazzo Buoncompagni Corcos (Scarinci)
Via del Governo Vecchio 3

Bibliography: Falda, *Nuovo teatro*, I, pl. 22; *Guide Rionali*, V, 3, p. 68.

Built, probably in the early 17th century, by Solomon Corcos, a Jew who was converted by the Oratorians in 1582 and took the name and arms of Gregory XIII (Buoncompagni). The Buoncompagni dragon appears in the capitals of the columns which flank the door.

Palazzo Buoncompagni Ludovisi
Via del Babuino 49

Bibliography: Architettura minora, I, pls 68, 69; D. Biolchi, 'Il ripristino della Fontana del Babuino', *Capitolium*, XXXII, 12, 1957, p. 14; D'Onofrio, *Acque e Fontane*, p. 118; Elling, pl. 115.

The remarkable rusticated door of this palace is composed of the surround of a fountain which stood here against the wall of the Palazzo Buoncompagni Ludovisi. It was originally set in a simple late 16th-century rusticated arch, but was given the present elaborate setting in 1738. In 1877 in order to clear the pavement of the via Babuino the basin was moved to the villa of Pius IV on the via Flaminia. The recumbent figure of a satyr which formed the central feature of the fountain was first moved to the court of the Palazzo Cerasi and later – in 1957 – set up next to the church of S. Atanasio dei Greci on the other side of the street. The rock forms of the base are inspired by Bernini's Palazzo di Montecitorio.

See also Palazzo de Carolis.

Palazzo della Cancelleria
Piazza della Cancelleria

Bibliography: E. Lavagnino, *Il Palazzo della Cancelleria*, Rome, n.d.; A. Schiavo, *Il Palazzo della Cancelleria*, Rome, 1963.

Begun in 1485 for Cardinal Raffaello Riario, together with the church of S. Lorenzo in Damaso by an unknown architect probably trained in Urbino. The design for the door was originally made by Vignola (engraving in the *Regole delli Cinque Ordini*) but it was not executed till the time of Sixtus V (1589) after a design by Domenico Fontana. The palace became the regular residence of the papal vice-chancellors.

Within the palace is a small chapel with fine stuccoes and frescoes by Perino del Vaga and a large hall with frescoes by Vasari representing episodes from the life of Paul III, called the Sala dei Cento Giorni, because the artist is said to have completed the decoration of the room in a hundred days. The Gran Sala was decorated for Clement XI in 1718. The main elements of the decoration are the cartoons made by Marcantonio Franceschini in 1711–12 for the decoration of the vault of the bay outside the Cappella del Coro in St Peter. The larger ones represent the *Heavenly Host* and the smaller ones scenes from the *Old Testament*. They are interspersed with six medallions representing the arts, probably by Nasini, and a series of *vedute* by the otherwise unrecorded Tyrolese artist Andreas Spängl, representing buildings restored by Clement. They also incorporate, on the end wall, an *Allegory of Time*, with a clock, which survived from a decoration carried out by Baciccio for Cardinal Francesco Barberini who was vice-chancellor from 1632 to 1679. The room was heavily restored in the 19th century and again in 1943 (Enggass, 'Baciccio: A new fresco and two modelli', *Burlington Magazine*, CXVIII, 1976, p. 589, and S. Rudolph, 'The "Gran Sala" in the Cancelleria Apostolica', ibid., CXX, 1978, p. 593; F. de Federico, 'The mosaic decoration for the chapel of the Choir in St Peter's', *Storia dell'Arte*, 32, 1978, p. 71).

Capitoline Palaces

Bibliography: Ferrerio, *Palazzi*, pls 9, 10; Tessin, p. 188; Rodoconachi, *Le Capitole romain antique et moderne*, Paris, 1904; H. Siebenhüner, *Das Kapitol*, Munich, 1954; Ackerman, *Michelangelo*, London, 1961, p. 54; C. Pietrangeli and A. Ravaglioli, *Il Campidoglio*, Rome, 1965; J. Wilde, *Michelangelo*, Oxford, 1979, p. 174; *Guide Rionali*, X, 2.

The history of the palaces on the Capitol falls almost entirely outside the Baroque period, but their influence was so great that they cannot be ignored, and they contain a certain number of works of art of the Baroque period.

The Capitol has been since ancient times the centre of the civil administration of Rome. In the 12th century a senate house was built on the site of the ancient Tabularium and in the early 15th century a second palace was built on the site of what is now the Palazzo dei Conservatori. In 1538 the statue of Marcus Aurelius was moved here from the Lateran and about the same time Michelangelo was commissioned to design a complete lay-out for the area. By the time of his death in 1564 the staircase in front of the Palazzo del Senatore had been built and the Palazzo dei Conservatori begun. The work was continued by Giacomo della Porta who freely altered Michelangelo's designs and was responsible for the giant pilasters on the façade of the Palazzo del Senatore, the tower of which was rebuilt in 1578 by Martino Longhi the Elder. The central window of the Conservatori was inserted in 1568. It is generally ascribed to Giacomo della Porta, but stylistically there is much to be said for Baglione's attribution (p. 58) of it to Giacomo del Duca (cf. windows in the dome of S. Maria di Loreto). It was violently criticized by Visentini (*Osservazioni*, p. 3). The third palace, the Palazzo Nuovo, was begun in 1603, but was not completed till the pontificate of Innocent X who, over a period of ten years (1644–54), provided funds for the building. In gratitude for this the Senate commissioned a statue of him to be set up in the Palazzo dei Conservatori (see below).

The decoration of the rooms in the three palaces continued over a long period. The main room in the Conservatori was frescoed by the Cavaliere d'Arpino in 1595 and the name of Clement XII and the date 1734 appear in the main room of the Palazzo Nuovo, which contains a part of the Capitoline collection of sculptures.

In the Conservatori is Bernini's seated statue of Urban VIII (1635–40; Wittkower, *Bernini*, p. 206) and that of Innocent X, originally commissioned from Mochi in 1645 but actually executed in 1646–50 by Algardi (Heimbürger Ravalli, *Algardi*, p. 85) and in the Sala dei Capitani are statues of generals of the papal armies, including one of Carlo Barberini which consists of an ancient torso restored and completed by Algardi (ibid., p. 60), though the head may be by Bernini.

The Conservatori also contains the Capitoline Collection of paintings including many works of the Baroque period, of which the most important come from the collection formed by the Sacchetti who were among the earliest patrons of Pietro da Cortona.

In the garden behind the Conservatori is a door, which now leads to the garden of the former Villa Caffarelli. It was originally the entrance to the Casino of Pietro Zacone near the Forum of Trajan but was removed when the via dei Fori Imperiali was made in 1930 and set up here in 1950. The architect was Giovanni Battista Mola, the author of one of the early guidebooks to Rome (C. Pietrangeli, 'Un opera di G. B. Mola trasferita in Campidoglio', *Bollettino dei Musei Comunali di Roma*, XXIII, 1976, p. 15).

See plate 51.

Palazzo Capizucchi (Gasparri)
Piazza Campitelli 3

Bibliography: Baglione, p. 82; Mola, p. 130; Martinelli, pp. 235, 257; Falda, *Nuovo teatro*, I, pl. 32; *Guide Rionali*, X, 1, p. 42.

Built by Giacomo della Porta for Muzio Capizucchi at the end of the 16th century (it is shown in a map of 1593). The windows of the *piano nobile* were altered in the late 17th or early 18th century by the addition of Borrominesque pediments with oval panels. At the same time a blind arch with false perspective pilasters and soffit was set up on the right-hand wall of the court. See plate 31.

Palazzo Capodiferro. See Palazzo Spada
Piazza Capodiferro

Palazzo Capponi
Via degli Orsini 32

Bibliography: Guide Rionali, V, 3, p. 64.

The palace, which is on the corner of the Piazza dell'Orologio, belonged to the Orsini but passed in the 17th century to the Capponi. It has two impressive doors which appear to date from the early 17th century.

Palazzo Carbognano. See Palazzo Sciarra
Via del Corso 239

Palazzo Cardelli
Piazza Cardelli

Bibliography: Ferrari, *Lo Stucco*, pl. CLXIV: G. Scano, 'Palazzo Cardelli', *Capitolium*, XXXVI, 1961, 10, p. 22; Torselli, *Palazzi*, p. 78 (who reproduces it but confuses its history with that of the Palazzo di Firenze).

Built 1592–6 for Giovanni Pietro Cardelli by Francesco da Volterra and completed in 1601–2 by Gaspare Guerra. Further work was done by Francesco Peparelli in 1633, who constructed the staircase. The model for these additions was the palace belonging to Asdrubale Mattei, a cousin of Cardelli. Carlo Cardelli (1626–62) decorated the staircase with ancient bas-reliefs set in elaborate stucco panels and commissioned Pietro Paolo Naldini to make the statue of *Apollo*, set in a rusticated niche in the garden. The main *salone* on the ground floor has a ceiling fresco by G. B. Modanino depicting an allegory of the sciences and the arts.

Palazzo Carpegna (Accademia di S. Luca)
Via della Stamperia

Bibliography: Hempel, *Borromini*, p. 127; M. Tafuri, 'Borromini in Palazzo Carpegna', *Quaderni*, 14, 1957, p. 85; Blunt, *Borromini*, p. 161.

In the early 1630s Conte Ambrogio Carpegna, a protégé of the Barberini, bought the Palazzo Vaini at the north end of the block on the east side of the piazza in front of the Fontana di Trevi. Between 1638 and 1640 he bought the other houses on the island site. He commissioned Borromini to plan a new building when he only owned part of the site, but after 1640 the architect produced a series of plans of extraordinary ingenuity and variety for the whole area, one of which actually involved an extension across the road to the east of the block which was to be linked with it by a bridge. Unfortunately none of these grandiose schemes was executed and in the event Borromini simply added to the old palace a loggia leading to an oval spiral ramp. (For a discussion of Borromini's projects see Blunt, loc. cit.) Old engravings and plans show that the main entrance to the palace was through a gate in the wall facing the loggia, but this has now been abandoned and the visitor enters the palace through the door to the Palazzo Vaini. The palace is now the seat of the Accademia di S. Luca.

See plate 97, 98; see also Palazzo Baldinotti-Carpegna.

Palazzo Cavallerini
Via dei Barbieri 6

Bibliography: L. Salerno, 'Il Palazzo Cavallerini a via dei Barbieri', *Palatino*, VIII, 1964, p. 13; Guide Rionali, VII, 1, p. 30.

Probably built for Cardinal Giovanni Giacomo Cavallerini (1629–99) before 1664. The rooms on the *piano nobile* have ceiling frescoes by the two Gimignani: the *Chariot of Venus*, *Aurora*, and *Time discovering Truth* by Giacinto and *Justice* by Lodovico (U. Verena Fischer, *Giacinto Gimignani* (Dissertation, Freiburg, 1973) p. 170).

Palazzo Celsi (Viscardi)
Corso Vittorio Emanuele 18

Bibliography: Pascoli, I, p. 317; De'Rossi, *Architettura Civile*, I, pl. 139; Spagnesi, *G. A. De Rossi*, p. 121; Guide Rionali, IX, 1, p. 86.

Pascoli ascribes the door and the staircase of this palace to G. A. de'Rossi and the attribution is confirmed by an engraving of the door in Rossi's *Architettura Civile* (I, pl. 139). The staircase is unusual in having at the end of each flight an opening on to a small light-well – as in Sangallo's staircase at the Palazzo Farnese – with ancient statues in niches.

In the early 18th century the palace passed to the Viscardi who added the second floor. The eagles and swords of their coat-of-arms appear in the cornice and in the pediments over the windows.

Palazzo Cenci-Bolognetti (Petroni)
Piazza Gesù

Bibliography: Vasi, *Magnificenze*, pl. 135; Magni, II, pl. 98; Matthiae, *Fuga*, p. 79; Pane, *Fuga*, p. 116 and figs 98, 99; *Guide Rionali*, IX, 1, p. 36.

The palace was enlarged in 1737 by Conte Alessandro Petroni who commissioned Ferdinando Fuga to design a new façade for it. The design of this is based on Bernini's Palazzo Chigi (Odescalchi), with a giant order of pilasters over a rusticated ground floor, but with the difference that, as in the Consulta, Fuga continues the pilasters across the whole façade whereas Bernini made a contrast between the pilastered central block and the plain flanking sections. The palace is now the seat of the Social-Democrat party.
See plate 21.

Palazzo Cesi. See Palazzo Mellini
Via del Corso

Palazzo Chigi. See Palazzo Aldobrandini-Chigi
Piazza Colonna

Palazzo Chigi (Odescalchi)
Piazza SS. Apostoli

Bibliography: Falda, *Nuovo teatro*, I, pls 14, 15 and IV, pl. 26; Ferrerio, *Palazzi*, II, pl. 16; Tessin, p. 176; Vasi, *Magnificenze*, pl. 64; Magni, II, pls 52, 53; T. Ashby, 'The Palazzo Odescalchi in Rome', *Papers of the British School at Rome*, VIII, 1916, p. 55 and IX, 1920, p. 67; Hibbard, *Maderno*, p. 213; Fagiolo dell'Arco, *Bernini*, No. 200; Schiavo, *Fontana di Trevi*, p. 239.

In 1622 Cardinal Ludovico Ludovisi bought a palace on this site from Pierfrancesco Colonna, who, however, bought it back a year later, when the cardinal became vice-chancellor and therefore had official lodgings. Although Ludovisi only owned the palace for a year he carried out considerable alterations on it, particularly to the court which was begun by Maderno.

62. *Palazzo Chigi-Odescalchi. Engraving by Falda showing on the right its original form as built by Bernini. On the left is the church of SS. Apostoli and next to it the Palazzo Colonna before it was remodelled by Specchi. At the end of the* piazza *is the Palazzo Bonelli (Valentino), and beyond it to the right the dome and campanile of S. Maria di Loreto.*

In 1661 the palace was bought by Cardinal Fabio Chigi who had rented it since 1657. He at first asked Felice della Greca to make plans for its completion, but these were not carried out and in 1664 Bernini was called in and built the façade. Originally this consisted of seven bays articulated by giant pilasters on a rusticated ground floor, flanked at each end by three bays without an order. This use of a giant order meant a radical break with the Roman tradition of palace building, which almost invariably followed the model of the Palazzo Farnese with a series of pedimented windows without any articulation. The one exception was Michelangelo's Palazzo dei Conservatori (see Capitoline Palaces), which must certainly have been in Bernini's mind, but there the pilasters spring from the ground.

In 1746 the palace was bought by Prince Odescalchi who greatly increased the length of the palace (the pilastered section now has 15 bays) and added a second entrance, thus entirely destroying the proportions of Bernini's design. The architect of the extension was Nicola Salvi.

Palazzo Cimarra
Via Panisperna 200

Bibliography: Golzio, *Palazzi*, p. 123; Elling, pl. 97.

A large and undistinguished building, opposite the church of S. Lorenzo in Panisperna, which probably originally stood in a garden. According to Valesio's diary it was begun in 1736.

Palazzo del Cinque
Via Colonna Antonina 52

Bibliography: Magni, II, pl. 110; Portoghesi, *Roma Barocca*, pls 304, 305; Mallory, *Rococo*, fig. 50; *Guide Rionali*, III, 2, p. 74; Elling, pl. 120.

An impressive palace with elaborate window pediments probably dating from the early 18th century.

Palazzo Cini. See Palazzo Ferrini
Piazza di Pietra 26

63. *Palazzo Chigi-Odescalchi. Etching by Piranesi showing the palace as enlarged by the Odescalchi. On the extreme right the Palazzo Muti Papazzuri.*

Palazzo Clementi. See Palazzo Patrizi a S. Caterina
12 via dei Delfini

Palazzo Colonna
Piazza SS. Apostoli

Bibliography: Tessin, p. 175; De Brosses, II, p. 95; Vasi, *Magnificenze*, pl. 63; Magni, II, pls 88–90; Pollak, 'Antonio del Grande', *Kunstgeschichtliches Jahrbuch der K. K. Zentralkommission*, III, 1909, p. 135; E. Lavagnino, 'Palazzo Colonna e l'architetto romano Niccolò Michetti', *Capitolium*, XX, 1942, p. 139; Golzio, *Palazzi*, figs 99ff.

The palace was begun by Martin V (1417–31) and still contains at least one room with a vault frescoed by Pinturicchio, but the greater part of it dates from the 17th and 18th centuries.

The most important additions made to the palace in the 17th century were commissioned by Cardinal Girolamo Colonna and were continued after his death by the Contestabile Filippo. Their architect was Antonio del Grande who was responsible for the arcaded façade in the main court (the arches are now blocked up). His drawing for it in the Kunstbibliothek, Berlin, was published by S. Jacob (*Italienische Zeichnungen der Kunstbibliothek, Berlin*, Berlin, 1975, No. 365) who compares this façade stylistically with one built by the same architect for the Colonna palace at Palliano.

Del Grande also built the Galleria, the most splendid complete Baroque room in any Roman palace. It was begun in 1654, and vaulted by 1665. After del Grande's death in 1671, the work was continued by Girolamo Fontana. The ceiling frescoes, glorifying the victory of *Lepanto* in which Marcantonio Colonna was the Roman general, were painted by Giovanni Coli and Filippo Gherardi between 1675 and 1678. The decorative parts of the ceiling are by Giovanni Paolo Schor (1665–70; W).

From 1731 onwards Niccolò Micchetti added the wing along Piazza SS. Apostoli for Fabrizio Colonna, but this was altered in the 19th century so that only the two end pavilions remain as he designed them.

The palace contains rooms on the ground floor with landscape frescoes by Gaspard Dughet and Pieter Mulier, called Tempesta, both with painted and architectural settings by Giovanni Battista Magno, called Il Modanino

64. Palazzo Colonna. Engraving by Vasi showing the palace as remodelled by Specchi. Beyond it the church of SS. Apostoli and the Palazzo Muti Papazzuri.

(1667–8; cf. S. J. Bandes, 'Gaspard Dughet's frescoes in Palazzo Colonna, Rome', *Burlington Magazine*, CXXIII, 1981, p. 77). The rooms on the *piano nobile* contain an important collection of paintings, including many of the Baroque period. For the gardens behind the palace see Villa Colonna.
See plate 62.

Palazzo Colonna. See Palazzo Massimi di Rignano
Piazza Aracoeli 30

Palazzo Colonna di Sciarra. See Palazzo Sciarra
Via del Corso 239

Palazzo della Compagnia della Annunziata
Via della Annunziata

Bibliography: Baglione, p. 48; *Guide Rionali*, III, 2, p. 36.

Begun by Francesco da Volterra but left unfinished, and so much altered later that nothing remains of its original character.

Palazzo dei Conservatori. See Capitoline Palaces

Palazzo della Consulta
Piazza del Quirinale

Bibliography: Letarouilly, pls 29, 30, 57 (23, 24); Magni, II, pls 92–7; Matthiae, *Fuga*, p. 70; Pane, *Fuga*, p. 28 and figs 17–25; L. Bianchi, *Fuga*, p. 5; A. Agosteo and A. Pasquini, *Il Palazzo della Consulta*, Rome, 1959; Portoghesi, *Roma Barocca*, pls 428, 429; F. Borsi et al., *Il Palazzo della Consulta*, Rome, 1974; Elling, pl. 88.

The palace was built for Clement XII as the seat of the Consulta, the congregation which controlled the relations of the Holy See with secular powers. It was begun in 1732 on the designs of Ferdinando Fuga and was in the main finished by 1736. The sculptures over the doors and on the crowning balustrade are by Filippo della Valle and Paolo Benaglia. In the general design of the façade Fuga has followed Bernini's Palazzo Chigi with a tall order of pilasters over a – partly – rusticated ground floor but he has altered the proportions so that the two floors are of almost equal heights. The palace is ingeniously designed on a trapezoidal plan to fit the awkward site, and has on the inner side of the main block a staircase, originally open, which in many ways reflects those of Ferdinando Sanfelice in Naples, though it is much less subtle in its treatment of the openings which are defined by rectilinear forms as compared with Sanfelice's softly curved shapes. The arms of Savoy over the door are, of course, a late 19th-century addition.

The palace is now the seat of the Corte Costituzionale.
See plate 72.

Palazzo Cornaro (della Stamperia)
Via della Stamperia

Bibliography: Baglione, p. 82; Martinelli, p. 240; Ferrerio, *Palazzi*, I, pl. 36; Bellori, annotation to Baglione's *Vite*, facsimile 1935, p. 82; Titi, 1763, p. 354; M. Pierro, 'Il Palazzo della Stamperia', *Capitolium*, IV, 1928–9, p. 237; S. Benedetti, *Del Duca*, Rome, 1973, p. 226.

Ferrerio says that the palace was built in 1575, but in fact the two plots which formed the central part of the site were bought in 1579 and 1582 by the Venetian Cardinal Cornaro who built on it a small palace, consisting of the middle five bays of the existing front, and almost square in shape. After being occupied by a number of tenants, including Cardinal Mazarin, it was bought in 1647 by Donna Olimpia Maidalchini, sister-in-law of Innocent X, who enlarged it. In 1777 it was bought by Pius VI who installed in it the papal printing press.

The original palace is generally ascribed to Giacomo del Duca, Michelangelo's assistant at Porta Pia and author of the nearby church of S. Maria in Trivio. This attribution is based on the 18th-century guide-books (Titi, 1763, and others), but the first writers to mention the palace, Baglione and Martinelli, both ascribe it to Giacomo della Porta. On the other hand Bellori in a manuscript note to the *Vite* (p. 82) adds it to the list of del Duca's works.

Stylistic considerations confirm this attribution. An engraving in Franzini's *Descrittione di Roma antica* (Rome, 1643, p. 743) shows that the five central bays have not been basically altered and they contain several features which are too revolutionary for their time to be by the orthodox della Porta, notably the breaking of the tops of the windows, the scrolls under the straight pediments, and the treatment of the blocks over the columns supporting the balcony, the balusters of which are unusual in being nearly square in horizontal section. The masks under the cornice look much later but they appear in Franzini's engraving and if they date from the 16th century they must be by del Duca. A frieze over a landing on the staircase (Benedetti, fig. 194) contains masks which are purely Michelangelesque.

The palace is now the seat of the Direzione Generale delle Pensioni di Guerra.

Palazzo Corsini
Via della Lungara 10

Bibliography: Ferrerio, *Palazzi*, I, pl. 38; Tessin, p. 182; Vasi, *Magnificenze*, pl. 72; Percier and Fontaine, *Palais*, IV, pls 84, 85; Letarouilly, pl. 192 (148); Magni, II, pls 99, 100; Pane, *Fuga*, p. 58 and figs 39–46; Matthiae, *Fuga*, p. 73; L. Bianchi, *Fuga*, p. 42; Golzio, *Palazzi*, figs 107–10; *Guide Rionali*, XIII, 3, p. 70.

The first palace on this site was built in 1473 by Cardinal Cristoforo Riario. In the 17th century it was lived in by Queen Christina of Sweden. The present palace was begun for the Corsini in 1736 by Fuga. It is remarkable for a fine three-aisled vestibule leading to a passage which goes through to the garden at the back and is flanked by two flights of stairs. These unite at the half-landing to form a single flight which takes the visitor up to the *piano nobile*. This is the reverse of the normal 18th-century arrangement with a single flight dividing into two, but it has the advantage of allowing a carriage-way through to the garden and stables to be laid out on the main axis of the palace.

On the first floor (left) is a part of the Galleria Nazionale d'Arte antica, including much of the original Corsini Collection, acquired by the state with the palace.

The second floor (right) contains part of the library. The rooms have an important series of frescoed ceilings probably dating from the late 1730s, the authors of which have not been identified.

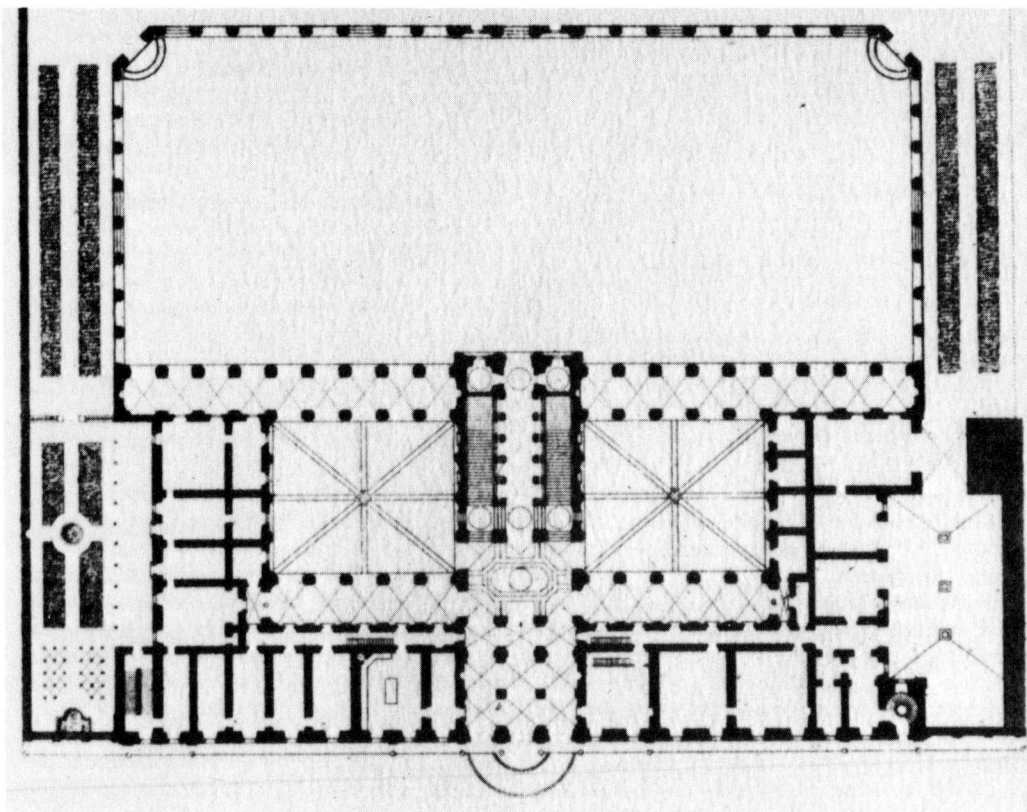

65. *Palazzo Corsini. Plan.*

Palazzo Costaguti
Piazza Mattei

Bibliography: Baglione, p. 166; Mola, p. 129; Titi, 1763, p. 90; Martinelli, p. 240; Letarouilly, pl. 22; Lotti, 'I Costaguti, Marchesi di Sipicciano e il loro palazzo di Piazza Mattei', *Palatino*, IV, 1960, pp. 108, 134 and V, 1961, p. 10; *Guide Rionali*, XI, p. 56.

The palace, which is of little interest architecturally, was built in the 16th century for the Patrizi family, according to Mola by Ascanio Rossi. It was bought in the early 17th century by Monsignor Vincenzo Costaguti who had it partly remodelled by Carlo Lambardi. He commissioned an important series of frescoes to decorate the rooms of the *piano nobile* from the principal artists of the day: Cavaliere d'Arpino (*Venus arming Aeneas*); Francesco Albani (*Hercules and Nessus*); Guercino (*Rinaldo carried away by Armida*); Domenichino (*Time and Truth*, with architectural surround by Agostino Tassi); Francesco Romanelli (*Arion*); Pierfrancesco Mola (*Bacchus and Ariadne*; W and Voss, pp. 504, 523ff., 549, 554, 559, 562); F. Allegrini (*Mars and Diana*).

Palazzo Crescenzi
Via della Rotonda 23

Bibliography: Falda, *Nuovo teatro*, II, pl. 3; Ferrerio, *Palazzi*, II, pls 16, 17; De'Rossi, *Architettura Civile*, I, pls 128–30; Mola, p. 127; Martinelli, p. 241; Titi, 1763, p. 184; I. Toesca, 'Pomarancio a Palazzo Crescenzi', *Paragone*, VIII, 91, 1957, p. 41; ibid, XIX, 1968, 221, p. 48; M. Roethlisberger, 'Les Fresques de Claude Lorrain', *Paragone*, X, 109, 1959, p. 41; ibid., XX, 233, 1969, p. 54.

Most authors say that the palace was built by Niccolò Sebregondi from the Valtellina, probably with the help of Giovanni Battista Crescenzi, who was an amateur architect, before 1617, when Crescenzi left for Spain. In the rooms on the first floor are frescoes by Cristofano Roncalli called Il Pomarancio, and friezes with landscapes, the latter executed for Giovanni Battista Crescenzi, probably between 1630 and 1635. These were ascribed by Roethlisberger to Claude Lorrain, but Ilaria Toesca rejected the attribution. Some rooms were also painted by G. B. Crescenzi himself.
See also Palazzo Serlupi Crescenzi.

Palazzo de Carolis
Via del Corso 307

Bibliography: Falda, *Nuovo teatro*, I, pl. 17; P. Ferri, *Roma ampliata*, Rome, 1725, p. 116; Rossini, *Mercurio Errante*, Rome, 1732, p. 64; Magni, II, pl. 107; Salerno, *Via del Corso*, p. 229; A. Bocca, *Il Palazzo del Banco di Roma*, Rome, 1961 and 1967; *Guide Rionali*, IX, 3, p. 40.

In 1714 Livio de Carolis bought a number of palaces and small houses which occupied the block facing S. Marcello, enclosed by the Corso, the via Lata, the Collegio Romano and the via del Caravita, and commissioned Alessandro Specchi to build him a palace to cover the entire site (finished 1724). The architect incorporated in the façade the famous 16th-century fountain called 'Il Facchino', showing a man holding a barrel from which the water flows (D'Onofrio, *Acque e Fontane*, p. 145). In 1872 this was moved to the façade facing via Lata in order to clear the pavement of the Corso. The palace passed through various hands, and was the French Embassy, presided over by the Cardinal de Bernis from 1769 to 1794 and by Chateaubriand from 1828 to 1830. In 1831 the palace was bought by Luigi Buoncompagni Ludovisi, Principe di Piombino, who added an attic and the heavy frieze containing the dragon of the Buoncompagni and the bends of the Ludovisi arms between the consoles. Since 1908 it has been the seat of the Banco di Roma. The interior has been much altered, but still contains Specchi's fine oval spiral staircase. There are painted ceilings by Sebastiano Conca, Francesco Trevisani, Andrea Procaccini, Benedetto Luti, Domenico Maria Muratori and Giovanni Odazzi dating from before 1732.
See plates 46, 47.

Palazzo del Bufalo
Via del Pozzetto

Bibliography: De'Rossi, *Architettura Civile*, I, pl. 104; Belli-Barsali, p. 48; Blunt, *Borromini*, p. 175.

The palace has been attributed to Giacomo del Duca but on little evidence and Benedetti in his monograph on the artist does not even mention it. The *casino* in the garden, which was destroyed in the 19th century, was famous for its frescoes by Polidoro da Caravaggio, but Borromini added to it a door which is known from an engraving in de'Rossi's *Architettura Civile*. Belli-Barsali shows a view of the *casino* with a fountain which certainly dates from the 17th century and might also be from the design of Borromini.

Palazzo del Bufalo Ferraioli (Niccolini)
Piazza Colonna

Bibliography: Ferrerio, *Palazzi*, II, pl. 47; Titi, 1763, p. 358; Salerno, *Via del Corso*, p. 206; G. Spagnesi, 'Palazzo del Bufalo-Ferraioli e il suo architetto', *Palladio*, N. S., XIII, 1963, p. 134; *Guide Rionali*, III, 1, p. 22.

Rebuilt by the del Bufalo family on the site of older houses about 1626 as part of the scheme to develop Piazza Colonna, on the north side of which the Palazzo Aldobrandini, later Chigi, was being constructed. Work on the palace was begun in 1626 and in the next year Francesco Peparelli was called in to design the whole scheme. Work was interrupted in 1635 by which time all but two bays of the present palace were complete and the whole palace was finished in 1645. In the 18th century it passed by descent to the Niccolini and then to the Ferraioli, to whom it still belongs. The balcony on the corner is a late addition, probably dating from the 19th century.

The – very crude – engraving of the palace in Fei's *Roma antica e moderna* of 1643 (II, p. 746) shows the palace with seven bays only, a round-headed rusticated door and the ground floor articulated with pilasters. Since at that time the palace was still unfinished it probably represents one of the earlier palaces on the site which was absorbed into the new building.
See plate 54.

Palazzo del Drago (Gentili)
Via in Arcione 71

Bibliography: Callari, p. 451; Elling, p. 282, pl. 105

Part of this palace was demolished when the Traforo running under the Quirinal was constructed in the late 19th century, but it still retains a fine early 18th-century door, with nervously carved capitals and entablature and unusually vigorous *barocchetto* hoods over the windows.

Said to have been built by Monsignor Antonio Gentile (made a cardinal in 1731). Later it was acquired by the del Drago family.
See also Palazzo Albani

Palazzo del Grillo
Via Tor de'Conti

Bibliography: De'Rossi, *Architettura Civile*, I, pls 140, 141; Visentini, *Osservazioni*, p. 40; Magni, II, pls 108, 109 and III, pls 26, 27; Ferrari, *Lo Stucco*, pls CLIIff.; Portoghesi, *Roma Barocca*, pls 350, 351; Elling, pls 178, 179.

The existing palace was built in the late 17th century round a much earlier nucleus. The architect is unknown but de'Rossi ascribes the two entrance doors to Carlo Rainaldi. Visentini picks out these doors for particularly vituperative criticism.

The garden, though small, is the most beautiful and the most perfectly preserved Baroque palace garden in Rome. It is on a higher level than the entrance, owing to the steep slope on which the palace is built, and contains a series of fine and elaborate late-Baroque fountains and doors which are traditionally ascribed to Carlo Rainaldi, but are stylistically more like the work of G. P. Schor (Hibbard, 'Palazzo Borghese studies. I: the garden and its fountains', *Burlington Magazine*, C, 1958, p. 205). Hibbard points out that the fountains are also close to one in the Palazzo Santacroce, the author of which is unknown.

The palace has a series of rooms with fine late-Baroque stucco ceilings.

Palazzo Donarelli (Ricci)
Via Giulia 97

Bibliography: Salerno, *Via Giulia*, p. 286

A small palace with an interesting entrance vestibule and oval staircase, probably dating from the early 18th century.

Palazzo Doria-Pamphili
Via del Corso

Bibliography: Falda, *Nuovo teatro*, I, pl. 38; id., IV, pl. 21, and *Fontane*, III, pl. 20; De Brosses, II, p. 106; Letarouilly, pls 59, 60, 67 (43–5); Magni, II, pls 80–7; Colosanti, pls 184ff.; Ferrari, *Lo Stucco*, pls CLXVff.; O. Pollak, 'Antonio del Grande', *Kunstgeschichtliches Jahrbuch der K. K. Zentralkommission*, III, 1909, p. 142; Salerno, *Via del Corso*, p. 250; Frommel, *Palastbau*, II, p. 88; A. Carandente, *Il Palazzo Doria-Pamphili*, Rome, 1975; Mallory, *Rococo*, p. 107; *Guide Rionali*, IX, 3, p. 56.

The first palace on this site was begun by Cardinal Niccolò d'Acciapacci about 1440 and completed by Cardinal Dionysius Zech (d.1465). It was enlarged by Cardinal Fazio Santori who acquired the palace between 1486 and 1489 and died in 1509, when it was given by Julius II to his nephew, Francesco Maria della Rovere, duke of Urbino. In 1601 the duke of Urbino sold the palace to Cardinal Pietro Aldobrandini. In 1647 his heir Donna Olimpia Aldobrandini married Innocent X's nephew Camillo Pamphili, and the palace passed to the Pamphili family. Camillo built a further section of the court and added a gallery. He also built a wing opposite the Collegio Romano, facing on a square formed by the demolition of the Palazzo

Salviati which was authorized by Alexander VII in 1659 to make an open space in front of the College. This wing, which was to contain the principal entrance to the palace, was finished in 1660, though the decoration of the interior went on till 1663. The documents prove that the architect was Antonio del Grande, though the old guide-books attribute it to Borromini, Bernini, Cortona and even Girolamo Rainaldi who died four years before it was begun.

Its principal interest lies in the arrangement of the vestibule and staircase. As at the Palazzo di Spagna, the axis of the staircase continues that of the vestibule and so creates a vista, which is here more striking than in the earlier building, because the vestibule is a more emphatically elongated rectangle and is free of the columns which tend to obstruct the view up the first flight of steps at the Palazzo di Spagna. The staircase leads to the vast Salone del Pussino in which hang big landscapes by Gaspard Dughet, brother-in-law of Nicolas Poussin.

Between 1731 and 1735 on the order of Camillo Pamphili the Younger the whole of the palace on the Corso was remodelled by Gabriele Valvassori, who closed the upper loggias of the court, turning them into galleries, and built the façade on the Corso, and the rooms of the palace were then redecorated. The Galleria degli Specchi was frescoed by Aureliano Milani, other rooms by Liborio Marmorelli, Pietro Angeletti, Tommaso Maria Conca, Stefano Pozzo, Pompeo Aldrovandini, Genesio del Barba, Filippo Catapani. In the Sala dei Velluti are busts of Innocent X and one of his brothers, probably Benedetto, by Algardi (Heimbürger Ravalli, *Algardi*, pp. 115, 121, who tentatively but unconvincingly identifies the second bust as representing Pamphilio).

In 1740–1 Camillo acquired the land facing on what is now the via del Plebiscito between the Palazzo Gottifredi and the Palazzo Aste and built on it an extension to the palace on the design of Paolo Ameli (finished 1744).

On the death of Girolamo Pamphili, brother of Camillo, the palace became the property of Prince Giovanni Andrea Doria, who was descended from a daughter of the elder Camillo Pamphili, and has since been known as the Palazzo Doria-Pamphili. In the second half of the 19th century many of the rooms were remodelled by the architect Andrea Busiri Vici. The palace contains one of the most important collections of paintings in Rome.
See plates 46, 47, 56.
See also Palazzo Pamphili.

66. *Palazzo Pamphili (now Doria-Pamphili). Etching by Piranesi showing the wing opposite the Collegio Romano, added by Antonio del Grande.*

Palazzo Este. See Palazzo Maffei
Via della Pigna

Palazzo Falconieri
Via Giulia

Bibliography: Ferrerio, *Palazzi*, II, pls 30–3; O. Pollak, 'Die Decken des Palazzo Falconieri', *Kunstgeschichtliches Jahrbuch der K. K. Zentralkommission*, V, 1911; Hempel, *Borromini*, p. 51; Wittkower, *Art and Architecture*, p. 225; Portoghesi, *Borromini nella cultura europea*, figs 32–7; id., *Borromini*, pls 136–43; Salerno, *Via Giulia*, p. 445; Battisti, 'Il Simbolismo in Borromini', *Studi sul Borromini*, I, p. 229; Blunt, *Borromini*, p. 169; *Guide Rionali*, VII, 3, pp. 42, 55. E. J. Howard, *The Falconerieri Palace in Rome* (Dissertation) New York, 1981.

The palace originally belonged to the Odescalchi, elements of whose arms can still be seen in the cornice. They sold it to Pietro Farnese, duke of Latera, in 1606, and he in turn sold it in 1638 to Orazio Falconieri. It then had a frontage of seven bays on via Giulia, running north from the church of S. Maria della Morte. In 1645 Falconieri acquired an adjacent palace and in 1646 he commissioned Borromini to remodel the whole complex.

Borromini systematized the street façade adding a second door and flanking it with pilasters ending in falcons' heads (in allusion to the owner's name). He also inserted a falcon in the key-stone of the second door, which is otherwise an exact copy of the original one in the 16th-century part of the palace. (The stucco rustication on this façade appears to date from the 19th-century restoration.) On the top of the south wing he constructed a Belvedere of unusual form with concave ends and Janus herms, forming – as seen across the Tiber – a clear challenge to Giacomo della Porta's loggia on the adjacent Palazzo Farnese.

In the interior Borromini decorated a number of small rooms with stucco ceilings (Portoghesi, *Roma Barocca*, pls 122–4), some almost neoclassical in their detail, based on complicated symbolism (cf. Battisti, who has traced the sources of several of them). These ceilings were almost certainly intended to be white – perhaps with some gilding – but some of them have suffered from having painted decoration added during the 19th-century restoration.

The wing between the block containing the loggia and the Tiber was rebuilt in the 19th century when the present staircase was constructed. In the process the chapel built and decorated by Borromini was destroyed, but its appearance is known from an old photograph and some of Borromini's drawings for it survive.

Drawings by Borromini for the exterior of the palace and for several of the ceilings are in the Kunstbibliothek, Berlin (S. Jacob, *Italienische Zeichnungen der Kunstbibliothek Berlin*, Nos 332–45). A drawing by Andrea Sacchi at Windsor (Blunt and Cocke, *The Roman Drawings at Windsor Castle*, London, 1960, No. 771) shows the big *salone* of the palace with a banquet taking place, but the room seems to be completely undecorated.

The palace is now the seat of the Hungarian Academy.

Palazzo Fani (Pecci-Blunt)
Piazza Campidoglio 3

Bibliography: Baglione, p. 82; *Guide Rionali*, X, 1, p. 20.

A palace on this site originally belonged to the Albertoni but was bought in the later 16th century by Mario Fani who married Olimpia Astalli and rebuilt the palace to the designs of Giacoma della Porta (finished before 1600). One room has a frieze frescoed by Gaspard Dughet.

Palazzo Farnese
Piazza Farnese

Bibliography: Tessin, p. 186; Letarouilly, pls 115–39 (89–113); R. de Broglie, *Le Palais Farnèse à Rome*, Paris, 1953; Ackerman, *The Architecture of Michelangelo*, London, 1961, p. 75; J. R. Martin, *The Farnese Gallery*, Princeton, 1965; Frommel, *Palastbau*, II, p. 103.

Begun 1516 for Cardinal Alessandro Farnese (later Pope Paul III) by Antonio da Sangallo the Younger, continued after his death in 1546 by Michelangelo who is responsible for the top floor of the *cortile*, the frieze on the façade and the window over the entrance. After Michelangelo's death the court and façade over the river were altered by Giacomo della Porta, who closed the open, three-bay loggia on the first floor of the rear block and built another loggia facing the river – but closed on the court side – on the second floor.

In connection with later (Baroque) developments the false perspective introduced by Sangallo at the court end of the main vestibule is of interest.

INTERIOR

In the first *salone* on the *piano nobile* is a fireplace designed by Vignola and statues by Guglielmo della Porta from the tomb of Paul III in St Peter's, which were removed and set up here when the tomb was moved. The *salone* next door was frescoed by Salviati and Taddeo Zuccaro with scenes from the history of the Farnese family. Under Ranuccio Farnese, Annibale Carracci, with his brother Agostino and other assistants, including Domenichino and Lanfranco, were commissioned to fresco first the *Camerino* and then the *Galleria*. In the latter Annibale created one of the most harmonious decorative schemes in any Roman palace, which was to exert a profound influence on all such schemes throughout the 17th and 18th centuries (J. R. Martin, *The Farnese Gallery*, Princeton, 1965; D. Posner, *Annibale Carracci*, London, 1971, I, p. 93 and II, p. 49). The palace is now the French Embassy.

Palazzo Ferraioli. See Palazzo del Bufalo-Ferraioli
Piazza Colonna

Palazzo Ferrini (Cini)
Piazza di Pietra 26

Bibliography: Baglione, p. 156; Martinelli, p. 243; Titi, 1763, p. 358; *Guide Rionali*, III, 2, p. 18; Elling, pl. 94.

Built by Onorio Longhi for Domofonte Ferrini in the early 17th century but left unfinished. Ferrini bequeathed it to the nuns of S. Maria in Aquiro, and in the 19th century it belonged to Conte Giuseppe Cini whose name appears over the door, which, however, is decorated with the elements of the arms of Ferrini and his wife Aurelia Grana.

Palazzo Gabrielli. See Miscellaneous, Seminario Romano
Via del Seminario 120

Palazzo Gaetani. See Palazzo Ruspoli
Largo Goldoni

Palazzo Galoppi (Volpi di Misurato)
Via del Quirinale 21

Bibliography: Torselli, p. 311, *Guide Rionali* II, p. 226.

Little information is available about the history of this palace, which has only belonged to the Volpi family since 1939. On stylistic grounds it is clear that it was built in the first half of the 18th century, by an architect who in his treatment of the two doors – one on the façade in the side street to the left – shows a remarkable understanding of Borromini's inventions.

Palazzo Gambirasi
Piazza S. Maria della Pace

Bibliography: Falda, *Nuovo teatro*, I, p. 126; De'Rossi, *Architettura Civile*, I, pl. 114; Spagnesi, *G. A. De Rossi*, p. 80.

The palace belonged to the church of S. Giacomo degli Spagnuoli, to which G. A. de'Rossi was architect. It was remodelled when the Piazza in front of S. Maria della Pace was altered by Cortona in 1656–7 (see S. Maria della Pace). The lower floors are typical of de'Rossi's severe style, but the pediments over the windows of the second floor are unlike his normal style and may be based on designs by Cortona to whom de'Rossi ascribes them. Falda shows the palace complete in 1665. See plate 41.

Palazzo Gasparri. See Palazzo Capizucchi
Piazza Campitelli 3

Palazzo Gentili. See Palazzo del Drago
Via in Arcione 71

Palazzo Giangiacomo
Via Monserrato 105

Bibliography: Guide Rionali, VII, 2, p. 44.

The palace is dated 1582 on the façade, but the author is unknown. Next to it at No. 103 via Monserrato is a small palace with a characteristic early 18th-century façade of good quality.

Palazzo Giustiniani
Piazza S. Luigi dei Francesi

Bibliography: Baglione, p. 130; Martinelli, p. 243; Mola, p. 124; Falda, *Nuovo teatro*, IV, pl. 41; Ferrerio, *Palazzi*, II, pls 40, 41; De'Rossi, *Architettura Civile*, I, pls 102, 103; Tessin, p. 174; De Brosses, II, p. 115; Percier and Fontaine, *Palais*, IV, pl. 21; Magni, II, pl. 27; Letarouilly, pl. 340 (220); Hibbard, *Maderno*, p. 114; I. Toesca, 'Note sulla storia del Palazzo Giustiniani a San Luigi dei Francesi', *Bollettino d'Arte*, XLII, 1967, p. 296.

The palace – apparently newly built for the Vento family – was bought in 1590 by the Giustiniani, a branch of the Genoese family who had settled in Rome. It is attributed in the early sources to Giovanni Fontana. In the early 17th century it housed the great collection formed by the marchese Vincenzo Giustiniani (d.1638), of which the ancient sculpture is recorded in engravings in the two volumes of the *Galleria Giustiniani*. The palace was slightly modified or extended by Maderno (*c.*1590–1) and between 1650 and 1655 Borromini produced plans for extensive alterations for Prince Andrea Giustiniani, Vincenzo's adopted son and heir, but these were not carried out and his only addition to the palace seems to have been the door facing the piazza. Ferrerio and de'Rossi show this with the eagles and tower of the Giustiniani arms over the door and similar motifs appear in a drawing for the door in the Albertina, but as it stands today the area over the door is plain.

The collections were sold in the early 19th century (but see Villa Giustiniani), the paintings being bought by the Berlin Museum. The palace is now a dependency of the Senate (Palazzo Madama).

Palazzo Gomez
Via della Croce 78A

Bibliography: Spagnesi, *G. A. De Rossi*, p. 162.

Built by G. A. de'Rossi, probably about 1678. It has a delicately fluted door and a picturesque courtyard, apparently laid out in the 19th century.

Palazzo Grazioli (Gottifredi)
Via Plebiscito 102

Bibliography: Falda, *Nuovo teatro*, I, pl. 16; Ferrerio, *Palazzi*, II, pl. 51; De'Rossi, *Architettura Civile*, I, pl. 174; Titi, 1763, p. 483; Portoghesi, *Roma Barocca*, pls 238, 241; *Guide Rionali*, IX, 1, p. 72

Originally built by Giacomo della Porta for the Gottifredi family, but enlarged in the pontificate of Alexander VII by Camillo Arcucci. The palace was much altered in the 1870s when a completely new façade was erected at the back, facing Piazza Grazioli, and the court was remodelled, but Arcucci's façade survives little altered.

See plates 55, 56

Palazzo Graziosi. See Palazzo Mastrozzi
Piazza S. Caterina della Rota

Palazzo Lancellotti
Piazza Lancellotti

Bibliography: Baglione, p. 48; Martinelli, p. 244; Ferrerio, *Palazzi*, II, pls 48, 49; De'Rossi, *Architettura Civile*, I, pl. 132; Titi, 1763, p. 407; Hibbard, *Maderno*, p. 123; Blunt, 'The other side'; *Guide Rionali*, V, 2, p. 12.

Begun by Francesco da Volterra (*c.* 1591) probably for Cardinal Scipione Lancellotti (d. 1598) and finished by Maderno for Cardinal Orazio under Paul V. The door, also commissioned by Orazio, was designed by Domenichino. It is the only work in architecture that he is known to have executed. Two drawings for it are at Windsor (Blunt, *Supplement to the Catalogue of the Italian Drawings at Windsor Castle*, London, 1971, p. 78, Nos 158, 159). Somewhat surprisingly this door is sharply criticized by Visentini (*Osservazioni*, p. 43). In the interior are *quadratura* frescoes by Agostino Tassi in collaboration with Guercino (J. Hess, *Tassi*, Munich, 1935, p. 18, and S. Jacob, 'Pierre de Cortone et la décoration de la galerie d'Alexandre VII au Quirinal', *Revue de l'Art*, XI, 1971, p. 48, fig. 12).

Palazzo Lante
Piazza dei Caprettari

Bibliography: Frommel, *Palastbau*, II, p. 224.

Built by the Medici in the 16th century and acquired by the Lante family, after complicated negotiations in 1585. The ceiling of the *galleria* has frescoes of allegorical subjects and scenes from the early history of Rome by Romanelli (1653; W).

Palazzo del Laterano

Bibliography: Ferrerio, *Palazzi*, I, pl. 10; De Brosses, II, p. 321; Letarouilly, II, pl. 223; Magni, II, pls 22–5; A. Schiavo, *Il Laterano. Palazzo e Battistero*, Rome, 1969; *Guide Rionali*, I, l, p. 60.

Mainly built by Domenico Fontana for Sixtus V between 1585 and 1590, but the east wing was not finished till the 18th century. The vaults of loggias, staircase and rooms were frescoed with *grotteschi*, interspersed with small religious subjects and the arms of the pope, by a team of artists under the direction of Giovanni Guerra (Colosanti, pls 100ff.).

At the south end of the west arm of the cloister is a double door leading to the church, designed by Borromini and dated 1650 (Portoghesi, *Borromini*, pl. 121). The stucco decoration over it consists of an orb – of the world – on which are displayed the arms of Innocent X, supported by a cherub. Two of his wings are spread out, like curved pediments over the doors, while with the other four he actually supports the orb. The fingers of one hand appear over the moulding between the two doors. The whole composition is a beautiful example of Borromini's use of sculpture to perform the function of architecture (cf. the niche with the statue of *S. Carlo Borromeo* on the façade of S. Carlo alle Quattro Fontane).

The palace now contains offices connected with the administrative services of the Vatican.

Palazzo Lazzarini
Via dei Lucchesi 20

Bibliography: Callari, p. 447.

Little is known of the history of this palace which has a fine late 17th-century door.

Palazzo Lovatelli
Piazza Lovatelli

Bibliography: Baglione, p. 82; Mola, p. 131; *Guide Rionali*, XI, p. 78.

Begun c.1580 for Gregorio Serlupi, probably from the designs of Giacomo della Porta, and finished after 1619 for his son by another, unnamed architect. Passed later to the Ruspoli and then to the Lovatelli.

Palazzo Ludovisi. See Palazzo Almagià
Via del Corso and Piazza S. Lorenzo in Lucina

Palazzo Macchi di Cellere
Piazza Montecitorio 115

Bibliography: *Architettura minora*, I, pl. 64; Callari, p. 470; *Guide Rionali*, III, 2, p. 76.

An inscription over the rather elaborately formed late-Baroque door states that Clement XII opened up the street – in effect the Piazza Montecitorio – in 1733, which is presumably the date of the palace in its present form. The architect is said to have been Tommaso Mattei.

Palazzo Madama
Piazza Madama

Bibliography: Martinelli, p. 293; Mola, p. 131; Falda, *Nuovo teatro*, IV, pl. 10; Ferrerio, *Palazzi*, I, pls 11, 12; De Brosses, II, p. 115; Magni, II, pls 28–32; G. Chierici, *Il Palazzo italiano*, 1957, p. 314; Portoghesi, *Roma Barocca*, pls 240–2; V. del Gaizo et al., *Palazzo Madama*, Rome, 1969; Connors, *Borromini*, p. 109.

Built on the site of a 16th-century Medici palace which took its name – like the Villa Madama – from Madama Margherita, natural daughter of Charles V, who married Alessandro de'Medici and later Ottavio Farnese. The palace was enlarged in 1610 by Ludovico Cardi, called Il Cigoli, who built a new façade. It was completed by Paolo Maruscelli for Ferdinand II, grand duke of Tuscany, in 1642. The mouldings and carved decoration of the windows, which include the lily of Florence, are unusually rich for Maruscelli, whose style is normally restrained and non-Baroque. The palace was bought by Benedict XIV to house the lawcourts, and since 1871 has been the seat of the Senate.

Palazzo Maffei (Sannesi, Este, Marescotti)
Via della Pigna

Bibliography: Baglione, p. 81; Totti, p. 388; Martinelli, p. 245; Mola, p. 129; Ferrerio, *Palazzi*, II, pls 20, 21; Roisecco, 1750, I, p. 530; Vasi, *Magnificenze*, pl. 78; Titi, 1763, p. 358; Magni, II, pl. 72; Hibbard, *Maderno*, p. 25; Wasserman, *Mascarino*, p. 111; *Guide Rionali*, IX, 2, p. 104.

Begun about 1580 for Cardinal Marcantonio Maffei, probably by Giacomo della Porta. In 1605 the palace, still unfinished, was sold to the duca Clemente Sannesi, in 1668 to the Este, in 1714 to the Acciaioli and in 1746 to the Marescotti who commissioned Ferdinando Fuga to make some alterations to the court. The façade

67. Palazzo Madama. Engraving by Vasi.

Palazzo Magnani
Via Campo Marzio 46

Bibliography: Guide Rionali, III, 2, p. 116.

Built, probably in the late 17th century, for the marchesi Magnani, the palace has a fine, if somewhat ponderous, door.

Palazzo Mancini
Via del Corso 271

Bibliography: Falda, *Nuovo teatro*, IV, pl. 40; Vasi, *Magnificenze*, pl. 170; Salerno, *Via del Corso*, p. 244; A. Schiavo, *Palazzo Mancini*, Rome, 1969.

The palace belonged to the Mancini family since at least the 16th century but the building owes its present form to Cardinal Mazarin, whose sister had married Lorenzo Mancini. His heir, the duc de Nevers, who had married one of Mazarin's nieces, commissioned Carlo Rainaldi to enlarge and remodel it in 1660. It was famous as the home of Mazarin's nieces whom he used in a complicated game of marriages for aggrandizement, one becoming Princess Colonna, another duchesse de la Meilleraye, the third duchesse de Nevers. In 1725 the palace was bought by the duc d'Antin, on behalf of Louis XV, for the French Academy, which had its seat there till the disturbances of the Napoleonic War. During this time many of the most important French artists of the period were lodged there as students or directors. It is now the seat of the Banco di Sicilia.

Architecturally it is unremarkable, though its wide entrance, flanked by four Doric columns, is a conspicuous feature of the Corso, but seems tame compared with Valvassori's lively façade of the Palazzo Doria-Pamphili opposite.

Palazzo Marescotti. See Palazzo Maffei
Via della Pigna

Palazzo Massimi. See Palazzo Albani
Via Agostino de' Pretis

Palazzo Massimi di Rignano (Colonna)
Piazza Aracoeli 30

Bibliography: Falda, *Fontane*, III, pl. 27; Coudenhove-Erthal, p. 57; *Guide Rionali*, X, 1, p. 22.

The palace probably dates from the late 16th or early 17th century, but the door and the fountain in the court were added in the later 17th century, almost certainly by Carlo Fontana. When the via del Mare (now via del Teatro di Marcello) was made in 1939 two bays of the palace were cut off at the left.

Palazzo Mastrozzi (Graziosi)
Piazza S. Caterina della Rota

Bibliography: Guide Rionali, VII, 2, p. 44; Elling, p. 311, pl. 118.

An early 18th-century palace with *barocchetto* windows incorporating a door – probably dating from the 16th century – with columns surrounded by bands of laurel leaves, like those recommended for the 'French Order' by Philibert de l'Orme.

Palazzo Mattei. See Palazzo Albani
Via Agostino de' Pretis

Palazzo Mattei di Giove
Piazza Mattei

Bibliography: Falda, *Nuovo teatro*, IV, pl. 43; Ferrerio, *Palazzi*, II, pl. 42; Letarouilly, pls 107, 108, 165, 166 (85, 86, 131, 132); Magni, II, pls 33–5; Golzio, *Archivi d'Italia*, S. II, IX, 1942, p. 46; Colosanti, pls 171ff.; G. Panofsky-Soergel, 'Zur Geschichte des Palazzo Mattei di Giove', *Römisches Jahrbuch*, XI, 1967-8, p. 109; Hibbard, *Maderno*, p. 127.

Built by Asdrubale Mattei (1556–1638), a member of a wealthy Roman family who acquired the whole of a large island site between the via delle Botteghe Oscure and the via dei Funari.

Between 1598 and c.1611 the main block of the palace on via dei Funari and six bays round the corner on via Gaetani were built to the designs of Maderno. Between 1613 and 1617 the east wing of the palace was extended to include the *Galleria*, and a wall added closing the court,

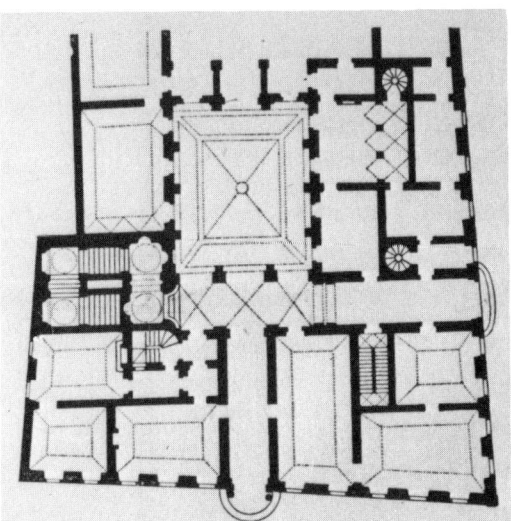

68. *Palazzo Mattei di Giove. Plan.*

with an arched opening leading to the garden, which joined that of the Palazzo Alessandro Mattei, later Gaetani, in the via delle Botteghe Oscure.

In its basic plan the palace goes back to Peruzzi's Palazzo Massimo alle Colonne, with an entrance passage leading to a loggia facing a narrow *cortile* and a staircase at one side, but in the Palazzo Mattei Maderno has taken advantage of the fact that the palace is on a corner site to make a second entrance from the via Gaetani which is on the axis of the loggia and leads directly on through it to the staircase. This is unusual in its plan because instead of leading straight on along the axis of the loggia it turns to the right and goes round a square so that the visitor arrives at the *piano nobile* with a view along the upper loggia. The arch leading to the staircase on the ground floor has canted sides with sloping panels, creating an effect of false perspective which foreshadows that in the top windows in the loggia of the Palazzo Barberini.

INTERIOR

On the ground floor, to the right of the main entrance is a room with a ceiling fresco of *Jupiter fulminating the Giants* by Gaspare Celio.

The first floor, which is occupied by an Italo-American Institute, contains a series of rooms with fine stuccoes in the same style as those in the old Palazzo Strozzi rooms of the Palazzo Barberini, enclosing *quadri riportati*.

In the *Salone* is Celio's fresco of *Moses giving thanks after the Crossing of the Red Sea*.

To the right (west) of this are three rooms, each with a single fresco on the ceiling: first,

Domenichino's *Jacob and Rachel* (Borea, *Domenichino*, p. 163); second, Albani, *Jacob's Dream*; third, Albani, *Isaac blessing Jacob*.

To the left (east) is a room with frescoes representing stories of the life of *Joseph* by Antonio Pomarancio and grotesques by Prospero Orsi.

Leading out of this room (to the north) are rooms with ceiling frescoes by Lanfranco (*Joseph and Potiphar's Wife* and *Joseph interpreting Dreams*, 1614).

These lead to the *Galleria* which has a vault entirely frescoed with subjects from the life of *Solomon*, early works of Pietro da Cortona, and *grisaille* and coloured decorations by Paolo Bonzi, called Il Gobbo dei Carracci (1621–2; Briganti, *Cortona*, p. 160 and Hess, 'Tassi, Bonzi e Cortona a Palazzo Mattei', *Commentari*, V, 1954, p. 303).

Asdrubale Mattei began collecting ancient sculpture as early as 1604, and he used some of the finest reliefs to decorate the staircase and the court of the palace (the inscription dates the decoration to 1616), setting them in stucco frames presumably designed by Maderno. In this he was following a fashion set at the Villa Medici in the late 16th century and followed at the Borghese, Giustiniani and Pamphili villas. In the years 1634–6 he commissioned the architect Gasparo de'Vecchi to design a series of bas-reliefs of later emperors from Heraclius to Ferdinand II mostly based on engravings after Goltzius which he inserted in the walls of the court between the ancient reliefs. The object of this curious addition was to proclaim that Asdrubale was related to the reigning emperor, Ferdinand II, through the marriage of the latter with Eleanora Gonzaga, to whom Asdrubale claimed to be related. To confirm the connection he offered hospitality to the Imperial ambassador, Principe di Bozzolò, during the years 1633–6.

Palazzo Mazzarino. See Palazzo Rospigliosi-Pallavicini
Via XXIV Maggio

Palazzo Mellini (Cesi, Salviati)
Via del Corso

Bibliography: Elling, p. 310, pl. 119; Salerno, *Via del Corso*, p. 219.

A palace on this site belonged to the Salviati family in 1533 and later passed to the Cesi, the Bentivoglio and finally to the Mellini. In the mid-18th century Cardinal Mario Mellini remodelled and enlarged the palace on the designs of Tommaso de'Marchis.

Palazzo Monaldeschi. See Palazzo di Spagna
Piazza di Spagna

Palazzo di Montecitorio
Piazza di Montecitorio

Bibliography: Falda, *Nuovo teatro*, I, pls 14, 15 and IV, pls 31, 32; De'Rossi, *Architettura Civile*, I, pls 105, 106; De Brosses, I, p. 49; Magni, II, pls 47, 48; Fagiolo dell'Arco, *Bernini*, 137; F. Borsi, M. del Piazzo et al., *Montecitorio*, Rome, 1972; *Guide Rionali*, III, 2, p. 84.

Begun in 1650 by Bernini on the orders of Innocent X who intended to present the palace to the Ludovisi, but having quarrelled with Cardinal Ludovico Ludovisi in 1654 he gave orders that work should be stopped. The palace was completed by Carlo Fontana in 1694 for Innocent XII as the seat of the papal law courts (Curia Innocenziana). In 1871 it was extended at the back to become the seat of the Chamber of Deputies and the whole of the interior was remodelled. For the very complete series of preparatory drawings by Fontana at Windsor see Braham and Hager, p. 112. Bernini's design for the façade is recorded in a painting preserved in the palace, dating from before 1655 (Fagiolo dell'Arco, *Bernini*, No. 137, and for a good detail *Pictures of Montecitorio* (no author), Rome, 1971).

Bernini's design included two novelties: first the line of the façade is not straight but is broken into three parts, of which the two side ones slope back slightly; second Bernini constructed the façade on a base composed of huge blocks of travertine cut to look like natural rock – a device he was to repeat a decade and a half later in his design for the Louvre.

See plate 54.

Palazzo Montoro
Via Montoro 7

Bibliography: Guide Rionali, VII, 2, p. 40.

Built by a member of the Chigi Montoro family. The style suggests the early 18th century and it is likely that the palace was built before 1736 when Giovanni Chigi Montoro married the heiress of the Patrizi family, since the heraldic features over the windows – *monti* and stars –

69. *Palazzo di Montecitorio. Engraving by Vasi showing the piazza before the obelisk was set up by Pius VI. In the distance on the right part of the Palazzo Aldobrandini-Chigi is just visible.*

refer to the Montoro and Chigi arms and not to the Patrizi. The ground floor shows unusually ingenious *barocchetto* forms for the doors and the openings of the *botteghe*, but unfortunately the name of the architect is not known.

Palazzo Muti Bussi all'Aracoeli
Piazza d'Aracoeli

Bibliography: Baglione, p. 82; Pascoli, I, p. 317; Letarouilly, pl. 342 (222); Magni, II, pl. 68; Spagnesi, G. A. De Rossi, p. 123; Elling, pl. 96; *Guide Rionali*, X, 1, p. 10.

Built on an ingenious plan designed to fit the island site which formed an irregular hexagon. The palace is attributed to Giacomo della Porta by Baglione, but Pascoli says it is by G. A. de'Rossi who was certainly in charge of the building for many years. The arrangement of vestibule and staircase is typical of him (cf. Palazzi Aste-Buonaparte and Celsi).

The palace contains frescoes by Gaspard Dughet (M. Boisclair, 'Gaspard Dughet: une chronologie révisée', *Revue de l'Art*, 34, 1976, p. 32).

Palazzo Muti Papazzuri (Balestra)
Piazza SS. Apostoli

Bibliography: Ferrerio, *Palazzi*, I, pl. 42; Titi, 1763, p. 317; Letarouilly, 28 (22); Torselli, p. 25.

According to the inscription on the plate in Ferrerio the palace was built in 1644 by Giovanni Battista Muti Papazzuri, probably to his own designs. It was later lived in by Henry Stuart, Cardinal of York, who died there in 1767.

The interior contains frescoes by Charles Mellin (D. Wild, 'Charles Mellin ou Nicolas Poussin', *G. B. A.*, 1966, ii, p. 177).

See plates 63, 64.

Palazzo Muti Papazzuri
Piazza della Pilotta 32

Bibliography: Falda, *Nuovo teatro*, IV, pl. 45; V. Lotti, 'Il Palazzo Muti Papazzuri alla Pilotta', *Alma Roma*, XIV, 1973, p. 9; D. Batorska, 'Grimaldi and the Galleria Muti-Papazzuri', *Antologia delle Belle Arti*, 7/8, 1979, p. 204.

Built between 1660 and 1678 by Mattia de'Rossi; now the Istituto Biblico. Much restored in the 19th century, but the *galleria* still has frescoes by G. F. Grimaldi and Ciro Ferri.

Palazzo Nari
Piazza S. Maria in Campo Marzio

Bibliography: Pascoli, I, p. 317; De'Rossi, *Architettura Civile*, I, pl. 135; *Architettura minora*, I, pl. 137; Spagnesi, *G. A. De Rossi*, p. 162.

According to Pascoli and de'Rossi the fine portal is by G. A. de'Rossi, an attribution which is stylistically convincing owing to the similarity of certain details (e.g. the shell) to features on the door of the Palazzo Celsi. Pascoli also says that he altered the staircase and the courtyard.

Palazzo Nari
Via di Monterone 2

Bibliography: A. Mezzetti, 'La Pittura di Antonio Gherardi', *Bollettino d'Arte*, XXXIII, 1948, p. 157.

A room on the first floor has frescoes of *Esther and Ahasueras* by Antonio Gherardi.

Palazzo Nerli. See Palazzo Albani
Via Agostino de'Pretis

Palazzo Niccolini. See Palazzo del Bufalo Ferraioli
Piazza Colonna

Palazzo Nuñez (Torlonia)
Via Condotti, via Bocca di Leone

Bibliography: Falda, *Nuovo teatro*, IV, pl. 46; Pascoli, I, p. 317; Spagnesi, *G. A. De Rossi*, p. 72.

Built by G. A. de'Rossi in 1658–60 for the marchese Nuñez and acquired in the 19th century by the Torlonia family. Typical of the severe 'non-Baroque' style of this architect.

Palazzo Odescalchi. See Palazzo Chigi-Odescalchi
Piazza SS. Apostoli

Palazzo Orsini. See Palazzo dei Piceni (Via Parione 7) and Pio di Savoia da Carpi (Piazza del Biscione 95)

Palazzo Ottoboni. See Palazzo Almagià
Via del Corso and Piazza S. Lorenzo in Lucina

Palazzo Pallavicini. See Palazzo Rospigliosi-Pallavicini
Via XXIV Maggio

Palazzo Pamphili
Piazza Navona

Bibliography: Falda, *Nuovo teatro*, IV, pl. 22; Ferrerio, *Palazzi*, pl. 9; De'Rossi, *Architettura Civile*, I, pls 125, 126; Vasi, *Magnificenze*, pl. 66; De Brosses, II, p. 120; Magni, II, p. 37; D. Frey, 'Borrominis Künstlerischer Anteil am Palazzo Pamphili auf der Piazza Navona', *Wiener Jahrbuch für Kunstgeschichte*, III, 1924–5, p. 41; Hempel, *Borromini*, p. 134; Portoghesi, *Borromini nella cultura europea*, p. 58; id., *Borromini*, pls XCV–CII, 145, 146; Salerno, *Piazza Navona*, p. 145; Golzio, *Palazzi*, figs 130–47; Blunt, *Borromini*, p. 173; Güthlein, *Familienarchiv Spada*, p. 218; *Guide Rionali*, VI, I, p. 40.

In 1645, the year after his election, Innocent X commissioned Girolamo Rainaldi to make plans for the extension of the family palace in Piazza Navona. Work began in 1646, but after a year Rainaldi was replaced by Borromini who made a series of drawings for the project (reproduced by Frey and Portoghesi), but unfortunately none of them was carried out, and Rainaldi's conservative and pedestrian design was preferred. Borromini was only able to decorate the *Salone* and build the Gallery. This is unusual in that it runs through the whole block – at the point adjacent to the church – and is mainly lit at the ends where Borromini inserted large Serliana windows. His other contribution to the Gallery is the series of doors which link it to the other rooms in the palace. These are curious in design and may incorporate features from designs by Cortona who in 1651–5 painted the frescoes on the ceiling – his last major commission as a decorative painter and perhaps the most completely successful of his secular fresco decorations – illustrating stories from the *Aeneid* (the Pamphili claimed descent from Aeneas). Borromini was also responsible for the stucco decoration in the *Salone* of the palace. The palace was completed by Girolamo Rainaldi's son, Carlo.

For a discussion of the iconography of the Gallery and for reproductions of Borromini's drawings for it see R. Preimesberger, 'Pontifex Romanus per Aencam praesignatus', *Römisches Jahrbuch*, XVI, 1976, pp. 221ff. The frescoes were restored in 1965. The vault of the gallery had first been decorated in 1647 by Giovanni

Antonio Galli, called Il Spadarino, with scenes from the life of Innocent X. The other rooms on the *piano nobile* of the palace have friezes with frescoes by Gaspard Dughet, Giacinto Gimignani (U. Verena Fischer, *G. Gimignani* (Dissertation, Freiburg, 1973, p. 147), Agostino Tassi, Andrea Camassei, G. Brandi and Francesco Allegrini.

The palace is now the Brazilian Embassy (for the restoration carried out since it was bought in 1961, see H. Gouthier de Oliveira Gondim, *Casa do Brazil em Roma*, 1963).

De'Rossi (pl. 126) states that the windows of the top floor of the main façade are by Giovanni Maria Baratta and (pl. 125) that the door opening on Piazza di Pasquino is by Niccolò Sebregondi.

See also Palazzo Doria-Pamphili.

Palazzo Pannuccelli and Pannuccelli-Toni. See Palazzo dei Pupazzi
Via Capo le Case 2

Palazzo Patrizi
Piazza S. Luigi dei Francesi

Bibliography: Mola, p. 127; Hibbard, *Maderno*, p. 135; Wasserman, 'The Palazzo Patrizi in Rome', *J.S.A.H.*, XXVII, 1968, p. 99; Vecchi, p. 47; Torselli, p. 209.

A 16th-century palace on this site was bought in 1605 by Olimpia Aldobrandini and enlarged to the design of either Carlo Maderno, Giovanni Fontana or, according to Mola, Giacomo della Porta. The façade, as remodelled, consisted of seven bays, but in the 19th century it was reduced to the present narrow form with only four. In 1642 the palace was sold to the Patrizi family who modified the staircase and the loggia on the court to the designs of Giovanni Battista Mola, probably about 1657. The palace is now the seat of the Argentine Embassy to the Holy See.

See also Palazzo Costaguti.

70. *Palazzo Pamphili. Engraving showing the banquet given in the Gallery of the palace by Lord Castlemaine, ambassador extraordinary of James II to Innocent XI in 1685. The engraving shows the doors designed by Borromini and part of the vault frescoes by Cortona. The ornaments on the table were carried out in sugar. The engraving of which this plate only shows a part comes from Michael Wright,* An Account of his Excellence Roger Earl of Castlemaine's Embassy, *London, 1688. The engraving is by A. van Westerhout after a drawing by G. B. Lenardi.*

Palazzo Patrizi a S. Caterina (Clementi)
12 via dei Delfini

Bibliography: Guide Rionali, xi, p. 36; S. Neuburger, 'Giovanni da San Giovanni im palazzo Patrizi-Clementi in Rom', Mitteilungen des Kunsthistorischen Instituts in Florenz, XXIII, 1979, p. 337.

A late 16th-century palace with one room on the *piano nobile* with a frieze decorated with frescoes by Giovanni da San Giovanni illustrating the life of *Abraham*, executed between 1626 and 1628. The palace is now the seat of the Soprintendenza ai Monumenti del Lazio.

Palazzo Pecci-Blunt. See Palazzo Fani
Piazza Campidoglio 3

Palazzo Perettini. See Palazzo Almagià
Via del Corso and Piazza S. Lorenzo in Lucina

Palazzo Petroni. See Palazzo Cenci-Bolognetti
Piazza Gesù

Palazzo dei Piceni
Via Parione 7

Bibliography: C. Astolfi, *La nuova sede del Palazzetto dei Piceni*, Rome, 1931; Benedetti, *Duca*, p. 359; Guide Rionali, VI, 1, p. 88.

The early 16th-century palace was restored about 1590 by an Orsini, probably Corradino, son of Vicino the creator of the gardens at Bomarzo. The principal addition made at this time was a small *giardino pensile* the walls of which are decorated with blind arches and niches of unusually complicated forms which have led to its being ascribed – convincingly – to Giacomo del Duca. The decoration of the rooms on the *piano nobile* was originally commissioned from Federico Zuccaro but actually executed by the Cavaliere d'Arpino.

Palazzo Pichini (Roccagiovine)
Piazza Farnese

Bibliography: Roisecco, 1750, I, p. 612; Titi, 1763, p. 108; Portoghesi, *Roma Barocca*, figs 285–7, plan on plate IX.

Built by Alessandro Specchi. The open staircase in the courtyard is like half of Fuga's double staircase in the Palazzo della Consulta.

Palazzo Pio di Savoia da Carpi (Orsini)
Piazza del Biscione 95

Bibliography: Mola, p. 131; De'Rossi, *Architettura Civile*, I, pls 116–18 and III, pl. 79; Roisecco, 1750, II, p. 41; Visentini, *Osservazioni*, p. 27; Vasi, *Magnificenze*, pl. 75; Titi, 1763, p. 168; Magni, II, pl. 36; Portoghesi, *Roma Barocca*, pl. 239; Guide Rionali, VI, 2, p. 150.

The palace on this site originally belonged to the Orsini but passed in the 17th century to the Pio di Savoia da Carpi who commissioned Camillo Arcucci to build a new façade. Later it belonged to the Righetti and is now the seat of the Istituto 'Tata Giovanni'. The elaborate pediments over the windows and the cornice are decorated with the lions' heads and rosettes of the Pio arms. Roisecco, writing in 1750, describes it as unfinished.

Palazzo di Propaganda Fide. See under Miscellaneous, Collegio di Propaganda Fide
Piazza di Spagna and Via di Propaganda Fide

Palazzo dei Pupazzi (Pannuccelli-Toni)
Via Capo le Case 2

Bibliography: Magni, II, pl. 111; Torselli, p. 283; F. Fasolo, 'Ritardi e anticipo nel tardo Barocco Romano', *Quaderni*, 2, 1953, p. 1; Portoghesi, *Roma Barocca*, pl. 307.

A small palace built by Francesco Rosa (recorded 1732–42) for the conte Centini. Its most unusual feature, the herm-caryatids supporting the pediments over the window of the *piano nobile*, are akin to those on the fountains in the Palazzo Borghese and the Palazzo del Grillo, the former associated with the name of Giovanni Paolo Schor.

71. *Palazzo Pio di Savoia da Carpi. Engraving by Vasi.*

Palazzo del Quirinale
Piazza del Quirinale

Bibliography: Falda, *Nuovo teatro*, I, pl. 13 and IV, pls 4, 5; *Giardini*, pls 5, 6; Ferrerio, *Palazzi*, I, pl. 1 and II, pls 5–8; Percier and Fontaine, *Palais*, IV, pls 63–6; Magni, II, pls 61–7, 91; J. Wasserman, 'The Quirinal Palace in Rome', *Art Bulletin*, XLV, 1963, p. 205; id., *Mascarino*, p. 142; Hibbard, *Maderno*, p. 194; G. Briganti, *Il Palazzo del Quirinale*, Rome, 1962; F. Borsi et al., *Il Palazzo del Quirinale*, Rome, 1973; Coffin, p. 181.

The *vigna* on the site was owned from the first years of the 16th century by the Carafa family but was leased by Cardinal Ippolito d'Este and used as a summer retreat by various popes. The existing palace was begun by Gregory XIII who built a *casino* at the north end of the site, incorporating parts of the earlier villa and surmounted by the Torre dei Venti, between 1583 and 1585 to the design of Ottaviano Mascarino, who planned a larger scheme including a forecourt. This *casino* contains an oval spiral staircase with coupled Tuscan columns which is the earliest of its kind (the next in date is Ponzio's at the Palazzo Borghese). In 1587 Sixtus V bought the *vigna* and continued the building under the direction of Domenico Fontana, who constructed the west wing facing the piazza and began that on the Strada Pia (via del Quirinale). In 1608 Paul V began the east wing which was to contain a private chapel. This section was built by Flaminio Ponzio, but on his death in 1613 Maderno took over. In 1614–15 he built the Cappella Paolina and the Sala dei Corazzieri in the wing along Strada Pia and the main door on the piazza (statues of *St Peter* and *St Paul* by Stefano Maderno and Guillaume Berthelot and *Madonna* by Pompeo Ferrucci). He was also responsible for enlarging and levelling the square. Urban VIII commissioned Bernini to make the Benediction Loggia over the main entrance in 1638 (Fagiolo dell' Arco, *Bernini*, No. 88). The long range of buildings along the via Pia (the 'Manica Lunga') which was used to house the pope's family was begun by Bernini for Alexander VII, extended by Specchi for Innocent XIII and completed for Clement XII by Fuga who also built the Palazzetto del Segretario delle Cifre at the end of the range. From 1870 to 1944 the Quirinal was the palace of the kings of Italy. It is now the residence of the President of the Republic.

INTERIOR

Sala dei Corazzieri (Colosanti, pl. 158): The

Palazzo del Quirinale

72. *Palazzo del Quirinale. Engraving by Vasi. On the extreme left a corner of the Stables of the Quirinal; next to it the statues of the* Horse-tamers *set up here by Sixtus V. On the right Fuga's Palazzo della Consulta. The engraving shows the* piazza *before Pius VI set up the obelisk which now stands between the two* Horse-tamers.

73. *The Quirinal. Engraving by Vasi, showing the 'Coffee House' by Fuga on the right.*

relief over the door to the Cappella Paolina is by Taddeo Landini and the angels supporting the arms of Paul V are by Pietro Bernini (left) and Guillaume Berthelot (right). The frescoed frieze by Agostino Tassi, Lanfranco, Carlo Saraceni and Orazio Gentileschi is an important example of *quadratura* illusionism as it was practised in the early 17th century (E. Schleier, 'Les Projets de Lanfranc pour le décor de la Sala Regia au Quirinal et pour la loge des Bénédictions à Saint-Pierre', *Revue de l'Art*, VII, 1970, p. 40).
Cappella Paolina: The ceiling was designed by Martino Ferrabosco (1616; Colosanti, pl. 92).
The Gallery: Decorated for Alexander VII by a group of artists under the direction of Pietro da Cortona. It was broken up by Napoleon into three rooms, but the frescoes survive (N. Wibiral, 'I pittori della Galleria di Alessandro VII nel Palazzo Quirinale', *Bollettino d'Arte*, XLV, 1960, p. 123, and S. Jacob, 'Pierre de Cortone et la décoration de la galerie d'Alexandre VII au Quirinal', *Revue de l'Art*, XI, 1971, p. 42).

The frescoes which form a cycle illustrating the Old Testament (with two scenes from the New) are as follows:
Sala degli Ambasciatori: *Adam and Eve* (Lazzaro Baldi), *The Expulsion from Eden* (Bartolomeo Colombo), *Cain and Abel* (Lauri and Gaspard Dughet), *The Judgment of Solomon* (Carlo Cesi), *Cyrus freeing the Jews* (Ciro Ferri), the *Annunciation* (Baldi), the *Nativity* (Carlo Maratta).
Sala del Trono: *The Ark* (G. P. Schor), *The Flood* (Baldi), *Sacrifice of Isaac* (Angelo Canini), *Victory of Joshua* (Guglielmo and Giacomo Cortese), *Gideon* (Filippo Lauri), *David and Goliath* (F. Murgia).
Sala Gialla: *Jacob and the Angel* (G. P. Schor), *The Reconciliation of Jacob and Esau* (Giuseppe Chiari), *The Burning Bush* (Giovanni Francesco Grimaldi), *The Crossing of the Red Sea* (Jan Miel), *The Spies with the Grapes* (Grimaldi), *Jacob sold by his brethren* (G. P. Schor), *Joseph recognizing his brethren* (Pierfrancesco Mola).

The private chapel (*Cappella dell'Annunziata*) was frescoed for Paul V by Guido Reni (1610).

Some of the furnishings of the Quirinal come from the palaces of the dukes of Savoy in Turin and elsewhere in Piedmont, but the greater part were taken from those of the dukes of Parma at Parma and Colorno, including very fine pieces made in Paris for Louise Elisabeth, daughter of Louis XV who married the Infante Philip, son of Philip V who was created duke of Parma in 1734. After the unification of Italy the contents of the two palaces were moved first to Florence, where they were housed in the Palazzo Pitti, and then when the capital was moved from Florence to Rome, were brought to the Quirinal (C. Briganti, *Curioso Itinerario delle Collezioni ducali parmensi*, Milan, 1969).

For the gardens, which are not accessible to visitors, see Belli-Barsala, p. 299. Architecturally their most interesting feature is the 'Coffee House' built for Benedict XIV by Ferdinando Fuga, which was finished in 1743 (Mathiae, *Fuga*, p. 39; Pane, *Fuga*, p. 94 and fig. 73) and decorated by A. Masucci (W).
See plate 97.

Palazzo Ricci. See Palazzo Donarelli
Via Giulia 97

Palazzo Roccagiovane. See Palazzo Pichini
Piazza Farnese

Palazzo Rondinini (Sansevero)
Via del Corso 518

Bibliography: Magni, II, pl. 73; Salerno, *Via del Corso*, p. 123; id., *Palazzo Rondinini*, Rome, 1965; Torselli, p. 241.

In 1744 the marchesa Margherita Ambra Rondinini bought a palace which the painter Giuseppe Cesari, Cavaliere d'Arpino, had built for himself about 1600 to the designs of Flaminio Ponzio. The palace was remodelled and enlarged by the architect Alessandro Dori and was completed by 1754. It was designed as much to contain the great collection of sculpture formed by Giuseppe Rondinini as to be a private residence. It has an impressive staircase and rooms decorated by a number of artists of the 1760s, mainly unknown but including the Frenchman Jacques Gamelin. Like the exactly contemporary Villa Albani it marks the end of the Baroque, as it begins to be qualified by neo-classical restraint.

After passing through various hands the palace is now the seat of the Banca Nazionale dell'Agricoltura.

Palazzo Rospigliosi-Pallavicini (Bentivoglio, Mazzarino, Pallavicini)
Via XXIV Maggio

Bibliography: Vasi, *Magnificenze*, pl. 62; Magni, II, pl. 26; Hibbard, 'Scipione Borghese's Garden Palace on the Quirinal', *J.S.A.H.*, XXIII, 1964, p. 163; id., *Maderno*, p. 192; L. Lotti, 'Il Palazzo Rospigliosi-Pallavicini di Montecavallo', *Alma Roma*, XV, 3/4, p. 1; Torselli, p. 200; Golzio, *Palazzi*, figs 197–216.

The palace was begun in 1611 on a site bought by Paul V for his nephew, Cardinal Scipione Borghese. In 1616 he sold it, still unfinished, to the duca d'Altemps. Later it was bought in by Cardinal Guido Bentivoglio (1619), the Lante family, Cardinal Mazarin (1641) and finally by the Rospigliosi-Pallavicini family to whom it still belongs.

The architects involved in the building of the palace were Flaminio Ponzio, Vasanzio, Carlo Maderno and possibly Cigoli and in the present state of knowledge their exact shares cannot be distinguished. The palace itself is awkwardly planned and bleak in appearance, and the most attractive features are the gardens with fountains and curved steps designed by Maderno, and above all the Casino dell'Aurora with the middle room decorated on its ceiling with Guido Reni's *Aurora* (1615) and frescoes by Paul Bril, Antonio Tempesta, Cherubino Alberti, Domenico Passignano and Giovanni Baglione. The palace contains frescoes by Giovanni da San Giovanni (1627) and a notable collection of pictures; the Casino delle Nove Muse was decorated by Agostino Tassi and Orazio Gentileschi and the Loggia di Psiche by Cigoli. The palace and the two latter casinos are not accessible but the Casino dell'Aurora is open on the first day of each month.

For an account of the magnificent furniture in the palace see A. Gonzalez Palacios, 'La Mobilia del Palazzo Pallavicini', *Arte Illustrata*, IV, 1971, p. 64.

Palazzo Rucellai. See Palazzo Ruspoli
Largo Goldoni

Palazzo Ruggeri
Corso Vittorio Emanuele II 20

Bibliography: Martinelli, p. 252; Mola, p. 227; M. V. Brugnoli, 'Un Palazzo Romano del tardo '500', *Bollettino d'Arte*, N. S. XLV, 1960, p. 223; id., *Palazzo Ruggeri*, Rome, 1961; C. Pietrangeli, 'Palazzo Ruggeri', *Archivio della Società Romana di Storia Patria*, XCIV, 1971, p. 169; id., 'Il Palazzo del Leone Rampante', *Capitolium*, XLV, 1970, p. 25; *Guide Rionali*, IX, 1, p. 90.

Built between 1588 and 1591 by Giacomo della Porta for Pompeo Ruggeri, several times Conservatore of Rome, but enlarged and altered in the 18th and 19th centuries. The *Salone* is decorated with frescoes illustrating the life of *Pompey* attributed to Giovanni and Cherubino Alberti.

Palazzo Ruspoli (Gaetani, Rucellai)
Largo Goldoni

Bibliography: Baglione, p. 346; Totti, p. 334; Mola, p. 129; Martinelli, p. 242; Falda, *Nuovo teatro*, IV, pl. 38; Ferrerio, *Palazzi*, I, pl. 23; Titi, 1763, p. 370; Magni, II, pl. 11; Salerno, *Via del Corso*, p. 153; Torselli, p. 243.

Built in the late 16th century by the Florentine architect Bartolomeo Ammanati for the Florentine family of Rucellai. The gallery was decorated, between 1586 and 1590, by Jacopo Zucchi, another Florentine, with an elaborate cycle of allegorical frescoes (F. Saxl, *Antike Götter in der Spätrenaissance*, Leipzig-Berlin, 1927). The palace was later bought by Cardinal Ulrico Gaetani for whom it was enlarged by Bartolomeo Breccioli, who added the cornice and the belvedere, and Martino Longhi the Younger, who built the spacious but simple staircase. In the 18th century it was bought by the Ruspoli family to whom it still belongs.

Palazzo Sacchetti
Via Giulia 66

Bibliography: Callari, p. 256; Frommel, *Palastbau*, II, p. 292; Dumont, *Francesco Salviati au Palais Sacchetti de Rome*, Rome, 1973; Torselli, p. 245.

Begun in 1542 by Antonio da Sangallo the Younger for his own use, but left unfinished at his death in 1546. Bought in 1552 by Cardinal Giovanni Ricci who finished it to the designs of Nanni di Baccio Bigio.

The *Salone* (now part of a bank) was frescoed by Francesco Salviati, probably in 1552–4. Like his cycle in the Oratory of S. Giovanni Decollato, this decorative scheme incorporates many illusionistic devices later used by Baroque artists, showing the main scenes as if they were framed paintings and the smaller ones as if depicted on hanging scrolls, suggesting Chinese roll paintings (cf. Hirst, 'Salviati's Chinoiseries in Palazzo Sacchetti', *Burlington Magazine*, CXXI, 1979, p. 791). It contains a bust of Cardinal Giulio Sacchetti by Giuliano Finelli probably dating from 1638 (cf. Nava Cellini, 'Un tracciato per l'attività ritrattistica di Giuliano Finelli', *Paragone*, 131, 1960, p. 22).

Palazzo Salviati. See Palazzo Mellini
Via del Corso

Palazzo San Calisto
Piazza di S. Maria in Trastevere

Bibliography: Falda, *Nuovo teatro*, I, pl. 33; Ferrerio, *Palazzi*, I, pl. 35; Titi, 1686, p. 37; Martinelli, p. 246; de'Rossi, 1697, p. 128; Magni, II, pl. 72; Torselli, p. 254.

The palace which was originally built for Cardinal Morone was given in 1615 – together with the adjacent church of S. Calisto – by Paul V to a body of Benedictine monks in exchange for their buildings on the Quirinal, the site of which he wanted for his nephew Scipione Borghese who was building his palace nearby (now the Palazzo Rospigliosi-Pallavicini). According to Titi and the other early sources it was 'rifabricata' for the monks by Orazio Torriani in 1615 (the date is given in de'Rossi's engraving) but the façade conforms to the regular type of Roman palace façade and has nothing monastic about it.

The arms on the façade, as shown in the engraving in Ferrerio, were those of Paul V but they have been replaced by those of Pius XI. The palace now belongs to the Holy See.

Palazzo de Sangro. See Palazzo Buoncompagni Corcos
Via del Governo Vecchio 3

Palazzo Sannesi. See Palazzo Maffei
Via della Pigna

Palazzo Sansevero. See Palazzo Rondinini
Via del Corso 518

Palazzo Santacroce
Piazza S. Carlo ai Catinari

Bibliography: Martinelli, p. 252; Titi, 1763, p. 98; Hibbard, *Maderno*, p. 129; S. Sinnisi, 'Il Palazzo Santacroce ai Catinari', *Palatino*, S. III, VII, 1963, p. 13; Spagnesi, *G. A. De Rossi*, p. 127; Torselli, p. 260; Elling, pls 121, 177; *Guide Rionali*, VII, 1, p. 48.

The palace was mainly built by F. Peparelli in the years 1630–40. The crude woodcut in Fei's *Roma antica e moderna* of 1643 (II, p. 726) shows the palace without the two left-hand bays, and this was probably its form before it was extended by G. A. de'Rossi about 1672. Probably about the same time a narrow court was added on the other side of the road running along the right-hand side of the palace, so that it continued the cross axis of the courtyard from which it could be seen through a gate, closed by an iron grille. At the end of this area stands a little terrace with a fountain below it in a somewhat fancy style which recalls those in the Palazzo Borghese and the Palazzo del Grillo. Spagnesi apparently accepts this as the work of G. A. de'Rossi, but Sinnisi states that the documents show it is by Alessio de'Rossi, who is also recorded as working on the interior of the palace (Spagnesi, p. 132, note 7).

The vault of the *Salone* was frescoed by Giovanni Francesco Grimaldi with allegorical groups and scenes from the *Old Testament* (D. Batorska, 'Grimaldi and the Salone Santacroce', *Storia dell'Arte*, 18, 1973, p. 173). The gallery is generally ascribed to Ruggieri but Waterhouse attributes it mainly to Grimaldi.

Palazzo Scarinci. See Palazzo Buoncampagni Corcos
Via del Governo Vecchio 3

Palazzo Sciarra (Carbognano)
Via del Corso 239

Bibliography: Titi, 1763, p. 326; Mola, p. 132; Martinelli, p. 253; Baglione, p. 135; Falda, *Nuovo teatro*, IV, pl. 37; Ferrerio, *Palazzi*, II, pl. 37; Letarouilly, pls 143, 144 (119, 120); Magni, II, pl. 12; Salerno, *Via del Corso*, p. 211; Carlo Pietrangeli, *Palazzo Sciarra*, Rome, 1972; Torselli, p. 265; C. De Seta, 'Disegni di Luigi Vanvitelli', in De Fusco *et al.*, *Luigi Vanvitelli*, Naples, 1973, p. 241.

Palazzo del Senatore

The palace was begun probably about 1590 by Francesco Colonna di Sciarra, duke of Palestrina. The architect is variously named as Martino Longhi the Elder (Ferrerio, who engraved the façade), Flaminio Ponzio (Baglione and Martinelli) and Orazio Torriani (Mola). In 1728 Guilio Cesare Colonna married the Barberini heiress, Cornelia Costanza, and his brother, Cardinal Prospero, made some notable additions to the interior including a library and a mirror room both designed by Vanvitelli in a style nearer to the true rococo than anything else to be found in Rome. The drawings for these are at Caserta. The palace was extensively altered about 1875, but the façade survived as one of the most harmonious of those erected in the last years of the 16th century. Titi ascribes the fine door to Antonio Labacco which cannot be correct because Labacco died many years before the palace was begun, but in its general design it is close to the engraved title page to his *Libro appartenente a l'architettura*.

Palazzo del Senatore. See Capitoline Palaces

Palazzo Serlupi Crescenzi
Via del Seminario 113

Bibliography: Baglione, p. 82; Ferrerio, *Palazzi*, II, pl. 55; *Guide Rionali*, III, 2, p. 28.

Begun by Giacomo della Porta for Ottaviano di Francesco Crescenzi. In the early 17th century it passed to Francesco Serlupi who took the name and arms of Crescenzi. The palace was continued by Onorio Longhi but never finished, only the left four bays and the central bay with the door being completed. The impressive façade includes one novel feature in that the windows are spaced unevenly, the two outer ones being separated from each other and the middle ones by wider intervals than in the central group, thus getting away from the rigid regularity of most mid and late 16th-century palaces.
See also Palazzo Lovatelli.

Palazzo Sinibaldi
Via del Mascherone

Bibliography: Torselli, p. 269.

Torselli says that this palace, which stands to the left of the Palazzo Farnese, was built for the Knights of the Teutonic Order, but was sold by the Emperor Leopold to the Sinibaldi family. Its most interesting feature is the door, of which the lower rusticated part might date from the 16th century but which ends above in a broken pediment enclosing swags and a coat of arms, making a whole of unusual complexity.

Palazzo Spada (Capodiferro)
Piazza Capodiferro

Bibliography: Ferrerio, *Palazzi*, I, pls 32, 33; Letarouilly, pls 243–6 (175–8); Magni, II, pls 13–16; Frommel, *Palastbau*, II, p. 61; L. Neppi, *Palazzo Spada*, Rome, 1975; Heimbürger Ravalli, *Archivio Spada*, p. 118; K. Güthlein, review of Heimbürger Ravalli, *Zeitschrift für Kunstgeschichte*, XLI, 1978, p. 336; J. Connors, review of Neppi and Heimbürger Ravalli, *J.S.A.H.*, XXXVIII, 1979, p. 193.

The palace was built originally by Cardinal Girolamo Capodiferro, a protégé of Cardinal Alessandro Farnese, later Paul III, who made him a cardinal in 1544. He spent the years 1541–3 at the court of Francis I, and visited France again in 1547 and 1553, and it is significant that he added the coat-of-arms of Henry II of France to

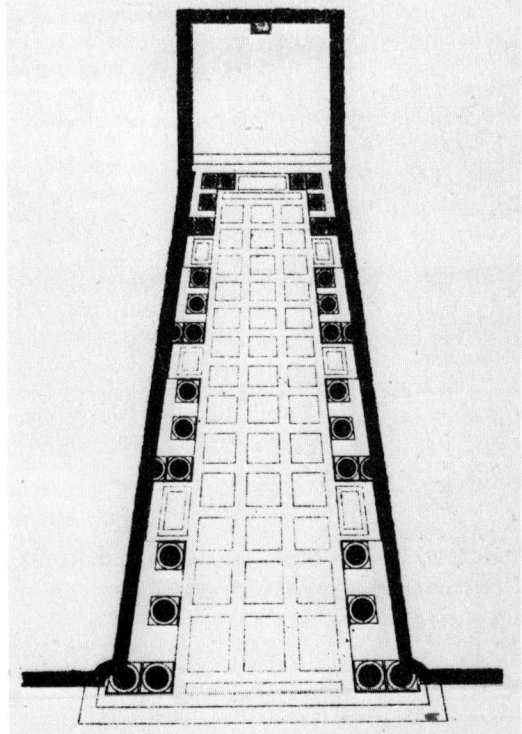

74. *Palazzo Spada. Plan of the false perspective portico.*

those of Paul III and Pius IV on the façade of his palace. The building of the palace was probably begun in 1549 and the decoration went on till the death of the cardinal in 1559.

Various names have been suggested for the architect of the palace, but Frommel has shown that Giulio Merigi da Caravaggio, given as the architect in Totti's guide of 1638, is the most convincing. The stucco decoration on the court façades is by Giulio Mazzoni of Modena who is also responsible for the decoration of the Galleria degli Stucchi. This is the earliest *galleria* to be found in a Roman palace and the closest imitation of the Galerie François I at Fontainebleau to be found in Italy, and it was no doubt directly inspired by Capodiferro's admiration for the work of Rosso and Primaticcio which he saw during his visits to France.

At the end of the 16th century the palace passed to the Mignanelli family, from whom it was bought in 1632 by Cardinal Bernardino Spada, the brother of Borromini's patron Virgilio Spada. He commissioned Paolo Maruscelli to make substantial alterations and additions to the palace, including the enlargement of the entrance vestibule (1633–4) and the creation of a drive from the via Giulia through the garden which he laid out anew on a much grander scale. In 1633–5 he called in two Bolognese experts in quadratura painting – the Spada family came from Faenza but had recently established themselves in Bologna – Agostino Mitelli and Angelo Michele Colonna, to fresco the Sala Grande, of which the chief ornament was a more than life-size statue believed to represent Marcellus. In 1644 the Galleria with a famous meridian clock, designed by Emmanuel Maignan, a French Minim of the Trinità dei Monti, was decorated with frescoes by G. B. Ruggieri. After Maruscelli's death in 1649 Borromini was called in to replace him, aided by his assistant Francesco Righi. They were responsible for the addition of two wings on the garden side and for the execution of the famous false perspective colonnade in the left-hand court (1653). This has always been attributed to Borromini but it is now clear that the original design is due to an Augustinian priest, Giovanni Maria da Bitonto, and that it replaced a painted perspective carried out in 1642–4 on the designs of Maruscelli. Bitonto had already executed a similar colonnade on a miniature scale for the High Altar of S. Paolo Maggiore at Bologna for the Spada family (1647). It is recorded however that the cardinal's appetite had been whetted by a false perspective structure which Borromini had made for the celebration of the Quarant'Ore in 1646, of which unhappily we have no record.

Borromini was also involved in the extension of the staircase, which now leads in a single flight right up to the Sala Grande – a very unusual arrangement – and in a project for the piazza in front of the palace, of which only the fountain was carried out (now destroyed). After the cardinal's death in 1661 two further additions were made to the palace: the concave wall with an arch in the middle leading to the garden, built by Camillo Arcucci in 1665, and the terrace over the colonnade, built by Tommaso Mattei in 1700–02.

In addition to the Sala Grande and the Galleria degli Stucchi the palace contains rooms decorated in the late 17th century. One of these has a vault frescoed with an allegory of the *Four Seasons* and the *Four Continents* by Giacomo Wernle.

The history of the palace has only become clear since the mid-1970s, when the Spada archives were made accessible. Earlier writers were often in serious error over both dates and attributions, which can however now be checked in the works by Heimbürger Ravalli and Neppi, of which an excellent survey is to be found in the review of both books by J. Connors (see bibliography). The palace is now the seat of the Consiglio di Stato. It also contains the collection of paintings formed by Cardinal Spada, probably the most important group of Baroque paintings in any public gallery in Rome.

See also Palazzo dello Spirito Santo.

Palazzo di Spagna (Monaldeschi)
Piazza di Spagna

Bibliography: Pascoli, I, p. 301; O. Pollak, 'Antonio del Grande', *Kunstgeschichtliches Jahrbuch der K. K. Zentralkommission*, III, 1909, p. 133; Hempel, *Borromini*, p. 131; Salerno, *Piazza di Spagna*, p. 89; Vecchi, p. 383.

In 1647 the palace belonging to the Monaldeschi family was bought by the count of Oñate for the Spanish Embassy. In discussing the staircase of the Oratory in the *Opus architectonicum* Borromini (or his spokesman Virgilio Spada) wrote that he had built it with a single vault covering both flights 'come io ultimamente ho pratticato nel Palazzo dell'Eccellentissimo Sig. Ambasciadore di Spagna'. Pascoli writes that Borromini made plans for the enlargement of the palace, and adds that though these were not carried out the king made him a knight of the Order of St James of Compostela. These two statements seem at first sight contradictory but they can be reconciled by supposing that Borromini made plans for large-scale rebuilding and expansion of which only a part, including the staircase, was carried out. Pollak – followed by Salerno – attributes the vestibule and staircase to del Grande, but he misinterpreted the document on which he based his argument.

The existing staircase dates from the 19th century, but the vestibule has several features which point to Borromini's authorship. The Tuscan columns linked by an abacus-architrave are like those in the cloister of S. Carlino. Two other features are borrowed from the Palazzo Farnese: one – the depressed arch over the central aisle of the vestibule – is taken from the corridor on the *piano nobile* of the palace, designed by Sangallo, the other – the asymmetrical jambs of the side openings – is based on Sangallo's entrance to the palace. Both these features are in accordance with the taste of Borromini but have – as far as I know – no parallel in the work of Antonio del Grande.

In the apartments of the ambassador are the two busts – *Anima Beata* and *Anima Dannata* – by Bernini which were made about 1619, probably on a commission from Pedro di Montoya (Wittkower, *Bernini*, p. 177 and Fagiolo dell'Arco, *Bernini*, No. 12).

Palazzo Spinola. See Palazzo Albertoni
Piazza Campitelli 2

Palazzo dello Spirito Santo (Spada)
Piazza di Montegiordano

Bibliography: Falda, *Nuovo teatro*, I, pls 22, 23; Hempel, *Borromini*, p. 176; Donati, *Artisti ticinesi*, p. 186 and fig. 221; Portoghesi, *Borromini*, p. 183; Blunt, *Borromini*, p. 175; Heimbürger Ravalli, *Archivio Spada*, p. 275; Blunt, 'Two neglected works by Borromini', *Römisches Jahrbuch*, 1982; *Guide Rionali*, V, 3, p. 66.

Commissioned from Borromini in 1661 by Virgilio Spada for the Ospedale di Spirito Santo of which he was *commendatore*, but left unfinished at his death in 1663 when Alexander VII ordered his nephew Orazio to buy the incomplete building and finish it at his own expense. This order was carried out by 1669. The exterior of the palace was completely remodelled in the 19th century, but its original appearance is known from drawings and the

75. *Palazzo dello Spirito Santo (Spada). Engraving by Falda, which shows on the left the* Torre dell'Orologio *of the Oratorio di S. Filippo Neri.*

engravings by Falda. It was articulated by four giant pilasters. The vestibule and the court contain elements which are certainly earlier than the 19th century and, as Donati points out, probably still show traces of Borromini's original project. In particular the ingenious arrangement of the court with superimposed arcaded loggias – now all blocked up – and the neat arrangement of the vestibule leading to a fountain in the left-hand bay of the main façade of the court are reminiscent of his method of designing.

Palazzo della Stamperia. See Palazzo Cornaro
Via della Stamperia

Palazzo Strada. See Palazzo Antamoro
Via della Panetteria 15

Palazzo Testa-Piccolomini
Via dei Lucchesi (next to S. Croce)

Bibliography: Elling, p. 303, pl. 116.

An early 18th-century palace, by an unknown architect with elegant *barocchetto* pediments over the windows.

Palazzo Torlonia. See Palazzo Nuñez
Via Condotti, via Bocca di Leone

Palazzo Trano. See Palazzo Almagià
Via del Corso and Piazza S. Lorenzo Lucina

Palazzo Valdambrini
Via Ripetta 142

Bibliography: Magni, II, pl. 74; Callari, p. 468.

Apparently dates from the mid or late 17th century, and has a fine door.

Palazzo Valentino (Bonelli, Alessandrino)
Piazza SS. Apostoli 119

Bibliography: Falda, *Nuovo teatro*, IV, pl. 39; Martinelli, pp. 232, 236; Mola, p. 132; Ferrerio, *Palazzi*, I, pls 27–8; G. F. Eminente, 'Dopo 100 Anni radicali restauri a Palazzo Valentini', *Rassegna del Lazio*, N.S. XX, 7, 1973, p. 6; Wasserman, *Mascarino*, p. 93.

Originally owned by the Sambeccari family; sold by them in 1585 to the Buoncampagni who immediately sold it again to Michele Bonelli (Cardinal Alessandrino) who rebuilt it to the plans of Fra Domenico Paganelli. Both Martino Longhi the Elder and Mascarino made plans for the rebuilding, but these seem to have been rejected. The palace was altered in the first half of the 17th century by Francesco Peparelli for the Principi di Francavilla. It was completely restored in the 19th century and has lost almost all of its original character. The palace is now the seat of the Administrazione Provinciale of Lazio.
See plate 62.

Palazzo Varese
Via Giulia 16

Bibliography: Salerno, *Via Giulia*, p. 440; Hibbard, *Maderno*, p. 207; Donati, *Artisti ticinesi*, figs 104–7.

The site was acquired between 1611 and 1616 by the Milanese Monsignor Diomede Varese who commissioned Carlo Maderno to rebuild the houses which stood on it. At the end of the court nearest the entrance is a four-storey loggia with two storeys of arcaded openings and two with flat entablatures all of the Tuscan order, and at the other end an impressive door, the effect of which is now damaged by its being set against a block built over what was probably originally a small garden running down to the Tiber.

Palazzo Venezia
Piazza Venezia

The palace built mainly by Pietro Barbo, later Pope Paul II, in the later 15th century, has no Baroque features except the fountain in the court, erected by Benedict XIII in 1730 to the designs of Carlo Monaldi (see D'Onofrio, *Acque e Fontane*, p. 524; Enggass, *Sculpture*, p. 185).
See also Madonna delle Grazie.

Palazzo Verospi
Via del Corso 374

Bibliography: Baglione, p. 156; Martinelli, p. 253; Ferrerio, *Palazzi*, II, pl. 50; Mola, p. 130; Titi, 1763, p. 349; H. Bodmer, 'Die Fresken des Francesco Albani im Palazzo Verospi in Rom', *Pantheon*, XVIII, 1936, p. 366; Wasserman, *Mascarino*, p. 121; Salerno, *Via del Corso*, pp. 175, 255; *Guide Rionali*, III, 1, p. 72.

Begun by Girolamo Rainaldi, finished by Onorio Longhi in 1606 and altered by Alessandro Specchi in the early 18th century.

The gallery on the first floor – originally an open loggia – has on its vault frescoes by Francesco Albani. The central panel shows *Apollo with the Four Seasons* and on the cove are painted *Day* and *Night* and the gods associated with the days of the week: *Diana, Mars, Mercury, Jupiter, Juno* and *Venus*. The decorative scheme is based on Raphael's Sala di Psiche in the Farnesina. The date of the frescoes has been the subject of dispute but they were certainly executed before 1623.

The palace is now the seat of the Credito Italiano.

Palazzo Viscardi. See **Palazzo Celsi**
Corso Vittorio Emanuele 18

Palazzo Volpi di Misurato. See **Palazzo Galoppi**
Via del Quirinale 21

Unnamed palace at 64 Piazza delle Coppelle

Bibliography: Architettura minora, I, pl. 131.

The façade of this palace is decorated with fine stuccoes much in the manner of those of the Palazzo del Grillo.

Unnamed palace at 103 Via del Governo Vecchio

Bibliography: Architettura minora, I, pl. 102; Portoghesi, *Roma Barocca*, pl. 22; *Guide Rionali*, VI, 1, pl. 102.

Nothing seems to be known of the history of this palace which appears to date from the late 15th or early 16th century. Its façade was decorated in the 18th century with a series of oval stucco medallions containing portraits of eminent lawyers.

III
THE VATICAN

76. *Vatican. Scala Regia. Engraving by Falda. The engraving greatly enlarges the width of the staircase in relation to the human beings walking up and down it, and also falsifies the effect by implying that light falls on the staircase from the left side, where there are in fact no windows, except at the first and second landings.*

The Vatican

Bibliography: G. P. Chattard, *Nuova descrizione del Vaticano*, Rome, 1762; D. Redig de Campos, *I Palazzi Vaticani*, Rome, 1967.

The building history of the Vatican lies mainly outside the Baroque period but can be briefly summarized as follows. In the first centuries after the establishment by Constantine of Christianity as the official religion of the Roman Empire the Lateran palace was the principal residence of the popes and the Vatican consisted of a relatively small building, though it was enlarged by Innocent III (1198–1216). When Gregory XI returned from Avignon, however, in 1377, he established his main residence there and the palace was enlarged by successive popes in the following two centuries till it attained its present extent, the last important addition before the 19th century being the block begun by Domenico Fontana for Sixtus V and finished under Clement VIII (J. Wasserman, 'The Palazzo Sisto V in the Vatican', *J.S.A.H.*, XXI, 1962, p. 26).

The visitor to the Vatican museums will not have his mind on the Baroque, though the Pinacoteca contains many paintings of the period. He will see many works, both of antiquity and of the Renaissance, which profoundly influenced the evolution of the style, and a number of frescoed rooms or corridors – such as the chapels of Pius V or the Galleria delle Carte Geografiche – which are iconographically the immediate predecessors of many Baroque projects, but he will encounter very few actual Baroque works: Pietro da Cortona's fresco of the *Pietà* in the chapel of Urban VIII (near the Stanze), and a number of *bozzetti* by Bernini and others in the galleries leading to and from the Library of Sixtus V; one bay of the vault of the Galleria delle Carte Geografiche, frescoed by F. Romanelli and G. A. Canini, and Guido Reni's vault frescoes in the Sala delle Nozze Aldobrandini (J. Hess, *Kunstgeschichtliche Studien*, I, p. 95, II, pls 29–35).

If the door of the Sistine Chapel is open the visitor will get a view of the Sala Regia and a glimpse of the Sala Ducale (see below).

The situation will be different, however, if he obtains permission to visit parts of the palace not normally accessible to visitors, where he will see Bernini's Scala Regia, with the equestrian statue of Constantine, and the Sala Ducale, with Bernini's ingenious invention for joining together the two rooms which went to form it, as well as the Sala Regia and the Sala Clementina which mark essential stages in the evolution towards Baroque decoration.

Entering by the door at the end of the right half of the Colonnade he will find himself in the corridor built by Bernini (finished 1662; Portoghesi, *Roma Barocca*, pl. 101) which leads to the Scala Regia, the grand approach to the papal apartments, at the bottom of which is Bernini's equestrian statue of Constantine the Great, situated at the point where the vestibule of St Peter's meets the corridor. (The statue and the arch leading to the staircase can also be seen through a glass door from the vestibule.) The statue was originally designed for the interior of the church under Innocent X in 1654 but executed for the present position under Alexander VII in 1662–8 (Wittkower, *Bernini*, p. 251, and Fagiolo dell'Arco, *Bernini*, No. 198).

The Scala Regia itself was built between 1663 and 1666 (Wittkower, *Bernini*, p. 245; Fagiolo dell'Arco, *Bernini*, No. 197). The space available was narrow and the walls enclosing it were not parallel to each other. Bernini solved the difficulties which faced him by placing his columns on converging lines, and reducing their height as they got further up the lower flight, as had been done in the Palazzo Spada colonnade; but he did so in a restrained manner not making the most of the perspectival effect as Borromini and his colleagues had done, but allowing the columns to stand further away from the wall at the bottom than at the top, thus making it possible to create a sort of triumphal arch at the bottom of the flight, over which he set the arms of the pope carried by two trumpeting stucco angels. Bernini increased the dramatic effect of the staircase by breaking it half way up by a landing strongly lit from a window invisible from the bottom of the staircase (the landing at the top of the first flight should also be strongly lit, but this effect is now nullified by the dark stained glass in the window). For an analysis of the perspective effects used by Bernini in the staircase see E. Panofsky, 'Die Scala Regia im Vatikan und die Kunstanschauungen Berninis', *Jahrbuch der preussischen Kunstsammlungen*, XI, 1919, p. 241. The stucco angels over the entrance to the staircase and the decoration on the vault in front of them are by Ercole Ferrata (1664) and the stuccoes on the landing are by Naldini.

SALA REGIA

Used for the reception of kings and emperors. Built within a 13th-century shell by Antonio da Sangallo the Younger for Paul III (begun 1538). However the wall opposite the entrance to the Pauline chapel has a Serliana inserted in the old building by Bramante in 1508 (the name of Julius II is inscribed on the outside). The decoration of the room was begun by Paul III. The vault was stuccoed by Perino del Vaga but the frames of the wall-frescoes were executed by Daniele da Volterra after Perino's death in 1547.

The cycle of frescoes begun in 1563 by Salviati and Taddeo Zuccaro for Pius IV illustrates themes emphasizing the temporal power of the popes, such as the submission of the Emperor Henry IV to Gregory VII and of Barbarossa to Alexander III, Peter of Aragon offering his kingdom to Eugenius III, Pippin giving Ravenna to the church, and the Donation of Charlemagne. The marble dado was also executed under Pius IV, but the remaining frescoes were not carried out till the time of Pius V (by Vasari and assistants, 1572) and refer to the great event of the pontificate: the *Victory of Lepanto*.

The series was completed under Gregory XIII who included subjects from the Massacre of St Bartholomew (1572).

THE SALA DUCALE

Formed of two rooms, not exactly aligned, the first of which was used for the reception of important but non-royal personages. The vault of this room was frescoed before 1565 with scenes from the *Labours of Hercules* by Raffaellino da Reggio.

In 1656–7 Bernini was commissioned to throw the two rooms into one and in order to mask the awkward transition from one to the other he inserted the arms of Alexander VII, enclosed in stucco drapery supported by putti, executed by Antonio Raggi (Wittkower, *Bernini*, p. 234; Fagiolo, *Bernini*, Cat. No. 164).

The Sala Ducale leads to the loggias of Gregory XIII decorated by Raffaellino da Reggio, Paris Nogari and others, which bring the visitor to the Sala Clementina. This was built for Clement VIII probably by Giacomo della Porta and frescoed by Giovanni and Cherubino Alberti with the *Glory of St Clement*. The work was mainly carried out between 1596 and the Holy Year of 1600. The frescoes on the walls were carried out after Giovanni Alberti's death (1601) by his brother Cherubino with the assistance of Baldassare Croce, but the *Shipwreck of St Clement* is by Paul Bril (M. C. Abromson, 'Clement VIII's Patronage of the Brothers Alberti', *Art Bulletin*, LX, 1978, p. 535; V. Hermann-Fiore, 'Giovanni Albertis Kunst und Wissenschaft der Quadratura', *Mitteilungen des kunsthistorischen Institutes in Florenz*, XXII, 1978, p. 61; and 'Studi sui disegni di figure di Giovanni e Cherubino Alberti', *Bollettino d'Arte*, VI, No. 5, 1980, p. 39).

Less easily accessible are the Sala di Carlo Magno with frescoes by Guidobaldo Abbatini (1635–7; W), the Sala della Contessa Matilda, decorated by Francesco Romanelli and Abbatini (1637–42; W and Hess, op. cit., I, p. 105, II, pls 43ff.), and the Sala delle Dame with a vault frescoed by Reni (Hess, op. cit., I, p. 95, II, pl. 32).

For the gardens see Belli-Barsali, p. 203. They contain the *casino*, built by Pirro Ligorio for Pius IV (Coffin, p. 267).

IV
THE VILLAS

Of the two general books on Roman villas the better is I. Belli-Barsali, *Le Ville di Roma* (Milan, 1970). Torselli's book with the same title is only useful for its plates. For the villas of the 16th century, and for a general discussion of the origins of the villa, see D. R. Coffin, *The Villa in the life of Renaissance Rome*, Princeton, 1979. For villas outside Rome see I. Belli-Barsali and M. G. Braschetti, *Ville della Campagna,* Milan, 1975. Many of the villas are engraved in the third part of Falda's *Le Fontane di Roma.*

Villa Albani (Torlonia)
Via Salaria

Bibliography: Vasi, *Magnificenze*, pl. 190; Magni, III, pls 61–6; Belli-Barsali, p. 313; J. Gaus, *Carlo Marchionni*, Cologne, 1967, p. 19.

At some date before 1748 – when it appears in Nolli's map with his name – Cardinal Alessandro Albani, nephew of Clement XI, acquired a *vigna* between via Salaria and via Nomentana, and began to lay out new gardens, mainly to contain his collection of ancient sculpture. Between 1756 and 1761 or 1762 the main palace was built and decorated to the design of Carlo Marchionni, though no doubt the cardinal had a good deal to do with the planning and particularly the disposition of the individual rooms for the display of the sculpture. His librarian, Winckelmann, described the cardinal as 'The first antiquarian in the world' and he was the centre of the revived enthusiasm for antiquity of which Winckelmann was the great exponent in writing. In this respect the Villa Albani belongs to the neo-classical movement, but the palace which Marchionni built for it must count as a very late – and not very distinguished – work of Baroque architecture. It is only in the decoration – both external and internal – of the palace and in the temples and pavilions in the garden that the new spirit is apparent. In 1761 Anton Raphael Mengs painted his *Parnassus* on the vault of one of the rooms in the palace and this became a symbol of the classical revival fostered by the cardinal (Voss, p. 655).

Curiously enough in the last gasp of Roman Baroque the architect turned back in many respects to the earliest stage of the movement. The portico with its heavy, free-standing columns recalls the nave arcade of S. Ignazio and the loggia in the court laid out by Ponzio and Vasanzio beside the main building of the Villa Mondragone at Frascati, with which the so-called coffee-house at the Villa Albani also has affinities in its lay-out.

In 1866 the villa was bought by Prince Alessandro Torlonia, to whose descendants it still belongs, but there are constantly rumours that it is to be bought by the state.

Villa Aldobrandini
Via Panisperna

Bibliography: Falda, *Nuovo teatro*, I, pl. 12; Belli-Barsali, p. 395.

The villa originally belonged to the Vitelli family who built a small *casino* on it in 1575. In 1600 it was given by Clement VIII to his nephew,

77. *Villa Albani. The Casino. Engraving by Vasi.*

Cardinal Pietro Aldobrandini, who enlarged it to the design of Carlo Lambardi and filled it with a collection of works of art including the famous ancient fresco called the *Aldobrandini Wedding*, now in the Vatican. The villa suffered greatly in 1876 when the via XXIV Maggio was made. Part of the garden was cut off and the level of the road was lowered. One of the pavilions was destroyed and replaced by the two modern copies which exist today. In 1920 the *casino* was extended down the via Panisperna. It is now the seat of the Istituto Internazionale del Diritto Privato. A few of the rooms survive with their original decoration.

The garden (entrance via Mazzarino 11) has lost all its original character.
See plates 15, 16.

Villa Altieri
Viale Manzoni 47

Bibliography: Falda, *Nuovo teatro*, IV, pl. 30; Percier and Fontaine, *Maisons de Plaisance*, p. 35, pls 44, 45; Spagnesi, *G. A. De Rossi*; p. 158; Belli-Barsali, p. 406; Torselli, *Ville*, p. 37; Elling, p. 463, pls 186–7; D. Helsted *et al.*, *Roma dei fotografi al tempo di Pio IX 1846–78*, Rome, 1900, pl. 200; S. Negro, *Nuovo album Romano*, Rome, 1964, pl. 166; *Guide Rionali*, XV, p. 158.

Built for Cardinal Paluzzo Albertoni-Altieri (see Palazzo Altieri) in 1674 by G. A. de'Rossi. A simple block-like building with a double-curved staircase leading to the *piano nobile*. It is now used as a school, all the surrounding gardens having been sold, and its original appearance can best be judged from the engraving in Falda (Spagnesi, fig. 82).

Villa degli Arcadi (Bosco Parrasio)
Via Porta S. Pancrazio 32

Bibliography: Elling, p. 471, pls 194, 195.

The gardens were laid out by Antonio Canevari in 1725 for the Academy of the Arcadians with elaborate steps and an open-air theatre in which the members of the Academy declaimed their compositions.

Villa Astalli
Via Emanuele Filiberto, at corner of viale Manzoni

Bibliography: Belli-Barsali, p. 404; *Guide Rionali*, XV, p. 160.

A late 17th-century villa of no great distinction, now deprived of all its gardens and standing on a major crossroads. It has simple façades decorated with oval niches containing busts.

78. *Villa Altieri. Engraving by Vasi.*

Villa Aurelia
Via Garibaldi

Bibliography: Belli-Barsali, p. 452.

Built by Cardinal Gerolamo Farnese (d.1668) round an earlier *casino* put up by Paul III. The name of the architect is not known. The villa was badly damaged during the siege of 1849 but is recorded in an engraving by Vasi and was rebuilt immediately in its original form. It now belongs to the American Academy.

Villa Barberini
Via del Gianicolo 4A

Bibliography: Percier and Fontaine, *Maisons de Plaisance*, p. 15, pl. 19; R. Battaglia, *Il Palazzo di Nerone e la villa Barberini al Gianicolo*, Rome, 1943; Golzio, *Palazzi*, p. 57; *Guide Rionali*, XIII, 1, p. 168; Belli-Barsali, pp. 42, 43.

Originally built by Cardinal Bonifacio Ferreri (d.1535). Bought in 1641 by Taddeo Barberini, who enlarged it to the designs of Francesco Contini. The appearance of the *casino*, which was destroyed in the siege of Rome in 1849, is recorded in an early 19th-century engraving, and two small pavilions by Francesco Contini, the Casino della Palma and the Palazzetto Vercelli, survive, the latter more or less intact.

The villa is now included in the Casa Generalizia dell'Istituto di S. Dorotea.

Villa Benedetti *(Il Vascello)* (destroyed)

Bibliography: M. Meyer, *Villa Benedetta*, Rome, 1677; J. G. Keysler, *Travels through Germany ... Italy and Lorrain*, London, 1756, II, p. 407; Vasi, *Magnificenze*, pl. 199; Torselli, *Ville*, p. 271; Belli-Barsali, p. 408; Fagiolo dell'Arco and Carandini, *L'Effimero barocco*, II, fig. 401.

Built by Louis XIV's and Mazarin's agent in Rome, the abbé Elpidio Benedetti, about the middle of the 17th century near the Porta di S. Pancrazio. The architect was Basilio Bricci, helped by his sister Plautilla, who was a painter. It was almost completely destroyed in the siege of 1849 but is recorded in engravings.

Villa Bolognetti (destroyed)

Bibliography: Percier and Fontaine, *Maisons de Plaisance*, p. 37.

Built in 1743 outside the Porta Pia on the via Salaria for Cardinal Mario Bolognetti on the designs of Nicola Salvi.

79. *Villa Benedetti. Engraving by Vasi showing, on the left, the Villa Corsini (destroyed)*

Villa Borghese

Bibliography: Falda, *Nuovo teatro*, IV, pls 12, 13; id., *Fontane*, III, pls 13–15; id., *Giardini*, pls 15, 16; Ferrerio, *Palazzi*, II, pls 26, 27; D. Montelatici, *Villa Borghese fuori di Porta Pinciana*, Rome, 1700; Magni, III, pls 29–32; P. della Pergola, *Villa Borghese*, Rome, 1967; A. Ravaglioli and C. Pietrangeli, 'Villa Borghese. Storia e immagini', *Capitolium*, XLIII, 1968, p. 37; Belli-Barsali, p. 254; C. H. Heilmann, 'Die Entstehungsgeschichte der Villa Borghese in Rom', *Münchner Jahrbuch*, XXIV, 1973, p. 97.

With the election of Cardinal Camillo Borghese to the papacy, as Pope Paul V, in 1605, his nephew Scipione Caffarelli, who took the name of Borghese and was made a cardinal in the same year, undertook a number of building schemes, which included the construction of the garden palace, now the Palazzo Rospigliosi-Pallavicini and the extension of the Palazzo Borghese in the centre of the town, and at the same time began to buy land adjoining the family *vigna* on the Pincio, with the result that within a few years he had acquired a considerable part of the vast area known today as the Villa Borghese.

As the centre of the villa he constructed the *Casino*, which was designed and begun by Flaminio Ponzio and continued after his death in 1613 by the Fleming Jan van Santen, called Vasanzio, who was mainly concerned with the decoration of the building. In plan Ponzio followed the type used by Peruzzi at the Farnesina with two projecting wings joined by a loggia on the ground floor, with the difference that at the Farnesina the wings project beyond the loggia, whereas at the Villa Borghese it runs flush with them. Ponzio also added two towers on the garden façade. In the decoration of the exterior he followed the fashion set at the Villa Medici of decorating the four façades with ancient busts and reliefs, surrounded by fluted frames. Many of these were removed in the late 18th or early 19th century and, as we know from engravings and painted views, the effect was originally one of much greater richness, and an account of the villa written in 1700 states that there were 140 bas-reliefs, 70 busts and 40 statues.

The ground floor contains a central *salone* running through two floors and five other rooms which were devoted to the cardinal's collection of sculpture, including not only works of antiquity, but a number of single figures and groups by Bernini, of whom the cardinal was one of the earliest sponsors, including the *David*, *Pluto and Proserpine*, *Aeneas and Anchises* and *Apollo and Daphne*. The vault of the room at the back on the first floor, which was once an open loggia, was decorated by Giovanni Lanfranco with a fresco of the *Council of the Gods* surrounded by fictive architecture supported by pairs of atlantes

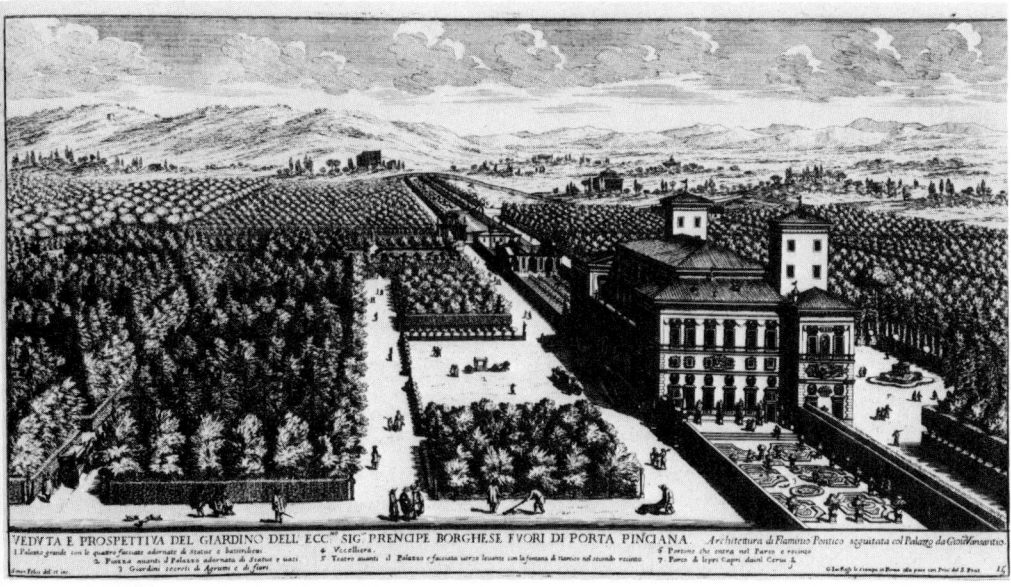

80. *Villa Borghese. Engraving by Falda.*

(1624–5; H. Hibbard, 'The Date of Lanfranco's Fresco in the Villa Borghese', *Miscellanea Bibliothecae Hertzianae*, 1961, p. 353). This and the other rooms on the first floor contain the great collection of paintings formed by Cardinal Scipione which includes not only masterpieces by Raphael, Titian, Correggio and Veronese and Caravaggio but important paintings by Roman artists of the next generation, notably Giovanni Lanfranco, and several of the few paintings ascribed to Bernini.

At the end of the 18th century considerable alterations were made to the interior of the *casino*. The vault of the *salone* was frescoed in 1782 by Mariano Rossi with a splendid composition representing a scene from Roman history: *Marcus Furius Camillus breaking the peace with Brennus*, one of the last examples of the full Baroque style in fresco painting, in which the artist has recovered to an extraordinary extent the spirit of Pietro da Cortona (A. Clark, 'Painting in Italy in the eighteenth century', exhibition catalogue, Chicago, Minneapolis, Chicago, 1970, p. 210). A few years later the walls were painted in the new 'Pompeian' style by a team of painters directed by Antonio Asprucci. The redecoration of the other rooms was carried out in a style which is clearly neo-classical, under the direction of Giovanni Battista Marchetti.

The formal gardens in front and to the south of the *casino* were laid out in 1617–19 by Girolamo Rainaldi who at the same time made an open air theatre in the area to the east of it. In 1688 two further pavilions – the Palazzo della Meridiana and an aviary – were constructed at either end of a *giardino segreto* to the north of the *casino* (Ferrari, *Lo Stucco*, pls Cff.). The name of Tommaso Mattei occurs in the accounts for these buildings, but it is not known whether he was the designer or the builder.

There were two entrances to the villa. One, consisting of two massive piers decorated with the dragon of the Borghese arms while the eagle stands on top, originally stood opposite the Muro Torto – part of the Aurelian walls between Porta Pinciana and Porta del Popolo – and led to the *vigna* owned by the family since the 16th century. The piers have now been moved to the entrance opposite Porta Pinciana. The other, a massive gate built by Girolamo Rainaldi, stands on the via Pinciana. Here the visitor passed through a semi-circle of hedges, which originally were cut with niches containing ancient statues, and then after a few hundred yards turned to the right and found himself on the main axis of the formal garden in front of the *casino*. To the right of the entrance is a small oval building with open arcades designed by Ponzio which was used for open-air meals. Below it was the wine-cellar. Further to the east are the stables.

In the last decades of the 18th century and the first half of the 19th, major alterations were made in the gardens. The formal gardens were swept away, together with many of the fountains; new gardens, including the enchanting Giardino del Lago, were laid out; and a number of pavilions and sham ruins in the neo-classical style were set up. In 1807 Prince Camillo Borghese sold a part of the collection of ancient sculpture to the Louvre, but he continued to extend the park by the acquisition of adjacent *vigne*. The bases decorated with the eagle and dragon of the Borghese arms which stood round the formal garden in front of the *casino* were sold in the 19th century and now stand on the terrace at Cliveden. They have been replaced by copies (cf. P. Hoffmann, 'Recenti ristauri a Villa Borghese', *Capitolium*, XXXV, 3, 1960, p. 3). In 1901 his descendant was compelled to sell the villa, with the *casino* and the collection of paintings and sculpture, to the state. The *casino* was made into a museum and the gardens were opened as a public park.

Villa Bosco Parrasio. See Villa degli Arcadi
Via Porta S. Pancrazio 32

Villa Carpegna
Via Aurelia

Bibliography: Elling, p. 465, pls 190–3; Belli-Barsali, p. 396.

Built and laid out by Cardinal Gasparo Carpegna (d.1714). The name of the designer is not known, but Elling has suggested that of Giovanni Antonio de'Rossi. The villa, which has fallen into decay but still retains many of its most important features, was bought by the state in 1979 and will, it is to be presumed, be restored.

Villa Celimontana. See Villa Mattei
Piazza Navicella

Villa Chigi
Via Salaria

Bibliography: Belli-Barsali, p. 334.

In 1763 Cardinal Flavio Chigi bought from Vincenzo Pucci a *vigna* on the via Salaria with a small *casino* which he enlarged on the designs of Tommaso Bianchi and Pietro Camporese the Elder, the building being completed by 1766. Architecturally it is of no great distinction, but it contains on the upper floor a flight of five rooms with remarkable painted decorations by Francesco Natale for the landscapes – some of which represent Chigi properties – and Giacomo Rubini for the decorative settings. The most remarkable is the room which leads to the chapel which is completely painted with a *trompe-l'oeil* rendering of hermits in the Thebaid, a scheme possibly suggested by Clérisseau's frescoes in the convent of SS. Trinità dei Monti.

Villa Colonna
Via XXIV Maggio

Bibliography: Vasi, *Magnificenze*, pl. 193; Magni, III, pls 42, 43; D'Onofrio, *Scalinate*, p. 59; Belli-Barsali, p. 402.

The Villa Colonna is in effect the gardens which stretch behind the Palazzo Colonna – to which they are joined by bridges – up the slope of the Quirinal. There was a separate entrance from the Quirinal side through an elaborate gate built in 1617. It now stands at the top of a double flight of steps which had to be added when the level of the street was lowered in the 1870s. The gardens, which are not normally accessible, were laid out about 1713.

Villa Corsini ai Quattro Venti (destroyed)

Bibliography: Belli-Barsali, pp. 43, 45, 56, 91, n. 3, 409.

The villa stood on the top of the Janiculum, near the Porta S. Pancrazio. It was probably originally built by Mattia de' Rossi in the last years of the 17th century but was rebuilt by Simone Salvi for Clement XII before he became pope in 1730.

81. *The gardens of Villa Colonna. Engraving by Vasi, showing the gardens laid out in the late 17th century on the slope behind the Palazzo Colonna, leading up to the Quirinal. The engraving shows the three bridges which join the garden to the palace.*

It was destroyed in the siege of 1849 but is recorded in engravings.
See plate 79.

Villa della Porta Radiani
Via Portuernse

Bibliography: Belli-Barsali, p. 402.

Of this villa attributed to Girolamo Rainaldi only the gate remains, a rather striking structure with the polygonal top to the main opening used by Michelangelo in the Porta Pia.

Villa de'Rossi (destroyed)

Bibliography: Ferrerio, II, pl. 61.

Ferrerio includes, as the last plate in his two volumes, an engraving of a *casino* built for Giovanni Giacomo de'Rossi by Giovanni Maria Baratta. It is described as being 'sul Gianicolo alla Lungara', but its exact site has not been determined.

Villa Farnese
On the Palatine

Bibliography: Baglione, p. 8; Falda, *Fontane*, III, pl. 10; id., *Giardini*, pls 9, 10; Vasi, *Magnificenze*, X, p. XLII; Letarouilly, pls 263–5 (181–3); M. Walcher Casotti, *Il Vignola*, Trieste, 1960, p. 185; H. Giess, 'Studien zur Farnese-Villa am Palatin', *Römisches Jahrbuch*, XIII, 1971, p. 179; *Guide Rionali*, X, 3, p. 102 and 4, pp. 24, 62.

The site was acquired between 1542 and 1565 by Cardinal Alessandro Farnese and his brothers Ottavio and Ranuccio. The lay-out of the gardens and the designing of the two pavilions have been ascribed to Vignola since the time of Baglione, but there are no documents to confirm the attribution and there is reason to think that the pavilions were constructed after his death in 1573. The name of Michelangelo's assistant, Giacomo del Duca, has also been suggested, but without documentary evidence. The gardens were almost completely destroyed in the late 19th-century excavations on the Palatine, but the two pavilions survive and the fine entrance gate which originally stood in the wall separating the villa from the Forum or Campo Vaccino was pulled down in 1882 but re-erected in 1957 on the via S. Gregorio. It was originally the centre of a long wall opened up by windows, but it now stands in rather unhappy isolation. Old photographs showing the gate and the gardens are reproduced by H. Giess.

Baglione attributes the gate to Vignola, but it is not mentioned by Danti in the biography of the architect published in 1587. Milizia (*Vite* II, p. 26) suggested that the upper part must be later than Vignola and this has led some writers to attribute it to Girolamo Rainaldi, who is named by Falda as the designer of the gardens and to whom payments are recorded between 1626 and 1635; but this cannot be correct, since the gate appears complete in Dupérac's map of 1577. Walcher Casotti has provided good evidence to suggest that it cannot have been planned before 1565, and the lower part was probably built between that date and Vignola's death in 1573.

Stylistically the lower part conforms to Vignola's style (cf. the door to the Villa Giulia), but the upper part is entirely different. It may have been added after Vignola's death by his son Giacinto, but Benedetti (*Giacomo del Duca*, p. 17) has suggested that it may be due to Giacomo del Duca who was working for the Farnese from 1565 onwards. The hypothesis is tempting. There are echoes of the Porta Pia in the general design and in that of the windows which existed in the wall in which the gate was set. Further, the shield is not unlike that on Porta Pia which is documented as being by del Duca, and the broken pediment and herm-caryatids occur in a drawing in the Victoria and Albert Museum ascribed to del Duca (Benedetti, pl. 154).
See also Villa Aurelia.

Villa Giustiniani (Massimo, Lancellotti)
Via Boiardo

Bibliography: Titi, 1763, p. 435; Letarouilly, pl. 328 (217); K. Gerstenberg, *Die Wandgemälde der deutschen Romantiker im Casino Massimo zu Rom*, Berlin, 1934; R. Battaglia, 'Le Ville Giustiniani a Roma e l'opera di Carlo Lambardi', *L'Urbe*, V, 1940, No. 12, p. 2; *Guide Rionali*, XV, p. 124; Blunt, 'Two neglected works by Borromini', *Römisches Jahrbuch*, 1982.

The existing *casino* was built between 1607 and 1618 by the marchese Vincenzo Giustiniani. On his death in 1637 it passed to his adopted son, Prince Andrea Giustiniani, who in 1640 married Maria Pamphili, niece of Cardinal Giovanni Battista Pamphili, later Pope Innocent X.

The *casino* was originally a plain rectangular building with two open loggias, one on the ground floor on the garden side and one on the upper floor of the entrance front. An engraving of about 1640 shows the latter in this form, but with the addition of the existing cornice which includes the eagle and tower of the Giustiniani arms, and the *guilloche* string-course below it. In 1649 Prince Andrea redecorated the outside of the building, incorporating in it many of the finest ancient reliefs from the celebrated collection formed by his adoptive father which was mainly housed in the palace opposite S. Luigi dei Francesi but parts of which were in the garden of a villa outside the Porta del Popolo from which they were transferred to the Lateran villa by Prince Andrea. The reliefs were set in elaborately designed frames, accompanied by laurel and oak wreaths, leafy branches twined into ovals, palmettes and dropping bands of bell-shaped flowers. Below the windows of the upper storey runs a decorative frieze incorporating the Giustiniani eagle and the Pamphili dove standing on garlands of laurel. This decoration is almost certainly by Borromini, to whom it is ascribed in the 1763 edition of Titi, and who is recorded as working for Andrea Giustiniani at the relevant period, mainly on plans for altering and enlarging the town palace, but also on one occasion on the gardens of the Lateran villa. Titi's attribution has been rejected by modern writers about Borromini on stylistic grounds, but the general disposition of the decoration is subtle enough to be by him and all the decorative motifs used on the villa can be paralleled in his work either in the Palazzo Falconieri (palmettes and ribbons), at S. Ivo and the Oratory (laurel wreaths), or in the vestibule leading from the church of the Lateran to the palace (leafy branches, Pamphili dove, and garlands). The similarity between the decoration in the Lateran and that on the *casino* is indeed so close that it suggests that the same team of stucco workers was used in both cases.

In the early 19th century the villa was bought by Prince Massimi and the main rooms on the ground floor were decorated by Overbeck and other members of the German Nazarene School.

Villa Lancellotti. See Villa Giustiniani
Via Boiardo

Villa Ludovisi, Casino dell'Aurora
Via Lombardia

Bibliography: Falda, *Giardini*, pls 11, 12; De Brosses, II, p. 63; Belli-Barsali, p. 239; G. Felici, *Villa Ludovisi in Roma*, Rome, 1952; Hibbard, *Maderno*, p. 212; Golzio, *Palazzi*, figs 175ff.; Coffin, p. 235; *Guide Rionali*, IV, 1, p. 63.

In 1621 Cardinal Ludovico Ludovisi bought a garden on the Pincio from Cardinal Francesco Maria del Monte and soon acquired other adjacent gardens, including one belonging to the Orsini. On this site he built a large palace and a small *casino*, called the Casino dell'Aurora from the famous ceiling fresco by Guercino of that subject. The architecture of the main palace is attributed by some early sources to Domenichino who was appointed by Gregory XV (Ludovisi) as his official architect, but Maderno certainly had a hand in the design.

In the early 19th century the villa was enlarged by the acquisition of the adjacent Villa Belloni, by Prince Antonio Buoncompagni Ludovisi, but in 1883 his heirs sold almost the whole of the villa, keeping only the Casino dell'Aurora and the main *casino*, part of which was incorporated in the new palace on via Veneto, built by Prince Rodolfo Buoncompagni Ludovisi and now the American Embassy. The present network of streets around via Veneto was laid out on the remainder of the grounds.

The Casino dell'Aurora is basically a late 16th-century building constructed by Cardinal Cecchino del Nero. The architect is not known. The vault of the central room was decorated for Cardinal Ludovisi by Guercino – in collaboration with Agostino Tassi – in 1621 with the fresco of *Aurora* which marked a crucial step towards the illusionism of the full Baroque (its novelty can best be realized by comparing it with Guido Reni's *quadro riportato* of the same subject in the *casino* of the Palazzo Rospigliosi-Pallavicini of 1615). In another room the same two artists painted a fresco of *Fame* on the vault, only slightly less striking in its illusionism than the *Aurora*. On the walls are landscapes by G. B. Viola, Domenichino, Guercino and Paul Bril.

Villa Massimo. See Villa Giustiniani
Via Boiardo

82. *Villa Ludovisi. Etching by Piranesi.*

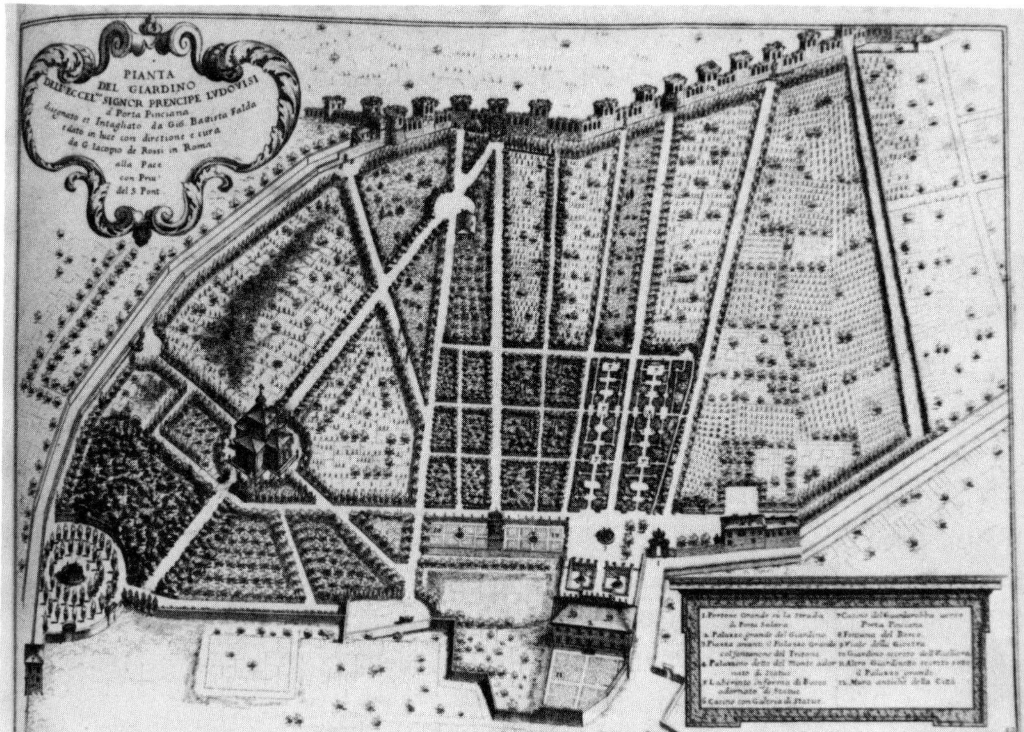

83. *The Villa Ludovisi. Engraving by Falda showing on the left the Casino dell'Aurora and at the bottom, near the panel with the inscription, the main palace. At the top, surrounding the garden, is a section of the Aurelian wall near to the Porta Pinciana.*

Villa Mattei (Celimontana)
Piazza Navicella

Bibliography: Falda, *Fontane*, III, pls 18, 19; id., *Giardini*, pls 17, 18; Tessin, p. 187; Benedetti, *Del Duca*, p. 308; Torselli, p. 95; Belli-Barsali, p. 384; Elling, pl. 174.

In 1553 Giacomo Mattei bought a *vigna* near the church of S. Maria in Domnica and between 1583 and 1586 his heir Ciriaco built on it a *casino* to the designs of Giacomo del Duca. This was enlarged and remodelled in later periods to such an extent that its original form cannot now be accurately determined. The original formal gardens were also transformed in the 'English' style in the 19th century.

The most important works of ancient sculpture were sold but the Egyptian obelisk and many fine architectural fragments survive, as well as one fountain, the oval Fontana del Fiume, inaccessible but visible from the terrace which overlooks the *viale* which runs beside the Baths of Caracalla.

The entrance gate to the villa is one made by Carlo Lambardi for the Villa Giustiniani near the Lateran, but moved here when the grounds of the villa were sold in the 1880s.

Villa Medici
Piazza Trinità dei Monti

Bibliography: Falda, *Giardini*, pls 7, 8; Magni, III, pls 9–11; Belli-Barsali, p. 185; C. Mignot, 'Les loggias de la Villa Médicis à Rome', *Revue de l'Art*, 19, 1973, p. 50; Torselli, p. 215; G. M. Andres, *The Villa Medici in Rome*, New York and London, 1976; Coffin, p. 219.

In 1540 the nephews of Cardinal Giovanni Ricci bought a *vigna* from the Crescenzi family and began to build a *casino* on it to the designs of Giovanni Lippi, called Nanni di Baccio Bigio, who died in 1568 and was succeeded by his son, Annibale Lippi. In 1576 it was acquired by Cardinal Ferdinando de'Medici who made additions to the building. The garden façade is inlaid with ancient bas-reliefs, an arrangement that was later followed at the Borghese, Giustiniani and Pamphili villas and at the Palazzo Mattei di Giove. The rooms were probably decorated at this time, but in the main *casino* only a

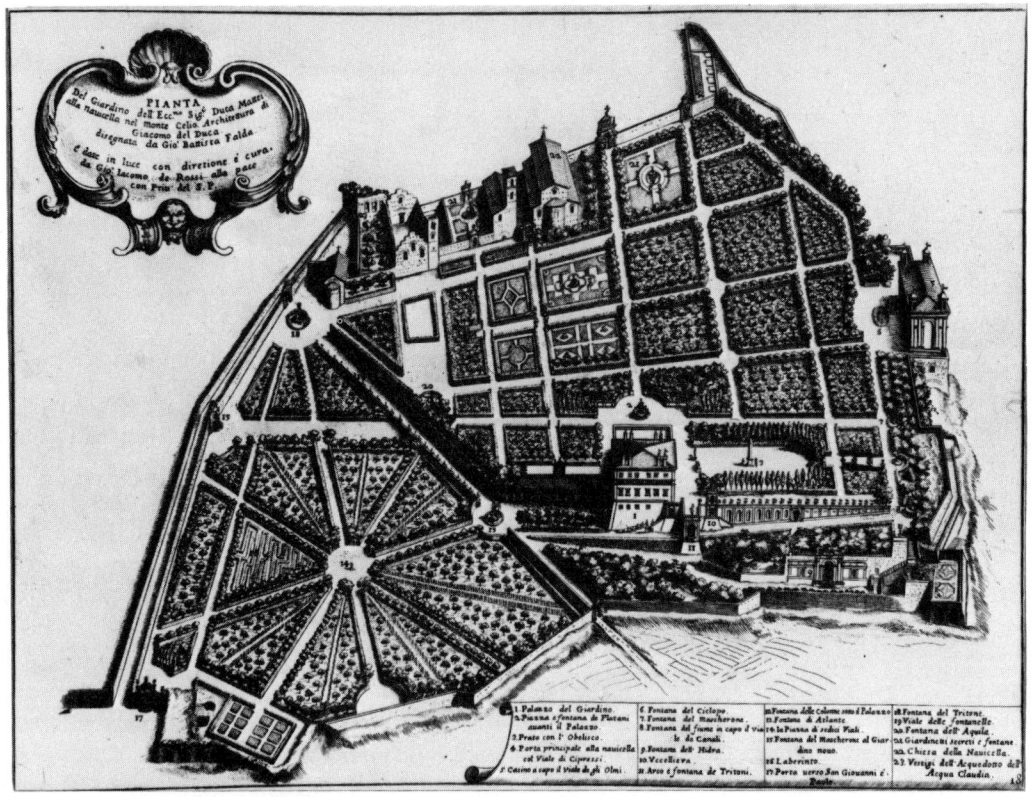

84. *Villa Mattei (Celimontana). Engraving by Falda.*

few frescoed friezes survived the alterations of the 19th century.

In the garden, however, is a small *studiolo* decorated for Ferdinando which survives intact (cf. E. Darragon, 'Le Studiolo du Cardinal Ferdinand à la Villa Médicis', *Revue de l'Art*, 19, 1973, p. 63).

The collection of sculpture was removed to Florence in the 1780s when the villa had passed to the house of Lorraine, as grand dukes of Tuscany. In 1804 the villa was taken over by the French authorities and is today the seat of the Académie de France à Rome, founded by Colbert in 1666, which had hitherto been housed in the Palazzo Mancini. The villa is the most complete example surviving of a late 16th-century *villa suburbana* with superb views over Rome. For the pavilions in the gardens (painted by Velázquez on his visit to Rome in 1649–50) see C. Mignot.

Villa Pamphili

Bibliography: Falda, *Nuovo teatro*, IV, pl. 23; id., *Fontane*, III, pls 21–6; id., *Giardini*, pls 19–21; De' Rossi, *Architettura Civile*, III, pls 74–7; De Brosses, II, p. 185; L. Frati, 'Giovanni Francesco Grimaldi detto il Bolognese', *Arte e Storia*, XIV, 1895, p. 35; O. Pollak, 'Alessandro Algardi (1602–54) als Architekt', *Zeitschrift für Geschichte der Architektur*, IV, 1910–11, p. 49; Magni, III, pls 21–2; A. Schiavo, *Villa Doria Pamphilij*, Milan, 1942 (for plates); Mallory, *Rococo*, p. 113; Belli-Barsali, p. 274; Güthlein, *Familienarchiv Spada*, p. 221; O. Reggio, 'Alessandro Algardi e gli Stucchi di Villa Pamphili', *Paragone*, 251, 1971, p. 3; D. Batorska, 'Additional comments on the Iconography of the Sala di Ercole at the Villa Pamphili in Rome', *Paragone*, 303, 1975, p. 22; Hoffmann, *Villa Doria Pamphili*, Rome, 1976 (reviewed by O. Osti Francisi in *Antalogia di Belle Arti*, 9–12, 1979, p. 181).

In 1630 Pamfilio Pamfili bought a small *vigna* outside the Porta S. Pancrazio, and when Cardinal Giambattista Pamphili became pope, as Innocent X, in 1644, he immediately decided to enlarge and embellish the property. The *vigna* contained a small *casino*, facing the via Aurelia,

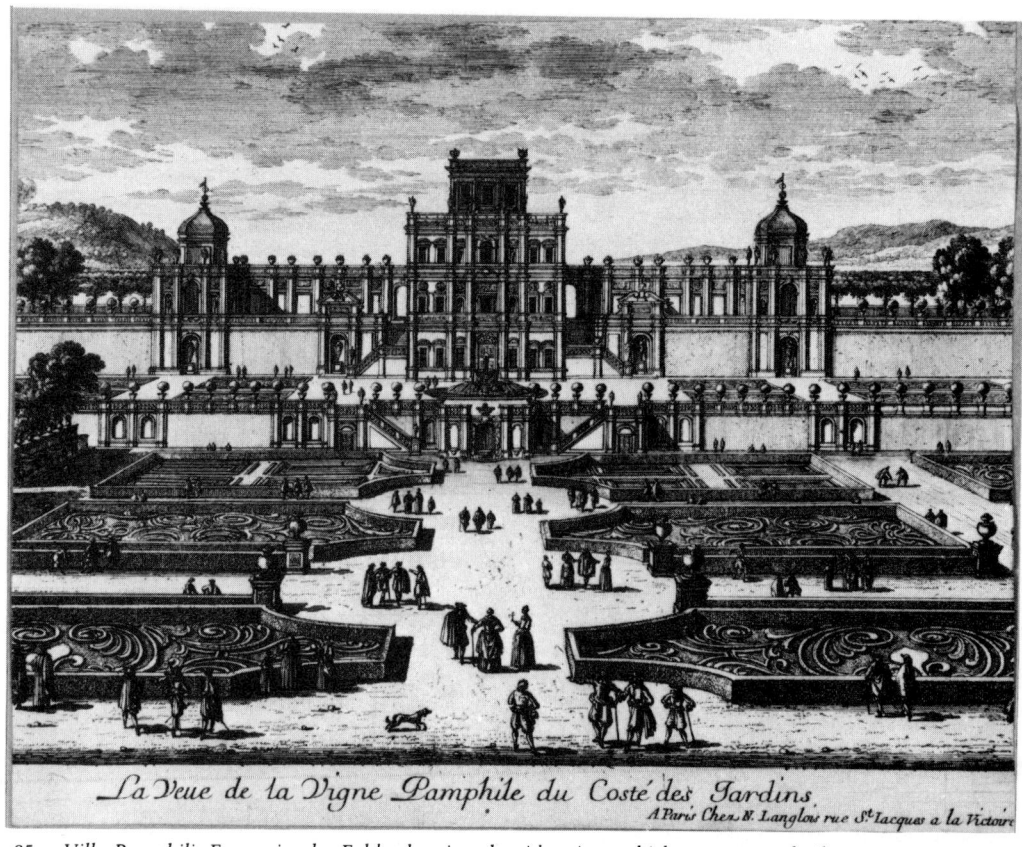

85. Villa Pamphili. Engraving by Falda showing the side wings which were never built.

86. Villa Pamphili. The Fountain of Venus. Engraving by Falda.

which survives and served as a lodging for members of the family even when the larger *casino* was built, because the latter contained no bedrooms and was designed purely for entertainment and the display of the collection of ancient sculpture, many pieces of which are set into the outer walls of the building as at the Medici, Borghese and Giustiniani villas and the Palazzo Mattei. The park, which was laid out at the same time as the *casino* was built, though much altered in the 19th century, is one of the largest in Rome, exceeded in size, but not in beauty, only by the Villa Borghese.

The *casino* was begun in 1645 and built very rapidly, being completed in 1647. The authorship of the building has given rise to much discussion. It was traditionally ascribed to the sculptor Alessandro Algardi, who probably supervised the design with the help of a professional architect (possibly Carlo Rainaldi) with Giovanni Francesco Grimaldi in charge of the actual construction. As it stands the *casino* is unusual in consisting of a single, almost cubical block, with slight projections on the main front, but it was originally intended that there should be wings. In the centre of the block on the ground floor is a circular *salone* round which are grouped the main rooms. The basic idea of this plan is taken from Palladio, but the arrangement of the rooms is freer and less symmetrical than in his villas.

All the rooms on this floor, except the vestibule, have stucco reliefs by Algardi, originally white on white (the blue ground is a later addition), some illustrating ancient Roman scenes, allegories alluding to Camillo Pamphili and episodes from the life of *Hercules*. The last are accompanied by much damaged frescoes on the same theme by Grimaldi.

The garden contains a number of grottoes and fountains, including the Grotto of Venus with stuccoes from Algardi's own hand (in the Giardino Segreto) and what is probably a late 19th-century copy of Bernini's *Lumaca*, of which the original, made for the fountain at the south end of the Piazza Navona, is now (in a ruined state) in the Palazzo Doria-Pamphili in the Corso (Heimbürger Ravalli, 'Bernini's shell decoration for Della Porta's Fountain at Piazza Navona', *Paragone*, 357, 1979, p. 83).

In the 1730s Gabriele Valvassori added the gate between the Giardino delle Delizie and the park, the enclosure to the Giardino dei Cedrati and the fountain of the Tiber, the two latter being attached to the Villa Vecchia.

Villa Patrizi

87. Villa Patrizi. Engraving by Vasi.

Villa Patrizi (destroyed)

Bibliography: Vasi, *Magnificenze*, pl. 191; Belli-Barsali, p. 46.

According to Vasi built by two brothers of Cardinal Giovanni Patrizi in 1717. The villa stood outside Porta Pia and was presumably pulled down in the late 19th century.

Villa Peretti (destroyed)

Bibliography: Falda, *Giardini*, pls 13, 14; Vasi, *Magnificenze*, pl. 195; D'Onofrio, *Acque e Fontane*, p. 202.

This villa, which must have been one of the grandest of all Roman villas, was laid out by Sixtus V on the designs of Domenico Fontana. It covered an area running east from S. Maria Maggiore and including the whole of the present Termini Station. It was sold up and built over in the 19th century and the only feature to survive from it is a fountain which was reconstructed on the lower slopes of the Janiculum (see Fontana della Prigione).

Villa Sacchetti (The Pigneto) (destroyed)

Bibliography: L. Berrettini, letter to Ciro Ferri in Campori, *Lettere Artistiche*, Modena, 1866, p. 505; Sandrart, p. 416; Falda, *Nuovo teatro*, IV; Vasi, *Magnificenze*, pl. 183; Fabbrini, *Vita del Cavaliere Pietro Berrettini da Cortona*, Cortona, 1896; Briganti, *Cortona*, p. 190; Noehles, *SS. Luca e Martina*, p. 15; Belli-Barsali, p. 40.

At an undetermined date, probably in or just after 1632, a number of the Sacchetti family commissioned Cortona to build a *casino* as the centre piece of his villa behind St Peter's, called the Pigneto (Cortona had already decorated, and probably built, Sacchetti's villa at Castelfusano). The *casino* was unfortunately allowed to fall into decay within a few decades and has now completely disappeared. It is however recorded in paintings, drawings and engravings which show it to have been a very precocious building for its time, with a bold use of contrasting curves unknown in the 1620s. Specchi's engraving (in Falda) is misleading in showing two double flights of steps which probably never existed and the curved wings as if they were almost quadrants, whereas in fact they were drawn according to Cortona's favourite form,

Villa Sacchetti

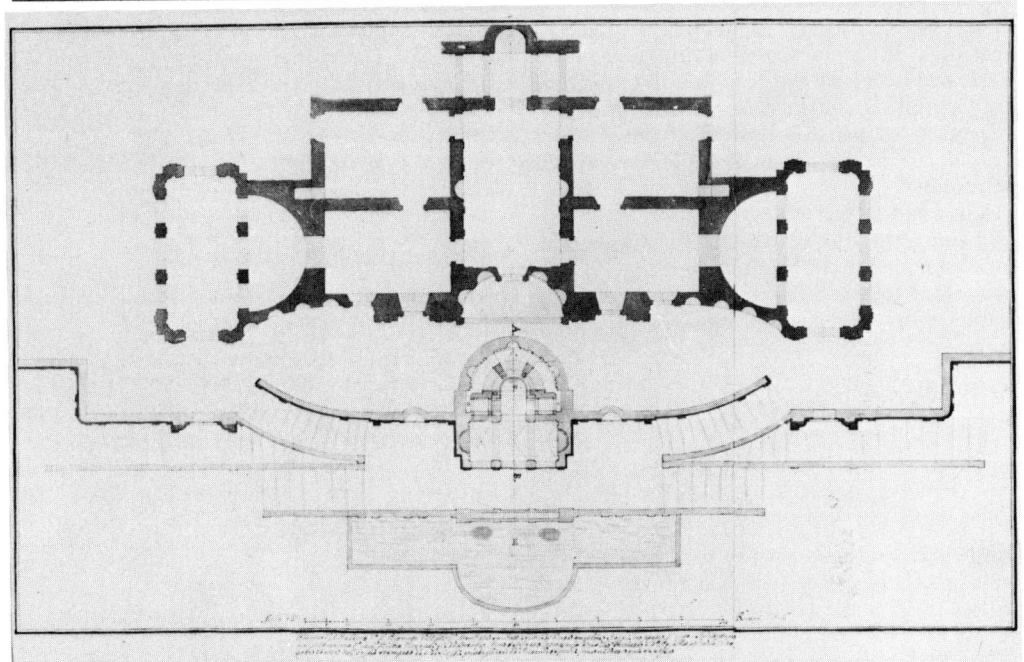

88. Villa Sacchetti (The Pigneto). Drawing by Pier Leone Ghezzi (author's collection).

89. Villa Sacchetti. Drawing by Hendrik van Lint, showing the tomb of a favourite donkey in the foreground (Earl of Leicester, Holkham Hall).

almost straight in the middle but curving sharply at the ends. Cortona's frescoes on the vault of the Salone are recorded in engravings by G. Audran and F. Carocci, and replicas of the principal panels, illustrating the story of *David*, are preserved in the Vatican and the Quirinal.

On a hill facing the *casino* stood an ancient urn containing the remains of a favourite donkey belonging to the Sacchetti, which used to be sent alone to market with a shopping list in its basket and returned with the provisions needed.

Villa Sforza ai Quattro Cantoni
Via dei Quattro Cantoni

Bibliography: Vasi, *Magnificenze*, pl. 158; *Architettura minora*, II, pls 72, 73; Belli-Barsali, p. 398; Elling, p. 68.

Little seems to be known of the history of this villa which is visible in Falda's plan of 1667. About 1700 it passed to the Oratorian Sisters and is now the seat of the Ufficio Tecnico delle Imposte di Fabbricazione. The treatment of the windows is unusual. Those on the lower floor have double pediments, those above are broken at the top by shells and at the bottom by a cusped panel enclosing a star. The style of the upper windows is very close to Borromini's in the 1650s. The rooms on the ground floor have late Mannerist frescoes of mythological subjects treated as *quadri riportati* on ceilings with white coves. There is also a chapel with a frescoed vault in the same style, but with stuccoes.

Villa Spada (destroyed)

Bibliography: S. Negro, *Nuovo Album Romano*, Rome, 1964, pl. 16; Belli-Barsali, p. 451.

The villa stood near the Porta San Pancrazio. It was built before 1668. The villa was Garibaldi's last headquarters in the Siege of Rome in 1849 and was largely destroyed in the siege. It is recorded in old photographs, and was rebuilt in its original form. It is now the seat of the Irish Embassy to the Holy See.

Villa Torlonia. See Villa Albani
Via Salaria

Villa Il Vascello (destroyed). See Villa Benedetti

90. *Villa Sforza ai Quattro Cantoni. Engraving by Vasi.*

Villa La Vignola
Via S. Gregorio

Bibliography: P. Guidi, 'La Ricostruzione della "Vignola"', *Ausonio*, VIII, 1912, p. 207; Coffin, p. 19; Belli-Barsali, p. 374.

This small but elegant *casino* originally stood on the southern slope of the Aventine between the Baths of Caracalla and the church of S. Balbina. In 1909 it was announced that it was to be pulled down, but owing to protests it was decided to rebuild it on its present site (this was done in 1911). The *casino* was built by Prospero Boccapaduli, in whose time as conservatore the Palazzo dei Conservatori was built and the Palazzo Senatorio remodelled, and who acquired the *vigna* in 1538. The date of the building is not recorded but it was probably soon after that of the acquisition of the site and it is shown in Paciotti's map of 1557. Its name 'La Vignola' suggests a connection with the architect of that name with whom it has no link, but may be a corruption of 'La Vignuolo', the little vineyard.

V
THE FOUNTAINS

Since antiquity the supply of water to Rome has been a matter of the greatest practical importance, as is attested by the remains of aqueducts which today form such an important feature of the Campagna immediately around Rome. When the popes returned to Rome from Avignon in 1377 they immediately began to reconstruct these aqueducts which had fallen into decay. They concentrated on restoring the Acqua Vergine, the one source which had never been wholly cut off, which came from springs at Salone, some 10 kilometres to the south-east of the Porta Maggiore. Nicholas V, Paul II and Sixtus IV (the last for the Holy Year of 1475) brought the water to the site of the present Trevi Fountain. Further extensions to the system were made by various popes during the 16th century, but the most important move was the decision, taken in 1570, to set up 18 new fountains over the whole area from the Piazza del Popolo to the Piazza di S. Maria (Piazza Venezia) and from the Piazza di Spagna to the via Giulia. Not all these were made and not all survive, but many of them, designed by Giacomo della Porta as 'Architetto del Popolo Romano', will be discussed below (see fountains in Piazzo Navona, Piazza Colonna, Piazza della Rotonda, etc.).

These fountains were largely erected owing to the energy of Gregory XIII who in 1583, two years before his death, decided in conjunction with the civic authorities of the Capitol to restore the aqueduct of Alexander Severus which brought water from a point in the Alban Hills between Montecompatri and Colonna to some of the higher areas of the city, including the Quirinal where the pope had begun to build his palace. This project was favoured by his successor, Sixtus V, perhaps because it would also have supplied water to his villa on the Esquiline. The water was brought to the fountain erected by Sixtus on the Quirinal (opposite the church of S. Maria della Vittoria) called – after his own Christian name – Acqua Felice, but it was also distributed to other fountains including those at the Quattro Fontane, the Madonna dei Monti, the Piazza Campitelli, the Piazza Montana, the Piazza Giudea in the ghetto, Trajan's column, and three on and below the Capitol. All these were designed by Giacomo della Porta, by right of his office, and Domenico Fontana was only allotted the fountain in front of the Quirinal.

On his election in 1605 Paul V immediately began planning to bring to Rome water from the lake of Bracciano (64 kilometres distant) to supply Trastevere and the Vatican where water was rare, using in part the aqueduct built by Trajan. The architects and engineers involved were Pompeo Targone, Giovanni Fontana and Carlo Maderno. At the end of the aqueduct on the top of the Janiculum Paul V erected the Acqua Paola in direct competition with the Acqua Felice of Sixtus V.

This was the last serious move made by any pope to bring water to the parts of Rome where it was really needed. In the 18th century the great event in connection with the erection of fountains was the completion of the Fontana di Trevi, a major event architecturally, but one which merely added a beautiful setting to an already constructed conduit.

The most complete account of the fountains of Rome is to be found in Cesare d'Onofrio's *Acque e Fontane* (Rome, 1977) but H. V. Morton's *The Waters of Rome* (London, 1966) is valuable as an account of the history of the water supply from antiquity onwards and the artistic products to which it gave rise. Many fountains are engraved in Falda's *Le Fontane di Roma* (parts I and III). The Spada archives contain a series of documents dealing with the complicated negotiations carried out by Virgilio Spada for Innocent X and Alexander VIII in connection with the distribution of water to various districts of Rome (Güthlein, *Familienarchiv Spada*, pp. 195–200.

Acqua Acetosa
Viale dei Parioli

Bibliography: Martinelli, p. 206; Falda, *Nuovo teatro*, I, pl. 35; id., *Fontane*, pl. 33; *Architettura minora*, II, pl. 155; N. Wibiral, 'A proposito di Andrea Sacchi architetto', *Palladio*, N.S., V, 1955, p. 56; D'Onofrio, *Acque e Fontane*, p. 514.

The fountain was built on the orders of Alexander VII in 1661–2 to the designs of Andrea Sacchi. It was for long ascribed to Bernini on the basis of 17th-century engravings but the documents, as well as a stylistic analysis, show that this is impossible, and the fountain must count, with the room of St Catherine of Siena in S. Maria sopra Minerva, as one of the rare works of architecture which can safely be attributed to Sacchi.

Acqua Felice
Piazza S. Bernardo

Bibliography: Baglione, p. 85; Falda, *Fontane*, I, pl. 8; Magni, III, pl. 17; D'Onofrio, *Acque e Fontane*, p. 222.

Built (1585–7) by Domenico Fontana for Sixtus V. It was executed by two of Fontana's assistants, Matteo da Città di Castello, and the architect's brother Giovanni Fontana. The figure of *Moses* is by Prospero Antichi and Leonardo Sormani. The reliefs represent *Aaron leading the Israelites to Water* and *Joshua making them cross the Jordan dry-foot*. The first is by G. B. Della Porta and the second by Flamineo Vacca and Pier Paolo Olivieri.
See plate 53.

Acqua Paola
Via Garibaldi

Bibliography: Falda, *Fontane*, I, pls 11, 12; Magni, III, pls 18, 22; Hibbard, *Maderno*, p. 198; C. H. Heilmann, 'Acqua Paola and the urban planning of Paul V Borghese', *Burlington Magazine*, CXII, 1970, p. 656; D'Onofrio, *Acque e Fontane*, p. 350.

In 1605 Paul V began plans to reconstruct the ancient *Acqua Traiana* to supply water to Trastevere, the area around via Giulia and the Vatican. To receive this the Acqua Paola fountain was constructed on the Janiculum 1610–11 and a smaller one against the Ospizio de'Mendicanti at the end of the via Giulia (see Fontana di Ponte Sisto). The Acqua Paola was probably designed by Flaminio Ponzio who with Giovanni Fontana was responsible for the engineering works

91. Acqua Felice. Etching by Piranesi showing the door to the villa of Cardinal du Bellay. On the extreme left, the corner of the façade of S. Maria della Vittoria.

92. *Acqua Paola. Etching by Piranesi showing the large basin added by Carlo Fontana.*

on the aqueduct. The design is based on that of Sixtus V's Acqua Felice – to which it was a conscious rival – but whereas the latter is a completely closed wall-like structure, the Acqua Paola stood free, with openings in the three middle arches which give a view of the loggia and garden on to which it backs. The Acqua Paola was intended to be the climax of a dramatic piece of town planning – or landscape gardening – since the pope intended to make a road leading to it from the Ponte Sisto through what was then an unbuilt-up, tree-covered slope, but this project was never put into effect. This road would have crossed the street planned as the main axis of Trastevere which was to run from S. Francesco a Ripa to join the via Lungara, but this was never completed, only the section from S. Francesco to S. Calisto being laid out.

The area behind the Acqua Paola was made by Alexander VII into a botanical garden, and in 1690 the fountain was altered by Alexander VIII who commissioned Carlo Fontana to construct the large basin in front of the fountain to replace the original narrow one shown in 17th-century engravings.

Fontana delle Api
Piazza Barberini, at the corner of via Veneto

Bibliography: Wittkower, *Bernini*, p. 265; Fagiolo dell'Arco, *Bernini*, No. 109; D'Onofrio, *Acque e Fontane*, p. 439.

This fountain was erected by Urban VIII in the last year of his pontificate (1644) against the corner of a palace where the via Sistina abuts on Piazza Barberini. In 1865 it was removed and the pieces stored till 1915 when it was reconstructed, disconsolate and *in vacuo*, on the pavement of the via Veneto. The upper shell – with the inscription – is part of the original, but the lower is a complete and arbitrary reconstruction. Only the *concetto* of the double shell, a symbol of life and fertility, with the Barberini bees, survives of what must have been a peculiarly concentrated invention of Bernini.

Fontana delle Api
Vatican, next to S. Anna dei Palafrenieri

Bibliography: Magni, III, pl. 23; Wittkower, *Bernini*, p. 265; Fagiolo dell'Arco, *Bernini*, No. 43; D'Onofrio, *Acque e Fontane*, p. 408; Blunt, *Borromini*, pp. 17, 225.

In 1626 Borromini was paid for carving this fountain which had been set up by Urban VIII in the Cortile di Belvedere. The design has been attributed to Bernini, and this is confirmed by the testimony of his son, but the fountain bears little resemblance to his other early works and the documents show that it came from the workshop of Maderno.

The main feature of the fountain is a rock, over which crawl the bees of the Barberini arms, while above it is a tablet on which is inscribed a distych by the pope himself. This idea of a rock fountain is connected with reconstructions of ancient fountains made by 17th-century archaeologists of which some, very similar to this, are recorded in drawings attributed (probably wrongly) to Pietro Testa in the Uffizi. Fountains of this type in mosaic occur in some ancient Roman villas.

Fontana del Babuino. See Palazzo Buoncampagni-Ludovisi
Via del Babuino

The Barcaccia Fountain
Piazza di Spagna

Bibliography: Falda, *Fontane*, I, pl. 15; Magni, III, pl. 34; H. Hibbard and I. Jaffé, 'Bernini's "Barcaccia"', *Burlington Magazine*, CVI, 1964, p. 159; Wittkower, *Bernini*, p. 265; D'Onofrio, *Roma vista*, p. 317; id., *Acque e Fontane*, p. 412.

The fountain was constructed in 1627–9 as part of Urban VIII's plan to bring some of the water of the Acqua Vergine to the area between the Piazza di Spagna and the Porta del Popolo which was becoming increasingly built up. The fountain had to be designed to be low because the pressure of the water was slight.

Both the authorship and the iconography of the fountain have given rise to much discussion. On the first point most modern authorities are agreed that the invention of the fountain is due to the young Gianlorenzo Bernini and not to his father who was old and hardly active any more as a sculptor when the fountain was carved (for the opposite point of view, however, see D'Onofrio, loc. cit.).

Hibbard and Jaffé have suggested that the

93. *The Barcaccia. Engraving by Falda showing the Piazza di Spagna before the building of the Spanish Steps. In the distance on the right the Trinità dei Monti and on the left the Villa Medici. For another view of the fountain, see plates 106–8.*

boat is partly an allusion to the ship of the Church, as immortalized in Giotto's *Navicella*, and partly an allusion to symbols used by Urban VIII himself in one of his poems, in which the guns of the Barberini ship fire not cannon balls but water to calm the troubles of the world (the boat has bees and suns, both emblems of the Barberini family). D'Onofrio, on the other hand, points out that the fountain was set up on the supposed site of Domitian's Naumachia, which was used for sham sea-fights, and maintains that the allusion is purely archaeological. There seems no difficulty in supposing that both hypotheses are correct, since it was normal practice with Seicento artists, patrons and writers of programmes, to combine in a single work of art *concetti* of various different types. The actual form of the fountain was no doubt suggested by ancient Roman ship fountains, of which one of the most famous stood in front of the church of S. Maria in Domnica, on the Celian, till it was replaced under Leo X by a copy.
See plates 106–8.

Fontana della Chiesa Nuova. See La Terrina
Piazza della Chiesa Nuova

Fountain of the Lateran
Piazza del Laterano

Bibliography: Falda, *Fontane*, pl. 9; D'Onofrio, *Acque e Fontane*, p. 290; id., *Obelischi*, p. 160.

The obelisk – the largest in Rome – was set up by Domenico Fontana on the order of Sixtus V in 1588. The fountain was begun by Clement VIII between 1600 and 1605 and was finished by Paul V who inserted the eagle and dragon of the Borghese arms. On stylistic grounds it is safe to say that the steps and the two basins belong to the earlier scheme of Clement VIII since they are much simpler than the richly carved superstructure with the arms of Paul V, but the designer's name is not known in either case.

Fountain of the Madonna dei Monti
Via Madonna dei Monti

Bibliography: Baglione, p. 82; Falda, *Nuovo teatro*, III, pl. 30; *Fontane*, pls 24, 31; D'Onofrio, *Acque e Fontane*, p. 256.

Constructed in 1588–9 by Giacomo della Porta but altered later when the original flower-shaped upper section was replaced by the present flat basin.

Fontana del Pantheon
Piazza della Rotonda

Bibliography: Baglione, p. 82; Falda, *Nuovo teatro*, I, pl. 31; id., *Fontane*, I, pl. 24; Magni, III, pl. 38; D'Onofrio, *Acque e Fontane*, p. 164; id., *Obelischi*, p. 250; T. Marder, 'Piazza della Rotonda e la Fontana del Pantheon', *Arte Illustrata*, VII, 1974, p. 310.

Designed in 1575 by Giacomo della Porta as part of the scheme to distribute the Acqua Vergine in the Campo Marzio. Of the original fountain only the basin remains. In 1662 Alexander VII added the steps that now surround it. In 1711 Clement XI decided to pull down the low buildings which surrounded the fountain and to clear an area corresponding to the present piazza, and he carried out this project in spite of the protests of the canons of S. Maria ad Martyres (the Pantheon) to whom they belonged and for whom they represented an important source of income. To make the fountain commensurate with its new and more open setting he added the obelisk, brought from the Piazza di S. Ignazio (shown in that position in an engraving of 1589, cf. *Guide Rionali*, IX, 2, p. 47), supported on a base designed by Filippo Barigioni, a somewhat unhappy design in which the base seems too big for what it carries, a point which is brought out by the fact that in the commemorative medals the obelisk is made to look much higher than it is in reality. Della Porta's original masks were replaced by copies in 1886.

Fountain in Piazza d'Aracoeli

Bibliography: Baglione, p. 82; Falda, *Fontane*, pl. 18; D'Onofrio, *Acque e Fontane*, p. 276.

Constructed by Giacomo della Porta in 1589 with three putti who pour out the water, round the three *monti* of the Peretti arms. In the 19th century the steps around it, planned in broken curves, were replaced by the present circular basin of water.

Fountain in Piazza Campitelli

Bibliography: D'Onofrio, *Acque e Fontane*, p. 280.

This fountain, of rather unusual shape, was executed by Giacomo della Porta in 1589, and paid for by three private individuals who had palaces in the square, Maria Capizucchi, Giacomo Albertoni and Giovanni Battista Ricci. In 1679 when the church of S. Maria in Campitelli was built it was moved from its original site to the other end of the piazza, because of the noise made by the servants and coachmen who congregated round it and disturbed the services.

Fountain in Piazza Colonna

Bibliography: Baglione, p. 82; Falda, *Nuovo teatro*, I, pls 14, 15; id., *Fontane*, pl. 22; D'Onofrio, *Acque e Fontane*, p. 174.

Constructed by Giacomo della Porta in 1575 to distribute part of the Acqua Vergine to the area round the Corso. Della Porta originally planned to have the fountain next to the base of the column of Marcus Aurelius, against which would have been set the ancient statue called 'Il Marforio' which in the event was placed in the fountain in the court of the Palazzo Nuovo on the Capitol. The actual fountain and the groups with dolphins were added by Alessandro Stocchi in 1830.

Alexander VII commissioned Pietro da Cortona to build a fountain as the central feature of a palace to face the Palazzo Chigi on the Piazza Colonna but the project was never carried out (Schiavo, *La Fontana di Trevi*, p. 79; D.'Onofrio, *Acque e Fontane*, p. 536).

See plate 54.

Fountain in Piazza Giudea

Via del Progresso

Bibliography: Baglione, p. 82; Falda, *Fontane*, pl. 28; Vasi, *Magificenze*, pl. 29; D'Onofrio, *Acque e Fontane*, p. 284.

Erected in 1591 by Giacomo della Porta in the Piazza Giudea at the centre of the ghetto, in front of the Portico of Octavia.

Fountains in Piazza Navona

Bibliography: Falda, *Fontane*, pls 19–21; Magni, III, pls 35–6; Wittkower, *Bernini*, p. 219; Fagiolo dell' Arco, *Bernini*, Nos 132, 143, 144; D'Onofrio, *Acque e Fontane*, pp. 152, 450, 504; Martinelli, *Piazza Navona*, Rome, 1970, passim.

In 1574 Gregory XIII decided to distribute water from the Acqua Vergine to four fountains in the most thickly populated areas of Rome, two in Piazza Navona, one in front of the Pantheon and one in the Piazza Colonna. The two in Piazza Navona – at the north and south ends – were designed by Giacomo della Porta who was also responsible for the sculptures which were to form the actual carriers of the water. For the southern fountain he used four figures which had been commissioned for the fountain in the Piazza del Popolo but which proved unsuitable for it. It is clear that he intended a similar sculptural decoration for the fountain at the north end of the piazza, but this was not carried out till the late 19th century, when the original 16th-century statues in the southern fountain were removed to the Giardino del Lago in the Villa Borghese and replaced by copies.

When Innocent X embarked on his ambitious scheme for turning the Piazza Navona into a monument to his family his plans included from an early stage the completion of the two fountains. The first step was due to Borromini who removed the steps round the two fountains and replaced them by the broad area of water which we now see. A little later Bernini, who had recaptured the favour of the pope, was commissioned to make a central feature for the southern fountain. This took the form of a shell – called somewhat contemptuously *La Lumaca*, the snail's shell – supported by dolphins, but when the central fountain of the Four Rivers was made this was felt by Donna Olimpia Maidalchini, the pope's sister-in-law, to be too small and it was replaced by the Triton swinging round a dolphin which we see there today (1653–5). The original is now in the Palazzo Doria-Pamphili in the Corso and a copy of it stands in the garden of the Villa Pamphili (Fagiolo dell'Arco, *Bernini*, No. 141; D'Onofrio, *Acque e Fontane*, p. 141; Heimbürger Ravalli, 'Bernini's shell decoration for Della Porta's Fountain at Piazza Navona', *Paragone*, 257, 1979, p. 83). The fountain at the north end of the Piazza was to have had a central figure of *Neptune* by Bernini, the design of which is known from a drawing at Windsor, but this was not executed, and the present statues were set up in 1878 (Blunt and Cooke, *Roman Drawings at Windsor Castle*, London, 1960, p. 24, No. 42).

As the central feature of the piazza Innocent planned a great fountain, to replace the drinking fountain set up there in the 16th century (and now in the Borghese Gardens). This was to be designed round an ancient obelisk which lay in the Circus of Maxentius, near the via Appia. Initially the commission was to go to Borromini who made an austere design known from a drawing (Hempel, *Borromini*, pl. 51), but owing to the intervention of Prince Niccolò Ludovisi Bernini's rival design was shown to the pope who immediately accepted it. The result was the present magnificent fountain of the Four Rivers, a masterpiece in which sculpture, architecture and iconographical allusion combine in a whole which only Bernini could have conceived and which forms the climax to one of the grandest of Baroque projects.

The obelisk is supported by statues of the four rivers, designed by Bernini but executed by studio assistants – the *Danube* by Antonio Raggi, the *Nile* by Giacomo Fancelli, the *Ganges* by Claude Poussin and the River *Plate* by Francesco Baratta – which symbolize the four continents over which extended the power of the papacy, symbolized by the papal keys and tiara over the arms of the pope on all four sides of the base, and the Pamphili dove with the olive branch on the top of the obelisk, converting it from a pagan monument into the symbol of triumphant Christianity – as Sixtus V had converted the columns of Trajan and Marcus Aurelius by setting the figures of St Peter and St Paul on them. For a detailed discussion of the iconography of the fountain see Preimesberger, 'Obeliscus Pamphilius', *Münchner Jahrbuch*, 3rd series, XXV, 1974, p. 77). Bernini's original *modello* in terracotta is still in the possession of his descendants (E. Sestieri, *La Fontana dei Quattro Fiumi e il suo bozzetto*, Rome, 1970.) See plate 102.

Fountain in Piazza del Popolo

Bibliography: Baglione, p. 82; Falda, *Nuovo teatro*, I, pls 6, 7; id., *Fontane*, pl. 14; D'Onofrio, *Acque e Fontane*, p. 102; id., *Obelischi*, p. 173.

The fountain set up in the Piazza del Popolo in 1572 by Giacomo della Porta for Gregory XIII was the first public fountain of Rome and the first to receive the water of the restored and extended Acqua Vergine. It was a simple octagonal structure with a circular basin. When the obelisk of Augustus from the Circus Maximus was set up in the centre of the piazza the fountain was moved slightly towards the Corso, but when in 1823 Giuseppe Valadier carried out the complete renovation of the piazza and the slope of the Pincio it was moved to the terrace in front of S. Pietro in Montorio. At an unknown date it was once more dismantled and in 1950, after a long spell in a warehouse, set up again in the Piazza Nicosia.

Valadier constructed a neo-classical fountain round the base of the obelisk, with four recumbent lions at the corners, spouting water. See plate 37.

Fontana di Ponte Sisto
Piazza Trilassa

Bibliography: Martinelli, p. 286; Falda, *Fontane*, pl. 22; Vasi, *Magnificenze*, pl. 178; Magni, III, pl. 19; R. Antioli, *Il Fontanone di Ponte Sisto*, Rome, 1899; Donati, *Artisti ticenesi*, fig. 55; Salerno, *Via Giulia*, p. 519; D'Onofrio, *Acque e Fontane*, p. 294.

This fountain originally stood against the Ospedale dei Mendicanti at the end of the via Giulia. It was built by Paul V in 1613 to transmit part of the water brought to the Acqua Paola on the Janiculum. Salemo ascribes the design of the fountain to Vasanzio who is mentioned in the documents together with Giovanni Fontana. The latter was certainly responsible for the engineering part of the job, but Martinelli also attributes the design to him. In 1879, when the Lungotevere was being constructed, the fountain was taken down and was reconstructed in its present position in 1898.

Fountain of the Porto di Ripetta
Via di Ripetta

Bibliography: D'Onofrio, *Acque e Fontane*, p. 520.

The fountain, designed by Alessandro Specchi, was erected by Clement XI in 1703–4 at the top of the steps leading up from the Ripetta, in front of the church of S. Girolamo degli Schiavoni. When the steps were swept away for the construction of the Lungotevere in the late 19th century the fountain was removed to an adjacent site.

Fontana dei Quattro Fiumi. See Fountains in Piazza Navona

Quattro Fontane

Bibliography: Baglione, p. 85; Martinelli, p. 282; Falda, *Fontane*, I, pl. 7; Magni, III, pl. 28; D'Onofrio, *Acque e Fontane*, p. 233.

The fountains were planned by Sixtus V in 1588 at the point where the strada Pia (via XX Settembre) crossed the Strada Felice (via delle Quattro Fontane) which he himself had laid out to the design of Domenico Fontana. They were to be paid for by a private individual, Muzio Mattei, who was building the palace (later Palazzo Albani) on the south-east corner of the crossroads. The fountain against his palace contains a statue of the *Nile*, that at the south-west corner (where the church of S. Carlo alle Quattro Fontane was later built) has the *Tiber*, while the two on the other corners have statues of goddesses – *Juno* at the north-west against the later Palazzo Galoppi and *Diana* at the north-east against the garden of the Palazzo Barberini. This was the last to be built; it was designed by Pietro da Cortona and appears still unfinished in a drawing by Lieven Cruyl dated 1665, but Falda shows it complete in 1691. It was intended, like the door next to it in via XX Settembre – which was the main entrance to the palace – to stand in a wall of the same height as the fountain and has lost much of its effect by being set in modern buildings, put up in the 1920s.

The iconographical scheme is curious, with two rivers and two goddesses and it may have been originally planned with four rivers and changed later – perhaps in order not to compete with the Four Rivers Fountain in Piazza Navona. It is even possible that the generally accepted identification of the goddess at the north-west corner as Juno may not be correct as she is shown with a swan instead of her usual peacock and leaning on a crowned lion, no doubt a heraldic allusion which has not so far been clarified. Further, the figure in the Cortona fountain may be Night rather than Diana, since she holds poppies in her left hand.

94. *The Quattro Fontane. Drawing made by Lieven Cruyl (1665) (Albertina). It shows the Strada Pia (left), leading to the Porta Pia, and the Strada Felice (right) leading to S. Maria Maggiore. On the extreme left is the garden of the Palazzo Barberini with the entrance gate and unfinished fountain by Cortona. In the middle is the Palazzo Albani and on the right S. Carlo alle Quattro Fontane with the unfinished fountain and Borromini's original belfry. In the distance along Strada Pia one can just distinguish the Acqua Felice and the churches of S. Susanna and S. Maria della Vittoria.*

Fountain and Obelisk of the Quirinal

95. The Quattro Fontane. Engraving by Falda showing Cortona's entrance gate and his fountain finished. The effect is now completely altered by the fact that fountain and gate have been absorbed into a modern office block.

Fountain and Obelisk of the Quirinal

Bibliography: Falda, *Nuovo teatro*, I, pl. 13; id., *Fontane*, I, pl. 6; Magni, III, pl. 39; D'Onofrio, *Acque e Fontane*, p. 246; id., *Obelischi*, p. 256.

In the square in front of the Quirinal stands a group of sculptures round an obelisk. The ancient Roman statues of *Castor* and *Pollux* with their horses (called the Horse-tamers), traditionally ascribed to Phidias and Praxiteles (see inscription), were set up here for Sixtus V in 1588 by Domenico Fontana who also made the fountain. Pius VI added the obelisk brought from the Mausoleum of Augustus, and the piazza with its balustrade was laid out by Pius IX in 1866.
See plate 72.

Fountain in front of S. Andrea della Valle

Bibliography: D'Onofrio, *Acque e Fontane*, p. 324.

Originally set up by Maderno in the Piazza Scossacavalli, the fountain was moved to the piazza in front of S. Andrea della Valle when the Piazza Scossacavalli was swept away in the making of the via della Conciliazione. At the same time the upper basin was removed and replaced by the present one.

Fountain in front of S. Maria Maggiore

Bibliography: Falda, *Fontane*, pl. 9; Hibbard, *Maderno*, p. 201; D'Onofrio, *Obelischi*, p. 219; Gigli, p. 27.

The monolithic column from the Basilica of Maxentius was transported by Maderno on the orders of Paul V in 1613 to the area in front of S. Maria Maggiore and crowned with a statue of the *Virgin*. It implied the dedication of a monument of pagan antiquity to Christian purposes analogous to Sixtus V's action in setting statues of St Peter and St Paul on the columns of Trajan and Marcus Aurelius. The statue of the *Virgin* is by Guillaume Berthelot.
See plates 34, 35.

Fountain in front of S. Maria in Trastevere

Bibliography: Martinelli, p. 281; Falda, *Fontane*, pl. 32; Magni, III, pl. 40; D'Onofrio, *Acque e Fontane*, p. 334.

An octagonal fountain of unusual size is shown on this site in Pietro da Massaio's plan of Rome dating from about 1471 and in 1598 it was planned to bring to it the waters of Acqua Felice by pipes running across the Ponte S. Maria, just downstream from the Isola Tiberina, but this bridge was swept away in a flood in December of that year and the waters did not actually reach the fountain till 1604, on which occasion it was reconstructed, probably to the design of Girolamo Rainaldi who had become 'architetto del Popolo Romano' on the death of della Porta in 1602. In 1659 it was remodelled on the orders of Alexander VII to the design of Bernini, who added four double shells at the corners of the main basin. In 1692 these were replaced by others of the form which we see today designed by Carlo Fontana. In 1873 the whole fountain was reconstructed with copies of Fontana's shells in grey marble (*bardiglio*) instead of the original travertine.

96. *The fountain in front of S. Maria in Trastevere. Engraving by Falda showing the fountain as it was remodelled by Bernini in 1659, and before the alteration made by Carlo Fontana in 1692.*

Fountain near S. Rocco

Bibliography: D'Onofrio, *Acque e Fontane*, p. 91.

Erected in 1774 by the Confraternity to which the church belonged. Water from the Acqua Vergine had been brought to the spot since 1580 for the use of the hospital attached to the church.

Iconographically this fountain is an 18th-century version of the 'Facchino' attached to the Palazzo de Carolis.

Fontana di S. Sebastiano
Via di S. Sebastianello

Bibliography: D'Onofrio, *Acque e Fontane*, p. 91; Elling, pl. 128.

A small fountain, carrying part of the Acqua Vergine, stood here from an early date, but the present structure, which bears the arms of France, was built when the Spanish Steps were constructed in 1723–8. The name of the architect is not known, but the fountain shows a clear and individual adaptation of Borrominesque motifs.

Fontana delle Tartarughe
Piazza Mattei

Bibliography: Baglione, p. 82; Martinelli, p. 277; Falda, *Fontane*, I, pl. 23; Magni, III, pl. 16; D'Onofrio, *Acque e Fontane*, p. 186.

One of the most famous and the most elegant of all 16th-century Roman fountains. The basic design is probably due to Giacomo della Porta, but the character of the decorative detail is so purely Florentine that it seems likely that the sculptor, Taddeo Landini, who made the bronze figures and was a Florentine by training, played a considerable part in it. The tortoises were added by Alexander VII perhaps at the suggestion of Andrea Sacchi. According to the original design there were four dolphins, but these were removed to the Terrina (see next entry).

La Terrina
Piazza della Chiesa Nuova

Bibliography: D'Onofrio, *Acque e Fontane*, p. 193.

This fountain, which originally stood in the centre of the Campo dei Fiori, had to be designed, like the Barcaccia, to be low because the pressure of the water was inadequate. In this case Giacomo della Porta, who made it (before 1590), actually set it in a dug-out area in the market place. It was originally decorated with four dolphins, designed for the Fontana delle Tartarughe, but removed from it in 1658 to be replaced by the bronze tortoises. In 1622 the present heavy cover was added, leading to the nickname of the fountain 'La Terrina'. In 1889 it was removed from the Campo dei Fiori to make way for the statue to Giordano Bruno and re-erected outside the Chiesa Nuova.

Fontana di Trevi

Bibliography: Falda, *Nuovo teatro*, III, pl. 25; De Brosses, II, p. 57; Magni, III, pls 44–7; A. Schiavo, *La Fontana di Trevi*, p. 63; H. L. Cooke, 'The Documents relating to the Fountain of Trevi', *Art Bulletin*, XXXVIII, 1956, p. 149; D'Onofrio, *Acque e Fontane*, p. 526; M. Rotili, 'I Progetti di Luigi Vanvitelli per la Fontana di Trevi', *Studi Romani*, XXI, 1973, p. 314; Braham and Hager, p. 162; J. R. Pinto, 'An early Project by Nicola Michetti for the Trevi Fountain', *Burlington Magazine*, CXIX, 1977, p. 853.

The Aqua Virginis or Acqua Vergine was brought to a site in the Campo Marzio in BC 19, but the conduit was broken after the Barbarian invasions. It was restored by Adrian I (771–95) and brought to a fountain almost on the present site by Nicholas V who caused Alberti to set up an inscription in 1453. Under Pius IV a new basin was made and in the late 16th century various projects for completing the fountain were made but none was carried out.

In 1629 Urban VIII commissioned Bernini to design for the present site a fountain which was to rival Sixtus V's Acqua Felice nearby and Paul V's Acqua Paola on the Janiculum. In 1643 the piazza was enlarged, the fountain was moved to its present position (Gigli, p. 232) and its substructure built, but nothing further was done, and there is no reason to suppose – as is often asserted – that his designs influenced later projects.

Nothing further is recorded about the fountain till the pontificate of Clement XI, who for a time, about 1704–5, was considering setting up the Antonine column recently discovered near the Palazzo di Montecitorio as the central feature of the fountain, a scheme for which the young Niccolò Michetti, Filippo Juvarra and others made designs. A further set of designs at Windsor do not incorporate the column and probably date from 1706, by which time it had been moved to the Piazza di Montecitorio where Clement intended to set it up.

In 1706 the design of a fountain was set as the subject for the Concorso Clementino, but none of the designs was approved. Benedict XIII ordered a further design from a Neapolitan

97. The Fontana di Trevi. Drawing made by Lieven Cruyl in 1665 (Albertini). It shows the basin made in the late 16th century. In the background is the façade of SS. Vincenzo e Anastasio, built by Martino Longhi the Younger in 1645–50. Above it in the distance is the Quirinal and to its right the Palazzo Rospigliosi-Pallavicini. The low buildings along the east side of the square had been acquired by the Carpegna family for the palace which they planned to build to the designs of Borromini but which was never carried out.

98. The Fontana di Trevi. Etching by Piranesi. On the right are the buildings belonging to the Carpegna.

sculptor and stucco worker, Paolo Benaglio, but again nothing was built.

In 1732 Clement XII opened a further competition in which the contestants were Vanvitelli, Bracci, Salvi, Maini and two Frenchmen, Lambert Sigisbert Adam and Edme Bouchardon (Vanvitelli's designs for the fountain are published by Rotili). After many hesitations Salvi's design was chosen and work was begun immediately. Four sculptors were chosen to execute the statues of the *Four Seasons* on the attic: Bartolomeo Pincellotti, Agostino Corsini, Bernardo Ludovisi and Francesco Queirolo. On either side of the central niche are reliefs: *Agrippa approving the design of the Aqueduct* by Andrea Bergondi and the *Virgin Trivia pointing out the source to Agrippa's Soldiers* by G. B. Grassi, and statues of *Abundance* and *Salubrity* by F. della Valle. The inscription below the arms of Clement XII is dated 1735 and when he died in 1740 the fountain was nearly complete, but only a full-scale model of the central figure (*Oceanus*) had been made by G. B. Maini and set up, and the rock base was not finished. The work was continued under Benedict XIV who added an inscription dated 1749, and was completed by Clement XIII in 1762 (inscription). The actual statue of *Oceanus* was carved by P. Bracci who probably followed Maini's model closely. The iconographical scheme and the particular significance attached to *Oceanus* are explained in a memorandum by Salvi published by Cooke.

Fontana del Tritone
Piazza Barberini

Bibliography: Falda, *Fontane*, I, pl. 16; Magni, III, pl. 33; Wittkower, *Bernini*, p. 200; Fagiolo dell'Arco, *Bernini*, No. 108; D'Onofrio, *Acque e Fontane*, p. 428; D. Helsted *et al.*, *Roma dei fotografi al tempo di Pio IX 1846–78*, Rome 1977, pls 49–64; *Guide*

The fountain was made in 1642–3 (Gigli, p. 251) for Urban VIII and incorporates the Barberini arms in the base composed of dolphins. It is Bernini's first free-standing public fountain –

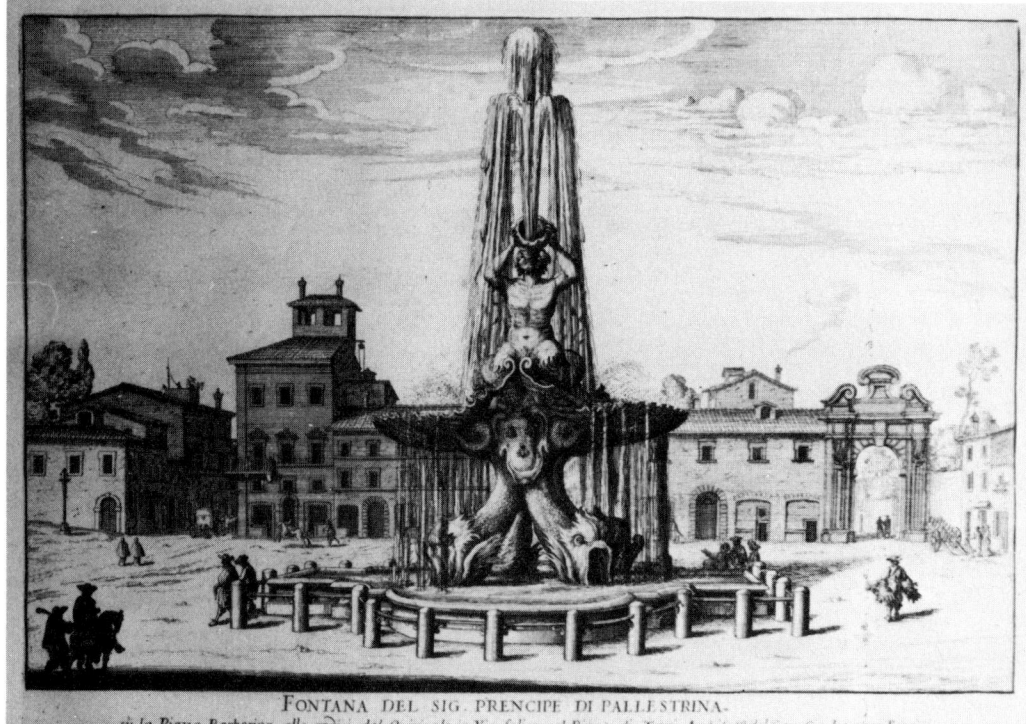

99. *Fontana del Tritone. Engraving by Falda showing the buildings which originally stood on the east side of the Piazza Barberini (where the Hotel Bernini now stands). On the right is Cortona's entrance to the stables of the Palazzo Barberini.*

the Fontana delle Api in the Vatican was a wall-fountain and the *Neptune* (now in the Victoria and Albert Museum, London) stood over a basin in the Villa Montalto – and Bernini has broken with previous tradition by eliminating all architectural features, except a minimal surround to the basin, and created a purely sculptural whole, which, as Wittkower points out, almost looks like a natural growth in which dolphins and shell fuse with the coat of arms, which appears to be cut on a piece of natural rock, into a single animated whole. It is also the first time that he attains a really Michelangelesque monumentality in his figure sculpture. The fountain suffers from being seen against the modern buildings on the north-east side of the square, but it has the advantage over many fountains that the actual size of the piazza in which it stands has not been altered. It was an act of great boldness to design such a small fountain for such a large piazza, but by its grandeur it amply fills the space.

Fontana dei Tritoni
Piazza S. Maria in Cosmedin

Bibliography: Magni, III, pl. 41; D'Onofrio, *Acque e Fontane*, p. 522; Mallory, *Bizzacheri*, pp. 42, 46; id., *Rococo*, p. 50.

Built in 1717–19 to the designs of Carlo Bizzacheri. The plan of the basin is related to the eight-pointed star of the arms of Clement XI (Albani) which appears under the shell carried by the two tritons, obviously inspired by Bernini's Triton Fountain in the Piazza Barberini.

VI
MISCELLANEOUS BUILDINGS

Accademia di S. Cecilia. See Conservatorio di S. Cecilia
Via Vittoria

Accademia di S. Luca. See Palazzo Carpegna
Via della Stamperia

Arch of Paul V
Via Aurelia Antica

Bibliography: Architettura minora, III, pl. 144; Brizzi, *Roma cento anni fa nelle fotografie della Raccolta Parker*, Rome, 1980, p. 211.

Near the Villa Pamphili is an arch built by Paul V and dated 1610 to carry the water of the Acqua Paola over the ancient via Aurelia to the Janiculum.

Biblioteca Casanatense
Via S. Ignazio 52

Bibliography: Coudenhove-Erthal, p. 81; *Guide Rionali*, IX, 2, p. 48

Founded in 1698 by a bequest by Cardinal Domenico Casanate who bequeathed his library to the Dominicans of S. Maria sopra Minerva. The main hall of the library was built by Carlo Fontana in 1700. At the end is a statue of the cardinal by Pierre Legros.

Carceri nuove
Via Giulia

Bibliography: Mola, p. 132; Salerno, *Via Giulia*, p. 359; *Guide Rionali*, VII, 3, p. 13.

In 1652 Innocent X decided to build new prisons on the via Giulia to replace the old Corte Savella. The project was inspired partly by a desire to improve the appalling conditions under which prisoners lived, but also to affirm the supremacy of papal justice by removing a last trace of mediaeval independence by which the ancient Savelli family still claimed to administer their own justice according to feudal practice.

Innocent deputed the planning of the new prison to his almoner, Virgilio Spada, who was probably responsible for one innovation, namely the introduction for the first time of the modern cell system. The architect was Antonio del Grande but it is possible that Spada also consulted his friend Borromini (he had a habit of consulting everyone available and then trying to combine what he thought the best ideas of each adviser). The building was finished in 1655. The prisons were enlarged by Leo XII in the 1820s to the designs of Giuseppe Valadier.

Casa di Carlo Maderno
Via dei Banchi Nuovi 3

Bibliography: Hibbard, *Maderno*, p. 208; Donati, *Artisti ticinesi*, fig. 137.

Maderno was given a house on this site in 1601 and in 1607 acquired another small house adjacent to it. It was probably at this date that he added the cornice and the windows in the upper storey.

Casa Giannini
Piazza Capranica 95

Bibliography: *Guide Rionali*, III, 2, p. 50; Elling, pl. 169

An interesting early example of an apartment block built in 1748 by Carlo Giannini on the site of a number of smaller houses demolished with the approval of Benedict XIV. The ground floor contained on the right a book-shop, 'All'insegno di S. Benedetto'. Each of the six original floors – the attic was added later – has its distinctive decoration.

Collegio Calasanzio. See Collegio Nazzareno
Piazza dei Massimi 31

Collegio Ghislieri
Via Giulia 38

Bibliography: Salerno, *Via Giulia*, p. 405; *Guide Rionali*, VII, 3, p. 22

This college, founded by the Roman doctor, Giuseppe Ghislieri in 1565, was transferred in 1670 to a palace on this site which belonged to the Confraternity of the Spirito Santo dei Napoletani, but was rebuilt and enlarged for the college. The palace was pulled down in 1936 to make way for the Liceo Virgilio, leaving only the façade of which the most remarkable feature is the door.

Collegio Inglese (S. Tommaso di Canterbury)
Via Monserrato

Bibliography: Anon., *The Venerable English College*, Rome, 1967.

The college was founded by Gregory XIII and was entrusted to the Jesuits for the training of young English Catholics. It was built at the expense of the Cardinal of Norfolk in about 1575. The church dates from the later 19th century, but the Oratory of the Sodality of Our Lady and the Refectory have late Seicento Baroque painted ceilings. The church retains the original altarpiece of *God the Father with the dead Christ* by Durante Alberti, and the tomb of Thomas Dereham (d.1739) by Filippo della Valle (H. Honour, 'Filippo della Valle', *Connoisseur*, CXLV, 1959, p. 176).

Collegio Innocenziano
Piazza Navona

Bibliography: Hempel, *Borromini*, p. 151, pl. 95; Salerno, *Piazza Navona*, p. 239.

The college was founded by Innocent X, possibly at the instigation of his sister-in-law, Donna Olimpia, for the religious education of young men from the Pamphili estates. It was designed by Borromini, probably between 1652 and 1658, and its façade on the Piazza Navona balances that of the *Galleria* of the Palazzo Pamphili on the other side of the church. It was however in the main actually built by Carlo Rainaldi (cf. Preimesberger, 'Pontifex Romanus per Aeneam praesignatus', *Römisches Jahrbuch*, XVI, 1976, p. 221). The *Cortile* (entrance via dell'Anima, 30) has a triple loggia, of which the two lower storeys have flat trabeations and the top one a Serliana. The *Salone* has a coved ceiling with frescoes by Francesco Cozza, representing *Liberality*, *Justice* and *Faith*.

Collegio Nazzareno (Calasanzio)
Piazza dei Massimi 31

Bibliography: Vasi, *Magnificenze*, pl. 161; Venuti, 1767, p. 667; Elling, pp. 223ff., pl. 84.

The college belongs to the Scolopi, or Congregazione della Scuole Pie, created in 1617 by S. Giuseppe Calasanzio, and established here in 1747 in a building designed by Tommaso de'Marchis, an impressive block articulated only with giant pilasters of undefinable order at the corners.

Collegio di Propaganda Fide
Piazza di Spagna and via di Propaganda Fide

Bibliography: Pollak, I, p. 211; Mola, pp. 120, 132; Falda, *Nuovo teatro*, I, pl. 9 and IV, pls 51, 52; Ferrerio, *Palazzi*, II, pl. 59; De' Rossi, *Architettura Civile*, I, pls 72–84 and II, pls 8–11; Titi, 1686, p. 313 and 1763, p. 344; Hempel, *Borromini*, p. 157; G. Antonazzi, 'La Sede della Sacra Congregazione e del Collegio Urbano', in *Sacrae Congregationis de Propaganda Fide memoria rerum*, ed. J. Meller, Rome, 1971, p. 306; Portoghesi, *Roma Barocca*, pls 156–63; id., *Borromini*, pls CIX–CXXIV, 157–77; Blunt, *Borromini*, p. 183; Güthlein, *Familienarchiv Spada*, p. 217.

In 1622 Gregory XV created a Congregation of Propaganda Fide to organize the missionary activities of the various Orders, and in 1627 Urban VIII attached to it a college for the training of young missionaries. (It is often said that the Congregation and College were controlled by the Jesuits, but this is not the case.) The Congregation was established in a palace (Palazzo Ferratini) at the south end of the Piazza di Spagna presented by a Spanish priest, Juan Bautista Vives. In 1634 Bernini built a small chapel called Re Magi. In 1642 it was decided to rebuild the façade on Piazza di Spagna on the design of the Theatine Padre Valerio, modified by Bernini. Between 1639 and 1645 a wing for the seminarists was begun by Gaspare de'Vecchi along the via Due Macelli. By 1646 the College had acquired the whole island and in that year Borromini was appointed architect. He proposed various plans for the completion of the building (Hempel, figs 55–9) which involved the destruction of Bernini's church. This was an oval with the short axis leading to the altar (cf. S. Andrea al Quirinale) the plan of which is recorded in Borromini's first drawing (Hempel, fig. 56) and the façade in an elevation (R. Pacini, 'Alterazioni dei monumenti borrominiani', *Studi sul Borromini*, fig. 32). Borromini first designed a longer oval with the main entrance on the street, but then chose a rectangle with rounded corners running parallel with the street, with the altar at the north-west end and the entrance from the vestibule of the College at the south-east. To the right (south-east) of the chapel he designed a court which was to have been made symmetrical by the insertion of a curved arcade which was never fully built. The façade, first designed with five and finally with seven bays, covers part of the chapel, the entrance to the College and the main staircase. Its relation to the interior is as arbitrary as in the Oratory. Many drawings are known for the windows, fireplaces and other details (Hempel, pls 104, 105). The door and windows on the

Collegio di Propaganda Fide

100. *Collegio di Propaganda Fide. Engraving by Falda, who has distorted the width of the street on which the Collegio faces so that he can present an almost frontal view of the façade. It shows the College with an open terrace over the main order of pilasters. This disappeared when the building was enlarged under Clement XI who added a floor to the right-hand part of the building. Beyond the College is the church of S. Andrea delle Fratte showing the upper half of the façade unfinished (as it remained till the 19th century) and the scaffolding still standing on the top of Borromini's dome, perhaps in preparation for constructing the lantern which in the event was never built.*

façade show a great variety of forms, and Martinelli (p. 201) calls attention to the fact that on the *piano nobile* Borromini has used the true Roman Doric without a base (though in fact this is invisible from the street). For a severe criticism of the architecture of the Collegio see Visentini, *Osservazioni*, p. 8.

The construction of the College went on long after Borromini's death in 1667, and the top floor of the right-hand half was added in 1705 (inscription at the top of the staircase) and has the arms of Clement XI on the outside.

INTERIOR
CHAPEL (RE MAGI)

For the vaulting of the chapel Borromini used a more sophisticated version of the scheme which he had used at the Oratory of S. Filippo Neri. The difference is that whereas at the Oratory the ribs abut on the central oval fresco, at Re Magi they run right across the vault of the chapel to form a hexagonal central panel which encloses a gilt stucco radiance.

1 to R: Carlo Pellegrini, *Conversion of St Paul* (1635, from the earlier church; W).

2 to R: Carlo Cesi, *Sts Charles Borromeo and Philip Neri* (W).
High Altar: Giacinto Gimignani, *Adoration of the Kings* (1634, from the old church); in the arch over it Lazzaro Baldi, *Christ's charge to St Peter* (before 1674; W); stuccoes by Cosimo Fancelli (Lavagnino, *Altari*, p. 127).
2 to L: Lodovico Gimignani, *The Crucifixion* (W).

In the niches are busts of benefactors of the College and Congregation: *Vives, Cardinal Antonio Barberini, Giovanni Savenir, Agostino Galamino, Cardinal Robert Ubaldini* and *Federico Corneli*.

Within the college the staircase and the corridor on the first floor contain fine stucco work certainly designed by Borromini. Off it opens the old oratory, now called the Cappella Newman (Cardinal Newman celebrated his first Mass there) the vault of which (partly frescoed by Giovanni Venturo Borghesi) is articulated into a remarkably formed series of panels on the design of Borromini.

Collegio Romano
Piazza del Collegio Romano

Bibliography: Falda, *Nuovo teatro*, I, pl. 183; Ferrerio, *Palazzi*, I, pls 43, 44; Letarouilly, pls 173, 174 (274, 275); E. Beltrane Quattrocchi, *Il Palazzo del Collegio Romano*, Rome, 1956; P. Pirri, *Giuseppe Valeriano*, Rome, 1970, pp. 52, 260; *Guide Rionali*, IX, 3, p. 16.

In 1551 the Jesuits set up a free school for Grammar, Humanities and Theology in a house below the Capitol, which was to be the nucleus of the Collegio Romano, but it was not till the pontificate of Gregory XIII that it was established, on a much larger scale, on its present site. The foundation stone was laid in 1582.

The biographers of artists from Baglione to Milizia attribute the design of the College to Bartolomeo Ammanati, but the early historians of the College all ascribe it to the official Jesuit architect, Giuseppe Valeriano, who designed the Jesuit churches in Genoa, Naples and elsewhere, and this attribution is confirmed by the documents. The only other architect mentioned in the documentation is Giacomo della Porta who appears as 'consultatore'.

The exact shares of the two architects are difficult to determine but the following points may be made. The elevation of the main court, with two superimposed loggias with pilasters, is very close to Valeriano's court of the Gesù Vecchio in Naples, except that the orders are Ionic and Corinthian instead of Doric and Ionic. The façade on the piazza (which, incidentally, was not enlarged to its present size till the 1660s; see under Palazzo Doria-Pamphili) has no exact parallel in the works of either Valeriano or della Porta, but the rather clumsy elevation with three mezzanines is unlike such a professional architect as della Porta and the high attic with a belfry has a parallel in the court of the Gesù Vecchio at Naples. On the other hand the Michelangelesque doors may well have been designed by della Porta, and he may have been responsible for the novel and impressive idea of introducing two staircases symmetrically placed at either end of the *cortile*.

The vault of the Old Pharmacy in a room on the ground floor to the left of S. Ignazio used as a store was frescoed in 1629 by Andrea Sacchi and Emilio Savonanzi. The main fresco represents the *Madonna with Sts Ignatius, Francis Xavier, Cosmas and Damian*, with lunettes of ancient doctors (Sutherland Harris, *Sacchi*, p. 57).

Conservatorio (Accademia) di S. Cecilia
Via Vittoria

Bibliography: Roisecco, 1750, p. 151; Donati, *Artisti ticinesi*, p. 381, fig. 325; Buchowiecki, III, p. 518.

Formerly the convent of S. Orsola, founded in 1599. The church (now used as a theatre) was rebuilt in 1750 by Mauro Fontana.

Dogana di Terra
Piazza di Pietra

Bibliography: Falda, *Nuovo teatro*, IV, pl. 33; Coudenhove-Erthal, p. 69; *Guide Rionali*, III, 2, p. 10.

Built round the ruins of the ancient Hadrianeum erected in AD 145 by Antoninus Pius in honour of his father Hadrian. It was converted into the Dogana di Terra by Carlo Fontana on the order of Innocent XII in 1695, but was altered in 1879, to house the Camera di Commercio.

The Granary of Clement XI
Via delle Terme di Diocleziano

Bibliography: Magni, II, pl. 102; Braham and Hager, p. 152.

The Granary, which faces the Baths of Diocletian, was built by C. Fontana for Clement XI in 1703–5, as part of the pope's scheme to control the supply of grain in case of famine. It was never completed and is now converted for modern uses (including a post-office), but the drawings at Windsor show that it would have contained some interesting architectural features, particularly a type of double staircase later much imitated in Austria and South Germany (e.g. by Fischer von Erlach at Klesheim).

Monte di Pietà
Piazza del Monte di Pietà

Bibliography: Baglione, p. 99; De'Rossi, *Altari*, pl. 46; Titi, 1763, p. 100; D. Tamilio, *Il Sacro Monte di Pietà*, Rome, 1900; Magni, I, pls 97–9 and II, pl. 59; Hibbard, *Maderno*, p. 218; Spagnesi, *G. A. De Rossi*, p. 165; M. Tosi, *Il Sacro Monte di Pietà*, Rome, 1937; A. Schiavo, *La Fontana di Trevi*, p. 167; Wasserman, *Mascarino*, p. 116; Portoghesi, *Roma Barocca*, pls 251, 252; Salerno, *La Cappella del Monte di Pietà*, Rome, n.d.,; Mallory, *Bizzacheri*, pp. 34, 45; id., *Rococo*, p. 39; Marina Costa, 'C. F. Bizzacheri e la cappella del Monte di Pietà', *Bollettino d'Arte*, S.VI, No. 6, 1979, p. 49.

101. *The Dogana di Terra. Etching by Bellicard (1750), showing the building after the restoration by Carlo Fontana (1695) but before the 19th-century alterations.*

The Roman Monte di Pietà, which lent money on security, was founded by Paul III in 1539. It was moved to its present site in 1605 and installed in the Palazzo Santacroce, built by Ottaviano Mascarino. The palace was enlarged by Maderno who was responsible for the tabernacle and coats of arms on the façade. It was again greatly enlarged about 1740 by Nicola Salvi to whom it owes its present appearance externally.

The most interesting part of the building is the chapel. Hibbard has shown that Maderno's chapel was in a different part of the palace and the present chapel was almost certainly designed by G. A. de'Rossi. It was finished structurally by 1641 but it was decorated from 1659 onwards. In that year Domenico Guidi designed the relief of the *Pietà* over the altar; its execution was – for unknown reasons – stopped and the relief was carried out on a new model in 1676 (J.M.). By 1686 the walls had been marbled with *giallo antico* and Sicilian jasper, but the decoration of the dome was not completed till the late 1690s when Bizzacheri was in charge, and Ottoni was paid for executing two medallions and two putti. The decoration of the walls included two large reliefs representing *Joseph giving grain to the Egyptians* by J. B. Théodon, and *Tobit lending money to Gabael* by P. Legros (1703–5; Enggass, *Sculpture*, pp. 71, 139), and four statues: *Faith* by Francesco Moderati, *Hope* by Agostino Cornacchini, *Almsgiving* by Bernardino Cametti (Enggass, pp. 156, 177, 202) and *Charity* by Giuseppe Mazzuoli.

With its rich marbles on the walls, elaborate gilt and white stuccoes on the dome, and white marble high reliefs and life-size statues, the chapel is one of the most splendid late Roman Baroque ensembles. It is however surprising as a work designed by G. A de'Rossi whose style is generally simple and severe. It may well be that the chapel was originally planned to be simple and that the rich decoration was only imposed on the architect by the wealthy commissioning body. In the vestibule is a bust of *S. Carlo Borromeo* by Domenico Guidi (c.1660).

Niche with statue of the Virgin.
Corner of Arco di S. Margherita and via del Pellegrino

Bibliography: Guide Rionali, VI, 2, p. 68.

Commissioned by Cardinal Pietro Ottoboni in 1716 and executed by Francesco Moderati. One of the finest examples of this typically Roman feature.

Obelisk and Elephant
Piazza della Minerva

Bibliography: Magni, III, p. 37; W. Heckscher, 'Bernini's Elephant and Obelisk', *Art Bulletin*, XXIX, 1947, p. 155; Wittkower, *Bernini*, p. 247; Fagiolo dell'Arco, *Bernini*, No. 206; D'Onofrio, *Obelischi*, p. 230.

The obelisk was found in the garden of the Dominican monastery of S. Maria sopra Minerva in 1665 and immediately on his return from Paris Bernini was commissioned by Alexander VII to erect it in the square in front of the church. The actual execution was entrusted to Ercole Ferrata, and the monument was unveiled in July 1667. Bernini was taking up an earlier project which he had proposed to Urban VIII to erect a similar monument in the garden of the Palazzo Barberini. The symbolism of the monument which is explained by the inscription on the base has been interpreted by Heckscher. The elephant had been for long a symbol of divine wisdom, but it is here used in a quite specific relationship to the place where it was found. The inscription on the base reads, translated: 'In the year of salvation 1667 Alexander VII dedicated to Divine Wisdom the ancient obelisk; sacred to the Egyptian Pallas, this monument was wrested from the earth so that it might be erected in Minerva's Piazza which now belongs to the Theotokes', alluding to the fact that the obelisk originally came from a temple of Isis and was found in one dedicated to Minerva. In this way the wisdom of Egypt and Rome was consecrated and Isis and Minerva made into symbols for the Virgin Mary to whom the church was dedicated. The inscription on the other side alludes to the virtue generally associated with the elephant, strength, which by analogy could refer to the mind as much as to the body.

Ospedale delle Donne
Piazza di S. Giovanni in Laterano

Bibliography: Vasi, *Magnificenze*, pl. 172; Spagnesi, G. A. De Rossi, p. 76; *Guide Rionali*, I, 1, p. 112.

Chapel built by G. A. de'Rossi in 1655–6. The severe façade is typical of the artist, a representative of the 'non-Baroque' tendency in the mid-17th century. The interior, a single very long barrel-vaulted chamber with a small vestibule, is now used as a ward of the hospital.

Ospedale di S. Gallicano
Via di S. Gallicano

Bibliography: Vasi, *Magnificenze*, pl. 174; Venuti, p. 1017; *Architettura minora*, II, pls 68, 69; P. de Angelis, *L'Ospedale di Santa Maria e San Gallicano*, Rome, 1966; M. Rotili, *Raguzzini*, p. 34; Portoghesi, *Roma Barocca*, pl. 359; Elling, pls 81, 83.

The hospital was founded by Benedict XIII in 1724 and built by F. Raguzzini. One of his simplest buildings, consisting of a long, straight front, broken only by the projecting façade of the church, the side bays of which are on concave curves, but which is topped by a somewhat fanciful attic composed of scrolls supporting a cross. Internally the church is a simple Greek cross with very shallow arms.

Ospedale di S. Giovanni (Ospedale del Salvatore)
Piazza S. Giovanni in Laterano

Bibliography: Mola, p. 78; Falda, *Fontane*, pl. 10; *Architettura minora*, II, pls 64–6, 108; Donati, *Artisti ticinesi*, figs 307–12; Spagnesi, *G. A. De Rossi*, p. 76; *Guide Rionali*, I, 1, pp. 88, 112; G. Curcio, 'L'Ospedale di S. Giovanni in Laterano', *Storia dell'Arte*, 36/37, 1979, p. 103.

According to Mola the men's hospital, facing the square, is by G. B. and Giacomo Mola.

The chapel of the men's hospital, SS. Andrea e Bartolomeo (open only for funerals), was also built by the two Molas but contains nothing of interest of the Baroque period.

Ospedale del Salvatore. See Ospedale di S. Giovanni
Piazza S. Giovanni in Laterano

Ospizio di S. Michele
Lungotevere Ripa

Bibliography: Falda, *Nuovo teatro*, IV, pl. 35; De'Rossi, *Architettura Civile*, III, pls 55–7; Donati, *Artisti ticinesi*, figs 273–8; Braham and Hager, p. 137; Elling, pls 78, 79.

Founded by Innocent XI in 1686 to house the poor, including children, and built on a vast site just above the port of the Ripa Grande. The architect of the first part, which was opened in 1688, was probably Mattia de'Rossi, who had been Bernini's assistant for many years. A further wing, probably designed by Carlo Fontana, was opened in 1698 under Innocent XII. The work was actively pursued by his successor, Clement XI. In 1701–4 he built the Casa Correzionale, which still serves as an institution for juvenile delinquents. On Fontana's death in 1714 he was succeeded by Niccolò Michetti acting jointly with Filippo de'Romanis. In 1735 Clement XII added a prison for women facing on to Porta Portese and designed by Fuga. The building was still being enlarged in 1790 and was probably intended to be extended by two further courts. In the history of poor houses it takes its place between the Albergo dei Poveri in Genoa, begun by Stefano Scaniglia in 1654, and that in Naples designed by Fuga in 1751; but it is a purely functional building with little architectural character. It is very fully documented by some forty drawings in the Royal Library, accompanied by an extensive written explanation dedicated to Clement XI.

Ospedale dello Spirito Santo. See S. Spirito in Sassia
Borgo S. Spirito

Pantheon. See S. Maria ad Martyres

Piazza di Montecitorio

Bibliography: D'Onofrio, *Obelischi*, p. 280; *Guide Rionali*, III, 2, p. 76.

The central feature is the obelisk, which was discovered in the early 16th century near S. Lorenzo in Lucina but was not fully excavated till 1748 on the order of Benedict XIV who intended to erect it in front of the Palazzo di Montecitorio. The project was not however actually carried out till 1788 when Pius VI caused the obelisk to be erected and topped it with unexpectedly Baroque bronze decorations, including allusions to his own arms (Braschi).

See also Palazzo Macchi di Cellere.

Piazza Navona

Bibliography: Salerno, *Piazzo Navona*, Rome, 1970; Armando Ravaglioli, *Piazza Navona*, Rome, 1973.

Built on the site of the Circus of Domitian the Piazza Navona has always been the scene of festivals organized by the Romans, but it owes its present appearance to Innocent X and his relatives, who made of it a sort of monument to the Pamphili family.

Before their time the piazza was surrounded by relatively small houses, though at the south end it was closed by the Palazzo de Torres, later Lancellotti, and the Palazzo Orsini later absorbed into the Palazzo Braschi. Part of the east side was occupied by the Spanish church of S. Giacomo degli Spagnuoli, built in the early 16th century, and at the ends were two fountains, designed by Giacomo della Porta in 1574, of which only that at the south end had figure sculptures, in the form of four tritons blowing water through conches (these are now in the Giardino del Lago in the Borghese Gardens).

When Cardinal Giovanni Battista Pamphili was elected pope in 1644 he made ambitious plans for remodelling the piazza. He enlarged the family palace which occupied part of the south end of the west side, rebuilt the church of S. Agnese, which was originally a modest church with its entrance in the via dell'Anima, and its choir backing on the piazza, on a much grander scale and facing the piazza; added a college to balance the palace to the north of the church; and commissioned Bernini to make the dramatic fountain of the Four Rivers in front of the church and to make sculpture for the two existing fountains. This work was not nearly finished at the time of Innocent's death in 1655, but it was carried on energetically by members of his family, of whom the most important were his sister-in-law Donna Olimpia Maidalchini, and his nephew Camillo. The scheme was carried through in spite of great difficulties, personal and financial. Only the fountain at the north end of the piazza was left without its statues which were not added till 1878.

The palace, church and fountains are discussed separately, see pp. 188, 3, 233.

Piazza del Popolo. See S. Maria di Montesanto

102. *Piazza Navona. Engraving by Vasi showing the* piazza *partially flooded for the August festival. On the left the Palazzo Pamphili and the church of S. Agnese. On the right S. Giacomo degli Spagnuoli. In the foreground Bernini's Fontana del Moro and beyond it his fountain of the Four Rivers.*

Piazza di S. Ignazio

Bibliography: Rotili, *Raguzzini*, p. 51; Portoghesi, *Roma Barocca*, pls 361–4; *Guide Rionali*, III, 1, p. 22.

Planned and built in 1727–8 by F. Raguzzini. One of the most ingenious and lively pieces of town-planning in Baroque Rome. The design, with its streets leading off the piazza symmetrically, suggests that the architect had been looking at stage designs – even perhaps at the Teatro Olimpico at Vicenza by Palladio and Scamozzi – but also at Cortona's remodelling of the piazza in front of S. Maria della Pace.

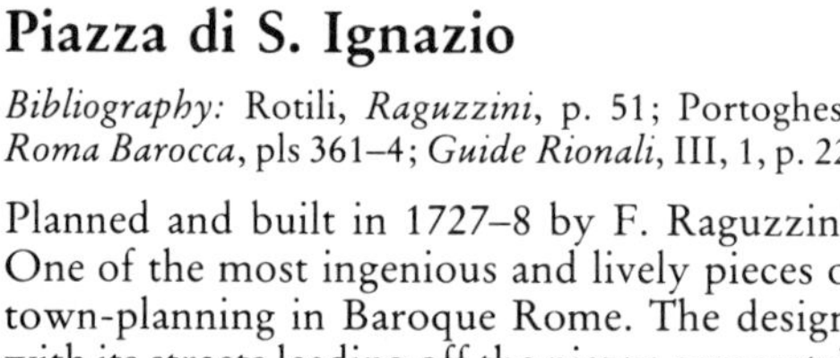

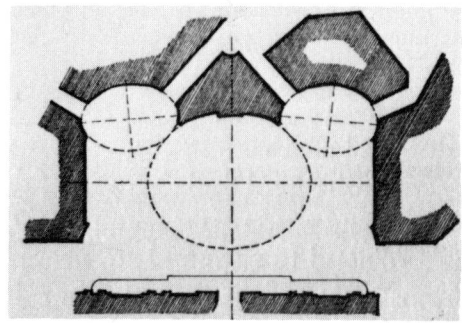

103. *Piazza di S. Ignazio. Plan.*

Ponte S. Angelo

Bibliography: M. S. Weil, *The history and decoration of the Ponte S. Angelo*, Pennsylvania State University Press, 1974.

The bridge (called the Pons Aelius) was built in AD 134 to lead to the Mausoleum of Hadrian, now the Castel S. Angelo. The *castello* and the bridge take their name from the miraculous appearance in 590 on the top of the mausoleum of an angel sheathing his sword to signify the end of a plague. In 1530 on the occasion of the visit of the Emperor Charles V two statues of *St Peter* and *St Paul* by Lorenzetto and Paolo Romano respectively were set up at the south end of the bridge, bearing on their bases the arms of Clement VII. In 1667 the newly elected Clement IX commissioned Bernini to make eight statues of angels carrying the symbols of the Passion to be set up over the piers of the bridge. In 1892 when the Lungotevere was made the arched ramps leading up to the bridge at each end were destroyed.

The angels were all designed by Bernini but were executed by assistants except for two, those carrying the *Superscription* and the *Crown of Thorns*, which were carved by the artist and his son. These were never set up and copies were made to replace them. Clement IX at one point intended to send them to his native town of Pistoia, but in the event they remained in the artist's house and were given by his grandson to the church of S. Andrea delle Fratte in 1729. Clement IX died in 1669 before the work was finished, but it was completed in 1672 by his successor Clement X who recorded the fact in an inscription on one of the bases at the north end of the bridge.

The sculptors of the individual statues are as follows:
The Angel carrying the Column, Antonio Raggi; *Crown of Thorns* and *Robe and Dice*, Pietro Paolo Naldini; *Nails*, Girolamo Lucenti; *Superscription*, Giulio Cartari; *Cross*, Ercole Ferrata; *Sponge*, Antonio Giorgetti; *Lance*, Domenico Guidi.

Porta del Popolo

Bibliography: Titi, 1686, p. 363; Vignola, *Regola delli Cinque Ordini d'Architettura*, Rome, n.d.; C. D'Onofrio, ' "Felici faustoque ingressui". Significato e origini dell'epigrafe di Porta del Popolo per l'ingresso della regina Cristina', *L'Urbe*, N.S., XXXVIII, 1975, 6, p. 3; Fagiolo dell'Arco, *Bernini*, No. 158, and p. 223, fig. 20.

The inscription on the outside of the gate states that it was built by Julius III in the third year of his pontificate, that is to say 1553. All the old and new guide-books record the tradition that it was designed by Michelangelo and built by Vignola. This is presumably based on the fact that an engraving of the outside of the gate is included in the *Nuova et ultima aggiunta delle Porte d'Architettura di Michelangelo Buonaroti* added to later editions of Vignola's *Regola delle Cinque Ordini d'Architettura*, but this publication contains a number of designs certainly not by Michelangelo and Vignola does not claim any connection with them in the inscriptions. Stylistically a connection with Michelangelo is out of the question and one with Vignola at least very dubious.

The gate was restored for the arrival of Queen Christina of Sweden in 1655 by Bernini who added the inscription on the inside of the gate together with the scrolls and the arms of Alexander VII above it. The statues of *St Peter* and *St Paul* on the outer face of the gate by Francesco Mochi were originally made for S. Paolo fuori le Mura but rejected and bought from his widow.

Porta Portese

Bibliography: Roisecco, 1750, I, p. 201; Venuti, 1767, p. 1047; Vasi, *Magnificenze*, pl. 12; Vasi, 1820, II, p. 406.

This gate was rebuilt by Innocent X on the site of the ancient Porta Portuensis, so-called because the road from it led to the port of Ostia. The name of the architect is not known, but the arms of Innocent X appear on the outer face of the gate.

Porta S. Giovanni

Bibliography: Benedetti, *Del Duca*, p. 95.

In 1573 Gregory XIII decided to enlarge the ancient Porta Celimontana on the approach to the new road which he was laying to enable him – and others – to reach the villas at Frascati. The work was finished in 1574, the date inscribed on the outside of the gate, which was renamed Porta S. Giovanni.

The architect in charge was Giacomo del Duca and not, as one would have expected, Giacomo della Porta who was 'Architetto del Popolo Romano'. The documents refer vaguely to previous work on the gate dating from the time of Pius IV for whom Michelangelo built the Porta Pia and who asked the artist to prepare drawings for other gates of the city. It is possible that such a drawing was known to del Duca; indeed one in the Casa Buonarroti, Florence (Benedetti, pl. 77) may be connected with this gate rather than with Porta Pia with which it is usually associated.

The hypothesis that a design by Michelangelo lies behind the gate as built might explain the choice of del Duca as executant architect, since he had been Michelangelo's assistant on Porta Pia and completed it after the master's death. It seems certain, however, that the main feature of the gate, its monumental rustication, is due to del Duca, who was without question the most inventive of Michelangelo's followers in architecture, and the only one who can be regarded as a link between him and Borromini.

Porta S. Pancrazio

On the Janiculum

Bibliography: Vasi, *Magnificenze*, pl. 13.

Built by Urban VIII as part of the fortifications of the Janiculum and dated by the inscription to 1644. Seriously damaged in the Siege of Rome in 1849 and rebuilt by Vespignani in 1857.

Porto di Ripetta

104. *The Porto di Ripetta. Engraving by Falda showing the port as it was in the 1660s. In the middle is the church of S. Girolamo degli Schiavoni and on the right the Palazzo Borghese with its loggia and hanging garden overlooking the Tiber.*

105. *The Porto di Ripetta. Anonymous etching from the Varie Vedute di Roma of 1748 showing the steps added in 1707 by Alessandro Specchi. The etching shows S. Girolamo degli Schiavoni and to the left S. Rocco before the façade was added by Giuseppe Valadier. The Palazzo Borghese has been altered by the addition of a closed balcony supported by columns which veils the entrance gate shown in Falda's engraving.*

Porta di Sisto Quinto
Via Marsala

A gate in the Aurelian walls bearing the arms of Sixtus V, but no date.

Porto di Ripetta (destroyed)

Bibliography: Falda, *Nuovo teatro*, II, pl. 38; Vasi, *Magnificenze*, pl. 85; *Architettura minora*, I, pls 4–7; D. Helsted et. al., *Roma dei fotografi al tempo di Pio IX 1846–78*, Rome, 1977, pl. 142; D'Onofrio, *Scalinate*, p. 322; id., *Il Tevere a Roma*, 1970, p. 86; Elling, pl. 127; *Guide Rionali*, VI, 2, p. 93; T. A. Marden, 'The Porto di Ripetta in Rome', *J.S.A.H.*, XXXIX, 1980, p. 28.

This was the port of Rome for those coming from up the Tiber, the opposite number to the Port of Ripa Grande (near the Ospizio di S. Michele, now destroyed) which served those coming up the river from Ostia and the sea. In 1707 a magnificent double flight of ingeniously curved steps leading down to the water was constructed by Alessandro Specchi, but they were destroyed when the Lungotevere was made in the late 19th century. They are however recorded in engravings, drawings and old photographs.

Seminario Romano (Palazzo Gabrielli)
Via del Seminario 120

Bibliography: Guide Rionali, III, 2, p. 26.

The palace was built in the late 16th century by Girolamo Gabrielli but was sold in 1607 and became the Seminary of the Jesuits, to whom it has belonged, except for short periods, ever since.

The Spanish Steps

Bibliography: Falda, *Fontane*, pl. 15; Salerno, *Piazza di Spagna*, p. 95; Lotz, 'Die Spanische Treppe', *Römisches Jahrbuch*, XII, 1969, p. 41; M. Laurain-Portemer, 'Benedetti et l'Escalier de la Trinità dei Monti', *Gazette des Beaux-Arts*, 1968, II, p. 273; D'Onofrio, *Scalinate*, pp. 131, 277; Mallory, *Rococo*, p. 36; Jacob, *Zeichnungen*, No. 377.

The Spanish Steps take their name from the fact that they run from the Piazza di Spagna to the church of the Trinità, in spite of the fact that they were conceived by a French first minister for the glory of the French king and paid for out of a bequest from a French diplomat. The architect was an Italian, but he was the choice of the French monks of the Trinità dei Monti and imposed on the pope over the head of his own candidate.

In 1494 Charles VIII bought a villa on the Pincio belonging to Daniele and Alvise Barbaro and established there a group of Minims, an order founded in France by S. Francesco di Paola. The church of the Trinità was begun in 1502; the façade is dated 1570 and the steps leading up to it were built in 1587. At the same time – at least as early as 1577 – the idea was mooted of linking the church with the square below – then called the Piazza della Trinità – by means of a flight of steps.

In 1655 Etienne Gueffier, chargé d'affaires at the French Embassy in Rome, promised 2,000 scudi for the construction of the staircase (the actual bequest in 1661 was of 10,000), and in 1660 Mazarin instructed his agent Benedetti to open a competition for the design of the steps. Four architects, including Carlo Rainaldi and François Dorbay, who was in Rome at the time, were asked to submit designs, and Benedetti was instructed to approach Bernini directly, which he did slowly and reluctantly. In fact Bernini made a model which was seen in 1687 by Tessin and which may be recorded in drawings (Lotz, figs 29, 30), though Benedetti claimed that these were of his own invention (see Lotz, p. 94 and Laurain-Portemer). Another project, tentatively ascribed to Giovanni Francesco Grimaldi, is in Berlin (Jacob).

Dorbay's projects survive (Lotz, 27a–d) and it is clear from them and from the Bernini–Benedetti set that the scheme was to be an affirmation of the power of the French monarchy, with an equestrian statue of the king at the centre, obviously a direct challenge to the Marcus Aurelius on the Capitol. Not unnaturally Alexander VII, who was constantly suffering humiliation from Louis XIV, rejected the scheme, which would have represented an intolerable assertion of the power of a foreign sovereign in papal territory; added to which the statue would have looked straight down on the Embassy of Spain, to which the pope looked for support against Louis.

Benedetti was still pressing the project on Colbert in 1664 and 1672 and at one point even hoped to get Bernini's rearing horse as the centrepiece of the design. Up to this point the story reads like a dress-rehearsal for the competition organized by Colbert a few years later for the completion of the Louvre. Nothing was done, however, and in 1717 Clement XI insisted that a decision should be made. He proposed as the designer the official papal architect, Alessandro Specchi, but the monks preferred their own architect, the little known Francesco de'

Sanctis, and the pope was forced to accept him. Specchi's own designs survive and it is clear that de' Sanctis incorporated several features of them into his final version, which was carried out between 1723 and 1728, the statue of the king having been omitted.

The obelisk at the top of the steps, which came from the gardens of Sallust, was set up by Pius VI in 1786. Standing as it does at the end of Sixtus V's via Felice (via Sistina) it balances the one which Sixtus erected below the apse of S. Maria Maggiore at the other end of the street.

De Sanctis' steps are so well-known and so loaded with associations that it is difficult to judge them objectively, but it is possible that Specchi's design might have been more precise and yet more lively in its movement, as he proved in his brilliant designs for the port of Ripetta.

See also plate 93.

106. *Piazza di Spagna and the site of the Spanish Steps. Etching by Israël Silvestre (c. 1640) showing the rough steps leading from the piazza to the Trinità dei Monti.*

107. *The Spanish Steps. Etching by J. L. Le Geay from the* Varie Vedute di Roma *of 1748. In the foreground is the Barcaccia.*

The Spanish Steps

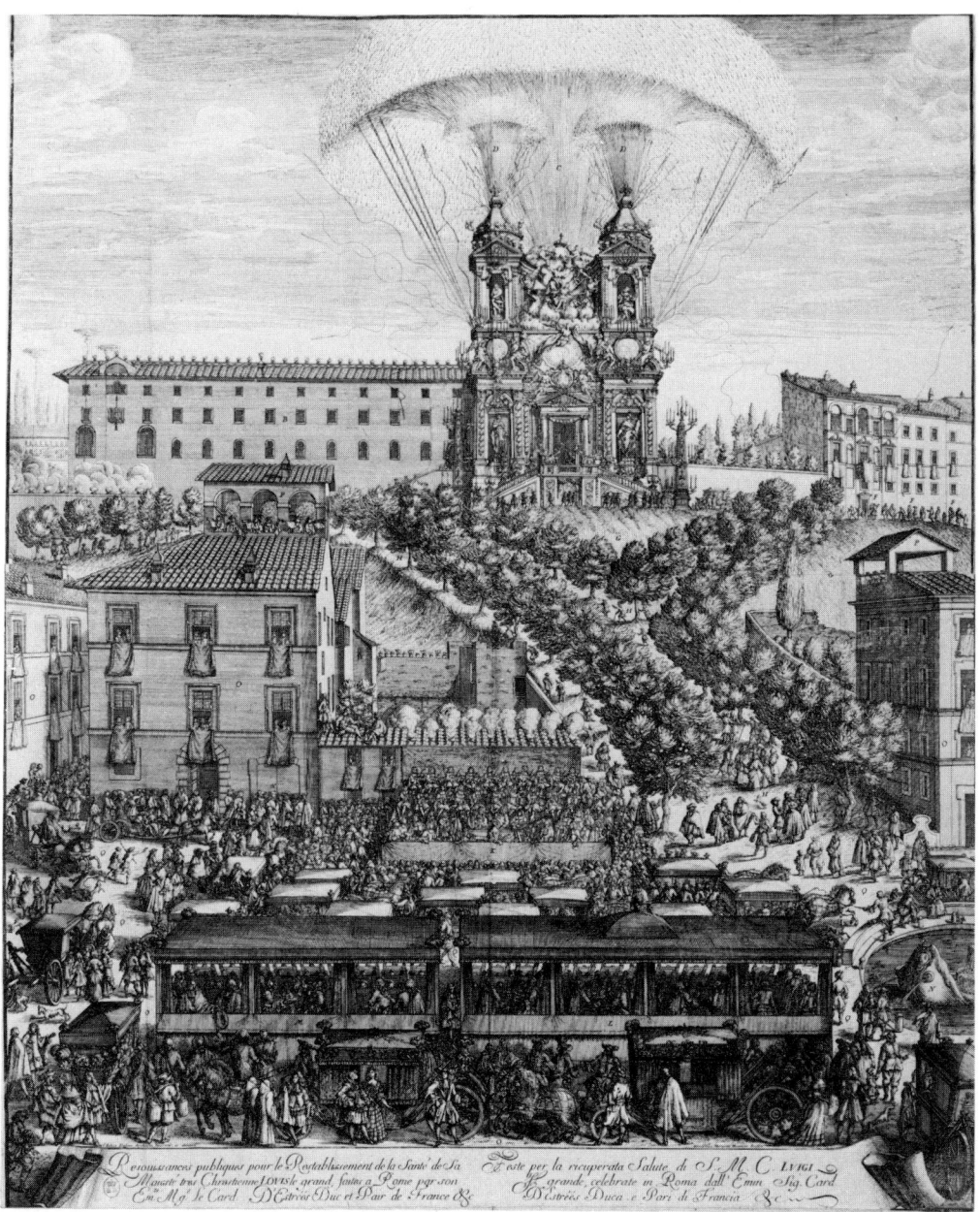

108. *Piazza di Spagna and the site of the Spanish Steps. Etching by Vincenzo Mariotti recording a display of fireworks ordered by Cardinal d'Estreés, French ambassador to Pope Innocent XI in 1687 in celebration of the recovery of Louis XIV after a serious illness.*

VII
THE ALBAN HILLS

This book is intended to cover the Baroque of Rome itself and not to include monuments of the period scattered over the province of Lazio. On the other hand the buildings on the Alban Hills, particularly the Villas of Frascati and Bernini's two churches at Ariccia and Castelgandolfo, are almost an extension of Roman Baroque and it seemed reasonable to include a few notes on them.

109. *Ariccia. Engraving by Falda showing the* piazza *in its original form before the viaduct was built. On the left is the church of the Assunta and on the right the Palazzo Chigi.*

ARICCIA

Bibliography: B. M. Apolloni-Ghetti, 'Il Palazzo Chigi all'Ariccia', *Quaderni*, 2, 1953, p. 10; Belli Barsali and Braschetti, p. 244.

In 1661 Cardinal Flavio Chigi, brother of Alexander VII, together with two of the pope's nephews, bought the estate of Ariccia from Giulio Savelli, principe di Albano. They set about enlarging and improving the old palace, mainly by frescoing the ceilings of the main rooms, in which context the names of Bastiano Ciardi and Pietro Tempesta are mentioned in the documents. In 1740 Augusto Chigi built the tower on the north-west corner of the palace, thus completing the effect of a mediaeval *castello*. The interior of the palace is not normally accessible.

The layout of the square in front of the palace and the construction of the church of the Immaculata opposite were assigned to Bernini who was prevented from making it perfectly symmetrical, with church and palace on the same axis, by the fact that the ground falls away rapidly behind the church, the back part of which had to be built upon a high substructure.

To judge the effect which Bernini intended in the piazza it must be remembered that till the viaduct which now carries the main road from the north into the town was built in about 1850, the piazza was a closed space, with a balustrade at the north end (as it appears in an engraving in Falda, *Nuovo teatro*, II, see pl. 109), not a thoroughfare, and was approached by the road which winds round the park and arrives at the gate to the right of the palace. From there it turned left to follow the line of the present via Appia to the south.

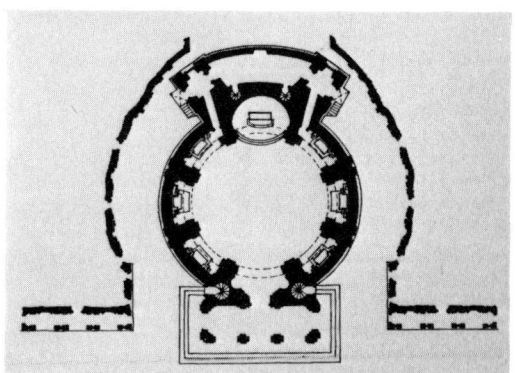

110. *Ariccia, Church of the Assunta. Plan.*

Collegiata dell'Assunta

Bibliography: De' Rossi, *Architettura Civile*, II, pls 56–8; Fagiolo dell'Arco, *Bernini*, No. 188; Portoghesi, *Roma Barocca*, pl. 78.

Built by Bernini in 1662–4 for Alexander VII opposite the Palazzo Chigi.

The conception of the whole, with a circular church enclosed in a semi-circle of subsidiary buildings, may derive from one of Montanus' reconstructions of ancient Roman temples (*Le Cinque Libri di Architettura*, Rome, Book II, 1621, pl. 28; Blunt, in *Studies in Western Art. Acts of the twentieth international Congress of the History of Art*, Princeton, 1963, III, p. 8) but it is boldly Baroque in character. On the other hand in detail the architecture is simple, even dry, with a straight unbroken pediment over the entrance portico, and no mouldings round the arches (cf. S. Bibiana of nearly 40 years earlier).

Stuccoes in the dome by P. P. Naldini. The apse was decorated by Guglielmo Cortese with a fresco of the *Assumption* (1664–6; W), but Bernini's structure suggests that he must have intended an architectural High Altar.

2 to R: Bernardino Mei, *St Augustine* (1665; W).

3 to L: Raffaelle Vanni, *St Thomas of Villanova* (1665; W).

2 to L: Lodovico Gimignani, *Riposo* (1664; W).

1 to L: Giacinto Gimignani, *St Anthony Abbot* (1665; W).

Santuario della Madonna, Galloro

Near Ariccia

Bibliography: Fagiolo dell'Arco, *Bernini*, No. 189.

Built 1624 and restored by Bernini in 1661–2 for Alexander VII. He built the façade and the dome, and may have designed the High Altar.

1 to R: Giacinto Gimignani, *St Thomas of Villanova* (1662; W).

CASTEL GANDOLFO

S. Tommaso da Villanova

Bibliography: Fagiolo dell'Arco, *Bernini*, No. 185; Portoghesi, *Roma Barocca*, pls 79, 80, 82.

Built by Bernini in 1658–61 for Alexander VII and dedicated to St Thomas of Villanova (1488–1555), a man of great piety, humility and charity who was canonized by Alexander in 1658, a typical example of the 'new saints' of the Counter-reformation.

This church is an extraordinary example of the severity of Bernini's architecture. The plan is a pure Greek cross and the walls are articulated with flat pilasters, with the result that externally the church is nearer in character to Giuliano da Sangallo's S. Maria delle Carceri at Prato than to contemporary Roman buildings. Internally the severity is mitigated by the ingenious treatment of the dome.

111. *Castel Gandolfo. Engraving by Falda showing the church of S. Tommaso da Villanova and in the background the papal palace.*

INTERIOR

Stuccoes of dome by Raggi including *tondi* with scenes from the life of *St Thomas* based on designs by G. P. Schor.

Altar to R: G. Gimignani, *St Thomas* (1661; W).

High Altar: Cortona, *Crucifixion* (1661; W).

Altar to L: Guglielmo Cortese, *The Assumption* (1660; W).

Papal Palace

Bibliography: Mignosi, p. 263.

The summer residence of the pope and not easily accessible. Built, mainly by Urban VIII, between 1623 and 1626 round a mediaeval castle belonging to the Savelli, but the building was enlarged, probably to the designs of Bernini, by the acquisition of neighbouring land in the following years. The interior was mainly decorated under Alexander VII. The gallery has frescoed landscapes by P. L. Ghezzi.

FRASCATI

Bibliography: for the villas see C. Franck, *The Villas of Frascati*, London, 1966, and Belli Barsali and Braschetti; Coffin, p. 40; A. T. Mignosi, *Villa e Paese. Dimore nobili del Tuscolo e di Marino*, catalogue of exhibition at the Palazzo Venezia, Rome, 1980; for engravings see Falda, *Fontane*, part 2, *Le Fontane delle Ville di Frascati*, Rome, 1675.

As early as Republican times wealthy Romans began to establish villas at Tusculum, on the Alban Hills and during the Empire the whole area was occupied and developed. After the Barbarian invasions the villas fell into decay, but in the Middle Ages the counts of Tusculum established themselves as a power threatening that of Rome itself. In 1191 Celestine III destroyed Tusculum, but some of the inhabitants settled in an area lower down the slope, on the site of the modern Frascati.

In the 16th century the Romans began once again to build villas in the area. Cardinal Alessandro Rufino founded one villa (later Falconieri) in 1548, and Cardinal Ricci of Montepulciano another in 1550, now the Villa Vecchia. They were followed by the humanist Annibale Caro who in 1563 built a further villa (later Torlonia). Others followed suit and by the mid 17th century Frascati had become another Tusculum. Several of the villas suffered severely when Frascati, which was an important headquarters of the German army, was bombed in 1943. Most of the villas are still private property and are not normally accessible, but some, such as Falconieri, are owned by semi-public organizations and can usually be visited if permission is applied for in advance.

112. *Frascati, General view. Engraving by Greuter (1620). Left half: bottom left, Villa Vecchia; above, Villa Mondragone; below right, Villa Borghese; slightly above right, Villa Falconieri; top right, Villa Rufinella.*

Cathedral

Bibliography: H. Hager, 'Girolamo Fontana e la facciata della Cattedrale di San Pietro a Frascati', *Commentari*, XXVIII, 1977, p. 273.

Built 1598–1610 by local architects, after a design by Mascarino had been turned down. The church has the form of a near-Greek Cross enclosed in a rectangle. To this stage belongs the right-hand campanile (except the curved top section) and the Doric pilasters of the lowest storey, from which one can conclude that the façade would have followed the model of S. Atanasio dei Greci. It was completed in a less severe style from 1696 onwards by Girolamo Fontana, nephew of Carlo, in spite of the fact that Frate Andrea Pozzo had put forward a design for it. Girolamo Fontana's model for the façade is preserved in the Sacristy. The relief over the middle door, representing *St Peter walking on the Waters*, is by Bernardino Cametti (1704) and the statues in the niches are by Andrea Fucigna (*Sts Peter and Paul*), Girolamo Gramignoli (*St Sebastian*), Vincenzo Felice (*St Philip*), Francesco Napoleoni (*St James the Less*), G. P. Mauri (*St Roch*).

The fountain (Hager, op. cit. p. 274) in the piazza del Duomo was built 1697–1700 probably to the design of Girolamo Fontana. Badly damaged by bombs but reconstructed after the war.

Hermitage of Camaldoli (S. Romualdo)

Bibliography: Mignosi, p. 233.

Founded in 1606. The church, which was rebuilt in the 18th century, has stucco decoration by Tommaso Righi.

S. Maria Assunta (Jesuit Church)

Bibliography: Braham and Hager, p. 66.

Built 1696–1700 probably from the designs of Andrea Pozzo, possibly modifying a plan prepared by Carlo Fontana. The church was certainly decorated by Pozzo, though Kerber (p. 47) is in error in dating this work to 1681–4.

Villa Aldobrandini

Bibliography: Falda, *Nuovo teatro*, IV, pls 24, 25; id., *Fontane*, II; Magni, III, pls 12–15; Franck, *Villas*, p. 115; K. Schwager, 'Kardinal Pietro Aldobrandinis Villa di Belvedere in Frascati', *Römisches Jahrbuch*, IX–X, 1961–2, p. 289; D'Onofrio, *La Villa Aldobrandini di Frascati*, Rome, 1963; Hibbard, *Maderno*, p. 131; Fagiolo dell'Arco, 'Villa Aldobrandini Tusculana', *Quaderni*, 62–6, 1964, p. 61; Belli Barsali and Braschetti, p. 178; Mignosi, p. 165.

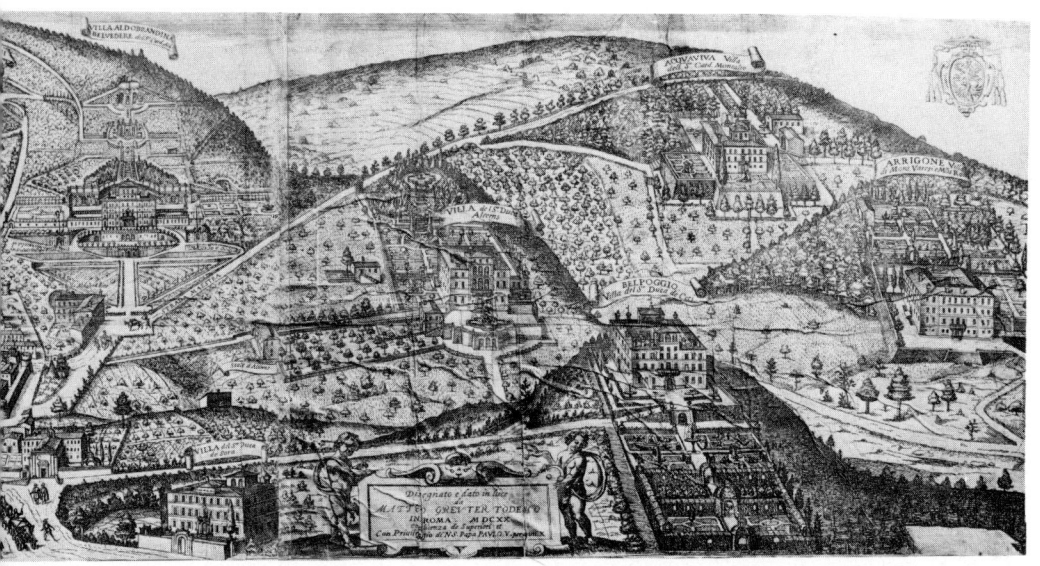

Right half: extreme left, Villa Lancellotti; above right, Villa Aldobrandini; middle, Villa Torlonia; further to right, Villa Pallavicini; above, Villa Grazioli; extreme right, Villa Arrigoni-Muti.

Villa Arrigoni-Muti

113. *Frascati, Villa Aldobrandini. Engraving by Falda showing the water-theatre and the cascade.*

A small villa was built on this site by Pier Antonio Contugi soon after 1560. In 1598 this was given to Cardinal Pietro Aldobrandini by his uncle Clement VIII as a reward for his share in the reconquest of Ferrara. In 1683 the villa passed to the Pamphili family by the marriage of Olimpia Aldobrandini to Camillo Pamphili, and when that family became extinct in 1760 it came under the ownership of the Borghese, a member of which had been Olimpia's first husband. In 1843 the title of Prince Aldobrandini was created for Don Camillo Borghese.

The construction of the present *casino*, which incorporated that of Contugi, was begun soon after the villa came into the possession of Cardinal Aldobrandini. It was designed by Giacomo della Porta, who however died the next year and the actual building was supervised by Maderno and Giovanni Fontana. The villa was habitable by 1603.

In 1600 plans were made to bring water for the construction of a cascade and water-theatre. This appears to have been designed by Maderno and executed jointly by him and Giovanni Fontana, who was a specialist in water-works. (For the iconography of the water-theatre see D'Onofrio, op. cit., and R. M. Steinberg, 'The Iconography of the Teatro d'Acqua in the Villa Aldobrandini', Art Bulletin, XLVII, 1965, p. 453.) The screen at the entrance from the piazza of the town was added by C. F. Bizzacheri before 1699 (Mallory, *Bizzacheri*, pp. 30, 45).

Some of the rooms on the *piano nobile* were decorated by the Cavaliere d'Arpino, but the most important frescoes were those by Dome-nichino in the *nymphaeum* on the right of the water-theatre which are now in the National Gallery, London.

Villa Arrigoni-Muti

Bibliography: Mignosi, p. 179

The villa was built on the site of one constructed by Ludovico Cerasoli before 1579. In 1595 the estate was bought by Monsignor Pompeo Arrigoni (1552–1616) who was made a cardinal in the next year by Clement VIII, and built the existing villa. The villa later belonged to the Muti, Amadei and Cesarini.

The interior contains frescoes by Ludovico Cigoli, Domenico Passignano, Lanfranco and the young Pietro da Cortona.

Villa Borghese

Bibliography: Magni, III, pl. 8; Franck, *Villas*, p. 73; Belli Barsali and Braschetti, p. 281; Mignosi, p. 217.

The villa was built in 1604–5 by Monsignor Ferdinando Taverna, governor of Rome under Clement VIII, but he sold it in 1614 to Cardinal Scipione Borghese. In the following years he enlarged it to the designs of Girolamo Rainaldi, who added the heavily rusticated porticoes which flank the *casino* on the front facing the Campagna and the semi-circular staircase leading to the garden. The villa remained in the Borghese family till 1896 when it was sold to Saverio Parisi. It contains some frescoes by G. and D. Valeriani and I. Heldmann dating from the 1730s.

Villa Falconieri

Bibliography: Magni, III, pls 50–4; Hempel, *Borromini*, p. 173; Franck, *Villas*, p. 133; Portoghesi, *Borromini nella cultura europea*, p. 343; Belli Barsali and Braschetti, p. 206; Coffin, p. 42; Blunt, *Borromini*, p. 177; Mignosi, p. 83.

The villa, built in the mid-16th century by Cardinal Ruffino, came in the 1650s into the possession of the Falconieri who in the 1660s enlarged it on the design of Borromini, encasing the existing *casino* in the middle pavilion and adding two long wings. The villa was unfinished at Borromini's death and several details are due to Ciro Ferri who completed the work and almost certainly built the entrance gate, which is a variant on Cortona's destroyed gate to the stables of Palazzo Barberini. The building was later altered by Fuga who inserted a mezzanine floor. The villa is now the seat of the Centro Europeo dell'Educazione.

The villa was damaged by bombing in 1943 but the principal rooms survived. Their decoration was mainly carried out in the 1670s. The *Salone* was frescoed by Niccolò Berrettoni; in other rooms the ceilings are decorated with frescoes representing the seasons, including *Spring* and *Autumn* by Ferri, *Summer* by Calandrucci (W). The wall decorations are by Grimaldi (landscapes, 1672). In the early 18th century Pier Leone Ghezzi added portraits of members of the Falconieri family and the walls of the Sala della Primavera were frescoed by Francesco Ignazio Borgognone, Il Bavarese (Busiri-Vici, *Orizzonte*, Rome, 1975, p. 176).

Villa Grazioli

Bibliography: Mignosi, p. 141.

The villa was built about 1580 by the learned Cardinal Antonio Carafa (1538–91) who was made a cardinal by Pius V in 1568 and was closely connected with the translation into practice of the decrees of the Council of Trent. On his death it passed to Cardinal Ottavio Acquaviva and later to various other owners, including the Odescalchi and their heir, Baldassare Erba, who added a gallery at some date between 1723 and 1743, till it was bought in 1843 by the Grazioli family.

The decoration of the main rooms was carried out for Cardinal Acquaviva by Agostino Ciampelli and his assistants, but the Gallery has brilliant illusionist frescoes by G. P. Pannini.

Villa Lancellotti

Bibliography: Franck, *Villas*, p. 153; Belli Barsali and Braschetti, p. 216; R. Lefèvre, 'Appunti sulla prima construzione di Villa Lancellotti a Frascati', *L'Urbe*, XXXVIII, 1975, p. 36; Mignosi, p. 191.

The villa was originally built about 1586 by the Oratorians as a summer retreat, but was enlarged by Cardinal Alfonso Visconti about 1600 for the benefit of the fathers. It later passed to the Mattei, Borghese and Piccolomini and was finally acquired in 1866 by Filippo Lancellotti who redecorated much of the interior. The ceiling frescoes executed by Cherubino Alberti for Visconti survive however.

The garden was certainly laid out before 1620 and its semi-circular water-theatre is the earliest of its kind at Frascati (cf. Villa Aldobrandini and Villa Mondragone). The gate, which is dated 1877, is a remarkably good pastiche of the early Baroque style.

Villino Mergé-Mastrofini

Bibliography: Mignosi, p. 249

A small villa of no great architectural interest but with interesting frescoed friezes by Agostino Tassi and his studio.

Villa Mondragone

Bibliography: Baglione, p. 176; Mola, p. 127; Falda, *Nuovo teatro*, IV, pl. 16; id., *Fontane*, II; Magni, III, pls 4–8; Franck, *Villas*, p. 57; Hibbard, *Maderno*, p. 191; Belli Barsali and Braschetti, p. 164; Coffin, p. 54; Mignosi, p. 107.

The Villa Mondragone stands on the highest point of the hills above Frascati and has the widest and most magnificent view of any of the villas.

In 1573 Cardinal Marcus Psiticus (Marco Sitico) Altemps, who had just completed the Villa Vecchia, bought a site above the villa, on which had stood the villa of the Quintilii, and commissioned Martino Longhi the Elder to build there a *casino* (finished 1575). He gave it the name of Mondragone after the dragon which was the emblem of his friend Gregory XIII (Buoncom-

Villa Rufinella

114. Frascati, Villa Mondragone. Engraving by Falda showing the teatro added by Cardinal Scipione Borghese.

pagni). In 1577–8 the cardinal had a new wing called the Ritirata built for his illegitimate son Roberto, to the south of the *casino*, through which the visitor now approaches the villa.

In 1613 the heirs of the cardinal sold the villa to Cardinal Scipione Borghese. Between 1615 and 1620 he built two wings to link the *casino* to the Ritirata, and added a whole section to the east consisting of a loggia and a water-theatre. The architects involved were the Dutchman, Jan van Santen, called Giovanni Vasanzio, and Giovanni Fontana, who was mainly responsible for the fountains and water conduits. It is often said that Flaminio Ponzio was involved, but in fact he died a few months before the acquisition of the villa.

The frescoes in the interior of the villa and the Ritirata date mainly from the period of Cardinal Altemps, but the stuccoes in the chapel were made by Annibale Durante for Cardinal Borghese (1619).

Villa Rufinella

Bibliography: Franck, *Villas*, p. 159; Belli Barsali and Braschetti, p. 276; Coffin, p. 51; Mignosi, p. 137.

In 1564 Cardinal Alessandro Farnese, titular abbot of Grottaferrata, ceded a part of the estate which the abbey owned near Frascati to Cardinal Alessandro Ruffino who also owned the Villa Rufina, later Falconieri. It changed hands many times and in 1740 was bought by the Jesuits of the Collegio Romano, as a summer resort. It was completely rebuilt for the Society on the designs of Luigi Vanvitelli on an unusual T-shaped plan, dictated by the need to provide a large number of small rooms – almost monastic cells – for the fathers. He also added a beautifully designed oval chapel. On the suppression of the Society in 1773 the villa fell back to the Camera Apostolica, was ceded by Pius VII to Lucien Bonaparte, bought by a Savoy and then by a Lancellotti. In 1966 it was bought by the Salesian fathers who have restored it after the serious damage which it received from bombs in 1943.

Villa Sora Buoncompagni

Bibliography: Mignosi, p. 209.

The villa was built in the late 16th century by the Moroni family and was sold in 1600 to Giacomo Buoncampagni, an illegitimate son of Gregory XIII, who was responsible for the decoration of the main rooms by the Cavaliere d'Arpino and his assistants. The frescoes in the chapel have been ascribed to G. Calandrucci.

Villa Torlonia

Bibliography: Falda, *Fontane*, II; Franck, *Villas*, p. 88; Hibbard, *Maderno*, p. 210; Belli Barsali and Braschetti, p. 164; Coffin, p. 48; Mignosi, pp. 77, 109.

The original villa was laid out by Annibale Caro in 1563. In 1607 it was bought by Cardinal Scipione Borghese, who commissioned Carlo Maderno and Giovanni Fontana to make the waterfall (1607–10). In 1614 it was sold to the duca d'Altemps and in 1621 to Cardinal Ludovico Ludovisi who carried out extensive work on the gardens under the direction of Maderno, with the assistance of Jacques Sarrazin for the sculpture. In 1680 the villa came into the possession of Lotario Conti, who built the magnificent series of staircases in the terraced gardens. The *casino* itself was destroyed by bombing in 1943, but the gardens have been restored and are now open to the public.

Villa Vecchia

Bibliography: Franck, *Villas*, p. 53; Coffin, p. 45; Mignosi, pp. 18, 107.

The *vigna* was bought in 1550 by Cardinal Giovanni Ricci who began building but sold the estate in 1562 to Cardinal Ranuccio Farnese. From him it passed to his brother Cardinal Alessandro who sold it to Cardinal Marcus Psiticus Altemps in 1567. The latter employed Vignola to enlarge the original *casino*. Its plan, which is known from a drawing in the Archivio di Stato, Florence (Mignosi, fig. 7), is more like a Venetian palace than any work of Vignola, with a long *salone* leading right through the building, lit only at the ends, and flanked by two ranges of smaller rooms.

In 1613 the villa was sold with the Villa Mondragone to Cardinal Scipione Borghese and it has remained ever since a part of the Mondragone estate. It was enlarged in the 17th and 18th centuries.

115. *Frascati, Villa Torlonia. Engraving by Falda showing the cascade added by Cardinal Ludovico Ludovisi.*

GENZANO

A fief of the Colonna and later the Cesarini and Sforza-Cesarini families.

S. Maria della Cima

Bibliography: Spagnesi, *G. A. De Rossi*, p. 97.

The parish church is a very early work by G. A. de'Rossi.

GROTTAFERRATA

An abbey of Basilian monks of Greek-Catholic rites founded by S. Nilo in 1004. It was restored and fortified by Giuliano de Sangallo for Cardinal Giuliano della Rovere, later Pope Julius II, who was abbot from 1473 onwards, as an outpost to resist possible attacks on Rome from the kingdom of Naples. The church, consecrated in 1025, was redecorated in the 17th century. The Baroque iconostasis was executed between 1659 and 1668 by Antonio Giorgetti (Montagu, *Giorgetti*, p. 283). Opening off the right aisle is the Cappella di S. Nilo, restored by Cardinal Odoardo Farnese and decorated from 1608 onwards with a fine series of frescoes by Domenichino representing scenes from the lives of Sts Nilus and Bartholomew (Borea, *Domenichino*, p. 144). The altarpiece of the *Madonna with the two saints* is from the studio of Annibale Carracci (D' Posner, *Annibale Carracci*, London, 1971, II, p. 75). It is likely that the rather unusual arrangement with a Serliana cutting off the end of the chapel to form a choir, covered by an oval dome, frescoed with *grisaille* acanthus patterns, like those in the Camerino of the Palazzo Farnese, is due to Domenichino (Lavin, *Bernini*, pls. 74–6).

MARINO

SS. Rosario

Bibliography: S. Benedetti, 'La chiesa del SS. Rosario in Marino', *Quaderni*, XII, 67–70, 1965, p. 7; Portoghesi, *Roma Barocca*, pls 333–6.

The Dominican convent was founded by a Princess Colonna in 1675, but the church was not built till 1712 to the designs of Giuseppe Sardi. It is circular in plan with the addition of a short choir and a longer nave, both rectangular. Its most unusual feature is the dome which is decorated with a series of rib-like bands which interlace to form a highly complicated pattern. At first sight these have some resemblance to the ribs on the domes of Bernardo Vittone's churches in Piedmont, but they are fundamentally different in that Vittone's are functional whereas Sardi's are purely decorative.

S. Barnaba

Bibliography: Jacob, *Zeichnungen*, No. 364.

Built by Antonio del Grande; foundation stone laid in 1640; building still in progress after 1660. A drawing for the façade by del Grande is in the Kunstbibliothek, Berlin.

INTERIOR

Right hand altar: E. Ferrata (with the assistance of Rusconi), *St Anthony Abbot*.

BIBLIOGRAPHY

The bibliography of works on Baroque Rome is vast and it will only be possible here to list the most important items, particularly those which themselves contain bibliographies which will lead the reader to further sources.

Of modern books much the most useful is Rudolf Wittkower's volume in the Pelican History of Art, *Art and Architecture in Italy 1600–1750*, which gives a brilliant survey of the development of all three arts – architecture, sculpture and painting – for the whole of the period. It also has a very full bibliography. For the architecture I have presented a shorter account, written from a slightly different point of view, in the section devoted to Rome in *Baroque and Rococo. Architecture and Decoration* (London, 1978). Paolo Portoghesi in his *Roma Barocca* gives his version of the subject, which to English minds is often difficult to follow, and in the American translation is unintelligible; the plates are, however, invaluable. A strangely appealing, if sometimes rather naïve, account of Roman architecture of the later part of the period is given by the Danish scholar, Christian Elling, in his *Rome. The Biography of its Architecture from Bernini to Thorvaldsen*, of which an English translation appeared in 1975. His love of Rome and his knowledge of the city, built up over many years of residence there, led him to search out and photograph many buildings neglected by other writers on the Baroque. In an article entitled 'Roman Baroque architecture: the other side of the medal' (*Art History*, III, 1980, p. 61) I have examined some of the buildings discussed by Elling and have attempted to give an account of the vernacular works which were being produced by architects of talent rather than genius during the period. In a series of beautifully illustrated and well-documented volumes (listed below) Cesare d'Onofrio has dealt with many individual aspects of Roman Baroque architecture, notably fountains, obelisks and staircases. Nina Mallory has provided much the best available account of the *Barocchetto* in Rome, in a book which, however, she perversely insists on entitling *Roman Rococo Architecture* (London and New York, 1977), a misuse of the word *rococo* against which I cannot protest too strongly.

For plates of Baroque Rome much the best, clearest and most detailed are those in Magni's *Il Barocco a Roma* (Turin, 1911) which have the incidental advantage of showing Rome before the motor-car arrived and the cobbled streets were macadamized. Many useful plates of sculpture in marble or stucco are to be found in two volumes by G. Ferrari, *Lo Stucco* and *La Tomba* (Milan, n.d.). Nineteenth-century photographs of Rome, often of great interest, are to be found in the following volumes: B. Brizzi, *Roma cento anni fa*, Rome, 1975; D. Helsted *et al.*, *Roma dei fotografi al tempo di Pio IX 1846–78*, Rome, 1977.

Bibliography

As regards the historical background, Professor Francis Haskell's *Patrons and Painters* (2nd edition, London, 1980) gives a vivid and detailed account of the relations of artists – not only painters – to their patrons in Rome, but the student will always have to turn to that inexhaustible source, Pastor's *History of the Popes* for details drawn from a life-time of study in Roman archives.

The most concise account of Roman painting during the Baroque period is that given by Sir Ellis Waterhouse in *Italian Baroque Painting* (London, 1962) and in the introduction to his *Roman Baroque Painting* (2nd edition, Oxford, 1976) which contains the most reliable list of Baroque paintings in Roman churches. The student will, however, still be able to fill in gaps for information about painters not dealt with by Waterhouse by reference to Hermann Voss' *Die Malerei des Barock in Rom* (Berlin, 1924). For ceiling paintings see M. C. Gloton, *Trompe-l'oeil et décor*, T. Poensgen, *Die Deckenmalerei in italienischen Kirchen*, and R. England, *The Baroque Ceiling Paintings in the Churches of Rome*. The Caravaggisti are covered in Benedict Nicolson's *The International Caravaggesque Movement* (Oxford, 1979). For the iconography of the religious art of the period Emile Mâle's *L'Art religieux après le Concile de Trente* (Paris, 1932) is still invaluable.

Sculpture is the Cinderella of the story. No general study of the subject has been undertaken since Wittkower's Pelican volume, though Professor Enggass' *Early eighteenth-century Sculpture in Rome* (Pennsylvania State University Press, 1976) fills a part of the gap.

Among modern guide-books the most generally useful is that of the Touring Club d'Italia, though the *Guide Rionali*, which are being published by the City of Rome and are available at the Museo di Roma (Palazzo Braschi), will, when complete, provide a much fuller and more reliable coverage of the monuments of the city.

For the churches of Rome the most convenient – and in many cases the best – source is the series called *Le chiese di Roma illustrate*, each volume of which deals with an individual church. Some of the earlier volumes in the series are inadequately documented but in the later ones the level of scholarship is high. In addition there is Walther Buchowiecki's *Handbuch der Kirchen Roms*, which, when it is complete, will presumably cover all the churches of Rome. It contains detailed descriptions – down to the last pilaster – of every church, an exact account of its history and a description of all the paintings, tombs and other objects in the church, with the names of the artists to whom they are attributed. From the point of view of the art historian however, it suffers from one major disadvantage: in all the more than two thousand pages of the book so far published the author never gives the authority for his attributions or dating. Some are obviously correct, but many, alas! are based on a misunderstanding of the documents or an unreliable authority. A much briefer but in many ways more useful guide is Diego Angeli's *Le Chiese di Roma* of 1903 (though it must be added that it is not free from mistakes). The most complete list of Roman churches, existing or destroyed, is to be found in M. Armellini, *Le Chiese di Roma* (Rome, 1887, reprint of second edition, Rome, 1942), but the author is mainly interested in the Early Christian and mediaeval periods. For these periods the reader should also consult R. Krautheimer *et al.*, *Corpus basilicarum christianarum Romae*, Rome (Vatican), 1937–77.

The early sources of information about Baroque buildings in Rome are of four kinds. First come the actual documents, as far as they have been published from the Roman archives by Pollak, Orbaan, Golzio, Garms, Güthlein, and others (listed below), including a few diaries such as those of Pope Alexander VII and Valesio. Second come the lives of artists by Baglione (1642), Bellori (1672, other lives published in 1942), Baldinucci

(1681–1728), Pascoli (1730), and Passeri (written in the late seventeenth century but not fully published till 1934). The third group of sources is the guide-books of which the earliest relevant to the Baroque are Totti (1638), Mola (1663, but not published till 1966), Martinelli (c.1660 but not published till 1969). The most useful is that by Titi which appeared in various editions between 1674 and 1763. It is particularly valuable for the later part of the period in recording buildings or works of art which had been put up or made in the interval since the previous edition. The last edition of 1763 was edited by the great art historian and critic, Giovanni Bottari, who added much information not given in earlier editions. For palaces and their contents Pietro Rossini's *Mercurio Errante* (first published in 1693) gives fuller details than Titi. A full bibliography of these and all the other guide-books is given by L. Schudt in *Le Guide di Roma* (1930). I should record that in quoting these guides I have been arbitrary – or lazy – in mainly using those of which I happen to own copies. No doubt further information could be derived from others to be found, for instance in the much more complete collections in the British Museum, the British School at Rome and the Bibliotheca Hertziana, Rome.

Something may be gleaned from the woodcuts illustrating many of the seventeenth- and early eighteenth-century guide-books which appeared under various titles such as *Le cose maravigliose dell'alma città di Roma* and under the names of Franzini, Felini and others (see Schudt, op. cit., pp. 31ff., 185ff.). They sometimes show the façades of churches before they were restored in the Baroque period, but they have to be used with extreme caution, because when the publisher did not have to hand a block representing the church in question he simply inserted another. So, for instance, in the 1643 edition published by Franzini (Schudt, No. 214) one block is used for S. Giovanni Decollato, S. Antonio a S. Maria Maggiore and S. Pudenziana – and probably represents none of them!

The printed texts are supplemented by the volumes of engravings. The earliest of these are the volumes by Falda, *Nuovo teatro* (1665), *Fontane* (1691) and *Giardini* (about 1680). These give views of the buildings in question which, though not architecturally precise, are of great interest because they show them in their original settings which have often been changed in the rebuilding of Rome since the Risorgimento, by the cutting of new roads and the lowering of the levels of old ones. Ferrerio's engravings in the *Palazzi di Roma*, published by G. J. de'Rossi in the 1670s, consist of plans and elevations, measured, though not always accurately. The *Architettura Civile*, published in three volumes by Domenico de'Rossi between 1702 and 1721, provides more accurate plans of many churches and detailed engravings of windows, doors and other architectural features, which made the vocabulary of the Roman Baroque known throughout Europe. This is supplemented by two volumes on special aspects of church architecture from the same publishers, the *Altari* of 1713 and the *Insignium templorum prospectus* of 1684. Even more accurate are the plans and elevations in Letarouilly's *Palais, maisons et autres édifices modernes* (1798) and *Choix des plus célèbres maisons de plaisance de Rome* (1809) which remain an invaluable source for the study of Baroque as well as Renaissance buildings. Many of these works have been reissued in facsimile in the last twenty years.

An interesting if totally hostile view of Roman Baroque architecture is to be found in the *Osservazioni* of Antonio Visentini, published in Venice in 1771, with savage criticisms of buildings from Michelangelo's tribunes of St Peter's and Porta Pia through the works of Bernini, Cortona and Borromini to the doors on the Palazzo del Grillo. Visentini's approach is that of a Venetian brought up on Palladio and influenced by incipient neo-classicism. The same attitude is taken by Francesco Milizia in his *Vite dei più celebri architetti*, published in Rome in 1768. A brief account of the reaction against

Roman Baroque in the 18th and 19th centuries may be found in the last chapter of my book on Borromini, though it must be borne in mind that writers of this period reserved their harshest criticism for Borromini and even Milizia describes Bernini's S. Andrea al Quirinale as *elegantissima* in spite of its faults. Most travellers, particularly the French and the English, are harsh on the Baroque, the principal exception being the Président de Brosses who writes enthusiastically about Bernini and even has a good word for Borromini. In this book I have only quoted from two of the earliest, Tessin and De Brosses. It would be fascinating to work through all the others to trace variations of taste, but this would be a labour of several years. For an account of the comments by travellers of all nationalities on Rome see L. Schudt, *Italienreisen im 17. und 18. Jahrhundert*, Vienna–Munich, 1959.

There are valuable monographs on the major and some of the minor architects of the period. For Bernini the basic works are Wittkower's Phaidon volume for the sculpture and his book written in collaboration with Heinrich Brauer for the drawings (a new edition by Ann Sutherland Harris and Allan Braham is promised), but much useful information can be gleaned from Fagiolo dell'Arco's book which has a complete catalogue of the artist's works, whether buildings, sculpture, paintings or drawings. For an analysis of Bernini's ecclesiastical architecture up to and including the Cornaro Chapel see Irving Lavin, *Bernini and the Unity of the Visual Arts*. Much new material will no doubt be published in the Acts of the Bernini Congress held in Rome in January 1981. For Borromini the basic work is still Hempel's monograph of 1924, but a brief summary of his achievement, with bibliography, is to be found in the present writer's Penguin volume (1979). Good plates are to be found in Portoghesi's *Borromini* (1968), though the text is as difficult as that in his *Roma Barocca*. Hans Thelen began a complete publication of the artist's drawings, but so far only the first volume, covering the works up to the early 1630s, has appeared. A brilliant history and analysis of one of his most important buildings, the Oratory of St Philip Neri, is to be found in J. Connors, *Borromini and the Roman Oratory*.

Unhappily – and surprisingly – no general work exists on the architecture of Pietro da Cortona, though I hope myself to complete a short monograph in the near future. Karl Noehles' book on the church of SS. Luca e Martina contains a great deal of information not only about that church, but about Cortona's other buildings. Monographs or articles also exist on some of the lesser architects of the period. Fasolo's volume on the Rainaldis is whimsical but useful; Hibbard deals thoroughly with Maderno, as does Spagnesi with G. A. de'Rossi; and monographs exist on Raguzzini (Rotili) and Fuga's work in Rome (Matthiae). The catalogue of Carlo Fontana's drawings at Windsor by Allan Braham and Hellmut Hager covers a great part of his activity, and Nina Mallory has devoted a useful article to Bizzacheri. Hager has dealt with many individual buildings or problems in a series of articles in *Commentari* and other periodicals.

For monographs or important articles on individual painters the reader is referred to Waterhouse's *Roman Baroque Painting*. The number of monographs is remarkably small: Posner on Annibale Carracci, Sutherland Harris on Sacchi, Briganti on Cortona, Cocke on Mola, Enggass on Baciccio, Kerber on Pozzo, to which should be added Ursula Verena Fischer's dissertation on Giacinto Gimignani (Freiburg, 1973) and Salvagnini's book on the Cortesi, inadequate though it is; but there is nothing on Domenichino, Lanfranco, Romanelli, Sassoferrato, Maratta or Conca, though works on some of them are promised.

With the sculptors the situation is still worse. Apart from Bernini, who is well covered, there are at present only monographs on Algardi (Heimbürger Ravalli) and Bracci (Gradara) and articles on some of the minor figures, but Jennifer Montagu's further monograph on Algardi is nearing completion.

The eighteenth century has been much less well studied than the seventeenth. The best treatment of the painting is still Voss' *Die Malerei des Barock in Rom* and the sculpture of the early decades of the century is covered by Engass' *Early Eighteenth-century Sculpture in Rome*. The architecture is treated by Nina Mallory in her *Roman Rococo Architecture*, already referred to, and will, when complete, contain much new information on all the arts in Rome in the eighteenth century. Unfortunately Anthony Clark's *Studies in Roman Eighteenth-Century Painting* (Washington DC, 1981) appeared too late for me to incorporate in this book the very important material which it contains.

The following list only includes works quoted frequently and therefore referred to in abbreviated form.

Bibliography

Ackerman-Lotz	J. S. Ackerman and W. Lotz, 'Vignoliana', *Essays in Memory of Karl Lehmann*, Locust Valley, 1964, p. 1.
Angeli	D. Angeli, *Le Chiese di Roma*, Rome, 1903.
Architettura minora	*Architettura minora in Italia*, Associazione artistica fra i Cultori di architettura, Turin, 1925.
Armellini	M. Armellini, *Le Chiese di Roma*, second edition, Rome, 1942.
Baglione	Giovanni Baglione, *Le Vite de'pittori, scultori ed architetti*, Rome, 1642.
Baldinucci	Filippo Baldinucci, *Notizie de' Professori del Disegno da Cimabue in qua*, Florence, 1681–1728.
Belli-Barsali	I. Belli Barsali, *Ville di Roma*, Milan, 1970.
Belli Barsali and Braschetti	I. Belli Barsali and M. G. Braschetti, *Ville della Campagna*, Milan, 1975.
Bellori	Giovanni Pietro Bellori, *Le Vite de' pittori, scultori et architetti moderni*, Rome, 1672. Facsimile edition, Rome, 1931.
Bellori, II	Giovanni Pietro Bellori, *Vite di Guido Reni, Andrea Sacchi e Carlo Maratti*, edited by Michelangelo Piacentini, Rome, 1942.
Benedetti, *Del Duca*	Sandro Benedetti, *Giacomo del Duca e l'architettura del Cinquecento*, Rome, 1972.
Bianchi, *Fuga*	L. Bianchi, *Disegni di Ferdinando Fuga e di altri architetti del Settecento*, exhibition catalogue, Gabinetto Nazionale delle Stampe, Rome, 1955
Blunt, *Borromini*	A. Blunt, *Borromini*, London, 1979.
Blunt, *The other side*	A. Blunt, 'Roman Baroque Architecture. The other side of the medal', *Art History*, III, 1980, p. 61.
Borea, *Domenichino*	E. Borea, *Domenichino*, Florence, 1965.
Bousquet, *Recherches*	Jacques Bousquet, *Recherches sur le séjour des peintres français à Rome au XVIIe siècle*, Montpellier, 1980.
Braham and Hager	A. Braham and H. Hager, *Carlo Fontana. The Drawings at Windsor Castle*, London, 1977.
Brauer and Wittkower	H. Brauer and R. Wittkower, *Die Zeichnungen des Gianlorenzo Bernini*, Berlin, 1931.
Briganti, *Cortona*	G. Briganti, *Pietro da Cortona*, Florence, 1962.
Buchowiecki	W. Buchowiecki, *Handbuch der Kirchen Roms*, Vienna, 1967.
Callari	I. Callari, *I Palazzi di Roma*, second edition, Rome, 1944.
Cartari-Febei	Manuscript diary in the Vatican Library. References to it were kindly supplied to me by Mr Marc Worsdale.
Cocke, *Mola*	R. Cocke, *Pier Francesco Mola*, Oxford, 1972.
Coffin	D. R. Coffin, *The Villa in the life of Renaissance Rome*, Princeton, 1979.
Colosanti	A. Colosanti, *Volte e Soffiti italiani*, Milan, 1923.
Connors, *Oratory*	J. Connors, *Borromini and the Roman Oratory. Style and Society*, New York/Cambridge (Mass.)/London, 1980.
Coudenhove-Erthal	E. Coudenhove-Erthal, *Carlo Fontana und die Architektur des römischen Spätbarocks*, Vienna, 1930.
De Brosses	C. de Brosses, *Lettres familières sur l'Italie*, edited by Y. Bézard, Paris, 1931.

De'Rossi, *Altari*	G. G. de'Rossi, *Disegni di vari Altari e Cappelle nelle Chiese di Roma*, Rome, 1713. Facsimile edition, London, 1970.
De'Rossi, *Architettura Civile*	D. de'Rossi, *Studio d'architettura civile*, Rome, 1702–21.
De'Rossi, *Prospectus*	D. de'Rossi, *Insignium Romae templorum prospectus*, Rome, 1684. German edition by Sandrart (Nuremberg, n.d.). The plates in the Italian edition are un-numbered and the numbers given in the entries below are those of Sandrart's reprint, which contains a few plates not in de'Rossi's volume. The plates are also reprinted in Sandrart's *Des alten und neuen Roms Grosser Schau-Platz*, Nuremberg, 1685. See also Rossi.
Del Piazzo	M. del Piazzo, *Pietro da Cortona. Mostra documentaria*, Archivio di Stato, Rome, 1969.
Diary of Alexander VII	R. Krautheimer and R. B. S. Jones, 'The Diary of Alexander VII', *Römisches Jahrbuch*, XV, 1975, p. 199.
Donati, *Artisti ticinesi*	U. Donati, *Artisti ticinesi a Roma*, Bellinzona, 1942.
D'Onofrio, *Acque e Fontane*	C. D'Onofrio, *Acque e Fontane di Roma*, Rome, 1977.
D'Onofrio, *Obelischi*	C. D'Onofrio, *Gli Obelischi di Roma*, Rome, 1967.
D'Onofrio, *Roma vista*	C. D'Onofrio, *Roma vista da Roma*, Rome, 1967.
D'Onofrio, *Scalinate*	C. D'Onofrio, *Scalinate di Roma*, Rome, 1973. See also Martinelli.
Eimer, *S. Agnese*	G. Eimer, *La Fabbrica di S. Agnese in Piazza Navona*, Stockholm, 1970.
Elling	C. Elling, *Rome. The Biography of its Architecture from Bernini to Thorvaldsen*, English translation, Tübingen, 1975.
Enggass, *Baciccio*	R. Enggass, *The Painting of Baciccio*, Pennsylvania State University Press, 1964.
Enggass, *Ottoni*	R. Enggass, 'Lorentius Ottoni Rom. Vat. Basilicae sculptor', *Storia dell'Arte*, 15/16, 1972, p. 315.
Enggass, *Rusconi*	R. Enggass, 'Rusconi and Raggi in Sant'Ignazio', *Burlington Magazine*, CXVI, 1974, p. 258.
Enggass, *Sculpture*	R. Enggass, *Early eighteenth-century Sculpture in Rome*, Pennsylvania State University Press, 1976.
England	R. England, *The Baroque Ceiling Paintings in the Churches of Rome, 1600–1750. A Bibliography*, Hildersheim/New York, 1979.
Fagiolo dell'Arco, *Bernini*	Maurizio and Marcello Fagiolo dell'Arco, *Bernini*, Rome, 1967.
Fagiolo dell'Arco and Carandini, *L'Effimero barocco*	M. Fagiolo dell'Arco and S. Carandini, *L'Effimero barocco*, Rome, 1977–8.
Falda, *Fontane*	G. B. Falda, *Le Fontane di Roma*, Rome, 1691.
Falda, *Giardini*	G. B. Falda, *Li Giardini di Roma*, Rome, c.1680.
Falda, *Nuovo teatro*	G. B. Falda, *Il nuovo teatro delle fabriche di Roma*, Rome, 1665–99.
Fasolo, *Rainaldi*	F. Fasolo, *L'opera di Hieronimo e Carlo Rainaldi*, Rome, 1961.

Bibliography

Fasolo, *Trastevere*	F. Fasolo, *Le Chiese di Roma, Trastevere*, Rome, 1949.
Ferrari, *Lo Stucco*	G. Ferrari, *Lo Stucco nell'arte italiana*, Milan, n.d.
Ferrari, *La Tomba*	G. Ferrari, *La Tomba*, Milan, n.d.
Ferrerio, *Palazzi*	P. Ferrerio, *Palazzi di Roma*, n.d.
Forcella	V. Forcella, *Iscrizioni delle Chiese ed altri Edifici di Roma*, Rome, 1869ff.
Franck, *Villas*	C. Franck, *The Villas of Frascati*, English translation, London, 1966.
Frommel, *Palastbau*	C. L. Frommel, *Der römische Palastbau der Hochrenaissance*, Tübingen, 1972.
Gallaccini, *Trattato*	T. Gallaccini, *Trattato sopra gli errori degli Architetti*, Venice, 1767. Facsimile reprint, London, 1970.
Garms	J. Garms, *Quellen aus dem Archiv Doria-Pamphili*, Vienna, 1972.
Gigli	G. Gigli, *Diario Romano (1608–72)*, Rome, 1958.
Gloton	M. C. Gloton, *Trompe-l'oeil et décor plafonnant dans les églises romaines de l'âge baroque*, Rome, 1965.
Golzio, *Chigi*	V. Golzio, *Documenti artistici sul seicento nell'Archivio Chigi*, Rome, 1939.
Golzio, *Palazzi*	V. Golzio, *Palazzi romani della Rinascita al neo-classicismo*, Bologna, 1970.
Gradara, *Bracci*	C. Gradara, *Pietro Bracci Scultore Romano*, Milan/Rome, 1920.
Grioni	J. S. Grioni, *Le Edicole Sacre di Roma*, Rome, 1975.
Guide Rionali	*Guide Rionali di Roma*, edited by Carlo Pietrangeli, published by the Assessorato Antichità, Belle Arti e Problemi della Cultura of the city of Rome. In progress.
Güthlein, *Familienarchiv Spada*	K. Güthlein, 'Quellen aus dem Familienarchiv Spada zum Römischen Barock', *Römisches Jahrbuch*, XVIII, 1979, p. 173, XIX, 1981, p. 173 (in progress).
Heimbürger Ravalli, *Algardi*	M. Heimbürger Ravalli, *Alessandro Algardi scultore*, Rome, 1973.
Heimbürger Ravalli, *Archivio Spada*	M. Heimbürger Ravalli, *Architettura Scultura e Arti Minori nel Barocco Italiano. Ricerche nell'archivio Spada*, Florence, 1977.
Hempel, *Borromini*	E. Hempel, *Francesco Borromini*, Vienna, 1924.
Hibbard, *Licenze*	H. Hibbard, 'Di alcune licenze rilasciate dai maestri di strade per opere di edificazione a Roma', *Bollettino d'Arte*, LII, 1967, p. 99.
Hibbard, *Maderno*	H. Hibbard, *Carlo Maderno*, London, 1972.
Jacob, *Zeichnungen*	S. Jacob, *Italienische Zeichnungen der Kunstbibliothek Berlin*, Berlin, 1975.
J.M.	Information from unpublished documents kindly given to me by Dr Jennifer Montagu.
J.S.A.H.	*Journal of the Society of Architectural Historians.*
Kerber	B. Kerber, *Andrea Pozzo*, Berlin/New York, 1971.
Kitson	M. Kitson, *The Complete Paintings of Caravaggio*, London, 1969.

Lavagnino, *Altari*	E. Lavagnino, G. R. Ansaldi and L. Salerno, *Altari barocchi di Roma*, Rome, 1959.
Lavin, *Bernini*	I. Lavin, *Bernini and the Unity of the Visual Arts*, Oxford, 1980.
Letarouilly	P. M. Letarouilly, *Edifices de Rome moderne*, Paris, 1869–74. References to the reprint (London, n.d.) are given in brackets.
Lotz, *Die ovalen Kirchenräume*	W. Lotz, 'Die ovalen Kirchenräume des Cinquecento', *Römisches Jahrbuch*, VII, 1956, p. 7.
Magni	G. Magni, *Il Barocco a Roma*, Turin, 1911.
Mâle	E. Mâle, *L'Art religieux après le Concile de Trente*, Paris, 1932.
Mallory, *Bizzacheri*	V. Mallory, 'C. F. Bizzacheri', *Journal of the Society of Architectural Historians*, XXXIII, 1974, p. 27.
Mallory, *Notizie*	V. Mallory, 'Notizie sulla Pittura a Roma nel XVIII secolo (1718–80)', *Bollettino d'Arte*, LXI, 1976, p. 102.
Mallory, *Rococo*	N. A. Mallory, *Roman Rococo Architecture from Clement XI to Benedict XIV*, New York and London, 1977.
Martinelli	C. D'Onofrio, *Roma nel Seicento*, Florence, 1969, published the manuscript of Fioravante Martinelli's *Roma ornata*.
Matthiae, *Fuga*	G. Matthiae, *Ferdinando Fuga e la sua Opera Romana*, Rome, 1951.
Melchiorri	G. Melchiorri, *Guida metodica di Roma*, Rome, 1840.
Mémoires d'Histoire et d'Archéologie	Published by the Ecole Française de Rome.
Mignosi	A. T. Mignosi, *Ville e Paese. Dimore nobili del Tuscolo e di Marino*, Catalogue of exhibition at Palazzo Venezia, Rome, 1980.
Mola	G. B. Mola, *Breve racconto delle miglior opere d'Architettura, Scultura e Pittura fatte in Roma*, edited by Karl Noehles, Berlin, 1966.
Montagu, *Giorgetti*	J. Montagu, 'Antonio and Giuseppe Giorgetti', *Art Bulletin*, LII, 1970, p. 278.
Münchner Jahrbuch	*Münchner Jahrbuch der bildenden Kunst.*
Nicolson	B. Nicolson, *The International Caravaggesque Movement*, Oxford, 1979.
Noehles, *Fasolo*	K. Noehles, review of Fasolo, *L'Opera di Hieronimo e Carlo Rainaldi*, in *Zeitschrift für Kunstgeschichte*, XXV, 1962, p. 116.
Noehles, *SS. Luca e Martina*	K. Noehles, *La Chiesa dei SS. Luca e Martina nell'opera di Pietro da Cortona*, Rome, 1969.
Orbaan	J. A. Orbaan, *Documenti sul Barocco a Roma*, Rome, 1920.
Pane, *Fuga*	R. Pane, *Ferdinando Fuga*, Naples, 1956.
Pascoli	L. Pascoli, *Vite de'Pittori, Scultori, et Architetti moderni*, Rome, 1730.
Passeri	G. B. Passeri, *Vite de'Pittori, Scultori et Architetti Dall'Anno 1641 sino all'Anno 1673*, edited by J. Hess, *Die Künstlerbiographien von G. B. Passeri*, Leipzig and Vienna, 1934.
Percier et Fontaine, *Maisons de Plaisance*	C. Percier and P. F. L. Fontaine, *Choix des plus célèbres maisons de plaisance de Rome et de ses environs*, Paris, 1809.

Bibliography

Percier et Fontaine, *Palais*	C. Percier and P. F. L. Fontaine, *Palais, maisons, et autres édifices modernes dessinés à Rome*, Paris, 1798.
Pio, *Vite*	N. Pio, *Le Vite di Pittori Scultori et Architetti*, edited by R. and C. Enggass, Vatican, 1977.
Poensgen	T. Poensgen, *Die Deckenmalerei in italienischen Kirchen*, Berlin, 1969.
Pollak	O. Pollak, *Die Kunsttätigkeit unter Urban VIII*, 1928–31.
Portoghesi, *Borromini*	P. Portoghesi, *Borromini*, Rome, 1967. American translation, London, 1968.
Portoghesi, *Borromini nella cultura europea*	P. Portoghesi, *Borromini nella cultura europea*, Rome, 1964.
Portoghesi, *Roma Barocca*	P. Portoghesi, *Roma Barocca*, Rome, 1966. American translation, London, 1970.
Pugliese-Rigano, *Lunghi*	A. Pugliese and S. Rigano, *Martino Lunghi il Giovane*, Rome, 1972.
Quaderni	*Quaderni dell'Istituto di Storia dell'Architettura*, Rome.
Ragguagli	*Ragguagli Borrominiani. Mostra documentaria*, Archivio di Stato, Rome. Catalogue by M. Del Piazzo, Rome, 1968.
Roisecco	G. Roisecco, *Descrizione di Roma moderna*, Rome, 1739. Later editions 1745, 1750, 1765. Based on the text of Rossi.
Römisches Jahrbuch	*Römisches Jahrbuch für Kunstgeschichte*. Published by the Bibliotheca Hertziana, Rome.
Rossi	F. de'Rossi, *Ritratto di Roma moderna*, Rome, 1645. Later edition 1652. Other editions revised by M. and P. Rossi. Those of 1697 and 1727 are quoted here. See also de'Rossi.
Rotili, *Raguzzini*	M. Rotili, *Filippo Raguzzini e il Rococò Romano*, Rome, 1951.
Salerno, *Piazza Navona*	L. Salerno, D. Redig de Campos, *et al.*, *Piazza Navona. Isola dei Pamphily*, Rome, 1970.
Salerno, *Piazza di Spagna*	L. Salerno, *Piazza di Spagna*, Cava dei Tirreni, 1967.
Salerno, *Via del Corso*	G. Lugli, L. Salerno, M. Zocca *et al.*, *Via del Corso*, Rome, 1961.
Salerno, *Via Giulia*	L. Salerno, L. Spezzaferro, and M. Tafuri, *Via Giulia*, Rome, 1973.
Sandrart	J. von Sandrart, *Academie der Bau-, Bild- und Mahlerey-Künste*, Nuremberg, 1675. Edition here quoted by A. R. Peltzer, *Munich, 1925*. See also de'Rossi. Prospectus.
Schiavo, *La Fontana di Trevi*	A. Schiavo, *La Fontana di Trevi e le altre opere di Nicola Salvi*, Rome, 1956.
Sestieri, *Conca*	G. Sestieri, 'Contributi a Sebastiano Conca', *Commentari*, XX, 1969, pp. 317, 328.
Spagnesi, *G. A. De Rossi*	G. Spagnesi, *Giovanni Antonio De Rossi Architetto Romano*, Rome, 1964.
Studi sul Borromini	Accademia Nazionale di San Luca, *Studi sul Borromini. Atti del convegno promosso dall'Accademia Nazionale di San Luca*, Rome, 1967.

Sutherland Harris, *Sacchi*	A. Sutherland Harris, *Andrea Sacchi*, Oxford, 1977.
Tessin	*Nicodemus Tessin d.y:s studienresor*, edited by O. Siren, Stockholm, 1914.
Thelen, *Borromini*	H. Thelen, *Francesco Borromini. Die Handzeichnungen*. Only the first volume has so far appeared. Graz, 1967.
Thieme-Becker	Thieme and Becker, *Allgemeines Lexikon der bildenden Künstler*, Leipzig, 1907–50.
Titi	F. Titi, *Studio di Pittura, Scoltura et Architettura nelle Chiese di Roma*, Rome, 1674. Enlarged editions with slightly different titles, 1686, 1708, 1721. The 1763 edition, much enlarged and remodelled by Giovanni Bottari, has the title *Descrizione delle Pitture, Sculture, ed Architetture esposte al pubblico in Roma*.
Torselli	G. Torselli, *Palazzi di Roma*, Milan, 1965.
Totti	P. Totti, *Ritratto di Roma moderna*, Rome, 1638.
Valesio	V. Golzio, 'Notizie sull'arte romana del Settecento tratte del Diario del Valesio', *Archivi d'Italia*, second series, III, 1936, p. 119.
Varriano, *Longhi*	J. Varriano, *Martino Longhi the Younger*, Dissertation.
Vasi	G. Vasi, *Itinerario istruttivo . . . per ritrovare . . . le antiche e moderne magnificenze di Roma*, Rome, 1763. Later editions by G. Vasi, 1765, 1770, 1777. Reissued with additions by M. Vasi, 1791, etc., and by Nibby, 1818, etc.
Vasi, *Magnificenze*	G. Vasi, *Delle Magnificenze di Roma antica e moderna*, Rome, 1747–61.
Vecchi	M. Vecchi, *Ambasciate estere a Roma*, Milan, 1971.
Venuti	R. Venuti, *Accurata e succinta descrizione . . . di Roma moderna*, Rome, 1766 (second edition 1767).
Vignola	*La Vita di Jacopo Barozzi da Vignola nel quarto centenario della morte*, Vignola, 1974.
Visentini, *Osservazioni*	A. Visentini, *Osservazioni . . . che servono di continuazione al trattato di Teofilo Gallaccini*, Venice, 1771. Facsimile edition, London, 1970.
Voss	H. Voss, *Die Malerei des Barock in Rom*, Berlin, 1924.
W	E. Waterhouse, *Roman Baroque Painting*, London, 1937; second edition Oxford, 1976.
Wasserman, *Mascarino*	J. Wasserman, *Ottaviano Mascarino*, Rome, 1966.
Weil, *Ponte S. Angelo*	M. S. Weil, *The History and Decoration of the Ponte S. Angelo*, Pennsylvania State University, 1974.
Wittkower, *Art and Architecture*	R. Wittkower, *Art and Architecture in Italy 1600–1750* (Pelican History of Art). References are to the paperback edition of 1975.
Wittkower, *Bernini*	R. Wittkower, *Gianlorenzo Bernini. The Sculptor of the Roman Baroque*. References here to the second edition of 1966.

Wittkower, *Italian Baroque*	R. Wittkower, *Studies in the Italian Baroque*, London, 1975.
Wittkower and Jaffé, *Baroque Art; the Jesuit Contribution*	R. Wittkower and I. Jaffe, *Baroque Art: The Jesuit Contribution*, New York, 1972.

INDEX OF ARTISTS

This index contains a list of architects, painters, sculptors and craftsmen and the particular works with which they were associated in Rome listed in the order in which they appear in this book. The dates of the artists are given where known. Names beginning with *del* or *della* are put under D.

Abbatini, Guidobaldo (c. 1600/5–56)
   S. Agostino 6
   S. Maria della Vittoria 123
   S. Pietro in Montorio 130
   S. Spirito in Sassia 147
   Vatican 204
Adam, Lambert Sigisbert (1700–59)
   Fontana di Trevi 240
'Adamo Lorenese', see Brefort, Adam Claude
Agellio, Giuseppe (1570–c. 1650)
   S. Silvestro al Quirinale 146
Agresti, Livio (active c. 1550–c. 80)
   S. Lucia del Gonfalone 74
Agricola, Luigi (b. 1750, recorded 1801)
   S. Antonio dei Portoghesi 16
Albani, Francesco (1578–1660)
   S. Maria della Pace 106
   Palazzo Costaguti 177
   Palazzo Mattei di Giove 186
   Palazzo Verospi 200
Alberti, Cherubino (1553–1615)
   S. Giovanni in Laterano 56
   S. Maria sopra Minerva 95
   S. Maria in Via (Largo Chigi) 119
   S. Silvestro al Quirinale 145
   S. Vitale 153
   Palazzo Rospigliosi-Pallavicini 194
   Palazzo Ruggeri 194
   Vatican 204
   Frascati, Villa Lancellotti 267
Alberti, Durante (1538–1613)
   S. Maria dei Monti 100
   S. Maria in Vallicella 116
   Collegio Inglese 246
Alberti, Giovanni (1558–1601)
   S. Giovanni in Laterano 56
   S. Silvestro al Quirinale 145
   S. Vitale 153
   Palazzo Ruggeri 194
   Vatican 204

Albertini, Matteo (recorded 1638–40)
   S. Maria sopra Minerva 96
Aldovrandini, Pompeo (1677–1735)
   Palazzo Doria-Pamphili 179
Alessi, Galeazzo (1512–72)
   Il Gesù 41
Alfani, Emanuele (active in the 1730s)
   S.S. Celso e Giuliano 29
Algardi, Alessandro 1598–1654
   S. Agnese in Agone 5
   S. Carlo ai Catinari 22
   SS. Carlo e Ambrogio al Corso 26
   S. Francesco a Ripa 40
   Il Gesù 45, 46
   S. Giovanni dei Fiorentini 51
   S. Giovanni in Laterano 54
   S. Ignazio 63
   SS. Luca e Martina 74
   S. Marcello 78
   S. Maria dell'Anima 81
   S. Maria in Campo Marzio 85
   S. Maria Maggiore 90, 91
   S. Maria del Popolo 108
   S. Maria della Scala 110
   S. Maria in Trastevere 112
   S. Maria in Vallicella and Oratory 116, 118
   S. Maria della Vittoria 123
   S. Nicola da Tolentino 126
   S. Pietro in Vaticano 136
   S. Silvestro al Quirinale 146
   SS. Trinità dei Pellegrini 151
   Capitoline Palaces 170
   Palazzo Doria-Pamphili 179
   Villa Pamphili 219
Allegrini, Francesco (1587–1663)
   SS. Cosma e Damiano (via dei Fori Imperiali) 30
   SS. Domenico e Sisto 35
   S. Marco 79
   S. Maria sopra Minerva 96
   S. Maria dell'Umilta 113

Index of Artists

Allegrini, Francesco (*contd*)
   Palazzo Costaguti 177
   Palazzo Pamphili 189
Altobelli, Gaetano (recorded 1734–5)
   S. Giovanni dei Fiorentini 50
Amato, Paolo (1634–1714)
   S. Maria Maddalena 89
Ameli, Paolo (recorded 1744)
   Palazzo Doria-Pamphili 179
Ammanati, Bartolommeo (1511–92)
   Il Gesù 43
   S. Pietro in Montorio 130
   Palazzo Ruspoli 194
   Collegio Romano 248
Amorosi, Antonio (1660–after 1736)
   S. Rocco 141
Angeletti, Pietro (active *c*. 1758–86)
   S. Caterina da Siena (via Giulia) 27
   Palazzo Doria-Pamphili 179
Anguier, Michel (1612–86)
   S. Giovanni dei Fiorentini 51
Antichi, Prospero (Bresciano) (d. 1592)
   S. Giovanni dei Fiorentini 52
   S. Pietro in Vaticano 134
   Acqua Felice 229
Antonini, G. B. (active *c*. 1700)
   Il Gesù 46
Aprile, Francesco (active 1642 onwards)
   S. Anastasia 8
   Gesù e Maria 47
Arconio, Mario (1575–1623)
   S. Eufemia 37
   S. Isidoro 65
   S. Maria in Vallicella, Oratory 117
   S. Maria della Vittoria 122
Arcucci, Camillo (active 1642–67)
   S. Maria del Rosario sul Monte Mario 110
   S. Maria in Vallicella and Oratory 115, 118
   Palazzo Grazioli 182
   Palazzo Pio di Savoia da Carpi 190
   Palazzo Spada 197
Arigucci, Luigi (active 1624–32)
   S. Anastasia 7
   SS. Cosma e Damiano (via dei Fori Imperiali) 30
   S. Giacomo alla Lungara 49
   S. Sebastiano al Palatino 144
Arpino, Cavaliere Giuseppe Cesare d' (1568–1640)
   S. Cesareo 29
   S. Giovanni in Laterano 55, 56
   S. Lucia in Selci 75
   S. Luigi dei Francesi 76
   S. Maria di Loreto 88
   S. Maria Maggiore 93
   S. Maria in Traspontina 111
   S. Maria in Vallicella 116
   S. Maria in Via (Largo Chigi) 119
   S. Onofrio 127
   S. Prassede 139
   SS. Trinità dei Pellegrini 151
   Capitoline Palaces 170
   Palazzo Costaguti 177
   Palazzo dei Piceni 190
   Palazzo Rondinini 193
   Frascati, Villa Aldobrandini 266
   Frascati, Villa Sora Buoncompagni 268
Asprucci, Antonio (1723–1808)
   Villa Borghese 212
Asprucci, Mario (1764–1804)
   S. Salvatore in Lauro 143
Avellino, Onofrio (d. 1741)
   S. Francesco di Paola 39
   S. Lorenzo in Lucina 69
   S. Maria delle Grazie alle Fornaci 87
   S. Maria della Luce 88

Baburen, D. van (before 1595–1624)
   S. Pietro in Montorio 130
Baciccio, Giovanni Battista Gaulli (1639–1709)
   S. Agnese in Agone 5
   S. Andrea al Quirinale 10
   SS. Apostoli 17
   S. Francesco a Ripa 40
   Il Gesù 43, 45
   S. Margherita in Trastevere 79
   S. Maria in Campitelli 84
   S. Maria Maddalena 89
   S. Maria sopra Minerva 94, 95
   S. Maria di Montesanto and S. Maria dei Miracoli 99
   S. Marta 123
   S. Nicola da Tolentino 126
   S. Rocco 141
   Palazzo della Cancelleria 170
Badalocchio, Sisto (1581/5–1647)
   S. Gregorio al Celio 62
Baglione, Giovanni (1571–1644)
   S. Bernardino ai Monti 19
   S. Cecilia 28
   SS. Cosma e Damiano (via dei Fori Imperiali) 30
   S. Luigi dei Francesi 76
   S. Maria della Consolazione 86
   S. Maria Maggiore 93
   S. Maria dell'Orto 102, 103
   S. Nicola in Carcere 125
   S. Onofrio 127
   Palazzo Rospigliosi-Pallavicini 194
Balassi, Mario (1604–67)
   S. Maria della Concezione 85
Baldi, Lazzaro (*c*. 1623/24–1703)
   S. Anastasia 7, 8
   S. Andrea delle Fratte 9
   S. Angelo in Pescheria 14
   Oratorio del Caravita 21

Index of Artists

S. Croce dei Lucchesi 33
Gesù e Maria 47
S. Giovanni Calabita 50
S. Giovanni in Laterano 54
S. Giovanni in Oleo 58
SS. Luca e Martina 74
S. Marcello 78
S. Maria in Campo Marzio 85
S. Maria sopra Minerva 94
S. Maria del Pianto 106
S. Maria in Vallicella 116
S. Pudenziana 139
S. Silvestro al Quirinale 146
SS. Sudario dei Piemontesi 148
Palazzo del Quirinale 193
Collegio di Propaganda Fide 247
Balducci, Giovanni (1560–1603)
    S. Prassede 139
Balestra, Antonio (1666–1740)
    S. Gregorio al Celio 62
Baratta, Andrea (active 1665–90)
    S. Agnese in Agone 4
Baratta, Francesco (d. 1666)
    Fountains in Piazza Navona 234
Baratta, Giovanni Maria (recorded 1654–66)
    S. Agnese in Agone 4
    S. Agostino 6
    S. Nicola da Tolentino 126
    Palazzo Pamphili 189
    Villa de' Rossi 214
Barattone, Luigi (early 18th century)
    S. Maria dell'Orto 102, 103
Barbalonga, Antonio (1600–49)
    S. Silvestro al Quirinale 145
Barbieri (Barberi), Pietro Andrea (recorded 1727)
    SS. Giovanni e Paolo 58
    S. Marcello 78
    S. Maria della Quercia 110
Barigioni, Filippo (1690–1753)
    S. Andrea delle Fratte 9
    S. Gregorio a Ponte Quattro Capi 63
    S. Marco 78, 79
    S. Pietro in Vaticano 136
    Palazzo Albani 158
    Fontana del Pantheon 232
Barocci, Federico (1526–1612)
    S. Maria sopra Minerva 95
    S. Maria in Vallicella 116
Barozzi, Giacinto and Jacopo, see Vignola
Bassano, Francesco (c. 1549–92)
    Il Gesù 46
    S. Luigi dei Francesi 76
Batoni, Pompeo Girolamo (1708–87)
    SS. Celso e Giuliano 29
    S. Eligio dei Ferrari 36
    Il Gesù 45
    S. Gregorio al Celio 62

S. Maria degli Angeli 80
S. Maria Maggiore 91
Battisti, Antonio de (early 17th century)
    SS. Trinità dei Pellegrini 151
    Palazzo Borghese 168
Beinaschi, Giovanni Battista (1638–88)
    S. Bonaventura al Palatino 20
    SS. Carlo e Ambrogio al Corso 26
    S. Maria del Suffragio 111
Belli, Pasquale (1752–1833)
    S. Maria della Consolazione 86
Benaglia, Paolo (first half of the 18th century)
    S. Giovanni dei Fiorentini 50
    S. Maria ad Martyres (Pantheon) 94
    Palazzo della Consulta 175
    Fontana di Trevi 240
Benefial, Marco (1684–1764)
    SS. Giovanni e Paolo 58
    S. Lorenzo in Lucina 69
    S. Maria d'Aracoeli 83
    S. Maria della Quercia 110
    Stimmate di S. Francesco 148
    SS. Trinità degli Spagnuoli 152
Bercari, Salvatore (recorded c.1743–4)
    S. Marco 79
Berettoni, Luigi (18th century)
    S. Cecilia 28
    S. Francesco di Paola 39
Bergondi, Andrea (recorded 1743–71)
    S. Agostino 6
    SS. Alessio e Bonifazio all'Aventino 7
    S. Marco 79
    SS. Nome di Maria 127
    S. Paolo Primo Eremita 129
    Fontana di Trevi 240
Bergonzoni (Borgonzoni), Padre Giovanni Battista (c.1628–92)
    S. Paolo alla Regola 129
Bernini, Gianlorenzo (1598–1680)
    S. Agnese in Agone 5
    S. Agostino 6
    S. Andrea delle Fratte 9
    S. Andrea al Quirinale 10
    S. Andrea della Valle 13
    S. Bernardino ai Monti 19
    S. Bibiana 19, 20
    S. Calisto 21
    S. Crisogono 31
    SS. Domenico e Sisto 35
    S. Francesca Romana 38
    S. Francesco a Ripa 40
    Il Gesù 45, 47
    S. Giacomo alla Lungara 49
    S. Giovanni dei Fiorentini 51, 52
    S. Isidoro 65
    S. Lorenzo in Damaso 68
    S. Lorenzo in Fonte 68
    S. Lorenzo in Lucina 69

Index of Artists

Bernini, Gianlorenzo (*contd*)
  S. Maria d'Aracoeli 82
  S. Maria Maggiore 90, 91, 92
  S. Maria ad Martyres (Pantheon) 94
  S. Maria sopra Minerva 95, 96
  S. Maria di Monserrato 97
  S. Maria di Montesanto and S. Maria dei Miracoli 98, 99
  S. Maria del Popolo 107, 108
  S. Maria in Via Lata 120, 122
  S. Maria della Vittoria 123
  S. Pietro in Montorio 130
  S. Pietro in Vaticano 132, 133, 134, 135, 136, 137, 138
  S. Prassede 139
  S. Spirito in Sassia 147
  SS. Trinità dei Pellegrini 151
  Palazzo Antamoro 160
  Palazzo Barberini 163
  Palazzo Bernini 166
  Capitoline Palaces 170
  Palazzo Chigi-Odescalchi 173
  Palazzo Doria-Pamphili 179
  Palazzo di Montecitorio 186
  Palazzo del Quirinale 191
  Palazzo di Spagna 198
  Vatican 203, 204
  Villa Borghese 211, 212
  Villa Pamphili 219
  Acqua Acetosa 229
  Fontana delle Api (Piazza Barberini) 230
  Fontana delle Api (Vatican) 230
  Barcaccia Fountain 231
  Fountains in Piazza Navona 233, 234
  Fountain in front of S. Maria in Trastevere 237
  Fontana di Trevi 238
  Fontana del Tritone 240
  Collegio di Propaganda Fide 246
  Obelisk and Elephant 250
  Piazza Navona 251
  Ponte S. Angelo 252
  Porta del Popolo 253
  Spanish Steps 255
  Ariccia, Collegiata dell'Assunta, Piazza 262, 263
  Ariccia, Santuario della Madonna, Galloro 263
  Castel Gandolfo, S. Tommaso da Villanova 263
  Castel Gandolfo, Papal Palace 264
Bernini, Pietro (1562–1629)
  S. Andrea della Valle 13
  Il Gesù 45
  S. Giovanni dei Fiorentini 51
  S. Maria Maggiore 90
  Palazzo del Quirinale 193
  Barcaccia Fountain 231

Berrettini, Luca (active 1635–79)
  SS. Luca e Martina 72, 73
  S. Marco 79
Berrettini, Pietro, see Pietro da Cortona
Berrettoni, Niccolò (1637–82)
  S. Maria di Montesanto and S. Maria dei Miracoli 99
  S. Maria del Suffragio 111
  Palazzo Altieri 160
  Frascati, Villa Falconieri 267
Bertholet, Guillaume (1570/80–1648)
  S. Maria Maggiore 93
  S. Maria in Vallicella 116
  Palazzo del Quirinale 191, 193
  Fountain in front of S. Maria Maggiore 237
Betti, Biagio (*c.* 1545–1615)
  S. Silvestro al Quirinale 146
Bianchi, Pietro (1694–1740)
  S. Maria degli Angeli 80
  S. Maria delle Grazie alle Fornaci 87
Bianchi, Tommaso (second half of the 18th century)
  Villa Chigi 213
Bianchini, Francesco (recorded 1702)
  S. Maria degli Angeli 80
Bicchierai, Antonio (active *c.* 1706–57)
  S. Lorenzo in Panisperna 70
  S. Maria degli Angeli 80
Bigot, Trophime (*c.* 1600–after *c.* 1650)
  S. Maria in Aquiro 82
Bitonto, Giovanni Maria da (recorded 1647–55)
  Palazzo Spada 197
Bizzacheri, Carlo Francesco (1656–1721)
  SS. Carlo e Ambrogio al Corso 25
  Gesù e Maria 47
  S. Isidoro 65
  S. Lorenzo in Lucina 69
  S. Luigi dei Francesi 76
  S. Marcello 78
  S. Maria Maddalena 89
  S. Maria di Montesanto and S. Maria dei Miracoli 99
  S. Pietro in Vincoli 138
  S. Salvatore in Lauro 143
  SS. Vincenzo e Anastasio 152
  Fontana dei Tritoni 241
  Monte di Pietà 249
  Frascati, Villa Aldobrandini 266
Bolgi, Andrea (1605–56)
  S. Agostino 6
  S. Antonio dei Portoghesi 16
  S. Francesco a Ripa 40
  S. Maria Maggiore 92
  S. Maria sopra Minerva 96
  S. Maria in Via Lata 122
  S. Pietro in Vaticano 133

Index of Artists

Bolini (early 17th century)
   Palazzo Borghese 168
Bolongier, Flaminio, see Boulanger, Flamen
Bonatti, Giovanni (c. 1635–81)
   S. Croce in Gerusalemme 32
   S. Maria dell'Anima 81
Bonfreni, Giovanni Battista (recorded c. 1757)
   S. Gregorio al Celio 62
Bonifazi, Ennio (recorded 1633)
   S. Maria sopra Minerva 95
Bonzi, Pietro Paolo (Il Gobbo dei Carracci) (c. 1573/84–1633/44)
   Palazzo Mattei di Giove 186
Borghesi, Giovanni Ventura (c. 1640–1708)
   S. Ivo della Sapienza 66
   S. Nicola da Tolentino 126
   Collegio di Propaganda Fide 247
Borgianni, Orazio (c. 1578–1616)
   S. Carlo alle Quattro Fontane 24
   S. Salvatore in Lauro 143
   S. Silvestro in Capite 145
Borgognone, Francesco, Giacomo and Guglielmo, see Cortese
Borgognone, Francesco Ignazio (Il Bavarese) (early 18th century)
   Frascati, Villa Falconieri 267
Borgonzoni, see Bergonzoni
Borromini (1599–1667)
   S. Agnese in Agone 3, 4, 5
   S. Anastasia 8
   S. Andrea delle Fratte 8, 9
   S. Carlo alle Quattro Fontane 23, 24
   SS. Carlo e Ambrogio al Corso 25
   S. Eustachio 37
   S. Giovanni Calabita 49
   S. Giovanni dei Fiorentini 51
   S. Giovanni in Laterano 53, 54, 55, 56, 57
   S. Giovanni in Oleo 58
   S. Girolamo della Carità 59
   S. Ignazio 63
   S. Ivo della Sapienza 66, 67, 68
   S. Lucia in Selci 75
   S. Maria Maggiore 92
   S. Maria ad Martyres (Pantheon) 94
   S. Maria sopra Minerva 95
   S. Maria dei Sette Dolori 110
   S. Maria in Vallicella and Oratory 114, 117, 118
   S. Pietro in Vaticano 133, 134, 136
   S. Sabina 142
   Palazzo Barberini 163
   Palazzo Carpegna 171
   Palazzo del Bufalo 177
   Palazzo Falconieri 180
   Palazzo Giustiniani 182
   Palazzo del Laterano 183
   Palazzo Pamphili 188
   Palazzo Spada 197
   Palazzo di Spagna 197
   Palazzo dello Spirito Santo 198
   Villa Giustiniani 215
   Fontana delle Api (Vatican) 231
   Fountains in Piazza Navona 233
   Carceri nuove 245
   Collegio Innocenziano 246
   Collegio di Propaganda Fide 246, 247
   Frascati, Villa Falconieri 267
Boselli, Orfeo (1597–after 1667)
   S. Adriano 3
   S. Ambrogio della Massima 7
   S. Carlo ai Catinari 22
   S. Maria dell'Umiltà 113
Bouchardon, Edme (1698–1762)
   Fontana di Trevi 240
Boulanger, Flamen (Bolongier, Flaminio) (second half of the 16th century)
   S. Maria d'Aracoeli 82
Bracci, Pietro (1700–73)
   S. Agostino 6
   S. Andrea delle Fratte 9
   S. Antonio dei Portoghesi 16
   S. Caterina da Siena a Magnanapoli 27
   S. Crisogono 31
   S. Giovanni dei Fiorentini 50
   S. Giovanni in Laterano 53
   SS. Giovanni e Paolo 58
   S. Girolamo della Carità 60
   S. Ignazio 64
   S. Marcello 78
   S. Maria degli Angeli 81
   S. Maria Maggiore 90
   S. Maria sopra Minerva 95
   S. Pietro in Vaticano 135, 136
   Stimmate di S. Francesco 148
   Fontana di Trevi 240
Bramante, Donato (1444–1514)
   S. Biagio della Pagnotta 19
   SS. Celso e Giuliano 28
   SS. Faustino e Giovita 37
   S. Maria della Pace 103
   S. Maria del Popolo 107
   S. Pietro in Montorio 129
   S. Pietro in Vaticano 130
   Vatican 203
Brandi, Giacinto (1621–91)
   S. Agostino 6
   S. Andrea al Quirinale 10
   S. Carlo ai Catinari 21
   SS. Carlo e Ambrogio al Corso 26
   S. Francesca Romana 38
   Gesù e Maria 47
   S. Margherita in Trastevere 79
   S. Maria del Suffragio 111
   S. Maria in Trastevere 112
   S. Maria in Via Lata 122

Brandi, Giacinto (*contd*)
   S. Rocco 141
   S. Silvestro in Capite 145
   Stimmate di S. Francesco 148
   Palazzo Pamphili 189
Brandini, Tommaso (active 1716–c. 1745)
   S. Croce in Gerusalemme 32
Breccioli, Bartolomeo (d. 1637)
   S. Giuseppe a Capo le Case 61
   S. Maria della Scala 110
   SS. Trinità dei Monti 150
   Palazzo Ruspoli 194
Breccioli, Filippo (d. 1627)
   S. Maria in Aquiro 82
Brefort, Adam Claude ('Adamo Lorenese')
   (mid-17th century)
   S. Pudenziana 140
Bresciano, Prospero, see Antichi, Prospero
Breton, Luc-François (1731–1800)
   SS. Claudio e Andrea de' Borgognoni 30
Bricci, Basilio (active mid 17th century)
   Villa Benedetti 210
Bricci, Plautilla (active mid 17th century)
   Villa Benedetti 210
Bril, Paul (1554–1626)
   S. Cecilia 28
   S. Maria Maggiore 91
   S. Vitale 153
   Palazzo Rospigliosi-Pallavicini 194
   Vatican 204
   Villa Ludovisi 215
Brughi, G. B. (c. 1660–1730)
   S. Angelo in Pescheria 14
Brunetti, Francesco (recorded c. 1690)
   S. Giacomo degli Incurabili 48
Bucci, Michele (late 17th century)
   S. Dorotea 36
Bufalini, Francesco (active 1670–94)
   S. Maria delle Grazie alle Fornaci 87
Buonarroti, Michelangelo the Younger (1568–1646)
   Palazzo Barberini 163
Buonvicino, Ambrogio (c. 1552–1622)
   S. Andrea della Valle 13
   S. Maria Maggiore 93
   S. Maria sopra Minerva 94
   S. Pietro in Vaticano 132
Buratti, Carlo (active c. 1702–32)
   Bambino Gesù 17
   SS. Luca e Martina 74
Busiri Vici, Andrea (1817–after 1896)
   Palazzo Doria-Pamphili 179
Buzzi, Carlo (d.1658)
   Gesù e Maria 47
Buzzi (Buzio), Ippolito (d. 1634)
   S. Maria Maggiore 93
   S. Maria sopra Minerva 95

Caccianiga, Francesco (1700–81)
   SS. Celso e Giuliano 29
Cades, Giuseppe (1750–99)
   S. Antonio dei Portoghesi 16
   SS. Apostoli 17
   S. Nicola da Tolentino 126
Cafà, Melchiorre (1635–67)
   S. Agnese in Agone 5
   S. Agostino 6
   S. Caterina da Siena a Magnanapoli 27
   S. Maria in Campitelli 84
Calandra, Giovanni Battista (1586–1644)
   S. Lorenzo fuori le Mura 70
   S. Maria sopra Minerva 96
Calandrucci, Giacinto (1645–1706/7)
   S. Antonio dei Portoghesi 15
   S. Bonaventura al Palatino 20
   S. Maria dell'Orto 102
   S. Maria del Suffragio 111
   S. Maria in Traspontina 112
   S. Paolo alla Regola 129
   Frascati, Villa Falconieri 267
   Frascati, Villa Sora Buoncompagni 268
Calcagni, Giuseppe (recorded 1602)
   S. Andrea della Valle 14
Calcagni, Tiberio (1532–65)
   S. Giuseppe dei Falegnami 61
   S. Maria Maggiore 93
Camassei, Andrea (1602–49)
   S. Egidio 36
   S. Giovanni in Laterano 57
   S. Maria della Concezione 86
   S. Sebastiano al Palatino 144
   Palazzo Barberini 165
   Palazzo Pamphili 189
Camassei, Giacinto (active c. 1670–after 1679)
   Palazzo Barberini 165
Cametti, Bernardino (1682–1736)
   Il Gesù 46
   S. Giovanni Calabita 50
   S. Giovanni in Laterano 55
   S. Marcello 78
   S. Maria ad Martyres 94
   S. Pietro in Vaticano 135
   Monte di Pietà 249
   Frascati, Cathedral 265
Campi, Pietro Paolo (active 1702–35)
   S. Agnese in Agone 5
   S. Salvatore in Lauro 143
Camporese, Pietro the Elder (1726–81)
   S. Brigida 20
   S. Maria in Aquiro 82
   Villa Chigi 213
Camporese, Pietro the Younger (1792–1873)
   S. Giacomo degli Incurabili 48, 147
Camuccini, Vincenzo (1771–1844)
   S. Girolamo della Carità 59

Canevari, Antonio (1681–c. 1751)
  S. Eustachio 37
  SS. Giovanni e Paolo 58
  Stimmate di S. Francesco 148
  Villa degli Arcadi 209
Canini, Giovanni Angelo (c. 1617–66)
  S. Francesca Romana 38
  S. Giovanni dei Fiorentini 52
  S. Marco 79
  S. Maria Maggiore 94
  S. Martino ai Monti 124
  Palazzo del Quirinale 193
  Vatican 203
Canini, Marc Antonio (early 17th century)
  SS. Domenico e Sisto 35
Canova, Antonio (1757–1822)
  SS. Apostoli 17
  Gesù 46
  S. Pietro in Vaticano 135, 136
Canuti, Domenico Maria (1626–84)
  SS. Domenico e Sisto 35
  Palazzo Altieri 160
Caporale, Francesco (recorded 1608–11)
  S. Maria Maggiore 90, 91
Carapecchia, Romano (active 1711–41)
  S. Giovanni Calabita 49
Caravaggio, Michelangelo Merisi, called (1571–1610)
  S. Agostino 6
  S. Anna dei Palafrenieri 15
  S. Luigi dei Francesi 76
  S. Maria del Popolo 108
  S. Maria della Scala 110
  S. Maria in Vallicella 115
  See also Merigi
Carcani, Filippo (recorded 1677–86)
  S. Giovanni in Laterano 55, 56
  Madonna delle Grazie 77
  S. Marco 79
  S. Maria Maggiore 94
  S. Maria di Montesanto and S. Maria dei Miracoli 99
Cardi, Ludovico, see Cigoli, Il
Carlone, Andrea (1639–97)
  Il Gesù 45
  Palazzo Altieri 160
Carnevale (recorded 1722)
  SS. Cosma e Damiano (via dei Barbieri)
Caroselli, Angelo (1585–1652)
  S. Francesca Romana 38
  S. Pietro in Vaticano 135
Carosi, G. A. (c. 1600–after 1659)
  S. Rocco 141
Carracci, Agostino (1557–1602)
  Palazzo Farnese 181
Carracci, Annibale (1560–1609)
  S. Caterina dei Funari 26
  S. Gregorio al Celio 62
  S. Maria di Monserrato 97
  S. Maria del Popolo 108
  S. Onofrio 127
  Palazzo Farnese 181
  Grottaferrata, Abbey 270
Carracci, Antonio (d. 1618)
  S. Bartolomeo all'Isola 18
  S. Maria in Monticelli 100
Cartari, Giulio (recorded 1665–78)
  S. Isidoro 65
  Ponte S. Angelo 253
Casali, Andrea (1720/24–after 1778)
  S. Gregorio a Ponte Quattro Cappi 63
  S. Lorenzo in Damaso 68
  SS. Trinità degli Spagnuoli 152
Casolani, Cristofano (early 17th century)
  S. Maria dei Monti 100
  S. Stefano del Cacco 148
Casolano, Giovanni (early 17th century)
  S. Pietro in Vaticano 134
Casone, Felice Antonio (1559–1634)
  S. Isidoro 65
  S. Lucia in Selci 75
  S. Marcello 78
  S. Maria della Concezione 85
Cassani, Alessandro (recorded 1677–9)
  S. Maria di Montesanto and S. Maria dei Miracoli 99
Cassignola (Cottignola), Giovanni Battista (second half of the 16th century)
  S. Agostino 6
  S. Maria sopra Minerva 95
Castellamonte, Carlo di (1560–1641)
  SS. Sudario dei Piemontesi 148
Castello, Bernardo (painter) (1557–1629)
  S. Maria sopra Minerva 96
Castello, Bernardo (architect) (1643–1709)
  S. Carlo alle Quattro Fontane 24
  S. Sabina 142
Castello, Domenico (active 1619–58)
  S. Anastasia 7
  SS. Cosma e Damiano (via dei Fori Imperiali) 30
  S. Francesco di Paola 39
  S. Giacomo alla Lungara 49
  S. Girolamo della Carità 59
  S. Isidoro 65
  S. Lorenzo in Fonte 68
  S. Lucia del Gonfalone 74
Catapani, Filippo (recorded c. 1735)
  Palazzo Doria-Pamphili 179
Caterinazzo (of Subiaco) (recorded 1652)
  S. Maria in Via Lata 121
Cati, Pasquale (c. 1550–c. 1620)
  S. Lorenzo in Panisperna 71
  S. Maria in Trastevere 112
Cavallini, Francesco (late 17th century)
  SS. Carlo e Ambrogio al Corso 26

Index of Artists

Cavallini, Francesco (*contd*)
  Gesù e Maria 47
  S. Marcello 78
  S. Maria del Popolo 107
  S. Maria dell'Umiltà 113
Celio, Gaspare (1571–1640)
  S. Carlo ai Catinari 22
  S. Francesco a Ripa 40
  Il Gesù 45
  Palazzo Mattei di Giove 185
Censore, Orazio (active 1569–1622)
  SS. Trinità dei Pellegrini 151
Cerrini, Giovanni Domenico (1609–81)
  S. Agata dei Goti 3
  S. Carlo ai Catinari 21
  S. Carlo alle Quattro Fontane 24
  S. Francesca Romana 38
  S. Isidoro 65
  S. Maria in Traspontina 111
  S. Maria in Vallicella 115
  S. Maria della Vittoria 122
Cerruti, Francesco (recorded *c.* 1747)
  S. Ignazio 64
Cerruti, Michelangelo (1666–1748)
  S. Anastasia 7
  S. Maria Maddalena 89
  S. Maria dell'Umiltà 113
  S. Pietro in Montorio 130
Cesari d'Arpino, see Arpino, Cavaliere Giuseppe Cesari d'
Cesi, Carlo (1626–86)
  S. Maria Maggiore 94
  S. Maria della Pace 106
  Palazzo del Quirinale 193
  Collegio di Propaganda Fide 247
Challe, Simon (1719–65)
  S. Luigi dei Francesi 76
Champaigne, Jean de (recorded 1676–9)
  SS. Trinità dei Monti 150
Chènevière, Jean de (recorded 1518–24)
  S. Luigi dei Francesi 75
Chiari, Fabrizio (*c.* 1615–95)
  S. Anastasia 8
  S. Marco 79
  S. Martino ai Monti 124
  Palazzo Altieri 160
Chiari, Giuseppe (1654–1727)
  S. Andrea al Quirinale 11
  SS. Apostoli 17
  SS. Carlo e Ambrogio al Corso 26
  S. Clemente 30
  S. Francesco di Paola 39
  S. Francesco a Ripa 40
  S. Giovanni in Laterano 54
  S. Ignazio 64
  S. Maria delle Grazie alle Fornaci 87
  S. Maria di Montesanto and S. Maria dei Miracoli 99

  S. Maria del Suffragio 111
  S. Silvestro in Capite 145
  Palazzo del Quirinale 193
Chiari, Tommaso (1665–1733)
  S. Clemente 30
Ciampelli, Agostino (before 1577–1642)
  S. Bibiana 19
  Il Gesù 45
  S. Giovanni dei Fiorentini 51, 52
  S. Giovanni in Laterano 56
  S. Prassede 139
  S. Vitale 153
  Frascati, Villa Grazioli 267
Ciardi, Sebastiano (*c.* 1602–after 1673)
  Ariccia, Palazzo Chigi 262
Ciarpi, Baccio (1578–1644)
  S. Giovanni dei Fiorentini 52
  S. Lucia in Selci 75
  S. Maria della Concezione 86
  S. Silvestro in Capite 145
Cignani, Carlo (1628–1719)
  S. Andrea della Valle 13
Cigoli, Il, Ludovico Cardi (1559–1613)
  S. Giovanni dei Fiorentini 51
  S. Maria Maggiore 93
  Palazzo Madama 183
  Palazzo Rospigliosi-Pallavicini 194
  Frascati, Villa Arrigoni-Muti 266
Ciolli, Giacomo (d. 1734)
  S. Paolo alla Regola 129
Cippitelli, Michele (active *c.* 1700)
  S. Pudenziana 139
Cipriani, Sebastiano (active 1696–1736)
  SS. Apostoli 17
  S. Maria in Campitelli 84
Circignani, Antonio, called Il Pomarancio (recorded 1623–44)
  S. Maria della Consolazione 86
  S. Maria in Traspontina 111
  S. Maria in Via (Largo Chigi) 119
  Palazzo Mattei di Giove 186
Circignani, Niccolò (Il Pomarancio) (?1517–after 1596)
  Oratorio del SS. Crocifisso 33
  Il Gesù 46, 47
  SS. Giovanni e Paolo 58
  S. Maria di Loreto 88
  SS. Nereo e Achilleo 125
  S. Pietro in Montorio 130
  S. Pudenziana 139
Clérisseau, Charles-Louis (1722–1820)
  SS. Trinità dei Monti 151
Cobaert, Jacob Cornelisz. (d. between 1609 and 1621)
  SS. Trinità dei Pellegrini 151
Coccetti, Liborio (recorded 1796)
  S. Maria della Concezione 85

Index of Artists

Coli, Giovanni (1636–81)
   S. Croce dei Lucchesi 33
   S. Nicola da Tolentino 126
   Palazzo Colonna 174
Colombo, Bartolomeo (active 1657–72)
   S. Giuseppe dei Falegnami 61
   Palazzo del Quirinale 193
Colonna, Angelo Michele (1600–87)
   Palazzo Spada 197
Commodi, Andrea (1560–1638)
   S. Carlo ai Catinari 21
   S. Vitale 153
Conca, Giovanni (active 1706–54)
   S. Maria della Luce 88
Conca, Sebastiano (1680–1764)
   S. Agostino 6
   Oratorio del Caravita 21
   S. Cecilia 28
   S. Clemente 30
   S. Lorenzo in Damaso 68
   SS. Luca e Martina 74
   S. Maria in Campitelli 83
   S. Maria in Campo Marzio 85
   S. Maria della Luce 88
   S. Maria Maddalena 89
   Palazzo de Carolis 177
Conca, Tommaso Maria (d. 1815)
   S. Caterina da Siena (via Giulia) 27
   SS. Giovanni e Paolo 58
   Palazzo Doria-Pamphili 179
Consalvi, V. (recorded 1742)
   S. Maria Maddalena 89
Contini, Francesco (active c. 1648–59)
   SS. Carlo e Ambrogio al Corso 25
   Palazzo Barberini alla Giubbonara 166
   Villa Barberini 210
Contini, G. B. (1641–1723)
   S. Agostino 6
   SS. Alessio e Bonifazio all'Aventino 7
   SS. Claudio e Andrea de' Borgognoni 30
   S. Ivo della Sapienza 66
   Madonna delle Grazie 77
   S. Maria d'Aracoeli 82
   S. Maria in Campitelli 84
   S. Maria di Monserrato 96
   S. Maria dei Sette Dolori 110
   S. Maria del Suffragio 111
   S. Maria della Visitazione 122
   S. Maria della Vittoria 123
   S. Sabina 142
   Stimmate di S. Francesco 148
   SS. Trinità dei Pellegrini 151
Corbelli, Giovanni (d. c. 1695)
   S. Francesco a Ripa 40
Corbellini, Sebastiano (late 17th century)
   S. Agnese in Piazza Navona 5
Cordier, Nicolas (1567–1612)
   S. Andrea della Valle 13
   S. Giovanni in Laterano 55
   S. Gregorio al Celio 63
   S. Maria Maggiore 93
   S. Maria sopra Minerva 95
Cornacchini, Agostino (1685–after 1754)
   SS. Carlo e Ambrogio al Corso 26
   S. Giovanni in Laterano 56
   S. Pietro in Vaticano 132, 133
   Monte di Pietà 249
Cornaro, G. (recorded 1734–5)
   S. Giovanni dei Fiorentini 50
Corsini, Agostino (1688–1772)
   S. Cecilia 28
   S. Croce in Gerusalemme 32
   S. Francesco di Paola 39
   S. Maria della Vittoria 123
   Fontana di Trevi 240
Cortese (Courtois), Francesco (second half of the 17th century)
   S. Andrea delle Fratte 10
Cortese (Courtois), Giacomo, called Il Borgognone (1621–75)
   Il Gesù (Casa Professa) 47
   S. Ignazio 64
   Palazzo del Quirinale 193
Cortese (Courtois), Guglielmo, called Il Borgognone (1628–79)
   S. Andrea delle Fratte 9
   S. Andrea al Quirinale 10
   Il Gesù 43, 47
   S. Giovanni in Laterano 56
   S. Marco 79
   S. Paolo Primo Eremita 128
   S. Prassede 139
   SS. Trinità dei Pellegrini 151
   Palazzo del Quirinale 193
   Ariccia, Collegiata dell'Assunta 263
   Castel Gandolfo, S. Tommaso da Villanova 264
Cortona see Pietro (Berrettini) da Cortona
Cortosi (recorded 1758)
   SS. Trinità degli Spagnuoli 152
Corvara, Cesare (active 1650–1708)
   S. Antonio dei Portoghesi 15
   S. Eustachio 37
Corvi, Domenico (1721–1803)
   S. Caterina da Siena (via Giulia) 27
   S. Marcello 78
Costantini, Ermengildo (active 1764–91)
   S. Stanislao dei Polacchi 147
Costanzi, Placido (c. 1690–1759)
   S. Apollinare 16
   SS. Claudio e Andrea de' Borgognoni 30
   S. Giovanni in Laterano 55
   S. Gregorio al Celio 62
   Madonna del Divino Amore 77
   S. Maria degli Angeli 80
   S. Maria in Campo Marzio 85

Constanzi, Placido (*contd*)
   S. Maria Maddalena 89
   S. Pietro in Vaticano 135
Costanzi, Simone (recorded 1698–1702)
   S. Carlo ai Catinari 21
Cottignola, G. B., see Cassignola, Giovanni Battista
Courtois, see Cortese
Cousin, Louis, see Gentile, Luigi
Cozza, Francesco (1605–82)
   S. Ambrogio della Massima 7
   S. Andrea delle Fratte 9, 10
   S. Francesco di Paola 39
   S. Maria ad Martyres (Pantheon) 94
   S. Maria della Pace 106
   S. Rocco 141
   Palazzo Altieri 160
   Collegio Innocenziano 246
Crecolini, Giovanni Antonio (1675–*c.* 1736)
   S. Clemente 30
   SS. Cosma e Damiano (via dei Barbieri) 31
   S. Francesco di Paola 39
   S. Lorenzo in Lucina 69
Crescenzi, Giovanni Battista (1577–1660)
   Palazzo Crescenzi 177
Cresti, Domenico (Il Passignano) (*c.* 1560–1636)
   S. Andrea della Valle 13
   S. Giovanni dei Fiorentini 51
   S. Maria Maggiore 93
   S. Maria della Pace 106
   S. Maria in Vallicella 116
   S. Prisca 139
   Palazzo Rospigliosi-Pallavicini 194
   Frascati, Villa Arrigoni-Muti 266
Croce, Baldassare (*c.* 1558–1628)
   Il Gesù 45
   S. Giovanni della Pigna 58
   S. Maria dei Monti 100
   S. Prassede 139
   S. Susanna 149
   SS. Trinità dei Pellegrini 151
   Vatican 204
Czechowiecz, S. (1689–1775)
   S. Stanislao dei Polacchi 147

Daniele (Ricciarelli) da Volterra (1509–66)
   S. Luigi dei Francesi 76
   S. Marcello 78
   S. Pietro in Montorio 130
   SS. Trinità dei Monti 150, 151
   Vatican 204
Daria, Simone (recorded 1600–07)
   S. Pietro in Vaticano 134
David, Marco (recorded 1758–63)
   S. Lucia del Gonfalone 74
   SS. Trinità degli Spagnuoli 152

Delaborde, Jean (recorded 1669–83)
   S. Andrea al Quirinale 11
Delattre, Pierre (1606–83)
   S. Ignazio 64
Del Barba, Genesio (1691–1736)
   Palazzo Doria-Pamphili 179
Del Colle, G. P. di Francesco di Michelangelo (recorded 1551)
   S. Marcello 78
Del Conte, Jacopino (1510–98)
   S. Giovanni Decollato 50
Del Duca, Giacomo (*c.* 1520–1604)
   S. Giovanni in Laterano 56
   S. Maria d'Aracoeli 82
   S. Maria di Loreto 88
   S. Maria in Trivio 113
   Capitoline Palaces 170
   Palazzo Cornaro 175, 176
   Palazzo del Bufalo 177
   Palazzo dei Piceni 190
   Villa Farnese 214
   Villa Mattei 217
   Porta S. Giovanni 253
Del Duca, Ludovico (active 1551–92)
   S. Giovanni in Laterano 56
Del Grande, Antonio (active 1652–71)
   S. Giuseppe dei Falegnami 61
   S. Maria dei Sette Dolori 110
   Palazzo Colonna 174
   Palazzo Doria-Pamphili 179
   Palazzo di Spagna 198
   Carceri nuove 245
   Marino, S. Barnaba 270
Del Sole, Giovanni Giuseppe (1654–1719)
   SS. Giovanni e Petronio dei Bolognesi 59
Del Vaga, Perino (1501–47)
   S. Marcello 78
   S. Stefano del Cacco 148
   SS. Trinità dei Monti 151
   Palazzo della Cancelleria 169
   Vatican 204
Della Cornia, Antonio (recorded 1634)
   S. Francesco a Ripa 40
   S. Maria dell'Umiltà 113
Della Cornia, Fabio (*c.* 1600–43)
   S. Caterina di Siena a Magnanapoli 28
Della Greca, Felice (*c.* 1626–77)
   SS. Angeli Custodi 14
   S. Rita da Cascia 140
   Palazzo Aldobrandini-Chigi 159
   Palazzo Chigi-Odescalchi 173
Della Greca, Vincenzo (active 1616–after 1650)
   S. Caio 20
   SS. Domenico e Sisto 35
Della Porta, Giacomo (1532/3–1602)
   S. Andrea della Valle 12
   S. Atanasio dei Greci 17
   S. Caterina dei Funari 26

Index of Artists

S. Cesareo 29
Oratorio del SS. Crocifisso 33
SS. Domenico e Sisto 33, 35
Il Gesù 41, 43, 45
S. Giovanni dei Fiorentini 50
S. Giovanni in Laterano 55, 56
S. Ivo della Sapienza 66
S. Luigi dei Francesi 75
S. Maria della Consolazione 86
S. Maria Maggiore 93
S. Maria sopra Minerva 95
S. Maria di Montesanto and S. Maria dei Miracoli 98
S. Maria dei Monti 100
S. Maria in Via (Largo Chigi) 119
S. Nicola in Carcere 125
S. Paolo alle Tre Fontane 129
S. Pietro in Vaticano 132
SS. Trinità dei Monti 150
Palazzo Albani 158
Palazzo Albertoni 158
Palazzo Aldobrandini-Chigi 159
Capitoline Palaces 170
Palazzo Capizucchi 170
Palazzo Cornaro 175
Palazzo Fani 180
Palazzo Farnese 180
Palazzo Grazioli 182
Palazzo Lovatelli 183
Palazzo Maffei 183
Palazzo Muti Bussi all'Aracoeli 187
Palazzo Patrizi 189
Palazzo Ruggeri 194
Palazzo Serlupi Crescenzi 196
Vatican 204
Fountain of the Madonna dei Monti 232
Fontana del Pantheon 232
Fountain in Piazza d'Aracoeli 232
Fountain in Piazza Campitelli 233
Fountain in Piazza Colonna 233
Fountain in Piazza Giudea 233
Fountains in Piazza Navona 233
Fountain in Piazza del Popolo 234
Fontana delle Tartarughe 238
La Terrina 238
Collegio Romano 248
Frascati, Villa Aldobrandini 266
Della Porta, Giovanni Battista (c. 1542–97)
S. Pudenziana 140
Acqua Felice 229
Della Porta, Guglielmo (d. 1577)
S. Pietro in Vaticano 135
S. Silvestro al Quirinale 145
Palazzo Farnese 180
Della Porta, Teodoro (1567–1638)
S. Giovanni in Laterano 56
Della Porta, Tommaso (c. 1520–67)
S. Maria sopra Minerva 95

Della Riviera, Egidio, see van der Vliet, Gillis
Della Valle, Filippo (1697–1768)
S. Antonio dei Portoghesi 16
SS. Apostoli 17
Il Gesù 46
S. Giovanni dei Fiorentini 50, 52
S. Giovanni in Laterano 53, 56
S. Ignazio 64
SS. Luca e Martina 73
S. Luigi dei Francesi 76
S. Maria Maggiore 89
S. Maria della Scala 110
S. Maria in Trastevere 112
S. Pietro in Vaticano 134
Palazzo della Consulta 175
Fontana di Trevi 240
Collegio Inglese 246
Dérizet, Antoine (1697–1768)
SS. Claudio e Andrea de' Borgognoni 30
S. Luigi dei Francesi 76
SS. Nome di Maria 127
De' Rossi, see Rossi
Dini, Lorenzo (recorded 1666)
S. Carlo alle Quattro Fontana 24
Diol, Giacomo (c. 1690–1759)
S. Paolo alla Regola 129
Domenichino (Domenico Zampieri) (1581–1641)
S. Andrea della Valle 11, 12
S. Carlo ai Catinari 21
SS. Giovanni e Petronio dei Bolognesi 59
S. Girolamo della Carità 59
S. Gregorio al Celio 63
S. Ignazio 63
S. Lorenzo in Miranda 69
S. Luigi dei Francesi 76
S. Maria degli Angeli 80
S. Maria della Concezione 86
S. Maria in Trastevere 112
S. Maria della Vittoria 122
S. Onofrio 127
S. Pietro in Vaticano 134, 135
S. Pietro in Vincoli 138
S. Silvestro al Quirinale 146
Palazzo Costaguti 177
Palazzo Farnese 181
Palazzo Lancellotti 182
Palazzo Mattei di Giove 186
Villa Ludovisi 215
Frascati, Villa Aldobrandini 266
Grottaferrata, Abbey 270
Dominicis, Carlo de (active 1716–70)
S. Agata dei Goti 3
S. Bartolomeo e Alessandro dei Bergamaschi 18
SS. Celso e Giuliano 28
S. Eligio dei Sellari 36
S. Salvatore delle Coppelle 142

Index of Artists

Dono, Giovanni Cesare (late 17th century)
  S. Carlo alle Quattro Fontane 24
Dorbay, François (1634–97)
  Spanish Steps 255
Dori, Alessandro (active c. 1732–71)
  S. Maria dell'Umiltà 113
  Palazzo Rondinini 193
Dosio, Giovanni Antonio (1533–after 1609)
  S. Lorenzo in Damaso 68
  S. Silvestro al Quirinale 145
Dughet, Gaspard (1615–75)
  S. Martino ai Monti 124
  Palazzo Borghese 168
  Palazzo Colonna 174
  Palazzo Doria-Pamphili 179
  Palazzo Fani 180
  Palazzo Muti Bussi all'Aracoeli 187
  Palazzo Pamphili 189
  Palazzo del Quirinale 193
du Jardin, François (Francesco Giardini) (active 1625–61)
  S. Nicola dei Lorenesi 125
Duqesnoy, François (1597–1643)
  S. Ambrogio della Massima 7
  S. Giovanni Decollato 50
  S. Lorenzo fuori le Mura 70
  S. Maria dell'Anima 81
  S. Maria di Loreto 88
  S. Onofrio 127
  S. Pietro in Vaticano 133
Durante, Annibale (active 1601–21)
  Frascati, Villa Mondragone 268

Elia, Alessio d' (recorded 1764–70)
  S. Andrea della Valle 13
Evangelisti, Filippo (1684–1761)
  SS. Marcellino e Pietro 77
  S. Maria d'Aracoeli 83
  S. Maria della Quercia 110

Fancelli, Cosimo (1620–88)
  S. Andrea della Valle 12
  SS. Carlo e Ambrogio al Corso 26
  Il Gesù 46
  S. Giacomo degli Incurabili 48
  S. Giovanni in Laterano 57
  S. Girolamo della Carità 59
  SS. Luca e Martina 74
  S. Marco 79
  S. Maria Maggiore 90
  S. Maria sopra Minerva 95
  S. Maria di Montesanto and S. Maria dei Miracoli 98
  S. Maria della Pace 104, 106
  S. Maria in Vallicella 115
  S. Maria in Via Lata 121, 122
  S. Nicola da Tolentino 126, 127
  Palazzo Borghese 167
  Collegio di Propaganda Fide 247
Fancelli, Giacomo Antonio (1619–71)
  S. Bernardo alle Terme 19
  SS. Carlo e Ambrogio al Corso 26
  Il Gesù 46
  S. Maria sopra Minerva 96
  Fountains in Piazza Navona 234
Fanzago, Cosimo (1591–1678)
  S. Agostino 6
  SS. Annunziata a Tor de'Specchi 15
  S. Girolamo della Carità 59
  S. Giuliano dei Fiamminghi 60
  S. Isidoro 65
  S. Lorenzo in Lucina 69
  S. Maria in Traspontina 111
  S. Maria in Via Lata 120
  Spirito Santo dei Napoletani 146
  SS. Trinità dei Pellegrini 151
Fedeli da Fossombrone, Tommaso (recorded 1627–9)
  S. Andrea della Valle 14
Felici, Vincenzo (recorded 1667–after 1701)
  S. Maria in Traspontina 111
  S. Maria in Trastevere 112
  S. Maria dell'Umiltà 113
  S. Silvestro in Capite 145
  Frascati, Cathedral 265
Fernandi, Francesco (called Imperiali) (active 1722–37)
  S. Eustachio 37
  S. Gregorio al Celio 62
Ferrabosco, G. B. (mid 17th century)
  S. Nicola da Tolentino 126
Ferrabosco, Martino (active c. 1616–23)
  S. Pietro in Vaticano (Piazza) 137
  Palazzo del Quirinale 193
Ferrari, Francesco (active 1721–44)
  S. Agata dei Goti 3
  S. Gregorio al Celio 62
  S. Ildefonso 65
  S. Marcello 78
  S. Prassede 139
  SS. Sergio e Bacco 144
  S. Stanislao dei Polacchi 147
Ferrata, Ercole (1610–86)
  S. Agnese in Agone 5
  S. Agostino 6
  S. Anastasia 8
  S. Andrea della Valle 12
  S. Francesca Romana 38
  S. Francesco a Ripa 40
  Gesù e Maria 47
  S. Giovanni dei Fiorentini 51
  S. Girolamo della Carità 59
  S. Maria dell'Anima 81
  S. Maria in Campitelli 84
  S. Maria Maggiore 90
  S. Maria sopra Minerva 95

Index of Artists

S. Maria di Montesanto and S. Maria dei Miracoli 98
S. Maria della Pace 106
S. Maria del Popolo 107
S. Maria in Vallicella and Oratory 115, 119
S. Nicola da Tolentino 126
S. Pietro in Vaticano 135
Vatican 203
Obelisk and Elephant 250
Ponte S. Angelo 253
Marino, S. Barnaba 270
Ferreri, Antonio (recorded c. 1632)
   S. Maria della Consolazione 86
Ferreri, Girolamo (recorded c. 1657–61)
   S. Giovanni in Laterano 53
Ferrerio, Domenico (d. 1630)
   SS. Alessio e Bonifazio all'Aventino 7
Ferri, Ciro (1634(?)–89)
   S. Agnese in Agone 5
   SS. Carlo e Ambrogio al Corso 26
   S. Giovanni dei Fiorentini 51
   S. Giovanni in Laterano 57
   SS. Luca e Martina 73, 74
   S. Maria sopra Minerva 94
   S. Maria dell'Orazione e della Morte 102
   S. Maria in Vallicella 116
   S. Nicola da Tolentino 126
   S. Pietro in Vaticano 134, 136
   S. Prassede 139
   S. Sebastiano fuori le Mura 143
   Palazzo Borghese 168
   Palazzo Muti Papazzuri (Piazza della Pilotta) 188
   Palazzo del Quirinale 193
   Frascati, Villa Falconieri 267
Ferroni, Giuseppe (active in the 1760s)
   SS. Vincenzo e Anastasio 152
Ferrucci, Pompeo (c. 1566–1637)
   SS. Luca e Martina 74
   S. Maria di Loreto 88
   S. Maria Maggiore 93
   S. Maria della Vittoria 123
   SS. Trinità dei Pellegrini 151
   Palazzo del Quirinale 191
Ferruzzi, F. (recorded 1718)
   S. Maria Maddalena 89
Fiammeri, Giovanni Battista (after 1530–1606)
   S. Vitale 153
Finelli, Giuliano (1601–57)
   S. Agostino 6
   S. Bibiana 19
   S. Caterina da Siena a Magnanapoli 27
   S. Giovanni in Laterano 56
   S. Isidoro 65
   S. Maria dell'Anima 81
   S. Maria di Loreto 88
   S. Maria Maggiore 92
   S. Maria sopra Minerva 96

S. Maria del Popolo 108
S. Maria in Via Lata 122
S. Silvestro al Quirinale 146
Palazzo Sacchetti 194
Fiori, Francesco (recorded 1774–80)
   SS. Gioacchino e Anna (via in Selci) 49
Fioriti, Bernardo (second half of the 17th century)
   SS. Luca e Martina 74
   S. Maria degli Angeli 80
Fontana, Antonio (second half of the 17th century)
   S. Maria di Montesanto and S. Maria dei Miracoli 98
   S. Maria in Vallicella 115
Fontana, Carlo (1638–1714)
   S. Andrea della Valle 12, 13
   SS. Apostoli 17
   S. Carlo ai Catinari 22
   S. Egidio 36
   SS. Faustino e Giovita 37
   S. Francesco a Ripa 39
   Il Gesù 46
   S. Giovanni in Laterano 54
   SS. Luca e Martina 74
   Madonna delle Grazie 77
   SS. Marcellino e Pietro 77
   S. Marcello 77
   S. Margherita in Trastevere 79
   S. Maria Maddalena 89
   S. Maria di Montesanto and S. Maria dei Miracoli 98, 99
   S. Maria del Popolo 107
   S. Maria in Traspontina 111
   S. Maria in Trastevere 112
   S. Maria dell'Umiltà 113
   S. Maria in Vallicella 115
   S. Marta 123
   S. Pietro in Vaticano 133, 134, 136, 138
   S. Rita da Cascia 140
   S. Sebastiano fuori le Mura 143
   Spirito Santo dei Napoletani 146
   S. Teodoro al Palatino 150
   Palazzo Altieri 160
   Palazzo Massimi di Rignano 184
   Palazzo di Montecitorio 186
   Acqua Paola 230
   Fountain in front of S. Maria in Trastevere 237
   Biblioteca Casanatense 245
   Dogana di Terra 248
   Granary of Clement XI 248
   Ospizio di S. Michele 251
Fontana, Carlo Stefano (active c. 1700–19)
   S. Clemente 30
   S. Eusebio 37
   S. Giuseppe a Capo le Case 61

Index of Artists

Fontana, Domenico (1543–1607)
  S. Giovanni in Laterano 53, 57
  S. Luigi dei Francesi 75
  S. Maria Maggiore 91, 92
  S. Maria di Montesanto and S. Maria dei Miracoli 98, 99
  S. Pietro in Vaticano (Piazza) 137
  S. Sabina 142
  S. Silvestro al Quirinale 145
  S. Susanna 148, 49
  SS. Trinità dei Monti 150
  Palazzo Albani 158
  Palazzo della Cancelleria 169
  Palazzo del Laterano 183
  Palazzo del Quirinale 191
  Vatican 203
  Villa Peretti 220
  Acqua Felice 229
  Fountain of the Lateran 232
  Quattro Fontane 235
  Fountain of the Quirinal 236
Fontana, Francesco Antonio (1668–1708)
  SS. Apostoli 17
  S. Carlo alle Quattro Fontane 24
  S. Maria di Montesanto and S. Maria dei Miracoli 98
  S. Maria della Neve 100
  S. Pietro in Vincoli 138
  Vatican 203
Fontana, Giovanni (1540–1614)
  S. Angelo in Pescheria 14
  S. Girolamo degli Schiavoni 60
  Palazzo Giustiniani 182
  Palazzo Patrizi 189
  Acqua Felice 229
  Acqua Paola 229
  Fontana di Ponte Sisto 234
  Frascati, Villa Aldobrandini 266
  Frascati, Villa Mondragone 268
  Frascati, Villa Torlonia 269
Fontana, Girolamo (active 1690–1714)
  Palazzo Colonna 174
  Frascati, Cathedral 265
  Frascati, Fountain in Piazza del Duomo 265
Fontana, Lavinia (1552–1614)
  S. Sabina 142
Fontana, Mauro (1701–67)
  S. Carlo ai Catinari 22
  SS. Nome di Maria 127
  Conservatorio di S. Cecilia 248
Fontebuoni, Anastasio (c. 1580–1626)
  S. Giovanni dei Fiorentini 51
  S. Lucia in Selci 75
Fortini, Alberto (recorded 1762)
  S. Marcello 78
Franceschini, Marcantonio (1648–1729)
  S. Pietro in Vaticano 136
  Palazzo della Cancelleria 169

Francesco da Volterra (d. 1594/5)
  S. Andrea della Valle 12
  S. Chiara 30
  S. Giacomo degli Incurabili 48
  S. Gregorio al Celio 62
  S. Lorenzo in Panisperna 70
  S. Macuto 76
  S. Maria in Aquiro 82
  S. Maria della Consolazione 86
  S. Maria di Monserrato 96
  S. Maria dell'Orto 102
  S. Maria della Scala 110
  S. Pudenziana 139
  S. Silvestro in Capite 145
  S. Susanna 148
  S. Tommaso in Parione 150
  Palazzo Cardelli 171
  Palazzo della Compagnia della Annunziata 175
  Palazzo Lancellotti 182
Francucci, Francuccio (active 1620–56)
  Il Gesù 46
Frémin, René (1672–1744)
  Il Gesù 46
Fucigna, Andrea (recorded 1702–3)
  SS. Alessio e Bonifazio all'Aventino 7
  S. Sabina 142
  Frascati, Cathedral 265
Fuga, Ferdinando (1699–1781)
  S. Apollinare 16
  Bambino Gesù 17
  S. Cecilia 28
  S. Francesco di Paola 39
  S. Giovanni dei Fiorentini 52
  S. Giovanni in Laterano 58
  S. Maria Maggiore 89, 90, 91, 92, 93
  S. Maria dell'Orazione e della Morte 101
  S. Maria della Vittoria 123
  S. Pietro in Vaticano 134
  S. Spirito in Sassia 147
  Palazzo Cenci-Bolognetti 172
  Palazzo della Consulta 175
  Palazzo Corsini 176
  Palazzo Maffei 183
  Palazzo del Quirinale 191
  Ospizio di S. Michele 251
  Frascati, Villa Falconieri 267
Fuga, Giacomo (18th century)
  S. Andrea delle Fratte 9

Gagliardi, Bernardino (1609–60)
  S. Bernardino ai Monti 19
  S. Marco 79
  S. Sebastiano al Palatino 144
Gagliardi, Filippo (active 1640–57)
  S. Martino ai Monti 124
Galilei, Alessandro (1691–1736)
  SS. Celso e Giuliano 29

S. Giovanni dei Fiorentini 50
S. Giovanni in Laterano 53, 56
Galli, Giovanni Antonio (Lo Spadarino) (c. 1580–after 1649)
  S. Caterina della Rota 27
  SS. Cosma e Damiano (via dei Fori Imperiali) 30
  S. Omobono 127
  Palazzo Pamphili 189
Gamelin, Jacques (1738–1803)
  Palazzo Rondinini 193
Garzi, Luigi (1638–1721)
  SS. Carlo e Ambrogio al Corso 26
  S. Caterina da Siena a Magnanapoli 27
  S. Croce in Gerusalemme 32
  S. Giovanni in Laterano 54
  S. Giovanni della Pigna 58
  S. Ignazio 64
  S. Marcello 78
  S. Maria in Campo Marzio 85
  S. Maria di Montesanto and S. Maria dei Miracoli 99
  S. Maria del Popolo 107
  S. Maria in Traspontina 112
  S. Paolo alle Regola 129
  S. Silvestro in Capite 145
  Stimmate di S. Francesco 148
  Palazzo Borghese 168
Garzi, Mario (active c. 1700)
  S. Maria dell'Orto 103
Gaulli, Giovanni Battista, see Baciccio
Gennaroli, Andrea (d. 1650)
  S. Giovanni Calabita 50
Gentile, Luigi (Louis Cousin) (1606–67)
  SS. Domenico e Sisto 35
  S. Marco 79
Gentileschi, Orazio (1562–1647)
  S. Maria della Pace 106
  S. Silvestro in Capite 145
  Palazzo del Quirinale 193
  Palazzo Rospigliosi-Pallavicini 194
Gessi, Francesco (1588–1649)
  SS. Giovanni e Petronio dei Bolognesi 59
Gesuelli, Francesco (recorded 1756)
  S. Maria Maddalena 89
Gherardi, Antonio (1644–1702)
  S. Carlo ai Catinari 21
  S. Maria d'Aracoeli 82
  S. Maria in Traspontina 112
  S. Maria in Trastevere 112
  S. Maria in Trivio 113
  SS. Sudario dei Piemontesi 148
  Palazzo Nari (Via di Monterone) 188
Gherardi, Filippo (1643–1700)
  S. Croce dei Lucchesi 33
  S. Nicola da Tolentino 126
  S. Pantaleo 128
  Palazzo Colonna 174

Ghetti, Santi (mid 17th century)
  Il Gesù 45
Ghezzi, Giuseppe (1634–1721)
  S. Cecilia 28
  S. Giuseppe dei Falegnami 61
  S. Maria d'Aracoeli 82
  S. Maria del Suffragio 111
  S. Maria in Vallicella 115
  S. Maria in Via Lata 122
  S. Salvatore in Lauro 143
  S. Silvestro in Capite 145
Ghezzi, Pier Leone (1674–1755)
  S. Calisto 21
  S. Clemente 30
  S. Giuseppe dei Falegnami 61
  S. Marcello 78
  S. Maria dell'Orazione e della Morte 102
  S. Maria in Via Lata 122
  S. Sebastiano fuori le Mura 143
  Castel Gandolfo, Papal Palace 264
  Frascati, Villa Falconieri 267
Ghioldo, Battista (recorded 1567)
  S. Maria in Traspontina 111
Ghisleni, G. B. (d. 1672)
  S. Maria del Popolo 108
Giaquinto, Corrado (1703–66)
  S. Croce in Gerusalemme 32
  S. Giovanni Calabita 50
  S. Lorenzo in Damaso 68
  S. Maria dell'Orto 103
  S. Nicola dei Lorenesi 125
  SS. Trinità degli Spagnuoli 152
Giardé, Arrigo (recorded 1659)
  S. Maria del Popolo 107
Giardini, Francesco, see du Jardin, François
Giardoni, Francesco (1692–1757)
  S. Maria Maddalena 89
Giarguzzi, P. (late 17th century)
  S. Carlo alle Quattro Fontane 24
Gillet, Nicolas (1709–91)
  S. Luigi dei Francesi 76
Gimachi, Carlo (recorded 1708–22)
  S. Anastasia 7
Gimignani, Giacinto (1611–81)
  S. Agostino 6
  S. Carlo ai Catinari 22
  S. Crisogono 31
  S. Giovanni in Laterano 57
  S. Lorenzo in Lucina 69
  S. Maria dell'Anima 81
  S. Maria dei Monti 100
  S. Silvestro al Quirinale 145
  Palazzo Cavallerini 171
  Palazzo Pamphili 189
  Collegio di Propaganda Fide 247
  Ariccia, Collegiata dell'Assunta 263
  Ariccia, Santuario della Madonna, Galloro 264

Gimignani, Giacinto (contd)
  Castelgandolfo, S. Tommaso da
    Villanova 265
Gimignani, Lodovico (1643–97)
  S. Andrea delle Fratte 9
  SS. Carlo e Ambrogio al Corso 26
  S. Lorenzo in Lucina 69
  S. Luigi dei Francesi 76
  S. Maria in Campitelli 84
  S. Maria Maggiore 94
  S. Maria di Montesanto and S. Maria dei
    Miracoli 99
  S. Maria delle Vergini 119
  S. Pudenziana 139
  S. Silvestro in Capite 145
  Palazzo Cavallerini 171
  Collegio di Propaganda Fide 247
  Ariccia, Collegiata dell'Assunta 263
Giordano, Luca (1632–1705)
  S. Maria in Campitelli 84
  S. Maria Maddalena 89
  Spirito Santo dei Napoletani 146
Giorgetti, Antonio (mid 17th century)
  S. Girolamo della Carità 59
  S. Lorenzo fuori le Mura 70
  S. Maria dell'Anima 81
  Ponte S. Angelo 253
  Grottaferrata, the Abbey 270
Giorgetti, Gioseppe (active 1658–79)
  S. Andrea della Valle 14
  SS. Luca e Martina 72
  S. Rocco 141
  S. Sebastiano fuori le Mura 143
Giorgi, Simone (mid 17th century)
  S. Carlo alle Quattro Fontane 24
Giorgini, Simone (active 1686–1706)
  S. Ignazio 64
  S. Isidoro 65
  S. Maria dell'Orto 102
  S. Maria della Scala 110
Giorgio da Coldrerio (first half of the 16th
    century)
  S. Giacomo degli Incurabili 48
Gismondi, Paolo (1612–c. 1685)
  S. Agata dei Goti 3
  S. Agnese in Agone 5
Giulio (Pippi) Romano (1492–1546)
  S. Maria dell'Anima 81
  S. Maria dell'Orto 102
  S. Prassede 139
Gonelli, Archangelo (recorded 1628–9)
  S. Croce in Gerusalemme 32
Gramiccia, Lorenzo (1702–95)
  S. Dorotea 36
Gramignoli, Girolamo (active c. 1680–1700)
  Frascati, Cathedral 265
Grammatica, Anteveduto (1571–1626)
  S. Salvatore in Lauro 143

  S. Stanislao dei Polacchi 147
Grandjacquet, Guillaume Antoine (1731–1801)
  SS. Claudio e Andrea de' Borgognoni 30
Grassi, Giovanni Battista (mid 18th century)
  Fontana di Trevi 240
Grassi, Orazio (1583–1654)
  Il Gesù 45
  S. Ignazio 63
Grassia, Francesco (Franco Siciliano)
    (recorded 1670)
  S. Girolamo degli Schiavoni 60
  S. Ildefonso 65
  S. Maria sopra Minerva 95
Graziani, Ciccio (17th century)
  S. Antonio dei Portoghesi 16
Graziani, Ercole, the Younger (1688–1765)
  S. Apollinare 16
Gregorini, Domenico (c. 1690–1777)
  S. Croce in Gerusalemme 31, 32
  S. Lorenzo in Damaso 68
  S. Maria in Via (Oratory) 120
Grimaldi, Alessandro (c. 1630–c. 1663)
  S. Maria in Publicolis 109
Grimaldi, Fabrizio (often called Francesco)
    (1543–1613)
  S. Andrea della Valle 12
Grimaldi, Giovanni Francesco (1606–80)
  S. Maria dell'Anima 81
  S. Maria in Publicolis 109
  S. Maria della Vittoria 123
  S. Martino ai Monti 124
  Palazzo Almagià 159
  Palazzo Borghese 167
  Palazzo Muti Papazzuri (Piazza della
    Pilotta) 188
  Palazzo del Quirinale 193
  Palazzo Santacroce 195
  Villa Pamphili 219
  Spanish Steps 253
  Frascati, Villa Falconieri 267
Grossi, Giovanni Battista (mid 18th century)
  SS. Apostoli 17
  S. Croce in Gerusalemme 32
  S. Nicola dei Lorenesi 126
Guercino (Giovanni Francesco Barbieri)
    (1591–1666)
  S. Agostino 6
  S. Crisogono 31
  S. Maria in Vallicella 116
  S. Maria della Vittoria 123
  S. Pietro in Vaticano 135
  S. Pietro in Vincoli 138
  Palazzo Costaguti 177
  Palazzo Lancellotti 182
  Villa Ludovisi 215
Guerra, Gaspare (c. 1560–1622)
  S. Andrea delle Fratte 8, 9
  S. Antonio dei Portoghesi 15

Palazzo Cardelli 171
Guerra, Giovanni (c. 1540–1618)
    Palazzo del Laterano 183
Guglielmi, Gregorio (1714–73)
    S. Agostino 7
    SS. Trinità degli Spagnuoli 152
Guidetti, Guidetto (active 1556–64)
    S. Caterina dei Funari 26
    S. Maria dell'Orto 102
Guidi, Domenico (1625–1701)
    S. Agnese in Agone 5
    S. Agostino 6
    SS. Alessio e Bonifazio all'Aventino 7
    S. Andrea della Valle 12, 13
    S. Francesco a Ripa 39
    Il Gesù 46
    Gesù e Maria 47
    S. Giovanni dei Fiorentini 51
    S. Giovanni in Laterano 55
    S. Ivo della Sapienza 68
    S. Maria dell'Anima 81
    S. Maria Maggiore 90
    S. Maria sopra Minerva 94
    S. Maria del Popolo 108
    S. Maria della Scala 110
    S. Maria dell'Umiltà 113
    S. Maria in Vallicella, Oratory 119
    S. Maria della Vittoria 123
    S. Nicola da Tolentino 126
    S. Pudenziana 140
    Spirito Santo dei Napoletani 146
    Monte di Pietà 249
    Ponte S. Angelo 253
Guidotti, F. (recorded 1682)
    S. Maria d'Aracoeli 83
Guidotti, Paolo (c. 1560–1629)
    S. Girolamo degli Schiavoni 60
    S. Maria dei Monti 100

Haan, David de (c. 1585–1622)
    S. Pietro in Montorio 130
Haerts, Jodocus (recorded 1634)
    S. Giuliano dei Fiamminghi 60
Haffner, Enrico (1640–1702)
    SS. Domenico e Sisto 35
    Palazzo Altieri 160
Hallet, Gilles (1620–94)
    S. Maria dell'Anima 81
Heldmann, I. (active 1736–51)
    Frascati, Villa Borghese 267
Honthorst, Gerrit van (1590–1656)
    S. Maria della Concezione 85
    S. Maria della Scala 110
    S. Maria della Vittoria 123
Houdon, Jean Antoine (1741–1828)
    S. Maria degli Angeli 80

Imperiali, see Fernandi, Francesco

Jacopo, maestro (early 17th century)
    S. Maria in Aquiro 82
Juvarra, Filippo (1678–1736)
    S. Girolamo della Carità 60
    Fontana di Trevi 238

Kent, William (1684–1748)
    S. Giuliano dei Fiamminghi 60
Krahe, Lambert (1712–99)
    S. Pasquale Baylon 129
Kuntz, Thaddeus (1731–93)
    S. Caterina da Siena (via Giulia) 27
    S. Stanislao dei Polacchi 147

Labacco, Antonio (c. 1495–after 1567)
    Palazzo Sciarra 196
Labruzzi (recorded 1753–55)
    S. Maria della Luce 88
Lambardi (or Lombardo), Carlo (1554–1620)
    S. Francesca Romana 38
    S. Maria in Via (Largo Chigi) 119
    S. Prisca 139
    Palazzo Costaguti 177
    Villa Aldobrandini 209
    Villa Mattei 217
Lamberti, Bonaventura (1661/2–1721)
    S. Maria sopra Minerva 94
    S. Maria della Vittoria 123
    Spirito Santo dei Napoletani 146
Landini, Taddeo (c. 1550–96)
    Palazzo del Quirinale 193
    Fontana delle Tartarughe 238
Lanfranco, Giovanni (1582–1647)
    S. Agostino 6
    S. Andrea della Valle 11, 13
    S. Carlo ai Catinari 21
    S. Giovanni dei Fiorentini 52
    S. Gregorio al Celio 63
    S. Lucia in Selci 75
    S. Maria della Concezione 85
    S. Maria Maggiore 93
    S. Maria dell'Orazione e della Morte 102
    S. Pietro in Vaticano 132, 134, 135
    Palazzo Farnese 181
    Palazzo Mattei di Giove 186
    Palazzo del Quirinale 193
    Villa Borghese 211, 212
    Frascati, Villa Arrigoni-Muti 266
Lapiccola, Nicola (c. 1730–90)
    SS. Apostoli 17
    S. Caterina da Siena (via Giulia) 27
    S. Lorenzo in Panisperna 71
Lapis, Gaetano (1706–76)
    S. Caterina da Siena (Via Giulia) 27
    SS. Celso e Giuliano 29
    S. Marcellino e Pietro 77
Laureto, Tommaso (c. 1530–1602)
    S. Susanna 149

Index of Artists

Laurenzi, Filippo (probably early 18th century)
  S. Nicola da Tolentino 125
Laurenziano, Giacomo (active 1607–50)
  S. Giovanni in Laterano 56
Lauri, Filippo (1623–94)
  S. Francesca Romana 38
  S. Maria della Pace 106
  Palazzo Borghese 168
  Palazzo del Quirinale 193
Lavaggi, Giacomo Antonio (recorded 1683–9)
  S. Ignazio 64
  S. Maria in Traspontina 112
Lebrun, André-Jean (1736–1811)
  SS. Carlo e Ambrogio al Corso 26
Le Doux, Jean (mid 18th century)
  S. Marco 79
Legnani, Stefano Maria (1660–1715)
  S. Francesco a Ripa 40
Legros, Pierre the Younger (1666–1719)
  S. Andrea al Quirinale 11
  S. Apollinare 16
  SS. Apostoli 17
  Il Gesù 46
  S. Giacomo degli Incurabili 48
  S. Giovanni in Laterano 54, 56
  S. Girolamo della Carità 60
  S. Ignazio 64
  Biblioteca Casanatense 245
  Monte di Pietà 249
Lemoyne, Paul (1784–1873)
  S. Luigi dei Francesi 76
Lenardi, Giovanni Battista (1656–1704)
  S. Andrea delle Fratte 9
  S. Giovanni Calabita 50
  S. Paolo alla Regola 129
Leoni, Ottavio (c. 1578–1630)
  S. Eustachio 37
Lestache, Pierre (c. 1688/9–1774)
  S. Croce in Gerusalemme 32
  S. Luigi dei Francesi 76
Leti, Filippo (active 1680–1711)
  S. Francesco a Ripa 39
Ligorio, Pirro (c. 1500–83)
  S. Giovanni Decollato 50
  S. Giovanni in Laterano 53
  S. Ivo della Sapienza 66
  S. Maria sopra Minerva 95
  Vatican 204
Ligustri, Tarquinio (da Viterbo) (early 17th century)
  S. Marcello 78
Lilio, Andrea (1555–1610)
  S. Agostino 6
  S. Girolamo degli Schiavoni 60
Lint, Pieter van (1609–90)
  S. Maria del Popolo 108

Lippi, Annibale (active 1563–81)
  S. Marcello 77
  Villa Medici 217
Lippi, Nanni di Baccio Bigio di Bartolomeo, see Nanni
Lironi, Giuseppe (?1679–?1749)
  S. Giovanni in Laterano 56
  S. Maria Maggiore 90
  S. Maria della Scala 110
  S. Pietro in Vaticano 133
Lobel (Lobelli), Claude (recorded c. 1696)
  Il Gesù 46
Locatelli, Pietro (c. 1634–1710)
  S. Agostino 6
Lombardo, Carlo, see Lambardi
Lombardo, Francesco (late 16th century)
  S. Maria in Via (Largo Chigi) 119
Lombardo, Leonardo (late 17th century)
  S. Marta 123
Longhi (Lunghi), Martino the Elder (active 1570–91)
  S. Atanasio dei Greci 17
  S. Bartolomeo all' Isola 18
  S. Girolamo degli Schiavoni 60
  S. Macuto 76
  S. Maria degli Angeli 80
  S. Maria della Consolazione 86
  S. Maria Maggiore 89, 93
  S. Maria dell'Orto 102
  S. Maria in Trastevere 112
  S. Maria in Vallicella 114
  S. Maria in Via (Largo Chigi) 119
  S. Prassede 139
  SS. Trinità dei Pellegrini 151
  Palazzo Altemps 160
  Palazzo Borghese 166
  Capitoline Palaces 170
  Palazzo Sciarra 196
  Palazzo Valentino 199
  Frascati, Villa Mondragone 267
Longhi (Lunghi), Martino the Younger (1602–60)
  S. Adriano 3
  S. Antonio dei Portoghesi 15
  S. Carlo ai Catinari 22
  SS. Carlo e Ambrogio al Corso 25
  S. Giovanni Calabita 49
  S. Girolamo della Carità 59
  S. Maria sopra Minerva 95
  S. Maria dell'Umiltà 113
  SS. Vincenzo e Anastasio 152
  Palazzo Ruspoli 194
Longhi, Onorio (c. 1569–1619)
  SS. Carlo e Ambrogio al Corso 25
  S. Eusebio 37
  S. Francesco a Ripa 39
  S. Giovanni in Laterano 56
  S. Maria Antiqua 81

S. Maria d'Aracoeli 83
S. Maria in Trastevere 112
S. Maria in Vallicella 116
S. Maria in Via (Largo Chigi) 119
Palazzo Ferrini 181
Palazzo Serlupi Crescenzi 196
Palazzo Verospi 200
Longhi, Silla (active 1568–1619)
   S. Maria Maggiore 93
Longhi, Stefano (d. 1635)
   S. Cesareo 29
Loo, J. B. van (1684–1745)
   S. Maria in Monticelli 100
Lorenzetto (Lorenzo di Ludovico di
    Guglielmo) (1490–1541)
   S. Maria del Popolo 108
   Ponte S. Angelo 252
Lorrain, Claude (1600–82)
   Palazzo Crescenzi 177
Lorrain, Nicolas (active 1627 onwards)
   S. Antonio dei Portoghesi 16
   S. Maria della Vittoria 123
   S. Nicola dei Lorenesi 126
Lucenti, Girolamo (1627–98)
   S. Maria Maggiore 90
   S. Maria di Montesanto and S. Maria dei
    Miracoli 99
   Ponte S. Angelo 253
Ludovisi, Bernardino (1713–49)
   SS. Apostoli 17
   S. Croce in Gerusalemme 32
   Il Gesù 46
   S. Giovanni in Laterano 53
   S. Ignazio 64
   S. Maria Maggiore 90
   S. Salvatore delle Coppelle 142
   SS. Trinità dei Pellegrini 151
   Fontana di Trevi 240
Luini, Tommaso (c. 1600–c. 1635)
   SS. Carlo e Ambrogio al Corso 26
   S. Maria in Via (Largo Chigi) 119
Lunghi, see Longhi
Luraghi, G. and G. B. (recorded 1718)
   S. Maria Maddalena 89
Luti, Benedetto (1666–1724)
   SS. Apostoli 17
   S. Caterina da Siena a Magnanapoli 27
   S. Giovanni in Laterano 54
   Palazzo de Carolis 177
Luzi, Filippo (1665–1720)
   S. Francesco di Paola 39

Maccarano, P. (recorded 1643–6)
   S. Maria dell'Umiltà 113
Maderno, Carlo (1556–1629)
   S. Ambrogio della Massima 7
   S. Andrea della Valle 12, 13
   S. Chiara 30

SS. Domenico e Sisto 35
S. Giacomo degli Incurabili 48
S. Giovanni dei Fiorentini 50, 51
S. Giovanni in Laterano 56
S. Gregorio al Celio 62
S. Ignazio 63
S. Lucia in Selci 75
S. Luigi dei Francesi 76
S. Maria in Aquiro 82
S. Maria ad Martyres 94
S. Maria sopra Minerva 94, 95
S. Maria della Pace 106
S. Maria della Vittoria 122
S. Paolo fuori le Mura 128
S. Pietro in Montorio 130
S. Pietro in Vaticano 132, 133, 137
S. Pudenziana 139
S. Silvestro in Capite 145
S. Susanna 149
Palazzo Aldobrandini-Chigi 159
Palazzo Almagià 159
Palazzo Barberini 163
Palazzo Barberini alla Giubbonara 166
Palazzo Borghese 167
Palazzo Chigi-Odescalchi 172
Palazzo Giustiniani 182
Palazzo Lancellotti 182
Palazzo Mattei di Giove 185
Palazzo Patrizi 189
Palazzo del Quirinale 191
Palazzo Rospigliosi-Pallavicini 194
Palazzo Varese 199
Villa Ludovisi 215
Fontana delle Api (Vatican) 231
Fountain in front of S. Andrea della
   Valle 236
Fountain in front of S. Maria Maggiore 237
Casa di Carlo Maderno 245
Monte di Pietà 249
Frascati, Villa Aldobrandini 266
Frascati, Villa Torlonia 269
Maderno, Stefano (c. 1576–1636)
   S. Cecilia 28
   SS. Domenico e Sisto 35
   S. Lorenzo in Damaso 68
   S. Maria di Loreto 88
   S. Maria Maggiore 90, 93
   S. Maria della Pace 106
   S. Susanna 149
   Palazzo del Quirinale 191
Maggi, Giovanni Paolo (d. 1613)
   SS. Trinità dei Pellegrini 151
Maglia, Francesco (late 17th century)
   Il Gesù 46
Maglia, Michele (Michel Maille) (active 1678–
   after 1702)
   Gesù e Maria 47
   S. Giovanni dei Fiorentini 51

Maglia, Michele (Michel Maille) (*contd*)
   S. Maria d'Aracoeli 82
   S. Maria in Campitelli 84
   S. Maria di Montesanto and S. Maria dei Miracoli 98
   S. Maria in Traspontina 112
   S. Maria in Trastevere 112
   S. Silvestro in Capite 145
Magno, Giovanni Battista (Il Modanino) (recorded 1667–8)
   Palazzo Colonna 174
Magnoni, Carlo (d. 1653)
   S. Giovanni in Laterano 57
Maignan, Emmanuel (recorded 1637)
   SS. Trinità dei Monti 151
   Palazzo Spada 197
Maille, Michel, see Maglia, Michele
Mainardi, Lattanzio (active *c.* 1585–after 1605)
   S. Maria dei Monti 100
Maini, Giovanni Battista (1690–1752)
   S. Agnese in Agone 5
   S. Agostino 7
   S. Andrea delle Fratte 9
   S. Giovanni in Laterano 53, 56
   SS. Luca e Martina 73
   S. Luigi dei Francesi 76
   S. Maria Maggiore 90
   S. Maria in Publicolis 109
   SS. Nome di Maria 127
   Fontana di Trevi 240
Maioli, Clemente (*c.* 1625–after 1664)
   S. Bernardino ai Monti 19
Malavista, Carlo (recorded *c.* 1676)
   S. Pudenziana 140
Mancini, Francesco (*c.* 1694–1758)
   S. Gregorio al Celio 62
   S. Maria degli Angeli 80
   S. Maria della Scala 110
   S. Pietro in Vaticano 136
Mangone, Giovanni (d. 1543)
   S. Luigi dei Francesi 75
Manno, Francesco (1752–1831)
   SS. Apostoli 17
Mannozzi, see San Giovanni, Giovanni da
Mantinovese, Pietro (active *c.* 1700)
   SS. Sudario dei Piemontesi 148
Maraldi, Pietro (recorded 1645)
   S. Rocco 140
Maratta, Carlo (1625–1713)
   S. Andrea al Quirinale 11
   SS. Carlo e Ambrogio al Corso 26
   S. Croce in Gerusalemme 32
   Il Gesù 43
   S. Giovanni dei Fiorentini 51
   S. Giovanni in Laterano 54, 57
   S. Giuseppe a Capo le Case 61
   S. Giuseppe dei Falegnami 61
   S. Isidoro 65
   S. Marco 79
   S. Maria degli Angeli 80
   S. Maria sopra Minerva 95
   S. Maria di Montesanto and S. Maria dei Miracoli 99
   S. Maria della Pace 106
   S. Maria del Popolo 107
   S. Maria dei Sette Dolori 110
   S. Maria in Vallicella 116
   S. Pietro in Vaticano 132, 136, 137
   Palazzo Altieri 160
   Palazzo del Quirinale 193
Maratta, Francesco (active 1700–19)
   S. Agostino 6
   S. Giovanni in Laterano 54
   S. Marco 79
   S. Maria degli Angeli 80
Marchetti, Giovanni Battista (1730–1800)
   S. Caterina da Siena (via Giulia) 27
   Villa Borghese 212
Marchionni, Carlo (1702–86)
   S. Apollinare 16
   S. Croce in Gerusalemme 32
   S. Maria Maddalena 89
   S. Maria sopra Minerva 95
   S. Pietro in Vaticano 136
   Villa Albani 208
Marchis, Tommaso de' (1693–1759)
   SS. Alessio e Bonifazio all'Aventino 7
   Palazzo Mellini 186
   Collegio Nazzareno 246
Marcillat, Guillaume de (d. 1529)
   S. Maria del Popolo 107
Mare, Mattia de (recorded 1764–70)
   S. Andrea della Valle 13
Mari, G. A. (mid 17th century)
   S. Maria sopra Minerva 95
   S. Maria del Popolo 107, 108
   S. Pudenziana 140
Mariani, Camillo (1556–1611)
   S. Bernardo alle Terme 19
   S. Maria Maggiore 93
   S. Maria sopra Minerva 95, 96
   S. Pudenziana 140
Marini, Pasquale Andrea (d. *c.* 1712)
   S. Andrea delle Fratte 9
   S. Maria in Campo Marzio 85
Marmorelli, Liborio (mid 18th century)
   S. Dorotea 36
   Palazzo Doria-Pamphili 179
Maron, Anton (1733–1808)
   S. Eusebio 37
Martines, Simone (active 1707–63)
   S. Giovanni dei Fiorentini 50
Martorana, Gioacchino (d. 1782)
   S. Dorotea 36
Maruscelli, Paolo (1596–1649)
   S. Andrea della Valle 14

S. Carlo ai Catinari 22
SS. Gioacchino e Anna (via del
   Quirinale) 49
S. Maria sopra Minerva 96
S. Maria dell'Umiltà 113
S. Maria in Vallicella, Oratory 117, 118
Palazzo Madama 183
Palazzo Spada 197
Marzio di Colantonio (c. 1560–c. 1620)
   S. Maria della Consolazione 86
Mascarino, Ottaviano (1524–1606)
   S. Caterina della Rota 27
   SS. Giovanni e Petronio dei Bolognesi 59
   SS. Luca e Martina 71
   S. Maria della Scala 110
   S. Maria in Traspontina 111
   S. Marta in Vaticano 124
   S. Salvatore in Lauro 142, 143
   S. Silvestro al Quirinale 146
   Spirito Santo dei Napoletani 146
   S. Spirito in Sassia 147
   Palazzo Albani 158
   Palazzo del Quirinale 191
   Palazzo Valentino 199
   Monte di Pietà 249
   Frascati, Cathedral 265
Massari, Francesco (recorded 1659–72)
   S. Lorenzo in Piscibus 71
Massarotti, Angelo (c. 1645–1732)
   S. Salvatore in Lauro 143
Massei, Girolamo (c. 1540–c. 1614)
   S. Prassede 139
Massi, Giovanni Antonio (recorded shortly
   before 1686)
   S. Dionigi alle Quattro Fontane 33
Massimano, Padre (recorded c. 1591)
   S. Salvatore in Lauro 142
Masucci, Agostino (1692–1758)
   S. Francesco di Paola 39
   S. Marcello 78
   S. Maria Maggiore 91
   S. Maria dell'Orazione e della Morte 102
   S. Maria del Popolo 108
   S. Maria in Via Lata 122
   SS. Nome di Maria 127
   Palazzo del Quirinale 191
Masucci, L. (d. 1785)
   SS. Nome di Maria 127
Mattei, Ambrogio (recorded 1764)
   S. Eligio dei Ferrari 36
Mattei, Tommaso (recorded 1700–33)
   S. Maria di Montesanto and S. Maria dei
      Miracoli 99
   Palazzo Macchi di Cellere 183
   Palazzo Spada 197
   Villa Borghese 212
Matteis, Paolo De (1662–1728)
   S. Maria sopra Minerva 95

Matteo (Bastonali) da Città di Castello (c.
   1525–after 1614)
   S. Andrea della Valle 13
   S. Giovanni dei Fiorentini 51
   S. Maria della Scala 110
   S. Maria in Vallicella 114
   S. Susanna 149
   Acqua Felice 229
Matteo (Pérez) da Lecce (c. 1547–c. 1600)
   S. Eligio degli Orefici 36
Mauri, Giovanni Pietro (active c. 1680–1700)
   Frascati, Cathedral 265
Mazzanti, Lodovico (c. 1679–1775)
   S. Andrea al Quirinale 16
   S. Apollinare 16
   S. Ignazio 64
Mazzoni, Giulio (c. 1525–1618)
   S. Maria del Popolo 108
   Palazzo Spada 197
Mazzuchelli, see Morazzone
Mazzuoli, Giuseppe (1644–1725)
   S. Cecilia 28
   S. Francesco a Ripa 40
   Gesù e Maria 47
   S. Giovanni in Laterano 54
   S. Maria in Campitelli 84
   S. Maria Maddalena 89
   S. Pietro in Vaticano 135
   S. Silvestro in Capite 145
   Monte di Pietà 249
Meder, Christian (late 17th and early 18th
   centuries)
   S. Andrea delle Fratte 10
Mei, Bernardino (c. 1615–76)
   S. Maria della Pace 106
   S. Maria del Popolo 108
   Ariccia, Collegiata dell'Assunta 263
Melchiorri, Giovanni Paolo (1664–1745)
   S. Maria in Traspontina 112
Mellin, Charles (c. 1597–1649)
   S. Luigi dei Francesi 76
   Palazzo Muti Papazzuri (Balestra) 187
Mellone, Carlo Francesco (active 1695–1726)
   S. Pietro in Vaticano 135
Menghini, Niccolò (c. 1610–55)
   SS. Luca e Martina 74
   S. Rocco 141
Mengs, Anton Raphael (1728–79)
   S. Eusebio 37
   Villa Albani 208
Mercati, Giovanni Battista (1600–after 1637)
   S. Bartolomeo all'Isola 18
   S. Maria delle Vergini 119
Merigi da Caravaggio, Giulio (active c. 1550)
   Palazzo Spada 197
Merlini, Lorenzo (1666–after 1736)
   Il Gesù 46
   S. Giovanni dei Fiorentini 51

Merlini, Lorenzo (contd)
   S. Pantaleo 128
Meucci, Vincenzo (1699–1766)
   S. Dorotea 36
Michelangelo (1475–1564)
   S. Andrea della Valle 13
   Il Gesù 41
   S. Giovanni dei Fiorentini 50
   S. Gregorio al Celio 63
   S. Maria degli Angeli 80
   S. Maria d'Aracoeli 82
   S. Maria Maggiore 93
   S. Maria sopra Minerva 95
   S. Pietro in Montorio 130
   S. Pietro in Vaticano 134
   S. Pietro in Vincoli 138
   S. Silvestro in Capite 145
   Capitoline Palaces 170
   Palazzo Farnese 180
   Porta S. Giovanni 253
   Porta del Popolo 253
Michele da Bergamo (early 17th century)
   S. Maria della Concezione 86
Michele, Monsù (second half of the 17th century)
   S. Giovanni dei Fiorentini 51
Michetti, Niccolò (active 1710–59)
   SS. Apostoli 17
   S. Francesco a Ripa 40
   S. Ignazio 64
   Palazzo Colonna 174
   Fontana di Trevi 238
   Ospizio di S. Michele 251
Miel, Jan (1599–1663)
   S. Maria dell'Anima 81
   Palazzo del Quirinale 193
Mignard, Pierre (1612–95)
   S. Carlo alle Quattro Fontane 24
Milani, Aureliano (1675–1749)
   SS. Bartolomeo e Alessandro dei Bergamaschi 18
   SS. Giovanni e Paolo 58
   S. Marcello 78
   Palazzo Doria-Pamphili 179
Milone, Vincenzo (recorded 1767)
   S. Omobono 127
Mitelli, Agostino (1609–60)
   Palazzo Spada 197
Mochi, Francesco (1580–1654)
   S. Andrea della Valle 13
   S. Bernardo alle Terme 19
   S. Giovanni dei Fiorentini 51
   S. Maria Maggiore 90, 93
   S. Maria sopra Minerva 94
   S. Paolo alla Regola 129
   S. Pietro in Vaticano 133
   S. Silvestro al Quirinale 146
   Capitoline Palaces 170

Porta del Popolo 253
Modanino, called Il, Giovanni Battista Magno (active 1647–70)
   Palazzo Cardelli 171
   Palazzo Colonna 174
Moderati, Francesco (c. 1680–after 1727)
   S. Agnese in Agone 5
   S. Maria ad Martyres 94
   S. Pietro in Vaticano 133
   Monte di Pietà 249
   Niche with statue of the Virgin 250
Mola, Giacomo (active 1615–37)
   S. Francesco a Ripa 40
   S. Maria del Pianto 106
   Ospedale di S. Giovanni 250
Mola, Giovanni Battista (c. 1588–1665)
   S. Eligio dei Ferrari 36
   S. Maria del Pianto 106
   S. Nicola da Tolentino 126
   Capitoline Palaces 170
   Palazzo Patrizi 189
   Ospedale di S. Giovanni 250
Mola, Pierfrancesco (1612–66)
   S. Anastasia 7
   SS. Carlo e Ambrogio al Corso 26
   SS. Domenico e Sisto 35
   Il Gesù 47
   S. Marco 79
   Palazzo Costaguti 177
   Palazzo Quirinale 193
Monaldi, Carlo (c. 1683–1760)
   S. Giovanni in Laterano 57
   S. Marco 79
   S. Maria Maddalena 89
   S. Maria ad Martyres 94
   S. Salvatore in Lauro 143
   Palazzo Venezia 199
Monaldi (or Moraldi), G. P. (recorded 1645–50)
   S. Francesco di Paola 39
Mondelli, Filippo (active 1740–54)
   S. Carlo ai Catinari 22
Monnot, Pierre Etienne (1657–1733)
   SS. Apostoli 17
   Il Gesù 46
   S. Giovanni in Laterano 54
   S. Ignazio 64
   S. Maria del Popolo 108
   S. Maria della Vittoria 123
   S. Pietro in Vaticano 136
Monosilio, Salvatore (active 1744–76)
   S. Caterina da Siena (Via Jiulia) 27
   S. Paolo alla Regola 129
   S. Pasquale Baylon 129
   S. Stanislao dei Polacchi 147
Montagna, Marco Tullio (active 1618–40)
   S. Giuseppe dei Falegnami 61

Index of Artists

Montano, Giovanni Battista (1534–1621)
  S. Giovanni in Laterano 55
  S. Giuseppe dei Falegnami 61
  SS. Luca e Martina 71
Montauti, Antonio (d. c. 1740)
  S. Giovanni in Laterano 57
Montesanti, Giuseppe (d. 1779)
  S. Lorenzo in Panisperna 71
Moraldi, G. P., see Monaldi
Morandi, Giovanni Maria (1622–1717)
  S. Maria dell'Anima 81
  S. Maria della Pace 104
  S. Maria del Popolo 107
  S. Maria in Vallicella 115
  S. Sabina 142
  S. Stefano del Cacco 148
Morandi, G. P. (early 17th century)
  S. Ambrogio della Massima 7
Morazzone, Mazzuchelli, Francesco, called Il Morazzone (1571/3–1626)
  SS. Carlo e Ambrogio al Corso 26
Morelli, Lazzaro (1608–90)
  S. Marco 79
  S. Maria di Montesanto and S. Maria dei Miracoli 98, 99
  S. Maria del Popolo 107
  S. Pietro in Vaticano 135
Morelli, Paolo (first half of the 18th century)
  S. Maria Maddalena 89
Moretto, see Somazzi
Mostaert, Nicolas (d. 1601/4)
  S. Maria dell'Anima 81
Mulier, Pieter, see Tempesta, Pietro
Multò, Francesco (recorded 1727)
  S. Maria delle Grazie alle Fornaci 87
Muratori, Domenico Maria (c. 1661–1744)
  SS. Apostoli 17
  Bambino Gesù 17
  S. Croce dei Lucchesi 33
  S. Francesco a Ripa 40
  S. Giovanni in Laterano 54
  S. Prassede 139
  S. Sabina 142
  Spirito Santo dei Napoletani 146
  Stimmate di S. Francesco 148
  Palazzo de Carolis 177
Murena, Carlo (1713/4–64)
  SS. Alessio e Bonifazio all'Aventino 7
  S. Antonio dei Portoghesi 16
  SS. Michele e Magno 124
Murgia, F. (c. 1612–73)
  Palazzo del Quirinale 193
Muti, Cristoforo (recorded 1692)
  S. Antonio dei Portoghesi 15
Muti Papazzuri, Battista (recorded 1644)
  Palazzo Muti Papazzuri (Balestra) 187
Muziano, Girolamo (1528–92)
  S. Agostino 6
  S. Caterina della Rota 27
  S. Maria degli Angeli 80
  S. Maria d'Aracoeli 82, 83
  S. Maria dei Monti 100
  S. Maria in Vallicella 115
  S. Martino ai Monti 124
  S. Pietro in Vaticano 135

Naldini, Pietro Paolo (c. 1615–91)
  Il Gesù 45
  Gesù e Maria 47
  S. Giacomo degli Incurabili 48
  S. Giovanni in Laterano 56, 57
  S. Girolamo della Carità 59
  S. Marcello 78
  S. Maria ad Martyres (Pantheon) 94
  S. Maria di Montesanto and S. Maria dei Miracoli 99
  S. Maria del Popolo 107
  S. Maria del Suffragio 111
  S. Martino ai Monti 124
  S. Nicola da Tolentino 126
  Palazzo Cardelli 171
  Vatican 203
  Ponte S. Angelo 253
  Ariccia, Collegiata dell'Assunta 263
Nanni di Baccio Bigio di Bartolomeo (d. 1568)
  Il Gesù 41
  Palazzo Sacchetti 194
  Villa Medici 217
Napoleoni, Francesco (active c. 1680–1700)
  Frascati, Cathedral 265
Napolino, Giuseppe (recorded c. 1705)
  SS. Apostoli 17
Nappi, Francesco (c. 1565–1630)
  S. Maria della Consolazione 86
Nasini, Giuseppe Nicola (1657–1736)
  SS. Apostoli 17
  S. Giovanni in Laterano 54
  S. Lorenzo in Lucina 69
  Palazzo della Cancelleria 169
Natale, Francesco (recorded soon after 1763)
  Villa Chigi 213
Natali, Giovanni Battista (active 1657–96)
  S. Maria del Suffragio 111
Natoire, Charles-Joseph (1700–77)
  S. Luigi dei Francesi 76
Navone, Francesco (d. 1804)
  S. Anna dei Palafrenieri 15
  S. Antonio dei Portoghesi 16
  S. Giuseppe alla Lungara 61
Navone, Giovanni Domenico (recorded 1733)
  S. Lorenzo in Piscibus 71
Nebbia, Cesare (1536–c. 1614)
  Oratorio del SS. Crocifisso 33
  S. Lucia del Gonfalone 74
  S. Maria dei Monti 100
  S. Maria in Vallicella 116

305

Index of Artists

Nebbia, Cesare (*contd*)
  S. Susanna 149
Nelli, Pietro (1672–1740)
  S. Caterina da Siena a Magnanapoli 28
Nessi, Antonio (active 1739–73)
  S. Lorenzo in Panisperna 70
  SS. Nome di Maria 127
Nicéron, Jean-François (1613–46)
  SS. Trinità dei Monti 151
Nicoletti, Francesco (active 1729–76)
  S. Maria Maddalena 89
Nocchi, Bernardino (1741–1812)
  S. Pudenziana 139
Nogari, Paris (*c.* 1536–1601)
  S. Andrea delle Fratte 9
  S. Maria dei Monti 100
  S. Prassede 139
  S. Susanna 149
  SS. Trinità dei Monti 150
  Vatican 204
Nolli, Giovanni Battista (1692–1756)
  S. Dorotea 36
Nuvolone, Francesco (active 1686–96)
  Il Gesù 46
  S. Ignazio 64

Odazzi, Giovanni (1663–1731)
  S. Andrea delle Fratte 9
  S. Andrea al Quirinale 11
  SS. Apostoli 17
  S. Bernardo alle Terme 19
  S. Clemente 30
  S. Giovanni dei Genovesi 52
  S. Giovanni in Laterano 55
  S. Maria degli Angeli 80
  S. Maria d'Aracoeli 82
  S. Maria della Scala 110
  S. Maria in Via Lata 122
  S. Prisca 139
  S. Sabina 142
  S. Stefano del Cacco 148
  Stimmate di S. Francesco 148
  Palazzo Albani 158
  Palazzo de Carolis 177
Olivieri, Padre Paolo (*c.* 1551–99)
  S. Giovanni in Laterano 56
  S. Maria d'Aracoeli 82
  S. Pudenziana 140
  Acqua Felice 229
Omodei, Cardinal Luigi (1608–85)
  SS. Carlo e Ambrogio al Corso 25, 26
Orazi, Andrea Antonio (1670–after 1749)
  S. Maria dell'Orto 102
  S. Maria della Vittoria 122
Orazi, Giuseppe (early 18th century)
  S. Maria dell'Orto 102
  S. Maria della Vittoria 122

Orlandi, Clemente (1694–1775)
  S. Paolo Primo Eremita 128
Orsi, Prospero (*c.* 1558–1633)
  Palazzo Mattei di Giove 186
Ottoni, Lorenzo (1648–1736)
  S. Francesco a Ripa 40
  Il Gesù 46
  Gesù e Maria 47
  S. Giovanni in Laterano 54
  S. Maria in Campitelli 84
  S. Maria ad Martyres (Pantheon) 94
  S. Maria in Publicolis 109
  S. Maria in Trastevere 112
  S. Silvestro in Capite 145
  Monte di Pietà 249
Overbeck, Friedrich (1789–1869)
  Villa Giustiniani 215

Pacetti, Camillo (1758–1826)
  S. Andrea delle Fratte 9
Pacetti, G. B. (1693–1743)
  S. Maria in Monticelli 100
Pacetti, Vincenzo (*c.* 1746–1820)
  SS. Michele e Magno 124
  S. Salvatore in Lauro 143
Pacilli, Carlo (?recorded 1734–5)
  S. Giovanni dei Fiorentini 50
Pacilli, Pietro (1716–after 1769)
  SS. Carlo e Ambrogio al Corso 26
  S. Giovanni dei Fiorentini 50
  S. Marco 79
  SS. Trinità dei Spagnuoli 152
Paganelli, Domenico (1545–1624)
  Palazzo Valentino 199
Paglia, Giuseppe (recorded 1662–82)
  S. Ildefonso 65
  S. Maria sopra Minerva 95
Paladino, Giuseppe (1721–94)
  SS. Trinità degli Spagnuoli 152
Palazzi, Giuseppe (*c.* 1740–1810)
  S. Caterina da Siena (via Giulia) 27
Palladio, Andrea (1568–80)
  S. Spirito in Sassia 147
Panaria, Matteo (mid 18th century)
  S. Pasquale Baylon 129
Pannini, Giovanni Paolo (1691/2–1765)
  S. Maria in Publicolis 109
  S. Maria della Scala 110
  Palazzo Albani 158
  Frascati, Villa Grazioli 267
Paolo Romano (recorded 1530)
  Ponte S. Angelo 252
Papaleo, Pietro (*c.* 1642–1718)
  SS. Apostoli 17
  S. Maria della Scala 110
  S. Sebastiano fuori le Mura 143
Paracca, Giovanni Antonio, called Valsoldo, see Valsoldo

Paradisi, Domenico (active 1691–1721)
   S. Cecilia 28
Parisi, Ambrogio (d. 1719)
   S. Barbara dei Librai 18
Parker, John (d. c. 1765)
   S. Gregorio al Celio 62
Parodi, Domenico (1668–1740)
   S. Maria dell'Orto 103
Parodi, Giovanni Battista (1674–1730)
   S. Pietro in Vincoli 138
Parrocel, Etienne (1696–1776)
   S. Caterina da Siena (via Giulia) 27
   S. Gregorio a Ponte Quattro Capi 63
   S. Luigi dei Francesi 76
   S. Maria Maddalena 89
   S. Maria in Monticelli 100
   S. Prassede 139
Passalacqua, Melchiorre (mid 18th century)
   S. Croce in Gerusalemme 31
   S. Eustachio 37
Passalacqua, Pietro (active 1706–48)
   Oratory of the SS. Annunziata 15
   S. Croce in Gerusalemme 31, 32
   S. Francesco d'Assisi a Monte Mario 38
Passeri, Giuseppe (1654–1714)
   S. Barbara dei Librai 18
   S. Caterina da Siena a Magnanapoli 27
   S. Croce in Gerusalemme 32
   S. Francesco a Ripa 40
   S. Giacomo degli Incurabili 48
   S. Maria d'Aracoeli 82
   S. Maria in Campitelli 84
   S. Pietro in Vaticano 137
   S. Sebastiano fuori le Mura 143
   Spirito Santo dei Napoletani 146
   S. Tommaso in Parione 150
   Palazzo Barberini 165
Passignano, Domenico, see Cresti
Patriarca, Pietro (early 18th century)
   S. Brigida 20
Pavoni, Stefano (recorded 1499–1500)
   S. Maria del Popolo 107
Pécheux, Laurent (1729–1821)
   S. Caterina da Siena (via Giulia) 27
Pellegrini, Carlo (1605–49)
   S. Pietro in Vaticano 135
   Collegio di Propaganda Fide 247
Penna, Agostino (active 1768–1800)
   S. Eustachio 37
   S. Maria del Popolo 108
Peparelli, Francesco (active 1614–40)
   S. Brigida 20
   S. Caio 20
   S. Francesco a Ripa 40
   Il Gesù 45
   S. Girolamo della Carità 60
   S. Maria in Traspontina 111
   S. Maria delle Vergini 119
   S. Salvatore in Campo 142
   Palazzo Cardelli 171
   Palazzo del Bufalo-Ferraioli 178
   Palazzo Santacroce 195
   Palazzo Valentino 199
Pérez, see Matteo da Lecce
Perfetti, Giovanni Antonio (active 1717–54)
   S. Biagio della Pagnotta 19
Peroni, Giuseppe (1626–63)
   S. Maria del Popolo 107
Perrier, François (1590–1650)
   Palazzo Almagià 159
Perrugini Stefano (recorded 1645)
   S. Francesco di Paola 39
Peruzzi, Baldassare (1481–1536)
   S. Giacomo degli Incurabili 48
   S. Maria dell'Anima 81
   S. Maria della Pace 106
Peruzzi, Salustio (d. 1573)
   S. Maria in Traspontina 111
Peruzzini, Giovanni (c. 1629–94)
   S. Salvatore in Lauro 143
Pesci, Girolamo (1684–1759)
   S. Giuseppe alla Lungara 61
Petrarca, Antonio (late 16th century)
   S. Giovanni in Laterano 55
Piastrini, G. D. (1678–1740)
   S. Clemente 30
   SS. Giovanni e Paolo 58
   S. Maria in Via (Largo Chigi) 119
   S. Maria in Via Lata 122
   S. Prassede 139
Piccioni, L. (recorded 1757)
   S. Giovanni in Laterano 57
Picconi, Niccolò (recorded 1753–9)
   S. Eusebio 37
Pieri, S. (1542–1629)
   S. Giovanni dei Fiorentini 51
Pietrasanta, Jacopo da (active 1452–c. 1495)
   S. Agostino 6
Pietri, Pietro de' (1663 (or 1665)–1716)
   S. Clemente 30
   S. Maria delle Grazie alle Fornaci 87
   S. Maria in Via Lata 122
Pietro (Berrettini) da Cortona (1597–1669)
   S. Agnese in Agone 3, 4
   S. Bibiana 19
   S. Carlo ai Catinari 22
   SS. Carlo e Ambrogio al Corso 25
   Il Gesù 43, 45, 46
   S. Giovanni dei Fiorentini 51
   S. Girolamo della Carità 59
   S. Ivo della Sapienza 66
   S. Lorenzo in Damaso 68
   S. Lorenzo in Miranda 69
   S. Lorenzo fuori le Mura 70
   SS. Luca e Martina 71–4
   S. Marco 79

Pietro (Berrettini) da Cortona (contd)
  S. Maria della Concezione 86
  S. Maria ad Martyres (Pantheon) 94
  S. Maria sopra Minerva 96
  S. Maria della Pace 103, 104, 106
  S. Maria in Vallicella 115, 116
  S. Maria in Via Lata 121
  S. Martino ai Monti 124
  S. Nicola da Tolentino 126
  S. Pietro in Vaticano 134
  S. Salvatore in Lauro 143
  Palazzo Barberini 164, 165
  Capitoline Palaces 170
  Palazzo Gambirasi 181
  Palazzo Mattei di Giove 186
  Palazzo Pamphili 188
  Palazzo del Quirinale 193
  Vatican 203
  Villa Sacchetti 220, 222
  Fountain in Piazza Colonna 233
  Quattro Fontane 235
  Castel Gandolfo, S. Tommaso da Villanova 264
  Frascati, Villa Arrigoni-Muti 266
Pilotti, Giovanni (recorded 1637)
  Il Gesù 45
Pincelotti, Bartolomeo (d. 1740)
  S. Agostino 6
  S. Giovanni in Laterano 56
  S. Maria sopra Minerva 95
  Fontana di Trevi 240
Pino, Marco (1525–87/8)
  S. Maria d'Aracoeli 82
Pinson, Nicolas (1640–after 1672)
  S. Luigi dei Francesi 76
Pinturicchio (c. 1454–1513)
  S. Maria d'Aracoeli 82
  S. Maria del Popolo 107
  S. Onofrio 127
  S. Pietro in Montorio 130
  Palazzo Colonna 174
Piombo, Sebastiano del (1485–1547)
  S. Maria della Pace 106
  S. Maria del Popolo 108
  S. Pietro in Montorio 130
Pippe, Nicolas (late 16th century)
  S. Luigi dei Francesi 76
Piranesi, Giovanni Battista (1720–78)
  S. Giovanni in Laterano 55
  S. Maria del Priorato 109
Poletti, F. (recorded 1727)
  S. Eligio dei Ferrari 36
Polidoro (Caldara) da Caravaggio (1490/1500–43)
  S. Silvestro al Quirinale 146
  Palazzo del Bufalo 177
Pomarancio, see Circignani and Roncalli

Pontelli, Baccio (c. 1450–after 1492)
  S. Agostino 6
  SS. Apostoli 16
  S. Maria della Pace 103
  S. Pietro in Montorio 129
Ponzio, Flaminio (1560–1613)
  S. Andrea della Valle 13
  S. Gregorio al Celio 63
  S. Maria Maggiore 90, 91, 92
  S. Sebastiano fuori le Mura 143
  Palazzo Barberini alla Giubbonara 166
  Palazzo Borghese 166
  Palazzo del Quirinale 191
  Palazzo Rondinini 193
  Palazzo Rospigliosi-Pallavicini 194
  Palazzo Sciarra 195
  Villa Borghese 211
  Acqua Paola 229
  Frascati, Villa Mondragone 268
Pordenone, Giovanni Antonio de Lodesan (c. 1484–1539)
  S. Maria dei Sette Dolori 110
Posi, Paolo (1708–76)
  S. Agostino 6
  S. Andrea delle Fratte 9
  S. Caterina da Siena (via Giulia) 27
  S. Maria dell'Anima 81
  S. Maria ad Martyres (Pantheon) 94
  S. Maria dell'Orazione e della Morte 102
  S. Maria del Popolo 108
Poussin, Claude (active 1644–61)
  Fountains in Piazza Navona 234
Poussin, Gaspard, see Dughet
Poussin, Nicolas (1594–1665)
  S. Luigi dei Francesi 76
  S. Pietro in Vaticano 135
Pozzi, Domenico (recorded 1624)
  SS. Trinità dei Pellegrini 151
Pozzo, Andrea (1642–1709)
  S. Andrea al Quirinale 11
  S. Apollinare 16
  S. Fraucesca Romana 38
  Il Gesù 43, 45, 46, 47
  S. Ignazio 63, 64, 65
  SS. Trinità dei Monti 151
  Frascati, Cathedral 265
  Frascati, S. Maria Assunta 265
Pozzo, Giovanni Battista (1561–89)
  S. Susanna 148
Pozzo, Stefano (c. 1707–68)
  S. Apollinare 16
  S. Francesco di Paola 39
  S. Ignazio 64
  S. Maria Maggiore 91
  SS. Nome di Maria 127
  S. Silvestro al Quirinale 146
  Palazzo Doria-Pamphili 179

Index of Artists

Prata, Battista (recorded 1600–03)
   S. Cesareo 29
Preciado de la Vega, Francisco (d. 1789)
   S. Pasquale Baylon 129
   SS. Trinità degli Spagnuoli 152
Prenner, Gaspar von (c. 1720–66)
   S. Dorotea 36
Preti, Gregorio (d. 1672)
   S. Carlo ai Catinari 21
   S. Rocco 141
Preti, Mattia (1613–99)
   S. Andrea della Valle 11, 13
   S. Carlo ai Catinari 21
   S. Giovanni Calabita 50
Prinoti, G. (17th century)
   S. Maria in Monticelli 100
Procaccini, Andrea (1671–1734)
   S. Giovanni in Laterano 55
   S. Maria degli Angeli 80
   S. Maria sopra Minerva 95
   S. Maria dell'Orto 103
   S. Maria in Trastevere 112
   S. Pietro in Vaticano 137
   Palazzo de Carolis 177
Puccini, Biagio (1675–1721)
   S. Agata in Trastevere 3
   S. Brigida 20
   S. Caterina da Siena a Magnanapoli 27
   S. Croce dei Lucchesi 33
   S. Eustachio 37
   S. Giovanni in Laterano 56
   S. Maria Maddalena 89
   S. Maria di Montesanto and S. Maria dei Miracoli 99
   S. Maria in Traspontina 112
   S. Paolo alla Regola 129
Puglia, Giuseppe (called Il Bastaro) (d. 1636)
   S. Girolamo degli Schiavone 60
Pulzone, Scipione (before 1550–98)
   S. Maria in Vallicella 115

Quadri, Carlo (recorded 1696)
   S. Maria Maddalena 89
Quattrini, E. (20th century)
   S. Cecilia 28
Queirolo, Francesco (1704–62)
   S. Andrea delle Fratte 9
   S. Giovanni dei Fiorentini 50
   Fontana di Trevi 240

Raffaele, P. (late 18th century)
   S. Nicola da Tolentino 126
Raffaellino (Motta) da Reggio (c. 1550–78)
   Vatican 204
Raggi, Antonio (1624–86)
   S. Agnese in Agone 5
   S. Andrea al Quirinale 10
   S. Andrea della Valle 13

   S. Carlo alle Quattro Fontane 24
   SS. Domenico e Sisto 35
   Il Gesù 45
   S. Giovanni dei Fiorentini 51
   S. Marcello 77
   S. Marco 79
   S. Maria sopra Minerva 95
   S. Maria di Montesanto and S. Maria dei Miracoli 99
   S. Maria del Popolo 107, 108
   S. Maria dell'Umiltà 113
   S. Nicola da Tolentino 126
   Vatican 204
   Fountains in Piazza Navona 234
   Ponte S. Angelo 253
   Castel Gandolfo, S. Tommaso da Villanova 264
Raguzzini, Filippo (c. 1680–1771)
   SS. Bartolomeo e Alessandro dei Bergamaschi 18
   S. Filippo Neri 37
   Madonna del Divino Amore 77
   S. Maria d'Aracoeli 82
   S. Maria sopra Minerva 94, 95
   S. Maria della Quercia 109
   S. Maria in Trastevere 112
   SS. Quirico e Giulitta 140
   S. Sisto Vecchio 146
   Ospedale di S. Gallicano 250
   Plazza S. Ignazio 252
Rainaldi, Carlo (1611–91)
   S. Agnese in Agone 3, 4, 5
   S. Andrea della Valle 12
   SS. Angeli Custodi 14
   S. Antonio dei Portoghesi 15
   SS. Apostoli 16
   S. Carlo ai Catinari 21
   Gesù e Maria 47
   S. Giovanni in Laterano 57
   S. Girolamo della Carità 59
   S. Ignazio 64
   S. Lorenzo in Lucina 69
   S. Maria d'Aracoeli 83
   S. Maria in Campitelli 83, 84
   S. Maria Maggiore 90
   S. Maria sopra Minerva 95
   S. Maria di Montesanto and S. Maria dei Miracoli 98, 99
   S. Maria della Scala 110
   S. Maria del Suffragio 111
   S. Maria in Vallicella and Oratory 116, 118
   S. Maria in Via (Largo Chigi) 119
   S. Silvestro in Capite 145
   SS. Sudario dei Piemontesi 148
   Palazzo Borghese 167, 168
   Palazzo del Grillo 178
   Palazzo Mancini 184
   Palazzo Pamphili 188

Index of Artists

Rainaldi, Carlo (contd)
  Villa Pamphili 219
  Spanish Steps 255
Rainaldi, Francesco (second half of the 17th century)
  S. Ignazio 64
Rainaldi, Girolamo (1570–1655)
  S. Agnese in Agone 3, 4
  S. Carlo ai Catinari 22
  S. Cecilia 28
  Il Gesù 45, 47
  S. Giovanni in Laterano 56
  S. Maria Maggiore 93
  S. Maria sopra Minerva 95
  S. Maria della Scala 110
  S. Rocco 140
  Palazzo Albertoni 158
  Palazzo Pamphili 188
  Palazzo Verospi 200
  Villa Borghese 212
  Villa della Porta Radiani 214
  Villa Farnese 214
  Fountain in front of S. Maria in Trastevere 237
  Collegio Innocenziano 246
  Frascati, Villa Borghese 266
Rambotti, Sebastiano (recorded 1718)
  SS. Apostoli 17
Ranucci, Giuseppe (recorded 1736–49)
  SS. Celso e Giuliano 29
  S. Lorenzo in Panisperna 71
  S. Maria dell'Orto 103
Raphael (Rafaello Santi) (1483–1520)
  S. Agostino 6
  S. Eligio degli Orefici 36
  SS. Luca e Martina 74
  S. Maria di Montesanto and S. Maria dei Miracoli 97
  S. Maria della Pace 106
  S. Maria del Popolo 107, 108
  S. Pietro in Montorio 130
  S. Pietro in Vaticano 132, 136
Raspantini, Antonio Liborio (recorded between 1670 and 1676)
  SS. Venanzio e Ansovino 152
Ravasi, M. A. (recorded 1691)
  S. Giuseppe dei Falegnami 61
Recalcati, Giacomo Onorato (recorded 1710)
  S. Agata in Trastevere 3
Reiffi, Pietro Paolo (active 1677–99)
  Il Gesù 46
Reni, Guido (1575–1642)
  S. Cecilia 28
  S. Giovanni in Laterano 56, 57
  S. Gregorio al Celio 63
  S. Lorenzo in Lucina 69
  SS. Marcellino e Pietro 77
  S. Maria della Concezione 85

S. Maria Maggiore 93
S. Maria dell'Orazione e della Morte 102
S. Maria in Vallicella 116
SS. Maria della Vittoria 123
S. Pietro in Montorio 130
S. Pietro in Vaticano 135, 136
SS. Trinità dei Pellegrini 151
Palazzo del Quirinale 193
Palazzo Rospigliosi-Pallavicini 194
Vatican 203, 204
Reti, Leonardo (active 1670–1709)
  S. Giovanni dei Fiorentini 51
  S. Maria dell'Orto 102
Ricci da Novara, Giovanni Battista (1537–1627)
  S. Agostino 6
  S. Francesco a Ripa 40
  S. Gregorio al Celio 62
  S. Marcello 78
  S. Maria Maggiore 92
  S. Maria del Popolo 108
  S. Maria in Traspontina 112
  S. Onofrio 128
  S. Pietro in Vaticano 132, 136
  SS. Trinità dei Pellegrini 151
Ricci, Sebastiano (1659–1734)
  SS. Apostoli 17
Ricciarelli da Volterra, Daniele, see Daniele da Volterra
Ricciolini, Niccolò (1687–after 1763)
  S. Giuseppe alla Lungara 61
  S. Maria degli Angeli 80
  S. Maria delle Grazie alle Fornaci 87
  SS. Michele e Magno 124
  SS. Nome di Maria 127
Righi, Francesco (recorded 1649–61)
  Palazzo Spada 197
Righi, Tommaso (1727–1802)
  S. Brigida 20
  SS. Luca e Martina 74
  S. Maria del Priorato 109
  Frascati, Hermitage of Camaldoli 265
Rinaldi, Antonio (c. 1709–94)
  S. Francesco a Ripa 40
Rinaldi, Giovanni (recorded 1670)
  S. Andrea al Quirinale 10
Ripoli, Tommaso (mid 17th century)
  S. Anastasia 8
Riviera, Egidio della, see Vliet, Gillis van der
Rocca, M. (1670/75–after 1751)
  S. Maria Maddalena 89
  S. Paolo alla Regola 129
Rodriguez, Emanuele (recorded 1733)
  SS. Trinità degli Spagnuoli 152
Romanelli, Giovanni Francesco (1610–62)
  S. Agostino 6
  S. Carlo ai Catinari 22
  S. Carlo alle Quattro Fontane 24

SS. Domenico e Sisto 35
S. Eligio degli Orefici 36
S. Giacomo alla Lungara 49
S. Marco 79
S. Maria degli Angeli 80
S. Maria dell'Anima 81
S. Maria in Vallicella, Oratory 117
S. Pietro in Montorio 130
S. Pietro in Vaticano 135, 136
Palazzo Altemps 160
Palazzo Barberini 165
Palazzo Costaguti 177
Palazzo Lante 182
Vatican 203, 204
Romanis, Filippo de' (active 1704–39)
Ospizio di S. Michele 251
Romano, Giovanni Francesco (mid 18th century)
S. Lorenzo in Panisperna 71
Romoli, Marcantonio (mid 18th century)
S. Andrea delle Fratte 9
Roncalli, Cristofano (Il Pomarancio) (1552–1626)
S. Gregorio al Celio 63
S. Maria degli Angeli 80
S. Maria d'Aracoeli 82, 83
S. Maria della Consolazione 86
S. Maria in Vallicella 116
S. Silvestro in Capite 145
Palazzo Crescenzi 177
Rondone, Alessandro (late 17th century)
S. Andrea della Valle 13
S. Maria di Montesanto and S. Maria dei Miracoli 98
S. Maria in Traspontina 112
Rosa, Francesco (d. 1687)
S. Agostino 6
SS. Carlo e Ambrogio al Corso 26
S. Caterina da Siena a Magnanapoli 27
S. Rocco 141
SS. Vincenzo e Anastasio 152
Rosa, Francesco (recorded 1732–42)
S. Maria Maddalena 89
Palazzo dei Pupazzi 190
Rosa, Salvator (1615–73)
S. Giovanni dei Fiorentini 51
Rosa, Sigismondo (early 18th century)
Madonna del Divino Amore 77
Rosati, Rosato (c. 1560–1622)
S. Carlo ai Catinari 21
Rossi, Alessio de' (second half of the 17th century)
Palazzo Santacroce 195
Rossi, Angelo de' (1671–1715)
Il Gesù 46
S. Giovanni in Laterano 54
S. Pietro in Vaticano 136

Rossi, Ascanio de' (late 16th century)
Palazzo Costaguti 177
Rossi, Domenico de' (recorded 1627–34)
S. Maria di Loreto 88
Rossi, Domenico de' (late 17th century)
S. Giacomo degli Incurabili 48
S. Silvestro in Capite 145
Rossi, Francesco de' (recorded 1593–6)
S. Susanna 149
Rossi, Giovanni Antonio de' (1616–95)
S. Francesco di Paola 39
S. Giacomo degli Incurabili 48
S. Giovanni in Laterano 56
S. Maria in Campitelli 83, 84
S. Maria in Campo Marzio 85
S. Maria Maddalena 89
S. Maria in Publicolis 109
S. Pantaleo 128
S. Rocco 140, 141
Palazzo Altieri 160
Palazzo Astalli 161
Palazzo Aste-Buonaparte 161
Palazzo Baldinotti-Carpegna 162
Palazzo Celsi 171
Palazzo Gambirasi 181
Palazzo Gomez 182
Palazzo Muti Bussi all'Aracoeli 187
Palazzo Nari (Piazza S. Maria in Campo Marzio) 188
Palazzo Nuñez 188
Palazzo Santacroce 195
Villa Altieri 209
Villa Carpegna 212
Monte di Pietà 249
Ospedale delle Donne 250
Genzano, S. Maria della Cima 270
Rossi, Giovanni Battista de' (first half of the 18th century)
S. Maria degli Angeli 80
S. Pietro in Vaticano 133
Rossi, Giovanni Francesco (active 1640–77)
S. Agnese in Agone 5
S. Caterina da Siena a Magnanapoli 27
S. Maria del Popolo 107
Rossi, Lazzaro de' (17th century)
S. Giacomo degli Incurabili 48
Rossi, Mariano (1731–1807)
S. Giuseppe alla Lungara 61
S. Paolo alla Regola 129
Villa Borghese 212
Rossi, Mattia de' (1637–95)
SS. Angeli Custodi 14
S. Croce dei Lucchesi 33
S. Francesco a Ripa 39, 40
S. Marcello 78
S. Maria in Campitelli 84
S. Maria Maddalena 89

Index of Artists

Rossi, Mattia de' (contd)
   S. Maria di Montesanto and S. Maria dei Miracoli 99
   S. Maria in Portico 108
   S. Maria delle Vergini 119
   S. Maria della Vittoria 122
   S. Pietro in Vaticano 135
   S. Silvestro in Capite 145
   Palazzo Muti Papazzuri 187
   Villa Corsini 213
   Ospizio di S. Michele 251
Rosso, Zanobi del (1724–98)
   S. Marcello 78
Rubens, Peter Paul (1577–1640)
   S. Croce in Gerusalemme 31
   S. Maria in Vallicella 116
Rubini, Giacomo (recorded c. 1766)
   Villa Chigi 213
Ruggieri, G. B. (recorded 1644)
   Palazzo Almagià 159
   Palazzo Santacroce 195
   Palazzo Spada 197
Rughesi, Fausto (recorded 1593–1606)
   S. Maria in Vallicella 114
Rusconi, Camillo (1658–1728)
   S. Agostino 6
   S. Francesco a Ripa 40
   S. Giovanni in Laterano 54, 56
   S. Ignazio 64
   S. Maria della Concezione 86
   S. Maria sopra Minerva 96
   S. Pietro in Vaticano 135
   S. Salvatore in Lauro 143
   S. Silvestro in Capite 145
   Marino, S. Barnaba 270
Rusconi, Giuseppe (1687–c. 1738)
   S. Ignazio 64
   SS. Luca e Martina 73
   S. Prassede 139
Rusconi Sassi, L, see Sassi, Ludovico Rusconi

Sacchi, Andrea (1599–1661)
   S. Bernardo alle Terme 19
   S. Carlo ai Catinari 22
   Il Gesù 43
   S. Giovanni in Laterano 56, 57
   S. Giuseppe a Capo le Case 61
   S. Isidoro 65
   S. Maria della Concezione 86
   S. Maria sopra Minerva 95
   S. Maria in Monticelli 100
   S. Maria del Priorato 109
   S. Pietro in Vaticano 135, 136
   Palazzo Barberini 165
   Palazzo Falconieri 180
   Acqua Acetosa 219
   Fontana delle Tartarughe 238
   Collegio Romano 248
Salé, Nicolas (Niccolò Sale) (active c. 1635–50)
   S. Pietro in Montorio 130
Salimbeni, Ventura (c. 1567/8–1613)
   Il Gesù 46
Salini, Tommaso (c. 1575–1625)
   S. Agostino 6
Salvi, F. (early 19th century)
   S. Cecilia 28
Salvi, Nicola (1697–1751)
   S. Eustachio 37
   S. Lorenzo in Damaso 68
   S. Pantaleo 128
   Palazzo Chigi-Odescalchi 173
   Villa Bolognetti 210
   Fontana di Trevi 240
   Monte di Pietà 249
Salvi, Simone (early 18th century)
   Villa Corsini ai Quattro Venti 213
Salviati, Francesco de' Rossi (1510–63)
   S. Francesco a Ripa 40
   S. Giovanni Decollato 50
   S. Marcello 78
   S. Maria dell'Anima 81
   S. Maria del Popolo 108
   Palazzo Farnese 180
   Palazzo Sacchetti 194
   Vatican 204
Sanctis, Domenico Antonio de (recorded 1715)
   S. Maria in Monticelli 100
Sanctis, Francesco de (1693–1731)
   SS. Trinità dei Pellegrini 151
   Spanish Steps 255, 256
Sandrart, Joachim von (1606–88)
   S. Francesco a Ripa 40
Sangallo, Antonio da, the Younger (1483–1546)
   S. Giacomo degli Incurabili 48
   S. Giovanni dei Fiorentini 50
   S. Giovanni in Oleo 58
   S. Luigi dei Francesi 75
   S. Marcello 77
   S. Maria di Loreto 88
   S. Maria sopra Minerva 95
   S. Maria di Monserrato 96
   S. Maria di Montesanto and S. Maria dei Miracoli 97
   S. Maria della Pace 106
   S. Pietro in Vaticano 132
   S. Spirito in Sassia 147
   Palazzo Farnese 180
   Palazzo Sacchetti 194
   Vatican 203
Sangallo, Giuliano da (1451/2–1516)
   Grottaferrata, Abbey 270
San Giovanni, Giovanni da (Mannozzi) (1592–1636)
   S. Maria dei Monti 100

S. Maria del Popolo 108
SS. Quattro Coronati 140
Palazzo Patrizi a S. Caterina 189
Palazzo Rospigliosi-Pallavicini 194
Sanni, S. (recorded 1734–5)
S. Giovanni dei Fiorentini 50
Sanquirico, Paolo (1565–1630)
S. Giovanni dei Fiorentini 52
Sansovino, Andrea Contucci (c. 1460–1529)
S. Agostino 6
S. Maria del Popolo 107
Sansovino, Jacopo Tatti (1486–1570)
S. Agostino 6
S. Croce in Gerusalemme 31, 32
S. Giacomo degli Incurabili 48
S. Marcello 77, 78
Santen, Jan van, see Vasanzio, Giovanni
Santi di Tito (1536–1603)
S. Giovanni dei Fiorentini 51, 52
Saraceni, Carlo (1585–1620)
S. Bernardo alle Terme 19
S. Lorenzo in Lucina 69
S. Maria dell'Anima 81
S. Maria in Aquiro 82
S. Maria sopra Minerva 95
S. Maria della Scala 110
Palazzo del Quirinale 193
Sardi, Giuseppe (1680–1753)
S. Lorenzo in Lucina 69
S. Maria in Cosmedin 86
S. Maria delle Lauretane 88
S. Maria Maddalena 89
S. Maria in Monticelli 100
S. Paolo alla Regola 129
S. Pasquale Baylon 129
SS. Trinità dei Spagnuoli 152
Marino, SS. Rosario 270
Sarrazin, Jacques (1592–1660)
S. Andrea della Valle 12
S. Lorenzo in Miranda 69
Frascati, Villa Torlonia 269
Sarti, Antonio (1797–1880)
Il Gesù 44
Sassi, Ludovico Rusconi (1678–1736)
SS. Apostoli 17
S. Giuseppe alla Lungara 61
S. Lorenzo in Damaso 68
S. Marcello 78
S. Salvatore in Lauro 143
Sassi, Matteo (1646–1723)
S. Maria in Monticelli 100
Sassoferrato, Giovanni Battista Salvi (1609–85)
S. Francesco di Paola 39
S. Giovanni in Laterano 57
S. Sabina 142
Savonanzi, Emilio (1580–1660)
S. Lorenzo fuori le Mura 70
Collegio Romano 248

Scala, Giovanni Battista (recorded 1654–7)
S. Girolamo della Carità 59
Scaramucci, Domenico (recorded 1735)
S. Giovanni dei Fiorentini 50
Schor, Cristoforo (1655–1701)
S. Antonio dei Portoghesi 15
Schor, Johannes Paul (Giovanni Paolo) (1615–74)
S. Caterina da Siena a Magnanapoli 27
S. Giovanni Calabita 50
S. Maria in Campitelli 84
Palazzo Borghese 167, 168
Palazzo Colonna 174
Palazzo del Grillo 178
Palazzo del Quirinale 193
Castelgandolfo, S. Tommaso da Villanova 264
Sebastiano Fiorentino (recorded 1483)
S. Agostino 6
Sebregondi, Niccolò (active 1612–51)
S. Maria del Pianto 106
Palazzo Crescenzi 177
Palazzo Pamphili 189
Secondo da Roma, Fra (recorded 1746)
S. Francesco a Ripa 40
Seiter, Daniel (1647/9–1705)
S. Maria degli Angeli 80
S. Maria d'Aracoeli 82
S. Maria di Montesanto and S. Maria dei Miracoli 99
S. Maria del Popolo 107
S. Maria del Suffragio 111
S. Maria in Traspontina 111
S. Maria in Vallicella 115
Semenza, Giovanni Giacomo (1580–1636)
S. Carlo ai Catinari 21
Serodine, Giovanni (1594–1631)
S. Lorenzo fuori le Mura 70
Serratini, Fra Giuseppe Antonio (recorded 1725)
S. Gregorio al Celio 62
Severoni, A. (recorded 1717)
S. Prassede 139
Sibilla, Gasparo (d. 1782)
SS. Trinità degli Spagnuoli 152
Sicciolante da Sermoneta, Girolamo (1521–c. 1580)
S. Eligio dei Ferrari 36
S. Giovanni in Laterano 55
S. Maria dell'Anima 81
S. Maria Maggiore 93
S. Maria della Pace 106
Siciliano, Franco, see Grassia, Francesco
Sillani, Sillano (second half of the 17th century)
S. Carlo alle Quattro Fontane 24
S. Maria di Montesanto and S. Maria dei Miracoli 98

Silvestro, Giuseppe (recorded 1755)
  Il Gesù 45
Slodtz, René-Michel (Michelange) (1705–64)
  S. Giovanni dei Fiorentini 52
  S. Luigi dei Francesi 76
  S. Marco 79
  S. Maria della Scala 110
  SS. Nome di Maria 127
Smigliewicz, Franz (1745–1807)
  S. Stanislao dei Polacchi 147
Soccorsi, Angeli (early 18th century)
  S. Prassede 139
Somazzi, Giovanni (Il Moretto) (mid 17th century)
  S. Andrea delle Fratte 9
Sorbi, Giovanni (b. c. 1695)
  S. Pasquale Baylon 129
Soria, Giovanni Battista (1581–1651)
  S. Carlo ai Catinari 21
  S. Caterina da Siena a Magnanapoli 27
  S. Crisogono 31
  SS. Domenico e Sisto 35
  S. Giuseppe dei Falegnami 61
  S. Gregorio al Celio 62
  S. Maria della Vittoria 122
  Palazzo Borghese 168
Sormani (Leonardo Milanese) (d. after 1589)
  S. Maria Maggiore 90
  S. Pietro in Montorio 130
  SS. Trinità dei Monti 150
  Acqua Felice 229
Spada, Gregorio (mid 17th century)
  S. Maria Maggiore 92
Spada, Orazio (mid 17th century)
  S. Andrea delle Fratte 9
Spada, Virgilio (d. 1662)
  S. Andrea delle Fratte 9
  S. Girolamo della Carità 59
  S. Maria in Vallicella, Oratory 117
Spadarino, Lo, see Galli, Giovanni Antonio
Spagna, Carlo (recorded 1677–8)
  S. Giovanni in Laterano 57
Spängl, Andreas (early 18th century)
  Palazzo della Cancelleria 170
Specchi, Alessandro (1668–1729)
  S. Anna dei Palafrenieri 15
  Bambino Gesù 17
  S. Maria ad Martyres (Pantheon) 94
  Palazzo Albani 158
  Palazzo de Carolis 177
  Palazzo Pichini 190
  Palazzo del Quirinale 191
  Palazzo Verospi 200
  Porto di Ripetta 234
  Spanish Steps 253
Specchi, Michelangelo (c. 1684–after 1750)
  S. Marco 79
  S. Maria del Carmine alle Tre Cannelle 85

Speranza, Giovanni Battista (c. 1600–40)
  S. Lucia in Selci 75
Sperone, Alessandro (recorded 1716–19)
  S. Eustachio 37
Spinazzi, Innocenzo (recorded 1755–98)
  S. Croce in Gerusalemme 32
Stanghellini, Antonio (recorded 1650)
  S. Maria d'Aracoeli 82
Stati, Cristoforo (1556–1619)
  S. Andrea della Valle 13, 14
  S. Maria Maggiore 93
Stella, Jacques (1596–1657)
  S. Maria sopra Minerva 95
Stern, Ignazio (1680–1748)
  S. Anna dei Palafrenieri 15
  S. Marcello 78
  S. Maria dell'Anima 81
  SS. Sergio e Bacco 144
Stern, Ludwig (1709–77)
  SS. Michele e Magno 124
  S. Prassede 139
Stocchi, Alessandro (recorded 1830)
  Fontana di Piazza Colonna 233
Subleyras, Pierre (1699–1749)
  S. Francesca Romana 38
  S. Maria degli Angeli 80
  S. Pietro in Vaticano 135

Tacconi, Innocenzo (active 1607–25)
  S. Maria del Popolo 108
Targone, Pompeo (1575–1630)
  S. Giovanni in Laterano 56
  S. Maria Maggiore 93
Tarquinio da Viterbo, see Ligustri, Tarquinio
Taruffi, Emilio (1633–96)
  S. Andrea della Valle 13
Tassi, Agostino Buonamici (c. 1580–1644)
  Palazzo Costaguti 177
  Palazzo Lancellotti 182
  Palazzo Pamphili 189
  Palazzo del Quirinale 193
  Palazzo Rospigliosi-Pallavicini 194
  Villa Ludovisi 215
  Frascati, Villino Mergé-Mastrofini 267
Tavolaccio, Domenico (mid 17th century)
  SS. Luca e Martina 74
Tedesco, Lorenzo (late 16th century)
  S. Spirito in Sassia 147
Tempesta, Antonio (1555–1630)
  S. Maria Maggiore 93
  Palazzo Rospigliosi-Pallavicini 194
Tempesta, Pietro (Pieter Mulier) (c. 1637–1701)
  Palazzo Colonna 174
  Ariccia, Palazzo Chigi 262
Teodoli, Girolamo (1677–1766)
  SS. Marcellino e Pietro 77
  S. Nicola in Arcione 125

Index of Artists

S. Salvatore in Lauro 143
Testa, F. (recorded 1714)
   S. Giuseppe dei Falegnami 61
Testa, Giuseppe (mid 17th century)
   S. Maria del Popolo 107
Testa, Pietro (1611–50)
   S. Maria dell'Anima 81
   S. Martino ai Monti 124
Théodon, Jean-Baptiste (1646–1713)
   Il Gesù 46
   S. Maria in Trastevere 112
   S. Pietro in Vaticano 134
   Monte di Pietà 249
Tibaldi, Pellegrino Pellegrini (1527–96)
   S. Marcello 78
Tito, Santi di (1536–1603) see Santi di Tito
'Todesco' (late 17th century)
   S. Maria di Montesanto and S. Maria dei Miracoli 98
Tommasini, Gregorio (recorded 1684)
   S. Salvatore in Onda 143
Tornioli, Niccolò (active 1622–40)
   S. Maria in Vallicella 116
Torriani, Carlo (recorded 1673)
   S. Marcello 78
Torriani, Niccolò (recorded c. 1621)
   SS. Domenico e Sisto 33, 35
   S. Maria di Monserrato 97
Torriani, Orazio (active 1601–57)
   S. Agostino 6
   S. Ambrogio della Massima 7
   S. Andrea della Valle 13
   S. Bartolomeo all'Isola 18
   S. Calisto 20
   SS. Cosma e Damiano (via dei Fori Imperiali) 30
   SS. Domenico e Sisto 33, 35
   S. Lorenzo in Miranda 69
   S. Marco 78, 79
   Palazzo San Calisto 195
   Palazzo Sciarra 196
Torrone, Angelo (recorded 1669–90)
   S. Giovanni della Pigna 58
   SS. Luca e Martina 72
Tosi, L. (recorded 1747)
   S. Pasquale Baylon 129
Trémolières, Pierre-Charles (1703–39)
   S. Maria degli Angeli 80
Trevisani, Francesco (1656–1746)
   S. Anastasia 7
   S. Andrea delle Fratte 9
   S. Giovanni in Laterano 55
   S. Ignazio 64
   S. Maria degli Angeli 80
   S. Maria d'Aracoeli 83
   S. Maria in Via, Oratory 120
   S. Onofrio 127
   S. Pietro in Vaticano 136

S. Silvestro in Capite 145
Stimmate di S. Francesco 148
Palazzo de Carolis 177
Triga, Giacomo (active 1710–46)
   SS. Celso e Giuliano 29
   S. Clemente 30
   S. Francesco di Paola 39
   SS. Giovanni e Paolo 58
   S. Marcello 78
Tristano, Giovanni (active 1558–75)
   Il Gesù 41, 43
Trometta, Niccolò (active 1565–1620)
   S. Maria dell'Orto 103
Troppa, Girolamo (active 1661–c. 1711)
   S. Agata in Trastevere 3
   SS. Carlo e Ambrogio al Corso 26
   S. Croce alla Lungara 33
   S. Maria del Suffragio 111
   S. Marta 123
Troy, J. F. de (1679–1752)
   SS. Alessio e Bonifazio all'Aventino 7
   SS. Claudio e Andrea de' Borgognoni 30
Turchi, Alessandro (1578–1649)
   S. Maria della Concezione 86
   S. Salvatore in Lauro 143
Turini, Pietro (recorded 1510)
   S. Omobono 127
Turriani, see Torriani

Ubaldini, Pietro Paolo (active 1630–c. 1670)
   SS. Domenico e Sisto 35
   S. Giacomo degli Incurabili 48
   S. Isidoro 65
   S. Nicola da Tolentino 126

Vacca, Flamineo (1538–1605)
   Acqua Felice 229
Valadier, Giuseppe (1762–1839)
   S. Lorenzo in Damaso 68
   S. Maria della Consolazione 86
   S. Maria Maggiore 90
   S. Maria di Montesanto and S. Maria dei Miracoli 98
   S. Pantaleo 128
   S. Pietro in Vaticano 132
   S. Rocco 141
   Fountain in Piazza del Popolo 234
   Carceri Nuove 245
Valadier, Luigi Maria (b. 1791)
   S. Maria in Via, Oratory 120
Valentin de Boullogne (1594–1632)
   S. Pietro in Vaticano 135
Valeriani, Domenico (active c. 1730–1771)
   Frascati, Villa Borghese 267
Valeriani, Giuseppe (active c. 1730–61)
   SS. Celso e Giuliano 29
   Frascati, Villa Borghese 267

Index of Artists

Valeriano, Giuseppe (1542–96)
  Il Gesù 43, 45
  Collegio Romano 248
Valerio, Padre (early 17th century)
  Collegio di Propaganda Fide 246
Valloni, Silvio (18th century)
  S. Maria della Scala 110
Valsoldo, Giovanni Antonio Paracca, Il (active 1572–1642)
  S. Andrea della Valle 13
  S. Maria Maggiore 90, 93
  S. Maria del Popolo 107
  S. Maria in Trastevere 112
  S. Pudenziana 140
  S. Susanna 149
Valvassori, Gabriele (1683–1761)
  S. Agnese in Agone 5
  SS. Bartolomeo e Alessandro dei Bergamaschi 18
  S. Maria della Luce 88
  S. Maria dell'Orto 102, 103
  SS. Quirico e Giulitta 140
  Palazzo Doria-Pamphili 179
  Villa Pamphili 219
Vannelli, G. B. (recorded 1714)
  S. Giuseppe dei Falegnami 61
Vanni, Curzio (active c. 1585–1613)
  S. Giovanni in Laterano 56
Vanni, Francesco (1563–1610)
  S. Maria degli Angeli 89
Vanni, Giovanni Battista (1599–1660)
  S. Giovanni dei Fiorentini 52
Vanni, Raffaelle (1587–1674)
  S. Croce in Gerusalemme 32
  S. Maria della Pace 106
  S. Maria del Popolo 107, 108
  S. Maria in Publicolis 109
  S. Maria in Vallicella, Oratory 117
  Ariccia, Collegiata dell'Assunta 263
Vanvitelli, Luigi (1700–73)
  S. Agostino 6
  S. Andrea delle Fratte 9
  S. Antonio dei Portoghesi 16
  S. Cecilia 28
  S. Maria degli Angeli 80, 81
  S. Pantaleo 128
  Palazzo Sciarra 196
  Fontana di Trevi 240
  Frascati, Villa Rufinella 268
Vasanzio, Giovanni (Jan Van Santen) (c. 1550–1621)
  S. Sebastiano fuori le Mura 143
  Palazzo Borghese 167
  Palazzo Rospigliosi-Pallavicini 194
  Villa Borghese 211
  Fontana di Ponte Sisto 234
  Frascati, Villa Mondragone 267

Vasari, Giorgio (1511–74)
  S. Pietro in Montorio 130
  Palazzo della Cancelleria 169
  Vatican 204
Vasconi, Filippo (c. 1687–1730)
  S. Caterina da Siena a Magnanapoli 27
Vasconio, Giuseppe (recorded 1657)
  S. Agostino 6
Vecchi, Gaspare de' (d. 1643)
  S. Maria dei Monti 100
  SS. Vincenzo e Anastasio 152
  Palazzo Mattei di Giove 186
  Collegio di Propaganda Fide 246
Vecchi, Giovanni de' (1536–1615)
  S. Bernardino ai Monti 19
  Oratorio del SS. Crocifisso 33
  S. Eligio degli Orefici 36
  Il Gesù 43
  S. Pietro in Montorio 130
Vecchiarelli, Pietro (recorded c. 1639)
  S. Maria dell'Umiltà 113
  S. Pietro in Vincoli 138
Velázquez, Antonio (mid-18th century)
  SS. Trinità degli Spagnuoli 152
Venturi, Sergio (c. 1584–1646)
  S. Crisogono 31
  Palazzo Borghese 168
Venusti, Marcello (1512/15–79)
  S. Maria sopra Minerva 95
  S. Maria della Pace 106
Verschaffelt, Peter Anton (1710–93)
  S. Croce in Gerusalemme 32
Vespignani, Virgilio (1808–82)
  Porta di S. Pancrazio 253
Vici, Andrea Busiri, see Busiri Vici, Andrea
Vicinelli, Odoardo (c. 1683–1755)
  S. Maria in Monticelli 100
Vignola, Giacinto Barozzi da (c. 1540–after 1584)
  S. Anna dei Palafrenieri 15
  Il Gesù 43
  S. Maria dell'Orto 102
  Villa Farnese 214
Vignola, Jacopo Barozzi da (1507–73)
  S. Andrea in via Flaminia 14
  S. Anna dei Palafrenieri 14, 15
  Oratorio del SS. Crocifisso 33
  Il Gesù 41, 43
  S. Giovanni in Laterano 55
  S. Lorenzo in Damaso 68
  S. Maria dell'Orto 102
  S. Maria in Traspontina 111
  Palazzo Borghese 166
  Palazzo della Cancelleria 169
  Palazzo Farnese 180
  Villa Farnese 214
  Villa La Vignola 223
  Porto del Popolo 253

Frascati, Villa Vecchia 269
Viola, Giovanni Battista (1576–1662)
   Villa Ludovisi 215
Vitale, Alessandro (recorded 1662)
   S. Marco 79
Viviani, Antonio (1560–1620)
   S. Girolamo degli Schiavoni 60
   S. Gregorio al Celio 63
Vliet, Gillis van der (Egidio della Riviera) (d. 1602)
   S. Maria dell'Anima 81
Vos, Martin de (1532–1603)
   S. Francesco a Ripa 40
Vouet, Simon (1590–1649)
   S. Francesco a Ripa 40
   S. Lorenzo in Lucina 69
Wehrle, Hans Conrad (early 18th century)
   S. Maria Maddalena 89
Wernle, Jacob (early 18th century)
   Palazzo Spada 197

Zaccolini, Padre Matteo (c. 1590–1630)
   S. Silvestro al Quirinale 146
Zoboli, Giacomo (1681–1767)
   S. Antonio dei Portoghesi 16
   S. Apollinare 16
   Bambino Gesù 17

S. Eustachio 37
S. Giovanni della Pigna 58
Zuccaro, Federico (1540–1609)
   Il Gesù 45
   S. Lucia del Gonfalone 74
   S. Marcello 78
   S. Maria dell'Orto 103
   S. Pudenziana 140
   S. Sabina 142
   SS. Trinità dei Monti 150, 151
   Palazzo dei Piceni 190
Zuccaro, Taddeo (1529–66)
   S. Marcello 78
   S. Maria della Consolazione 102, 103
   S. Maria dell'Orto 103
   S. Sabina 142
   SS. Trinità dei Monti 151
   Palazzo Farnese 180
   Vatican 204
Zucchetti, Filippo (active 1694–1712)
   S. Maria dell'Orto 102
   S. Maria della Scala 110
Zucchi, Francesco (c. 1570–1627)
   S. Cesareo 29
Zucchi, Jacopo (1541–89)
   S. Spirito in Sassia 147
   SS. Trinità dei Pellegrini 151
   Palazzo Ruspoli 194